D1827748

1 MONTH OF
FREE
READING

at
www.ForgottenBooks.com

By purchasing this book you are eligible for one month membership to ForgottenBooks.com, giving you unlimited access to our entire collection of over 1,000,000 titles via our web site and mobile apps.

To claim your free month visit:
www.forgottenbooks.com/free448195

ISBN 978-0-365-11932-6
PIBN 10448195

APPROBATION

The Archbishop and Bishops of the Province have indorsed the ILLINOIS CATHOLIC HISTORICAL SOCIETY and its work, and proffered their assistance. Following are extracts from their letters:

I give hearty approval of the establishment of a Catholic Historical Society that will not be confined to the limits of this Diocese only, but will embrace the entire province and State of Illinois, and to further encourage this movement, I desire you to enroll me among the life members of the Society.
Sincerely yours in Christ,

GEORGE W. MUNDELEIN, *Archbishop.*

The Bishop desired me to write you that he is pleased to accept the Honorary Presidency, and cordially approves of the good work undertaken by the ILLINOIS CATHOLIC HISTORICAL SOCIETY.
Faithfully yours in Christ,

M. A. TARRANT,
Secy. to the Bishop of Alton.

I am glad to have your letter about the CATHOLIC HISTORICAL SOCIETY, and will gladly serve in the capacity suggested. This will be a depository and will fill a much felt need.

P. J. MULDOON, *Bishop of Rockford.*

The sole aim of the Society, namely, 'To make known the glories of the Church,' should certainly appeal to all our Catholic people. I confidently hope that the Society may meet with the generous encouragement it richly deserves from everyone under my jurisdiction.

EDMUND M. DUNNE, *Bishop of Peoria.*

I wish to assure you that I am willing to give you every possible assistance in the good work you have undertaken, and in compliance with your request, I am likewise willing to be one of your Honorary Presidents.
Wishing God's blessing, I remain,

HENRY ALTHOFF, *Bishop of Belleville.*

CONTENTS

LOYOLA UNIVERSITY PRESS

CHICAGO, ILLINOIS

Illinois
Catholic Historical Review

VOLUME III   JULY, 1920   NUMBER 1

THE DOUBLE JUBILEE
A Memorable Page in History

I.

The 8th, 9th and 10th days of June, 1920, in Chicago, and the 12th of the same month and year in Joliet, witnessed the commemoration of some of the most interesting facts in the history of Mid-America. The great services, exercises and ceremonies enacted on those days centrally concerned the Catholic Church, its establishment, growth and progress in this region, but have a distinct bearing also upon civilized progress in all its phases.

ESTABLISHMENT OF THE CHURCH IN THE ILLINOIS COUNTRY

Two hundred and forty-five years ago, counting backward from April 11, 1920, Father James Marquette, S. J., on a plain near the the modern city of Utica in LaSalle County, with due solemnity, instituted the Catholic Church in Illinois, and careful study indicates that from that day to the present no decade has passed without showing substantial growth and progress.

For more than a century, although the population had increased in the territory now known as Illinois according to the claims of some to ten thousand, and certainly to as many as three thousand white men, there is no evidence that a single white man professing any but the Catholic faith ever set foot upon the soil of Illinois.

The best evidence indicates also that the great bulk of the native Indians who lived and died in Illinois during the eighteenth century embraced the faith and it seems not unreasonable to estimate that the number of Indians of the various tribes who came under the influence of the missionaries within the confines of the present state

5

and embraced Christianity would total ten thousand. It has been asserted that Father Claude Jean Allouez, S. J., who spent many years of his missionary life in Illinois and near Chicago, preached the gospel to one hundred thousand savages during his life-time and himself baptized ten thousand.[1] Letters of missionaries preserved to the present time state that as early as 1709 the four thousand savages dwelling near Peoria Lake were virtually all Christians and amongst the two thousand two hundred then settled at or near the second Kaskaskia in Randolph County, Illinois, "hardly forty may be found who do not profess the Catholic faith with the greatest piety and constancy."[2]

THE TRANSITION PERIOD

But time sweeps on and gradually white men mingle with the savages and in the missions both races join in the services and sacrifices. As the white men increased—especially after the French regime—sad commentary upon the humanity of the white race— the Indians decreased, but the gap is filled up and the old Church continues its growth.

PROTESTANTISM IS INTRODUCED

By the year 1800, and to any extent not until then, Protestantism in one form or other enters upon the scene. Call it competition or what you will, advocates of the various sects displayed a spirit of the bitterest animosity to Catholicism.[3] Quarreling desperately amongst themselves they agreed completely in their opposition to the Catholic Church and openly proposed to throttle it.[4] In their ambition for the destruction of the Catholic Church these sectarians had the sympathy and assistance of all those who wished to come into leadership in public and commercial affairs and to that end proposed to drive out the French who were old settlers or at least to minimize their influence and subordinate them. This combined opposition centered upon the French residents told severely for many years and indeed largely succeeded in discrediting everything French. Had there been no other element in the conflict and had it

---

[1] Campbell, *Pioneer Priests of North America*, Vol. III, p. 164.
[2] Gravier to Tamburini, *Jesuit Relations*, Vol. LXVI, p. 121.
[3] See Cofoid in Publication No. 10 *Illinois Historical Library*.
[4] *Home Missionary*, November, 1845.

been humanly possible, the hopes and ambitions of the newcomers for the destruction of the Church might have been realized.

THE IRISH COME TO ILLINOIS

As has so frequently happened in all parts of the world the Irish came to the defense of the Church and, too, of the downtrodden in Illinois. It is true that many Irishmen who came to Illinois had, either of themselves or through their ancestors, lost the faith but in that early day if through lack of opportunity or for other causes many Irish had ceased to practice their religion, yet they were imbued with the principles of charity and justice, Catholic attributes that frequently remain when the practice of the faith is abandoned. Where the French were compelled to leave off, the Irish began; nor were they long alone in upholding the standard of the Church for soon the Germans also came in numbers and to their great credit sustained the traditions of their countrymen whose faith survived the onslaught of the reformation

GREAT LEADERS OF THE CHURCH

To the great leaders of the Church under Divine Grace must be attributed its remarkable progress in the exceedingly trying circumstances, which obtained during nearly the whole of the nineteenth century. In the very darkest days of the Church—1783 to 1850— not only did she hold her own against the violent attacks, individual and collective, of the Protestant sects, but attracted to her communion as converts many of the most highly educated and accomplished men and women of the day.[5]

Much has been made in sectarian—and indeed in non-sectarian— writings of the "circuit rider" (preacher) of the first half of the nineteenth century, and a few men, perhaps a half dozen, have been glorified as great "circuit riders" who travelled about on horseback preaching the Baptist, Methodist or Presbyterian doctrine. In the same period the Catholic Church was represented by a galaxy of some fifty learned men coming from homes of ease and opulence frequently, trained in the best schools, capable of assuming the highest positions in public, commercial or professional life, who literally rode the circuit year after year until the last spark of life was extinguished by their exertions. In his day Father Pierre Gibault's circuit em-

---

[5] Such converts include William Morrison, Mrs. Robert Morrison, John Hay, Gov. William S. Bissell and Stephen A. Douglas.

braced Kaskaskia, Vincennes, Detroit, Michilimackinac, Peoria, Cahokia and all tribes and settlements intervening. In like manner Father Donatien Olivier travelled from Cahokia to St. Louis, from St. Louis to Kaskaskia, from Kaskaskia to Shawneetown, Vincennes, Ouatanon (now Fort Wayne) and circuitously back again. Father Elisha Durbin was for sixty years constantly in the saddle except when celebrating Mass, hearing confessions, administering the sacraments or stealing a few hours of sleep. Father Stephen Theodore Badin covered the whole of Kentucky and Indiana and one-half of Illinois. His brother, Father Vincent Badin, labored in the Galena district. Rev. Charles Felix Van Quickenborne, S. J., re-evangelized Western Illinois. Father George John Alleman covered Rock Island County and nearly the whole of the Military Tract. Father Michael Carroll brought the gospel from Alton into every corner of the surrounding counties. Father Peter Paul Lefevere evangelized Quincy and the surrounding territory to be followed later by Father Augustus Brickweddie and Father Patrick T. McElhearne. Father Thomas Cusack spread the gospel all along the Illinois Central Railroad. Father Patrick McCabe was the apostle of Cairo; Father John Ryan, of the Mattoon country. Father John Blasius Raho, C. M., established the Church in LaSalle and Ottawa, and made a wide circuit of several counties. Father John Gueguen was the apostle of Lake County; Fathers James Plunket and Hippolyte Du Pontavice were the evangelizers of Joliet and of Will and the surrounding counties. Father John Mary Iraneaus St. Cyr was the father and founder of the Church in modern Chicago, and at intervening points throughout the state other zealous priests and missionaries brought the gospel to every group of settlers as fast as they came.[6]

During all these years since the territory became American, the Church in the Illinois country was directed by prelates living beyond the present borders of the State. In succession Rev. John Carroll, first as Prefect Apostolic and later as Bishop of Baltimore ruled. Then came Right Rev. Benedict Joseph Flaget as Bishop of Bardstown (Louisville). Next Right Rev. Joseph Rosati, Bishop of St. Louis and next for the eastern half of the state Right Rev. Simon William Gabriel Bruté, Bishop of Vincennes. Following the two last named came Archbishop Peter Richard Kenrick of St. Louis and Right Rev. Celestine De Haliandiere of Vincennes.[7]

---

[6] See *Archdiocese of Chicago, Antecedents and Development*, pp. 125 to 147.
[7] *Ib.*

St. Joseph's Church,
Prairie du Rocher, Ill.

PRESENT CHURCHES IN OLDEST PARISHES IN STATE

1. Immaculate Conception, Kaskaskia, established by Father Marquette, S. J., April 11, 1675.
2. Holy Family, Cahokia, established by Father Francis Pinet, S. J., September, 1699. 3. St.
Joseph's, Prairie du Rocher, established in 1722. 4. Old Holy Family, Cahokia, built in 1797,
still in use as school and meeting hall. 5. St. Patrick's, Ruma, formerly O'Hara's settlement,
1818. The first church with an English speaking congregation. (See *History of Diocese of
Belleville*, by Frederick Beuckman.)

1. St. Mary's Church, built in 1833 by Rev. J. M. I. St. Cyr. Stood at the Southwest corner of State and Lake. 2. The same building, removed in 1836 to the rear of the lot at the Northwest corner of Michigan Avenue and Madison Street, enlarged and altered by the addition of a belfry. 3. The germ of Mercy Hospital, "Tippecanoe Hall" on Kinzie Street opened as a County Hospital in 1847. Sisters of Mercy took charge in 1851. 4. The first Orphanage begun in 1849 stood on Wabash Avenue near Van Buren Street. 5. The new St. Mary's Church, stood at the Southwest corner of Wabash Avenue and Madison Street. Begun by Rev. Maurice de St. Palais, completed by Rt. Rev. William Quarter, D. D., dedicated on the first Sunday in October, 1845 and made the cathedral, and the first Convent of Mercy, built in 1847. 6. The first parochial and episcopal residence, built by Father De St. Palais in 1838, stood at the Northwest corner of Michigan Avenue and Madison Street. The first three bishops lived in this building. These buildings were destroyed by the fire of Oct. 9, 1871.

THE NEW ERA

So sparse was the population that the growth in the Church was greater than was preceptible and though the northern part of the state was more than one hundred years behind the southern part in settlement, yet as early as 1833 Chicago had become populous and important enough to merit, in the view of Bishop Rosati of St. Louis, a church and resident pastor. Accordingly in compliance with the request of some one hundred and twenty Catholics, who comprised almost the whole of the population of the place, the bishop sent Rev. John Mary Iraneaus St. Cyr to organize the Church and minister to the spiritual needs of the Catholics of Chicago. Father St. Cyr arrived in Chicago on the first of May, 1833, and celebrated his first Mass here on the succeeding Sunday, May 5th.[8]

The next ten years saw such a remarkable growth in the City of Chicago as to bring it into sufficient importance to be recommended by the Council of Bishops as the seat of a See which the bishops recommended should be established for Illinois, and accordingly the Holy See on the 28th day of November, 1843, erected the diocese of Chicago and appointed Rev. William Quarter, then of New York, as the first bishop.

Arriving in Chicago on the 5th of May, 1844, just eleven years from the day that the first Mass was celebrated here by Father St. Cyr, Bishop Quarter celebrated his first Mass in his new See.[9]

Taking stock of the surroundings the new bishop found himself in a frontier city of some 10,000 population, the shepherd of a flock of fifty thousand souls with but thirty-nine priests in the entire diocese and but two priests in the City of Chicago, ministering to the needs of the Catholics in one single church.

SEVENTY-FIVE YEARS IN RETROSPECT

The dominant note in the June, 1920, celebration was the Diamond Jubilee of the establishment of the Diocese. The Silver Jubilee of His Grace Most Rev. Archbishop George William Mundelein, D. D., was a coincidence that added immeasurably to the zest of the celebration and the observance of the Silver Jubilee was of the highest interest and gratification both to the people of the diocese and the contemporaries of the Archbishop.

By one means or another the record of the Church in Illinois

---

[8] Ib.

[9] See diary of Bishop Quarter in Feehan Souvenir, p. 64.

was reviewed during the festal season. Tender tributes were paid
to the sainted prelates who sheperded the flock in the past years, to
the faithful clergy and religious who bore the burdens from the
earliest day and to the loyal people who through opposition, stress
and storm, by their sacrifices and exertions carried forward the
essential works of progress.[10]

It has been a matter of some surprise that in such a short time
(preparations for the celebration were begun only in April) such
a complete and so well co-ordinated a program could have been arranged and successfully executed.

II.

THE ARCHBISHOP'S SILVER JUBILEE

The festal season was opened with the celebration of the silver
jubilee of Archbishop Mundelein's ordination to the priesthood. Exactly twenty-five years before, the then young divinity student was
ordained priest in Rome and it was a pleasant coincidence that his
silver jubilee occurred so near the seventy-fifth anniversary of the
great diocese over which he has been called to rule.

This magnificent ceremony presented to the eye and to the mind
a view such as is witnessed only in the great ceremonies of the
Catholic Church. An able clergyman, not of the Catholic faith,
writing of the ceremony said:

With all the pomp and beautiful ceremonial of the ancient church of Rome,
the three day celebration of the diamond jubilee of the archdiocese of Chicago
and the silver sacerdotal jubilee of the Most Rev. George William Mundelein,
Archbishop, started with the solemn pontifical High Mass at Holy Name Cathedral
yesterday.

Seated on the throne in the sanctuary and presiding at the service was the
senior prelate of the Roman Church in America, Cardinal Gibbons of Baltimore.
Opposite him sat the Most Rev. John Bonzano, apostolic delegate.

The celebrant was the jubilarian, Archbishop Mundelein. Assistant Priest,
Rev. John Webster Melody, D. D., pastor of St. Jarlath's Church. Deacons of
Honor, Rev. Thomas Bona, pastor of St. Joseph's Church, Summit, Ill., and Rev.
William H. Dettmer, pastor of St. Benedict's Church. Deacon of the Mass, Rev.
George McCarthy, chaplin United States Army. Sub-deacon of Mass, Rev. D. L.
McDonald, pastor of Immaculate Conception Church, Elmhurst, Ill. Assistants
to the Most Rev. John Bonzano, D. D., Apostolic Delegate to the United States
were: Rev. P. W. Dunne, pastor of St. James' Church, the Rev. Francis Gordon,

---

[10] See *Archdiocese of Chicago*, pp. 5 to 150.

C. R., pastor of St. Mary of the Angel's Church, and the Hon. Dennis Kelly, K. S. G. Assistants to His Eminence, James Cardinal Gibbons, D. D., Archbishop of Baltimore, were: The Right Reverend Monsignor M. J. FitzSimmons, V. G., Rector of the Cathedral of the Holy Name; Right Reverend Monsignor Francis C. Kelley, D. D., president Catholic Church Extension Society, Right Reverend D. J. Riordan, pastor of St. Elizabeth's Church, and the Hon. Edward Hines, K. C. S. G.

The sermon was preached by the Most Rev. Patrick J. Hayes of New York. In the sanctuary were all but three of the archbishops of America,[11] many bishops and other prelates.

Nearly a thousand priests of the diocese and hundreds of sisters sat in the nave of the church. Some two thousand five hundred people thronged the vast cathedral building to participate in the service. The choir, assisted by orchestra and grand opera soloists, under direction of Pietro Yon, sang the magnificent music of the church.

The various speakers recounted the rapid progress of the church from the time it first became a diocese in 1844 with the Rt. Rev. William Quarter as its first bishop, and sounded highest praise of Archbishop Mundelein for his achievements during the four years of his rule here.

The climax of the service was the reading of the message of congratulation from Pope Benedict XV.[12]

THE POPE'S LETTER

Venerable Brother: Greeting and the Apostolic Blessing!

With pleasure we have heard of the sacred solemnities which are about to be celebrated on the seventy-fifth anniversary of the foundation of the Diocese of Chicago, and our pleasure is all the greater because we learn that on this occasion also you are happily to commemorate the twenty-fifth year of your priesthood, and that the seminary recently erected by you in memory of your predecessor is to be dedicated. With good reason, then, there are to be, as we have heard, manifestations of public rejoicing, with a concourse of not a few of our venerable brethren. And indeed thanks are to be rendered to God because in such a short period not only has your city shown a remarkable growth in human affairs and worldly prosperity, but has flourished also in a wonderful manner in the propagation and the vigor of Catholic Faith. And to this end you yourself have contributed not a little, since in the five years of your pastorate you have left nothing undone to foster Christian life among the people by many works of faith and piety—among which we may reckon the seminary for the education of boys to the priesthood, as well as many monuments of your charity and your munificence.

And therefore, since we do not wish that our voice be silent in the assembly of those who congratulate with you, with an especial paternal affection, by these letters, we embrace you and your faithful; and we wish that under your able guidance for many years, the church of Chicago may prosper more and more. And we shall not cease to pray God—the Giver of all good gifts—to be ever

---

[11] The absentees were in Rome.

[12] Rev. F. L. Gratiot in *Chicago Daily Tribune*, June 9, 1920.

propitious towards you. And that we may give some token of our benevolence
towards you, we appoint you an Assistant to the Pontifical Throne, and command that an apostolic brief be sent you. And furthermore, for the sake of
increasing the splendor of your solemnities, we empower you to bless in our
name, and to grant a plenary indulgence under the usual conditions to all
who shall be present at the sacred function. And as a further testimony of our
benevolence, venerable brother, we grant to you, and to the clergy and the people
placed in your care, the apostolic benediction.

Given from St. Peter's, at Rome, May 5th, 1920, in the sixth year of our
pontificate.[13]

BENEDICT XV PÓPE.

ARCHBISHOP HAYES' ADDRESS

Most Rev. Patrick J. Hayes, Archbishop of New York, delivered
the address of congratulation which was a masterpiece of diction.
After reviewing the history of the Church in Illinois during the
missionary period and the creation of the diocese, the Most Reverend
Archbishop expressed mutual congratulations to the people and the
prelate of the diocese and closed with the following eloquent paragraphs:[14]

Our beloved jubilarian would be the first to disclaim that this day glorifieth
him personally rather than the Church of God, especially here in America. What
doth this solemn jubilation profit America? It brings to America ''the power
and the divinity and the wisdom and the strength and honor and benediction''
(Apoc. V:12) of Christ Our Lord, ''the head of all principality and power.''
(Col. II:10.) Jesus Christ is not only the great High Priest of the supernatural
order: He is the King—yea, ''Prince of the kings of earth'' (Apoc. I:5) the
supreme ruler of mankind, of all races and of all nations. The Prophet Isaias
cried out of old ''The nation and the kingdom that will not serve Thee shall
perish'' (LX:12). This is true today as it was when uttered centuries ago. It
applies to our beloved America, which is sadly in need today of spiritual light,
courage and strentgh in the domestic, industrial, social and political disturbances
that comfort only wicked men and make the law-abiding gravely anxious. Christ
lives in His Church, to which He gave a mission with power to protect the family,
to hallow the school, to purify the marketplace, to guide lawgivers, to teach
reverence for authority, to inculcate obedience, to stimulate patriotism—in a word,
to bless America.

America has no sincerer friend in thought, word and deed than the Catholic
Church. The most virulent foes of the Church are equally America's most dangerous ones. Let America and the Church make common cause in Christ and for
Christ. The Church stands ever at the portals of civilized society with the flaming
sword of the Cherubim lest evil might enter in. The Church also wings her flight

---

[13] This document was read from the pulpit in both Latin and English by
Right Rev. Msgr. Edward F. Hoban, D. D., Chancellor.

[14] Archbishop Hayes' sermon was printed in full in the *New World*, June 11,
1920.

from the rising to the setting sun, and again from dusk to dawn, bearing the. burning coals of the Seraphim to cleanse, purify and sanctify the children of men.

O thou, Holy Church of Chicago! clap thy hands in joy, raise thy voice in prayer, sing the canticle of praise; lift up thy gates that the King of Glory may enter in—on this thy day of solemn jubilee! Alleluia!

O thou priest of the Most High, shepherd of flocks! bend lowly thy mitred head for Christ's fullness of benediction and unction, while the revered representative of our Holy Father, thy consecrated brothers in the episcopal order, thy annointed priests, thy holy virgins, thy innocent children and thy faithful people acclaim thy jubilee day to thine own peace and consolation and to the greater glory of God! Alleluia!

TESTIMONIALS OF LOYALTY

At the conclusion of the Mass, Right Rev. Alexander J. McGavick, auxiliary bishop of Chicago, presented the Archbishop with a purse of $256,000. subscribed by the clergy of the archdiocese as a token of their esteem for the archbishop. On behalf of the laity, Count Dennis F. Kelly presented a purse of $750,000.

In response to the congratulations and the presentation of the purses the Archbishop addressed the assemblage as follows:[15]

ARCHBISHOP MUNDELEIN'S ADDRESS

Surely a demonstration such as this ought to gladden the heart of any mortal man. The manifestation of affection on the part of our Catholic people, the tribute of loyalty from a great body of clergy, the presence here of so many of my brethren of the episcopate, the assistance here of the Papal Legate, the coming, too, of America's best loved man, the Venerated Cardinal of Baltimore, and above all the loving words of congratulation and the blessing of our Holy Father, all serve to make this an unforgettable occasion for the Archbishop of Chicago, his clergy and his people. From the very first moment this festivity was suggested, I have steadfastly declined to regard it in any way as a personal tribute: I have looked upon it simply as an opportunity given the priests and people of Chicago to show their loyalty to their leader and their bishop, to do honor to the place that he holds rather than to the man who holds it. In troublous times like ours, in these days when respect for constituted authority of every kind is constantly growing less, a demonstration of obedience and affection such as this, is an object lesson to our fellow-citizens outside the fold, because it is given to a man whose only title to it comes from the position he holds by divine commission as the chief pastor of more than a million souls. And if in the few years I have spent among you I have contributed even a little to merit this demonstration then I fervently thank God today that he has moulded my thoughts, inspired my words and guided my footsteps for His own greater glory and the advancement of our Holy Faith.

The past twenty-five years have been uniformly happy for me, for they have

---

[15] Published in full in *New World*, June 11, 1920.

been filled with more blessings than are ordinarily given to even the favored among the children of God: but if this be so, the last four and a half years that were spent in your midst were literally crowded with many and splendid achievements for the promotion of God's honor and glory and the salvation of souls intrusted to our care. During a war that tore the world asunder, that roused racial and nationalistic hatreds and antipathies to a high pitch, here in this city, which was thought the danger spot of the country because of the multitude of elements that make up our population, we had the splendid spectacle of a united people, bound together by the noblest of all ties, the bond of our common faith and of love for one another, forming a cause of congratulation to our country and consolation and a credit to our Church. And during these troublous times the Lord has helped me ever to remember that while the people looked to me as their leader to guide them in their patriotic endeavors, yet many of them looked to me too as their father for sympathy, and today I feel that I have not failed them, and no word of mine added to the sorrow in their heart or to the burden they have had to bear. Perhaps what stands out most prominently in the diocese during the past few years is the fact that we have become more united, we are binding together our efforts, we have found our strength in union. In our organizations, in our schools, in our charities, we have striven for the unity the Lord had prayed for in His Church, ''that they may be one, as thou Father and I are one, that they may be one in us.'' And all this has helped to make the work of the Church more effective, to make our people prouder of its progress, and make our friends and neighbors better disposed towards the children of the Church. And for all of this there are no words that can tell the gratitude I feel to Almighty God on this day, for it has not been difficult to see with our own eyes the indwelling of the Divine Spirit in our midst and to see the evidences of His work on all sides. And I am equally grateful to the priests and religious of this diocese. I have never seen a more splendid loyalty, a more generous co-operation, a more unselfish obedience than they have shown in every work that was undertaken here. Whatever success has been attained is due entirely to them, after God's grace, for it would have been impossible without the one even as it would have been without the other.

DEVOTES GIFTS TO DIOCESAN USES ONLY

It is this same generous and loyal spirit that has actuated this wonderful testimonial on the part of the clergy, that has prompted them to dip into the meagre store of their savings and make their gift to their archbishop one unequalled and unforgettable both for its magnitude and its unselfishness. And it seems fitting that this, their gift, should be presented to me by the good bishop who has been such a loyal and affectionate helper to me and such an inspiring example and friendly counsellor to them. And this, your united gift, I receive deeply moved by a sense of gratitude for the devotion that prompted it and with an appreciation of the sacrifice your share thereof has meant for many of you. For that very reason, I shall keep none of it for myself or for any use of my own, but in its entirety I intend to devote it to the erection of the building in which the future priesthood of this diocese will be trained: so that should they themselves ever forget, the very stones of which it will be built will proclaim that loyal and generous spirit that bound together the present generation of our clergy.

Perhaps I have been even more deeply impressed by the continued, loyal, generous coöperation given me by the Catholic people of Chicago. Never in any spirit of criticism, rather in an unwavering attitude of filial obedience, responsive to every call they have merited the praise that nowhere have I met a people so Catholic, so practically Catholic as they. Their very position as to their parish schools, their readiness to support them, their reluctance to settle where there is none, demonstrates their appreciation of the value of religious education for their children. Their quick and almost lavish response to every appeal of their bishop and their pastor, whether for the Holy Father, for the sufferers abroad or the needy at home has proclaimed their broad charity as the inseparable companion of their deep faith. It is in entire conformity with their convictions and their uniform practice that they should signalize this jubilee day by the great gift they have presented to me today, and which will be devoted to the many corporal and spiritual works of mercy in their midst. But while we rejoice in the blessings of today we are mindful of our indebtedness to those who have gone.

The upbuilding of this great Church has been accomplished in an incredibly short time. Our diocese is only seventy-five years old, yet now we are one of the great churches of Christendom. Today there are more priests attached to this Cathedral Church than were then in all Chicago, there are more people in this one parish than were in the whole diocese when the first bishop came. Seventy-five years ago, why it is only yesterday; the venerable figure that presides at this ceremony had already taken his first steps towards the sanctuary, when Bishop Quarter undertook the long journey to his newly-made diocese, and there are those in the sanctuary today, there are some in the pews who looked on his face in life and in death. If so much has been accomplished in so short a time, who can tell what the future still has in store? And that is our hope and our consolation today, that while we are reaping in joy what others sowed in tears, others again will reap the fruits of our labors, that God has given us a mission such as has been given but to few people, that we are building the superstructure, where others have laid the foundations, for the golden age of the Church in America. And if sometimes I have seemed too exacting, too feverish in my anxiety to prosecute the work that lies before us, have patience with me, it is because there is so much to be done, so much more we might do were it not that we must wait for those who lag and tarry by the way, because at the best the twilight comes early when we must cease from labor. We celebrate today our diamond jubilee. In the beautiful hymn of today's Mass I was reminded of another jubilee that lies just ahead of all of us.

> Thou who feedest us below
> Source of all we have or know,
> Sitting at the feast of love
> We may see Thee face to face.

ENCHANTING MUSIC

The music rendered on this occasion by the combined choirs of priests, students and distinguished vocalists deserves special mention. A great organist hailing originally from Rome, Pietro A. Yon, com-

posed the Mass sung and participated personally in the service. The program included the following:

Prelude, Allegro Concerto Gregorian, Yon—Organ and orchestra; soloist, Pietro A. Yon.

Processional, Ecce Sacerdos Magnus, Yon—Grand Chorus (four male voices) priests and cathedral choir.

Proper of the Mass—Gregorian—Surpliced choir, sanctuary organ accompanist, Mr. L. Daly.

Missa Regina Pacis—(four-voice choir), with complete orchestra, organ and soloists, under the direction of the composer, P. A. Yon. Soloists—Mr. Vittorio Arimondi, basso; Mr. William R. Rogerson, tenor; Mr. Edouard V. Dufresne, barytone; at the organ, Rev. J. E. Bourget, D. M. D.

Offertory—O Sacrum Convivium. A capella—L. Viadana; grand chorus of priests, Cathedral choir and St. George choir of the Quigley Preparatory Seminary.

Postlude—Second part—Concerto Gregorian, Yon—Adagio and finale, for organ and orchestra. Soloist, Pietro A. Yon.

Recessional—Jubiliate Deo, op. 27—Carl Thiel. Four voices, organ and orchestra.

LUNCHEON

Following the service at Holy Name Cathedral the visiting prelates and clergy were entertained at luncheon served in the refectory of the Quigley Preparatory Seminary on Rush street.

The possibilities of the beautiful new building were demonstrated even beyond the hopes of the most sanguine of committees. The spacious corridors, assembly hall, class rooms, gymnasium and swimming tank were all day thronged with the hundreds of distinguished guests who were eloquent in their praise first of the architectual beauty, then of the practical arrangements which are the last word in educational service.

More than a thousand churchmen gathered at the luncheon.

The toastmaster was the Rt. Rev. Msgr. D. J. Riordan. Those who spoke were: His Eminence, Cardinal Gibbons; the Most Rev. Austin J. Dowling, D. D.; His Excellency, the Apostolic Delegate, the Rt. Rev. Msgr. P. J. McDonnell, and the most reverend jubilarian.

THE PAPAL LEGATE'S ADDRESS

The guests at the dinner had the great privilege of hearing a charming address by Most Rev. John Bonzano, Papal Delegate, which was so interesting as to require reproduction in permanent form:

It affords me genuine pleasure to meet so many members of the American hierarchy and clergy who have come here to honor the Archdiocese of Chicago and its chief pastor. If in every gathering of this kind it is befitting to speak

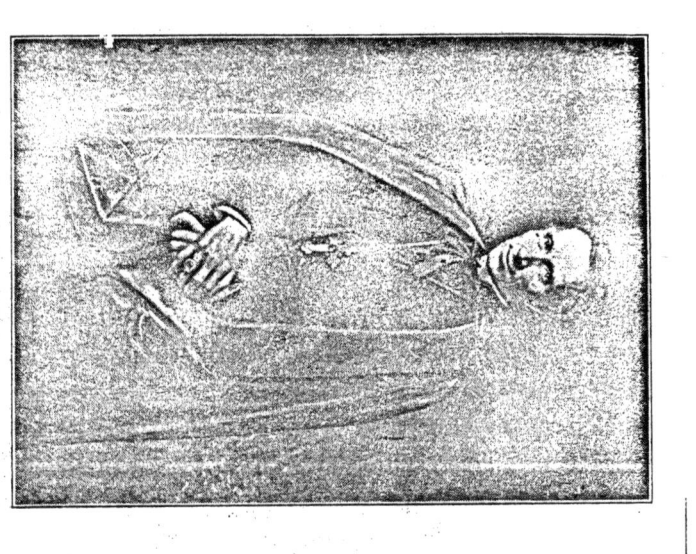

His Eminence, James Cardinal Gibbons, Baltimore, Md.

His Excellency, John Bonzano, Papal Delegate,
Washington, D. C.
Cuts by courtesy *New World*.

MOST REV. JOHN J. GLENNON, D. D., Archbishop of
St. Louis
Cuts by courtesy *New World*

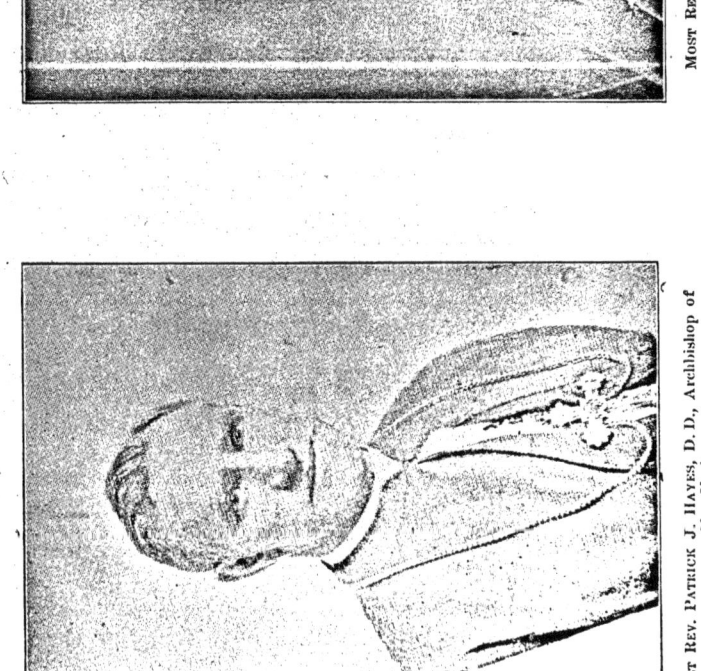

MOST REV. PATRICK J. HAYES, D. D., Archbishop of
New York

Most Rev. Henry Moeller, D. D., Archbishop of Cincinnati
Cuts by courtesy *New World*.

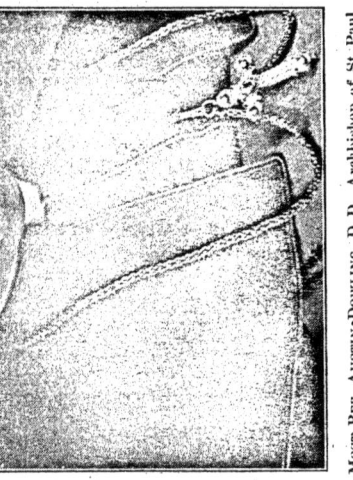

MOST REV. AUSTIN-DOWLING, D. D., Archbishop of St. Paul

Cuts by courtesy *New World.*

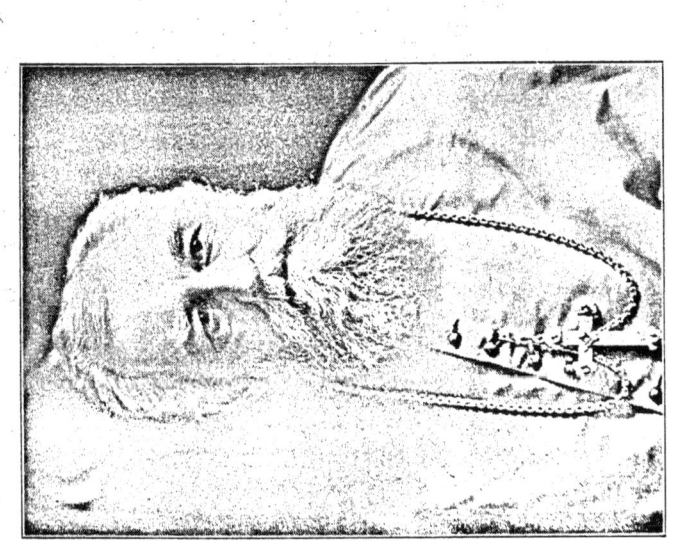

MOST REV. SEBASTIAN G. MESSMER, D. D., Archbishop of Milwaukee

of the Sovereign Pontiff, the present occasion surely invites us in a special manner to pay him the tribute of our loyalty and devotion.

It was my privilege last summer to visit the Holy Father, and I noted with heartfelt joy that in the midst of the agitation which is convulsing the world, he was calmly yet actively working in behalf of humanity, and especially in behalf of the millions who are suffering from the effects of the war.

Now that the great conflict is ended, and the passion of strife is subsiding, the people are coming to realize how much they owe to Benedict XV. They are awakening, as it were, from what was worse than a dreadful nightmare, and as they see more clearly the meaning of what has happened, they turn to the Universal Father for comfort and relief.

As I ascended the steps that lead to the halls of the Vatican, I seemed to hear the voices of the multitudes all over the world crying out in their distress. With their words of thankful appreciation, they mingled their prayers for help, for release from the burden of sorrow, for guidance toward peace. Like the trembling disciples on the storm-tossed sea, they cry out in any agony of fear—''Lord, save us, we perish.''

And not the multitudes only are looking to the Pope for assistance; the rulers of the earth are beginning to see that without his aid they are powerless in face of the present situation. They are at last giving heed to the call of the Psalmist: ''Et nunc, reges, intelligite; erudimini, qui judicatis terram.''

The heads of the new nations—those which have come into existence through the great upheaval—are seeking to establish relations with the Holy See. For even at the birth of their national organization they are wise enough to understand that they need the influence of the Holy Father, if they are to live and prosper.

But the older nations also are coming to see the light; they have learned through the bitter experience of war what they had forgotten in the pleasant days of peace. They acknowledge that there can be no thorough restoration of order and no permanent security of peace except through the coöperation of him who represents on earth the prince of peace.

And so it appears more plainly, day by day, that God, Who in the ways of His providence orders all things both in heaven and on earth, has been pleased to raise up our Holy Father, Pope Benedict XV, at this time, when the Church and all mankind have the greatest need of his wisdom. For he alone, surveying the world from his exalted position, has pointed the way in which the nations should walk, the way of justice and charity, marked out in the Gospel and sanctified by the footsteps of Christ our Savior.

Deeply concerned as he is for the welfare of Europe, the Holy Father looks beyond its confines, and beyond the ocean, to the Church of America. As you already know, he has declared that this country is to have a leading part in the reconstruction of the world. He earnestly hopes that the faithful in the United States, and especially the bishops and priests, will give him their hearty coöperation.

He has noted with gratification the progress of the Church and the expansion of its field in a hundred dioceses, and now that the importance of America in the temporal order is universally recognized, the Holy Father feels that in the cause of religion and charity, the Catholics of America will take the foremost place.

In the celebration of these days we have a further proof of the Pontiff's

good will. You have heard the words of congratulation which he was pleased to send His Grace, the Archbishop, the clergy and people of Chicago on this auspicious occasion. They express the paternal interest of the Sovereign Pontiff in the great archdiocese which is celebrating its diamond jubilee, and his affectionate regard for the distinguished prelate who within twenty-five years has so worthily borne the priestly, the episcopal and the archiepiscopal dignity.

I congratulate the diocese on the splendid progress which has marked these seventy-five years, on the zeal of the clergy and the generosity of its people. Chicago has shown its greatness not only in the increase of population and the growth of its material prosperity, but also in the development of its intellectual and spiritual life. And the Church of Chicago while building up its own institutions for the advancement of religion, has given proof of its Catholic spirit by providing for the needs of religion in many other sections of the country. You therefore have reason to be proud of your record, and I am glad to assure you that the Holy Father rejoices most heartily in your efforts and achievements.

And now, Your Grace, let me offer you my heartfelt congratulations and good wishes on this day of your priestly jubilee. With you I give thanks to Almighty God for the singular favors with which He has blessed you during these twenty-five years. He has made your labors fruitful both for His glory and for your comfort, so that as greater undertakings are now before you, you may feel assured, as I do, that the blessings of heaven will descend upon you more abundantly, and give you the joy of seeing an even more rapid development of the church over which you are placed.[16]

Rt. Rev. Msgr. P. J. McDonnell addressed the guests on "The Catholic Church in Chicago."[17]

III.

DEDICATION OF THE QUIGLEY MEMORIAL SEMINARY

One of the great features of the second day of the jubilee celebration was the dedication of the Quigley Preparatory Seminary. This interesting ceremony brought a notable gathering to St. James' Chapel where Solemn Pontifical Mass was celebrated and an eloquent sermon was preached by Most Rev. John J. Glennon, Archbishop of St. Louis. This ceremony was also attended by Cardinal Gibbons and the apostolic delegate, Very Rev. John Bonzano.

There are but few, if any, pulpit orators in America that excel the archbishop of St. Louis, and his sermons and addresses are always noted not only for brilliancy but as well for soundness. All of Arch-

---

[16] The Papal Delegate's address was published in the *New World*, June 11, 1920.

[17] Msgr. McDonnell's address was published in full in the *New World*, June 18, 1920.

Quigley Preparatory Seminary.

Gustavus Doane, Architect

Rt. Reverend Quigley, D.D.
President

at the erection Z. Davis, Architect

Quigley Preparatory Seminary.

Most Reverend George C. Mundelein, D.D.
Archbishop

Zachary G. Davis, Architect.

QUIGLEY PREPARATORY SEMINARY
DEDICATED JUNE 9, 1920

Cut by courtesy Z. Davis, Architect.

bishop Glennon's address was able and eloquently delivered but the historical part is of greatest interest here.

ARCHBISHOP GLENNON'S ADDRESS

He said, therefore, to what is the Kingdom of God like, and whereunto shall I resemble it? It is like unto a grain of mustard seed, which a man took and cast into his garden, and it grew and became a great tree and the birds of the air lodged in the branches thereof.

I am privileged to speak to you of the seventy-five years that have elapsed since the coming to Chicago of its first bishop; and as the one so privileged hails from the city of the Crusader King, St. Louis, an opportunity is given me to first of all extend the greetings of a mother to her daughter, to bring good wishes from the cradle to the throne. The mother's heart beats with pride, beams with love on her northern daughter, who has, under God's benediction, grown so great and so fair. Other cities there may be who cast a critical and envious eye because of what has been done, and will be done in Chicago. St. Louis, however, can watch with pride and affection every onward step—every added grace, of her spiritual daughter.

Of course there may be those who will set limitations to these claims of ours. A city that has grown so great and fair is naturally disposed to claim a prouder origin and a nobler lineage. They may seek, for instance, to recall the far-off days, the year 1674, the days when from out the northern mists, from the forests primeval of Canada there came to the shores of the lake the great missionary Marquette, who set up the standard of the cross by the banks of the Illinois, and preached to the tribes who dwelt there. They would tell of the cabin he built somewhere around; and how he and his missionaries, shod with the gospel of peace, wandered by the lake-side and through the swamp lands, the pioneers of Christ in all this western land.

A BRIEF HISTORY

From these early visitations a broken history may be constructed.

I should not be the one to disparage the efforts of these saintly pioneers. On the contrary to them should be given the fullest measure of acclaim—more than that, we may confidently assert that whatever be the greatness of the yesterdays and today of the Church of America—however heroic the faith and generous the sacrifices of our millions of today, yet for the splendid daring, great sacrifices, sufferings and achievements, these missionaries of the days of old outrank them all. Marquette, La Salle, Joliet, Allouez and the rest will stand for all time as the heads of the heroic band, who braving storm and stress, forest gnomes and savage men, sought to plant by the brimming river and along the wide sweep of the savannahs the cross of the Savior and bring to the savages who dwelt there the gospel of Christ.

But for Chicago theirs was only the acquaintance that the missionary makes in passing. Father Marquette built a cabin here; but did not himself remain. After him, Father St. Cosme and Gravier and other Jesuits came; but only to visit these then unhospitable shores. Later on, in the first quarter of the last century, we hear of Father Richard and Father Badin, who came to celebrate Mass and preach the Gospel, attracted, perhaps, by the presence of the few Catholics who dwelt around Fort Dearborn, which was erected here in 1804.

ESTABLISHMENT OF THE CHURCH

The year 1833 (eighty-seven years ago) marks the formal establishment of the Church in Chicago; for in that year there came in response to the petition made to Bishop Rosati of St. Louis from the Catholics scattered in these parts, Father St. Cyr, to be its first accredited pastor. He it was, who, under God's benediction, planted the seed spoken of in my text—the mustard seed, which was destined to grow in a few short years to a mighty tree. The land appeared unhospitable—naught but a marsh, swept by the swish of the waters and the winds of the lake; yet under the kindly providence of God, as grew the city, so grew the Church, until today in its hospitable shade the wanderers from many lands find protection and support.

OUR FIRST PASTOR

Father St. Cyr was a son of France, born during its Revolution; but fashioned and trained in the years of its religious reawakening; and had come, as so many of his compatriots, to the far west country. After two years of special preparation, he was ordained a priest in 1833 by Bishop Rosati and commissioned by him to go northward to the village known as Chicago to plant there the cross and gather around it the scattered inhabitants. The good Bishop also advised Father St. Cyr that if Chicago should be deflected from the Diocese of St. Louis, then he, Father St. Cyr, was to return home. Father St. Cyr reached the city in the Maytime of '33, celebrated Mass and prepared at once to build a church, acquiring property therefor on the corner of Lake and State streets. Here he erected a frame structure and dedicated it in October of that year. His congregation consisted of French and American traders, people from the Fort and three or four hundred Indians who dwelt around.

After a two year stay Father Cyr returned to St. Louis. Henceforth, however, there was to be a regular succession of pastors—Father O'Meara, and then Father St. Palais and the rest, to continue the formal life of the Church of Chicago.

Father St. Cyr returning to St. Louis received many important charges; and was given many years to labor as a devoted pastor and chaplain in that Diocese; yet his brightest memory and greatest achievement was that he was the prophet and founder of the Church of Chicago. In a reply to a letter which he received in the eighties making inquiry about the early Church of Chicago, he writes: "I was ordained priest the sixth of April, 1833, by Bishop Rosati, and twelve days afterwards was sent to Chicago by the same bishop, at which place I arrived May first." Note now the evident appreciation of his labors. He adds: "I had no predecessor; and I don't think much about my successor."

LATER HISTORY

The Church of Chicago prospered. Soon we hear of the "City" of Chicago; then in 1844, the "Diocese" of Chicago; and the coming as first Bishop of the Right Reverend Bishop Quarter, who, evidently inspired with its future greatness, both religious and commercial, established a university here, calling it "St. Mary of the Lake." He invited the Sisters of Mercy also to establish their schools and hospitals. However, after four short episcopal years, Bishop Quarter was called home by the Good Shepherd.

Cut by courtesy *Le Petit Séminaire*.

REV. FRANCIS A. PURCELL, D. D.,
Rector Quigley Preparatory Seminary

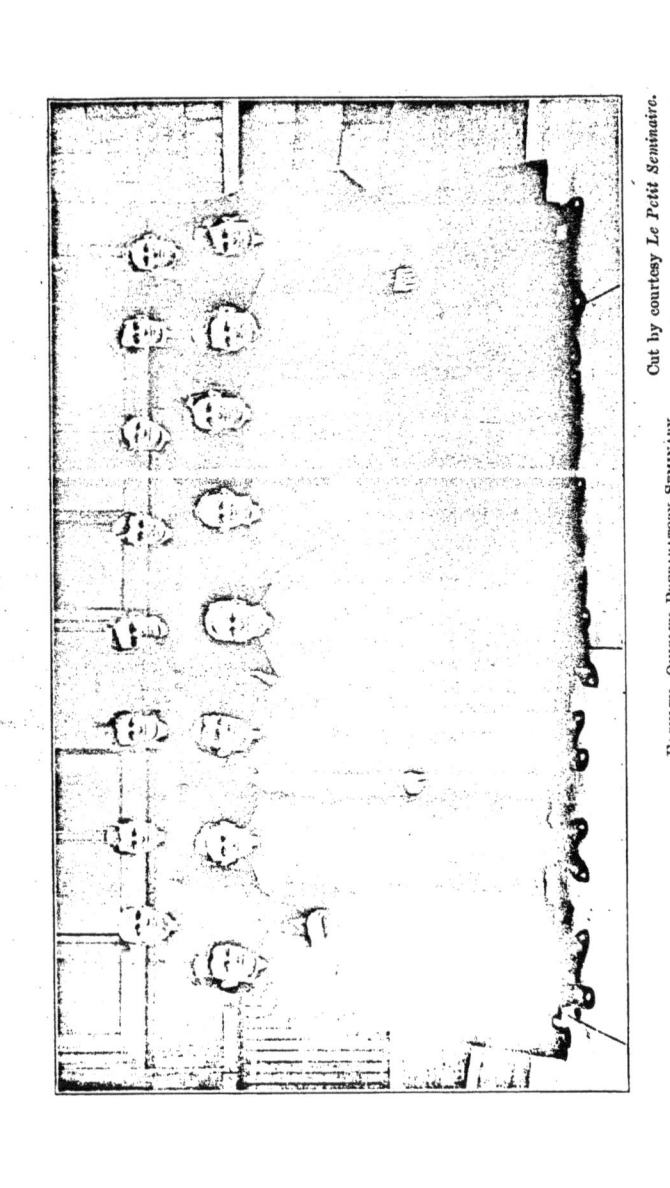

FACULTY, QUIGLEY PREPARATORY SEMINARY   Cut by courtesy *Le Petit Seminaire.*

Now from St. Louis comes the Jesuit, Father Van de Velde, as the second Bishop, soon to be succeeded by Bishop O'Regan; and he in turn by Bishop Duggan. These latter, like their predecessor, being from the city of the King.

Again, we turn to the east, and Chicago receives from Baltimore its courtly and gracious Bishop Thomas Foley, who, however, was soon to bend beneath his burden; for the burden of Chicago was becoming more grievous every day; and but too early he was called to his reward, resigning the see into the hands of the Right Reverend Patrick A. Feehan.

TWO PREDECESSORS

It was during Bishop Feehan's career that Chicago assumed in every sense its metropolitan proportions. By leaps and bounds the city grew. A world's congress is held to mark the quadricentennial of America's discovery; and the eyes of the world are turned towards the giant of the west. The Diocese with Illinois is now separated from the Province of St. Louis, and becomes metropolitan in fact as well as in name; and proudly and triumphantly Chicago stands today as in all its ways metropolitan—even cosmopolitan in its aspirations.

Archbishop Feehan! At that name we pause to recall today in grateful affection and appreciation that courage and sweetness, that stalwart faith and gracious courtliness, that native dignity and nobility, which made him prince and leader in the Church of God.

And now, again, from the east comes Archbishop Quigley, strong and calm and resolute, whose life and labors are still before us, and whose name is held in grateful benediction. We thought he was only resting in the midday of his labors, when the Master called him to his rest.

Of the successor of Archbishop Quigley, our present illustrious Archbishop, it is needless for me to speak today. His praises were spoken in grand acclaim by the many voices of yesterday, and perhaps more eloquently by the multitude of his achievements, and the even more splendid purposes which await a speedy accomplishment. We can readily yield to the record of the few years he has been in your midst to speak for him; and for immediate evidence we need not go beyond the buildings where we are assembled, which in all their refinement of art, nobility of purpose, gracefulness of outline, appear at once to symbolize and express the soul of the builder.

Chicago of seventy-five years ago, a straggling and struggling village, its one church and its two priests and twenty others scattered through the vast territory of the Illinois; and now after these years the great metropolis, moving onward with its millions to reach a topmost place among the first cities of the world— a city so great that its history cannot be written; for they who write it are too busy in making it. Difficult it is, if not impossible, to set down the record of a city moving so fast that each day has its own revelation. And for its Catholic life, who will tell the story of its varied deeds of charity and religion—its schools and scholars—its churches and congregations. In fact its commercial activities which have made the city famous are out-rivaled and surpassed by its spiritual energies. Look where you may over the vast territory where stands the city, and you will find outlined against its horizon the spires and domes that mark its churches, the towers and halls of its schools and colleges, and the many institutions that exemplify its thousand fold mercies and pities. Well, indeed, may be

applied to the prelates, priests and faithful of Chicago the claim made long ago
by the pagan poet:
"Quae regio in urbe nostri non plena laboris."[16]

The Quigley Memorial Seminary is noted as one of the handsomest buildings in Chicago and is the tribute which the Archbishop and his people have paid to the memory of the late archbishop. It is amongst the best equipped educational institutions in America and is officered by an eminent faculty of which Rev. Francis A. Purcell, D. D., is Rector.

IV.

THE SACRED CONCERT

On Wednesday evening the great musical festival occurred. This took the form of a sacred concert in the Cathedral.

The Church was filled to over-flowing long before the hour for the beginning of the concert and the highest expectations of the best musical critics were realized. The musical program was as follows:

SACRED CONCERT PROGRAM

Chorus—Entree—Jubilate Deo—Carl Thiel.
Organ—Sonata Cromatica—A. B. C.—Yon.
Ave Maria—Bossi.
Prelude et Fuga—J. S. Bach.
Soloist—Pietro A. Yon.
Tenor solo—Cujus Animan—Rossini. Mr. William H. Rogerson. Chorus—
De Profundus—Falso Bordono. Sung in memory of deceased Catholics of the Archdiocese of Chicago.
Gesu Bambino, Yon—Solo and chorus. (By request Mr. Yon played his beautiful improvisation of this greatly admired Christmas anthem).
Bass solo, Pater Noster—Vittorio Arimondi.
Organ solo—Fantasie sur des airs de Noel, Father De la Tombelle Echo, Yon. Christus Resurrexit, O Ravanello. Soloist—Pietro A. Yon.
Solemn Benediction of the Most Blessed Sacrament—Chorus, O Sacrum Convivium—A capella—L. Viadana. Tantum Ergo—Theodore DuBois. Solo and chorus.
Barytone solo—Edward Dufresne.
After Benediction the American Rhapsodie by P. A. You was played in memory of deceased soldiers and sailors of the Great War.

This grand sacred concert and organ recital took place under the leadership of the Reverend Fathers J. E. Bourget, D. M. D., and P.

---

[16] Archbishop Glennon's address was published in full in *New World*, June 18, 1920.

Mahoney, D. D., assisted by the world famous organist, Pietro A. Yon of New York. Mr. Vitorio Arimondi, basso; Mr. William R. Rogerson, tenor, of the Chicago Grand Opera Company; Mr. A. Edouard and H. Dufresne, tenor and barytone; priest choir of the Archdiocese of Chicago, Cathedral choir, St. George Choral Society of the Quigley Preparatory Seminary, and Holy Name school soprano boys' choir, under the direction of Professor A. Huguelet, second organist of the Cathedral.

V.

THE PAGEANT OF CHRISTIAN HISTORY

The daily press of Chicago wrote the history of the pageant of Christianity, staged on Thursday, June 10th, the third day of the jubilee celebration, in glowing words. One of these accounts was as follows:

For more than three hours yesterday the children of Chicago's parochial schools—thousands upon thousands of them—passed in review before Cardinal Gibbons along Lake Shore drive in a mighty, moving procession unequaled in the city's history of religious pageantry.

It is estimated that one hundred thousand persons lined the boulevard as the colorful and impressive procession depicting the rise and progress of Christianity, moved from the Municipal pier, passed the reviewing stand where stood the highest prelates of the Roman Catholic church in America, and marched on to Lincoln Park where it disbanded.

The pageant climaxed the three days' celebration of the diamond jubilee of the archdiocese of Chicago and the twenty-fifth of the priesthood of the Most Rev. George W. Mundelein, archbishop of Chicago.

Interspersed between the snow white ranks of marching boys and girls were one hundred and forty-seven elaborate floats representing the various incidents in the march of the Christian religion from the "Presentation of Mary in the Temple" to "1920 and the Diamond Jubilee."

The spectacle of the thousands of white clad children massed in preparation for the parade near the Municipal pier at eleven o'clock moved Col. Marcus Kavanaugh, the grand marshal and veteran of parades, to awe. "Never have I seen anything like this in my life," he exclaimed. "There must be fifty thousand children in line. It is the greatest event ever staged by the Church in Chicago."

Cardinal Gibbons, inured to the splendor of religious ceremonials, turned to Archbishop Mundelein as the rows of jubilant children passed and exclaimed: "It is truly magnificent! You are to be congratulated, as are all these splendid children for an achievement such as I rarely have had the privilege to witness."

And the rows of hot, perspiring girls and boys bore triumphant expressions as they trudged along in the burning sunlight. They seemed to be crusaders

marching determinedly but happily on their quest. As the pupils of St. Ignatius
school passed by the procession halted while a little girl, Dorothy Clark, leaped
lightly from a pony cart, climbed to the reviewing stand, and with a demure
little speech presented Cardinal Gibbons with a book, the gift of her schoolmates.
With Cardinal Gibbons in the stand was the Most Rev. John Bonzano,
apostolic delegate to America. At the right hand of Archbishop Mundelein sat
Eamonn de Valera, president of the "Irish Republic." Next to the standard
bearers, one holding aloft the flag, the other the crucifix, stood Bishops P. J.
Muldoon of Rockford and E. M. Dunne of Peoria.

Colonel John V. Clinnin was Colonel Kavanaugh's chief of staff. His aids
were Colonel James Ronayne, Major Edward H. White, Lieutenant Roger
Faherty, John C. Cannon, General James A. Ryan, Colonel John J. Garrity,
Colonel Daniel Moriarity, Major Frank T. Quilty, Major William J. Swift,
Captain John J. O'Hern, Captain Thomas Octigan, Captain William H. Sexton
and Captain John A. Hartman, Captain Walter J. Sullivan, Captain Cyril Larkin,
Captain John K. Murphy, Senator Francis Brady, Lieutenant William Corboy,
Lieutenant Maurice F. Dermel, Lieutenant Callistus J. Ennis, Frank Gorman,
Frank Igoe, Edward H. Kirchberg, William H. Lyman, Jr., John Farren
MacMahon, John J. McKenna, John O'Connell, Augustine O'Connor, Harry J.
Powers, Jr., John Pierre Roche, John A. Power, Jr., Harry M. Zimmer.

Each school's float depicted some incident in the life of its patron saint.
There was Ste. Anne Teaching the Blessed Mother; Christ Blessing Little
Children; The First Easter Morn; Trial Scenes of Ste. Agnes; St. George and
Companions; St. Ambrose and the Emperor Theodosius; Pope Celestine Com-
missioning St. Patrick; The Holy Grail; Brian Boru at Clontarf; Ste. Margaret,
Queen of Scotland; Joan of Arc's Triumphant Entry into Orleans; First Mass in
English America; Marquette on the Chicago River; and scores of others.

Among the larger schools represented in the parade were St. Martin, Ste.
Agatha, St. Mel, St. John the Baptist, Providence Academy, Presentation,
Annunciation, St. Philip High, St. Jerome, St. Finbar, St. Patrick, St. Ignatius,
Ste. Ita, St. Helen, St. Bride and St. Thomas Aquinas.[18]

Another Chicago publication commenting editorially on the
pageant said:

Whether or not it was the purpose of the great parochial school pageant displayed on the boulevard on June 10th last to visualize the importance of the
Catholic schools, that great display certainly suited well that purpose. From each
of one hundred and eighty-tree schools in Chicago came a few of the pupils of
the higher grammar grades, totaling in the aggregate at least thirty thousand.
The marchers were selected with closest attention to their qualifications to with-
stand the rigors of the trip, younger children and the less rugged being omitted.
Each of one hundred and forty-seven of the schools was also represented by one
or more floats, chariots or decorated vehicles, all of which were of artistic construction and amongst which were a large number more beautiful and meritorious
than anything of the nature ever before seen on the streets of Chicago.

In this splendid parade there was nothing crude, garish or in the slightest

Photo by E. Williams

ASSEMBLING AT MUNICIPAL PIER FOR PAGEANT.

ST. MARY'S HIGH SCHOOL FLOAT, AWARDED SECOND PRIZE

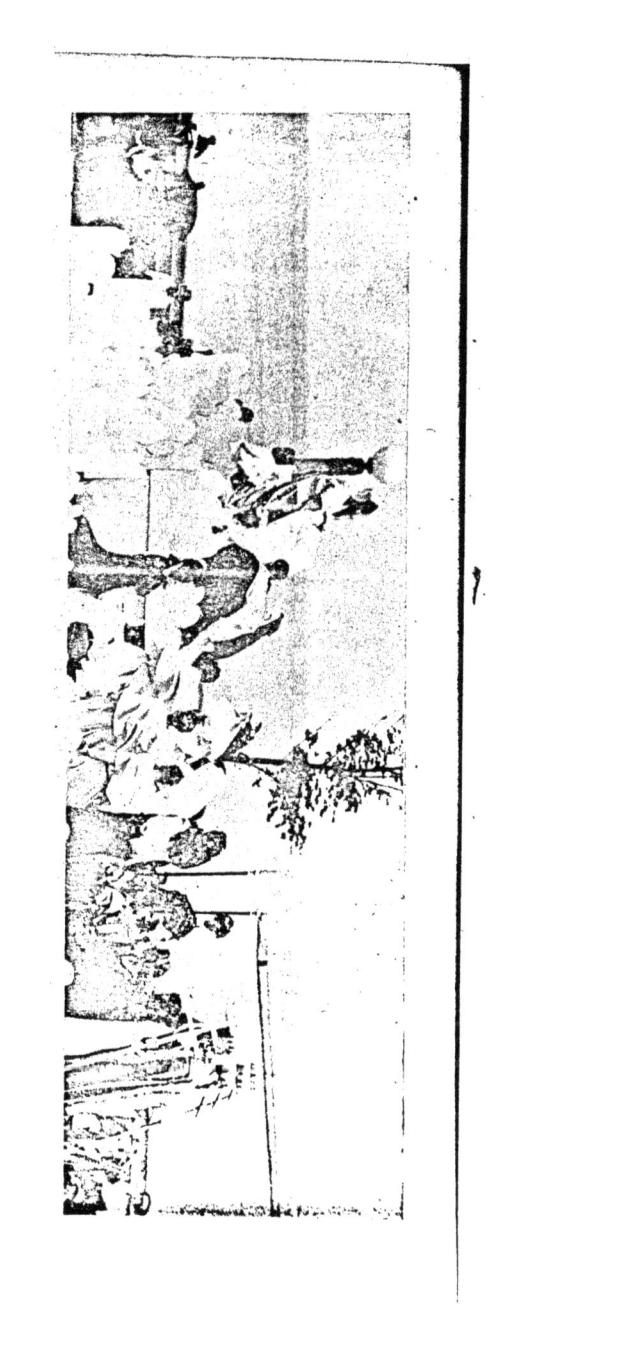

manner offensive to taste, sentiment or conviction, nor was there any of the silly, far-fetched allegory so frequently seen in nondescript pageantry. For the purpose no fiction or alleogry was necessary—the facts sought to be visualized were more enchanting, more beautiful and more romantic, if you please, than the broadest imagination could conceive.

The parochial school pageant was particularly notable in that it not only had the body or outer form of rare beauty but also had within it a radiant soul. From His Grace, the Archbishop, who conceived the pageant, to the men and women who perfected the plans and from them to the children who actually participated and indeed even to the designers of the costumes and the builders of the floats, came an inspiration that throbbed in every moment of the magnificent panorama. The boys who represented St. Ignatius as a courtier and warrior, were for the time such; the beautiful girls who paid court to the Queen of Heaven were truly in that attitude of mind. Without the slightest suggestion of impropriety every instrumentality of the great pageant fitted properly into its place.

No doubt long years will pass ere Chicago will witness such another demonstration, but should there never be a similar demonstration, the pageant of June 10, 1920, in honor of the seventy-fifth anniversary of the establishment of the Chicago diocese and of the twenty-fifth anniversary of the ordination of Archbishop George William Mundelein and as a representation of the parochial schools of Chicago, will live long in memory.[20]

THE PAGEANT MAKERS

First honors for the tremendous success of the great pageant are due to the patient ever-toiling sisters, who if they did not in all cases conceive the plans and designs, were wholly in some cases, and very largely in all cases, responsible for their success, and the purity of conception and beauty of execution were but reflections of the loftiness of their ideas and ideals.

The pastors and their able assistants come in for a large share of credit in connection with the conception and execution of the splendid plans, and finally the pageant committee with Right Reverend Msgr. Francis A. Rempe, D. P., as chairman, and Rev. Jos. A. Casey, Rt. Rev. F. C. Kelley, P. A., D. D., Rt. Rev. S. Nawrocki, D. P., Rev. John B. Furay, S. J., Rev. Francis Gordon, C. R., Rev. A. A. Quigley, O. S. M., Rev. H. P. Coughlin, Rev. J. J. Leddy, Rev. John McCarthy, Rev. T. Magnien, O. F. M., as associates, merited high praise.

It goes without saying of course, that the sturdy marchers, the ideally beautiful girls and the rugged wholesome boys who gave color, life and spirit to the scene, were the very heart of the pageant.

---

[20] *Columbian and Western Catholic,* June 18, 1920.

Several bands enlivened the pageant with martial and other suitable music.

All these have rendered a service to the Catholics of Chicago, and indeed to the people in general, which deserves to be long remembered.

THE PRIZE WINNERS

The three exhibits finally settled upon as entitled to preference were, in order those of St. Thomas the Apostle School; St. Mary's High School and Holy Name Cathedral School.

The great St. Dominic (with attendants) who, in the thirteenth century, won back the people of southern France to the Church, spread the devotion of the Rosary and founded the Order of Preachers was portrayed in the float presented by St. Thomas the Apostle School.

St. Mary's High School portrayed "Our Lady of Lourdes; Learning, Art, Science, Literature."

The exhibit of the Holy Name Cathedral School represented the Silver Jubilee of the Archbishop.

St. Thomas the Apostle's exhibit was number 50 in the processional order, St. Mary's High School was number 137, the Holy Name Cathedral School, number 112.

The prizes awarded were as follows: St. Thomas Apostle School, a trip to Europe for two sisters; St. Mary's high school, a trip to St. Anne de Beaupre; Holy Name Cathedral School, a trip to St. Anne de Beaupre.

Honorable mention was also given in order to the exhibits of St. Ignatius School, Extension Society, St. Jarlath's, SS. Cyril and Methodius, St. Stanislaus, Holy Innocents, Holy Trinity, St. Anselm, St. Mary's Training School, Our Lady of Pompeii, Slovaks and the Queen of the Holy Rosary, Holy Angels, Holy Family, St. Martin's, De La Salle Schools, St. Matthias, Our Lady of Mercy and Mt. Carmel Schools.

THE PROCESSIONAL ORDER OF THE FLOATS

The complete list of floats in processional order follows:

1. Presentation of Mary in the Temple.................Presentation School
2. Saint Anne Teaching the Blessed Mother............Providence Academy
3. The Annunciation ....Annunciation School
4. The Angels of the Nativity..........................Nativity School
5. St. John the Baptist.........................St. John Baptist School

Several bands enlivened the pageant with martial and other suitable music.

All these have rendered a service to the Catholics of Chicago, and indeed to the people in general, which deserves to be long remembered.

THE PRIZE WINNERS

The three exhibits finally settled upon as entitled to preference were, in order those of St. Thomas the Apostle School; St. Mary's High School and Holy Name Cathedral School.

The great St. Dominic (with attendants) who, in the thirteenth century, won back the people of southern France to the Church, spread the devotion of the Rosary and founded the Order of Preachers was portrayed in the float presented by St. Thomas the Apostle School.

St. Mary's High School portrayed "Our Lady of Lourdes; Learning, Art, Science, Literature."

The exhibit of the Holy Name Cathedral School represented the Silver Jubilee of the Archbishop.

St. Thomas the Apostle's exhibit was number 50 in the processional order, St. Mary's High School was number 137, the Holy Name Cathedral School, number 112.

The prizes awarded were as follows: St. Thomas Apostle School, a trip to Europe for two sisters; St. Mary's high school, a trip to St. Anne de Beaupre; Holy Name Cathedral School, a trip to St. Anne de Beaupre.

Honorable mention was also given in order to the exhibits of St. Ignatius School, Extension Society, St. Jarlath's, SS. Cyril and Methodius, St. Stanislaus, Holy Innocents, Holy Trinity, St. Anselm, St. Mary's Training School, Our Lady of Pompeii, Slovaks and the Queen of the Holy Rosary, Holy Angels, Holy Family, St. Martin's, De La Salle Schools, St. Matthias, Our Lady of Mercy and Mt. Carmel Schools.

THE PROCESSIONAL ORDER OF THE FLOATS

The complete list of floats in processional order follows:

1. Presentation of Mary in the Temple.................*Presentation School*
2. Saint Anne Teaching the Blessed Mother...........*Providence Academy*
3. The Annunciation ....*Annunciation School*
4. The Angels of the Nativity.........................*Nativity School*
5. St. John the Baptist........................*St. John Baptist School*

52. Troubadours at the Court of Frederick II.....*Our Lady of Victory School*
53. St. Louis Enters Paris With Crown of Thorns.*St. Clara and St. Cyril School*
54· The Golden Stairs, Dante and Beatrice.....................*St. Lucy School*
55. St. Catherine of Sienna............................*St. Catherine School*
56. Cathedral Age............................*Our Lady of Sorrows School*
57. St. Elizabeth with Roses............................*St. Elizabeth School*
58. Joan of Arc's Triumphant Entry into Orleans.........*St. Edmund School*
59. Joan of Arc at the Coronation of Charles VII..*St. Thomas Aquinas School*
60. Philip the Good, Order of the Golden Fleece.....*St. John Berchman School*
61. The Guilds...*Holy Angels School*
62. St. Casimir; The Spirit of Lithuania; Lithuanian Living Flag;
    First Baptism in the iLthuanian Nation; Silver Cross;
    Girls in National Costume........................*Lithuanian Schools*
63. St. Ignatius and Courtiers............................*St. Ignatius School*
64. St. Francis Xavier Preaching to the Heathen..........*St. Barbara School*
65. St. Stanislaus Kostka.......................................*Polish Schools*
66. The Battle of Lepanto....................*Holy Rosary School* (Pullman)
67. St. Vincent de Paul................................*St. Vincent Schools*
68. John Sobieski and Suite............................*Holy Innocent School*
    John Sobieski and His Victory Over the Turks........*Holy Trinity School*
69. Mary, Queen of Scots.................*St. Thomas of Canterbury School*
70. De La Salle Teaching the Nations..............*Christian Brothers' School*
71. The American Indian.............................*St. Veronica School*
72. Columbus Pleading with Isabella for Aid..............*St. Anselm Schools*
73. Columbus Planting the Cross of Castile in America..*Precious Blood School*
74. Columbus at the Court of Ferdinand and Isabella....*St. Alphonsus School*
75. First Mass in the New World..........................*St. Rita School*
76· First Mass in English America............*St. Mary School* (Lake Forest)
77. Discoveries ....*Our Lady of Lourdes School*
78. First Mass at Ville Marie, Montreal....................*St. Joseph School*
79. Ven. Marguerite Bourgeoys...........................*Notre Dame School*
80. Acadians—Evangeline ....*St. Bernard School*
81. Penn's Treaty with the Indians..................*St. Clare of Montefalco*
82. Charles Carroll Signing the Declaration
    of Independence ....*St. Viator School*
83. George Washington and Allies..............*St. Charles Borromeo School*
84. Franciscans in California............................*St. Augustine School*
85. Las Casas and the Indian Missions;
    Liberty, Justice, Mercy....................*Our Lady of Grace School*
86. Bishop Baraga at Marquette·.........................*St. Stephen School*
87. Lincoln and Emancipation·......................*St. Michael School*
88. Marquette on Chicago River·.............................*St. Anne School*
89. Father Pinet and Guardian Angel Mission.
    Immigrants from Trier to New Trier........*St. Joseph School* (Wilmette)
90. Fort Dearborn ....*All Saints School*
91. Bishop Quarter ....*Bishop Quarter School*
92. University of St. Mary of the Lake ....*St. Mary of the Lake*
93. Pioneer Sisters of Mercy..............................*St. Joachim School*
94. Chicago World's Fair..................................*St. Cecelia School*

NOTABLE JUBILEE VISITORS

From Florida to Alaska, and from California to Ontario, Canada, dioceses and religious communities were represented in the long list of prelates and dignitaries gathered at this epoch-making Jubilee of the Archdiocese of Chicago:

There were first of all Rt. Rev. Msgr. John Bonzano, Papal Legate, and His Eminence James Cardinal Gibbons. Cardinal O'Connell was in Rome and thus prevented from attendance. Amongst the hierarchy were Most Reverend S. G. Mesmer, Milwaukee; Most Reverend J. J. Keane, Dubuque; Most Reverend J. J. Glennon, St. Louis; Most Reverend P. J. Hayes, New York; Most Reverend Austin Dowling, St. Paul; Most Reverend H. Moeller, Cincinnati; Most Reverend J. W. Shaw, New Orleans; Most Reverend J. J. Harty, Omaha; the Most Reverend Alexander Christie, D. D., Archbishop of Portland, Ore.

Of the bishops there were The Right Rev. A. J. McGavick, Chicago; The Right Rev. P. J. Muldoon, Rockford; The Right Rev. T. Meerschaert, Oklahoma; The Right Rev. O. B. Corrigan, Baltimore; The Right Rev. J. J. Hennessey, Wichita; The Right Rev. J. M. Koudelka, Superior; The Right Rev. William Turner, Buffalo; The Right Rev. M. F. Burke, St. Joseph; The Right Rev. T. F. Shahan, Washington; The Right Rev. J. J. McNicholas, Duluth; The Right Rev. P. P. Rhode, Green Bay; The Right Rev. J. H. Tihen, Denver; The Right Rev. M. J. Hoban, Scranton; The Right Rev. M. J. Curley, St. Augustine; The Right Rev. D. J. O'Connell, Richmond; The Right Rev. H. Althoff, Belleville; The Right Rev. M. C. Lenihan, Great Falls; The Right Rev. P. R. Heffron, Winona; The Right Rev. J. Chartrand, Indianapolis; The Right Rev. M. F. Fallon, London, Ont.; The Right Rev. Frederick Eis, Marquette, Mich.; The Right Rev. James Davis, Davenport, Iowa; Rt. Rev. John J. Lawlor, D. D., Bishop of Lead, S. D., Right Rev. J. F. Busch, D. D., Bishop of St. Cloud, Minn.; Right Rev. J. Crimont, S. J., Vicar Apostolic of Alaska; Right Rev. Joseph F. McGrath, D. D., Bishop of Baker, Ore.; Right Rev. Joseph Schrembs, D. D., Bishop of Toledo, Ohio.

Monsignori from beyond the archdiocese who were present:
The Very Rev. J. T. O'Connell, Toledo; The Very Rev. Edward Dyer, S. S.,

Baltimore; The Very Rev. A. E. Manning, Lima, Ohio; The Very Rev. F. J. Van Antwerp, Detroit; The Very Rev. J. Rainer, Milwaukee; Right Rev. Msgr. E. B. Ledvina, vice-president Catholic Extension Society; Very Rev. Andrew Morrissey, C. S. C. (Provincial Superior), Notre Dame, Ind.; Very Rev. John Cavanaugh, C. S. C., Holy Cross College, Washington, D. C.; Very Rev. Thomas F. Burke, C. S. P., Superior General, New York; Rev. Boleslaus Puchalski, Brooklyn, N. Y.; Very Rev. T. W. Smith, O. M. O. (Provincial), Washington, D. C.; Very Rev. Mathias Faust, O. F. M. (Provincial), New York; Very Rev. Raymond Meagher, O. P. (Provincial), New York.²¹

V.

CHICAGOANS HONORED BY POPE

To further mark the jubilee the most distinguished honors so far conferred on Catholic laymen by the Holy See were awarded to Mr. Edward F. Hines and Mr. D. F. Kelly, on Monday evening, June 7, at the home of Archbishop Mundelein, by His Excellency, John Bonzano, Apostolic Delegate to the United States. Mr. Hines was created Knight Commander, Con Placa, of the Order of St. Gregory the Great, Civil Class. Mr. Kelly was made a Knight Companion of the Civil Class. The conferring of the honors was made in the presence of His Eminence, Cardinal Gibbons, Bishop O'Connel, Richmond, Mrs. Hines and her children, Mrs. Kelly and her daughter, and a small gathering of friends. His Grace, the Archbishop, spoke of the work of Mr. Hines and his recent princely gift, of Mr. Kelly as the man who aided him most powerfully in the work of charity. The remarks of His Grace may be summed up in the following statement:

> The two interests to which I hope to give the greatest attention are the work of education and the work of charity. One is wrapped up in the plans for the coördination of the Catholic colleges and universities. To these plans Mr. Hines has given the first and greatest impetus through his magnificent gifts and other valuable services. To the development and fostering of these plans Mr. Kelly has given services that can never be adequately acknowledged. The decorations conferred on these two men are not then merely personal distinctions; they are signs of the gratitude of the archbishop and the whole diocese.

EDWARD HINES, K. C. S. G.

Edward Hines, son of Peter and Rose (McGarry) Hines, was born in Buffalo, New York, July 29, 1863, and is the eldest of seven chil-

²¹ *New World*, June 11, 1920.

dren, he being the only son. He came with his parents to Chicago in 1865, and attended school until he was 14 years of age, when he was employed as tally-boy on the lumber market by the firm of Peter Fish & Bro. and rapidly rose from this position to that of president of the lumber company bearing his name, which he organized and started in 1892.

On June 12, 1895, Mr. Hines married Miss Loretta O'Dowd of Chicago, and has three charming children living, Ralph, Charles and Loretta. Lieutenant Edward Hines, Jr., the eldest son, died in France, June 4, 1918, while serving with the Second Machine Gun battalion.

It was in the name of his son that Mr. Hines recently made his princely gift of $500,000, towards the erection of the great Catholic University in Chicago, St. Mary of the Lake. The Catholic Church Extension Society also has known Mr. Hines' energetic generosity. Mrs. Hines has just concluded a very successful fund-raising campaign for Rosary College and the woman's part of the great new university.

DENNIS F. KELLY, K. S. G.

Dennis Francis Kelly, born in Chicago, August 23, 1868. Educated at St. Mary's School, Chicago, Illinois. Entered Mandel Brothers' employ as errand boy on June 6, 1879, now general manager.

Married Irene E. Sullivan on January 4, 1894. One daughter, Eileen Glassbrook Kelly. Member of the Chicago Athletic, Industrial and Exmoor Country Clubs. Was president of the Exmoor Country Club, 1912-13-14; president Chicago Athletic Club, 1917; president Chicago District Gold Association, 1916-17; president Associated Catholic Charities, 1918-19-20; director of the Continental and Commercial National Bank and Continental and Commercial Trust and Savings Bank, and the Employers' Association; member of the executive committee of the Chicago Association of Commerce. Commissioned lieutenant colonel in Illinois National Guard, by Governor F. O. Lowden, on December 28, 1918. Residence, Highland Park, Ill.

Mr. Kelly has been an outstanding figure in the inauguration and development of the Associated Catholic Charities, which has done such particularly creditable work throughout the limits of the archdiocese.

EDWARD HINES, K. C. S. G.

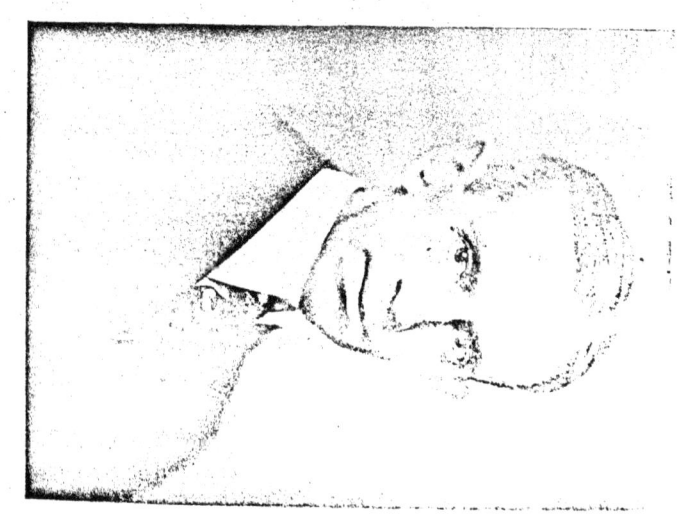

DENNIS F. KELLY, K. S. G.

VI.

THE CELEBRATION AT JOLIET

The counties of Will and Grundy both of which are in the Archdiocese of Chicago, joined in a celebration of the double jubilee on June 12, 1920. A correspondent of a Chicago paper writes of that celebration as follows:

Joliet, the second largest Catholic city in the State, turned out en masse last Saturday to greet the Right Reverend Monsignor John Bonzano, Apostolic Delegate, and Archbishop George W. Mundelein of Chicago.

It was with much cheering and hand-clapping that the two dignitaries were welcomed to the city to close the double celebration—the diamond jubilee of the Chicago archdiocese and the silver jubilee of the Most-Reverend Archbishop.

The celebration also had another significance, of which the inhabitants of Will and Grundy counties are particularly proud. The Archbishop was especially elated over the wonderful showing made in a recent half million dollar drive for a new orphanage to be located in the vicinity of Joliet, and stated that the city had many possibilities in which he might carry out his work.

Attended by more than fifty priests of the two counties and other nearby counties, the procession filed into St. Mary's church at 10:30 o'clock, where more than 1,000 people were assembled to witness the ceremony, having gathered there long before the distinguished guests arrived in Joliet from Chicago.

Guests of honor were His Grace, the Archbishop, the Most Reverend John Bonzano, D. D., Apostolic Delegate, together with prominent members of the hierarchy.

Marching units, horse-drawn units, and a motor division made up the procession which filed through the loop at eight o'clock and past the reviewing stand in front of St. Mary's church, where were seated Archbishop Mundelein, Monsignor John Bonzano and a host of dignitaries of the church.

Preceding the pageant, John W. D'Arcy, grand marshal of the day, placed a wreath of laurels on the statue of Louis Joliet in the courthouse yard.

Three bands accompanied the parade which took three quarters of an hour to pass the reviewing stand. The high school band headed the procession and the grade school players led the final unit of the demonstration. St. Patrick's fife and drum corps accompanied the float from St. Patrick's school.

The parade was led by a platoon of police commanded by Patrol Sergeant Beck. Behind the police came the grand marshal of the parade and the flag borne by William Redmond. Following the flag was the high school band and four boys from four of the parochial schools carrying the banners which were later given to the prize winning floats.

PLANTING OF CROSS REPRESENTED

The first float, representing the planting of the cross in America, was arranged by St. John's school. The St. Francis academy float, presented the founding of the Franciscan missions and a survey in tableau of the work of Padre Junipero Serra, preceded by children of the school.

A float arranged by the pupils of St. Raymond's, showing the arrival of

Marquette in Joliet, in 1673, which in turn was followed by a portrayal of early Catholicity in Lockport, by the St. Dennis and St. Joseph churches of that community. A replica of the first log church in Will county was carried on the Lockport float. The Lockport church was built in 1837, several years before the establishment of the archdiocese of Chicago.

FIRST CATHOLIC CHURCH

The first Catholic church erected in Joliet, St. Patrick's, was also shown in the parade, the first float bearing this being preceded by the St. Patrick's fife and drum corps and girls of St. Patrick's school dressed as spirits of early Catholicity in Joliet.

The Guardian Angels' Home entered two floats in the parade, one interpreting the Spirit of Charity and the other the work of St. Vincent de Paul, the father and protecting saint of the orphans.

St. Joseph's school and parish was represented by pupils of the school dressed in Slavick costumes. This contingent was led by Joseph Zalar, secretary of the Slavonic Catholic Union.

De La Salle institute portrayed the development of education in America. The float entered by the institute showed representatives of all nations in which Catholic educational institutions are established.

HAS TWO FLOATS

Holy Cross, the Polish parochial school, had two floats, Heroism and Catholicity in the war. War work was depicted by a float from Sacred Heart school, a Knights of Columbus Hut, bearing a sign, "The Real Guardians of Liberty," the only touch of humor in the procession.

St. Mary's Croatian school float, portraying the newest saint, Jeanne D'Arc, and the figures of St. Cyril and St. Methodius on the float entered by SS. Cyril and Methodius school, followed the Sacred Heart contingent.

The grade school band and St. Francis academy students concluded the parade. On the St. Mary's float was a tableau of Cardinal Gibbons blessing Columbia.

It is estimated that three thousand children marched in the parade.

Following the celebration of pontifical high Mass, by special permission William Redmond made an address on behalf of the laity of Joliet.

Commending the prelate's attitude during the war and his policy of reconstruction following the cessation of war, Mr. Redmond welcomed the Archbishop to Joliet.

"Representing the laity of Will and Grundy counties, we welcome Your Grace to Joliet. We are genuinely pleased to have a part in this celebration in honor of your sacerdotal silver jubilee.

"You came to this diocese a stranger to us. We were told you were a great worker in the interests of education and charity. This pleased our people because we were taught that sacrifice for education and charity constitute the essence of religion. We felt the diocese would take on new life; great accomplishments could be expected. These expectations are now facts.

NOTED FOR PATRIOTISM

"Your patriotism of peace has been no less renowned than your patriotism of war. You have shown your intense love of country in building up better

we are proud to share this great accomplishment with Your Grace.

"We know the dependent children placed in the care of this new orphanage will be properly educated and trained in domestic science or the manual arts so that each and every one will be able to step out and take his or her place as respectable worthy citizens of this great state and nation."

THE PRIZE WINNERS

St. Francis College, Lockport, Guardian Angels Home and De La Salle Institute, in the order named, were awarded prizes.

Four banners carried by couriers on horseback heading the procession were awarded as prizes by the judging committee made up of Commissioners Frank X. Friedrich, T. V. Gorey and Maurice F. Lennon. The winning floats represented "Columbia," the final number in the pageant, presented by St. Francis' College. It was awarded a banner bearing the United States shield. Lockport's float, showing early Catholicity in the community in a replica of the first log cabin church on the banks of the river, received second prize, the pope's banner. Third prize, typifying Catholic charity, went to the Guardian Angels' home. It was a banner of the archbishop's coat of arms. De La Salle claimed fourth honors, a shield of the city of Joliet, for a float representing Catholic education. There was close competition in the awarding of the emblems, according to the judges.[22]

ARRANGING FOR THE CELEBRATION

In April His Grace, the Most Reverend Archbishop, called a meeting of the pastors of Will and Grundy counties to launch forth a drive for $500,00, to be used in the erection of a new orphanage for the children of these two counties. Up to date the men of the different parishes have turned in $400,000.

His Grace further decided to give one full day of the jubilee celebration to the two counties, and set Saturday, June the 12th, as

---

[22] Charles E. Hassock in *New World*, June 18, 1920.

jubilee day. Accordingly the celebration was opened by a Solemn Pontifical Mass, which was sung by the Archbishop in St. Mary's church, Joliet, at 10:30, in the presence of the Apostolic Delegate. The sermon on the occasion was preched by the Right Reverend Francis C. Kelley, D. D., president of the Catholic Church Extension Society.

Msgr. Kelleys' Address

In the course of his classic sermon Msgr. Kelley said: "What does this Jubilee mean? It is an appeal to history. It means that what the great modern Church is not afraid to do, her children, gathered into small congregations keeping her faith and worshiping according to her laws are not afraid to do. A Jubilee of this kind is not only a day of rejoicing, but a confident challenge to all who, in any way, come within its influence. The chief glory of the Church is that each recurring Jubilee shows that, in a smaller way, the story of progress of the Church Universal applies to each and every section of it. The rise and growth of Christianity is duplicated in the rise and growth of each diocese and of each parish. The fate of the Church was indicated by Christ Himself. Its pains and labors were foretold. Its days of peace were known long in advance. Its days of sorrow were just as strongly outlined. But to the sanction of the past in all that concerned the Church was added the assurance of the Divine Promise. So the history of the Church and her churches is thus lifted far above the ordinary place of eminence. It thrusts its head into the bright clouds that veil the throne of the King from human eyes. In the history of a diocese or parish, as in the history of the Church Universal, there is a visible connection between earth and heaven. The historic Church becomes the Church of the eternal present, whose records are no longer the mere stones of a structure fastened one to the other, but those of a building of steel and iron, whose essential strength is independent of the material upon which its embellishments are carved, and is found rather in its imperishable framework, sunk deep into the caissons of Faith, rearing its great, graceful symmetry to the heavenly gate touched by the highest rung of the Ladder of Jacob. Before such a record the confidence is born that speaks in the words of Ecclesiasticus: 'O Wisdom, thou comest out of the mouth of the Most High; thou reachest from one end to the other.' "[23]

Following the Pontifical Mass a banquet was served to the visiting and local clergy.

At 2:00 p. m. His Grace, the Archbishop, and his guests took places on the reviewing stand to witness the parochial school children's pageant.

The Rev. Philip L. Kennedy, pastor of St. Patrick's church, was chairman of the pageant committee. John W. D'Arcy, prominent Joliet attorney, was the grand marshal. Music was furnished by

---

[23] Msgr. Kelley's sermon was printed in full in *New World*, June 18, 1920.

ıts Cyril and Methodius school band, Central school band, the
ı school band and St. Patrick's fife and drum corps.
Simultaneously with the beginning of the pageant came the an-
ncement from Chicago that the Illinois Steel Company had con-
ated $10,000 to the proposed orphans' home. Work on the in-
tion will begin this summer. The added contribution places the
l between $400,000 and $500,000.

VII.

THE LITERATURE OF THE JUBILEE

The importance attached to a public event is frequently indicated
he attention given it by the Press and the accounts and publica-
s that grow out of it. Judged from this standpoint, no single
lic event in Chicago or Joliet has attracted more general attention
left a more extended literature.

Perhaps the most appropriate of the literature for first mention
ıe beautiful ode written expressly for the Jubilee:

JUBILEE ODE

"Let voices rise in anthems clear and sweet;
    Let heaven's dome resound with jubilee;
Let breezes catch the note and bear it fleet;
    To meet the waves of our great inland sea.

"We stand where stood the Indian's quaint tepee;
    Where fleetest creatures ranged the forests through;
Where fields of maize waved ripe—a tawny sea—
    Where ruled his tribe the dusky Chicagou.

"Three hundred years have sped since urged by zeal
    To this low portage by the gleaming lake
Marquette's canoe slipped silent through the reeds.
    With cross upraised—the Black Robe's sole appeal—
He taught what Christ had suffered for their sake,
    And won each savage heart ere grazed his keel.

"Since that first Mass beside the river's brink,
    Its choir—the wind-swept branches tossing high—
A chain of Masses—this the initial link—
    Our city binds to heaven in holiest tie.

"This Garden City, doomed, it seemed, to die—
Fort Dearborn's awful massacre how tell?
Or that dread night when on October's breeze
Were blown the sparks that bore destruction fell?
Like phoenix rose a destiny to fulfill
Like eagle soars—its victory cry 'I will'.

"Three-quarters of a century have elapsed
Since first a shepherd came this flock to guide,
Commensurate with our civic strength today,
To growth religious, too, we point with pride.

"O tangled grass that o'er the waters bending,
Kissing the keel rough-hewn of his canoe,
Which conquered wind and wave with toil unending
Dost see Marquette's most sanguine dream come true?"[24]

Not less beautiful but more personal are the following lines inspired by the Jubilee:

"DOMINUS ADJUTOR MEUS"

With awe we learn his projects vast;
Ere morrow's sun long shadows cast,
Their execution see.
He shrinks from no Herculean tasks;
He leads the way before He asks
That we his followers be.
A tower of strength—nor hindrance knows;
He courts no friends; He fears no foes,
Whence comes such strength is plain.
What eye so keen? What heart so brave?
What soul so pitying to save?
His motto is not vain.[25]

THE NEW WORLD

The *New World* in its issue of June 4th supplied a remarkably
beautiful four-page supplement carrying cuts of Most Reverend
Archbishop George William Mundelein and many of the visiting
prelates, besides a 5,000 word sketch adapted from the Jubilee book,
"Archdiocese of Chicago, Antecedents and Development." The

[24] From the *New World*.
[25] From the *New World*.

beauty of design and color was notable and a large part of the regular issue was filled with description and announcements of the coming celebration. In its issue of June 11th the addresses of Archbishops Hayes and Mundelein were reproduced in full as well as a very complete account of the exercises to the time of going to press. In the issue of June 18th was published a complete description of the pageant with a list of the floats and the schools represented. The same number contained also the address of Most Reverend Archbishop John J. Glennon of St. Louis at the dedication of the Quigley Preparatory Seminary, and of Right Reverend Msgr. P. J. McDonnell on the same occasion, as well as many columns of description and comment on the great Jubilee both in Chicago and Joliet. The classic address of Right Rev. Msgr. Francis Clement Kelley delivered at Joliet was also published in this number.

The issue of June 18th also contained a full page of pictures of the individual floats.

This valuable publication is to be congratulated on its splendid treatment of the Jubilee celebration.

OTHER PERIODICALS

The daily Press, despite the press of news due to the Republican convention and other causes, devoted much space to the subject. The *Chicago Daily Tribune*, the *Evening Post*, the *Evening Journal*, and the *Daily News* all carried announcements and accounts of all the exercises. The *Herald and Examiner* printed a strong editorial and the *Tribune, Herald and Examiner, Daily News* and *Evening American* carried cuts.

The *Columbian and Western Catholic*, the official paper of the Knights of Columbus, also devoted considerable space to the celebration.

HANDBOOK OF THE PAGEANT

One of the most notable and pleasing pieces of literature published in connection with the Jubilee exercises was a handbook of the pageant, "The Rise and Progress of Christianity" prepared by Reverend Claude J. Pernin, S. J., under the direction of the pageant committee. In this beautiful booklet the 149 units are named in their processional order, making a very useful guide in viewing the procession. In a foreword to the booklet the author says:

"The floats succeed each other in historical order, beginning with

: portrayal of biblical scenes at and before the birth of Christ.
ey represent successive events in the great drama of Christian
)gress through all ages, in all countries and among all peoples
ere the One, Holy, Catholic and Apostolic Church has brought
ht and life to 'the nations that lay in darkness and the shadow of
ith.'
"The biblical and historical scenes recall the Miracle plays, the
nbolic - floats resemble the old Moralities which originated with
1 were fostered by the Church in the middle ages.
"The same spirit which produced them and the same purpose
ich animated them in former ages, produces and animates our
geant today. Born of the spirit of Faith, the purpose is to show
concrete form the enduring consequences of that Divine injunction:
" 'Going, therefore, teach all Nations whatsoever I have com-
nded you.' "
Father Pernin most happily presented the pageant by a headline
'erence to the historical significance, then the name of the float
:h the name of the school presenting it, and a surprisingly apt
)tation from the Scriptures or (in a few cases only), a pat stanza
m the poem of some distinguished writer. A very intimate knowl-
ge of the Scriptures and the best English writers is displayed in
s book.²⁶

A SOUVENIR FOR GUESTS

A beautiful memorial to the first bishop of Chicago, the Right
erend William Quarter, D. D. (1844-1848), was found in the
sentation to each guest at the luncheon, of a handsomely bound
'y of the pioneer bishop's life and the beginning of the Church
Chicago.
This charming volume is notable in both subject and author. The
ject is the saintly first bishop of Chicago and the author, the
test of Chicago's earliest physicians. Dr. John E. McGirr, the
hor, was the Murphy of the earlier day medical profession, a
fessor and lecturer of signal ability, the nestor of the science
ilty of the University of St. Mary of the Lake, and with his
er, Dr. Patrick McGirr, the sponsors of Mercy Hospital.
Bound in full limp leather, gilt top, printed on deckled edge
1 made paper, with illustrated plates, the name of each guest
ossed in gold thereon, this edition de luxe, from the press of

* Copies of this booklet are still available through the *New World*.

GENERAL VIEW OF COURT

ADMINISTRATION GROUP

LIBERAL ARTS HALL

RESIDENCE HALL

The Corner Stone of Rosary College was laid by Most Rev. George William Mundelein, D. D., Archbishop of Chicago, June 20, 1921.

St. Iary's Training School, Desplaines, Ill., will serve as a souvenir of an unusually brilliant event, while at the same time perpetuating the deeds of Chicago's first bishop and the memory of Chicago's early struggle for existence.

MOTION PICTURES OF THE PAGEANT

By permission of the pageant committee the complete display was filmed by Iatre's Library and will be available for schools and theatres and thus perpetuate the pageant in its original beauty. Special films of the several units separately will also be available.

THE JUBILEE HISTORY

The permanent memorial of the diocesan Jubilee is contained in a very comprehensive history of the diocese and archdiocese under the title "Archdiocese of Chicago; Antecedents and Development." This is a work of somewhat more than 800 pages including text and illustrations and so beautifully made up as to be almost an art book.

The various subdivisions of the book deal with the following subjects, consecutively: The Early Church; Former Ecclesiastical Jurisdiction; The Bishops and Archbishops of Chicago; The Early Clergy; Nineteenth Century Missionaries; The Parishes, Their Growth and Development; Catholic Education; The Benevolent Institutions, and the Catholic Societies.

The nearly three-hundred pages of half-tone cuts present most interesting representations of the Bishops and Archbishops, the churches and their pastors, the schools and benevolent institutions, besides other pictures of historical interest.

The book is printed on thin gloss paper and substantially bound in cloth. For more satisfactory results in illustration a large page and wide column has been used, the book over all measuring 9x12 inches.

The general history and the life and labors of the bishops and archbishops and the early clergy as well as the account of the early days of the older parishes were written by Joseph J. Thompson. Editor-in-chief of the ILLINOIS CATHOLIC HISTORICAL REVIEW. In general the accounts of the parishes and of the educational and benevolent institutions were prepared by the pastors or those in present charge, while the accounts of the societies were prepared by the officers or persons designated by them. The whole was supervised in the Chancellor's office, directly under the eye of the Right Rev.

Chancellor Msgr. Edward F. Hoban and the particular direction of Very Rev. Denis J. Dunne, D. D., to whose watchful care and untiring efforts the accomplishment of the task is largely to be credited. The book was printed and publishel by the press of St. Mary's Training School at Desplaines and is a credit to that department of the great benevolent institution which has developed the plant.[27]

Jubilee week of June, 1920, has taken a permanent place in history as one of the most notable periods in the creditable records of Chicago.

JOSEPH J. THOMPSON.

Chicago.

---

[27] See review in this number of ILLINOIS CATHOLIC HISTORICAL REVIEW.

REVEREND GASPAR HENRY OSTLANGENBERG

The life of Father Ostlangenberg is typical of a certain class of pioneer priests. They went forth into the battlefield of Christ with holy enthusiasm and heroically bore the greatest privations, but the irregularity of their lives unfitted them for the regular performance of pastoral duties under normal conditions. In those early days the unlimited possibilities of life, in this country, developed a great deal of self-reliance and individuality of character, both in. clergy and laity. It brought out in many of the missionaries traits of eccentricity which exposed them to misunderstandings with the laity. Under these circumstances they did not always show good judgment and prudence in pacifying factions and ensuring peace. As soon as the missions became stable parishes, these pioneers failed; like nomads they wandered from place to place, even from diocese to diocese, until the infirmities of old age brought them to rest in some quiet and obscure retreat.

Gaspar Henry Ostlangenberg was born March 4, 1810, of wealthy parents, the owners of Ostlangenberg manor, near Langenberg, Kreis Wiedenbrueck, diocese of Paderborn, in Westphalia. Probably he made a classical course in some Westphalian town, until he resolved to abandon his country and embrace the life of a poor missionary in some wilderness of the Mississippi Valley. At the age of twenty-three he crossed the ocean to enter St. Mary's Seminary at the Barrens, Perry Co., Missouri. He arrived there November 1, 1833[1]. February 24, 1835[2] Father Regis Loisel wrote to Bishop Rosati of St. Louis, that the student Ostlangenberg was grievously sick. In pioneer days when the ax of the colonist cleared the forest and his plow broke the virgin soil, fevers broke out even in the healthiest locations and drove many a tradesman and many a missionary back to his home in Europe.

March 4, 1835 Bishop Rosati wrote to Cardinal Franzoni:

Amongst them (the alumni of the Seminary) a German, a promising young man by the name of Gasp. H. Ostlangenberg, of the diocese of Paderborn in Prussia, has no dimissorial letters from his

[1] v. Rosati's *Statistics of the Seminary*, Archdiocesan Chancery, St. Louis.
[2] All the letters and other documents used in compiling this sketch are preserved in the Archives of the Archdiocesan Chancery Office of St. Louis. The English is Father Ostlangenberg's.

43

Ordinary; he cannot obtain them, because he left his country, when by law he was still subject to military conscription. The Bishops are prohibited from issuing such letters, unless the applicants have first satisfied their obligation. Wherefore I humbly ask Your Eminence to obtain for me from the Holy Father the faculty to ordain the aforesaid young man without the dimissorial letters from his Ordinary. When still a layman he left the diocese of Paderborn and emigrated to America. (*Archives, St. Louis*).

March 15, 1835, Pope Gregory XVI granted to Bishop Rosati the faculty he had asked for, but shortly after the Exeat for the young student arrived from Paderborn. Both documents, the Roman privilege and the Exeat from Paderborn are preserved in the office of the Rt. Rev. Chancellor in St. Louis. Ostlangenberg's friend and colleague at the Seminary was his countryman, Hy. Fortmann, later on well know at Chicago as pastor of Grosse Point. Ostlangenberg was ordained subdeacon July 22, 1837; the order of the Holy Priesthood was conferred upon him July 7, 1838:

On July 20, 1838, Bishop Rosati, according to his Diary, gave the major faculties to Rev. J. A. Lutz, the minor faculties to Rev. Gaspar Henry Ostlangenberg. Up to January, 1839 he kept the newly ordained priest who knew English fairly well at the Cathedral of St. Louis, to assist Father J. Fischer[3] in attending the several stations near St. Louis, where the services of a priest were required who could preach and hear confessions in both English and German. Before the year 1843 the Cathedral was the only Catholic church in the city of St. Louis. The Germans, since Septuagesima Sunday, 1834, had their services in St. Mary's chapel (formerly the entertainment hall of St. Louis Academy[4]) or in the basement chapel of the Cathedral; since 1835 German sermons were also preached by the Jesuit Fathers in St. Aloysius chapel on the grounds of St. Louis University. But since 1838 Bishop Rosati planned the erection of a second church, in honor of Our Lady of Victories, in the western part of the city (Reilly's Addition), to provide for the numerous German immigrants.[5] Probably he intended to employ Father Ostlangenberg at some work in connection with this new parish. But

---

[3] Father John Peter Fischer, a native of Lorraine, was ordained priest in St. Louis Cathedral, January 1, 1837; after having been pastor at New Madrid for about a year, he was appointed assistant to Father Lutz at the Cathedral; in 1843 he was appointed pastor of St. Mary's church. June 10, 1856 he left St. Louis and returned to his native country.

[4] v. *Centralblatt and Social Justice*, February and September, 1916.

[5] v. *Centralblatt and Social Justice*, November, 1917 and November, 1918.

the plan could not be carried out, partly because the Germans did not like the location, partly on account of the financial crisis of those days which paralyzed business for years.   •

On Little Muddy Creek, St. Clair County, Illinois, a few Irish immigrants had built their log cabins; they were joined by some North-Germans, mostly from the diocese of Paderborn. Because St. Liborius, Bp. C. is the patron of Paderborn, the colony was called, "Libory Settlement." In August 1838, B. Dingwerth and W. Harwerth went to St. Louis and asked the Bishop to send a priest to the new and promising colony, a priest who would speak both languages, English and German. He sent Father Ostlangenberg, to see what could be done for the Libory people. On August 5, 1838, Ostlangenberg said the first Mass for the colonists in the log house of Mr. W. Harwerth.[6] He encouraged them to build a chapel, then returned to St. Louis to direct the undertaking from there as well as he could. The ground for the new church was donated by B. Dingwerth. On October 21, 1838, Bishop Rosati writes in his diary:

Today I received the visit of a certain German man who lives on Little Muddy Creek, in St. Clair County. He asked for the permission to build a church which is to be called after St. Luke. At that place there are twenty German families and on the other side of the creek seven more, who also wish to build a church; finally at the little river called Shoal Creek, there are about sixty families, amongst whom a church must be built in honor of St. Boniface. If it be God's will, Mr. Ostlangenberg will have charge of these parishes.

The same diary enables us to follow the development of things:

On December 1, 1938: I told the German Catholics who live on Oka River, St. Clair County that after New Year's I would send to them Father Ostlangenberg, to reside in their midst.

On January 19 Bishop Rosati gave the papers of institution to the parish of S. Thaddeus on Silver Creek and to the mission of S. Liborius at Fayetteville and to S. Boniface, Shoal Creek, to Rev. Gaspar Henry Ostlangenberg, together with the major faculties.

On January 21, 1839 Rev. Mr. Gaspar Henry Ostlangenberg left St. Louis for the missions of S. Thaddeus and of S. Liborius at Fayetteville, St. Clair County, Illinois, distant from St. Louis thirty miles.

• v. *Pastoralblatt*, October, 1917, p. 146. The notices from Bishop Rosati's Diary on Father Ostlangenberg were copied from this sketch by Rev. Souvay of the Kenrick Seminary.

Arrived in the settlement, the young priest made his home in the sacristy of the unfinished church. On April 21, 1839, he wrote to Bishop Rosati from St. Libory:

The church is not blessed, no bell, no baptismal font, but there is a confessional and a tabernacle (not the Blessed Sacrament). No residence for the priest who lives in the Sacristy. He uses German and English in preaching, sings High Mass on Sundays (German hymns), in the afternoon Vespers and Catechism. Mission: St. Boniface on Shoal Creek, Clinton County. This mission has a church and a priest's house.

We will permit Father Ostlangenberg himself to tell the story of the Libory settlement from his letters which are all written in English:

Libory Settlement the 8th of March, 1839.

Most Rev. Father:

Since I did not receive an answer to my letter which I lately addressed to you, I think it necessary to write again; and I hope you will be at home now. Besides the things marked in my last letter, I beg leave to add some which I would be glad if you would deign to inform me of. The logs for the new church being ready to be put up, the people want me to lay the foundation. As the church will be only of wood, and as I hope we shall soon proceed to commence a stone one, I suppose it will not be necessary to perform any ceremony which otherwise I had not power to do; but now is the question whether You will bless the building before I could celebrate Mass in it, or You give me the permission to perform the Divine Sacrifice in it, without being blessed. I would like to perform divine service in a church, as soon as it can be fit for the purpose, for the place where I offer the sacrifice of Mass now, is not, as You will imagine, adapted neither convenient for such a function.

I also would ask whether I could hear confessions in a private house at the distance of six miles from our place, so that the few people who live about the said place might hold their Easter duty there? I also would ask whether I might and if You think it proper, bless the grave yard at Shoal Creek and at my place also? Other things of which You would like to have an information, the bearer of the letter can tell You better, than I write to You. I humbly beg pardon for my frankness.

I remain Your humble and obedient servant,

G. OSTLANGENBERG.

N. B.—I beg Your prayers for me.

Right Reverend Sir:

According to faculties which You have given me, I have blessed our church on Sunday last[7]; on which day also I read the pastoral

---

[7] Father Ostlangenberg dedicated the church in honor of St. Liborius, although

letter, both in English and in German. I beg leave of You for an information which to inquire I forgot, whilst I was in St. Louis. Our congregation, many of whom were joined and inscribed whilst in Europe, into several confraternities, desires ardently to have any confraternity in the parish. The confraternity which they would most like is: Confraternity of the agony of our Savior, in order to obtain a happy death, the prayers of which they have in their prayer books. Now, if You would approve of the institution of the kind, I would beg to tell me, how it should be conducted, and under what conditions, and whether any indulgence would be annexed to it. I remain with respect and humility.

Your humble and obedient servant,

G. OSTLANGENBERG.

Libory Settlement, 8 May, 1839,
St. Clair County, Illinois.

On April 17, 1839 twenty-one men of Shoal Creek sent a petition to Bishop Rosati, written in the German language, in which they asked the Bishop to appoint Father Ostlangenberg their first resident priest. Ostlangenberg would have been only too glad to transfer his residence from St. Libory to Shoal Creek (now Germantown). Since Bishop Rosati however neither read nor spoke German, his secretary, Father Joseph A. Lutz[3] translated the petition into English for him.

the Bishop had placed the mission under the protection of St. Thaddeus (Judas Thaddeus, the Apostle); in later documents, for some time, the church in Libory settlement appears under the title of St. Thaddeus.

Bishop Rosati systematically dedicated the churches of his Diocese to biblical saints. To Our Lady the church at the Barrens, to St. Joseph that of Apple Creek and Westfalia; St. Ann: Little Canada; St. Joachim: Old Mines; St. John the Bapt.: New Madrid; St. Michael: Fredericktown; St. Gabriel: Prairie du Chien; St. Raphael: Dubuque; St. Stephen: Richwoods and Indian Creek; St. Peter: Gravois and Dardenne; St. Paul: Salt River; St. Andrew: Teutonia; St. James the Elder: Potosi; St. James the Minor: Harrisonville; St. John Ap.: Springfield; St. Thomas: Johnson Settlement; St. Philip: French Village, Ill.; St. Bartholemew: North Santa Fe; St. Matthew: Alton; St. Simon: Fountain Green; St. Thaddeus: Libory; St. Matthias: Bloomsdale (Establishment); St. Barnaby: leville; St. Luke: Fayetteville; St. Mark: Cincinnati, Ralls Co., Mo. The church at Ottawa was dedicated to the Blessed Trinity, the mission at La Salle to the Holy Cross, those at Commerce and Peoria to the Holy Redeemer (Saint-Sauveur), that at Quincy to the Ascension of Christ.

[3] Joseph Antony Lutz, born June 9, 1801, at Odenheim, Baden, Germany and ordained at Paris, had arrived in St. Louis, November 5, 1826; since 1831 he was pastor of the Cathedral parish and Bishop Rosati's secretary. Being a South German and in full sympathy with the French regime at St. Louis, he was not a particular friend of the North German priests who about 1837 came to St. Louis, Fathers Meinkmann, Brickwedde, Ostlangenberg and Fortmann. Father Lutz left the diocese of St. Louis on April 15, 1847 and died at New York on February 6, 1861.

'or some reason, in the translation, he omitted Rev. Ostlangenberg's
ame and made the corresponding passage read: ''We beg therefor
ιost humbly His Lord's Grace to favor us with a German priest.''
'wo monτhs later Father Ostlangenberg himself, from Shoal Creek,
τote to the Bishop:

Shoal Creek, June 16, 1839.
;ight Reverend Sir:
    The great confidence I have in Your indulgent goodness which,
las, I have knowingly and unknowingly, perhaps, on account of
.y awkward behaviour, so often abused, beg humbly, have to address
.yself again to You. I am almost forced to write to You in the
eople's behaviour [Sic!] at this place. They also beg of me, to
rite for them, since they do not know the English. They long
ished to have a priest resident here. They are about 60 families,
:sides the single men. They have prudently made the account for
ιe support of a priest, which will be, I doubt, not sufficient. I find
solid piety in the congregation. They have been twice disappointed
γ my not calling at a promised time, which made them feel bad.
heir numerous children grow up in ignorance. Some sick persons
:quire frequently a priest. One of them complained to me that they
:ver could get a priest of You, and having been in some measure
ηkindly put back for days at St. Louis, before he could see You
ιd speak to You; he uttered some dispairing words of disdain.
hey would very much desire to have me, but I told them, that it
:rhaps should not be Your wish and also (ut dictum fuit apud vos
. secreto) that I could not well ride on horseback. They then prom-
:d to give me a horse with a carriage, and not let me suffer any-
ing; and that I might, with Your approbation, not every other
ιnday but less frequently visit the parish of Libory Settlement.
: viderer in favorem cujusdam haec scripsisse, ita, ut consequentia
.mnationi meae esset, dico quod accidit mihi. Nescio qua Dei bonitate
r totam hebdomadam quamvis toties equitando inter infirmos, non
pertus sum naturae lapsae infirmitatem. Hilari animo incedo dum
ligit me inimicus. Utinam Deo favente continuarem.[9] I was obliged
write this to-night, since to-morrow morning I intend to return
Libory. I expect to be here again Sunday after next. Fiat mihi.
ut vos scitis et sicut Vos vultis. Non mea sed Vestra fiat voluntas.
animae meae animarumque aeternam salutem.[10] I held an English

---

[9] ''That it may not appear as if I wrote this in anybody's favor, and that
blame for possible consequences may not be cast on me, I tell what experi-
e I made. By the unmerited goodness of God I did not feel the infirmities
my body, although I have been compelled to ride on horseback a great deal
ting the sick. Serene in mind 'I go while the enemy afflicteth me.' May God
ɔ me to hold out.''
[10] ''May it be done to me as You know best and as You wish. Not my
Your will be done to the eternal salvation of my own soul and of the souls
ɔthers.''

sermon here in the afternoon, where some Americans had collected
together. I instructed for a time a German Lutheran family, who have
also made confession, but not yet received communion.

Your humble servant,

C. H. OSTLANGENBERG.

Address for the kind answer to this letter would be: in care of
Mr. Hermann (?), Shoal Creek, Clinton County, Ill.

Libory Settlement, 2nd August, 1839.

Right Reverend Sir:

I have hardly a moment of time to write; however, I deem it
necessary to make use of the opportunity which just is offered to
me, since a man is starting for St. Louis. Your kind letter I received
and read it with a spirit of inexpressible gratitude, for the good
care and trouble You evinced for the honor of God and for my poor
soul. I have prayed to Almighty God to make known to me His
Holy will, but I hardly could seriously reflect on Your proposal, on
account of my manifold labours, and thus I could not yet make up
my mind for the result. As I in my last letter stated to You, has
my trouble (disclosed to You) ceased, but not quite. However, I
hope of the merciful God, that this will have, with the grace of God,
an end, if the condition which I have told You would be granted to
me; namely by the people of Shoal Creek offered me a carriage, so
that I had not so much to ride on horseback, but only if I would
live there. I beg humbly pardon for the complaint, which You so
patiently suffered, on account of the people at Shoal Creek. I did
not, perhaps, explain the matter in an expressible manner. They on
the contrary expressed to me an uncommon, most unexpected kind
audience. It was this they had been told by some others, perhaps,
in a hasty tone, to wait for a third day, where they knew, that You
were within and, probably, to speak on the same day, and that it
would have been hard for them, to pay an expense for three days'
stay in St. Louis. My labours are considerable, and there is a great
deal of inconvenience, stopping one-half week in one place and the
other half in another, as I can hardly take the books necessary for
my studies. I am called to Carlisle, 8 miles at a distance from Shoal
Creek. In its vicinity there are labouring some Catholicks on the
public roads, where there are some sick and many others who ought
to comply with their duties. At Shoal Creek there are nearly in
every house two or three persons sick. At Libory Settlement there
are some sick too; I am also called some twelve miles towards Kaskaskias where there are some Catholic families. Since I have scarcely
a little time to compose any instructions, and I meet frequently with
Protestants to whom I ought to speak some words, many of whom
come on Sundays to our meeting, as they call it, I would ardently
beg of You to procure me some short instructions which I might
learn by heart. There is another thing for which I would want information: A Catholic girl of about 16 years was carried off by a
Lutheran, to whom she has been married before a judge, without

the consent of her parents, who live within twelve miles from Libory Settlement, who requested me to do something to her, because they are much grieved on this account. I did not speak to her, but told her parents, that after two weeks I would speak to the couple; in the meantime they might leave it to Almighty God and make themselves easy about it. Now I would like to know how to behave in this circumstance.

One thing more: when I was at Carlisle I heard of a criminal in prison whom I understood to be a Catholic. Although he never called for a priest and he knew that I had been there and then was there, I went to see him. He is a Pole by nation, a Catholic; sentenced to be hung in about a month's time—this he knows—after he has committed murder. I found him rather in a despairing state. I inquired after his religion and reminded him to meditate on the eternal truths. He evinced a great coldness about his duties and consequently about his eternal welfare. I could do nothing to him then and he did not even request me to come another time, in order to comply with his duties. I spoke some words of consolation to him and promised him that I was ready at any time to visit him, in order to prepare him for receiving the sacraments; and since he had nothing of pious books, I promised him to send him or to bring to him good books above all a prayer-book. All the books he had to read were novels and romances and such like foolish, greatly protestant writings. I would beg of You, how I should go on with this man. I once more beg humbly Your kind advice with regard to my own salvation and the granting of the above petitions. I shall at all times and in every circumstance endeavor to comply with Your wishes.

I am and remain most respectfully Your obedient, humble and most unworthy minister,

G. OSTLANGENBERG.

But on the day of which Bishop Rosati received Ostlangenberg's letter, (Aug. 3) he appointed Father Henry Fortmann first pastor of Shoal Creek.[11] So Father Ostlangenberg had to remain at Libory; from there he served the missions of St. Luke at Fayetteville and of St. Barnabas at Belleville. His last letter to Bishop Rosati is dated February 19, 1840:

Right Reverend Sir:
Since the time of Lent is drawing near I beg leave by an opportunity of a man going to St. Louis, to address to You these few lines which, I hope, will meet You in a good state of health. I would

---

[11] John Henry Fortmann, born at Lohne, Oldenburg, diocese of Muenster, in 1802, entered the Seminary at the Barrens, June 3, 1833, after he had made two years of theology at Muenster. He was ordained November 1, 1837, but remained at the Seminary, attending the German colonists at Apple Creek, whilst Father Wiseman served the Kentuckians. Later on he was pastor of Grosse Point (Wilmette) near Chicago, and of Teutopolis. d. at Peoria, March 9, 1858.

beg of You to instruct me, how I should proceed to sanctify with my congregation this coming holy time? Or, perhaps You would approve of my intention which is: to preach on Sundays at Mass in English, if there be some persons who do not speak the German language; to have in the afternoon the Stations of the Cross with a Sermon in German; to invite the people to assist at Mass every morning and read to them the Epistle and Gospel with a short instruction; to have Mass on Fridays at 9 o'clock, the prayers and canticles according to the German Hymn- and prayer book, called Devotion for Lent, with a German instruction. I do not know how to perform the usual ceremonies on the three last days of Holy week, since we are wanting many things for this purpose. I would likewise beg of You to speak to the mother of the hospital to have the goodness to send to me something for the strengthening of my stomach, which is so much impaired that it refuses anything. I would have occasion to get this with Your kind answer by the same opportunity above mentioned.

Yours with respect, humble and obedient Servant,

G. H. OSTLANGENBERG.

Libory Settlement, the 19th of February, 1840.

In the spring of 1840 Father Peter Paul Lefevere, the stout-hearted missionary of northeastern Missouri and western Illinois, in company with Bishop Rosati and Father Joseph A. Lutz, left for Europe (April 27) in order to recuperate. Since the mission of Libory Settlement could now be provided for by Father Fortmann from Shoal Creek, Ostlangenberg was sent by the Vicar General P. Verhaegen, S. J., to serve the missions in Ralls, Warren, Pike, Monroe and Clarke Counties, Missouri; he resided at Indian Creek, Monroe County. The missionary life in this vast region was full of hardships, long and dangerous journeys, severe exposures and privations. Father Ostlangenberg, although a Westfalian, was not of the rugged strong Teuton type, so common in the northwestern provinces of Germany; he was undersized and feeble and very sensitive, seemingly little adapted for the rough pioneer life he was compelled to lead amongst the colonists of Father Lefevere's vast district.

In November, 1841 Father Verhaegen relieved Father Ostlangenberg of his difficult mission and sent him to Galena, Ill.,[12] where he was to assist Father Romigius Petiot in serving the different stations which were springing up everywhere near the boundary line of Illinois

---

[12] v. ILLINOIS CATHOLIC HISTORICAL REVIEW, October, 1919. Essay on the *Northwestern Missions in Illinois*, by Rev. J. Rothensteiner. The German parish at Galena was started by Father Rod. Heimerling in September, 1850 (Diary of Bp. Van de Velde).

and Wisconsin. Whilst living in Galena he attended St. Matthew's church at Shullsburg, from April, 1843, to March, 1844, in the neighboring county of Lafayette, Wis., where the famous Father Mazzuchelli, O. P., had inaugurated a mission on August 27, 1835.[13]

On November 28, 1843 the diocese of Chicago, comprising the entire state of Illinois was established. This fact, however, does not seem to have enhanced the chances of our hero for a quiet and indisturbed life and work in the Lord's vineyard. It was for him the beginning of a life of unrest and disappointment.

On May 5, 1844, Rt. Rev. Wm. Quarter, the first Bishop of Chicago, arrived in his episcopal city, accompanied by his brother, the Rev. Walter Quarter. He found at Chicago two priests from the diocese of Vincennes, Rev. Maurice de Saint-Palais[14] and Rev. F. Fischer,[15] and these were recalled to their own diocese by Bishop de la Hailandiere, on the separation of Illinois from the See of Vincennes. Chicago was then not much more than a large village, and an uninviting field. Ten weeks after the coming of Bishop Quarter both missionaries, according to the instructions given them by their Bishop, left Chicago: de Saint-Palais on August 23. Fischer one day later. Some time before, Bishop Quarter had sent orders to Father Ostlangenberg to leave Galena and to take charge of the Germans in Chicago. In 1832 only one German Catholic (Hondorf) had been in the city[16]; in 1844 the German colony had grown to be quite considerable. On the day when Father Fischer left (August 24), Ostlangenberg arrived in the Bishop's house at Chicago.[17]

---

[13] v. T. J. Sullivan, *History of the Church in Wisconsin*, p. 540.

[14] Maurice de St. Palais, later on Bishop of Vincennes.

[15] Father F. Fischer on December 5, 1848, was sent to Highland, Illinois, by Administrator Walter Quarter (Diary). He was pastor of Ste. Marie for many years.

[16] The original of the petition to Bishop Rosati, on which Hondorf's name is found, is preserved in the Archives of St. Louis.

[17] Diary of Bishop Quarter, printed in McGovern, *Souvenir of Archbishop Feehan Silver Jubilee*. p. 63 ss.

The Bishop had visited Galena in August, 1844. He writes in his Diary:

"8th of August: The Bishop set out in company of Rev. Walter J. Quarter for Galena; arrived about 12:30 A. M., Saturday morning. Rev. Mr. Ostlangenberg said an early Mass; after Mass saw Rev. Mr. Petiot; preached on Sunday at 10 o'clock, and in the afternoon at early candle light. On Monday morning at 9:00 o'clock administered the Sacrament of Confirmation; on Tuesday morning, the 12th, the Bishop and brother set out for Chicago." Later on he writes:

"24th day (August) Rev. Father Fischer took his final leave of this diocese, returning to his own at Vincennes. This evening, Rev. Mr. Ostlangenberg ar-

When the young and zealous priest had surveyed his new missionary field he saw at once that from the Pro-Cathedral the spiritual needs of the German immigrants could not be provided for in a satisfactory manner. He insisted that two churches should be built for them, one south, another north of the river. But he was not the man selected by Divine Providence to accomplish this task. He was called elsewhere.

War had broken out in the Catholic congregation at Belleville, St. Clair County, Illinois. In November, 1842 Bishop Kenrick of St. Louis had sent to Belleville the Rev. Joseph Kuenster[18] as the first resident pastor. In March, 1843, he started to erect a small stone church and on the following Christmas Day he celebrated in it the first Mass. The building, however, was unfinished: all it contained was an altar made of rough boards, and two candlesticks; no pews, no Communion railing, no stove. When the zealous but inexperienced pastor enforced some laws of the Church regarding sponsorship at baptism, etc., dissensions which culminated in open rebellion, arose between him and some of his parishioners. In the summer of 1845 the mutinous men held the poor priest a prisoner in a deserted blockhouse near Centreville, for 22 hours.[19] Utterly discouraged, Father Kuenster asked his new Bishop (of Chicago) to relieve him. He left Belleville to take charge of the congregation of Teutopolis.

Since Father Ostlangenberg personally knew most of the people of Belleville, Bishop Quarter thought that he would be the proper person to appease the turbulent spirits. He gave the care of the Germans at Chicago to Father Jung[20] who, on September 21, 1845,

rived from Galena, to take charge of the German congregation. 27th, today Rev. John Brady set out for Galena, where he is to officiate as assistant pastor to the Rev. Mr. Petiot."

"Holy Week, 1845, on Holy Thursday, Ostlangenberg was deacon; on Good Friday he officiated, on Holy Saturday he was deacon."

McGovern's Book is the property of Mr. F. Kenkel, editor of the *Amerika.*

[18] Father Kuenster had come to America from the diocese of Treves and had been ordained priest by Bishop Peter R. Kenrick, August 25, 1842; for a short time he had charge of St. Joseph's church, Apple Creek; he died as pastor of St. Boniface church, Quincy, Ill., in 1857.

[19] v. Theo. Brunner, *History of the Catholic Church in Quincy.*

[20] "21 September (1845). Today, about 1:30 P. M. Rev. Mr. Jong arrived in the Empire. He is from Strasburg, Germany, and is appointed pastor of the German congregation." (Diary of Bishop Quarter). Father Jung preached the German sermon at the dedication of the Cathedral of Chicago on October 5, 1845; on March 28, 1846 he signed the contracts for the erection of two German churches: St. Peter's on the South side (opened August 2, 1846) and St.

had arrived from Strassburg, Alsace, and sent Ostlangenberg to the mission of St. Barnabas at Belleville.

The parish of Belleville had increased and now numbered one hundred and thirty families, including several nationalities—German, French, Irish and Bohemians, but the new pastor was just to all. Peace returned and the young priest completed the church commenced by his predecessor. Thereupon Bishop Quarter visited the parish in May, 1847, and dedicated the church to St. Peter. At the same time the Bishop administered Confirmation to one hundred and twenty-three persons. In a short time Father Ostlangenberg liquidated three thousand two hundred dollars of the debt. One month before the dedication of his church Father Ostlangenberg had been at Chicago to take part in the first diocesan synod, April 18, 1847.[21]

On April 10, 1848 Bishop Quarter died. His successor, Bishop Van de Velde after his consecration (February 11), before going to Chicago, gave confirmation at Alton, on February 18. His Diary[22] gives a graphic account of his experiences in St. Clair and Clinton Counties:

On Sunday, February 25th the Bishop gave Confirmation at Belleville, St. Clair County to twenty-eight persons, of whom two were converts. It had thawed nearly all of the preceding week and the roads were almost impassible. The carriage which was sent out on Friday to St. Louis to take out the Bishop, could not reach one-half the distance. The omnibus vehicle did not run on Saturday and the Bishop had to leave St. Louis on Sunday morning, after celebrating Mass and found an omnibus on the Illinois side of the river which left about 9 o'clock and reached Belleville about two o'clock P. M. The people who attended in crowds at High Mass had mostly dispersed; the bell was rung for Vespers after which the Bishop gave confirmation.

On Monday, February 26th, the Bishop left in an open wagon for Germantown, Clinton County (called Shoal Creek Settlement), where he arrived at night-fall and was met at a distance of about three miles by fifty-two horsemen, and at the church by Rev. J. Marogna. On the following day the Bishop gave Confirmation to 103 persons and preached in German, and on the 28th left for the Libory Settlement; sixty horsemen came to meet him at the crossing of the Oka or Kaskaskia river and when in the neighborhood of the

Joseph's on the North side (opened August, 15, 1846). Later on he was pastor of Shoal Creek, Clinton County.

[21] v. F. Beuckmann, *History of the Diocese of Belleville*, St. John's Orphanage Edition, p. 28, and Diary of Bishop Quarter, p. 83.

[22] v. Diary of Bishop Van de Velde, *Souvenir of Silver Jubilee of Archbishop Feehan*, p. 89 ss.

ev. Mr. Ostlangenberg appeared at the head of a long
nd women, followed by all the children that had been
Confirmation.

lay March 1st, the Bishop administered Confirmation to
the small log church of Liborius, where he preached
t High Mass, and also said Mass next day. Arrange-
nade to build a new brick church, 80 by 40 feet, and
with four windows on each side, each 10 by 5, with
heads. Permission was also given to build a frame
t long by 26 wide and 16 high, at Fayetteville, St. Clair
ie bank of the Oka or Kaskaskia river.[23]

lay, March 4th, the Bishop was to have left for Prairie
ive Confirmation in St. Augustine's Church on Sunday,
lay, Tuesday and Wesnesday at O'Hara's Settlement,
and Waterloo, but the bad state of the weather and
which were impassible, rendered it scarcely possible
was therefore compelled to remain at Oka or Libory
l Monday—not being able for want of a chalice and of
rate Mass on Sunday or the following day—when with
y he returned to Belleville in a four-horse wagon.

ay, 6th of March, the Bishop returned to St. Louis in
the first that had ventured to make the trip for the
; four times did the leading horses break their gears,
wagon buried up to the axle-trees in the mud, and a
used to pull it out; when in sight of the river the axle-
twain. It had taken more than eight hours to travel
)f fourteen to fifteen miles.

to Bishop Van de Velde's Diary (p. 115) Father
ς, on November 13, 1849, arrived in Chicago on his way
th the Bishop's permission, and left Chicago on Novem-
as replaced at Belleville by Rev. Buschotts, S. J. On
the next year, the Bishop, returning from Detroit by
aukee, met Father Ostlangenberg, arrived from Europe
with him to Chicago on August 28. Ostlangenberg
er left Chicago for Belleville on August 30. (Diary,
28).

ter (1850) at Belleville, the cemetery on Walnut Hill

, 1849 the Libory Settlement again obtained a resident priest in
Father Brickwedde. Flor. Aug. Brickwedde was b. June 24,
nau in Hanover and was ordained priest on September 20, 1830,
He arrived at St. Louis in July 1837 and was appointed first
of the Mission (Ascension of Christ) at Quincy, Ill. After a
fight with an unruly faction in the parish, he resigned March 16,
Bishop Van de Velde to St. Louis and was there appointed pastor
ment. He died at Belleville, November 21, 1865. v. Pastoralblatt,

was purchased. On January 4, 1852, a Mutual Benefit Society was established, which, however, after a few years was discontinued.

Whilst he was pastor at Belleville, Father Ostlangenberg visited nearly all the missions in St. Clair County. In 1845 and 1846 he frequently went to Cahokia, since the parish after Father Loisel's death (May 10, 1845) was vacant for nearly three years. Also St. Thomas' church in Johnson Settlement was attended by him, until, in the year 1849, it was abandoned and the congregation was trans-.ferred to Centreville. In 1846 his name appears in the baptismal register of the German settlement (Teutonia) near Prairie du Long. . At Mascoutah and Fayetteville he sometimes said Mass in the houses of the colonists. In 1854 and 1855 he went to French Village (St. Philip) which parish had no resident priest at that time. He may justly be called the Apostle of St. Clair County.[24]

This was the glorious period in the life of Father Ostlangenberg, when he traveled over the forest trails and through the swamps and marshy prairies of St. Clair County. Such a life, considering the frailty of his constitution, demanded the courage of a deep-rooted faith and an indefatigable zeal for the salvation of souls.

The apostolate of Father Ostlangenberg at Belleville and St. Clair County in general lasted until November, 1855. Father G. H. Plathe, the pastor of the Germans of the southside of Chicago had moved the church of St. Peter's to Polk Street where the present church stands. This change was required by circumstances and was satisfactory to most of the members of St. Peter's congregation, but by no means to all. Discord in the parish rose to such a degree that Father Plathe resigned (September 23, 1855) and left the diocese. His successor was Rev. C. Schilling. But the incessant scrimmage with the trustees was so distasteful to him, that he threw up his hands after two weeks and also resigned. Bishop O'Regan who had been rector of the diocesan Seminary at Carondelet (St. Louis), was personally acquainted with Father Ostlangenberg the zealous pastor of Belleville. He called him to Chicago to restore peace and order there as ten years before he had done at Belleville. To strengthen

---

[24] 23 June, 1853: Anniversary of the Consecration of St. Liborius Church. Said first Mass (Van de Velde), at which the children made their first Communion. High Mass by Rev. J. G. Ostlangenberg of Belleville; Deacon H. Fortmann of Hanover, Subdeacon, Rev. H. Liermann of Centreville; Assistant deacons at the throne: Rev. F. Patschowski and Rev. A. Brickwedde, Pastor. Sermon by Rev. F. Patschowski.

July 5: He sang High Mass at French Village (Ostl.), 6th, at Waterloo, on the occasion of Confirmation. (Diary of Bishop Van de Velde).

his position, he gave him the title of Vicar General for the Germans of Chicago.[25]

But the hopes of Bishop O'Regan were not realized. Father Ostlangenberg failed to quench the fires of tumult in St. Peter's parish. He struggled with the trustees for one long year, then, irritated and despondent, he resigned, following the examples of his predecessors, Fathers Jung, Weikamp, Plathe and Schilling. The continual strife was too much for the impressible man. The Bishop sent him to a new field of activity.

When Father Bernard Weikamp who had been Pastor of St. Peter's before Ostlangenberg (1850-1853) had relinquished all hopes of pacifying the trustees of his parish, he left his unruly congregation. From means which he had brought from Europe and other money which he collected at Chicago, he built a frame church on the west side, in honor of St. Francis of Assisi. This new place of worship was intended for the use and benefit of a Franciscan community of the Third Order which he had undertaken to found whilst pastor of St. Peter's. To the church of St. Francis he retired in the summer of 1853. From all sides pious souls, men, women and children, flocked to him, to live in poverty, chastity and obedience, under his direction according to the spirit of St. Francis. Father Weikamp, by permission of the Bishop, in connection with his church, also formed a German parish, which was to have no trustees, since the church was property of the community.

But the severe zeal and almost eccentric piety of their pastor was offensive to some members of the parish. Father Weikamp also saw that the fast growing city of Chicago was not a place fit to establish a theocratic community according to his own peculiar ideas. Wherefore, in the fall of 1855, he accepted an invitation of Bishop Baraga of Sault-Ste-Marie, Michigan, and transferred his community to the Indian mission of Arbre Croche. He closed his church at Chicago and offered the property for sale. To this rather impetuous procedure Bishop O'Regan objected. However, by correspondence between Bishops Baraga and O'Regan the affair was finally settled,[26] and Father Duggan, Administrator of the diocese during Bishop

---

[25] v. F. Beuckmann, *History of the Diocese of Belleville*, 1914, St. Clair County, Necrology, p. 2. He may have enjoyed the title of Vicar General when still at Belleville.

[26] v. J. Rezek, *History of the diocese of Marquette*, I, p. 142. Much of the information about Father Weikamp I received through the kindness of P. Bernardin Abbink of Avilla, Ind.

58   F. G. HOLWECK

O'Regan's absence, reopened St. Francis church in January, 1857
with Father Ostlangenberg as pastor.

But the parish had hardly been organized along the lines of the
diocesan statutes, when the newly elected trustees, as most trustees
did in those times, rose in arms against their pastor. On the occasion
of a bazaar, in January, 1859, when Father Ostlangenberg's trusty
housekeeper pitched into the fight to defend her master, the ungallant
trustees threw her down the steps leading to the hall.[27] Now Father
Ostlangenberg was done with St. Francis parish, done with the
diocese of Chicago. He left the city at the end of January, 1859, a
few days, after the administrator of the diocese, Bishop Duggan, had
been transferred to See of Chicago. Otlangenberg's work in the
pioneer missions of St. Clair County, Illinois, had been eminently
successful, but amongst the shrewd city people of Chicago he help-
lessly failed and never after regained a strong foothold anywhere.

He did not return, however, to the south of Illinois, where the
See of Alton had been erected, on January 9, 1857, nor to his original home diocese, St. Louis, but he followed the example of his
friend, Father Simon Siegrist[28] of Sts. Peter and Paul's church in
St. Louis and sought admission in the diocese of Vincennes, Indiana.
Bishop Maurice de Saint-Palais who had preceded Father Ostlangenberg in the missionary field of Chicago before the coming of Bishop
Quarter, was soliciting for German priests to provide for the numerous
immigrants who from the Teutonic countries of Europe were flocking
into the State of Indiana. Father Siegrist probably brought about
the incardination of Ostlangenberg into the diocese of Vincennes.

Less than two months after his departure from Chicago, March
19, 1859, we find his name in the baptismal register of Richmond,
Wayne County, Indiana.[29] But his soft and restless soul would not

---

[27] Information given by Mr. Nicholas Dreher, the pioneer teacher of St.
Joseph's School at Chicago, who in his boyhood was a sort of a factotum to
Father Ostlangenberg and lived in his house at St. Francis Church.

[28] Rev. Simon Siegrist was b. at Stotzheim in Alsace in 1822; he came to
St. Louis with Vicar General Melcher in July 1847 and was ordained priest on
August 29 of the same year. After having been pastor of Mattese, St. Louis
County, he founded Sts. Peter and Paul's parish in St. Louis in 1849; January 1,
1858 he left for Vincennes and died at Indianapolis.

[29] "After Father Merl left in June, 1858 the congregation (of Richmond)
was without a resident priest until the following spring, when Rev. Ostlangenberg
was stationed here. Father Ostlangenberg stayed only a few months, and the
growing congregation was again left without a pastor until the newly ordained
Rev. J. B. H. Seepe arrived on Christmas Eve, 1859. The church was too small
to accommodate the faithful. It was therefore decided to erect a larger edifice,

t him to take root: In September of the same year his name
pears from the registers of St. Andrew's church at Richmond.
ould not fully hunt up the trail of Ostlangenberg through the
ern portion of Indiana; we traced him next to St. Joseph's
strong) near Evansville, where he baptized from November 1,
to April 7, 1861,[30] then to Madison on the Ohio, where he was
iistrator of St. Mary's German parish from May 26, 1861 to
nber 30, 1861, whilst the pastor, Rev. Leonard Brandt, was
t in Europe.[31] Then he was pastor of Jeffersonville, opposite
ville, Ky.[32] At last, since December, 1863 we find him at St.
el's church, Brookville, on the White River. His first entry in
iptismal book was made January 3, 1864, his last on December
8.[33] St. Michael's parish at Brookville, at that time, was mixed,
an and English. Father Ostlangenberg, however, had come to
na to work amongst his own countrymen and grew impatient,
se the Bishop would or could not offer him a purely German
n. Much against the advice of Father Scheideler, his friend,
t the diocese of Vineennes, in December, 1868, and offered his
es to Bishop Carrel of Covington, Ky.[34]
out this time he paid a visit to his old home in the North of
any, probably with the intention of remaining there to find
where there were no merciless trustees to rack the poor pastor,
urches to be built without funds, no contending nationalities
satisfied. But an American missionary, inured to the drudgery
neer life could no longer conform to the bureaucratic monotony
ropean conditions. He returned to the mission of America. In
atholic Directory of 1870 he appears as pastor of Four Mile,
he city of Covington[35]; in 1874 he was parish priest of Ludlow,

---

on the English speaking portion resolved to organize a parish for them-
For' History of Catholicity in Richmond, St. Andrew's church.'' Comed by Rev. F. A. Roell, Richmond.
ly the kindness of Rev. Th. J. Vollmer of Armstrong.
. Ch. Bilger, *History of St. Mary's Parish*, Madison, Ind., p. 11.
atholic Directory, 1863.
y the kindness of Rev. A. Schaaf, Brookville.
aformation received through the kindness of Rev. M. Fletschmann, Vin-
Ind. Also Father Schaaf writes: ''The reason assigned for his leaving
lle is given: This parish at that time, was mixed, German and English,
being a German, preferred a German parish.''
our Mile is now called Camp Springs. Ostlangenberg was appointed to
ish on December 12, 1868. (Reiter Sohematismus, p. 59.) He performed
baptism on January 22, 1869, his last September 19, 1873. Father Chas.

Kent County, and since May, 1875,[36] pastor of Augusta, Bracken County. When he came to Augusta, he was 65 years of age; bodily weakness precluded the possibility of further peregrinations. He died at Augusta, on August 9, 1885 and was buried in the cemetery of the Catholic parish of St. Augustine's.

F. G. HOLWECK.

St. Louis, Mo.

Woeste of Camp Springs writes to us (April 5, 1920): "He labored with great zeal in this parish, which at time numbered ninety families, paid off a considerable portion of the parish debt (as much as $1,300.00 in a single year of his regime) and through his kind disposition and his good example succeeded in winning the hearts of his people. He remained until September, 1873."

[36] By the kindness of Rev. R. Van der Vorst of Augusta.

THE NORTHEASTERN PART OF THE DIOCESE OF ST. LOUIS UNDER BISHOP ROSATI

(Continued from April, 1920)

The requirements of space forced us to break off in our account of Father Peter Paul Lefevere's aactivities in planting the church throughout the northwestern part of Illinois. We here resume the thread of our narrative, or rather the good Father's own narrative as contained in his letters to Bishop Rosati. Among the many cares thrust upon the devoted missionary by the dispensations of Divine Providence, were the three orphan children, concerning whom we have heard a few particulars in a former chapter. Father Lefevere now writes:

ST. PAUL'S, September the 26th, 1835.

To the Right Reverend Bishop Rosati:

RIGHT REVEREND SAR—The great interest I feel in the welfare of the orphan children of Wm. Carter, of whom I formerly wrote to you, as also their now unpleasant situation and the embarassment of those with whom they are living, compel me to importune you again with entreaties for their speedy admission into Orphan Asylum. Before my departure from St. Louis you promised to receive them as soon as the new building should be completed; and from the advertisements I see in the *Shepherd*,[2] this building must by this time be nearly finished. Therefore I hope, through your benevolence, that the long wished for time of their admission is now come. You would confer the greatest favor upon your humble servant and the tutors of these children, if you would be so kind as to write imme-

---

[1] Father St. Cyr has been repeatedly quoted as saying that President Lincoln was in youth a Catholic. What Father St. Cyr actually stated was taken down from the priest's own lips by Archbishop Ireland in 1866: "I visited several times the Lincolns in their home in Southern Illinois. The father and the step-mother of Abraham Lincoln both were Catholics. How they had become Catholics, I do not know. They were not well instructed in their religion; but they were strong and sincere in their profession of it. I said Mass repeatedly in their house. Abraham was not a Catholic; he never had been one, and he never led me to believe that he would become one. At this time Abraham was twenty years old, or thereabouts, a thin, tall young fellow, kind and good natured. He used to assist me in preparing the altar for Mass. Once he made me a present of a half-dozen of chairs. He had made those chairs with his own hands, expressly for me; they were simple in form and fashion as chairs used in country places then would be." *The American Catholic Historical Researches*, July, 1905, p. 208.

[2] *The Shepherd of the Valley*, the early St. Louis Catholic paper, founded in 1834, probably by Deodat Taylor, suspended before 1839. Next published in 1851 by E. A. Bakewell and discontinued in 1854.

61

diately, when and in what manner they might be sent. Mrs. Carter, the grand-mother and guardian of these orphans, is particularly anxious to bind them, if agreeable to your views, either to you or to their superior, for fear that after her death, some of their paternal relations might interfere with their happiness, being strenuously opposed to the Catholic religion.

I hope you still enjoy perfect health, and may God continue it for many years. I am well at present, but somewhat fatigued from the continual missionary courses I have performed ever since my departure from St. Louis, in which I had the pleasure of receiving into the pale of the Church three adult persons, one of whom I solemnly baptized before a great concourse of people, which, I hope, will have caused some good effect upon their minds. Nothing more at present, except that the Catholics on Salt River and throughout my mission are more than anxious to see and hear their beloved Bishop, whom they never as yet had the pleasure of seeing and hearing. Persons are daily inquiring, when, I should think, the Right Reverend Bishop will come, to administer confirmation, and I am almost wearied out telling them: he will, he will, he will, without ever being able to state the certain week or month of his coming. As I propose to set out this very morning for another mission, and expect to be absent for some length of time, I hope you will have the kindness of sending an immediate answer, in regard to these two orphans, to Mrs. Ann Carter (widow), directed to Dry Fork postoffice, Ralls County, Missouri. By this you will infinitely oblige, Right Reverend Sir,

Your most humble and obedient servant,

PETER P. LEFEVERE.

The next letters revert to the work to be done immediately for the rising settlements between the Lower Illinois and Mississippi Rivers:

ST. PAUL'S, October 6, 1836.

RIGHT REVEREND SIR—I have been deeply engaged in the constant exercises of the mission ever since my departure from St. Louis. When I reached Salt River after a mission of 18 days, I had no sooner received your letter of the 9th of August, conveying the doleful intelligence of the death of our much beloved Mr. Condamine,[19] but another one was handed to me which called me in all haste into the State of Illinois, to assist two persons at the point of death. So that, although much fatigued and thinking to be at my journey's end, I was obliged to set out again, and ride in full speed upwards of a hundred miles to the County of McDonough, where instead of two I found numbers of Catholics dangerously sick of the bilious and congestive fevers, which complaints were so prevailing there and in the adjacent counties, that I have been all this while so intensively engaged in visiting and assisting the sick in various parts of Illinois, that I could

---

19 The Rev. M. Condamine had on April 18, 1836, been entrusted with the care of souls in the congregation about Fever River, the principal places of which are mentioned as Galena, Prairie du Chien and Dubuque. But as Father Mazzuchelli at the same time received notice from his Dominican Superior that he might stay for a time at Fever River, the appointment of Condamine was revoked, and on May 18, 1836 Condamine was appointed Pastor of Cahokia, and two days later Bishop Rosati's Pro-Vicar General. On the 8th of August, 1836, Father Condamine died in Cahokia.

:isure, many. a time, to say my office, and have. often been in danger of
in the difficult crossing of swamps and high water-courses. But thanks
, I have escaped safe so far; sickness is now abating, and I hope to be
r sometime in attending the different stations here in Missouri.
ırospect of having a stone church erected at the head of the Des Moines
:ms to have failed. Mr. George Atcheson has sold out and his property
into the hands of an Eastern Company. But I hope that the congre-
ıich consists of 15 families, will shortly be able to build one themselves.
egation of Crooked Creek, hearing the good news of soon having a priest
amongst them, have purchased 40 acres of land in your name for the
which I hold the certificate. This congregation, being on the east line
k County, and west of McDonough, would be the most central place of
on, and would likewise offer the most suitable and convenient residence
:st. There are upward of 30 Catholic families, all zealous and much
religion; and as they all live tolerably compacted, there might soon be
establishment made and decently supported. From there he (Father
might extend his mission to the head of the Rapids and to the Half
eservation, which is only a distance of 25 to 30 miles. Also to the north-
r of Fulton County, at a distance of 40 miles, where there is a small
on of fervent Catholics, who, last Summer, have laid off a town named
tin, which from its situation must soon become a considerable inland
n he could now and then go to Peoria, McComb, Rushville, Meridocia,
n, Jacksonvlile, Naples, etc., where are here and there some number of
living." But principally to Quincy, which is 55 miles from Crooked
l where there is a large and still growing congregation of between 40
milies in and about town. When I was there last week, the Catholics
ansported with the prospects I gave them of being regularly visited,
became more anxious than ever to build a church. To this end we held
and appointed five trustees to draw and make up a subscription and
i the building of the church. A respectable gentleman, not a Catholic,
ind enough to give a lot of ground for the purpose, which was then
y surveyed and whereof the deed was to be made in your name the
day. More than half of this congregation are Germans, and they are
y desirous of having preaching in German now and then. The Lutheran
who have also formed a small congregation here, have got a German
rom Cincinnati to preach for them; and the Presbyterians, who con-
deavor to draw all on their side, have offered him their meeting house,
ıute largely towards his support. Even some of the Catholics, wearied
ithout Divine Service on Sundays, and desirous of hearing a sermon,
ed in making up his salary. Thus you see that this congregation
ve all, in need of immediate attendance. For the Catholics have now
good footing in Quincy, but if they be neglected, I greatly fear, that
l not be of long duration. I would therefore beg you, earnestly, to
ı that mission, if possible, a priest who speaks the German language
English, for there is another congregation of Germans in Beardstown
ıois River, 12 miles east of Rushvill, where he could do an immense

ıese places and many more will meet us again and again in the course
few years.

deal of good. If it be not possible, I hope you will endeavor to get someone to go from St. Louis at least two or three times a year to Quincy; Mr. Lutz, for instance, or Father Helias or anyone else, which might easily be done, for two boats are running regularly, every week, the trip from St. Louis and back. Moreover the Germans have promised to pay the priest who would go, for his trouble and expense. He might address himself to Adam Schmitt, opposite the Presbyterian meeting house, in Quincy. With full confidence therefore in your zeal and good will towards this mission, I am, Right Reverend Sir,

> Your most humble and obedient servant,
>
>   PETER P. LEFEVERE.

P. S.—Please send me an Ordo for next year, for I did not get any for this year.

Father Lefevere's anxiety in regard to the Catholics of Quincy was not without cause; for in the course of time one of the first and most influential promoters of the church there apostatized. Five months, however, passed by without anything more than an official enquiry as to conditions instead of a promise of assistance. And yet Father Lefevere was in urgent need of help, especiall for Illinois, as the following letter shows:

> ST. PAUL'S, March the 9th, 1837.

RIGHT REVEREND SIR—Your letter of the 5th of Jauuary, 1827, came to hand a few days since and I hasten, with the first opportunity to comply with your request, in answering the several interrogatories therein contained. I shall answer them severally and as precisely as possible. First, the number of Catholics I visit is from 1,000 to 2,000 souls. Second, in the mission which I have hitherto attended there are fourteen stations, id est, congregations, big and small; besides a great number of scattered families not belonging to any particular congregation, of these there are eight stations in the State of Missouri, four in the State of Illinois, and two in the Wisconsin territory. Viz.: in the State of Missouri, 1, in Pike County, on Pinno Creek; 2, in Lincoln County, between Troy and Louisville; 3, in Ralls County, on Salt River, fifteen miles northwest from New London; 4, on Cedar Creek; 5, in Monroe County, on Indian Creek, seven miles north from Florida; 6, on the South Fork of Salt River, six miles south from Florida; 7, in Marion County, in the town of Palmyra; 8, in Lewis County, on the Wyaconda River, ten miles northwest from Tully. In the State of Illinois, 1, in Adams County, in the town of Quincy; 2, in Hancock County, at the head of the Lower Rapids; 3, at the head of Crooked Creek, twenty-five miles east from Commerce; 4, in the northwest corner of Fulton County, on Cedar Creek. In the Wisconsin territory, 1, at Keokuk, in the Half Indian tract, between the River Des Moines and the Mississippi; 2, on Skunk River, ten miles west from Fort Madison. Third, the number of baptisms of infants is seventy-seven. Fourth, number of adults, eight. Fifth, number of converts, eight. Sixth, as to the number of deaths, I am not able to make a statement; but the number of burials I have performed, is nine. Seventh, number of marriages, thirty-six. Eighth, number of First Communions, about twenty-five. Ninth, number of Paschal Communions is 497. As to the number of dispensations for marriages, which I have granted, it is as follows:

l) Dispensations upon the impediment existing between baptized and non-bap-ted, fourteen. (2) Upon the impediment of consanguinity in the second degree, ro; of consanguinity in the third degree, one. Total, eighteen. Such is the atement, Right Reverend Sir, I can only give in answer to the several questions u have asked me. These stations above named, together with the numerous fam-es widely scattered in remote parts of the same and other counties, keep me ntinually traveling from one part of the country to another, and were I to go ither soever, Catholics, dispersed in the country, invite and beg me to come, one ip would take me six months steady riding. And although these Catholics ought be visited, yet it is absolutely out of my power. For no sooner have I ended e journey, than I have to commence another, and so on in rotation; so much so, at, in the course of the year, I cannot remain one week steady at home. And rticularly this last winter, during the coldest weather, at a time when I thought enjoy a few days for myself, I was called out to the sick; three times into the ate of Illinois, once to the River Des Moines, and once into the Wisconsin terri-ry, 150 miles north from Ralls County; and that at a time when the snow was out eighteen inches deep on the ground, and I had to ride a distance of twelve les on the ice on the Mississippi. Then on my return, the weather breaking up th a sudden thaw, the waters began to run so swiftly, that I was compelled to ivel all the night and day in full speed in order to get the start of the high iters, and it was then only by lucky circumstance, or special providence of God, at I several times escaped being drowned. I must finish this detail for fear of ing prolix. But if ever you have been on extensive missions, Right Reverend r, particularly in a newly settled country like this, where people are poor, with-t sufficient house room and destitute even of all the necessary conveniences of 'e, you must be acquainted with the hardships and privations to which a priest continually exposed, and the little decency with which the Sacred Rites can be rformed. To those unacquainted with its meaning, the celebration of Mass in tle log cabins, which serve for work-room, refectory, dormitory and kitchen, to merous families, must look more like a comedy than a religious action. For ' part, I am thoroughly acquainted with them. Four and a half years' con-nt exercise in this mission has made me taste so much of this bitter cup, that hout assistance, I am becoming unable to continue it any longer. Moreover,)erceive that, after much toil and labor, I have done but little good to others, l greatly endangered my own life and salvation. For I perceive but too well t, when I am attending one congregation, religion suffers in other congrega-as, for want of their being regularly attended and instructed. Whilst, on the er hand, the most of my time being spent in traveling, necessity must of course, ipel me to retrench from my own religious duties and devotional exercises; and h a necessity often repeated, is but too apt to engender a habit. As the money ch you have received at different times from several parts of Europe,[13] was

---

[13] Bishop Rosati did, indeed, during these trying years obtain great help from Leopoldine Society of Vienna in Austria. At least 54,500 florins (a fl. 40 cts.) e contributed by the Catholics of Austria to the support of the missions in Diocese of St. Louis. Other large sums came from the Society of the Propa-ion of the Faith of Lyons, France, and from the St. Ludwig's Missionary lety of Munich in Bavaria. It is well, especially in these ungracious days, to ill the true Christian charity of our foreign brethren in the faith, shown to n the years of our greatest need.

given for the very purpose of supporting the mission, I had always entertained great hopes that you would have lent some pecuniary aid to erect, here and there, a plain building, at least in places where it is indispensably necessary to celebrate the Divine Mysteries with any degree of becoming decency; and my hopes were so much the more confident, because I knew that you knew that this mission stood the most in need of it. But now my hopes look frustrated, and I begin to despair. From the little zeal and interest you have hitherto manifested towards this mission, it appears to me that you think it not worth your attention, and that all your object is to ornament St. Louis and care but little about the rest. But I must confess that, when I am in St. Louis, my heart sickens whenever I behold the superfluous splendor and luxe that is there displayed about the Cathedral, whilst religion here suffers from want of things indispensably necessary. This, in my opinion, looks pretty much like a father of a family arrayed in the most splendid apparel surrounded with a parcel of his children stark naked. I was also in hopes, Right Reverend Sir, that you would have stationed a priest on Crooked Creek, for the mission of Illinois and Wisconsin territory, as you promised me last Summer; and that you would have mentioned something about it to me in answer to a letter I wrote to you on the subject last Autumn. But as I have never received or heard a word about it, I must now also confess to you that I am tired and wearied out, and that what you tacitly seem to exact from me with regard to my continuing these long protracted journeys, seems to me unreasonable and impracticable. Wherefore, unless there be someone sent to divide with me the labors of this mission, I have resolved to abandon it and to retire to myself, or leave the Diocese. Not because I am not willing to labor in the ministry, but because I feel unable to continue what I have hitherto done. For let the work be ever so tilsome and fatiguing, I will cheerfully undertake it, provided, I am able to do to and do it with usefulness to the salvation of others without endangering my own. But in the present circumstances and upon other considerations not mentioned, I feel myself under no obligation to stay any longer. In finishing, I beg of you now, as a favor, to let me know by letter, whether and when you will send a priest to the Illinois. As to the different stations and other particulars of that mission you, no doubt, know them already from the last letter I wrote to you on the subject. In expectation then of a speedy answer, I remain, with great respect, Right Reverend Sir,

Your most humble and obedient servant,

PETER P. LEFEVERE.

McDonough County is an open prairie traversed by a stream of water called Crooked Creek. Its first settlement was Carter's, made in 1826. What had delayed its progress was the lack of timberlands, so necessary for building and fuel. The principal settlements in 1834 were Macomb and Fountain Green, the latter place about twenty-five miles from Commerce, on the Mississippi River, afterward called Nauvoo, the one-time home of the Mormons. The head of Des Moines Rapids, also called the Lower Rapids to distinguish them from the Upper Rapids at Nauvoo, is Warsaw, in Hancock County, just across the river from Keokuk, Iowa.

According to Father Lefevere there were a good number of German Catholics at Quincy, which, therefore, should have a German priest, and an entire settlement of German Catholics at Beardstown, on the Illinois River. Father Lutz, whom Lefevere wished to be sent to the Germans at Quincy, was the Indian missionary of a former chapter of this sketch. Father Helias, S. J., was the Apostle of Central Missions, where numerous German Catholics required his continual presence.

Father Lefevere has in his official report for 1836 given a statement of the "Number of *Catholics* living in the several respective counties, expressed here below, with the different churches therein built or proposed to be built":

STATE OF MISSOURI

County of Lincoln, a church proposed to be built at Louisville.............. 108
County of Pike.. 113
County of Ralls, one church already built (St. Paul's) in Salt River Township, and another one now a-building in the Town of Cincinnati........ 455
County of Monroe, a church (St. Stephen's) to be built in Sandy Creek, five miles north of Florida... 232
County of Marion 69
County of Lewis, a church proposed to be erected on the Wyaconda River, eight miles northwest of Tully.................................. 109
Half Indian Tract... 38

1124

STATE OF ILLINOIS

Adams County, a church proposed to be built in Quincy................... 205
Hancock County, a church is to be built at the Des Moines Rapids, and another at the headwaters of Crooked Creek, near Fountain River.............. 214
Schuyler County 29
Fulton County, a church proposed in the Town of St. Augustine........... 32
McDonough County 25
Peoria County 13

548

My address runs thus:
        PETER PAUL LEFEVERE,
            Dry Forks Postoffice,
                Ralls County, Mo.

It will be noticed that in this account the missions of the Northwest Territory, i. e., of Iowa, are wanting. The reason is because they, with Galena and Prairie du Chien, had been turned over to Father Samuel Mazzuchelli on June 24, 1835, in answer to his letter from Prairie du Chien, dated March 12, 1835:

MOST REVEREND BISHOP—I was informed a few days ago that the Territory of Wisconsin now forms a part of your Diocese, and as a consequence the two priests of this territory are under your ecclesiastical jurisdiction. For the last three months I have been making preparations to leave this place, intending to go to the State of Ohio. In the month of April I went down the Mississippi River in a steamboat, using the opportunity to inform myself concerning the state of these missions.

Bishop Rese has not yet received any reply from Rome regarding me, and now I, who wanted to do so much, am tired of being left alone among difficulties without any assistance, and of being exposed to so many dangers. I have started an association at Prairie du Chien for the building of a church; the men pay fifty cents each month, and the women twenty-five cents, but my church will not be built without the assistance of a priest. I am preparing many for first Communion and others to make their Easter. Father D. Vanderbrock, a Hollander of the Order of St. Dominic, is now the pastor of Green Bay, where there are no less than 500 French and about just as many Catholic Indians.

Asking your blessing, I have the honor to be

Your Reverence's most humble servant,

SAMUEL MAZZUCHELLI, O. P.

In his answer of July 27th of the same year Father Mazzuchelli informs Bishop Rosati that he had in the meantime visited his Dominican Superior Father Young at Somerset, Ohio, and obtained permission to remain, for a time, under the rule of the Bishop of St. Louis. But a difficulty arose, as the permission had been given orally, whereas Bishop Rosati required it in writing. But this slight difficulty was arranged pleasantly and Father Mazzuchelli entered the Diocese of St. Louis and labored therein with truly apostolic zeal and corresponding success, as we shall see later on.

Here is Father Mazzuchelli's letter:

GALINA, July 27, 1835.

MOST REVEREND BISHOP ROSATI—I would like to have seen you personally after my return from the State of Ohio, in order to acquaint you with the permission which Sig. Young gave me to remain yet a little while in this part (of the land) so that I might settle my personal affairs at Green Bay. I have personal debts which I am obliged to pay, and in Ohio I would not be able to find the necessary means to pay my just debts to my neighbors. Mr. Young did not give me this permission in writing, he gave it "viva voce." This is an abuse which the Dominicans have introduced into this country, and it is rare, as far as I know, that they give any commission in writing, when the person who commands and the person that should obey find themselves together. Yet the measures which Your Grace has taken do not offend me in the least; I ought rather to praise the exact observance of the laws of Mother Church in your Diocese, no less than the prudence with which your letter is filled. I was sick in bed for about a week with throat trouble and a bilious fever, but now I am convalescing. The present circumstances affect me very much, for the people were so good to me while I was sick. There are many families that contributed to the church and that say that

they belong to the parish of Galena. They live in the neighborhood, but in the Territory of Michigan. Again I want to observe that my honor, as well as the good of religion here, is in danger, because we have done for this church in fifteen days as much as was done for the past five years; and now, that we have the land, the money and the good will, all of a sudden the principal and necessary agent should be wanting. I will do all that is possible for me to continue the building of the church, without which the priests will not be able to remain here, and would always be embarrassed. I repeat that these circumstances touch my heart and make me cry, yet I hope that after this storm I will find mercy with men, as I see that I have found mercy with the Lord. My illness rendered me incapable of leaving for Prairie du Chien.

Be kind enough to remember me in your prayers. I am,

Your most humble servant,

SAMUEL MAZZUCHELLI.

P. S.—I received your Grace's letter the 26th of June while I was ill.

In the meantime Father Lefevere had received notice of the appointment of Father St. Cyr for the missions in northern Illinois. In his elation he answers at once:

DRY FORK P. O., March 17, 1837.

RIGHT REVEREND SIR—I have just received your letter of the 20th of February ult., eight days after I mailed my last, by which you give me the glad tidings of the arrival of Mr. St. Cyr, and of his destination for Crooked Creek. It is truly consoling to me, and will no doubt be the cause of much good in that mission. I feel sorry, very sorry, that I cannot go to St. Louis about the time you would wish me to go. But now I have made several appointments at different stations; also several persons have made preparations and fixed the time for marrying after Easter, so that my absence at this time would cause much interruption. For having caused some discontent among the people, by frequently disappointing them, on account of the many and distant sick calls, I had last Winter, I should not wish to disappoint them any more, if I could possibly avoid it. Moreover many persons are now preparing to make their Easter, and might perhaps neglect it, if I were to absent myself at this time. So that I shall not be able to leave here before the third or fourth Monday after Easter. I hope, therefore, that you will excuse me; I will give Mr. St. Cyr all the instruction and encouragement possible with regard to that mission. Should he desire to start to that mission sooner, and have my company, he might come to Salt River, and I will conduct him up and introduce him to the congregation on Crooked Creek; if not, he may expect me in St. Louis about the fourth week after Easter.

I am in great haste, Right Reverend Sir,

Your humble and obedient servant,

PETER P. LEFEVERE.

With the appointment of Father St. Cyr for Crooked Creek and Quincy, Father Lefevere's missionary activities were confined to Northeast Missouri. We will give the substance of his report for 1836, with some additional information derived from other unpublished sources:

Ralls County, Cincinnati Mission, St. Mark's Church 407
Ralls County, Salt River Mission, St. Paul's Church
Lincoln County, Louisville Mission, St. Simeon's Church............. 84
Pike County, Pinno Creek Mission 106
Pike County, Cedar Creek Mission
Monroe County, Indian Creek Mission, St. Stephen's Church......... 261
Marion County, Palmyra Mission.................................. 95
Lewis County, Wyaconda River Mission, St. John's Ev. Church 160
Clark County, West Santa Fe Mission, St. Bartholomew's Church

¯1113

Concerning the early settlers of St. Paul's, we have already given an account. At Cincinnati a church was building under the title of St. Mark. Concerning St. Simeon's Church at Louisville, in Lincoln County, we find that there was a frame building, thirty feet square, erected in 1838. The first Catholics of the place were Dr. Hayden, Enoch Emerson, coming there in 1830. The first priests to say Mass were the Jesuit Fathers, Felix Verreydt and Charles Van Quickenborne, in 1832.[13] Mass was said by these priests and by Father Lefevere in the house of Mr. Emerson and Dr. Hayden. The number of families in 1838 is biven as twenty.

Passing over Pike County we come to St. Stephen's, at Indian Creek, in Monroe County, which received its first Catholic settlers in the year 1832, in the families of Leonard Green and Alexander Winnsett. Mass was said and other services were held in the house of Leonard Green for three years, then at Raphael Yates' and Mr. Piersall's homes. The church, a log building, forty-eight feet by twenty-five feet, was erected in 1838. The first Mass was said in it on the third Sunday of August of the same year. There was eight acres of land belonging to the church and a graveyard, which were given by Vincent Yeates and James Murphy. In 1838 there were thirty-eight Catholic families at Indian Creek.

The following letter, written on December 26, 1837, is the last one received by Bishop Rosati from St. Paul's:

RIGHT REVEREND SIR—I received your letter of the 6th of September last, and in compliance with your request, as I am now on the eve of starting on mission to the northern boundary of the state, I hasten to send you, enclosed, the statistics of my mission for the year 1837, which I have made up to the best of my knowledge. You will perceive that the space under the head: *Nus. Confirmatum*, is

---

[13] As early as 1830 Louisiana, New London, Palmyra and Troy were visited by the Jesuit Father J. Van Lommel.

left blank. I have left it so, in hope that you will be so kind as to fill it up yourself, being fully persuaded that no one can know better than yourself the exact number of confirmations you have given in this mission, and how often you have visited this part of your Diocese during the five years that I have now attended it. With regard to your request under the head *Notatu digna*, I can only state that I arrived here on Salt River and took charge of this mission on the 5th day of January, in the year 1833, and have continued to attend it ever since. Previous to that period, no priest or missionary, that I know, has ever resided, or been stationary in this mission. But during the two or three years preceding, some of the Jesuits visited a small part of it, once or may be thrice a year. The church of St. Paul, in Ralls County, is the only one which with great difficulty I got, in a manner, completed in the year 1834 and in which Divine Service is now performed. Besides this church I have three other ones a building, viz.: One on Indian Creek, which is nearly completed; one in Lincoln County, in Louisville, and one in Clark County, on the Wyaconda River, which are commenced, but for want of means cannot go on. No church in my mission, that I know, has as yet been blessed, though I begged you several times to pay a visit to these poor congregations of your Diocese, and bless the church on Salt River.

As for the public lands, I can state with some certainty, that in and about the congregations in the counties of Pike, Ralls, Marion and Monroe there are none to be had. For Congress land in these settlements has been culled over and over, and the few 40 or 60 acres, that might here and there be vacant, are not worth entering. There is, however, some prairie yet vacant, but no timber to supply it. Land could now be purchased, at second hand, and very cheap from speculators. There is yet, I believe, a good deal of the choicest land vacant on the north fork of Salt River, and on Black's Creek (Shelby County) may be not more than 10 or 12 miles from the congregation on Indian Creek. Also, in the counties of Lewis and Clark there may yet here and there and be some choice spots of vacant land, and pretty convenient to the church now a building. In the County of Lincoln there is no public land that I know of, but there is a large scope of old claims in and about the congregation near Louisville, the improvements on which could be bought at the very lowest and almost insignificant price. These are the particulars I thought worthy of notice and in hope that they will satisfy your request, I remain, with profound sentiments of respect, Right Reverend Sir,

Your humble and obedient servant,

PETER P. LEFEVERE.

The sly sarcasm as to Bishop Rosati knowing best how many Confirmations there had been in Ralls County, was perhaps the means of bringing the overburdened Bishop to the fulfilment of Father Lefevere's great longings; but not before the month of October, 1838. In his letter to Father John Timon, October, 20, 1838, Bishop Rosati writes:

"VERY-REVEREND AND DEAR SIR—I returned to St. Louis last Thursday from my visit of the upper congregation of this State, which has been highly gratifying to me. I gave Confirmation to forty-five persons in St. Paul's, Salt River; to

twenty-eight in St. Stephen's, Indian Creek, where we gave a little Retreat of three days. Fr. Verhaegen and myself preached every day to a numerous congregation. We had many confessions. Mr. Lefevere keeps his churches and congregations in the best order. The people are very good, practical Catholics.'"⁴

REV. JOHN ROTHENSTEINER.

St. Louis.

---

⁴ Letter in Archives of Catholic Historical Society of St. Louis.

IRISH COLONIZATION IN ILLINOIS[1]

Those in this country who are sympathizing with the Irish fight for self-determination and an Irish republic will be interested to know that one hundred years ago among the pioneers of the region of the middle west, south of Lake Michigan, were Irish Sinn Feiners or Republicans. Most of them came from the South in the region of New Orleans, although there was a goodly number from New York, Philadelphia and Baltimore. They were as a rule men of education and initiative, strongly imbued with the love of liberty and the right of free speech. They left Ireland as a result of the failure of the uprising of 1798, to cast their fortunes with and lend their brain and brawn to the upbuilding of the young republic.

The New York Irish Emigrant Association led by such sterling Irishmen as Thomas Addis Emmett, Daniel McCormick, James Mc-Bride, Andrew Herris, John W. Mulligan, William Sampson and Dr. William J. Macnevan, directed the Irish families to the fertile farming country of the state of Illinois where their brain and brawn could be used in breaking the virgin soil for their own and the country's benefit.

In behalf of these emigrants from the old sod, in New York City, in December, 1817, the above Irishmen, with others influential in the councils of the Association, drew up a memorial and presented it to Congress. At the session in February the next year, 1818, it came before the members for consideration. Among other things, the As-sociation (it was called the New York Irish Emigrant's Association) asked, in the memorial, "for a portion of the unsold lands in the Illinois Territory (now the State of Illinois) and that the portion may be set apart or granted to the trustees for the purpose of being settled by emigrants from Ireland on an extended term of credit."

In part the memorial reads as follows:

Your memorialists, while they presume most respectfully to solicit your attention to the helpless and suffering condition of the numerous foreigners, who, flying from a complicated mass of want and misery, daily seek an asylum in the bosom of the United States, are embold-ened by the recollection that a liberal encouragement to the settlement, by meritorious strangers, has always characterized the Government, and constituted authorities of the Union. The wise and brave founders of its independence held out to the oppressed and suffering of every

[1] Apropos of our Article on "The Irish in Illinois" a number of communica-tions have been received of which the accompanying is very interesting.

73

nation consoling assurance that, in this country at least, they should find a refuge and a home. . . . . They come (the Irish emigrants) indeed, not to return and carry back the profits of casual speculations, but to dedicate to the land of their hopes, their all. . . . . The Irish emigrant, cherished and protected by the Government of the United States, will find his attachment to their interest increase in proportion to the benefits he has received. He will love, with enthusiasm, the country that affords him the means of honorable and successful enterprise and permits him to enjoy unmolested and undiminished, the fruits of his honest industry. Ingratitude is not the vice of Irishmen. Fully appreciating his comparative comforts and the source from whence they flow, he will himself cherish and inculcate. in his children, an unalterable devotion to his adopted, and their native country. Should hostilities approach her (the country) in that quarter, (Illinois) whether in the savage forms of the tomahawk and scalping knife, or with the deadlier weapon of civilized warfare, the Irish settlers, with their hardy sons, will promptly repel the invasion, drive back the war upon the enemy and give to our extended frontier, security and repose. . . . .

On behalf of the New York Irish Emigrant Association, New York, December, 1817.

> THOMAS ADDIS EMMETT, President.
> DANIEL McCORMICK, Vice-President.
> JAMES McBRIDE, Second Vice-President.
> ANDREW HERRIS, Treasurer.
> JOHN W. MULLIGAN, Secretary.

William Sampson, Wm. J. Macnevan, James Sterling, William Edgar, Jr., Matthew Carroll, John Mayhue, John Heffernan, Dennis McCarthy, Mat. L. Davis, J. Chambers, Thomas Kirk, D. H. Doyle, John R. Skidds. Robert Fox, Joseph R. Mullany, R. Swanton.[2]

---

[1] Most of the men who signed their names to the above memorial distinguished themselves later in New York and the country. Thomas Addis Emmett, the first on the list was a man at that time of international importance. He was the ablest leader of the United Irishmen during the uprising of 1798 in Ireland and was the oldest brother of Robert Emmett one of the leading spirits in that ill-fated attempt to throw off the shackles of England. With Dr. Macnevan, another of the signers, he was tried before a secret committee of the House of Lords in the year of the uprising but they and their companions, disclosed no information to their eager questioners. Thomas Emmett and Dr. Macnevan came to America after their release from Fort George in Scotland and settled in New York City where they speedily established themselves in the good graces of the authorities by their practical work for the betterment of the city and country. Dr. Macnevan came to New York in 1805. Soon after his arrival he began practice as physician and speedily showed that he had distinctive ability. In 1808 he was appointed professor of obstetrics in the College of Physicians and Surgeons and in 1811 filled the chair of chemistry and materia medica. He was the first to establish a chemical laboratory in New York City. In 1820 he resigned his professorship and, in company with Dr. Valentine Mott, Dr. John

Apparently, the prayer of the Irish memorialists received favorable consideration in Congress, for we read in the annals of that body that on December 16, 1818' thirteen days before Congress admitted Illinois as a state, one Mr. Clagett submitted to the House of Representatives the following resolution:

That it is expedient to authorize the Secretary of the Treasury to designate and set apart ...... townships, each of six miles square, in the State of Illinois, east of the military bounty lands, each alternate section thereof to be settled by emigrants from Ireland and sold to them at two dollars per acre, to be paid by three installments, as follows to wit: -One-third part thereof at the end of four years; one other third part thereof, at the end of eight years; and the residue thereof at the end of twelve years, from the day of sale, with interest on the said several sums. Provided,

1. That the Secretary of the Treasury may, and it shall be his duty to reject all applications of such emigrants for the lands afore-

---

W.-Francis, Dr. David Hosack and others, he founded a new medical school on Duane Street. He was president of the "Friends of Ireland," and nearly every Irish society in New York City. In connection with his great efforts to help his fellow countrymen to find homes in America, he published a pamphlet entitled: "Directions or Advice to Irishmen Arriving in America," and also established a bureau for Irish servant girls. Dr. Macnevan was born in Ballynahon, County Galway, March 21, 1763, and died in New York City July 12, 1841.

William Sampson, another one of the signers of the memorial, was an author and the son of a Presbyterian clergyman. He was born in Londonderry, Ireland, January 17, 1764 and died in New York City, December 27, 1836. When a young man he joined the Irish Volunteers. Later he entered Dublin University and became a barrister. While practicing his profession he acted frequently as counsel for members of the United Irishmen Society. After the failure of the rebellion of 1798, he was brought a prisoner to Dublin. He was released on condition that he went to Portugal. At the instance of the British government he was arrested there after some agitation. Finally he was set free and came to America where he established himself as a lawyer in New York City. Through his practice and writings he became famous and his criticisms of the common law procedure were influential in bringing about amendments and consolidations of the laws of the state. He published several books including "Discourses and Correspondence with Learned Jesuits upon the History of the Law."

Mat. L. Davis was born in 1766 and died in Manhattanville, N. Y., June 21, 1850. By trade he was a printer and later became a skillful writer and attached himself to the fortunes of Aaron Burr whom he supported for the candidacy of president. For many years he wrote letters to America, the *New York Courier* and *Enquirer* under the penname of "The Spy in Washington." He published the "Memoirs of Aaron Burr' and edited Burr's private journal during his residence in Europe.

James W. Mulligan, another of the signers, was Quartermaster-general of the U. S. Army in New York City, at that period.

said; unless the applicants shall have been satisfactorily recommended as moral and industrious men.

2.   That no contract shall be made with any emigrant as aforesaid unless he shall engage to improve at least twenty of each hundred acres to be transferred as aforesaid and also to erect a suitable dwelling house and barn thereon.

The fifth provision stated that "if the provisions of payment or improvement shall not be fully complied with at the expiration of the term of 12 years, the said premiums so forfeited shall revert to the United States" consideration being given for amounts paid in. For the first five years the lands were exempted from taxation.

In the spring of 1819, as the result of the liberal provisions of the above act, hundreds of emigrants of good character from Ireland, who landed at the ports of New York, Philadelphia, Baltimore and New Orleans, were directed into the new land of promise. From the first, the Emigrant's Association of New York took an active interest in weeding out the undesirable element that came over with the more promising farmers, laborers, tradesmen and mechanics. Most of the emigrants went overland—that is those who came by New York, Philadelphia and Baltimore. Others went by the Great Lakes and the Mississippi River.

GEORGE F. O'DWYER.

Lowell, Mass.

THE FRANCISCANS IN SOUTHERN
. ILLINOIS

(Continued from April, 1920)

The year 1875 was to be a most important one in the history of
Commissariat. In fact, it ushered in a new epoch marked by the
ction of the Province of the Sacred Heart and an increased
ivity in every field of labor over a great extent of the United
.tes. The event Providence made use of to bring about these
ults, which proved to be so beneficial in many ways, was the
lturkampf in Germany.
It is not the purpose of the writer to enlarge upon the causes
l effects of this destructive war on the Church, but a short account
the banishment of the Franciscans of the Province of the Holy
)ss and their coming to this country, will no doubt be of interest
the readers of the ILLINOIS CATHOLIC HISTORICAL REVIEW.
By the laws of July 5, 1872, and of May 13, 1873, the Jesuits
l the so-called affiliated Orders (the Redemptorists, Lazarists, the
nbers of the Congregation of the Holy Ghost, and the Sisters of
Sacred Heart), were banished from the German Empire. This
isure foreboded the fate of the remaining Orders and Congrega-
is. The government had already drawn up a list of these religious
lies together with an exposition of their organization and aims,
l prepared to make war on them also. The blow fell in May 1875,
n a law was passed, by which all Orders and Religious Congrega-
s, with the exception of those that devoted themselves exclusively
he service of the sick, were prohibited in all the domains of the
ssian monarchy; their foundation were to be dissolved within
months, while those of the religious who were permitted to remain
e placed under the supervision of the state. Thus thousands of
and women, who had labored with heroic self-devotion and with
t success for the welfare of their fellowmen, were obliged to
idon their peaceful homes and their country and seek an asylum
oreign lands.

The sources from which we have drawn in writing this sketch are: Letters
ev. Mark Thienel, O. F. M., and Rev. Anselm Puetz, O. F. M.—*Schematismus
inciae Saxoniae S. Crucis*, Warendorf, 1873;—*Catalogus Provinciae SS.
s Jesu in Statibus Foederatis Americae Septentrionalis*, St. Louis, Mo.,
; *Die Herz Jesu Provinz*, St. Louis, Mo., 1903.

Thus, too, the Franciscans of the Province of the Holy Cross went
into exile. This Province had, at the time (in Europe) nine convents
and six residences, and exclusive of the religious laboring in the
United States, about 95 priests, 54 clerics, and 137 brothers, of whom
about 42 were Tertiaries Regular.

"We most earnestly besought the Sacred Heart to avert the
worst," thus writes Father Anselm Puetz, one of the exiles. "What
we directly prayed for, the Sacred Heart refused us; we were driven
into exile, for we could not comply with the demand of the state,
to acknowledge no foreign superior, without proving traitors to
Mother Church and the Order. Our Lord, however, answered our
petitions in another and more sublime manner: besides admitting us
to assist him in carrying the cross, He, according to the designs of
His divine Providence, wished to use us as feeble instruments in
founding a new Province of the Order, dedicated to the Sacred Heart.

"God's blessing evidently rested on us. Not a single Father,
cleric, or brother, left the Order, although the temptation was alluring
enough. When Father Provincial Gregory Janknecht gathered the
novices about him and explained the state of affairs and offered them
the alternative of doffing the habit or of emigrating to the United
States, all, without the least hesitation, declared their readiness to
go into exile."[2]

Next to God's blessing, this happy result was due to the circum-
spection of the Very Rev. Gregory Janknecht. A man of extraordinary executive ability, he found a place of refuge for his brethren
in Holland and in the Commissariat which he had founded in the
United States. In the former country, he acquired an estate at
Harreveld, which was well adapted for the needs of a religious community. This convent also served as the novitiate. Another house
was opened at Watersleyde, near Sittard, in the diocese of Roermond,
to serve as a preparatory seminary for young men who wished to
become priests of the Franciscan Order.

The greater number of the religious who were destined to seek
refuge in the United States, met at Duesseldorf in the beginning of
June.[3]

---

[2] Letter of Rev. Anselm Puetz, O. F. M., to Rev. Eugene Hagedorn, O. F. M.,
in which the writer graphically describes the voyage of the banished religious
and their arrival at Teutopolis.

[3] On account of their large number, the religious were divided into two bands.
The *obedience* of the larger band which met at Duesseldorf, reads as follows:

lorf was in commotion. An immense crowd assembled
Franciscan monastery and did not mince words in
olicy of the 'liberal' government. Men, women, and
ing the streets, sang religious hymns. It was a
els and men to witness this spontaneous profession
:ouching testimonial of esteem for the Franciscans.''⁴
xiled religious, amid the liveliest manifestations of
pathy of the people who had gathered in large
ss their departure, went on board the river steamer
rdam, at about 1 o'clock a. m., on Friday, June 11.
ered 85 persons: 16 priests, 34 clerics (of whom
11 lay brothers (of whom 2 were novices), 5 Ter-
and 19 students who were preparing to enter the
voluntarily went into exile with the religious.
:he gigantic *Germania* on her pedestal in the Nieder-
after having been freed of 66 'dangerous char-
peaceful religious who sought only to serve God,
ı souls, and to benefit their fellow men, must have
es of the 'Law'. Some of them had fought in the
lozens of them had hastened to the battlefields to
:d and sick and to console the dying. They had even
decorations from the very government that now
ated them.''⁵
ached Rotterdam in the evening of the same day,
exiles went on board the *Rotterdam*, which was to
e United States. The ocean voyage began the next
ed uneventful, and on Wednesday, June 30, the
d the harbor of New York. News of the coming
ligious had preceded them, and several communities,

J. M. F.
ore sequentes Patres et Fratres: (......follow the names
)..
ostram Americanam dimitto, ut praesentiam A. V. P. Com-
sionis adeant, cujus obedientiae in posterum sint subjecti.
eutia uostra Monasteriensi sub meo Chirographo Officiique
)ma mensis Junii anni 1875.
F. GREGORIUS JANKNECHT, *Min. Provlis.*
Ord. FF. Min. S. Franc. Recoll. Prov. Saxouiae S. Crucis.
the smaller band is dated Paderborn, June 23. Originals
hives in St. Louis, Mo.
selm Puetz, O. F. M.

particularly the Capuchins and the Sisters of the Poor of St. Francis, had made extensive preparations to provide lodgings for them, until they could continue their journey westward. Their stay in New York lasted but one day. In the evening of July 1, they set out for Teutopolis via the Erie railway, by way of Buffalo, through Canada to Detroit, thence to Chicago, from which city they traveled to Effingham, where they arrived in the afternoon of July 3. The special car in which they had traveled from New York, was at once brought to Teutopolis. At the station, a procession was formed, which amid the ringing of bells, wended its way to the church. Here the Rev. Guardian, Gerard Becher, addressed a few appropriate words to his exiled brethren, whereupon the Benediction of the Blessed Sacrament was given. After a repast in the convent refectory, about fifty of the religious were lodged at the college, while the novices and the rest remained at the convent.

The other band of exiles, consisting of 11 priests, 5 clerics, and 9 brothers (of whom 2 were Tertiaries Regular), arrived on July 10. Others came during the following months and during the next year, so that the total number that came to the Commissariat in consequence of the *Kulturkampf* was 101 religious (32 priests, 42 clerics, and 27 brothers), and 23 students.

RESULTS

Already before the arrival of so many religious, the Rev. Provincial Gregory had authorized the Rev. Commissary, Maurice Klostermann, by cable, to accept new places; for a number of bishops, hearing of the coming of the banished friars to the United States, had invited them into their dioceses. A meeting of the councilors of the Commisariat was, therefore, held to deliberate on the new foundations, to assign superiors and other religious, and to regulate the courses of studies for the clerics. The following parishes were accepted: St. George's, Hermann, Mo., with four missions; St. John the Baptist, Jordan, Minn., with four mission; St. Peter's, Chicago, Ill.; and the parish of the Sacred Heart, Indianapolis, Ind. The next year, the Fathers accepted St. Mary's, Wien, Mo., with a number of missions, and St. John the Baptist, Joliet, Ill.

The students of theology were sent to St. Louis, Mo.; those of philosophy to Quincy, Ill., while the students continued their studies at the college in Teutopolis.[6]

---

[6] Of these students fifteen became priests (twelve Franciscans), and one became a lay brother.

The Very Rev. Provincial Gregory himself came to the United States in October, 1876,—this was his third visit—, to make provi- sions for the welfare of the Commissariat in the new circumstances. He remained eighteen months, and by his prudent measures con- tributed much to the future growth and successful labors of the Commissariat and Province. He called a meeting of the councilors at St. Louis, Mo., in January, 1877, at which the Fathers decided to take charge of the parishes at Columbus, Neb., Rhineland (Starken- burg), Mo., Chaska, Minn., and Radom, Ill. To these were added in 1878, Chillicothe, Mo., with several missions; and the missions among the Chippewa Indians in northern Wisconsin.

ERECTION OF THE PROVINCE OF THE SACRED HEART

The number of houses of the Commissariat had now increased to about sixteen, and that of the religious to about 235. Owing to the disturbed condition of the Province in Germany, to the peculiar needs of the houses in the United States, and to the distance which made an efficient government by the Provincial very difficult, it was deemed advisable to separate the houses in this country and to organize them into a custody, or small province. The Provincial and his council, accordingly, met at Puett, in Holland, on September 17, 1878, and drew up a petition to this effect to the Most Rev. General of the Order in Rome. The latter and his council approved of the separation, but decided to change the Commissariat into a province, and not a custody.[7] The superiors of the Commissariat having, ac- cording to orders, sent in the names of those Fathers whom they considered best qualified to discharge the office of Provincial and Definitors, or councilors, the Most Rev. General Bernardine a Portu Romatino, by letters patent, on April 26, 1879, separated the houses of the Commissariat from those in Europe and established them into a Province, under the title of "The Province of the Sacred Heart of Jesus." The superiors appointed for the first term of three years were: Vincent Halbfass, Provincial; Maurice Klostermann, Custos; Kilian Schloesser, Anselm Mueller, Damasus Ruesing, and Francis Moenning, Definitors.

At the same time, Father Maurice Klostermann was appointed Commissary General and commissioned to preside at the first chapter and to instal the new Provincial and his councilors. This chapter

---

[7] A custody is a small province, with from four to eight convents. It is gov- erned by a *custos*, who has all the rights and privileges of a provincial.

was held at Teutopolis, on July 2. One of the important measures decided upon at this meeting, was the transfer of the Provincial's residence to the convent in St. Louis, Mo.

MARVELOUS GROWTH

The new Province now entered upon an era of marvelous growth, especially in the western and northern states. In 1885, the Old Mission, at Santa Barbara, Cal., and the parish and orphan asylum at Watsonville, Cal., were placed in charge of the Province, and in the course of time, foundations were made in other parts of the state of California, and in Washington, Oregon, and Arizona. In the last-mentioned state, the Franciscans took charge of all the missions among the Pima and Papago Indians. In 1913, the Province numbered fifty houses (of which fourteen were convents and three colleges), 263 priests, 111 clerics, and 217 brothers. In 1915, the houses in the Pacific states and Arizona, seventeen in number, were separated and established into the Province of St. Barbara.

ST. PETER'S, CHICAGO

It remains to give a short account of the parishes in Illinois, in charge of the Franciscans after the year, 1875. The first of these is St. Peter's, Chicago.

This parish was founded in the spring of 1846, by the Rev. John Jung. A suitable site for a church was procured on Washington Street, between Wells and Franklin Streets, and on it was erected a frame church, 40x60 feet. A school and a rectory were built soon after. The parish then numbered about thirty German families.

In consequence of the expansion of the business district of the city, the church was, in 1853, moved to Clark and Polk Streets. The present church building was begun by the Rev. John Bapt. Jager in 1863 and completed by his successor, the Rev. Peter Fischer, in 1865. The latter also built the rectory. During his administration, the parish reached its greatest size: in 1870, it numbered over 1,200 families.

The increase in the number of priests, in consequence of the *Kulturkampf*, enabled the Franciscans to accept the invitation of the Rt. Rev. Bishop Thomas Foley to take charge of St. Peter's parish. Father Liborius Schaefermeyer, who had been pastor of St. Boniface parish, Quincy, Ill., and Vicar-General of the diocese of Alton, and who had entered the Order in 1874, was appointed

pastor and superior; his assistant was Father Maternus Mallmann. They arrived with two lay brothers at the end of July, 1875. The reception of the friars on the part of the majority of the people was far from cordial. Many were filled with distrust of the "monks", others were bitter in their opposition to them and declared: "We don't want men that were not good enough for Bismarck." It was even proposed to appoint a "vigilance committee" to hinder the Franciscans from taking possession of the rectory. But when Father Liborius and his assistant went about their work as if nothing were amiss and spared no pains in promoting the spiritual welfare of the people, the distrust and opposition gradually vanished and changed to love and veneration. In later years, the memory of these events, while causing regret, at the same time never failed to amuse.

In 1878, Father Liborius built the school at a cost of $7,000. His successor, Father Augustin Henseler (1879-1885), did much to embellish the interior of the church. During his administration there began an exodus of families to other parts of the city, which completely changed the character of the parish. This exodus was due to the growth of the business section of the city, the encroachment of the railroads, and the influx of a class of people of very questionable character. At the present day, St. Peter's not only ministers to the needs of the various nationalities of the district in which it is situated, but it is also much frequented by Catholics from all parts of the city.[8]

St. John the Baptist, Joliet, Illinois

In 1851, the Catholic Germans of Joliet, who up to this time had attended St. Patrick's Church, organized a parish of their own. They at once began to build a church and brought it under roof during the summer. Its dimensions were 40x80 feet. Services were held in it for the first time by the Rev. Christopher Zucker, of Naperville. Up to the year 1854, the people had no resident pastor, but their needs were attended to by the Rev. J. C. Regal, assistant at St. Patrick's Church, Rev. F. Köpp, of Chicago, Rev. C. Zucker, of Naperville, Rev. P. Fisher, Rev. G. H. Ostlangenberg, and Rev. Gipperich. At the end of the year 1854, the Rev. Kaspar Mueller was appointed first resident priest. In 1866, when the Benedictine

---

[8] Cf. For detailed account of St. Peter's, see *Archdiocese of Chicago—Antecedents and Development. Die kathol. Kirchengeschichte Chicago's,* p. 20, sqq.

Fathers of Chicago were in temporary charge, the parish undertook the building of the present church of stone. The structure was completed by the Rev. Ferdinand Algayer (1866-1867) and the Rev. Francis X. Nolte (1868-1876).

At the death of the latter, in 1876, Bishop Foley entrusted the parish to the care of the Franciscan Fathers. Father Gerard Becher was the first Franciscan in charge. The parish at that time numbered about 530 families, of whom 43 were Polish and 41 Slovenian. Besides making improvements on the church building, Father Gerard, in 1885, erected a new school of stone. His successor, Father Cyprian Banscheid (1885-1898), built a hall for the societies of the parish and enlarged the convent. At his time, the number of Slovenian and Polish families that attended St. John's, increased to such an extent that it was thought advisable to organize them in separate parishes. St. Joseph's parish for the Slovenians was established in 1890, and that of the Holy Cross for the Poles in 1893.

As elsewhere, the labors of the Fathers were not restricted to the parish. From 1883-1891, they had charge of the missions Strassburg, Will County, and Richton, Cook County. Both are now attended from Steger. The following institutions in Joliet are attended by the Franciscans: St. Francis Academy, since 1873; St. Joseph's Hospital, since 1882; Guardian Angel Home for Children, since 1897; and Illinois State Penitentiary, since 1877.[9]

St. Michael's, Radom

The town of Radom, Washington County, was founded in 1873. In that year, the Illinois Central Railroad issued an invitation to Polish immigrants to settle in Washington County, offering to sell its lands to them at acceptable rates. Regarding the matter, Father Bruno Torka, O. F. M., who, before joining the Franciscan Order, was the first teacher in the settlement, sent the writer the following information:

"The whole movement to settle Washington County was brought about by the Illinois Central R. R., under the direction of the Rev. Wotowski (if my memory serves me), a Polish priest who had lost an arm in the revolution in Poland. He was assisted by the Polish generals Michatowski, Malinowski, and the station agent, whose name I cannot recall. But the leader was a Russian general, Mr. Turcin,

---

[9] Cf. *Die Herz Jesu Provinz*, p. 74, sqq; *Die S. Johannes Gemeinde zu Joliet, Ill.*, 1902. See also *Archdiocese of Chicago—Antecedents and Development*.

and his wife, who was a well educated lady, and who built a large
house to serve as an academy, but it was never occupied."
    Many families in the cities accepted the invitation of the organ-
izers of the colony. As an inducement to others to join their countrymen, the railroad company donated a tract of land for church and
school purposes, supplied the building material, and authorized its
agent to begin the construction of the church. The trustees, who
had been chosen by the people, chose St. Michael as the patron of
the parish. Services were held occasionally by priests of neighboring
parishes, and after 1875, by Father Mark Thienel, O. F. M., of Teutopolis.
    In 1877, a delegation appointed by the people, went to Alton and
petitioned Bishop Baltes to place the parish in charge of the Franciscans. Their petition was granted, and in the summer of that year,
Father Desiderius Liss was sent to attend the spiritual needs of the
faithful. The small house which served as the rectory, consisted of
five apartments. Two of these were used as school rooms. Seventy
children attended. Mr. Joseph Torka was the first teacher—from
September 1877 to September 1878. He then continued his studies
at St. Joseph's College, Teutopolis, and in 1880 joined the Order,
receiving the name of Father Bruno. Amid many difficulties and
hardships, Father Desiderius succeeded in erecting a school and a
residence for Sisters. The Sisters de Notre Dame, of Milwaukee,
have charge of the school since 1879.
    In 1880, Radom was made a "residence", with Father Mark
Thienel as its first superior. His successor, Father Urban Stanowski,
enlarged the church by adding a transept and a sanctuary. In 1891,
Father Sebastian Cebulla (1887-1894) erected a school of brick; the
old school was thenceforth used as a society hall. A new rectory
of brick and a convent for the Sisters, likewise of brick, was erected
in 1895 and 1900, respectively.
    Since 1877 the Franciscans also had charge of the mission at
Dubois, a Polish settlement four miles south of Radom. They likewise
attended Sheller, Jefferson County, for many years. The secular clergy
took charge of the former parish in 1898, and of the latter in 1908.
    The parish at Radom was relinquished by the Franciscans in the
summer of 1914.[10]

_____

[10] *Die Herz Jesu Provinz*, p. 83, sqq.

CHURCH OF THE IMMACULATE CONCEPTION, PESOTUM

The Catholics of this settlement in Champaign County at first fulfilled their religious duties at Tolono. In 1875, a school was built in which the Rev. William Kuchenbuch, pastor at Danville, celebrated Mass for the first time on October 21. In 1876, the Franciscans were called upon to take charge of the mission. Father Casimir Vogt, of Teutopolis, was appointed in August of that year, and at once took steps to build a church. It was placed under the patronage of the Immaculate Conception, and dedicated on October 14, 1877. Services were henceforth held twice a month. This first church building was replaced by a new one during the administration of Father Fulgence Hansen. It was dedicated by the Rev. Provincial Vincent Halbfass, in January, 1882. In January, 1884, owing principally to its distance from Teutopolis, the parish was again placed in charge of the secular clergy. The Rev. Adolph Bergmann was the first resident priest.[11]

ST. AUGUSTINE'S, CHICAGO

The beginning of this parish dates back to the year 1879. In April of that year, Mr. Edward Koch and his wife donated four lots on Laflin and 49th Streets for church purposes. After two more lots had been purchased, a small frame church was erected and dedicated to St. Augustine. Services were held at first by the assistant of St. Anthony's Church, but as the number of German families increased, the Rev. Denis Thiele was, in 1882, appointed rector of the parish. He enlarged the church, so that the upper story was used for divine service and the lower for school purposes. The school, which had an attendance of thirteen children during the first year, was in charge of Miss Margaret Oswald and Mrs. Masquelet. These were succeeded, in 1884, by the Poor Handmaids of Jesus Christ, of Fort Wayne, Indiana.

In 1885, Father Thiele was appointed to organize Holy Trinity parish on West Taylor Street, and the Franciscans were asked to take charge of St. Augustine's. The first Franciscan pastor and superior was Father Symphorian Forstmann; his assistant was Father Anselm Puetz. They began their spiritual labors among the people by preaching a mission, which proved to be most beneficial.

The parish continued to grow, and it soon became necessary to build a larger church and school. Father Kilian Schloesser, pastor of St. Peter's Church (1885-1888), who had in many ways come to

---

[11] *Beitraege zur Geschichte von Teutopolis und Umgegend* (1901), p. 103, sqq.

the aid of the struggling parish, succeeded in procuring a whole block
of property on Laflin Street, between 50th and 51st Streets, at a cost
of $15,000. On this site, a larger church of frame was erected in
1887; the old church was transferred from its location on 49th streeet
and converted into a school. In a very short time, this second church
also proved too small to accommodate the families that continued to
affiliate themselves with St. Augustine's. In 1891, accordingly, plans
were drawn by Brother Adrian Wewer, O. F. M., for a church of
brick, 200x80 feet (transept 100 feet), with a steeple 225 feet in
height; it was decided, however, to build only the nave of the church
for the time being. Building operations were begun on July 29, 1891,
and on September 25, 1892, the finished structure was dedicated by
Archbishop Feehan. A new convent and rectory was built in 1899.

In 1903-1904, during the administration of Father Benignus
Schuetz, who succeeded Father Symphorian in 1900, the transept and
sanctuary of the church were built. The Sister's convent, which was
erected in 1897, was enlarged in 1904. Father Benignus also built a
larger school containing twenty-four class rooms, to accommodate the
number of children, who had increased from thirteen in 1879 to over
1,100.[12]

Little can be said at present of the activity of the Franciscans at
the *Cook County Infirmary* at Oak Forest, since it was only in 1912
that they, at the request of Most Rev. Archbishop James Edward
Quigley, began to minister to the needs of the sick in that public
institution. At first Father Hilary Kieserling alone daily brought the
consolations of religion to the sick and dying, but in 1913 a community, consisting of three Fathers and two Brothers, was established in a residence built for them close to the Infirmary. Ever
since, three Fathers daily make the rounds of the wards and night
and day answer the numerous calls for their ministrations.

Thus the blessing of God has been upon the labors of the Franciscans, and we pray that their endeavors in behalf of the people
entrusted to their charge may continue to meet with abundant fruit
in the future.

SILAS BARTH, O. F. M.

Teutopolis, Illinois.

---

[12] *Die Herz Jesu Provinz,* p. 46, sqq.; *Die kathol. Kirchengeschichte Chicago's,*
p. 143, sqq. See also *Archdiocese of Chicago—Antecedents and Development.*

THE LEOPOLDINE ASSOCIATION—THE GERMAN "PROPOGATION OF THE FAITH" SOCIETY

Since the happy termination of the World War in November, 1918, all countries of the revolutionized, pauperized and starving Europe are extending their pleading arms across the wide expanse of the Atlantic for immediate assistance from prosperous America in its present hour of desperation. In this World War America has nobly acquitted itself and fully paid its debt of gratitude toward chivalric France, which in its golden days of Catholicity espoused the cause of our colonies against their oppressor, England. It is also gratifying to learn how the United States by means of its relief organizations established throughout Austria has checked starvation's march through that distressed land and prevented death from taking toll of at least one million of its people. The French charge d' affaires assured us that our speedy work of relief, our immense supplies of food and medicines to starving Vienna has saved that populous city of two million inhabitants from death by starvation and disease. To quote the words of the French charge d'affaires: "It is one of the finest pages in American history."[1] The American relief administration for Austria was organized at Vienna, May 16, 1917, and thus Austria's enemy of yesterday is Austria's greatest friend and benefactor to-day. Kindness has completely effaced the hatred engendered by the war in the hearts of Austria's people. This sudden change in sentiment is difficult to understand if we do not look for its explanation in the Catholicity of its people. One hundred fifty thousand children in the city of Vienna alone are being fed by the children's fund of the United States Administration organized by Herbert Hoover which furthermore has established more than three hundred feeding stations throughout the country and provides one full meal daily for three hundred thousand children; not to speak of the hundreds of thousands of men and women who are being fed by the general relief board of the United States. This absolutely indispensible organization of the hour has also provided Austria with twenty-five tons of cod liver oil, one hundred thousand tons of soap, one hundred thousand overcoats, one hundred thousand pairs of shoes and woolen

---

[1] Paul Scott Mowrer in Special Cable to *Chicago Daily News*, Vienna, June 14, 1920.

stockings. About four millions of dollars worth of food drafts have
been sent from America to Austria during the past three months, *i. e.,*
since the inauguration of the food draft system, March 1, 1902.[2] To
become more local, it may be added that the Catholic Austrian Relief
Committee of Chicago has collected a total sum of thirty thousand
dollars and has sent 14 tons of clothing to somewhat relieve the
Austrian situation.[3] A collection for the children of Central Europe
taken up in the Chicago diocese alone amounted to fifty thousand
five hundred dollars.[4]

Thus America has generously repaid Austria for its invaluable aid
to the struggling Catholic Church of America in its infancy and for
the five hundred or more heroic sons who prior to 1890 submitted to
voluntary exile from their mother land to labor heroically here in the
middle west as missionaries, pastors and prelates, thereby conse-
crating their talents, their energies and their lives to the civilization
and christianizaton of this country.

Whilst we to-day may acclaim ourselves as the very saviours of
millions of Austria's people, it remains for us to prove by purely
documentary evidence drawn from but one historic source "The Leopoldine Annals" published by the "Leopoldine Association" at
Vienna from 1831 to 1886 in the interest of the American missions,
that America's present generation is merely reciprocating the charity
of Austria's generations of the past century toward the upbuilding
of the Catholic Church in these United States. To acquire a clear
perspective we will consider: (1) The Leopoldine Association, (2) The
Leopoldine Annals, (3) Austria's Aid to Chicago and the missions of
the Middle West.

1. THE LEOPOLDINE ASSOCIATION

Quis revolvet nobis lapiden? Who shall roll away the stone of
poverty as a hindrance to the growth of Christ's Church here in
America? This was the cry of the Catholics in the United States in
the first quarter of the last century. The chains of political serfdom
were forever broken at Yorktown by the surrender of Cornwallis to
George Washington through the aid of twenty-one thousand Catholic
Frenchmen as compared to the nine thousand soldiers that comprised

---

[2] *Ib.*
[3] Report: Catholic Austrian Relief Committee of Chicago.
[4] Arch-diocesan Chancellor's Report for 1919 (Chicago).

90   FRANCIS J. EPSTEIN

his own army;[5] and we can readily assert without fear of contra-
diction that of the latter at least four thousand were French, Irish or
German Catholics—truly a Catholic victory for America's Freedom!
And now the dawn of a glorious future for the Catholic Church in the
United States also arrived; it was about to arise from its early
grave, to which the missions established by the French and Spanish
Missionaries in the previous centuries were consigned by England
upon its acquisition of the vast territory to the west and south from
France and Spain respectively. And yet, unmindful of America's
Catholic origin, forgetful of the discoveries made by her intrepid and
resolute sons through the length and breadth of both North and South
America, ignoring the self-sacrificing labors of her missionaries: the
Jesuits in the North and Middle West, the Franciscans in California,
Arizona and New Mexico, and all this long before the English set foot
on the Atlantic coast, Lord Baxley speaking on the growth of the
Catholic Church in America during the first quarter of the nineteenth
century says: "That of all the parts of the world America was the
last country that Rome was expected to take possession of and strange
enough that now, when Rome was losing its strongholds in Eusope, it
was gaining new ones in the greatest stronghold of Protestantism. To
think of a Catholic bishopric in Boston, the cradle of American Protestantism, and then where only a few years ago there was but one
bishop in the Catholic colony of Maryland (created in 1790) and now
in a few years (1808) we have four bishoprics: Baltimore, New York,
Boston and Bardstown. Rome is not asleep but continues its aims at
the conquest of the world."[6]

At this juncture the French society for the "Propogation of the
Faith" was founded at Lyons in 1822 through the efforts of Bishop
Du Burg of New Orleans, but did not extend its branches into other
countries until a much later date. Still again the same cry went
forth: "*Quis revolvet nobis lapidem?* Who shall roll away the stone
of poverty, which is ever more and more proving a hindrance to the
growth of Christ's church here in America? · *Erat quippe magnus
valde!* This time the cry for urgent help was embodied in the person
of Father Frederic Rése, then vicar-general and later first bishop of
Detroit, who in 1828 was sent to Europe by his ordinary, Bishop
Edward D. Fenwick, the first bishop of Cincinnati and also the first
American-born Dominican, who introduced the Dominican Order into

---

Kenny, Rev. Lawrence, S. J., (ILLINOIS CATHOLIC HISTORICAL REVIEW, Vol.
II, N.o 4, p. 490.
[6] *Annals of the Leopoldine Association*, Vienna, Report III. Letter V (1892).

the United States (Kentucky, 1805). His mission was to solicit priests as well as funds for the poverty-stricken Ohio missions, which territory he told them was as large as all France and in which only sixteen priests were attending to forty thousand Catholics. He graphically narrated to the Viennese how he and Bishop Fenwick visiting the missions heard the evening Angelus ringing a mile distant from a small chapel in the dense forests, where only a short time previously sacrifices were offered to heathen gods. His zeal and enthusiasm, his earnest presentation of the needs of America's missions in a pamphlet entitled "Abriss der geschichte des Bisthums Cincinnati in Nord-America," (Vienna, 1829) an excerpt of Father Theodore Stephan Badin's history, won him friends among all classes, people as well as clergy and nobility. The Prince-Archbishop of Vienna, Leopold-Maxmilian, became much enthused over the project of organizing a special society for the support of the American missions and to this end obtained an audience for Father Rése with the emperor, Francis I. By a bull "Quamquam plura sint," dated January 30, 1829, Leo XII, then pope, sanctioned the proposed society.

Archduke Rudolph, Cardinal Archbishop of Olmutz, graciously took over the Protectorate of the newly planned mission society. The society was officially established on May 13, 1829, in the Archbishop's palace at Vienna, on which occasion Canon Joseph Pletz of the Cathedral delivered a magnificent oration on the divine and world-wide mission of the Catholic Church and the duty of all Catholics to assist in extending its civilizing and cultural influence to the uttermost bounds of the earth. "States come and go," he said, "accordingly as they respect or despise the religion of Christ or exchange the banner of the cross for that of a false prophet." In his address before that select assembly of dignitaries Father Rése said, "The Catholics of North America, especially of Ohio, Michigan and the Northwest, appeal to you through me, that you might become their helping angels, and even now in advance you may rest assured of the lasting heartfelt gratitude of the learned and to the Lord converted." The society was christened "Leopoldinen-Stiftung" to forever commemorate the beautiful life of the Archduchess Leopoldina, daughter of Francis I, who died in America as empress of Brazil, having been the wife of Pedro I of Brazil. The society's membership was restricted to the crownlands of the Austrian Empire and its first officers were Anton Carl Lichtenberg as Actuary with Dr. Caspar Wagner as Treasurer. The objects of the society are briefly stated in the first paragraph of its statutes, namely:

(1) The promotion of greater efficiency in the Catholic missions of America.

(2) The participation and the edification of the faithful in extending the church of Jesus Christ unto the remotest regions of the earth.

(3) To perpetuate the memory of her majesty, Archduchess Leopoldina of Austria, who died in America as Empress of Brazil.

The means selected to attain these ends were prayer and almsdeeds. Every member obliges himself to daily recite one Our Father and the Angelus, with the added petition: "St. Leopold; pray for us!"; to the faithful performance of which a plenary indulgence was attached on the day of admission, once every month and on the patron feast of the Immaculate Conception (December 8th). To collect funds for the upkeep of the missions, circles of ten members each were formed in all parishes throughout the empire and the promoter of each circle would deliver the colltected moneys to the respective pastor, who in turn would send them to the local dean and the latter would deliver these funds to the ordinary every three months. The bishops would then send their reports to the Central bureau at Vienna. The total receipts of the first year amounted to 49,823 fl. Every year the entire Austrian clergy was requested to appeal to their congregation on the feast of St. Leopold, for contributions toward the support of the American missions. [7] It has been carefully estimated that within the first decade of its existence (1829-1839) this society has contributed to the American missions the then enormous sum of $220,000.[8] Let us not forget that the bulk of these contributions came from the laboring classes and servant girls, although the nobility also contributed generously. Let us add that in addition to the actual funds, the Leopoldine Association sent trunkfulls of all sorts of religious articles every few months, such as books, chalices, capes, vestments, rosaries, oil stocks, paintings, bells, censors, altar linens, crucifixes, etc. Let us conclude by perpetuating the name of the first great benefactor of the Leopoldine Association. It was the Reverend Sebastian Bilinck, pastor in Knihiniz in Maehren (Moravia), who on December 16, 1829, willed his entire possessions to the Leopoldine Association and thereby to the American missions.[9] God rest his noble soul.

(To be continued)

Wheaton.   REV. FRANCIS J. EPSTEIN.

[7] Ib., Report I, Statutes (1831).

[8] Preuss' Fortnightly Review (1914), Vol. XXI, No. 15, Aug. 1.

[9] Annals of the Leopoldine Association, Vienna, (1831).

CORNERSTONE OF HISTORY-MAKING INSTITUTION LAID

On Sunday afternoon, June 20th, 1920, the cornerstone of the central building of Rosary College, located near River Forest on the outskirts of Chicago, was laid by Most Reverend Archbishop George William Mundelein, D. D.

The brief ceremony was impressive and the participation of the Archbishop himself in the principal role as well as the music furnished by the justly renowned Paulist choir and the large concourse of people attending, made the scene memorable.

＊ ＊ ＊

Archbishop Mundelein's addresses are uniformly excellent but that delivered on this occasion took on additional merit by reason of the inherent interest in the subject. His Grace rapidly but most understandingly sketched the history of Catholic education in Chicago and paid a genuine tribute, especially to Irish Catholic parents of Chicago who despite their sometimes meagre resources, made grievous sacrifices for the education of their daughters. "In this respect," said the Archbishop, "the Irish differ somewhat from other nationalities, whose principal interest usually centers in their sons." He expressed satisfaction that so much had been accomplished through the development, first, of the parochial schools and afterwards the high school and convent, and declared that for some time it had been a matter of much regret that after leaving the Catholic high school, it had been necessary for Catholic girls, if they desired a college education, to procure it in non-Catholic institutions. The want of a Catholic college for women has been recognized but the rapid, almost sudden changes through which women have been precipitated into the business world, made the need particularly urgent and one that could no longer be ignored. To fail to meet this need was to resign the contest for desired and desirable recognition. Hence, though the establishment of an institution of the character and capacity required involves heavy expenditures and possible sacrifices, if the well-being of coming generations is to be served, there is no choice but to undertake the work with all its burdens and responsibilities.

＊ ＊ ＊

The selection of a site not less than the splendid promise of excellent results to be attained, affords assurance that Rosary College

93

is destined to be a great educational institution. Not in all the County of Cook might a more beautiful site be found, and to its natural beauty is added the charm of suitable seclusion and selectiveness. It is sufficiently removed from the noise, discomforts and distractions of the great city. The opportunity for study and reflection so valuable to both teacher and student is found and can be embraced in this pleasing location. That it is not now closely connected as to transportation facilities, is a slight inconvenience that a very short time will remedy.

Out of a field of teaching orders, all admirably qualified, the religious of the Order of St. Dominic have been selected to assume the important duties and heavy responsibilities of Rosary College. Obedient to duty's call they have taken up the burden and look to their brothers and sisters in the world to sustain them in their stupendous but glorious undertaking.

Their special appeal is to the members of their own sex and in the exercise of infinite care an auxiliary organization of laywomen has been formed to assist in procuring the means for the construction and equipment of the college buildings. By universal agreement Mrs. Edward Hines has been selected as leader of the auxiliary and the organization most effectively inaugurated. The first request for funds made through this organization netted some one hundred and seventy-five thousand dollars; but as very much more is required the good women will still continue their endeavors until all the wants of the college are supplied.

* * *

There are, so to say, three classes of young women that Rosary College is well calculated to serve. There are first, those of well-to-do families who will want every comfort and convenience that without actual extravagance can be provided. Nothing that any such young woman should have is beyond the power of an institution like Rosary College to supply.

In the second class may be included those who are in a sense obliged to finance their resources, who cannot consistently with other claims upon them afford the advantage of continuous residence in the institution, but who wish to live with their families and assist in the daily routine of house work or other endeavors, but have means sufficient to make their way as day scholars. For such the institution will especially adapt itself.

In the third class will be included those who are virtually without means to prosecute a higher education. For such generous provision

is being made by means of endowments, and, as has been frequently
expressed, it is the earnest hope of His Grace the Archbishop and
the promoters of Rosary College that no young woman seeking a
higher education and qualified to pursue it, may see her ambition
thwarted for the want of resources.

* * *

Advancement to more eminent service has come to depend largely,
almost wholly, upon educational attainments as marked by collegiate
and university degrees and distinctions. Women, not content with
the humbler grades of employment will welcome Rosary College as a
solution of the difficult problem of advancement.

Rosary College finds a warm welcome also from all those who
cannot go far away from home and also from parents who have a
desire to have their daughters near them while they are pursuing
their studies.

It is most reasonable to assume that the excellent opportunities
which an institution like Rosary College can offer will increase appre-
ciably the number and percentage of women to enter the field of
higher education and hence there is excellent reason for believing that
the college will be well patronized.

* * *

Chicago, the entire country indeed and, in an especial manner
Catholics, are fortunate in the acquisition of Rosary College. A great
educational institution is an asset whose value increases and mag-
nifies with the flight of time,—a perpetual benefaction. And it is to
be remembered it is the heritage not of the Dominican Sisters nor
even of the Archbishop of Chicago but of the people.

The opportuneness of the launching of the project is to be judged
by the possibilities of success. Large funds are needed. Gifts are
required. An essential prerequisite of giving is having. Never have
those who may be expected to give and who have given been so well
able to give as now. And although there are numerous demands and
living expenses have very greatly increased especially for those who
demand extraordinary goods and services, yet all who can give at
all can now give more easily and with less real sacrifice than ever
before, so great is the general prosperity.

The time is opportune for another important reason. An institution blessed with the powerful and undaunted sponsorship of a champion like the great Archbishop of Chicago is fortunate indeed. It
may not always please a benign Providence to look with such favor

upon this locality and accordingly it is well to reap the harvest
during the sunshine.

*   *   *

The laying of the cornerstone of this great educational institution,
which means its virtual establishment, happily coincided with the
celebration of the seventy-fifth anniversary of the establishment of
the Chicago diocese which it is to serve. It may be confidently pre-
dicted that when the centennary of that historic event shall recur,
Rosary College will be reputed amongst the most noted and fruitful
of the institutions of the Archdiocese.

JOSEPH J. THOMPSON.

Chicago.

Illinois Catholic Historical Review

Journal of the Illinois Catholic Historical Society

617 Ashland Block, Chicago

EDITOR IN CHIEF
Joseph J. Thompson.........Chicago

ASSOCIATE EDITORS
Rev. Frederick Beuckman.......Belleville   Kate Meade ....Chicago
Rev. J. B. Culemans.............Moline   Rev. Francis J. Epstein..........Chicago
William Stetson Merrill .... Chicago

COMMENDATION OF MOST REVEREND ARCHBISHOP GEORGE W. MUNDELEIN

This publication is one we can be proud of. It is gotten up in an attractive form and its contents are interesting and instructive. I have been complimented on it and have heard it praised in many quarters. * * * The Society should receive encouragement from every source, and all who possibly can should enroll in its membership. * * * I need not add that your work has not only my blessing, it has my encouragement. It has every aid I can give it.

EDITORIAL COMMENT

Subscription Price Increased. At the last meeting of the governing board of the ILLINOIS CATHOLIC HISTORICAL SOCIETY it was decided after careful deliberation to increase the subscription price of the ILLINOIS CATHOLIC HISTORICAL REVIEW from two to three dollars per year.

It is of course wholly unnecessary to enter upon explanations. The fact that everything that enters into the production of the REVIEW has greatly increased in cost is well known to all. Of course our annual subscription did not pay the cost of the magazine at any time, but the disparity between cost and subscription price became so great that we were in the attitude of wholly disregarding all business dictates. Recent numbers of the REVIEW cost slightly above 70 cents per number while we were getting but 50 cents.

It is hardly to be expected that a periodical like the ILLINOIS CATHOLIC HISTORICAL REVIEW can be produced from the proceeds of annual subscriptions. Other sources of revenue must be found and interested readers who are in a position to render extraordinary help must be depended upon to do so.

The REVIEW has proven its value and has obtained the approval of those whose good opinion was necessary to its success. It has prospered through a most difficult period and everyone connected with it is filled with confidence for its future.

At the Threshold of Another Year. This issue of the ILLINOIS CATHOLIC HISTORICAL REVIEW is the initial number of Volume III. Two complete volumes have been issued and each succeeding number, we are grateful to be able to state, has been received with approval.

If we have not been able to produce much that is entirely new (we have

97

some claims in this direction) we feel that we have at least been able to
formulate many historical facts correctly. In putting an historical fact in form
there is the possibility of wide divergence and the manner in which a fact is
stated frequently exercises an important influence upon its reception. If, for
example, much labor is expended and many sacrifices made, the motive has
much to do with the quantum of sympathy or approval to be accorded. Hence,
if an historian shall recite heartrending tales of suffering and sacrifice by pioneer
priests and laymen and ascribe to the victims an unworthy or frivolous motive,
very little sympathy will result. If, on the other hand, the motive be worthy
and truthfully stated, the true sense of appreciation of all fair-minded readers
is aroused. It is, of course, a plain perversion of truth to ascribe unworthy
motives when neither the circumstances nor plain reason justify. Due to the
manner of previous treatment it is firmly believed that restatement of even the
most elementary and best known historical incidents is justified on this ground
alone. Catholics at least are entitled to a Catholic view on historical events.

Another thing we think we have done something in the direction of accom
plishing is the development of the historical spirit. Many who have given slight
attention to history in the past, through our feeble efforts, have first, possibly
out of sympathy, read casually some of the articles in the ILLINOIS CATHOLIC
HISTORICAL REVIEW, and have gradually become more and more interested. Some
have been influenced to study other historical works and some even have developed
a sufficient interest to wish to be well informed, reading with avidity not only
all that appears in the ILLINOIS CATHOLIC HISTORICAL REVIEW but reaching out
for every possible source of information.

Our greatest accomplishment, as we view it, however, is the success which
we have in some measure attained in bringing out writers of merit. Not all of
the contributors to the ILLINOIS CATHOLIC HISTORICAL REVIEW are tyros. The
splendid papers of Dr. Garraghan, Father Rothensteiner, Father Barth, Father
Souvay, Father Holweck and Father Kenny, seasoned students and writers on
historical themes, are of course, unsurpassed, but in addition we have introduced
a number of beginners whose productions have been gratifyingly received. In a
very early number we gave expression to this thought: ''We wish, if possible,
to create a large new circle of historians, if you please, at least of persons who
will take a constructive interest in history and in co-operation with them to
serve history not only in a true form but in a palatable diet.''

With each succeeding year we hope to be able to realize the same approval
and friendly interest that have marked the two years just closed.

An Historical Season. The first half of the year 1920 has been rich in
the making of Catholic history in the archdiocese of Chicago. Indeed the past
few years have been very active years in that regard. Since the advent of His
Grace, the Most Rev. Archbishop George William Mundelein, the progress of the
Church, always notable, has, if possible, been more marked.

An institution is generally—though not always correctly—estimated by
visible evidences and progress towards a higher and better civilization is generally
marked by the existence and multiplication of churches and educational and
charitable institutions. Judged in this way the progress of the Catholic Church
in recent years in the archdiocese of Chicago is phenomenal.

Not only have the individual parishes done wonders in the erection of

magnificent churches and commodious parochial schools, but the expansion of diocesan institutions has been marvelous.

At the very outset of his administration, the Archbishop announced the establishment of a preparatory seminary, designed primarily, of course, for the education of young men, but specifically to honor the memory of his renowned predecessor, the late Archbishop James Edward Quigley. In but little more than two years the splendid seminary was completed and on the 9th of June, 1920, was dedicated with impressive ceremonies.

Finding the necessity existing for a Catholic womens' college, His Grace set about the establishment of Rosary College, the cornerstone of which was laid on the 20th of June, 1920.

Responding to another need His Grace has entered upon the establishment of a maternity home for young mothers and children under the name of Misericordia which will prove a distinct addition to the benevolent institutions of the Church and of the City of Chicago.

The greatest of his tangible works yet undertaken is the greater university for which ground has been secured near the town of Area on the outskirts of Chicago, and future students of history will read with interest the manner in which the initial steps for this great institution were taken. That the half million dollars, the gift of one man, Mr. Edward Hines, the nucleus for the fund of the great institution, was the largest single donation for Catholic educational purposes up to the time it was made, is an important historical fact, and that it was followed shortly after by a donation of $256,000 from the priests of the archdiocese is scarcely less important.

These are some of the big undertakings that will make history and that indeed are history, and which with numerous other facts were brought out by the Diamond Jubilee Celebration.

A Chicago daily paper, commenting upon the celebration and these important works, said: ''Catholicism has today in Chicago its hundreds of churches, colleges, schools, orphanages, refuges, homes for boys, girls and the aged, settlements and social centers.

'' 'By their fruits ye shall know them.'

''Before Chicago's archdiocese is a century old it will, in all probability, contain the largest Catholic university in the United States. The Church leaders that are here have vision as well as retrospect. Seventy-five years is an honorable age, but it is a milestone of mere infancy in a hierarchy that is synonymous with the Christian era.''

A Remarkable Publication. In other columns of this issue will be found the first of a series of articles by Reverend Francis J. Epstein, dealing with the Leopoldine Association and the *Annals* or periodical publications of that association. These annals were published from 1829 to 1868 and considerable search throughout this country has disclosed but one full set. This set is in possession of St. Francis College, Milwaukee.

More than one hundred letters written from the central states during the period for which the annals were published, are to be found in these books. These letters were written by the early bishops and early missionaries and sent to the association whose headquarters were located at Vienna, Austria. All of the letters written by the first bishop of Chicago, Right Reverend William Quarter, D. D., have been translated by Father Epstein and published in the ILLINOIS

CATHOLIC HISTORICAL REVIEW. Those of later bishops and others will find place from time to time under the series of articles Father Epstein is developing.

The attention of the state historical societies has been drawn to these publications by mention in the Catholic Historical publications and the Historical Commission of Michigan has been sufficiently interested to institute a preliminary survey of the publications. The task has been assigned to Professor John W. Scholl of the University of Michigan who has made a preliminary report, in which amongst other things the Professor says:

The Leopoldinen-Stiftung was an association founded in Austria for the propagation of the Catholic faith in North America, principally among the heathen tribes of the Indians. It was named in honor of the late Empress of Brazil, born Archduchess of Austria.

Members bound themselves to say certain prayers for the Empress' soul and pay certain annual dues for support of the missions.

Archbishop Milde of Vienna was made President of the Central-Direction of the association. It undertook, as part of its activities, the publication of an Annual Report called *Berichte der Leopoldinen Stiftung*, Etc., for the information of its members in regard to the progress made in carrying out the aims of the organization. These reports were to be made *nach Massgabe Unserer Correspondenz Nachrichten*, i. e. in such measure and kind as reports of correspondents in the mission fields made possible.

So, in general, the series of annual "Hefte" published by the Society from 1829 to 1868 are made up of Letters, Extracts from Letters, Reports of Mission Journeys, Appeals for Funds for Various Church and School Needs, Letters of Thanks for Funds Received, etc., etc.

As the society was formed for mission work in North America, the Letters, Reports, etc., come in to the Central Direction of the Society, or to the Archbishop of Vienna in person, from all the Dioceses of the United States and parts of Canada, and generally deal with the local needs of the particular mission-station or diocese from which they are dated. Some few are most general in their reference.

For the most part, as was natural under the circumstances, the mass of the Letters is made up of appeals for financial aid for building church or school or hospital, or paying debts already contracted, or supporting the priests in comfort, in dioceses in which there was a rapidly growing but somewhat scattered Catholic population. These appeals often involved statistics of the Catholic population, its source, whether from Ireland or Germany, etc., its character, situation, danger of loss to the church from sectarian missions or mere isolation; they record missionary journeys to various towns, the confessions, baptisms, conversions of Protestants, communions, etc., at the various points visited. Such materials are frankly ecclesiastical, and if the missions had no other records they might prove important documents for the history of the founding of the Catholic churches and the development and spread of Catholicism throughout the country, which kept pace with the immigration from Europe that was almost the sole source of the membership ministered to.

Apparently the contents of the annals are too Catholic for Professor Scholl. His intimations that "such matters are frankly ecclesiastical" and "that secular history is reflected only here and there in these letters, and only incidentally," presages a decision against the translation and publication of the letters by the Historical Commission.

We have frequently urged that these letters should be translated into English and published. We cannot agree with the Professor that they have little bearing upon secular history, but even if that were true, they deal with the momentous subject of religious history, which is ample warrant for their translation and publication.

BOOK REVIEWS

!atholic Beginnings in Kansas City, Missouri—By Gilbert J.
aghan, S. J., Loyola University Press, Chicago.

Iany new chapters are being written on the romantic and color-
iistory of the pioneer period in the Mississippi Valley during the
iteenth and eighteenth centuries, a period hitherto rather neg-
d by the annal writer and romancer. This may be in part due
e fact that the pioneering was done by people of French origin
scent, and there have been few French writers in the field.
here is at present a revival of interest in this French phase of
arly history and personal correspondence, state papers, archives,
other data are being brought out that shed new light on the pic-
que story of those far-off days.
he settlement of Kansas City, Missouri, by the French, is the
e of a very interesting book, just off the Loyola University Press,
ago, written by Gilbert J. Garraghan, S. J. The author has
the letters of Father Roux, pioneer priest of Kansas City to
p Joseph Rosati of St. Louis, as a center around which the nar-
e is written; the situation of the settlement, at the junction of
Iansas and Missouri rivers, as an outfitting station for the Santa
ader, Rocky Mountain trapper, California gold-seeker, Oregon
r, and all those who swept across the great plain to the west,
the situation and setting admirable for a story of unique human
est.
his little book has in it material that could be elaborated into
books so full is it of leads into historical lanes and by-paths.
res an intimate view of life in those days of first rude contact
frontier conditions. It reveals the distinctly French atmosphere
e locality, and through all its pages, you feel the shadowy pres-
of the Indian hovering just outside the French settlement and
g local color to the picture. The intense yearning of the mis-
ry for the conversion and civilization of the Red man and the
bitter disappointments in his work with them are set down
vividly.
ouches of local color light up the pages of hard work and anxiety,
he list of names called off in the account are full of interest to
isians because of the family connections these names have with
on the roster of history-makers in Illinois.
ot the least remarkable are those passages telling of the strong

women of the time, women who left a record of gentle breeding, charity, patience. and a great Christian faith as their contribution to life,
to the end that what might have been utterly harsh and sordid, rose
into the realm of pure romance.

Read the book to learn of Daniel Morgan Boone, son of the great
Daniel Boone, whose two daughters were baptized by Father Roux;
of François Gesseau Chouteau, of the Chouteau family that has given
a score of distinguished names to Mississippi Valley history; of Prud-
homme, Bartholet, and Jesseret; of Vasquez, the Spaniard. And the
women....Mme. Vasquez, née Emilie Forestin Parent, a woman of
refinement and culture, a fervent Catholic, in whose house was said
the first Mass at Kansas City. Father Lutz writes that this lady
reared her children very carefully and that they consoled her in her
old age, a commentary on French family life. Her charity was notable.

So also, of Mme. Chouteau, the first white woman in Kansas City.
Née Therese Berenice Menard, daughter of Col. Pierre Menard, first
lieutenant-governor of Illinois, she came with her husband to start
civilization and society in this frontier settlement. The record of her
beautiful life, her charities, and of the family she reared to carry on
that work in frontier places, is one of the brightest chapters in the
book.

At a very early day came Mme. Grandlouis whose record is similar in kind to these other women of the future city.

This dash of color is only one of these compelling pages: ''West-
port was full of Indians whose shaggy ponies were tied by dozens
along the houses and fences, Sacs and Foxes with shaved heads and
painted faces, Shawnees and Delawares, in calico frocks and turbans,
Wyandottes dressed like white men, and a few wretched Kanzas
wrapped in old blankets, were strolling along the streets or lounging
in and out of the shops and houses.''

Here is something of the personal hardships of the pioneer priest:
''To get to my destination, I travel ten miles....on reaching my
presbytery, I find there neither breakfast, dinner, supper nor a fire.
An old mattress, a sheet, blankets, a pillow raised on a large wooden
support—such is my bed. If I want to eat, I must go in search of
food, often several miles away....I have the pleasure of seeing many
Americans present; they listen with the greatest patience to my poor
English....I must make another trip to the poor Kickapoo Indians.
They made me promise to go and visit them at the beginning of
spring. I had a visit from the Prophet on New Year's day. I instructed on the principal truths of our holy religion and on a few

moral principles also, and particularly on baptism....I was visited
by the chief of the Kaw's....a chief's son....the first warrior of the
nation. All three were daubed with red and black paint, and ornamented with bracelets, medals, collars and ear-rings, and decked with
plumes of feathers''....

The drunkenness of some of the Kickapoo Indians caused a visit
to the priest from the chief who begs his patience and forbearance
towards the wayward Indians and pleads that the priest, having cured
them of smallpox and been kind even to the wicked, should not yet
give them over to despair.

A closing vignette gives one more touch to the romance which the
French settler always found in the Indian—*mon frere sauvage.*

''Among the young persons who were invited to the ball was an
Iroquois girl of very attractive appearance,....yet as soon as she
knew that its pleasures would be attended with danger to her, she put
all thought of being present out of her mind. Not to be without a
reason for her refusal, she cut off her hair, a sign of deep mourning
among the Iroquois. Finally, so as not to anger her father, who
wished her to attend the ball, she would go only if accompanied by
him.''

G. C.

The Michigan Fur Trade. Ida Amanda Johnson, Michigan Historical Commission. University Series V.

The study of the Michigan fur trade by Ida Amanda Johnson
makes interesting reading.

In her preface the writer says: ''This little study aims to give
an account of the fur trader's regime in Michigan; to show the
trading policy of the various nations which successively held sway
over her territory and its results, and the gradual transition from
the influence and domination of one government to that of another;
to relate the story of the rise and growth of the various posts and
outposts within Michigan's borders, the influences to which they were
subjected and their fortunes in peace and war; to depict the life
of the traders, their relations to the red men and to each other; and
finally, to show what place these forest rovers, the frontier heroes
of the State, hold in her history.''

The book is divided into ten chapters as follows: Pioneer Trade;
Detroit, the Great Depot of Trade; Revival of Michilimackinac and
Other Posts; British Policy and Early Trade; Michigan Fur Trade
in Revolutionary Times; U. S. Policy and the Extension of Its Trade

into Michigan; Trade During the War of 1812 and Early Operations of the American Fur Company; Michigan Fur Trade at Its Height; The Closing Days of the Michigan Fur Trade; The Trader's Life.

Naturally though the study is particularly of Michigan, it is not and could not be confined strictly to the present limits of that state since the fur traders were also travelers and pursued their activities in various localities.

The writer in this interesting study names Medard Chouart, Sieur de Groseilliers, Pierre Radisson and Robert Cavelier, Sieur de La Salle as the forerunners of the Michigan fur trade.

The important part played by the missionaries in the pioneer days is thus alluded to. "Surely the Jesuit, that blackrobed priest of frontier life, who followed hard and fast in the footsteps of the trader, must be accorded a place among these early scouts of civilization. Wherever the fur trade went he followed, for both were interested in the savage,— one seeking him for his peltries, the other for the salvation of his soul. Though not a trader, yet, at times, this follower of the Cross did trade. He had his influence and certainly his say in this early commerce, and it is in his records that knowledge of pioneer trade must be sought."

And the manner in which they endeavored to reconcile the trade with morality is reviewed. "These men were not averse to trade, but helped to make it possible and profitable. By their kindness to the Indian they made him well disposed toward the French, and thus opened the way to many western tribes for their trade. Mackenzie says of them 'if these missionaries did not obtain their object, they were yet of great service to the commanders who engaged in those expeditions, and they spread the fur trade. They realized its value to their native country.' Father Carheil says, 'I desire the good of both religion and the Trade, which you are obliged to keep in accord one with the other, without ever separating one from the other.'"

The contrast between the treatment accorded the Indians by the French and the English is made very plain and the debauching of the Indians by the rum route is well described.

The chapter on "The Trader's Life" is especially interesting.

A feature of the study is the copious foot notes and references amongst which of necessity references to the letters of the missionaries contained in the *Jesuit Relations* are very numerous.

Archdiocese of Chicago—Antecedents and Development, by ·
Joseph J. Thompson, LL. D., issued by the Archdiocesan Chancery,
St. Mary's Training School Press.

A volume of rare historic value, of particularly appropriate interest is "The Archdiocese of Chicago, Antecedents and Development," just issued by the Chancery Office from St. Mary's Training
School Press, Des Plaines, Illinois.

The purpose of the publication explained in the foreword by
Joseph J. Thompson, author and compiler, "is to commemorate the
75th anniversary of the erection of the Chicago diocese, and to put
in permanent form the story of the founding and growth of the
Catholic church in this region."

Seventy-five years of diocesan achievement, founded upon pioneer
missionary activity makes interesting reading at this time. Then, as
pointed out, "for 170 years the Gospel had been preached on Illinois
soil before a diocese was established in Chicago."

Names and records of men like Father Marquette, S. J., (1673),
Father François Pinet, S. J., (1696), Father Pierre Gibault, (1768);
Rev. M. Levadeau and Rev. G. Richard, Sulpitianus, (1793); Rev.
Charles Lusson, (1798); Fathers John and Donatien Olivier, (1799;
Father St. Cyr, (1833); Rev. Bernard Shaefer; Rev. Timothy
O'Meara; Rev. Maurice de St. Palais; Rev. Francis J. Fisher; Rev.
J. F. Plunket; Rev. Hippolyte du Pontavice and Rev. John Guguen,
graphically tell the story of earlier priestly activity in the Illinois
district.

* * *

Rt. Rev. Bishop John Carroll, Baltimore, was first of the American heirarchy to exercise ecclesiastical authority over this district,
1789-1810. Bishop Flaget, Bardstown, succeeded in control on the
establishment of his diocese. In 1827 by arrangement Bishop Rosati,
St. Louis, administered affairs of the Church in western and northern
Illinois. In 1834, Bishop Bruté, Vincennes, Indiana, took over the
administration. Previous to this time, as early as 1659, affairs in
Illinois had been directed from Canada, making in all eleven bishops
who exercised control over Chicago before its elevation as a diocese.
Even after the revolution, Illinois affairs continued to be directed
from Quebec until a new arrangement was made, making the United
States a separate jurisdiction.

* * *

The Fifth Provincial Council of Bishops held May 14, 1843, passed
favorably upon a request for the establishment of a diocese in Chicago.

The territory then covered the entire state of Illinois. Alton diocese was created in 1857. Peoria was erected in 1877, and Rockford in 1908. At present the territory of Chicago diocese comprises the counties of Cook, Lake, Du Page, Will, Kankakee and Grundy.

* * *

The later story of Chicago is told largely in the lives of its bishops —The Right Reverend William Quarter, D. D., 1844-1848; Right Reverend James Oliver Van de Velde, 1849-1852; Right Reverend Anthony O'Regan, D. D., 1854-1858; Right Reverend James Duggan, D. D., 1859-1870; Right Reverend Thomas Foley, D. D., 1870-1879; Most Reverend Patrick Augustine Feehan, D. D., 1880-1902; Most Reverend James Edward Quigley, D. D., 1903-1915; Most Reverend George W. Mundelein, D. D., 1915.

* * *

A beautiful tribute is paid the pioneers of Illinois. Pastors and missionaries are here recorded, beginning with the Indian missionary period, 1673-1777. The list of martyr missionaries, includes only those who on our own territory suffered violent deaths at the hands of the Indians. Father Gabriel de la Ribourde, superior of the Recollects in 1680, was killed by the Kickapoo Indians on the Illinois River, not far from Morris, Illinois. Father Membre, another Recollect, with Father Ribourde at the time, was killed in Texas in 1687. Father de Saint Cosme was killed along the Mississippi in 1706. Father Gravier, S. J., vicar general of Illinois missions, was killed in 1708. Rev. Antonius Senat, S. J., who labored at Peoria was burned at the stake in 1736. Abbe Joseph Gagnon a short time later was martyred not far from the Holy Family Mission at Cahokia.

* * *

A complete list of the clergy who served Chicago before its establishment, as well as those ordained by the different bishops is appended. In the case of outstanding names a more complete biography is given, as, for instance, Father St. Cyr, founder of the first church in modern Chicago.

A similar tribute is paid the early bishops who displayed such evident zeal for the struggling community.

In the sketch of Chicago's development, affairs of general importance are carefully recorded. The story of our first Mass, the first church, school and convent makes interesting reading. It is shown that Madison Street, and the lake, by a coincidence, seems to have been the attractive center of early church activities. The coming of the religious orders, establishment of parishes with full particu-

lars and illustrations, the growth of educational and charitable institutions, all receive the greatest possible attention.

The havoc of the great fire of 1871, estimated at about one million dollars, is sketched. How the Church rose supreme from the ashes is graphically told. Present day status as compared with statistics given in various earlier periods illustrate the side by side development of the church with the marvellous growth of the city itself.

              *   *   *

The volume is the result of much diligent research and careful compilation. To the editor much credit is due. The binding is substantial, the letterpress first class, the whole mechanical arrangement redounding to the credit of the recently established St. Mary's Training School Press.

The Diamond Jubilee History of the Archdiocese of Chicago is a work which reads like fiction, by no means an accumulation of dry statistics. Catholics, and indeed, Chicagoan's interested in local history will find their home libraries incomplete without it. The volume has over 700 pages, 9x12 inches, is profusely illustrated, printed in de luxe form, bound in cloth, excellently finished. It may be obtained at the Chancery Office, 740 Cass Street, Chicago. Price, $5.00.—From *New World*, June 11, 1920.

NECROLOGY

ROGER C. SULLIVAN

Roger C. Sullivan was for many years one of the most influential men in the United States. No man of the Irish race and no Catholic layman has exercised locally and nationally more power than Roger Sullivan. In his lifetime, as is quite natural, there were those who · betimes found fault with some of his actions or activities, and since he was but human he of course possessed human imperfections. Many of the same people who criticised him in his lifetime have joined in the almost universal chorus of praise bestowed upon him since his death.

Roger Sullivan was born in Belvidere, Illinois, February 3, 1861. His father died when he was a child. His first employment was as a farmhand, in which capacity he labored for $8.00 a month. At the age of eighteen years he came to Chicago and worked in the old West Side railway shops for a time. He had an inclination to politics and after laboring faithfully in the ranks of the Democratic party for several years, was in 1890 elected probate clerk, and from that time became a political leader. He became also a business man of much ability, and accumulated a fortune.

His first important venture in the business world was the organization and establishment of the Ogden Gas Company about which much has been said and written, in criticism by his enemies and in commendation by his friends. The most notable of his own comments upon this venture was to the effect that the Ogden Gas Company brought about a reduction in the price of gas from $1.25 to $0.85 per thousand feet.

After the consolidation of the Ogden Gas Company with the Peoples' Gas Light and Coke Company, Mr. Sullivan centered his principal business in the Sawyer Biscuit Company. He also had large holdings in the Great Lakes Dock and Dredge Company.

From the time that the late John P. Hopkins came to Chicago until his death he and Mr. Sullivan were fast friends and were closely associated socially, politically and financially.

All who were favored as acquaintances of Roger Sullivan esteemed him as a genial and courteous gentleman, and his beautiful home life was the cause of genuine admiration.

In political dealings Roger Sullivan had a reputation of straightforwardness. He asserted only what he believed and he fulfilled what

ROGER C. SULLIVAN

Born, February 3, 1861. Died, April 14, 1920

he promised. As a result of his activities in politics, more recognition was accorded men of his own race and creed than had ever before been secured. That is not to say that there was favoritism but only that prior to Roger Sullivan's time such recognition was very meagre, if not positively withheld.

Though sometimes abused in his lifetime as a reactionary, the study of his record since his death shows him to have been connected with almost every valuable progressive movement inaugurated during his lifetime and to have exercised a potent influence in its success.

One of the incidents that gave him perhaps the greatest satisfaction of any thing he was ever connected with was the virtual selection of Woodrow Wilson as the nominee of the Democratic party in the Baltimore convention.

To the mind of the writer Roger Sullivan's near-election to the United States Senate from Illinois was his greatest achievement. His creed and nationality condemned him in the eyes of bigots of which Illinois has always possessed a large number. He was slandered and misrepresented for many years previous by the press and other enemies who could not worst him in politics or business and adopted questionable methods for revenge; besides his party was in the minority to the extent of some one hundred and fifty thousand. Despite all these obstacles, at the end of perhaps the most remarkable campaign ever made in the United States he was defeated by but a few thousand votes.

Not in recent years has a death in Chicago elicited such numerous and widespread expressions of regret. Almost every man who has attained to eminence in public life in the United States from the President down, sent letters of condolence.

Roger Sullivan's death occurred on the 14th day of April, 1920. He left a widow, one son and three daughters.

He was buried from the Holy Name Cathedral, his funeral obsequies being participated in by His Grace the Most Reverend Archbishop George William Mundelein and a concourse of clergymen who knew and highly respected him during his lifetime. His remains were buried in Mount Carmel Cemetery.

JOHN F. SCANLAN

John F. Scanlan. Born December 29th, 1839. Died June 12th,)20.

An enthusiastic member of the ILLINOIS CATHOLIC HISTORICAL OCIETY in the person of the late John F. Scanlan, was called to 1e reward of a virtuous and fruitful life, June 12th, 1920.

The deceased was the last survivor of a band of brothers, Patrick, dward, Mortimer, Timothy, Michael and John, the most prominent : whom perhaps were the late Mortimer and Michael and the de- :ased.

These sturdy men were born in Castle Mahon, County Limerick, ·eland, but came to America in 1848 when John F. was nine years d. He was therefore, more than seventy years a resident of Chicago, :ing at the time of his death amongst the very oldest residents.

The Scanlan brothers were men of distinction and in many respects ere unique. Of them it may truthfully be said that they marked it their own way. Entirely self-reliant they were without fear. hey prospered in business but never became rich. It is doubtful they ever had any desire to be rich. They attained much prom- ence but their prominence was incidental,—in a manner thrust)on them. They did not seek it through the usual channels in which ·ominence is pursued.

It is true that John F. Scanlan was once (1878) elected to the ite legislature, and as a matter of interest and conviction strongly ampioned on the platform and through the press the Republican ·rty and its doctrine of tariff protection. It is very plain how- er, that this course was not taken to add to his popularity. As a itter of fact, he was running counter to the views and political eferences of virtually all men of his own race and creed, and was ·erely criticised by the great majority of those. Dr. Cole, author of he Era of the Civil War", Vol. III, of the Centennial History of inois makes the Scanlan brothers the founders and leaders of the sh Republican contingent in Illinois and says that in 1868 the nois State Journal estimated there was not to exceed one Repub- in voter in every fifty Irish voters in the state. In the face of se overwhelming odds the Scanlans upheld the Republican ban- ·, assisted and seconded by Thomas Pope Hodnett and Alderman thur Dixon, not for temporal rewards, as the flight of more than y years has abundantly proven, but from conviction.

The friends of John F. Scanlan during his lifetime and since

his death claim more credit for him as the father and founder of the Catholic Order of Foresters than for any other of his achievements. Those well acquainted with his efforts for Irish freedom will however be inclined to differ somewhat with that view. Of all the men who have come to Chicago, and championed the cause of justice to Ireland, the Scanlan brothers perhaps exerted the greatest effort in that regard. The *Chicago Tribune* of November 2nd, 1866, according to Dr. Cole, in his work above mentioned, stated that P. W. Dunne of Peoria subscribed more money to the Fenian cause than any other man in America, but Cole attributes to the Scanlans the leadership of the Fenian movement. It is perhaps true that after General Thomas W. Sweeney, who led the Fenian forces into Canada, Michael and John F. Scanlan were the most active and influential men in the movement. According to Cole "Chicago had the finest regiment in the Fenian army, 1,000 strong and nearly all veterans. In a few hours the Irish of the city raised $40,000 for their mobilization. Companies from all parts of the state were concentrated in Chicago from which they moved eastward without any attempt at interference."

Though the Fenian movement later came to be looked upon by some as improper, it was not so regarded at the time by the rank and file of American citizens, and indeed was in a large sense a reflection of the belief that prevailed then and still obtains, in justice to Ireland. The same author tells how the Fenian movement was considered. "Oddly enough," says he, "there was little criticism of this attempt to accomplish by force in spite of American neutrality regulations, what might more lawfully have been attempted by political methods. . . . . So formidable had been this Irish movement that no attempt was made within the state to check it. The Democrats commended the zeal for liberty displayed by the Fenians and heaped encomiums upon the Irish while the Republicans saw no propriety in opposing it. Governor Yates and the state officers graced with their presence Fenian entertainments in Springfield and noticed invitations to other celebrations with letters of regret, commending the principles of the organization."

If John F. Scanlan loved his native land and was willing to fight for it and if necessary die for it, he proved that he had a similar affection for his adopted country. When the Civil War broke out he was one of the first to enlist in the service of the United States and did his full duty in service at Camp Douglas where he was assigned. Since the war he had been an honored member of U. S. Grant, Post 28

of the Grand Army of the Republic, the members of which paid his
memory a touching tribute at his bier.

The self-effacement of the deceased is well illustrated in his
relations with the Catholic Order of Foresters. Conceded by all to
be the inspiration, the father and founder of that society he per-
sistently put aside all preferment in that connection, serving under
draft as chief executive officer only until some one else could be
found properly qualified for the leadership. Throughout the long
years of his life, after the founding of the Order, he held the love,
almost veneration of all the officers and members, but never profited
pecuniarily nor sought honors or distinctions through the Order.

For more than twenty years prior to his death, deceased was a
trusted employee of the United States Revenue Department.

His splendid life was summed up in the funeral oration preached
by his lifelong friend Right Reverend Monsignor Daniel J. Riordan.
Msgr. Riordan told about his love for the land of his birth and of
his work, efforts and ideas for the welfare of Ireland, far in advance
of their time. He told of his patriotic love for this his adopted
country, of his love for its flag and how as a soldier he had drawn
his sword in its behalf during the conflict of the Civil War. He
related his love for his home and how well he had performed his
duty as a Christian. Father, how he and his good wife by their exemplary lives were not only revered and respected by their children
but averred that their christian lives were a worthy example and a
true exemplification of the Catholic Christian Home. How well he
"kept the word" was evidenced by one practice that he religiously
observed—daily visiting the Church and making the Stations of the
Holy Way of the Cross for the last twenty years and when prevented
from making his daily visit by sickness or other cause, reciting the
prayers and meditations at home. This practice was unknown to
even his family and friends until a short time before his death. He
told of his work as a Fraternalist and the part he had played in the
foundation of the Catholic Order of Foresters, paying glowing tribute
to the record of the Order and the excellent manner in which this
work had been carried on by those that succeeded him.

An impressive sight was the ceremony of the Grand Army of
the Republic. Members of General U. S. Grant Post No. 28 gathered
at his late residence and after reading an official copy of his war
record, draped his coffin with the American flag. The interment was
at Calvary Cemetery.

ILLINOIS
CATHOLIC HISTORICAL
REVIEW

Volume III   OCTOBER, 1920   Number 2

PUBLISHED BY

THE ILLINOIS CATHOLIC HISTORICAL SOCIETY

CHICAGO, ILL.

APPROBATION

The Archbishop and Bishops of the Province have indorsed the ILLINOIS CATHOLIC HISTORICAL SOCIETY and its work, and proffered their assistance. Following are extracts from their letters:

I give hearty approval of the establishment of a Catholic Historical Society that will not be confined to the limits of this Diocese only, but will embrace the entire province and State of Illinois, and to further encourage this movement, I desire you to enroll me among the life members of the Society.

Sincerely yours in Christ,

GEORGE W. MUNDELEIN, *Archbishop.*

The Bishop desired me to write you that he is pleased to accept the Honorary Presidency, and cordially approves of the good work undertaken by the ILLINOIS CATHOLIC HISTORICAL SOCIETY.

Faithfully yours in Christ,

M. A. TARRANT,
Secy. to the Bishop of Alton.

I am glad to have your letter about the CATHOLIC HISTORICAL SOCIETY, and will gladly serve in the capacity suggested. This will be a depository and will fill a much felt need.

P. J. MULDOON, *Bishop of Rockford.*

The sole aim of the Society, namely, 'To make known the glories of the Church,' should certainly appeal to all our Catholic people. I confidently hope that the Society may meet with the generous encouragement it richly deserves from everyone under my jurisdiction.

EDMUND M. DUNNE, *Bishop of Peoria.*

I wish to assure you that I am willing to give you every possible assistance in the good work you have undertaken, and in compliance with your request, I am likewise willing to be one of your Honorary Presidents.

Wishing God's blessing, I remain,

HENRY ALTHOFF, *Bishop of Belleville.*

CONTENTS

LOYOLA UNIVERSITY PRESS

CHICAGO, ILLINOIS

MARIE JEAN PAUL ROCH YVES GILBERT MOTIER DE LAFAYETTE

From a portrait by Sully in 1824 for the city of Philadelphia, now in
Independence Hall.

Cut by courtesy *Ohio Archaeological and Historical Quarterly*, C. B.
Galbreath, Editor.

Illinois
Catholic Historical Review

| VOLUME III | OCTOBER, 1920 | NUMBER 2 |

SOME FIRST LADIES OF ILLINOIS

A STUDY IN TYPES

No dynastic hue has ever tinged any section of the American people. In the forty-eight commonwealths, and particularly in those beyond the wash of the Atlantic, no governors and no governors' families have ever been other than good democrats. After their brief spell of eminence, they have gone back to plow in the fields of common citizenship and have lived truly as people of the people. Yet even so that fierce light which beats upon a throne stays focussed upon them and upon their off-spring, and they are marked among their fellows. History can follow them down through generations. They become thereby excellent types in which we may see more clearly and with a longer range of vision the mutations that are going on quietly, yet often deeply, in the family career, of the average American.

On at least three occasions in the early days of Illinois, it fell to the lot of a Catholic woman to be the "first lady" of that state; if this is the proper designation of the governor's wife. Not only Mrs. Bissell, but the governor also, was of the faith; before her, two other Catholic ladies presided over the executive mansion, the wives, namely, of Governors Reynolds and Ford.

Reynolds, Ford, and Bissell will accordingly become the titles to the three chapters in which we may study, as in types, what was the fortune and fate of Catholic life in the welter of pioneer days in the great West. Should the triple division offer a suggestion to the mind that we are to indulge in a Greek trilogy, it may be acknowledged that in some of the facts there are sufficiently intense dramatic elements that might be developed and visioned—not here—but in a play in accordance with Athenian standards; the second story is frightfully Greek. The dogs of the Erinnys run down their

helpless quarry with fatalistic relentlessness. The first chapter, albeit replete with matrimony, is rather tame. But there is nothing Hellenic in the third, for it concludes with so sweet a triumph of God that the sad stage of the pagans could never conceive of anything quite so divine.

MRS. JOHN REYNOLDS, 1830-1834

The figure of John Reynolds stands conspicuous in early Illinois. He was a giant of bland features, very ignorant of most things, and pompous in his assumed wisdom. For almost fifty years he won elections, and to him that game was about all there was worth while in life. He wrote books about everything within the circle of the political horizon of which he himself was the center; and thereby made it an easy task for subsequent writers to fill their pages with pictures of him and his times, and they have generously availed themselves of his bounty. Women at that time were not resident within the furthest verge of the political horizon, they lived in the world beyond, so that in the copious Reynolds' literature only the most meagre information may be found concerning the partner of his home. Fortunately we have other sources, and first among them the old Cahokia marriage records.

Here a multiplicity of matrimonial entanglements must be disposed of before there can be a reasonable hope of individualizing the lady we are seeking. Her name was successively Catherine Dubuque, (indicating a relationship with the founder of Dubuque, Iowa), then Pelletier dit Antaya, (this was never really her name, but that of her step-father), next Manegle, and finally Reynolds. Her mother was twice bound in the holy bonds of marriage, Catherine followed the good material precedent, and both her husbands indulged in double matrimonial ventures.

Before 1787, Catherine's mother, Susanne Cesire married (1st) John Baptiste Dubuque; on July 31, 1801, Catherine's mother married (2nd) Louis Pelletier dit Antaya; on April 28, 1782, Catherine's spouse-to-be, Joseph Managle, married Agnes Palmier Beaulieu; on February 28, 1814, Catherine herself is married to Joseph Manegle, a man twice her age; on February 3, 1818, Catherine marries John Reynolds. So far the Cahokia Church Records.—We learn elsewhere that, in May, 1836, Reynolds married Sarah Wilson in Georgetown, D. C.

For almost seventeen years Catherine Dubuque was the wife of John Reynolds. She died, aged 45, just a few days before—in search for more acceptable office—he resigned his governorship. No mem-

He prepared the prisoner for his dread ordeal so well that many an onlooker envied the dying man the bravery and the peace of his last moments. The priest himself was on this occasion so moved by the readiness of the people, with whom he came in contact, to hear the gospel that he shortly afterwards made long missionary tours through the state gaining rich fruit in souls. These visits were the harbingers of the second spring of Illinois' Catholicity.

An appreciation of Mrs. Reynolds that was sent as a contribution to the Shepherd of the Valley—and which is almost certainly the composition of the governor himself—ttells us the important fact of her life from the Catholic point of view. It says "she was raised and educated in the Holy Religion of God. She was a true believer in the faith and doctrine of the Roman Catholic Church, lived in obedience to its holy precepts, and died in that faith, praising God."

(Shepherd of the Valley, Nov. 15th, 1834).

There is no subsequent history of the Reynolds family. There do not seem to have been any descendants of the governor or of Mrs. Reynolds in either of their double marriages.

It might seem that I should include here Governor Thomas Carlin, whose administration covered the years from 1838 to 1842. His Irish parentage makes the probabilities that he was a Catholic about three to one. The further fact that his parents moved from Kentucky into Spanish Missouri, where they were obliged to have their children baptized as Catholics, increases the probability multifold. But this paper concerns ladies. Thomas married Rebecca Huitt, who bore him thirteen children, of whom seven grew to maturity. Save that the Huitt family seems to have originally lived near New Orleans, there is no other shadow of evidence available to indicate that Carlin's wife was ever of the true fold.

Mrs. Thomas Ford, 1842-1846

A sense of dismay, almost of disaster, spread from circle to circle of certain sections of Illinois society a few years when it was announced in the public press that Mrs. Anne E. Daviess, the last surviving daughter of Governor Ford, one of Illinois' great governors, had died on March 17th, 1910, practically an object of public charity.

Mrs. Daviess had lived with a daughter, Mrs. Gamble, in Middleton, Logan County, until that daughter's death in 1907. Mrs. Gamble dying left six little children to the care of her husband, a man of humble circumstances, who now found it impossible to give the necessary attention to the ailing old lady, Mrs. Daviess. He accordingly asked relief of the County. She was not sent to the poor farm, as is usual in similar cases, but to a hospital in Lincoln, the county seat. Lincoln boasts two excellent hospitals, one a Catholic institution, the other in charge of the Lutheran deaconesses. The latter was chosen as a home for Governor Ford's daughter, though on what principal of selection we are not informed. But we are told that, when it was learned she was an Episcopalian, a minister of that denomination attended her regularly. Despite special efforts of the good deaconesses to brighten her declining days, she resisted all attempts to secure from her any recital of her past life or any details of the home life of her distinguished father; she was so broken, it was said, by her sorrows, that death itself seemed a benison. Her body was taken to Peoria for burial and laid there to rest in the beautiful Springdale cemetery besides that of her father, the governor, and of her mother, and of an unmarried sister Julia.

Just at the time that Mrs. Daviess was cast upon her county for care, the legislature of Illinois, desirous of commemorating the exalted services of her father, ordered a splendid cenotaph be erected to his memory. It must have seemed a mockery to her at the time; and the traveller today who sees the one word "Ford" standing out on the rich sarcophagus looks to his guide for an assurance that it is not an ill-placed jest of an advertiser It was a cruel frivolity no doubt to the living daughter of Ford, but it is not such today, for much sorrow lies beneath that stone.

Eulogists at the time of the dedication of the monument in Peoria recalled the rare virtues of Governor Ford, and dwelt particularly on the fact, with its obviously much needed imitation today, that he retired from his governorship a poor man. That honesty is its own sufficient reward seemed to be the lesson of his life, until the revelation of the after careers of his family broke in upon the community and shocked the shallow moralizers.

For the death of Mrs. Daviess directed attention to the other members of the Ford family, and it brought to light, that—if rumor could be credited—the fate of the late daughter was radiant as compared with that of the two sons. Ford's elder son, Sewell, took part in the Civil War, and so distinguished himself for bravery that he lost an arm in his country's cause. Unable to find any other occupation after the conclusion of the civil strife, he served as a barkeeper, until he learned of the frightful death of his brother, Thomas, Jr., in Kansas. Thomas had gone west to seek his fortune, and report brought back the story that a vigilance committee somewhere west of Wichita hanged him as a horsethief. Sewell left for Kansas, perhaps to seek revenge for his brother's taking off, but the vigilance committee was beforehand with him, and he met his brother's fate. It must be repeated that these accounts are rumor. Correspondence with the Secretary of the Kansas Historical Society brings us the prompt reply that, owing to frequent inquiries as to the fate of the Ford boys, investigations have been made in the matter but that nothing in the line of historical proof has ever been secured.

There remains one more child of Ford. Mary Francis, his second daughter, died suddenly in the city of St. Louis, July 27th, 1906, the day after she had celebrated her 69th birthday. She was the wife of John Jay Bailey, and the mother of eight children, four of who survived her; these were Dr. Julia Mastler, an osteopath, and Mrs. Oliver F. Goodell of St. Louis; and Dr. Katherine B. Woodward, a homeopath, and Harry C. Bailey of Ft. Smith, Arkansas. Mrs. Bailey was incinerated at the St. Louis crematory.

There is the story: one daughter dies a public charge; another is committed to the flames by the science-dried hearts of her own children; and the two sons are listed as hanged. One cannot forbear from exclaiming with the apostles, in the ease of the blind man: Lord, whose was the sin?

It cannot be said that Ford was ever a child of the Church; but it is certain that his wife was. Her name was Frances Hambaugh. In the petition of the Belleville Catholics to Bishop Rosati for a pastor for their rising settlement, her father's name, Henry Hambaugh, heads the lists of signers. Frances, or Fannie as she was called, is everywhere described as a remarkably beautiful girl, and and as good hearted as she was fair. At the age of sixteen she was married to Ford by a Justice of the Peace in Belleville, but we find in the Cahokia Records that the sanction of the church was

placed upon the marriage by Father Regis Loisel of St. Louis oñ one of his visits across the Mississippi, three months later. The Hambaughs moved from Belleville soon after to a fine farm, near Ver· sailles, in what was then Schuyler, but now Brown County. There in 1833, Father Van Quickenborne was a guest of the family. Fannie's brother, Stephen, was married to a non-Catholic, Elmira Mary. Stone; this lady was baptized on the occasion, and her godparents were John Hambaugh, and Mrs. Frances (Hambaugh) Ford. The Hambaugh family were devoted to their Church. The Fords made their home with them most of the time, both before the election to the governorship and after. The Ford children all spent their childhood in the Hambaugh home, and it may be affirmed with little less than certainty that they were all baptized children of the Church. Who could ever have prophesied their ending! Have the powers of evil been so ruthless in their rage when exercising it against the children of unbelief! Is this story typical of the course of other Catholic families that drifted from their moorings in those desolate days for the faith? Let us hasten to a brighter page.

MRS WILLIAM H. BISSELL, 1857-1860

In the April number, 1909, of the Journal of the Illinois State Historical Society, two pages of editorial notes are devoted to the announcement that a Life of Governor Bissell is practically completed, but that material particularly for the years 1834-1837 is still desired. As more than ten years have since elapsed, that energetic society must have accumulated matter for an extended and very complete biography. We shall try to confine ourselves here to features of the story of the Bissell family that are likely to be passed over in the other periodical.

Bissell must have been a man of wonderfully attractive personality. He came to the west from New York as a stranger, but was here only a brief time when he was chosen to represent his section of the state in Congress; he was re-elected without opposition; he was re-elected the third time against powerful and able antagonism. He had been a Democrat, but joined the Republican party at the moment of its formation, and was its first nominee for the governorship of Illinois. It has been stated and repeated on good authority—among others by the late Charles Johnston of St. Louis and Judge B. Hay of Illinois—that had it not been for his already failing health, Bissell would have been the Republican nominee for the Presidency in place of Lincoln. The two were intimate friends;

their bodies lie not far apart in the Oak Ridge cemetery at Springfield, and it will not be our part to suggest posthumous rivalry. It
is clear to our readers that it fell to. Bissell to be recipient of the
greater gift, the pearl of great price. His dying moments—and of
course, there are no other such golden moments in any life—were
sanctified by the Divine Sacraments. His family and Father J.
Fitzgibbon were at his bedside, and his last instructions were that
his burial should be according to the ceremonial of the Church.

Even after his death, the Chicago Journal denied that Bissell
had died a member of the Catholic Church, but the St. Louis *Republic*
made this strange assertion subject of an editorial in its issue of
March 24th, 1860; it said, "he connected himself with the Catholic
Church in 1854, and has been a member of it ever since that time.
The question acquires importance only from the fact that it has been
denied, and hence the statement."

It should be stated for the credit of the great citizenship of
Illinois that at a time when Know-Nothingism was at its apogee,
despite the prominence of the Catholic features of the obsequies,
practically the whole state took part in the demonstration of sorrow.
Father Cornelius Smarius, an eloquent Jesuit, delivered the funeral
oration; extracts from this rather pompous pronouncement are still
to be seen in some of the popular elocution books in use in all American colleges. The veterans of the Mexican War, Bissell's fellow
soldiers, occupied the place of honor in the funeral cortege, then
followed the clergy of the city of all denominations, while Masons,
Odd Fellows, Turners and Sons of Temperance joined with the Catholic Societies in closing the procession, "the largest and most imposing" according to contemporary accounts, ever seen in Springfield.
Chicago military and civil organizations were unusually well represented.

Bissell's widow was the daughter of one of Illinois' most distinguished statemen, Senator Elias Kent Kane. Elizabeth Kane was
born in old Kaskaskia, September 29th, 1824. Her mother was
Felicite Pelletier dit Antaya, of an old French family that has been
already mentioned as giving a step father to Mrs. Governor Reynolds.
Miss Kane was Bissell's second wife, and they had no children. Three
of her nieces lived with her at Springfield; these and the two daughters of Bissell's first marriage were known as the Bissell girls, and
the five of them made the executive mansion the social center of
Illinois of that day. A poem addressed to one of them, "Remembered
Eyes," still holds a place in American literature.

Bissell's daughters were Josephine and Emily; the poem was in- . dited to the latter. They attended the Ursuline Convent near their home, but were slow in relinquishing the faith of their deceased mother, Emily James, for the new-found religion of their father, that of their step-mother. They responded at length, but not firmly.

The story of their defection is interesting. Mrs. Bissell did not long survive her husband, and the daughters lived for some time with the family of Lieut.-Governor Koerner, a man of great forcefulness of opinion but of no faith. Catholicity in Belleville seemed entirely foreign. The Sunday Mass was always accompanied by an unintelligible sermon seldom less than an hour in duration. Emily was married to a Swedenborgian, Charles W. Thomas, by a Presbyterian minister, and thus one of Bissell's two children seemed lost to the church. Three bright healthy children blessed this union, who were given the names Bissell, and Charles, and Josephine. In time a wave of Episcopalianism swept through Belleville, and the two boys, Bissell and Charles Thomas, together with their aunt, Josephine Bissell, succumbed to it, and Josephine died in 1904 out of the visible unity of the Church. This was the second of Bissell's daughters, and in her decease the knell of the Catholicity of the Bissell family seemed to have been tolled.

But there was a seed planted in fertile ground hidden deep and warm during those cold days of the faith. The other Josephine, the daughter of Mr. and Mrs. Thomas, was at this time studying at the Loretto Convent at Nerinx, Kentucky. She returned home in her 18th year a Catholic, and the tender Catholic branch will grow into a glorious tree.

Not long after this, her mother, Mrs. Thomas, visiting St. Louis, went to see a newly completed Catholic church—the College Church— whose doors are always open wide, and whose beauty makes it a Mecca for many who enter with little thought of prayer. While she was admiring the monolithic columns, a priest came out to one of the confessionals. It was Daniel McErlane, who at the time of his death was called "a sleuth of souls", owing to the fascination about him that brought all classes of the weary and the heavy laden to him for solace. At his entrance into the church, more people rose up and hastened towards him than Mrs. Thomas had imagined were in the building. One by one they came away from him with a look of heavenly peace that stirred her, and she knelt to pray. She too went to him, and she used to say afterwards that she walked back to Belleville that evening on the air. Of course no such physical

miracle occurred, but in reality a more marvellous and lasting one had been effected. For from that day until her holy death in 1912, she was a model of attention to all her religious duties. Meanwhile her husband, Mr. Thomas, was stricken down with a fatal illness, in the midst of a political campaign, wherein he was the candidate for the supreme judgeship of Illinois. He called for a priest shortly before the consummation and appeared before the Eternal Judge clothed in white robe of baptismal innocence.

And what of the two boys and of Josephine? Bissell Thomas married Anna McCabe, and made his home in San Francisco. When he went to France with the 16th Engineers, there was another Emily to be kissed good-bye, and to pray for his safe return. Charles Thomas married Eugenie Papin of an old Catholic family of St. Louis. They have now a little Catholic Japanese daughter, Mary Papin Thomas, in their home at Osaka, in the Flowery Kingdom.

Josephine married Bonaventure Portuondo, a physician of Spanish ancestry, and still resides at the old homestead, Belleville. Their living children are Rita, Josephine, Isabella, Bonaventure, and Sylvia Carmen. The first named is now Sister Rita of the Ursuline Convent at Springfield. From his post in Springfield, Governor Bissell swayed the destinies of Illinois for high and noble ends during his brief, incomplete term of power; but persons who realize how immeasurably higher a hidden handmaid in Nazareth elevated the world's civilization than the mightiest of the Caesars, may reasonably hope that Illinois will be no less blessed in the humble Ursuline of today than in her powerful progenitor.

In the third generation every descendant of Governor Bissell— in Illinois, in California, and in Japan—is a loyal child of the church. Who will gather back the sad progeny of Governor Ford and of the other thousands of wayfarers, bereft of their heavenly birthright in the wilderness of the strange new life of the early West! May we hope that the home-coming of the Bissells is typical of the things that are to be among these other thousands, millions, all over America! Fiat.

LAURENCE J. KENNY, S. J.

St. Louis University.

THE NORTHEASTERN PART OF THE DIOCESE OF ST. LOUIS UNDER BISHOP ROSATI

Among the most valuable documents in the archives of the St. Louis Archdiocese we must number the letters of Father Samuel Mazzuchelli, O. P., the founder of the Church in Iowa. They are all addressed to Bishop Rosati. Some are written in English, the bulk, however, is in Italian. They form an interesting commentary to the "Memoirs, Historical and Edifying of a Missionary Apostolic", (i. e., Father Mazzuchelli) published in 1915.[1] They have never before been printed. In retracing our steps to the northern missions of Galena and Dubuque and Prairie du Chièn, we will have occasion to print them all as a sort of documentary history of the early days of the Church in these parts. Father Mazzuchelli received his appointment from Bishop Rosati on June 12' 1835. As he was more closely identified with the Church of Iowa than that of Illinois or Wisconsin, we will open our article with the first and the chief city of that State.

"The little episcopal city of Dubuque, writes Father Mazzuchelli in his Memoirs, "dates its origin from the year 1813: Prior to that date all the present territory of Iowa was still inhabited by numerous Indian tribes. The Government, having bought from these tribes the land adjoining the river, after various treaties, or to speak more correctly, after the expenditure of generous sums of money, many thousands of the citizens of the Republic settled there within a few months, but especially in the vicinity of Dubuque on account of the lead mines. The traffic in this valuable metal erected the city of Dubuque, named for the last French trader (Julien Dubuque) who, after spending many years of his life in that place with the Indians, died in 1811. In 1835, the year in which the church lot was acquired in Dubuque, the village numbered about two hundred and fifty persons, the missions, including the miners, numbered about 750.

---

[1] This book, as Archbishop Ireland states, was originally written in Italian, and printed in Milan in 1844, during a visit of Father Mazzuchelli to his native land. It was translated by a Dominican Sister of Sinsinawa, Wisconsin, and published by the W. F. Hall Company, Chicago, 1915.

Almost 200 of this number were Catholics; almost all of Irish descent, so there seemed to be a very good prospect of a flourishing parish, both here and at Galena across the river.''[2] It was on June 24, 1835 that Bishop Rosati gave all faculties for Galena to Father Samuel Mazzuchelli. This included Dubuque; and accordingly, in July of the same year the missionary of the North visited the place for the first time. Mass was said at the home of P. Quigley: the people of the town showed the greatest interest and generosity, so that the cornerstone for the church to be called St. Raphael's, could be laid amid universal rejoicing on the Feast of the Assumption of the Blessed Virgin in the year 1835. But what were the antecedents of this man that instilled new life into these drooping missions of the North.

Father Samuel Charles Mazzuchelli, O. P., was born in Milan, Italy, in the year 1806 of a distinguished family. In 1822 he became a novice of the Order of St. Dominic in Rome. When the first bishop of Cincinnati, Edward Fenwick, himself a Dominican, came to Rome in 1828, seeking helpers for the missions in the wild Northwest, the youthful deacon, full of glowing dreams of religious triumphs and romantic adventures in the wilderness of America, obtained permission from his superiors to join the saintly Bishop Fenwick. In 1830 he was ordained priest, and immediately set out for the Island of Mackinac, the most north mission of the diocese of Cincinnati. Mackinac was the starting point for Father Marquette's voyage of discovery: it was to be the starting point also for Father Mazzuchelli's missionary journeys, which were to bring him in such close union with the northeastern part of Bishop Rosati's diocese of St. Louis.

Mackinac was the center of a parish that extended from Lake Huron to the Mississippi River. Here stood the only chapel in this wide territory, but the parishioners, Catholic Indians and half-breeds, Frenchmen from Canada and native Creoles, Irish miners and German farmers, scattered members of almost every nation, were settled down or wandered about in every part of it. To supply them spiritual necessities in life and in death the pastor was obliged to travel almost constantly in winter on snowshoes or in a sled, in summer on horseback or in a birch-canoe. Mass was said at times under a spreading greenwood tree, sometimes in the wigwam of a converted Indian, sometimes the rude dwelling of a trader, miner or trapper. In Green Bay Father Mazzuchelli built the first church and opened the first school, not only of the neighborhood, but of the entire

[2] *Memoir*, p. 190.

established at Prairie du Chien a school, as the most of our nation are here on the Benecault River, we are anxious to have the school placed among us. You are aware, and we wish our Great Father to know that many of us have joined the Catholic Church and have become Christians. Many men of our nation seem desirous of becoming civilized through the exertions of our friend here, the black-gown (Father Mazzuchelli), we, therefore, hope that our prayers may be granted by our Great Father; we will then be able to have our children educated among us and in the Catholic Faith. We have never had any one until lately to teach us the word of God. We begin to see light and we wish to know more of our Great Father above. We want Father Mazzuchelli to remain with us and the school established among us."[3] Next to the love of God as expressed in the burning zeal for souls, and naturally flowing from this fountain-head of all true wishes, come the distinctive qualities of our noble-minded apostle, his fearlessness in danger, his patience in adversity, his disinterestedness in all his undertakings. "In perils often," Father Mazzuchelli might say with the Apostle of the gentiles. One example only can we give: It was a morning in March that the priest was called from his home at Galena to bring the last sacraments to a dying person in Iowa Territory. The ice on the river was broken up by a sudden change in the temperature, and was carried along with the swift current. The priest found no other means of transport than a sort of narrow canoe hollowed out a single trunk of a tree, which had been lying on the bank all through the winter. Father Maz-zuchelli engaged four men to row him across the river. After pushing

[3] *The American Catholic Historical Researches*, Vol. XII, 2, p. 61

Cut by, courtesy *Rosary College.*

VERY REV. SAMUEL MAZZUCHELLI, O. P.

Missionary Apostolic amongst both Indians and White people
in Illinois, Iowa, Michigan, Wisconsin and Minnesota.

out about half a mile the water began to pour in through several cracks, soon made wider by collision with the drifting ice. The steersman courageously managed the frail craft, ordering all to remain seated and perfectly quiet. Father Mazzuchelli felt secure amid the seething rushing waters, bearing as he did, the Blessed Sacrament upon his breast. Kneeling in the water and paddling with a single oar, he followed the directions of the steersman, and when the water had risen to within four finger's length of the rim of the canoe, they reached a little island, where they repaired their boat and proceeded on their voyage. Of Father Mazzuchelli's patience his letters will give abundant examples: of noble disinterestedness, we would add a brief word. "It may be well to remark, says he, that the generosity of the faithful in these parts depends in a great measure upon the disinterestedness of the Priest. If he manifest any desire for money, then all is lost for the church, for he is the sole agent, secretary and treasurer. If he does not divest himself completely of self, and consecrate himself without reservation to the propagation of the Truth, that indispensible boundless confidence of his people loses itself in doubts and suspicions, and at last vanishes entirely. The great secret of finding money where it does not seem to exist, lies in the sincere disinterestedness of the Priest. . . . . In the United States the church is generally the poorst of the poor: for either one must be built, or it is in debt, or else it requires repairs, or necessary furnishings for the altar. So if the Priest desires to see the people liberal and full of confidence in his personality, he must himself lead the way. Keeping nothing for himself, and putting everything that he possesses in the treasury of the church. The same Providence that cared for him in the past will not fail him in the future: for ever true are those words of our Divine Master: "When I sent you without purse and scrip and shoes, did you want anything?" (Luke XXII, 35.)[4]

In July, 1835, when Father Mazzuchelli arrived at Galena, he found, as he himself says, "not a vestige of the sacred things necessary for the celebration of the Holy Sacrifice." In an upper room of the dwelling of one of the parishioners he erected an altar, probably of a dry-goods-box, which transformed the place into a church. In one corner, separated from the altar by a curtain was the bed of the Priest. So poor, yet so intimate with God, was this secong springtide of the church in Galena. But this beautiful promise of a rich

---

[4] *Memoir*, p. 219.

harvest seemed to be doomed to failure once more. On April 18, 1836, Bishop Rosati, on hearing that Father Mazzuchelli had been recalled by his Superior in the Order entrusted the parishes of Galena, Dubuque and Prairie du Chien to the Rev. ℈. Condamine. When Father Condamine arrived at his destination, Father Mazzuchelli's recall had been revoked, and Father Condamine was appointed to Cohokia, May 18, 1836. Father Mazzuchelli writes:

Dubuque, May. 11, 1836.

Rt. Rev. Bishop of St. Louis.

SIR—I send you a copy of a letter I received from the Rt. Rev. Cipoletti, General of the Order of St. Dominic. This letter is an answer to a petition made by the inhabitants of this place on the fourth of August last and, I believe, of another made by the people of Galina. Bishop Rese has written to Rome on the same subject. Now I beg of you those spiritual faculties which are necessary to perform my ministry. The deed of the Churches will be made over to you, but they cannot be altered this moment. I must pay $550.00 on the lot of Galina, and as Bishop Resé will probably be in this part of the New Territory this season, I shall be able to make over to you the deed of Dubuque. All I care is the good of religion and have no partiality to any diocese. To this day I have done every thing as I knew best; and I am always ready to acknowledge my faults.

Pray give me your Episcopal blessing.

Your very humble servant,

SAMUEL MAZZCHELLI, O. P.[1]

Bishop Rosati cherfully gave Father Mazzuchelli the faculties asked for and continued him as Pastor of the Northern Missions, May 14, 1836.

In the next letter there is a note of holy joy at seeing the sacrifices and labors blessed at last by a distinct success:

Galina, July 14, 1836.

Most Rev. Bishop Rosati.

SIR—After many a day of hard work and uneasiness, I succeeded, with the will of God to complete the stone walls of St. Raphael's Church at Dubuque as high as the roof. Every preparation is now made to raise the roof and two stone-cutters are at constant work to make a plain cornice round the building and to finish the front. On the 4th of July the church was used by the people of the town to hear the *Oration* delivered by a lawyer. I had to act the part of chaplain and say the prayer. The expenses of the building have been very great for one man like me agitated by many trials: I already paid $2,400.00. Want of time has hindered me from collecting the $800.00 due on the subscription, only $300.00 were lent to me to pay the last debts. I hope to say Mass in St. Raphael's church next Sunday. The church of Galina is as I left it last Fall, many things have entirely discouraged me in the undertaking; however

---

[1] Original in English. Archives.

last Saturday I took two of my men to this place, they now work in the quarry. I opened this quarry on the church lot; about 200 perch of stone are now ready round the foundation, lime and sand are also procured. All this is a great deal here where materials are very scarce. There is not a person here that can move a step for the building of the church. I have to procure every material to the amount of a cent. The most difficult part of the work is the collection. Althought I am confident of. the great attachment of the people to me, and of the knowledge they have of my disinterestedness, still it is with the greatest reluctance I do begin this work and sincerely wish to abandon if I could. My constant occupation in May and June about the church of Dubuque has prevented me from attending at the church of Mill-Seat, Wisconsin Territory, 15 miles from this place. Nearly all the materials for the building of it are now ready. Next week I shall spend three or four days about that place to gather all materials, make contracts, collect the money, and begin the work if possible. For many good reasons I abandon the mission of Prairie du Chien, Fort Winnebago; and I wish to see Bishop Resé in the ends of his diocese. The 3 Liguorian priests of Green Bay,[•] with about $3,000.00, got the possession of an establishment that cost $8,000.00, and is now worth at least $12,000.00. They have but one settlement to attend. I do not see why they should be left there in peace. Prairie du Chien and Fort Winnebago could be made part of their parish. I have to notify you, that I have received several invitations to visit the new towns below Galina on both sides of the Mississippi, in order to build chapels, but I cannot move from these parishes now. It is probable that in the Fall, with your consent, I shall visit those places to secure valuable lots for the good of religion. As I stay but a very short time in each parish, those who wish to get married are always in a very great hurry and, with many reasons, give no time for the publications. I do not know how to manage these cases. If I require the publications they would be compelled to go to a magistrate. I wish you to give me some directions in this particular. If I cannot see Bishop Resé this summer or some priest I shall be obliged to come to St. Louis. *ad confitendum.* This satisfaction was denied to me by M. Condamine. I should be much pleased to secure the holy oils and a Latin Ritual, with two altar stones. I left two of them in the hands of Mr. Borgna last winter, and got two or three made by the stone cutters on the church ground. I have not paid him yet; should you be so good as to pay them, consecrate them and send them to me; I shall with the utmost pleasure pay all expenses.

    Today I wrote the first letter to the General Superior Cipoletti since I left Rome.

Your most obedient servant,
SAMUEL MAZZUCHELLI, O. P.

    But the spiritual interests of the congregations[7] would, at times seem secondary to cares for the temporalities. There is a letter in

---

[•] The Liguorian priests of Green Bay were the Redemptorist Fathers. Simon Saenderl, F. X. Haetscher, and F. X. Tschenhens, who had come from Vienna, Austria. Cf. Father Holweck's articles in *Pastoral Blatt,* Vol 54, Nos. 7, 8 and 9.

[7] Original in English. Archives. Father Mazzuchelli always spells the city's name Galina.

the Archives of St. Louis written during a visit to the city, that throws light on such business transaction. It is in regard to the church lot in Dubuque, which, as we have seen, was obtained by Father Fitzmaurice from the United States Agent in 1834, but for the securing of which the proper steps do not seem to have been taken.

St. Louis, November 13, 1836.

Rt. Rev. Bishop Rosati.

Sir—Being necessary to give the power of attorney to some person residing about Dubuque in order to obtain from the U. S. Commission the title of a certain piece of ground on which your Rt. Reverence has a claim, the following remarks are required:

1. It was in the year, 1834, that the U. S. agency gave a permit to the Rt. Rev. Joseph Rosati to occupy a certain piece of ground adjoining the town of Dubuque for the use of a Catholic church and house and garden for the priest.

2. By an act of Congress, 1836, those individuals who have received a permit from the U. S. agent for the Lead Mines to occupy any lot — in the town of Dubuque, are entitled to a pre-emption of said lot.

3. As the Rev. Bishop cannot in person attend before the U. S. Commissioners, it is indispensable to appoint someone to act in his place. This may be done, either by giving a deed of all his claim on said ground to a confidential friend, or by appointing an attorney to act in his place before the Commissioners.

4. Should the Bishop think proper to give the deed to his priest, he shall be able to appoint an attorney himself, if so necessary. And if the Bishop prefer to give him only the power of attorney, it must be made so as to allow him to appoint another in his place.

5. The said ground or part of it has been unjustly claimed by a widow woman. She claims that some of the Catholics, when Rev. Fitzmaurice lived in Dubuque, left the decision of the case to an arbitration, which decided in favor of the widow (What she did not claim was neglected by the Catholics).

6. M. O'Farrel, a merchant of Dubuque, having bought the house and lot with all the claims of the widow, has considered all the ground as his own.

7. Some difficulties may arise in which the priest does not like to be.

8. Arrangements can be made with Mr. O'Farrel for what he has sold and, by giving him some profit, everything could probably be settled.

9. Although the permit gives more than four acres, still the act of congress does not give the pre-emption on any lot of larger size, so that the surplus of four acres has to be disposed before the commissioners will examine the claim.

10. A friendly arrangement with Mr. O'Farrel is the best course. He has caused that part of Dubuque, Iowa, to be valuable, and consequently he has an indirect claim on it.

Your humble Servant,
SAMUEL MAZZUCHELLI, O. P.[*]

[*] Original in English. Archives.

Galina, Ill., January 5, 1837.

Rt. Rev. Bishop—Knowing that you are not in a hurry to have that report I promised you of the various parishes of this country, and anxious to give correct information, I shall defer it for a few weeks longer. I hope you received 'that letter I wrote before I left St. Louis, and which I consigned to Mr. Walsh. Mr. Patrick Gray of this place who died in Pittsburg last summer has left in his will $250.00 for establishing the Sisters of Charity in this town. Now, as it is very improbable that the Sisters of Charity should come to this place shortly, it would be advisable to get that money from the Executors of Mr. Grey, while it is in their hands,—for it might disappear. One of the Executors is a Protestant, the other a Catholic (who cares very little about religion). I am informed that by getting a receipt of $250.00 from some Superior of the Sisters of Charity, the money will be paid by the Executors to the Church of Galina. The Protestant executor would have paid me long ago, if I had given him the receipt. While I set the circumstances before you, I write you that it is impossible to take the lot of the church from the hands of the four individuals who have the deed, without paying part of the money. We owe $600.00 on the lot. Should we now pay about one-half that amount I shall go security for the balance, and get the deed in your name. This is the best time, for now the town commissioners are sitting, and shortly the deed will be given to the actual owners by Government. In doing as I said, you shall have the deed from the U. S. My health is very good.

Please to give me your Episcopal Blessing.

Most Obedient Servant,

Samuel Mazzuchelli, O. P.[a]

Galina, February 9, 1837.

Rt. Rev. Bishop—On the 6th inst. after an absence of four weeks from Galina I received Your three letters of January last. I hope to comply with your wishes as far as I am able. The receiving of the $250.00 is still involved in some difficulties, but I have no doubts that by prudent exertions, the money will be paid and the deed properly made. In Dubuque I shall lay my claim very soon and expect to have some difficulties not easily surmounted. On Monday next I shall start for Rock Island. About that place there is a great preparation to be made for the establishment of our religion. From that place you shall receive a letter of mine.

Please to give me your Blessing.

Most Obedient Servant,

Samuel Mazzuchelli.[b]

Galina, Illinois, March 4, 1837.

Rt. Rev. Bishop—I have at last received the sum of $250.00 for the Sisters, not from the Executors, for the one who lives in Galina openly refused to pay

[a] Original in English. Archives.
[b] Original in English. Archives.

I board in various houses, for I have no means to pay regular boarding, a bad table, now and then. I have now good beds, but no furniture. No salary. Baptisms and marriages will give enough to buy clothes. I must say that a salary was offered to me in Dubuque last summer. I declined it, because I have no fixed place, and because the church could not be finished whilst the people are obliged to pay a salary. The pew rent will in time become an excellent support for the priest. Disinterestedness, patience and humility are indispensible with the people I have here. You know well the great faults of the nation I have to live with. Please to give your blessing.

Your obedient servant,

SAMUEL MAZZUCHELLI, O. P.[19]

Galina, Ill., April 16, 1837.

RT. REV. BISHOP ROSATI—Your letters have not reached me in time, for I was detained on the west side of the Mississippi for three weeks by the ice. Ten days after Easter I came to Galina and read your letter. The next day I started for St. Louis, where I expected to see you, in the meantime went to my duties. On my return I stayed at Rock Island to visit the poor Catholics of that place. Mr. Le Clair will probably build a very nice brick church of

---

[19] Original in English. Archives.

Rt. Rev. Bishop—The short letter I have just received gives me a very great pleasure. The congregation of Dubuque has much increased this summer; the church, with the assistance of God, will shortly be finished, except the inside plastering and pews. There is a large but humble room under the altar. Times are very difficult, and it will be with the greatest difficulty that I shall get four hundred dollars to continue the building of the wall of Galina Church. Protestants, after much preparation, have given up the idea of building their church this year. My occupations do not permit me to attend the building of the church of St. Gabriel at Davenport. I made and sent down to that place all necessary plans for a handsome church of brick. M. Leclaire has the means and the generosity, but he is unable to make contracts and does not understand building. He wrote me to go down and have the church built. Now I do not know what to do. We have no opposition here from the Protestants. I shall do my best to prepare a place for the new Bishop.

Your humble Servant,
SAMUEL MAZZUCHELLI.[11]

Who Mr. LeClaire was appears from the following passage from Father Mazzuchelli's "Memoirs":

"Among the most beautiful and charming sites on the western bank of the Mississippi is that one opposite the famous Rock Island, more than a hundred miles from Dubuque down the river. Nature itself seems to have shaped this regular verdant slope, girdled and shielded by hills, that man might raise a city there. A certain Antoine Leclaire, a devout Catholic, noted no less for his integrity than for his wealth, for many years had his happy home there, alone with his wife, and held his estate of a square mile along the river. This had been presented him as a free gift by the tribes of the Sacs and Foxes in their gratitude toward their faithful friend and interpreter and beneficent adviser on the occasion of the ceding of that section to the United States Government. It was in 1836 that Mr. Leclaire began to convert his estate into a city, which he named Davenport. His faith did not let him forget the cause of Religion: for in the city he was planning, he donated a square in an advantageous position for the erection of a church. The city sprang up as by magic and

---

[11] Original in English. Archives.
[11] Original in English. Archives.

extending beyond the confines of Leclaire's estate became the center. of trade for the southern part of Iowa.''

After hesitating a while Father Mazzuchelli came to the assistance of Mr. Leclaire, the principal proprietor of Davenport, and in April, 1831 laid the first stone of the church which was called St. Gabriels. The first bricks manufactured in the place were used in the construction of the building which was only forty by twenty-five and built with two stories, so as to accommodate on the lower floor, the priest who was to make his home there." Thus far the account given of the beginnings of Davenport, now an episcopal see.

The diocese of Dubuque, comprising the state of Iowa, was eestablished July 28, 1837, and its first bishop, Mathias Loras was consecrated as its first bishop December 10th, same year. Father Mazzuchelli became Vicar General of the new diocese, yet remained attached to St. Louis on account of his pastorship of Galina. As the building of the church of St. Michael was still in progress it was but natural that Father Mazzuchelli should continue his ministrations there, as we see from the following letter:

Dubuque, September 1, 1837.

MONSIGNOR—I happened to receive this morning your esteemed letter of the 17th of August. Hence I have prepared all the letters that I thought to be necessary concerning the subject of Mr. Ferdinand McCosker. Your Grace may rest assured that nothing will happen contrary to the canons of Holy Mother Church.

I have already done all that was possible for me to do concerning the welfare of religion in this country. The church of Dubuque is worthy of being a cathedral. I have obtained the claims of about three acres of land joined to the lot of the church. The commissioners have not yet begun to examine the claims of Dubuque, and as a consequence, the claim of the year 1834 is still in statu quo. I wrote some months ago to your Grace, telling you that the title to the church of Galina was given to the bishop, and on account of many difficulties with the trustees I did not have sufficient money to settle up. Mr. Dowling of Galina gave me $250.00 for the Sisters of Charity. But this man has not yet received one cent from the executors of Mr. Gray. On the 28th of the past month I finally accomplished my desire and I paid for the land of the church of Galina, $615.00, the title I had from the trustees is given to your Grace. 117 feet are being used for a church, and 100 feet is for the Sisters of Charity. All this was done by divine Providence in a time when money was scarce, and under many difficulties caused by perverse men. I have also paid 259 dollars for lumber, and there is left in the treasury of the church of Galina 141 dollars. Divine Providence will also assist me to build a small house for the resident priest. It is almost impossible for a priest to stay at Galina under the present circumstances. The papers of Dubuque and

" *Memoirs*, pp. 190, 191.

From October 10 to October 14, Father Mazzuchelli was in St. Louis, but failed to see the bishop who was at the Seminary of St. Mary's of the Barrens.

St. Louis, October 14, 1837.

MOST REVEREND BISHOP—I arrived at St. Louis the tenth day of this month with the hope of seeing your Grace, but as I did not have the time or the means of paying you a visit, it seems necessary for me to write you a few lines before I leave for my mission. The difficulties that I have to overcome with the government committee, now in session at Dubuque, on account of the land given by the agent, are very great, and are caused by some rich and powerful Americans who do not keep their promises. It would be of the greatest help to have an American priest here for a few days; he would be able to lessen the opposition. I am very uneasy about these affairs, the loss and the gain are of great value. I need money to employ two lawyers, and I hope that Providence will give it to me. Today I leave for my mission. The water of the Mississippi is very high, but with the grace of God I will arrive at the mission in three days. I have asked (Rev.) Mr. Jameson to visit my place, and he replied that he would come with much pleasure, if Your Grace grants him the permission. Wherefore I ask you to grant the afore mentioned Mr. Jameson the special permission to visit my people; for I think such visit to be necessary for the good of religion. I shall be absent eight or, at most ten days As I have not yet had the pleasure of seeing a priest at my mission, I hope that you will grant my request. Mr. Jameson expects a reply from

14 Original in Italian. Archives.

Your Grace. I would be very glad to be at the Seminary on the day of the consecration of the church, but my temporal affairs on account of the church will not permit such a long visit. I am alone with many expenses and without resources, the debts afflict me with remorse, and as a consequence I desire to begin the interior of the church without difficulty, and one day to receive the new bishop without any debts.

Not having had the consolation of seeing Your Grace in person I ask your blessing in writing.

Your Grace's humble Servant,

SAMUEL MAZZUCHELLI, O. P.[14]

P. S.—My health is very good.

Galina, December 28, 1837.

MONSIGNOR—This morning I received the instructions which you sent from Dubuque on the 11th inst. But as the mail will leave in a few hours it will be impossible for me to answer all the proposed questions. When the mail leaves next Monday I will send all the information which Your Grace deems necessary, and since I desire to receive your letters without any loss of time please be good enough to send my mail to Galina, where all my letters are addressed.

Your humble servant,

SAMUEL MAZZUCHELLI.[16]

March 4, 1838.

MY LORD BISHOP OF ST. LOUIS—A few days ago I received the instructions in which you gave me the precise information concerning the limits of the new diocese. Last year I had sent to Bishop Resé a description of the new diocese according to my idea, hoping that he would present it to the Fathers of the Council; but now that all has been settled by the authority of the church, it is useless to speak about it any more. As regards the faculty of pro vicar general, I wish you to know that it was my intention not to accept any dignity of such nature, but accidentally your letter fell into the hands of a man that knows a little Latin, and having seen the contents of it, he made them known to my friends. Hence it would not be prudent to reject the faculty. It was my purpose to do nothing more to the church of Dubuque, hoping that the bishop would arrive in the month of May. Now being informed that he will not be in his diocese until the month of November, it put me in many difficulties to finish the church before he comes. Yet I hope with the grace of God to have the church of St. Raphael prepared for the consecration next September, but it will be necessary for me to have a priest here after Easter. I hope that Your Paternity will be able to send one of those priests now in your diocese.

The parish of Galina in the State of Illinois contains about 400 Catholics. Many people of the Wisconsin Territory consider Galina their parish, hence

---

[14] Original in Italian. Archives. (The Reverend) Mr. Jamison was an accession fromt he East, and returned to Baltimore. In a letter at the end of this article Bishop Loras has a word to say in regard to Mr. Jamison.

[16] Original in Italian. Archives.

the reason why I have written about 600. Galina is about six miles from the territory.

Next month I shall pay a visit to Your Grace.

Your humble servant,

SAMUEL MAZZUCHELLI.[17]

December 3, 1838.

MONSIGNOR—I have received two letters from Bishop Loras. He wrote the second letter from Havre in which he tells me to rent a house, as he is to be in Dubuque about All Saints. Last month I took a house and paid the rent for a month, and I bought a bed with other things. I am not disposed to make any debts for the bishop, because a fatal experience has taught me not to trust the future. If he does not arrive before the middle of this month, I will give up the house which costs 25 dollars a month. Everything is dear in this place. Circumstances are such in Dubuque that the bishop will be obliged to take care of his own cooking. Monsignor Loras will find in my insignificant person a most humble and a most faithful servant. With the grace of God I hope to make my home with Bishop Miles towards the end of next year.

Your Paternities most humble servant,

SAMUEL MAZZUCHELLI.[18]

Bishop Loras arrived in St. Louis late in the year 1837, and was detained there the entire winter, as navigation on the river was blocked by the masses of ice coming down its majestic current. Father Mazzuchelli left Galina on March 19th by the first steamboat, to bring his bishop to the episcopal city of Dubuque. On the 21st day of April, 1838, the prelate took possession of his Cathedral. On the 28th day of April Bishop Loras officiated in the church of Galina. It was a great event in the town that had never before been visited by a bishop. On a former occasion Father Mazzuchelli had asked for an assistant: this request was now to be gratified, but in a manner not altogether satisfactory to the old missionary.

Galine, July 23, 1839.

RT. REV. BISHOP—The Rev. Mr. Lee arrived in Dubuque when Bishop Loras was still absent on a visit to St. Peter and Prairie du Chien. I advised him to remain in Dubuque last Sunday, while I would go to Galina to prepare everything for his reception. As the people of this place do not like a change of clergyman and felt quite displeased at the idea of it, so I deemed it more prudent to tell the congregation, that the Rev. Lee was sent up by you to be an assistant to me in this mission, as I was about to visit many other places; in this way they were sufficiently satisfied. Mr. Philip Barry will board him, and there he will be kept away from any place where his countrymen might

---

[17] Original in Italian. Archives.

[18] Original in Italian. Archives. Bishop Richard P. Miles of Nashville was a Dominican.

be an occasion of evil to him. I left for his use all those conveniences I have procured heretofore, and, if he does well, before winter he will be better fixed and liked by the inhabitants. Should he taste any liquor he is a gone man in this place. I shall continue to be responsible for all things belonging to the finishing of the church.

My respects to your worthy coadjutor, Bishop Timon.

Your most humble servant,

SAMUEL MAZZUCHELLI.[18]

Poor Father Constantine Lee did not last long at Galina. Undoubtedly a man of talent and capable of doing good work among his country men, he spoilt all by his lack of self-restraint. On September 13, three months after his coming to Galina, he wrote a long rambling letter to Bishop Rosati, full of self accusations and bitter complaints. We will give all the items of historical interest scattered through the five pages: leaving the rest to the oblivion it deserves:

"I am always at Bishop Loras' command whenever he requires my services. I preached the Consecration sermon of the Cathedral. The bishop preached on Friday, the day following. On Saturday I preached the funeral oration of Bishop Bruté, and the same day returned to my congregation in Galena. On Monday I attended a sick-call in the country. On Tuesday I commenced collecting for the new church and, notwithstanding a sick-call of twenty-two miles, I collected on Tuesday and Wednesday in paid money between three and four hundred dollars. I went to the homes of the people and found them generous indeed, no one refusing out of all I called upon, but four. When I got their names I would not leave the house until they had paid the money which they did freely, when they saw that I made it a rule. This small sum encouraged the workmen to proceed on Thursday. I was then obliged to ride thirty-eight miles under the heat of thee sun to attend a sick-call, and the next day I was thrown down with bilious fever, from the effects of which I have not as yet recovered..... I have every reason to believe that the great majority of the congregation are both very ignorant of and very careless in the practice of their religion. If it pleases Almighty God to restore me to my former strength, I intend to give them a retreat, and I have every reason to think that Bishop Loras will assist me. I know that it is impossible for you to come here this season. I will do all in my power to be ready for you next May. By that time I hope to have 150 communicants ready for confirmation, and the

---

[18] Father Mazzuchelli's greetings to "Bishop" Timon, Rosati's "coadjutor," was premature, as Father Timon sent back the bulls of his appointment. He became Bishop of Buffalo on September 5, 1847.

church ready for consecration. . . . . I wish to inform you as to
the present state of the new church at Galena. I do not know the
exact figures but I know that the church is deeply plunged in debt.
Mr. Mazzuchelli told me that he was giving the pews as security,
and that he would not go to any one to collect a dollar. The church
is neither ceiled nor plastered, a few crazy old boards supply the
place of an altar, and nothing but the stones and lime surround
it. . . . . The workmen are now hurrying up the pews in order to
sell them to pay themselves. For my part I have no more authority
regarding the affairs of the church than if you had never appointed
me. No doubt, Mr. Mazzuchelli is an excellent man, but he has by
far too many irons in the fire in the diocese of Dubuque to bestow
much attention here. Besides, the orders of Mr. Mazzuchelli differ
so widely from your instructions that I cannot, in conscience, obey
him. On my arrival he told me that there was no support for me
here, but that I might take my meals wherever I could get them. I
told him that was contrary to your orders. . . . . But he would make
no other arrangement. So dire necessity obliged me to do what I
never have done before. Many days have I remained in my lonely
habitation without tasting a morsel, ashamed to go to any one's
house to look for a meal. . . . . I was told that the people expected
that I would eat in one house, sleep in another, just as it might
happen, like Mr. Mazzuchelli. I take the Sunday collection which
amounts to five or six dollars, but this is a very small item when
everything is so extravagantly high. As to the other chances, *i.e.*,
baptisms, marriages, funerals, etc., they are not worth speaking
of. . . . . My furniture in the old chapel where I live, is a bed,
three chairs, a table large enough to hold my writing materials. I
have no knife, fork, spoon nor plate, but sooner than go to Mr.
Major Barry's or any other place to get my victuals for nothing,
I will buy a small cooking stove and cook for myself as well as I
can. The number of Catholic souls here, in town and country, of
age if instructed to approach the holy sacraments is, as near as I
can say, five hundred. The children, who are numerous, are extremely ignorant. I have made it my chief object every Sunday to
represent to the Catholic parents the sin they were guilty of in
allowing their children to grow up in ignorance of the very principles of religion. I have succeeded in bringing together a great
number, but I must use very great exertions with them, before they
will be fit for the sacrament of confirmation. There is a pious widow
here who teaches the Catholic school and helps to instruct the children

in Catholic doctrine. She is a convert, her name is Mrs. Farrar. She is rich, and built a fine school house on one of her lots, expecting that two Sisters of Charity would come and live with her, to teach in the Catholic school. She would give the house and lot: There are by far better prospects for the Sisters here than in Dubuque, and I think that, if the grand prospect be lost sight of, it may be long ere another present itself."[20]

And now having viewed conditions and prospects of the northern-most missions under Bishop Rosati's rule, through eyes somewhat dimmed and blurred by faults and misfortunes, let us listen to Father Mazzuchelli's final message to the beloved Bishop of St. Louis:

November 6, 1839.

RT. REV. BISHOP ROSATI—Having been the pastor of Galina for four years past and being now almost unable to combine my various duties in the Iowa Territory with the care of this place, I deem it necessary to write to you a few lines on this subject. I do sincerely regret that the Rev. C. Lee was not qualified for this parish and that he has confirmed the people in their unfavorable opinion of Irish priests. Our church and popularity here, being built upon zeal, disinterestedness and piety, nothing less is required in a clergyman to do good here, at least for a year or two longer, when everything will be completed. There is no doubt that, if this parish is well conducted, it will in two years be one of the most conspicuous of Illinois, and will much assist the Bishop of the State. The annual rent of fifty-six pews amounts to over fourteen hundred dollars, the collections on Sundays to over three hundred dollars. All this money is now given for the building of the church, which I hope to finish next year. So I take the liberty to advise you, my most esteemed Bishop to send to Galina a pious disinterested priest. If he is anxious, and the people are satisfied, I will give up to him forever all the credits, debts and cares of the church. Should this not please you or him, I will continue to do as I have done, and let him have all the private contributions; and if this is not satisfactory I will provide house, table and clothes and any other thing he should be in need of, provided he gives to the church treasury all that he shall receive in the parish. But aware of your many difficulties I dare suggest to you another plan, and this is to let the Bishop of Dubuque have full jurisdiction of the northwest corner of Illinois as long as you will have it yourself. The Bishop of Dubuque can easily send a priest to this place and come himself with the greatest facility. The people of Galina are now very much attached to Bishop Loras and would be much pleased with the arrangement. Your wisdom and zeal, however, are far superior to my word. Our retreat, which was to begin on the 6th of October, was by the inclemency of the weather, deferred to the 13th, and lasted until the 21st. A great many people were at church every day. One hundred and thirty-eight communions, thirty-six confirmations. My little share of the work was to preach the word and the superior call of my affectionate Bishop and companion in the missions was to communicate the spirit. I thank God that in all things

---

[20] Father Lee's letter is in Archives of St. Louis Archdiocese.

With the appointment of Bishop Loras to the new diocese of Dubuque, the territory west of the Mississippi and north of the Missouri line was detached from the diocese of St. Louis. But the neighboring Missions on the Illinois side were still under Bishop Rosati's jurisdiction. An arrangement was, however, made by which the Bishop of Dubuque was to provide for Galena, until other arrangements should be made. In ocnsequence we find Bishop Loras and his Vicar-General, Father Mazzuchelli, officiating at the East side of the river, as delegates of Bishop Rosati. We found two letters of Bishop Loras in our archives, which we will insert here as showing how the transition from St. Louis to Chicago was made at Galena, the city that had such a hold on Bishop Rosati.

Dubuque, December 17, 1839.

MONSIGNEUR AND VENERABLE BROTHER—I would have received this good Irishman, (a school-master) at Dubuque, but Mr. O'Reilly, who is doing very well suffices us. I have proposed him at Galena, but his quality as an Irishman has singularly cooled down the zeal, especially of the Irish, in his regard; nevertheless, since there is actually no Catholic school there, and since there is a multitude of children to instruct, he may come, but, (1) I cannot advance him anything; (2) An excellent Catholic lady, who is on the point of opening her school here, claims all the girls, at least those she can receive; (3) If we are lucky enough to have here the Sisters of Charity next year, it must be well understood, that they will have a right to all the Catholic children whom they can instruct. Under these conditions he can come and rely upon my support.

What you tell me in Your letter of 23 Sept., that I may regard Galina and its surroundings as forming part of my diocese, causes me pleasure, and I willingly consent to the arrangement, on account of the geographical situation of that part of Illinois; nevertheless I fear this new responsibility. I believe, however, that I need not do more for the place than I have done so far. I have established myself at Galina since Advent, in the absence of Mr. Mazzuchelli who is at Burlington, and I fill here, to the best of my power, the office of pastor. I shall pass Christmas here. The people are well disposed. I have daily more than 50 children or adults at my catechism class. The Mass is frequented on work days. On Sundays the Church is full to overflowing. I preach here once in *my* English. Mr. Cretin, who was a little lonesome, whilst I was in Dubuque, will have a grand chance to practice his English on young men likewise. I can absent myself freely, and this is absolutely necessary, if it were only for the Council, which really cannot be placed better than in Spring. I at first thought that it was of little consequence to me to be present,

²¹ Original in English. Archives.

but I can make such good use of the Journey that I decided to go. What you have the goodness to tell me about Kentucky, is quite consoling; how I wish to see the worthy Patriarch, (Bishop Flaget) at the Council!

I am waiting every day for details on the disaster of Mobile. How severely this poor bishop is tried! I am afraid that his poor Cathedral progresses but little. How immensely the loss of Mr. Mauverney is felt; he was the soul· of that college. You say that You have lost Mr. Jamison; what will all those good ladies do at St. Louis! As far as I am concerned, I do not think that this is such a great evil. The conduct of Mr. Lee here has raised the repugnance which our good Irish entertain against priests of their own nationality, to the utmost. There is in this, I feel, something providential. Our young men will do very well. I am very insistent on their acquiring the English language and mastering their Theology in Latin. They write to me from Davenport that Mr. Pelamoniques is doing very well, by virtue of his piety, his zeal and his polished manners. He already preaches in English every Sunday. After Christmas I shall push the construction of two churches, 20 and 18 miles from Dubuque. God will bless our efforts and our feeble beginnings.

I congratulate You on having with You, after Christmas, the Bishop of Nancy. If we were not at the ends of the earth, I would aspire to the same honor; but it is You whom he must visit first. Would You please tell the good Sisters Mary Angela, that I cannot send the money soooner than after Christmas, since I do not have the bills here, and that I thank her again for the lively interest she takes in me.

Please pray in a special manner for the last of Your confreres who so well feels his own indignity and who shall always bed evoted to You in Christ Our Lord,

MATHIAS, BISHOP OF DUBUQUE.[22]

Dubuque, December 31, 1839.

MONSEIGNEUR AND VENERABLE CONFRERE—I arrived from Galena, where I spent all Advent and Christmas to my satisfaction. I officiated alone on the holy day of Christmas, but the church was filled four times within 24 hours. At midnight it was crowded, without the least disorder; also at Dubuque. We are more happy here than in the South where there are men who give trouble. Next Sunday I shall ordain my poor deacons, and I shall conduct the best one to Galena, where he shall stay and where from time to time, he shall be replaced. . . . . I shall go there myself occasionally and shall keep You "au courant" on what is done there. We shall soon need a church.

The 12 Ordos have arrived and the twelve masses shall be persolved according to that intention, and we have enough of them for this year.

My answer on the subject of the Irish school teacher is on the way. I have rented for him at Galena a nice room for his school. A room at the Court House is offered gratis. There are so many children in this little town, that he may expect great success.

The reports concerning S. Viateur are very encouraging; I hope that the result will make themselves felt as far as here; this will, if You succeed, doubtlessly be, one of the most beautiful pearls in your crown.

The diocese of Dubuque is certainly still too young for the Madams of the

---

[22] Original in French. Archivos.

Visitation. We must commence with those of Charity. But we shall talk of this in Spring.

I shall propose to You a matter, which may appear new and strange. But please examine it before God and the Holy Canons. Could they not for a particular diocese or for an entire ecclesiastical province grant a lenten dispensation from some of the fast days, as they grant it from abstinence? This would rectify many consciences. *Nobody* fasts here, although several keep the abstinence, not only on Friday, but also obstinately on Wednesday, in spite of the dispensation. I really do not know what to do. I think that, by strictly exacting the fast in Lent on Wednesdays, Fridays and Saturdays, and the abstinence on Wednesdays and Fridays, we would preserve in the church something of the Fast in the strict sense of the term. What do you think of it. It is no Fast to take coffee and bread and nearly always something else besides. The faithful would familiarize themselves gradually with the Fast and a little later, it might perhaps be exacted in its entirety. Once more, would You consider this before God?

As far as the abstinence on Wednesday is concerned, I could hardly reprove the people for keeping it up, to do something more in Lent, than during the rest of the year, as is the case here amongst the Christians, who keep the abstinence on Fridays of the year.

You will tell me, that we can give particular dispensations; but hardly anybody asks for them, not at Mobile, nor at Dubuque, nor at St. Louis, I believe. A general dispensation for Lent would prevent many false consciences.

You see that I speak openly to You; would You continue to do the same towards me and to believe in my sentiments of esteem, of respect, and friendship, at the beginning of the New Year, for which I wish You all happiness.

MATHIAS, Bishop of Dubuque.[31]

The "best one" of the newly ordained priests was Father Remigius Petiot, a native of France. He was sent to Galena shortly after his ordination and for a number of years labored faithfully and successfully in that difficult mission. But as Bishop Rosati left St. Louis on April 27, 1840 to attend the Fourth Council of Baltimore, and then set sail for Europe, never again to see his diocese, we have no letters from the Rev. Petiot in our archives. As Bishop Loras writes, Galena became practically a part of Dubuque diocese until it passed under the jurisdiction of Chicago in 1844.

REV. JOHN ROTHENSTEINER.

St. Louis.

---

[31] Original in French Archives.

THE IRISH IN CHICAGO

(Continued from April, 1920)

In 1833-34 came a galaxy of brilliant lawyers; virtually all of them of Irish extraction, amongst whom may be named Edward W. Casey, who was the fourth lawyer to arrive in Chicago. Coming near the same time were Edward G. Ryan, James H. Collins, and William B. Snowhook.

Edward W. Casey was not admitted to the bar in this state until January 7, 1835 and did not remain long in the state, returning to the East from whence he came in 1838. Judge Goodrich says:

He was a thorough lawyer, a fine scholar, a most amiable man and a polished gentleman. Though he had acquired a good practice and had before him the highest promise of professional success, he abandoned his profession and returning to his Eastern home engaged in farming.[40]

James H. Collins came in 1834 and formed a partnership with John Dean Caton, afterward Judge, who had studied law under Collins in New York. The firm of Collins & Caton was dissolved in 1835 and Mr. Collins formed a partnership with Justice Butterfield.

In those early years of the Chicago Bar the firm of Butterfield & Collins was the most conspicuous, being usually engaged in every important law suit on one side or the other.

They were of counsel for the government in the celebrated Beaubien Land Claim. Collins defended Owen Lovejoy in 1842 in his celebrated trial for harboring a runaway slave and secured his acquittal. He was an early and most violent and extreme Abolitionist and in 1850 was the candidate of that party for Congress. He died in 1854 of Cholera. Isaac N. Arnold says of him that:

He was a good lawyer, a man of perseverance, pluck and resolution and as combative as an English bulldog.''[41]

Edward G. Ryan was born in Ireland in 1810, and arrived in Chicago in 1836. He formed a partnership with Henry Moore in 1837 and afterwards associated with Hugh T. Dickey but soon after turned his attention to journalism and as hereinafter stated became

---

[40] Andreas' *History of Cook County*, pp. 254, 255.
[41] *Ibid.* p. 255.

the editor of the *Tribune*. In 1842 he removed to Racine, Wisconsin becoming Chief Justice in 1874. He died October 19, 1880.[42]

At about the same time came Doctor Charles Volney Dyer the son of Daniel and Susan Dyer. Doctor Dyer was chiefly noted as an active officer of the celebrated "underground railroad" of Chicago and helped in rescuing from slavery and the fangs of human bloodhounds thousands of fugitives. To the opponents of slavery it is considered a sufficient eulogy of a man to say that he was prominently connected with the "underground railroad." Abraham Lincoln as a personal compliment gave Dyer the appointment of Judge of the Mixed Court for the suppression of the African slave trade.[43]

William B. Snowhook was born in Raheen, Queens County, Ireland, and came to New York when eight or nine years old. As he grew up he was employed in the office of Thomas McElrath where he worked with Horace Greeley. When sixteen years old he made a trip to Ireland and remained two years and then went to New Orleans and engaged in building levees by contract and afterwards had a contract for a portion of the Morris and Essex Canal in New York and a portion of the Maumee Canal. Upon the completion of this work he came to Chicago in 1836 and with William B. Ogden and others took a contract on the Illinois and Michigan Canal. He later went into the grocery and commission business in Chicago. Mr. Snowhook was instrumental in raising and equiping the Montgomery Guards, was commissioned Colonel by Governor Ford in 1846 and served on the Governor's staff during the Mormon troubles. He was admitted to the bar in 1857. At the outbreak of the Civil War he was commissioned Colonel and was largely instrumental in raising the famous Irish Brigade. In 1856 he formed the law partnership of Snowhook, Johnson and Gray in which he remained until the time of his death, May 5, 1882. He was the father of Patrick W. Snowhook, who also became a prominent lawyer at the Chicago Bar.[44]

The Chicago Directory of 1839 contained the names of the following Irishmen: Thomas, Allen, J. P.; Brock, John; Bannon, Andrew; Bartell, Thomas; Burke, M.; Busch, John B.; Bracken, John; Byrnes, Michael; Collins, John; Conley, John; Connell, I.; Carlin, Philip; Carney, James and Patrick; Corrigan, William; Carroll, Ed-

See Andreas' *History of Illinois*, Vol I, pp. 378, 442, 444, 276.

I have found no proof that C. Volney Dyer was Irish. It is an Irish name. For a sketch see Bennett, p. 64. See also Andreas' *History of Chicago*, Vol. I, pp. 176, 220, 273, 460, 461, 462, 522, 594, 597, 606, 607.

Andreas' *History of Chicago*, Vol. I, p. 244.

ward; Clark, Thomas; Casey, Edward, John, Patrick, Peter and Stephen; Clifford, Thomas; Cassidy, P. E.; Cunningham, H.; Cavanaugh, M.; Dalz, John and Thomas; Donlin, John; Doyle, James H. and Michel; Diversy, Michael; Doyle, Simon; Duffey, Pat and James; Dunlap, William; Dunlop, Hugh; Dempsey, John; Dwyer, Cornelius; Farley, A. U.; Farrell, Thomas; Fleming, William; Foley, Thomas; Finnerty, John, Peter and James; Fitzgibbons, John and P.; Fitzgibbons, M. and P.; Gallagher, William; Gavin, Edward and Isaac R. (sheriff); Gibbons, Edward; Gill, Edmund; Gillespie, John J. and E.; Gregg, David R.; Haffey, William, Michael and Edward; Hanlon; Hayden, James; Healy, Robert; Higgins, Pat; Hines, Austin; Hogan, John S. C. (first postmaster); Hogan, Charles P.; Horan, Owen; Hoyne, Thomas; Kane, Patrick and James; Keefe, James and Owen; Keenan, John J.; Kehoe, James and Michael; Kelly, James; Kelly, Capt.; Kelsey, Patrick; Laflin, M.; Lane, James; Lantry, Michael; Lynch, Patrick; Money, Michael and Peter; Moore, Joseph; Murphy, John; Murray, James; McAuley, P.; McBride, T.; McCabe, Patrick; McCarthy, Owen, McDermott, Mrs. A.; McDonnell, C. and M. and P.; McGovern, John; McGraw, James and Edward; McGuire, M.; McHale, John; McKay, Patrick; McLean, Thomas; McMahon, P.; O'Brien, George and James; O'Connor, J. and Martin; O'Malley, Charles; O'Meara, the Rev. T.; O'Neill, John and Michael; Prindiville, M. and R.; Raber, Philip; Reed, Thomas; Reis, John M.; Riley, Nicholas and Peter; Rogers, John; Rooney, William; Ryan, John; Sammons, Capt.; Savage, Maurice; Sherry, Thomas; Smith, Joseph F.; Snowhook, W. B.; Soraghan, Daniel and John; Sullivan, Owen; Sweeney, John; Tiernan, Hugh; Tinsouey, John and Patrick; Walsh, Patrick; West, Thomas; White, Christopher; Young, John.

IN THE SCHOOLS

Important events in the history of the Chicago schools occurred in this period. As has before been noted, William L. Cox, a discharged soldier, kept the first school as early as 1816. He seems to have been succeeded by Stephen J. Forbes. I have no means of knowing Mr. Forbes's nationality but the likenesses which have been preserved of him make him look very much like an Irishman. In 1832 Colonel Owen and Colonel Hamilton employed John Watkins as a teacher, of whom I find no reference as to nationality. Miss Eliza Chappel taught here beginning in 1833. Grenville T. Sproat, Thomas Wright, George Davis and some others taught at intervals, but an early historian has left us a picture of school conditions which is worth reproduction. He says:

"In 1836, and until March, 1837, John Brown taught a private school in the North Division, near the corner of Dearborn and Walcott Streets. Mr. Brown ceased to teach in consequence of being severely beaten by some of his pupils, and sold out his leases in March, 1837, to Edward Murphy, who took decided means to secure success. On opening his school with thirty-six pupils, he addressed them setting forth the necessity of observing the rules of the school and promising chastisement to those who should infringe them.

"The day after," says Mr. Murphy, "I placed an oak sapling an inch in diameter, on my desk. That afternoon a Mr. S. who owned the building, came into the school-room, and seeing the walls decorated with caricatures, and likenesses of almost every animal from a rabbit to an elephant, he got in a raging passion, and used rather abusive language. I complained, he became more violent. I walked to my desk, took the sapling and shouted 'clear out,' which he obeyed by a rapid movement. This trifling incident effectually calmed the ringleaders, some of whom now occupy honorable and respectable positions in society.

"Mr. Murphy's vigorous administration secured the admiration of the school officers, who rented the building and made him a public school teacher from August, 1837, to November, 1838, at a salary of $800 per annum.[45]

If Murphy was not the first teacher, he was apparently the most successful so far.

THE CHICAGO PRESS

In 1833 an epoch was marked in Chicago's history when John Calhoun came here and established the first newspaper, the *Chicago Democrat*, and though the expense of such an undertaking might be considered relatively small in comparison with the demands of such an institution at the present day, yet Calhoun's resources were not sufficient, and he was generously assisted by Thomas Joseph Vincent Owen. Calhoun was an able man, and proved a splendid representative of the fraternity of the Press, and for his day, published a meritorious paper.[46]

While upon the subject of papers, it may be permissible to call attention to the fact that James Washington Sheehan was a leading spirit in the establishment of what became the *Chicago Times* and that Edward G. Ryan with others established the weekly *Tribune* in 1840. Joseph K. C. Forest, James J. Kelly and John E. Wheeler organized the *Tribune* in 1847, which later became the property of Joseph E. Medill. Sheehan was one of the most talented newpaper

---

[45] Andreas' *History of Chicago*, Vol. I, p. 208.
[46] See cut and sketch, Andreas' *History of Chicago*, Vol. I, p. 360, et seq.

men ever entering that field and had a very noted subsequent career. Edward G. Ryan, whose first activities in this community were with the Weekly *Tribune*, after some years spent in Chicago, went to Detroit and became a leading lawyer and later on the leading jurist of the state, having been elected to the Supreme Court Bench, and recognized as one of the ablest judges of the entire West.[47]

Joseph K. C. Forest was descended from a family holding a prominent and influential position in business and political circles in Cork, Ireland, where he was born November 26, 1820. Shortly after the "*Tribune*" was started he became associate editor of the Chicago *Democrat* under the management of "Long John" Wentworth and was afterwards connected with the St. Louis *Democrat*, Chicago *Times*, Chicago *Republican* and the Chicago *Interocean*.[48]

James Washington Sheehan was born in Baltimore of Irish parentage and received his education at the Jesuit School in Frederick, Maryland. His first visit to Illinois was as a reporter of the Constitutional convention of Illinois, held in 1847, which resulted in the suggestion of Stephen A. Douglas that he start a Democratic newspaper in Chicago, whereupon he started the Chicago *Times* which he sold to Cyrus H. McCormick in 1860 and then began the publication of the *Post* which in April, 1865, he sold to the *Republican* Company. He joined the *Tribune* Editorial Staff in 1866 and remained with the *Tribune* until his death. In 1863 he was a member of the School Board of Chicago and labored untiringly to improve the school system.

A lawyer by early education, a politician by training, a student of trade and finance by predilection, no one could have been better fitted for the editorial duties which devolved upon him. Outside of the office, as well as in it he was the pleasantest and most genial of companions, the embodiment of jest and anecdote, and reminiscence and the delight of the circles in which he moved and of the houses at which he was an honored guest.[49]

Joseph E. Medill became, of course, the best known newspaper man of his day. He was a son of Irish parents who immigrated to America in 1819. He was admitted to the bar and practiced law for some time. He came to Chicago in 1854 and purchased the *Tribune*.

[47] See note 42.

[48] Andreas' *History of Chicago*, Vol. II, p. 498. See also Munsell's *History of Chicago*, Vol. II, pp. 38-39.

[49] For sketch see Andreas' *History of Chicago*. See also Munsell's *History of Chicago*, Vol. II, pp. 46-47. Vol. II, 494. Consult index for numerous references.

1872, and managing editor in 1888. He retired from the *Journal* in 1891 and was appointed by President Harrison U. S. Consul at Bermunda.[51]

John F. Finerty was the son of a leading Irish journalist, and was born in Galway, Ireland. When he first came to the United States he joined the 99th Regiment of New York Militia. In 1868 he became a reporter on the Chicago *Republican* and in 1871 was made editor of that paper. After the fire he joined the staff of the *Evening Post*, but soon went to the *Tribune* where he remained until 1876. For some years he was traveling correspondent for the *Times* and other papers. In 1881 he organized the first Irish National Land League. In 1882 he established the Chicago *Citizen* which is still published. In November, 1882, he was elected to Congress as an independent Democrat. During all his life in Chicago Mr. Finerty was a man of great prominence.[52]

Martin J. Russel became connected with the *Herald* at its first establishment. Mr. Russel had an interesting career. He was but sixteen years of age when the Civil War broke out, but accompanied James A. Mulligan, his uncle when he went with his Irish Brigade to the war. After the regiment was exchanged it was reorganized at Chicago in the winter of 1861 and 1862 as the 23rd Illinois Volunteers and young Russel was chosen Second Lieutenant of Company A, November 1, 1861, when he had not yet reached his sixteenth year. The regiment was ordered to Virginia in June 1862 and the following December Colonel Mulligan being assigned to the command of a

[50] Andreas' *History of Chicago*, Vol. II, p. 51. Consult index for many references. See also Munsell's *History of Chicago*, Vol. II, p. 48, 49.

[51] Munsell's *History of Chicago*, Vol. II, p. 42.

[52] Munsell's *History of Chicago*, Vol. II, pp. 73, 74.

brigade, Lieutenant Russel was appointed upon his staff as Assistant
Adjutant General and served through the various campaigns in
Virginia with him. In 1870 Mr. Russell became a city reporter of
the Chicago Evening Post where he remained until 1873 when he
joined the city department of the Times and was shortly afterward
advanced to the editorial staff as paragraphist. When Mr. Story
published the afternoon paper called the Telegram in 1876, Mr.
Russel was made editor of that paper. He was a member of the Board
· of Education of Hyde Park from 1874 to 1880, Village Clerk from
1876 to 1880 and commissioner of the South Parks from 1880 to
· 1890.[53]

At the same time that Martin J. Russell joined the Herald staff
Margaret B. Sullivan became Literary Editor of that paper and
attained a reputation of being one of the most gifted of all those
connected with the Press of Chicago. Of Margaret Sullivan Mr.
Onahan says:

The cleverest and most versatile writer on the Chicago Press in
my judgment and that of others was a woman—Margaret Sullivan.[54]

John R. Walsh was, for a great part of his life, connected with
the Press and though his life went out under a cloud of failure in
his banking enterprise, was a notable man. William J. Onahan, one
of the emost highly respected men in Chicago, has but recently paid
Mr. Walsh the following tribute:

"There is another man once and for long a power in Chicago
of whom I cannot forbear to speak, John R. Walsh. From a poor
boy he succeeded by his industry and unflagging perseverance to
attain to a position of wealth and influence. His life through the
long struggle was without blemish, he had no bad habits, and he was
held in highest repute by all. He became the head of three leading
financial institutions, he controlled an important daily paper, and by
his acuteness he was regarded as a power in all local affairs.

"John R. Walsh was boundless in his charities. No church, no
institution, no person need appeal to him in vain. He gave generously
and freely, as I can testify. He did not long survive his misfortune,
which beyond doubt hastened his death."[55]

THE ILLINOIS AND MICHIGAN CANAL

From the earliest days in which Illinois became known to white
men, a continuous waterway between Lake Michigan and the Missis-

[53] Munsell's History of Chicago, Vol. II, p. 58. His daughter, Ruth Russell,
has just published a most interesting book, "What's the Matter With Ireland!"
See review in this number.
[54] Sixty Years in Chicago, pub. 22, Illinois State Historical Library, p. 85.
[55] Ibid. p. 86.

GEORGE P. A. HEALEY
Noted Portrait Painter, Chicago's
Greatest Artist.

GEN. JAMES A. MULLIGAN
Of the "Irish Brigade" 23rd Illinois
Infantry.

sippi river was advocated. Joliet, in his report to the Governor of Canada, after his voyage of discovery with Father Marquette in 1673 according to Father Claude Dalbon, S. J., said:

The fourth remark (he had made three other suggestions) concerns a very important advantage, and which some will perhaps find it hard to credit; it is that we can quite easily go to Florida in boats, and by very good navigation. There would be only one canal to make by cutting only half a league of prairie to pass from the Lake of the Illinois (Lake Michigan) into the St. Louis river (the Des Plaines and Illinois). The route to be taken is this; the bark should be built on Lake Erie, which is near Lake Ontario, it would pass easily through Lake Erie to Lake Huron, from which it would enter the Lake of Illinois (Lake Michigan). At the extremity of this would be the cut or canal of which I have spoken to have a passage to the St. Louis river which empties into the Mississippi river.

Almost every public man after Joliet, talked about a canal for the purpose avoiding the portage, which, in the dry season was at times thirty or forty miles in length, but when the water courses were swollen, was about five or ten miles. While the country was still under territorial government, the subject was debated and legislative action begun as soon as the state was admitted into the Union, which culminated in the actual breaking of ground for a canal on the Fourth of July, 1836.

Upon this gala occasion, two very early Irishmen occupied prominent places—Dr. Wm. B. Egan was the orator of the day, and the eloquence with which he championed the cause of the canal, has been written about in every history and historical sketch which has come down to us. Dr. Egan was not only the proponent of the canal from the platform, but was one of its most earnest and effective advocates from the time he came to Chicago until the work was completed.[56]

In the parade and pageantry which accompanied the celebration of the breaking of ground for the canal, John Stephen Coates Hogan, of whom we have before spoken, was the officer of the day.[57]

Perhaps the construction of the Illinois and Michigan Canal was due more to the efforts of State Senator Michael Ryan than any other one man. He piloted the legislation under which the canal was built through the General Assembly. He was the principal power in financing the work both at home and abroad. It was he that succeeded in overcoming the technical engineering difficulties, and it

---

[56] See note 38. *Supra.*
[57] See note 35. *Supra.*

that the work was to go on, boat loads of Irishmen came to Chicago and scattered out along the route of the waterway, peopling the whole north-central part of the state, nor were the Irish confined to those who handled the pick and shovel alone, but the more difficult and technical work of the actual building was done in a large measure by Irish contractors. For the purpose of indicating to what extent Irishmen participated in the building of the Illinois and Michigan Canal, I am taking space to give the names of the contractors engaged upon the work in 1846, according to the report of the Canal Commissioners made to the Illinois State Senate on December 7th, of that year.[59]

The work was divided into sections and contracts for the sections were in existence that year as follows: Daniel Lynch, Section 22, Patrick Kinney & Co., Section 28, L. O'Connor, Section 31, Cosgrove & Lalor, Section 35, Gay, Gooding & Curry, Section 36, Erwin, Kittering & Norton, Sections 39 and 40, Thos. Lonergan, Section 41, Fealey & O'Neal, Sections 58 and 60, J. & T. Lonergan, Sections 62 and 63, Richard P. Morgan, Section 109, McDaniel & Williams, Sections 111, 12-30-32, M. Neary, Section 114, Tyrrell & Burns, Section 116, McDonald & Sons, Section 67, James Burke, Section 123, James Mulloy, Section 124, James Cronin, Section 127, T. O'Sullivan, Section 135, M. Costello, Section 138, Cosgrove & Kearney, Section 139, Hennessey, Brennan & Cody, Section 141, Redick & O'Sullivan, Section 142, Jeremiah Crotty, Sections 143-44-45-46, Kenedy & Kilduff, Sections 147-49-54, Locks No. 9 and 10, Timothy Kelly, Sections 152 and 153, William Byrnes, Lock No. 13, Byrnes & Cahill—the little Venetian Aqueduct, M. Kennedy & Co., Culvert 112, Campbell & McGir, Culvert Section 121, Conklin & Shields, Culvert Sections 149 to 154, McDonald & Maloney, sub-structure for bridge on Section 125.

---

[58] Andreas' *History of Chicago*, Vol. I, pp. 169-70.
[59] See Senate Report made at Session of General Assembly beginning December 7, 1846.

DISTINGUISHED IRISHMEN OF CHICAGO

Chicago has had many distinguished citizens of all nationalities and there is certainly no intention of belittling the great men of other nationalities by directing attention to some conspicuous representatives of the Irish race. As a very distinguished Irish-American, I have no hesitancy in naming Thomas Hoyne. In a volume published after his death as a memorial, containing somewhat less than one hundred and fifty pages, being the bare record of the resolutions and eulogies relating to Thomas Hoyne, I find an expression by another distinguished Irish-American, the late Judge Thomas A. Moran which fits the situation perfectly. At a memorial meeting which was addressed by Honorable Melville W. Fuller, Chief Justice of the Supreme Court of the United States, Honorable Lyman Trumbull, former Governor and United States Senator, Honorable Carter H. Harrison, Mayor of the City of Chicago, Honorable Murray F. Tuley, Mr. C. P. Kimball, Judge H. M. Shepard and Colonel Shirley, Judge Moran said:

Thomas Hoyne has, in my opinion, without attempting to give any fullsome or extraordinary praise, impressed himself more on the City of Chicago as a city than any other man in my knowledge. I know of no man now, I can think of none living or dead who has impressed himself on the City of Chicago and so markedly as Thomas Hoyne.

And in summing up the benefits conferred upon the city by Thomas Hoyne, the Honorable Isaac N. Arnold says:

"The Chicago University and Astronomical Observatory, the Public Library and the Historical Society were each the recipients of liberal contributions of money, as well as of his care and labor in administration."

To this summary may be added that he endowed the Chicago College of Law, afterwards the Northwestern University Law School, was the most effective proponent of the "Free Public Library," presided at the first meeting called to organize that institution, was chosen President of the Board of Directors and served in that capacity for several years. That he was an earnest advocate of the boulevard system, and in fact, if not the leader, at least the effective supporter of every public movement for the benefit of Chicago during his entire residence here. With reference to his character, Justice Fuller said:

Mr. Hoyne did not maintain his high character by taking refuge behind the entrenchments of caution, but by attacking the enemy in the open field. The simple honesty of his character was as marked

as its fearlessness. He, in a just sense, kept himself unspotted from the world. He hated corruption. He could not comprehend how men could wear their spots as if they were jewels. He absolutely abjured the theory that in politics or business, results cannot be reached except by processes that stain. He refused to regard public or business affairs as pitch that could not be handled without defilment. Impetuous in acton, his instincts naturally led him in the right direction. Impetuous in speech, his speech was naturally in support of that which was true and honest, and of good report.[60]

I have not found in reference to any single individual who has lived in Chicago, as universal and sincere encomium as has been pronounced upon Thomas Hoyne. Though Thomas Hoyne was all his life closely associated with non-Catholics, having married the daughter of a non-Catholic minister, he remained true to his faith, and was buried with all the rites of the church.

Nor did his greatness overshadow his brother Philip A. Hoyne, who was a distinguished lawyer at the Chicago Bar, and it was also reflected in his brilliant family, amongst whom there were several distinguished professional men.

Francis Adams for years a most successful and valuable aid to the city in the office of Corporation Counsel, was born in Enneskillen, Ireland, March 26th, 1829, and came to Chicago in 1855. When in 1883 he resigned the position of Corporation Counsel, the elder Harrison wrote him a letter saying:

I regret the necessity more than any one else. When difficult legal questions have come up, I have always felt myself safe in being guided by your opinion. When important matters of municipal interest have been in court, I have felt with your attending to such matters that the city was safe. There is no one else I can get to fill your place in whom I can put this trust.[61]

Daniel McIlroy for a long time a successful practitioner in Chicago was a native of Tyrone, Ireland, but before coming to Chicago kept a school in Boston. He was a graduate of Cambridge University, and afterwards studied law with Judge Story. He came to Chicago in 1844, was elected State's Attorney in 1849 and filled that office for eight years.[62]

John Alexander Jameson for eighteen years Judge of the Superior Court of Cook County, a noted jurist and law writer was of Irish

[60] *In Memoriam* Thomas Hoyne, for numerous references see Munsell's *History of Chicago*, Vol. II, pp. 164, 167, 452, 453, 463, 513, 515, 517, 556, 557, 630, 737.
[61] Andreas' *History of Chicago*, Vol. II, p .54.
[62] *Ibid.* p. 461.

extraction and was scarcely more noted than his father who was a man of rare ability and great prominence in Vermont.[63]

James Ennis, another distinguished lawyer of the Chicago Bar, was born at Enniscorthy, County Wexford, Ireland. He was admitted to the Bar in 1856 and his biographer says that:

His unimpeachable integrity accompanied with his knowledge and ability brought him a lucrative practice which constantly increased up to the time of his death, a period of nearly a quarter of a century.[64]

William C. Goudy was not only one of the most interesting characters in our early history, but a very distinguished lawyer. He was of Irish ancestry, and though born in Indiana and beginning his career down state, became a resident of Chicago, where he died in 1893.[65]

Amongst prominent business men there was one early book-man, Charles McDonnell, who was greatly beloved by all who knew him. He was born in Clonegal County Wexford, Ireland. His education was supervised by his brother Nicholas, a professor in St. Peter's College, Carlow. In his native land, he was a woods schoolmaster, but located in Chicago as early as 1836. He was one of the first members of St. Mary's Church, was one of the organizers of St. Patrick's Society, the Catholic Young Men's Association and the Union Catholic Library, and a generous patron of the University of St. Mary of the Lake. He was one of the earliest members of the Board of Education of the city, was an alderman in 1842-47-48-52-53, Justice of the Peace from 1862 to 1864 and was admitted to the Bar in 1867.[66]

Hugh Maher was born in Ireland in 1818 and came to Chicago in 1837. Here he rapidly amassed great wealth, and in later years was known in business circles as one of the boldest yet shrewdest speculators of his time. An idea of the extent of his possessions may be gained from the statement that he owned the dock frontage on both sides of the Chicago river from 12th to 18th Street. A small portion of this property he sold to the Lake Shore & Michigan Southern Railroad Co. for $205,000.00. In 1873 Mr. Maher moved to Hyde Park where he lived until his death in 1884.[67]

[63] *Ibid.* p. 457.

[64] Andreas' *History of Chicago*, Vol. II, p. 482.

[65] Ancestors from Armagh, County Tyrone, Ireland. See Ensley Moore, *A Notable Illinois Family* in Pub. No. 12, Illinois State Historical Library, p. 315, et seq.

[66] *Ibid.* p. 503.

John J. Shortall was born in the city of Dublin in 1838. The family moved to America when Shortall was six years old. After the death of his parents, the young lad was employed by Horace Greeley, and several years of his young life were passed in the office of the New York *Tribune* in daily contact with Horace Greeley, Charles A. Dana and Bayard Taylor. He came to Chicago in 1854. Here he was first employed upon the survey of the Illinois Central Railroad and next in the office of the Chicago *Tribune*. In 1856 he became an Abstractor, and in a remarkable manner preserved the records of his Abstract office during the great fire. Mr. Shortall devoted the greater part of his life in Chicago to philanthropic and humanitarian activities, and his biographer says of him:

It may be justly said that in religious, political, civil and social life, Mr. Shortall is one of the best representative men in the city he has made his home, and in comprehensive intellect, business ability, keen judgment and in the best social qualities, he is the peer of any citizen of the great city of Chicago.[68]

Cyrus Hall McCormick whose immediate ancestors migrated from the north of Ireland and settled in Virginia, is too well known as the Father of American Reaping Machines to need more extended mention.[69]

It will be interesting to note a few of the prominent physicians of Irish birth or ancestry and to recall that Doctors Patrick and John E. McGir came here in the early 40's and were physicians and chemists of rare ability. Dr. John McGir was a professor in the University established by Bishop Wm. Quarter immediately upon his arrival here.[70]

The McGirrs were amongst the worthiest Irishmen that have honored Chicago by residence here since the city was founded.

Dr. Patrick McGirr, the father, was a learned physician of the old school and was noted for both his ability and benevolence. Two of his daughters were religious of the Order of Mercy and both became very prominent in the work of that Sisterhood. Their father was an untiring friend of the Sisters of Mercy and a constant benefactor. In old age the father and mother came to live at the Mercy Hospital and

---

[68] *Ibid.* p. 587.

[69] Munsell's *History of Chicago*, Vol. II, p. 661.

[70] See *History of the Diocese of Chicago*, McGovern, New World, April 14, 1900. See also Andreas' *History of Chicago*, Vol. I, pp. 218, 298, 463, 520. For appreciative notices of the McGirrs see *Leaves from the Annuals of the Sisters of Mercy*, pp. 261-2 and 298.

West of Sulphuric Ether as an anaesthetic. The drug was then known as letheon, and this was the first city west of the Allegheny where it was given a practical test. In a short time, chloroform was discovered and the formula for its distillation was immediately procured by Dr. Quinlan, and he and Professor J. V. Z. Blaney (almost at the same time, but independent of each other) were the first to distill this anaesthetic in Chicago.[71]

I need only mention the name of Dr. John B. Murphy, so well is he known, as another distinguished representative of the Irish race.

A beautiful character in the history of Chicago was George P. A. Healy, who maintained a studio in Chicago several years following 1855.[72] Respecting this great artist the venerable Chicagoan, the late Wm. J. Onahan says:

My earliest familiarity with art, I may say, was acquired in my visits in early years to Geo. P. A. Healy's gallery, then on Lake

[71] Munsell's *History of Chicago*, Vol. II, p. 658 et req.
[72] Mr. Healy donated his art collections to the Chicago Public Library, Munsell's *History of Chicago*, Vol. II, p. 141. After becoming world famous he came to Chicago to make it his home. *Ibid.* 580. See sketch Andreas' *History of Chicago*, Vol. II, p. 559, 560. For activities consult index to Andreas, Vol. II.

Street, where was exhibited several of his most celebrated pictures including the Presentation or Reception of Franklin at the Court of Louis XVI. He had a liberal patron in Thomas B. Bryan—and in my boyhood friend Bishop Duggan. Many of Mr. Healy's pictures are in Chicago. Several in the Newberry Library.[72a]

Mention should be made of James McMullen who was born in Ireland and who for fifty years was one of the leading lumbermen of Chicago. Of James C. McMullen, the well-known railroad man; John V. Clark who was amongst the earliest and soundest bankers, the Cudahys, Michael and John, Thomas Agnew, William P. Rend and Thomas Lonergan. Of Mathew Laflin who came to Chicago in 1837 to forward the work of the Illinois and Michigan Canal and was the father of Lycurgus and George Hinman Laflin; Andrew Jackson Galloway, a very competent railroad engineer, state legislator and respected citizen, whose father was born on the Isle of Inch in the River Lough Swilly, County Donegal, Ireland; Peter F. Flood, the early sea-captain who came in 1831; John Prindiville, the early lake navigator who came in 1836 and was so familiarly known as the "Storm King"; Chief Dennis J. Sweenie, so long at the head of the Fire Department; Captain Joseph Wilson; Captain Walsh; William Buckley and James Ward of the fire fighters. Amongst worthy grain and commission men there were Patrick Moran, Robert Warren and William McCrea.[73]

In the theatrical world there were the Jeffersons, father, mother and son, the latter the lovable Joe Jefferson who won the world in Rip Van Winkle, and there was Uncle Dick Hooley, the patriarch among theatrical managers of Chicago.[74]

THE IRISH IN THE CIVIL WAR

The Irish element in Chicago can justly lay claim to creditable recognition with respect to the Civil War and "No class" says Cook, "was apparently more enthusiastic for the defense of the flag which symbolized the Union of States when fired upon at Sumter than the Irish." No regiments were more quickly filled than those recruited under Irish auspices, and that this enthusiasm was not a mere flash in the pan is well shown by the spirit in which discouragements

---

[72a] *Sixty Years in Chicago*, Pub. No. 22. Illinois State Historical Library, p. 83.

[73] Sketches or mention of all these worthy Irishmen will be found in Andreas' and Munsell's *History of Chicago*.

[74] *Ibid.*

Citizens.

MICHAEL CUDAHY
One of Chicago's Most Benevolent
Captains of Industry.

JOHN F. FINERTY
One of the Most Prominent and Popular Public Men of His Day.

were disregarded and obstacles overcome. As soon as war was a certainty, this call was issued:

Rally! All Irishmen in favor of forming a regiment of Irish volunteers to sustain the Government of the United States in and through the present war will rally at North Market Hall this evening, April 20th. Come all! For the honor of the Old Land, rally for the defense of the new.

The signers for this call were: James A. Mulligan, Aldermen Comisky and McDonald, Captains M. Gleason, C. Moore, J. C. Phillips, Daniel Quirk, F. McMurray, Peter Casey; Citizens, Daniel McIlroy, John Tully, Phillip Conley, T. J. Kinsella.[75]

The meeting so called was addressed by Colonel Mulligan and others, and the enrollment list was then opened. In an hour and a half, 325 names were signed, recruiting officers appointed and a committee appointed to secure equipment.[76]

The Shields Guards was the first Chicago Company that took measures to offer its services to the Government. This was done in accordance with resolutions passed at their armory on the evening of January 14th, 1861, while the excitement in regard to the treasonable proceedings at Charleston was at its heigth. The fourth of a series of resolutions then adopted read:

Resolved that we the Shield's Guards of the City of Chicago lay aside for the present our individual political predilections, and having in view only the interest and demands of our common country, tender our services as citizen soldiers to the Commander-in-Chief of the Army in the United States, to be by him placed in whatever position our country calls upon us to fill.[77]

The following companies filled and ready to march on short notice were drilling and equipping in Chicago, several having already been accepted by the War Department: The Emmet Guards, Captain C. R. Walsh; O'Mahony Rifles, Captain J. C. Phillips; Shields Guards, (two companies), Captains James and Daniel Quirk; Jackson Guards, Captain Francis McMurray; Montgomery Guards, Captain Michael Gleason. These seven companies were later covered into the "Irish Brigade."[78]

The Irish Brigade was not accepted in the first call, and upon receiving the intelligence that it could not be mustered into service

[75] See Curry's *Chicago—Its History and Its Builders*, Vol. II, p. 121.
[76] See *The Irish Element*, New World, April 14, 1900, j. 109.
[77] Andreas' *History of Chicago*, Vol. II, p. 161.
[78] *Ibid.* p. 164.

under the second call of the President, held a meeting at which the
entire force was present. After several patriotic speeches were made,
a vote was taken as to whether the "Brigade" should disband. Only
four out of 864 men voted aye, the rest determining to retain their
organization, continue their drilling and perfect their equipment.
Colonel James Mulligan visited Washington to urge the claims of his
command, and on the 17th of May, it was accepted by the President
as an independent regiment for the war.[79]

On the return of Colonel Mulligan from Washington, a brick
structure on Polk Street was secured and equipped as barracks by the
Regiment, under the name of "Fontenoy Barracks."[80]

Almost at once after its acceptance, the Regiment was sent to
Missouri and assisted in the advance on Lexington. Here they formed
a part of a Union force of four or five thousand men opposing a Rebel
force many times greater, and after a noble defense of some ten days,
the Union force was obliged to surrender. The entire Regiment was
taken prisoner, but soon afterwards exchanged and joined the army
of the Potomac.

It was the Siege of Lexington which inspired a poet, whose verses
were printed in "Putnam's Rebellion Record" in the following lines:

> "The Irish boys are bold and brave,
>   The Irish boys are true;
> They love the dear old stars and stripes,
>   The spangled field of blue.
> " 'Tis Mulligan can tell the tale
>   Of how they fought that day,
> When with the foe at Lexington
>   They met in bloody fray.
> "Fast flew the shot and murderous shell,
>   The bullets fell like rain;
> But dauntless stood his brave brigade—
>   The heroes of the plain."[81]

In a former paper an attempt was made to pay a tribute to the
gallant General Mulligan. Here, this brief mention of his service
and of his death only may be given. While opposing the forces of
General Early in the Valley of Shenandoah on the 24th day of July,
1864, Mulligan was wounded and fell. Some of his men came to his
assistance, but seeing that the Confederates were rapidly advancing
in overwhelming numbers, and that every man was needed to oppose

---

[79] *Ibid.* p. 165.
[80] *The Irish Element*, New World, April 14, 1890, p. 109.
[81] Curry's *Chicago—Its History and Its Builders*, Vol. II, p. 122.

their advance he said: "Never mind me boys, but save the flag of the "Irish Brigade." A song was composed by General George F. Rool soon after the death of General Mulligan entitled "Lay me Down and Save the Flag." Honorable E. D. Cook, a member of the Legislature said of him:

He was spotless in life, distinguished in ability, a lion in courage, a hero in battle and his memory should not die. His was no claptrap devotion, no simulated patriotism born of sordid motives or personal ambition. It had its promptings and inspiration in a more solid and generous foundation. It was based on an earnest and in-telligent love of his country, a loyal attachment to principle and a love of liberty.

Mr. Curry in his history of Chicago says that:

No part of the History of the Civil War has greater interest for the youth of Chicago and Evanston than the career of Colonel Mulligan, and there was no hero of that war whose memory we can cherish more fittingly on our annual Memorial Days.[82]

Another regiment organized early in the war was the 58th, or the McClellan Brigade as it was popularly known. It was organized on Christmas day, 1861, and the commanding officers were: Colonel William F. Lynch, Captain Company A, Robert W. Healy, Company B, Captain Thos. W. Griffin, Company H, Captain Lawrence Collins, Company K, Captain Patrick Gregg.

The Historian Andreas says:

The 58th Illinois was composed of the best material, its officers were educated men and many of them being men of means contributed largely to the support of the Regiment while in camp. Colonel Lynch was educated at the University of Notre Dame at South Bend, as was also Captain Robert W. Healy of Chicago; Captain Gregg, Company K, was a graduate of the Royal College of Surgery, Dublin.[83]

The Regiment was thrown into service at once without any preparation, but fought brilliantly under General Lew Wallace. It suffered at Ft. Donaldson more than other regiments which had been longer in service. The boys were unprovided with haversacks and fell short of rations, their arms were worthless, and they were without tents or fires, yet the new Regiment bore these hardships with courage and cheerfulness. It was in constant action, and on January 1st, 1864, was concentrated at Cairo where the men re-enlisted as veterans.

---

[82] *Ibid.* pp. 122, 123.
[83] *History of Chicago*, Vol. II, p. 222.

Colonel Lynch was promoted to be Commander of the First Brigade, Third Division, 16th Army Corps On January 21st, the Regiment proceeded to Vicksburg, where it joined General Sherman's forces and participated in the famous raid through Mississippi known as the "Meridian Raid." Captain Tobin of Company K was shot through the heart while leading his men in a charge at the Battle of Pleasant Hill. On January 23rd, 1865, the Veterans and recruits of the Regiment were consolidated into four companies under the designation of Battalion 58, Illinois Infantry, R. W. Healy commanding the Battalion. The privates in this regiment were not all Irish, but the Kelly's, Burke's and Sheas enlisted therein in large numbers, and the report of the Adjutant-General in reference to the fight at Ft. Donaldson reads:

> The conduct of the men on this occasion was remarkable. Raw men, without rations and armed with the most worthless guns, they behaved as well as veterans of a hundred battles.[84]

No less laudable, if not so well known, was the 90th Illinois Infantry, "The Irish Legion." The principal commanding officers of this war organization were: Col. Timothy O'Meara, Lieutenant-Colonel Smith McCleary, Major Owen Stewart, Adjutant Edward S. Davis, Quartermaster Redmond Sheridan, Sergeant Henry Strong, First Assistant Sergeant John B. Davidson, Chaplain, Father Thomas Kelly, Captains, Company A, Patrick Flynn, Company H, Michael M. Clark, Company I, Thomas Murray, Company K, John McAssey.

The 90th was organized at a meeting at St. Patrick's Church, August 8th, 1862, of which Very Reverend Father Dennis Dunne was Chairman, and James Washington Sheehan was Secretary. During the preceding months, Father Dunne, with the hearty approval of Bishop James Duggan, had conspicuously exerted himself in raising the Regiment and at this meeting he was by acclamation elected Temporary Colonel, the Regiment being long known as Father Dunne's Regiment. It was christened the "Irish Legion" and mustered into service September 22nd, 1862.

In a former paper I have given a sketch of the record of this "Irish Legion," and need only say that at the end of the War, after being welcomed in Chicago by Governor Richard Yates, it afterwards marched to the residence of Right Reverend Father Dunne, the "Father of the Regiment," from thence to the schoolhouse connected with St. Patrick's Church, where Father Dunne affectionately wel-

---

[84] *Ibid.* pp. 222-23-24.

comed his boys to their homes and Reverend Dr. Brennan read the resolutions of congratulations and respect to the "Irish Legion" passed at a meeting of Catholic Irish citizens of Chicago.[85]

Among the notable individuals of Irish birth or ancestry that were prominent in the War may be mentioned in addition, one of the greatest generals of the War, namely, John A. Logan,[86] who needs no comment. Another distinguished general was Wm. Sooy Smith. In private life, General Smith was a civil engineer. Upon the breaking out of the war, he entered the service and was commissioned Colonel of the 13th Regiment of Ohio Volunteer Infantry. During the progress of the war, he was made Chief of Cavalry of the Military Division of the Mississippi, attached to General Grant's Staff, and was also on staff duty with General Sherman in the same capacity. He was disabled by sickness in 1864, and resumed his professional work in Chicago. General Smith's reputation as a military man was excellent, but as a civil-engineer, he occupied the first rank.[87]

Charles Arthur Ducat was a well known officer of the Civil War, of Irish birth, having first seen the light of day in Dublin, February 24th, 1830. He came to Chicago in 1851 and in 1857 became Secretary and Chief Surveyor of the Board of Underwriters. Upon the firing on Fort Sumter, he threw himself heart and soul into the service of his adopted country, and first raised a corps of engineer soldiers, sappers and miners, whose services were not accepted, whereupon he enlisted as a private in the 12th Illinois Volunteer Infantry, but was quickly promoted by various stages until he reached the rank of Major, and in recognition of merit and gallantry exhibited in the battles of Ft. Henry and Ft. Donaldson, was advanced to the rank of Lieutenant-Colonel. He afterwards participated in all the battles of General Grant's campaign, displaying rare ability and distinguishing himself for his brilliant and gallant conduct. When General Rosecrans assumed command of the army, Lieutenant-Colonel Ducat became his Inspector-General. Later when General Rosecrans took command of the Army of the Cumberland, he became his Acting-Chief of Staff, Acting Inspector-General, and subsequently was ap-

---

[85] For a very complete sketch of the 90th Infantry, see Andreas' *History of Chicago*, pp. 249, 250, 251, 251. For history see Adjutant General's Report, 1860 to 1865, Vol. V, pp. 309-10-11.

[86] For a sketch of the Logan family giving place of birth of father as Ireland, see Judge Gillespie *Pioneer History of Illinois*, pp. 286, 287.

[87] Munsell's *History of Chicago*, Vol. I, pp. 690-1-2-3-4-5.

pointed Inspector-General of the Army and Department of the Cumberland. Ducat was disabled by sickness in 1863, and returned from
the army, engaging in private business, but was in June 1875 appointed by the Governor to the position now corresponding to
Adjutant-General, and in 1877, Governor Shelby M. Cullom appointed him Major-General.[88]

Major John Murphy was born in County Wexford, Ireland. He
raised a company for the 67th Illinois under Colonel Hough. He
was immediately commissioned Seecond Lieutenant, in which capacity
he served for four months at Camp Douglas . He then organized a
company for the 90th Illinois, recruited it in Chicago and was made
its Captain. In the battle of Mission Ridge, Captain Murphy distinguished himself in advancing the skirmish line, and as a reward
for his bravery, received what few men were ever honored with,
a general order from the Brigade Corps and Department, compli-
menting him on his efficient services. Major Murphy passed through
29 battles with "the consciousness of having rendered his country
service in the time of need, and of defending the flag which he had
chosen from all the world as his standard of free thought and
liberty." After the war he engaged in the grocery business and
lead an honorable and comfortable life.[89]

William H. Medill was a brother of Joseph Medill. On the 18th
of April, 1861, he joined Barker's Dragoons, and with that organization proceeded to Cairo, remaining at Camp Defiance, having been
selected by General McClellan as a Body-Guard, left to join him at
Clarksburg, Va., in June. With the Dragoons, young Medill participated in the engagements at Buchannan, Rich Mountain and Beverly
in July, and in August returned with them to Chicago. Medill
then recruited the Fremont Dragoons to the maximum, and it became Company G, 8th Illinois Cavalry. On September 10th. 1862,
Captain Medill was commissioned Major. At Gettysburg, with his
regiment, he held a whole division of the enemy in check for three
hours at the opening of the battle and until re-enforcements came up.
In the pursuit of Lee's Army on July 6th, 1863, Major Medill
received his death wounds while at the front leading his regiment
in an attempt to seize a bridge which the Confederates were throwing
over the Potomac in the vicinity of Williamsport. He died July 16th.
1863, and his remains were brought here by his brother and interred
with military honors in Graceland Cemetery. His biographer says:

---

[88] See sketch Andreas' *History of Chicago*, Vol. II, p. 179.
[89] Andreas' *History of Chicago*, Vol. II, p. 252.

Still other military men both in time of war and peace deserve notice, but I can only mention some of their names. Amongst them are Col. William P. Rend, Major John Lanigan, Major James Quirk, Majjor John E. Doyle, Adjt. John McKeogh, Quartermaster Irish Brigade, Thomas Brennan, Michael J. Dunne, Staff Officer of General Johnson, Captain Thomas L. Hartigan and Colonel Francis T. Colby.[91]

THE CHICAGO FIRE

As we have introduced at least three important epochs in the history of Chicago, namely: The Fort Dearborn Massacre, the Building of the Illinois and Michigan Canal and the Civil War, it would seem appropriate to speak of a fourth, the Great Fire of 1871. So much space has been consumed in other connections, however, that it would be unreasonable to dwell at any length on this most terrible of all the experiences of our city and state. There was one personage in connection with the Chicago Fire, however, so interesting as to demand some attention, and that is not (so as to relieve your troubleded anticipation) Mrs. O'Leary or Mrs. O'Leary's cow, either. In my opinion, Mrs. O'Leary was a good woman who has been basely slandered. I am referring to General Philip H. Sheridan, who, for some years prior to the fire, and for some years thereafter, was a resident of Chicago and in command of the Western Military Department, with headquarters here.

It will be remembered that as the fire raged night and day and got completely beyond the control of every agency within the city, and while the flames, like red monsters, were lapping up the substance of the city, and the people were in despair, a cry went up for help, and at least a second time in his life the presence of General Sheridan was eagerly sought, as when he was absent at the time of the attack on Winchester. Men breathlessly inquired: "Where is Sheridan? Find Sheridan! Sheridan can save us!" and the quest for the little General was as eager in '71 as it had been on that fateful day in '64 when:

Wider still those billows of war
Thundered along the horizon's bar;
And louder yet into Winchester rolled
The roar of that red sea uncontrolled,
Making the blood of the listener cold

[90] *Ibid.* p. 261.
[91] For sketch see *New World*, April 14, 1900, p. 109 et seq.

> As he thought of the stake in that fiery fray,
> With Sheridan twenty miles away.

Nor do we think the satisfaction felt on the Field of Winchester when Sheridan arrived was greater than that felt by the denizens of Chicago when it was at last reported that Sheridan had come, Sheridan was in charge, Sheridan can save us! and, as at Winchester, as:

> He dashed down the line with a storm of huzzas,
> And the wave of retreat checked its course then, because
> The sight of the master compelled it to pause.

With the singular skill and ability of which General Sheridan was abundantly possessed, he took charge of the situation, put the district under military rule, brought up tons of powder and blew up dangerous structures to prevent the spread of the fire; and all through the nights and days that the fire raged, Sheridan was the central figure in the prevention and rescue work, and of course did more than any single man, aye, more than hundreds of men combined in the great catastrophe.[92]

More Recent Notables

There have passed from the scenes of their temporal activities in Chicago during recent years, many worthy men of Irish birth or blood, whose memories deserve much more than I am able to give here, namely: mere mention, but that at least, I feel, in justice must be done.

Amongst such who have graced the bench here are: Judge Richard S. Prendergast, Judge Thomas A. Moran, Judge John Gibbons, Judge James Goggin, Judge Walter J. Gibbon, Judge James M. Doyle, and Judge Daniel Scully; and amongst lawyers, legislators and others: William J. Hynes, Miles Kehoe, Frank J. Lawlor, Edward P. Burke, Michael J. Corcoran, William P. Whelan, James J. McGrath, John Comisky, Michael B. Bailey, Henry F. Donnovan, Thomas J. Carney, Joseph J. Curran, Timothy Ryan, S. S. Hayes, Timothy Brennan, Daniel O'Hara, Daniel W. Ryan, William J. McJarigle, John M. Dunphy, James H. Ward, Lawrence A. Yore, Jeremiah J. Crowley, Thomas Barrett, John M. Smyth, Dr. John Juerin, Joseph Cremin, Thomas Brennan, Thomas Cannon, T. F. Kinsella, John Breen, B. O'Sullivan and John F. Scanlan.[93]

---

[92] For all the papers and documents in connection with Sheridan's activities in the Chicago Fire, see Governor John M. Palmer's Memoirs.

[93] I think I need cite no proof that the men named in this paragraph were all of Irish birth and parentage and I think everyone of them was proud of the fact.

It is to be noted that I have not attempted to write of the clergy or religious, large numbers of whom were of Irish birth or ancestry. These great and good men and women deserve better treatment than I could hope to give them here, and may be more properly dealt with in some other appreciation.

Thus hastily and very incompletely may be sketched the connection of representatives of the Irish race with the City of Chicago, and though the record here presented may read well, and though the list of names, incomplete though it be, may seem extended, how unfair it all is. The names that have been mentioned were of those more or less in the lime-light, who became known to a large number of their fellows. They do not include the multitudes amongst whom there were undoubtedly men and women of higher character, of purer ideals, of greater devotion to the best there is in life.

I have read somewhere of two rather acute individuals who were discussing the question of publicity. One made this suggestion: If you place a quantity of unwinnowed grain in a vessel and shake it thoroughly, the chaff and the poorest and lightest grain will come to the top; the other said: Yes, but if you put a quantity of new milk in a vessel and let it stand without agitation, the best part, the cream, will rise to the top.

As between them, I think it a draw. The one was no doubt right when he intimated that agitation brought to the surface and into the public view, many light individuals. There was too, some philosophy in what the other intimated as to settled conditions bringing forward the solid and substantial.

There is this comfort in connection with the representatives of the Irish race herein alluded to, that without exception they ran a true course, and like the great bulk of their confreres of the same race, they at least averaged up well, demonstrated their patriotism on all occasions and lived in a large measure exemplary lives. We of this generation may well wish for the grace and fortitude to live up to the standard they have set.

To this list prepared many months ago should be added several names of distinguished Irishmen who have died since, including, John P. Hopkins, Roger C. Sullivan, and John F. Scanlan.

Chicago.   JOSEPH J. THOMPSON.

ILLINOIS

(Continued from July, 1920)

The account of the activity of the Franciscans in Southern Illinois would be incomplete without a reference to their efforts in the field of education. This brings us to the history of the colleges founded by them at Quincy and Teutopolis. We shall, in this number, present a brief sketch of St. Francis Solanus College at Quincy, and conclude our series of articles on the labors of the Franciscans in the state with a sketch of St. Joseph's Seminary and College in the next number.

ST. FRANCIS SOLANUS COLLEGE

When the Franciscans were asked, in 1859, to make a foundation in Quincy, it was expressly stipulated that, besides engaging in parish work, they should open a high school for boys and young men. There was, indeed, urgent need of a Catholic high school and college in this part of the state, but owing to the scarcity of priests and religious, it was a matter of extreme difficulty, if not an impossibility, to obtain Catholics educators for such an institution. In these circumstances, the pioneer Franciscans, with characteristic zeal and energy, determined to accept the invitation of Rt. Rev. Bishop Juncker to supply the deficiency.

The arrival of Father Servatius Altmicks and his companions in Quincy and the beginning of their foundation, has already been told.[1] As soon as the friars had taken up their abode in the Jast House, at the end of December, 1859, they set aside the first floor for the purposes of the high school which they planned to open as soon as possible. This undertaking in the interest of education was attended with many difficulties. The Fathers were few in number, hampered by the lack of resources, and besides engaged in pastoral work. At this distant date, it is indeed a cause of wonderment that they succeeded so well in the face of so many difficulties; one cannot but admire the zeal and courage of these pioneers. It was naturally impossible under the circumstances, to begin with a complete course. The main point was to make a beginning; the course could be extended and perfected later as reinforcements would arrive from Germany and

---

[1] Cf. ILLINOIS CATHOLIC HISTORICAL REVIEW, April, 1920, p. 448.

as conditions in the mission would improve. This was the opinion of
Bishop Juncker, the Rev. H. Schaefermeyer, and of the Catholics of
Quincy. Accordingly, the Fathers resolutely set to work, and early
in the year 1860, probably in March, they were in a position to receive
the first students.

During the summer, the convent, built on the Borstadt property,
was ready for occupancy. Two apartments of the building were used
as class rooms. The school year 1860-1861 began in September with
three classes and three teachers: the Fathers Servatius Altmicks,
Maurice Klostermann, and Rayncrius Diekneite. On the first day,
about eighty students were enrolled. "All agree that they were a
fine, well-behaved set of boys and young men. But, alas, for the
high aspirations of the projectors. It soon appeared that Latin and
Greek, together with the other branches of a high school curriculum,
would not be much in demand till the younger students had reached
a suitable stage of development. As to the young men who formed
the majority of the student body, they were mostly such as had,
for some reason or other, failed to acquire an elementary education
in boyhood, and realizing their handicap too late to avail themselves
without embarrassment of the lower schools, gladly seized the opportunity of pursuing a rudimentary course under the pretence, albeit
false, of being "College students".[2]

This state of affairs, which naturally did not tend to arouse enthusiasm or even encouragement, was aggravated by various other
circumstances. "Many of the first students had undoubtedly been
attracted by the novelty of the thing; others had become discouraged;
still others were more than satisfied with the absorption of the most
rudimentary smattering of education; improvement in local public
schools and establishment of other private schools elsewhere, proved
strong drawing cards;—for one reason or other, the number of students rapidly dwindled."[3] The Order, moreover, found it next to
impossible to provide a sufficient number of teachers; the income was
entirely inadequate to meet current expenses, and hence the Fathers,
in 1863, seriously considered the advisability of closing the school.
This course would undoubtedly have been adopted, but for the
energetic protest of the Rev. H. Schaefermeyer and of many prominent citizens of Quincy, and the cool determination of the Rev.

---

[2] *Jubilee Souvenir of St. Francis Solanus College*, Quincy, Illinois, 1912,
p. 32, sq.

[3] *Ibid.*, p. 33.

Ferdinand Bergmeyer, at that time superior of the Franciscans in Quincy.

THE INSTITUTION ON A FIRM BASIS

After mature deliberation, it was decided to continue the school for a year or two, in the hope that conditions would improve. This hope was realized under the management of the new Rector, Rev. Anselm Mueller, who took charge in September, 1863.[4] During the next two years, the attendance continued to decrease; "but everywhere the presence of a master hand was evident, and in 1865, the tide began slowly to turn."[5] Confidence in the undertaking was restored. A growing efficiency in all departments was soon evident; an increase in the number of students was recorded from year to year, and by 1869 the College was on a firm basis.

A BOARDING SCHOOL

In the meantime, the institution had again been obliged to seek other quarters. In February, 1861, separation of the school and convent was deemed advisable, and two rooms were engaged in the neighboring orphanage. Classes were taught here until February, 1865, when the College found its fourth temporary home in the parish school building. Under the circumstances, only day scholars could be admitted. This restricted the student body to residents of Quincy or to such, naturally few, as could find convenient lodging in the town.

Thus matters stood until the year 1869, when, on the occasion of the canonical visitation by the Rev. Provincial Gregory Janknecht, a decision was reached which proved to be of far-reaching influence on the development of the institution. With his usual far-sightedness, Father Gregory perceived that, if the College was to fulfill the expectations of its founders, it would have to be placed in a position to admit boarders, and he gave orders to erect a building adapted for this purpose as soon as possible. Plans were, accordingly, drawn

---

[4] *Ibid.*, p. 34. Father Anselm Mueller was born at Bonn, in Germany, on November 22, 1838. After receiving an excellent education in the schools of his native city, he entered the novitiate of the Order in April, 1857. In May, 1862, he was sent to Teutopolis, and on December 19, of the same year, he was ordained a priest by the Rt. Rev. Bishop Damian Juncker. He was a member of the faculty of St. Joseph's Seminary and College, at Teutopolis, till the summer of 1863.

[5] *Ibid.*, p. 34.

St. Francis Solanus Church and Vicinity ~ 1884

ORPHANAGE   COLLEGE   CHURCH   SCHOOL

for a building of brick, 70x90 feet, four stories high, exclusive of basement, to be erected on a plot adjoining the convent to the east. The cornerstone was laid September 4; 1870, and on September 10, 1871, the completed structure was dedicated by the Rt. Rev. Bishop Peter J. Baltes. "St. Francis Solanus College ceased to be a mendicant and wanderer on the face of the earth, and finally had a roof of its own. It was now in a condition to receive boarders as well as day scholars, and it fame began to spread in the land."[6] The number of boarders increased from year to year, thus proving the correctness of Father Gregory's foresight. On several occasions, students apply-ing for admission had to be refused, as the available accommodations were taxed to the limit. These cramped conditions continued until 1886, when the College acquired possession of the first convent build-ing.[7]

Improvements went on constantly in the equipment as well as in the curriculum of the institution. Among the former improvements, we may note especially the installation of a more modern lighting and heating system, and the building of a steam laundry. Through the untiring efforts of Father Anselm and the faculty, the curriculum was enlarged and perfected, so that it at length embraced the Classical Course, divided into the Academic and Collegiate Departments, of four and three years respectively, and the Commercial Course, ar-ranged for a period of three years. The course of Philosophy em-bracing two years, the second and third of the Collegiate Course, was introduced in 1879. This course was discontinued about the year, 1894, but again introduced in 1897.

The twenty-fifth anniversary of the founding of the College was celebrated amid general rejoicing in 1885. Two year later, Father Anselm celebrated his silver sacerdotal jubilee, "and when, in 1892, after thirty years' guidance of the College destinies, he humbly bowed to the will of his superiors transferring him to another field of labor, he could depart with the assurance that he had done his duty and more than his duty, and that the future of the College was assured."[8]

NEW BUILDINGS

Father Anselm's successor in the management of St. Francis Solanus College was Father Nicholas Leonard. Born at Kerperich, in Alsace, on April 23, 1853, he came to this country with his parents

[6] *Ibid.*, p. 35.
[7] ILLINOIS CATHOLIC HISTORICAL REVIEW, April, 1920, p. 451.

in early youth.. After completing his preparatory studies at
Teutopolis, he entered the novitiate of the Order on June 30, 1870.
He was ordained a priest on February 1, 1877, and was at once
appointed to teach at the college at Teutopolis. He labored there with
great success until the summer of 1884, when he was appointed Vice-
Rector of St. Francis Solanus College. Father Nicholas was a man
of most lovable character and of eminent attainments,—an excellent
educator.

Soon after his appointment, the new Rector, to provide for the
needs of the constantly growing institution, undertook to carry out.
the long-cherished plan of replacing the western wing, consisting of
the old convent building, with more commodious and up-to-date
structures. The southwestern corner of the block, formerly occupied by the first church and parochial school, was added to the
College property, and a strip of land on the east side was purchased
from the St. Aloysius Orphan Society. The cornerstone of the wing
containing the study hall and the auditorium, was laid on September
20, 1893; the structure was ready for occupancy on Thanksgiving
Day, 1894. Simultaneously work was progressing on the western
wing, the cornerstone of which was blessed on March 13, 1894. It
was finished and occupied during the summer of 1895. In 1898, the
old convent building was torn down, and on its site the present central
structure was erected.

"Only one inexperienced in such matters can appreciate what all
this building and expense meant for Father Nicholas, who, at the
same time, was active in the educational work of the institution; in
fact, his claim to merit and fame rests chiefly on his labors in the
latter field. Everything, however, was prospering, and he was looking
forward with confidence in his ability to pay debts incurred and to
finish the proposed buildings, when a most unfortunate accident in
alighting from a street car in Omaha, Nebraska, August 25, 1900,
rendered necessary the amputation of his left leg and brought him
to death's door. He returned to the College after a few months,
but he was a broken man. Resigning his office in December, 1921,
he retired to St. Louis, where after suffering an attack of apoplexy,
he died, March 17, 1903. No student who enjoyed the privilege of
being educated under his direction, can ever forget his marvelous
ability to lead the young mind successfully along the stony road of

*Jubilee Souvenir of St. Francis Solanus College, p. 36.

knowledge, or his wonderful insight into the youthful heart. His
memory is in benediction.''[9]

Father Anselm Mueller was, after Father Nicholas' death, again
appointed Rector of the College, and despite his advanced years, he
guided its destinies with almost undimished vigor from January,
1902, until the summer of 1909. Under his successors, Father Samuel
Macke (1909-1910) and Father Fortunatus Hausser (1910-1915), the
Commercial Course was reorganized and improved, and at the same
time, many improvements were made in the equipment and buildings.
A beautiful chapel in the Romanesque style, begun in September,
1910, was solemnly dedicated on April 28, 1912. On this occasion,
the golden jubilee of the College and the silver sacerdotal jubilee of
Father Fortunatus were joyfully and enthusiastically celebrated by
the faculty and students, and a large concourse of alumni and friends
of the institution.

Very gratifying, indeed, are the results achieved in the field of
education by St. Francis Solanus College, or as its official title now
reads, Quincy College and Seminary. Through the efforts of excellent
professors, it has justly acquired the reputation of imparting a solid
secondary education, especially in the classical studies. It numbers
among its alumni over three hundred priests, secular and regular,
and a large number of teachers, lawyers, physicians, and successful
business men. Its future prospects are bright, and there is every
reason to hope that it will continue to contribute its share in the
education of Catholic youth.

SILAS BARTH, O. F. M.

Teutopolis, Illinois.

---

[9] *Ibid.,* p. 37.

LAFAYETTE IN ILLINOIS.

The birthday of Marie Jean Paul Roch Yves Gilbert Motier De Lafayette was observed on September 6th (he was born September 6, 1758) and a large delegation of Knights of Columbus, after having crossed the ocean for the purpose unveiled a statue of the patriot Frenchman which the order presented to France at Metz, his birth place.

This attempt at doing honor to the memory of a distinguished friend of America may or may not have inspired the article in the *Atlantic Monthly* for May, 1919 in which the great patriot is held up to ridicule and his admirers denominated dupes.

Fortunately the *Atlantic Monthly* article has not been permitted to pass unnoticed, but on the contrary Mr. C. B. Galbreath has, in a splendid article in the *Ohio Archeological and Historical Quarterly* for July, 1920, not only successfully refuted the *Atlantic Monthly* writer's inferences and innuendoes, for that is what the article consists of, but has given us a most interesting account of part of Lafayette's life.

Mr. Galbreath writes under the title "Lafayette's Visit to the Ohio Valley States" and for the benefit of our readers who may not have access to the Ohio Archeological and Historical Quarterly we are reproducing, with the permission of the author and publisher that part of the article describing Lafayette's visit to Illinois:

LAFAYETTE IN ILLINOIS

Lafayette first came to America in 1777, when he was a youth of nineteen years, when disaster seemed about to overwhelm the American cause. He joined Washington at the Brandywine and was wounded in the battle here, was with the commander in chief through the terrible winter at Valley Forge and fought without pay until the crowning triumph of American and French arms at Yorktown.

He first made a brief visit to the United States in 1784. Later when the young Republic had expanded westward and was fast becoming a nation wide and strong, after the French revolution, his long imprisonment in an Austrian dungeon and the downfall of Napoleon, Lafayette came again and as "the nation's guest" visited every state in the Union.

176

Cut by courtesy *New World.*

THE LAFAYETTE STATUE PRESENTED BY THE KNIGHTS OF COLUMBUS

Marshal Foch making his speech of acceptance after he had been presented with a golden diamond studded baton by the Knights of Columbus. The picture was made at Metz, during the presentation ceremonies of the Statue of Lafayette to France by Supreme Knight James A. Flaherty, of Philadelphia, who is shown on the Marshal's left. The presentation was made at the foot of the Lafayette Statue—*International Film Photo.*

In the latter part of February, 1825, he started on his southern nd western tour. Down the Potomac and the Chesapeake, through ʾirginia and the Carolinas he went, down to the sunny southland to ɪeet the early spring. Overland across Georgia he passed and down he Alabama. Out from the bay of Ϩobile the vessel steamed and ore him to New Orleans — the French-American city that welcomed ɪm in a delirium of joy. Up the "Father of Waters" he came, isiting new states, then the western frontiers of civilization, marvel- ɪg at the prodigies of progress in the wlderness.

As his delighted eyes dwelt upon the happy prospect, he forgot ge and fatigue and felt bounding through his veins again the en- husiasm of revolutionary days. In what had been the Northwest ʾerritory he rejoiced to see the principles that claimed his youthful ɪeart embodied in the structures of three noble states, prophetic of ɪhat the greater Republic was to be when slavery under the flag ɪould cease and liberty should become universal in America.

The fame of Lafayette's reception in the East gradually reached he frontier settlements of the West and stimulated a lively desire o see and greet the nation's guest. Late in November of 1824 the ɪgislature of Illinois appointed a committee who formulated the fol- owing address to Lafayette:

ADDRESS OF THE ILLINOIS LEGISLATURE

ʾo General Lafayette:

SIR:—The General Assembly now in session, in behalf of the people of the ːate of Illinois, feel it their duty to express to you, how largely its citizens ɑrticipate in the feelings of joy and gratitude, which your arrival in the ͂nited States has inspired. All our sentiments are in perfect harmony with ɪose of our fellow citizens of the East, who have so warmly greeted your visit ɪ this Republic. They have spoken the language of our hearts. The voice of ːatulation which has been sounded from Maine to Louisiana, is echoed from ɪe banks of the Mississippi. Remote as we are from the Atlantic states, we ɪve not been able to join with our fellow-citizens in their congratulations, and ɣ to the Guest of the Nation: "Welcome Lafayette." But though we have ɪt spoken it, we feel it. No sooner had the news of your arrival reached this ɪstant part of the country, than every eye sparkled with joy, every heart beat ɡh with gratitude, and every bosom swelled with patriotic pride, that Lafayette ɪs in America. With your name is associated everything that can command ɪ respect, admiration and esteem. Your early achievements in the war of the ɪvolution, and the uniform devotion to the cause of American liberty, have ːitten the name of Lafayette upon the tablet of our hearts, and secured to ɪ the brightest page of our history. The same pen that records the virtues ɪ glories of Washington, will perpetuate the name of Lafayette. Few of us, ɪllinois, have any recollection of the eventful scenes of the Revolution; but

our fathers have told us, and when they have rehearsed to us its interesting
events, the names of Washington and Lafayette have adorned the recital. There
are few men living, if any, who have such claims upon the gratitude of the
American people, as yourself. You largely contributed to lay the foundation,
on which are erected our present political institutions; and even here, in Illinois,
a thousand miles from the scenes of your early exploits, we reap the rich reward
of your toil and blood. When you were fighting by the side of Washington,
Illinois was scarcely known, even by name. It has now become an important
member of the great American family, and will soon assume a prominent rank
among the sister states.

The uniformity of your character particularly endears you to the hearts
of the American people. Whether we behold you amid the storms of revolution
or the oppressions of despotism, you appear the same consistent friend of
liberty and of man throughout the world.

We scarcely indulge the pleasing hope of seeing you among us; but if
circumstances should induce you to make a visit to the western country, be
assured, sir, that in no part of it will your reception be more cordial and
welcome than in Illinois; and you will find hearts deeply penetrated with that
gratitude which your visit to the United States has awakened in every part
of our happy country. We entreat heaven, that the evening of your life may
be as serene and happy, as its morning has been brilliant and glorious.

The invitation was forwarded, together with a letter by Governor
Coles. Under date of April 12, 1825, Lafayette writing from New
Orleans signified his eager desire to visit Illinois and suggested points
at which he might meet representatives of the state. Governor Coles
in his reply informed the General that Colonel Hamilton[1] would meet
him in St. Louis and arrange the details of his visit to Illinois.[2]

---

[1] William S. Hamilton was the son of Alexander Hamilton. His name was
William Stephen, not William *Schuyler*, as written by Governor Coles. He was
aid-de-camp to Governor Coles with the rank of Colonel. (For interesting sketch
of Colonel Hamilton see Washburne's "Sketch of Edward Coles.")

[2] The following letters passed between Lafayette and Governor Coles:

LAFAYETTE TO EDWARD COLES

New Orleans, April 12, 1825.

My Dear Sir: Notwithstanding many expostulations I have received on
the impossibility to perform between the 22 of February, and the fifteenth of
June, the tour of visits which I would have been very unhappy to relinquish,
we have arrived thus far, my companions and myself, and I don't doubt but that
by rapid movements, we can gratify my ardent desire to see everyone of the
western states, and yet fulfil a sacred duty as the representative of the Revolutionary Army, on the half secular jubilee of Bunker Hill. But to do it, my dear
sir, I must avail myself of the kind, indulgent proposal made by several friends
to meet me at some point near the river, in the state of Illinois — I would say,
could Kaskaskia or Shawneetown suit you to pass one day with me? I expect
to leave St. Louis on the 29th of April, but being engaged for a day's visit at
General Jackson's I might be at Shawneetown on the 8th of May, if you don't
take me directly from St. Louis to Kaskaskia or some other place. Excuse the

On Saturday, April 30, 1825, Lafayette and party accompanied by prominent citizens, chiefly from Missouri, on board the steamer *Natches*, arrived in Kaskaskia. The visit was entirely unexpected at that time and no military parade was attempted. The news of the arrival soon spread, and the streets and way leading to the landing were thronged with people. The party landed about one o'clock in the afternoon. The guests proceeded to the residence of General Edgar where a reception was held. After partaking of refreshments the General was welcomed by Governor Coles in the following address:

GOVERNOR COLES' ADDRESS

General Lafayette:

In the name of the citizens of Illinois, I tender you their affectionate greeting and cordial welcome. Entertaining for you the most sincere affection, veneration and gratitude, they have largely participated in the joy diffused throughout our extensive Republic by your arrival in it; and are particularly gratified that you have extended your visit to their interior and infant state. For this distinguished mark of respect, I tender you the thanks of Illinois. Yes, General, be assured I speak the feelings of every citizen of the state, when I tell you that we experience no common gratification on seeing you among us. We are not insensible to the honor done us by this visit, and only regret that we are not able to give you a reception more consonant with our feelings and wishes. But you will find our excuse in the recent settlement of the state, and the infancy of our condition as a people.

You will doubtless bear in mind that Illinois was not even conceived at the period of the Revolution, that she has come into existence but a few years

---

hurry of my writing, as the post is going, and receive in this private letter,—for indeed, to the Governor I would not know how apologize for this answer to so polite a proposal,—receive I say, my high and affectionate regards.

LAFAYETTE.

His Excellency, Governor Coles, Illinois.

GOVERNOR COLES TO LAFAYETTE

Edwardsville, Apr. 28, 1925.

Dear Sir: — This will be handed to you by my friend and aid-de-camp, Colonel William Schuyler Hamilton, whom I take particular pleasure in introducing to you, as the son of your old and particular friend, General Alexander Hamilton. As it is not known when you will arrive at St. Louis, or what will be your intended route thence, Colonel Hamilton is posted there for the purpose of waiting on you as soon as you shall arrive and ascertaining from you, and making known to me, by what route you purpose to return eastward, and when and where it will be most agreeable for you to afford me the happiness of seeing you and welcoming you to Illinois.

I am, with the greatest respect and esteem, your devoted friend,

EDWARD COLES.

General Lafayette.

since, and of course has not yet procured those conveniences and comforts which her elder sisters have had time to provide. But, General, though her citizens can not accommodate you as they would wish, believe me they receive you with all those emotions which swell the bosom of the affectionate child, when receiving its kind parent, for the first time, at its new and unfinished dwelling.

Your presence brings most forcibly to our recollections an era of all others the most glorious and honorable to the character of man, and most propitious to his high interests;—when our fathers aroused to a sense of their degradation, and becoming sensible of their rights, took the resolution to declare, and called into action the valor to maintain, and the wisdom to secure, the Independence of our country and the liberty of themselves and their posterity. In the performance of this noble but arduous service, you acted a distinguished part, —the more so as your conduct was prompted by no motive of self-interest. You were influenced by an enlarged philanthropy, which looked on mankind as your kindred, and felt that their happiness was near and dear to yours. You saw a far distant and alien people, young and feeble, struggling for their rights and liberties, and your generous and benevolent bosom prompted you to surmount the many restrictions and obstacles by which you were encompassed, and with a disinterested zeal, chivalrous heroism, and pure and generous philanthropy, surpassing all praise, flew to the assistance of the American patriots, and aided by your influence, counsel, services and treasure, a cause you had so magnanimously espoused.

The love of liberty, which is the most prominent trait in the American character, is not more strongly implanted in every bosom than is an enthusiastic devotion and veneration for the patriotic heroes and sages of the Revolution. We glory in their deeds, we consecrate their memories, we venerate their names, we are devoted to their principles and resolved never to abandon the rights and liberties acquired by their virtue, wisdom and valor. With these feelings, and looking upon you as one of the most virtuous and efficient, and the most disinterested and heroic champion of our rights and liberties, a Father of the Republic, an apostle of liberty, and a benefactor of the human race, our emotions can be more readily conceived than expressed.

Language can not describe our love for the individual, our gratitude for his services, our admiration of his character; a character which has under the most adverse and trying circumstances, throughout a long and eventful life, remained pure, consistent and unsullied by any act of injustice, cruelty, or oppression. Whether aiding the cause of liberty in a foreign and distant country, or in your own dear native France; whether at the zenith of power, commanding millions of men, and wielding the destinies of a great nation, or imprisoned by the enemies of fredom in a foreign dungeon, suffering for many years all the pains and privations which tyranny could devise, we still see displayed the same distinguished traits of character;—never tempted by power, nor seduced by popular applause; always devoted to liberty, always true to virtuous principles: never desponding, but ever firm and erect, cheering and animating the votaries of freedom; and when overtaken by adversity, beset with difficulties, the victim of your virtues, preferring the loss of wealth, of power, nay of liberty, and even of life itself, to the smallest sacrifice or compromise of your principles.

"I would not have ventured, on this occasion, to have said thus much, but for the difficulty I have met with in restraining my feelings when addressing

General Lafayette; and also from a belief that it would have a good effect on those of our countrymen about us, to hold up to their admiration the strong and beautiful traits of your character. In this view your visit to America will not only make the present generation better acquainted with the Revolution, but will, by exhibiting so perfect a model, render more attractive and impress more forcibly upon their recollections the republican principles, and the pure and ennobling virtues of that period.

I must be permitted to say, in addition to that joy which is common to all portions of the Union, there is a peculiar gratification felt in receiving you, one of the fathers of our political institutions and the friend of universal freedom, in the bosom of a state, the offspring of those institutions, which has not only inherited the precious boon of self government, but has been reared in the principles and in the practice of liberty, and has had her soil in an especial manner protected from oppression of every description.

In addition to this, what reflections crowd the mind when we consider who is our Guest, and when and where we are receiving him. Not half a century has elapsed since Jefferson penned the declaration of America's wrongs and of man's rights; Washington drew the sword to maintain the one and avenge the other; and Lafayette left the endearments of country and family to assist in the arduous contest. Then our population was confined to the sea-board and extended back no further than the mountains. Now our republic stretches from ocean to ocean, and our population extends 1200 miles into the interior of this vast continent. And here 1000 miles from the ocean and from the interesting scenes of your glorious achievements at Brandywine, Monmouth, and Yorktown, we, the children of your compatriots, enjoy the happiness of beholding the great friend of our country.

These reflections expand our imaginations, and make us delight in anticipating the future. And, judging from the past do I hazard too much in saying the time is not far distant when the descendants of the revolutionary worthies, inheriting the spirit of their fathers, and animated with the same attachment to liberty, the same enthusiastic devotion to country, and imbued with the same pure divine principles, will people the country from the Atlantic to the Pacific; irradiating this whole continent with the diffusion of intelligence, and blessing it by the establishment of self government, in which shall be secured personal, political and religious liberty? When, in the progress of our country's greatness this happy period shall arrive, the philanthropist may look with confidence to the universal restoration of man to his long lost rights and to that station in the Creator's works and to that moral elevation to which he was destined. And then, my dear General, the world will resound with the praises of Washington and Lafayette, of Jefferson and Franklin, of Madison and of the other patriots, sages, and heroes of the glorious and renovating era of 1776.

LAFAYETTE'S RESPONSE

To which General Lafayette replied:

It is to me, sir, an exquisite gratification to be in the state of Illinois, and in the name of the people, welcomed by their worthy governor, whose sentiments in my behalf, most kindly expressed, claim my lively acknowledgments, at the same time that his patriotic, liberal anticipations and observations excite the

warmest feelings of my sympathy and regard.—Obliged as I am by a sacred engagement well understood by all the citizens of the United States, to shorten my western visit, I will take with me the inexpressible satisfaction to have seen the growing prosperity and importance of this young state, under the triple guarantee of republican institutions, of every local advantage, and of a generous determination in the people of Illinois to improve those blessings, on the soundest principles of American liberty. To those cordial congratulations, my dear sir, I join my thanks for the honor you have done me, to associate my name with those of my illustrious, dear and venerated friends, and I request you to accept in behalf of the citizens of Illinois, of their representatives in both houses, and of their chief magistrate, my gratitude for their affectionate invitation, for the reception I now meet in this patriotic town of Kaskaskia, my best wishes, my devotion and respect.

After the address the crowd of citizens pressed forward to grasp the General by the hand. Among them were some old revolutionary soldiers who had fought with him at the Brandywine and at Yorktown. They were affectionately greeted by their old commander. The meeting of these revolutionary veterans deeply affected those who witnessed it. The company then proceeded to the tavern kept by Colonel Sweet where an ample dinner awaited them.[3] The decorations, though hastily prepared, were most appropriate. The walls of the room were hung round with the laurel wreath tastefully displayed, while over the chair of the guest was erected an arch of roses and other flowers which presented the form and colors of the rainbow.[4]

THE TOASTS

After dinner the following toasts were offered:

BY GENERAL LAFAYETTE—Kaskaskia and Illinois; may their joint prosperity more and more evince the blessings of congenial industry and freedom.

---

[3] Order of procession—General Lafayette, George Washington Lafayette, Colonel Levasseur, De Syon, Governor Coles; Colonel Morse and Colonel Ducros, aids of the Governor of Louisiana; Mr. Caire, Secretary of Governor of Louisiana; Mr. Prieur, Recorder of New Orleans; Colonel Scott, aid to Governor of Mississippi; General Gibbs, General Stewart, Colonel Rutledge, Colonel Balch, Tennessee Committee; Judge Peck, General Dodge, Colonel Wash, Colonel O'Fallon, St. Louis Committee; Citizens of Kaskaskia and vicinity; Committee of arrangements—General Edgar, Governor Bond, William Morrison, Sr. Capt. Stacy McDonald, Judge Pope, Hon. E. K. Kane, Col. Menard, Col. Greenup, Col. Mather, Major Maxwell, Major Humphreys, Doctor Betz, Pierre Menard, Jr.

[4] We joined the procession and took our place at the table, where the General was seated under a canopy of flowers prepared by the ladies of Kaskaskia with much skill and taste; and which produced by the blending of the richest and most lively colors the effect of a rainbow.

LEVASSEUR.

By G. W. LAFAYETTE—The grateful and respectful confidence of my father's children and grandchildren, in the kindness of his American family towards him.

By GOVERNOR BOND — General Lafayette—may he live to see that liberty established in his native country which he helped to establish in his adopted country.

By GENERAL EDGAR—John Quincy Adams.

By COL. SCOTT, of Mississippi—The memory of General Washington.

By COL. MORSE—Gratitude to an old soldier, which equally blesses the giver and receiver.

By GEN. DODGE—General Lafayette, the champion of the rights of man in the old world — the hero who nobly shed his blood in defense of American liberty.

By S. BREESE, ESQ. — Our illustrious Guest—in the many and trying situations in which he has been placed, we see in him the same consistent friend of liberty and of man.

By COL. STEWART—Bolivar, the South American liberator.

By S. SMITH—General Lafayette, the protector of American liberties.

By COL. O'FALLON — The states of Illinois and Missouri—united by the same interests, their citizens should regard each other as members of the same family.

By WM. MORRISON, ESQ.—The land we live in.

By COL. BALCH—Governor Coles—sound in his principles, amiable in his manners; his efforts to promote the interests of his state will be received with gratitude by the freemen of Illinois.

By WILLIAM ORR — The American revolution—May the patriotic feeling which distinguished that period never cease to exist in this Union.

THE GRAND BALL

The General and other guests now proceeded to the house of William Morrison, Sr., by whom a ball was given on this occasion. Here the ladies of the town and vicinity were presented to the General; and far into the night, in honor of the illustrious guest "youth and pleasure chased the glowing hours" that vanished all too soon.[5]

---

[5] The following account of the reception is given by Levasseur, the private secretary of Lafayette:

"In the escort which formed to accompany him, we saw neither military apparel nor the splendid triumphs we had perceived in the rich cities; but the accents of joy and republican gratitude which broke upon his ear was grateful to his heart, since it proved to him that wherever American liberty had penetrated there also the love and veneration of its people for its founders were perpetuated.

"We followed the General on foot and arrived almost at the same time at the house of General Edgar, a venerable soldier of the revolution, who received

him with affectionate warmth and ordered all the doors to be kept open that his fellow citizens might enjoy, as well as himself, the pleasure of shaking hands with the adopted son of America. After a few minutes had been accorded to the rather tumultuous expression of the sentiments which the presence of the General inspired, Governor Coles requested silence, which was accorded with a readiness and deference which proved to me that his authority rested not only on the law but still more on popular affection. He advanced towards Lafayette, about whom the crowd had increased, and addressed him with emotion in a discourse in which he depicted the transports his presence excited in the population of the state of Illinois, and the happy influence which the remembrance of his visit would produce hereafter on the youthful witnesses of the enthusiasm of their fathers for one of the most valiant founders of their liberty.

"During an instant of profound silence, I cast a glance at the assembly in the midst of which I found myself, and was struck with astonishment in remarking their variety and fantastic appearance. Besides men whose dignity of countenance and patriotic exaltation of expression readily indicated them to be Americans, were others whose coarse dresses, vivacity, petu₁ance of movement, and the expansive joy of their visages strongly recalled to me the peasantry of my own country; behind these, near to the door, and on the piazza which surrounds the house, stood some immovable, impassive, large, red, half-naked figures, leaning on a bow or a long rifle: these were the Indians of the neighborhood.

"After a pause of some seconds, the Governor resumed his address, which he concluded by presenting with great eloquence, a faithful picture of the benefits which America had derived from its liberty and the happy influence which republican institutions would one day exercise on the rest of the world. When the orator had finished, a slight murmur of approbation passed through the assembly, and was prolonged until it was perceived that General Lafayette was to reply, when an attentive silence was restored.

"After these reciprocal felicitations, another scene not less interesting commenced. Some old revolutionary soldiers advanced from the crowd and came to shake hands with their old general, while he conversed with them, and heard them, with thought and feeling, cite the names of their ancient companions in arms who also fought at Brandywine and Yorktown, but for whom it was not ordained to enjoy the fruits of their toils nor to unite their voices with that of their grateful country. The persons whom I have remarked as having some likeness in dress and manners to our French peasants, went and came with vivacity in all parts of the hall, or sometimes formed little groups, from the midst of which could be heard, in the French language, the most open and animated expressions of joy. Having been introduced to one of these groups by a member of the committee of Kaskaskia I was received at first with great kindness and was quickly overwhelmed with a volley of questions, as soon as they found I was a Frenchman, and accompanied General Lafayette." These were French Canadians who had emigrated to Illinois.

The attention of Levasseur was attracted to the Indians who were present in great number, several tribes being represented. It was the season of the year when they came to sell the furs that they had accumulated as the result of their winter's trapping and hunting. He soon engaged in conversation with these sons of the forest, many of whom could speak French. At the suggestion of Mr. Caire, private secretary of the Governor of Louisiana, the two visited an Indian camp about half an hour's walk distant. With the exception of an old woman cooking at a fire in the open air there was no one in the camp. She did not answer questions, and maintained a stolid indifference while they examined the huts and surroundings. When they were about to leave, Levasseur, on crossing a stream that ran through the camp, saw a small water wheel which appeared to have been thrown on the bank by the rapidity of the current. "I took it up," said he, "and placed it where I thought it had originally been put by the children, on two stones elevated a little above the water, and the current striking the wings made it turn rapidly. This puerility, which probably would have passed from my memory, if, on the same evening, it had not placed me before the Indians in a situation sufficiently extraordinary, excited the attention of the old woman, who by her gestures, expressed to us a lively satisfaction."

On returning to Kaskaskia, Levasseur met Mr. De Syon, a young Frenchman who at the request of Lafayette had accompanied the party from Washington. He also had made an excursion into the adjacent country and had met among the Indians a handsome young woman who spoke good French and asked if Lafayette was at Kaskaskia. When told that he was, she manifested a strong desire to see him. "I always carry with me," she said, "a relic that is very dear to me; I wish to show it to him; it will prove to him that his name is not less venerated in the midst of our tribes than among the white Americans for whom he fought." Thereupon she drew from her bosom a pouch, which contained a letter carefully wrapped in paper. "It is from Lafayette," she said. "He wrote it to my father a long time since and my father, when he died, left it to me as the most precious thing he possessed." This interested Mr. De Syon and he asked her to accompany him to the city. She declined the invitation but requested him to come to her camp that evening if he wished to speak further. "I am well known in Kaskaskia," she said. "Myn ame is Mary."

De Syon's story so impressed Levasseur that he determined to see the young Indian princess and bring about a meeting between

we were about to enter the enclosure, we were arrested by the fierce barking of two stout dogs which sprang at, and would probably have bitten us, but for the timely interference of our guide.

We arrived at the middle of the camp, which was lighted by a large fire, around which a dozen Indians were squatted, preparing their supper; they received us with cordiality, and, as soon as they were informed of the object of our visit, one of them conducted us to the hut of Mary, whom we found sleeping on a bison skin. At the voice of Mr. De Syon, which she recognized, she arose, and listened attentively to the invitation from General Lafayette to come to Kaskaskia; she seemed quite flattered by it, but said before deciding to accompany us that she wished to mention it to her husband.

While she was consulting with him, I heard a piercing cry; and turning round I saw near me the old woman I had found alone in the camp in the morning; she had just recognized me by the light of the fire and designated me to her companions, who, quitting immediately their occupations, rushed round me in a circle, and began to dance with demonstrations of great joy and gratitude. Their tawny and nearly naked bodies, their faces fantastically painted, their expressive gesticulations, the reflection of the fire, which gave a red tinge to all the surrounding objects, everything gave to the scene something of an infernal aspect, and I fancied myself for an instant in the midst of demons. Mary, witnessing my embarrassment, put an end to it, by ordering the dance to cease, and then explained to me the honors which they had just rendered me. *

"When we wish to know if an enterprise which we meditate will be happy, we place in a rivulet a small wheel slightly supported on two stones; if the wheel turns during three suns without being thrown, the augury is favorable; but if the current carry it away, and throw it upon the bank, it is certain proof that our project is not approved by the Great Spirit, unless, however, a stranger comes to replace our little wheel before the end of the third day. You are

---

* Known to Americans by the name "Chief Jean Baptiste Du Coigne," or "Du Quoin."

while her husband and those who were to accompany her to Kaskaskia, hastily took their supper of maize cooked in milk. She informed me that her father, who was a great chief of one of the nations that inhabited the shores of the great lakes of the north, had formerly fought with a hundred of his followers under the orders of Lafayette when the latter commanded an army on the frontiers; that he had acquired much glory, and gained the friendship of the Americans. A long time after, that is, about twenty years ago, he left the shores of the great lakes with some of his warriors, his wife and daughter; and after having marched a long time he stablished himself on the shores of the river Illinois.

"I was very young then," she said, "but have not forgotten the horrible sufferings we endured during this long journey, made in a rigorous winter, across a country peopled by nations with whom we were unacquainted; they were such that my poor mother, who nearly always carried me on her shoulders, already well loaded with baggage, died under them some days after our arrival; my father placed me under the care of another woman, who also emigrated with us, and occupied himself with securing tranquil possession of the lands on which we had come to establish ourselves, by forming alliances with our new neighbors. The Kickapoos were those who received us best, and we soon considered ourselves as forming a part of their nation. The year following my father was chosen by them with some from among themselves, to go and regulate some affairs of the nation with the agent of the United States, residing here at Kaskaskia; he wished that I should be of the company; for, although the Kickapoos had shown themselves very generous and hospitable towards him, he feared that some war might break out in his absence as he well knew the intrigues of the English to excite the Indians against the Americans. The same apprehension induced him to accede to the request made by the American agent, to leave me in his family, to be educated with his infant daughter. My father had much esteem for the whites of the great nation for which he had formerly fought; he never had cause to complain of them, and he who offered to take charge of me inspired him with great confidence by the frankness of his manners, and above all, by the fidelity with which he treated the affairs of the Indians; he, therefore, left me, promising to return to see me every year after the great winter's hunt; he came, in fact, several times afterwards; and I, notwithstanding the disagreeableness of sedentary life, grew up, answering the expectations of my careful benefactor and his wife. I became attached to their daughter who grew up with me, and the truths of the Christian religion easily supplanted in my mind the superstitions of my father, whom I had scarcely known; yet, I confess to you, notwithstanding the influence of religion and

188   C. B. GALBREATH

civilization on my youthful heart, the impressions of infancy were not entirely
effaced.

"If the pleasure of wandering conducted me into the shady forest, I
breathed more freely, and it was with reluctance that I returned home; when,
in the cool of the evening, seated in the door of my adopted father's habitation,
I heard in the distance, through the silence of the night, the piercing voice of
the Indians, rallying to return to camp, I started with a thrill of joy, and my
feeble voice imitated the voice of the savage with a facility that affrighted my
young companion; and when occasionally some warriors came to consult my
benefactor in regard to their treaties, or hunters to offer him a part of the
produce of the chase, I was always the first to run to meet and welcome them.
I testified my joy to them by every imaginable means, and I could not help
admiring and wishing for their simple ornaments, which appeared to me far
preferable to the brilliant decorations of the whites.

"In the meantime my father had not appeared at the time for the return
from the winter's hunting; but a warrior, whom I had often seen with him,
came and found me one evening at the entrance of the forest, and said to me:
'Mary thy father is old and feeble, he has been unable to follow us here; but
he wishes to see thee once more before he dies, and he has charged me to conduct
thee to him.' In saying these words he forcibly took my hand and dragged me
with him. I had not even time to reply to him, nor even to take any resolution,
before we were at a great distance, and I saw well that there was no part left
for me but to follow him. We marched nearly all night, and at the dawn of
day we arrived at a bark hut, built in the middle of a little valley. Here I saw
my father, his eyes turned towards the just rising sun. His face was painted
as for battle. His tomahawk, ornamented with many scalps, was beside him.
He was calm and silent as an Indian who awaited death. As soon as he saw me
he drew out of a pouch a paper wrapped with care in a very dry skin, and
gave it to me, requesting that I should preserve it as a most precious thing.

" 'I wished to see thee once more before dying,' he said, 'and to give this
paper, which is the most powerful charm (manitou) which thou canst employ
with the whites to interest them in thy favor; for all those to whom I have
shown it have manifested towards me a particular attachment. I received it
from a great French warrior, whom the English dreaded as much as the Americans loved, and with whom I fought in my youth.' After these words my father
was silent. Next morning he expired. Sciakape, the name of the warrior who
came for me, covered the body of my father with the branches of trees, and
took me back to my guardian."

Here Mary suspended her narrative and presented to me a letter a little
darkened by time, but in good preservation. "Stay," said she to me, smiling,
"you see that I have faithfully complied with the charge of my father; I have
taken great care of his manitou." I opened the letter and recognized the signature and handwriting of General Lafayette. It was dated at headquarters,
Albany, June, 1778, after the northern campaign, and addressed to Panisciowa,
an Indian chief of one of the Six Nations, to thank him for the courageous
manner in which he had served the American cause.

"Well," said Mary, "now that you know me well enough to introduce me
to General Lafayette, shall we go to him that I may also greet him who my
father revered as the courageous warrior and the friend of our nations!"

Willingly, I replied, but it seems to me that you have promised to inform us in what manner, after having tasted for some time the sweets of civilization, you came to return to the rude and savage life of the Indians?

At this question, Mary looked downwards and seemed troubled. However, after a slight hesitation, she resumed in a lower town: "After the death of my father, Sciakape often returned to see me. We soon became attached to each other; he did not find it difficult to determine me to follow him to the forest, where I became his wife. This resolution at first very much afflicted my benefactors; but when they saw that I found myself happy, they pardoned me; and each year, during all the time that our encampment is established near Kaskaskia, I rarely pass a day without going to see them; if you wish, we can visit them, for their house is close by our way, and you will see, by the reception they will give me, that they retain their esteem and friendship." Mary pronounced these last words with a degree of pride, which proved to us that she feared that we might have formed a bad opinion of her, on account of her flight from the home of her benefactors with Sciakape.

We accepted her suggestion and she gave the signal for departure. At her call, her husband and eight warriors presented themselves to escort us. Mr. De Syon offered her his arm, and we began our march. We were all very well reived by the family of Mr. Menard; but Mary above all received the most tender marks of affection from the persons of the household. Mr. Menard, Mary's adopted father, was at Kaskaskia as one of the committee charged with the reception of Lafayette, and Mrs. Menard asked us if we would undertake to conduct her daughter to the ball which she herself was prevented from attending by indisposition. We assented with pleasure; and, while Mary assisted Miss Menard to complete her toilet, we seated ourselves round a great fire in the kitchen. After we had spent some time talking to a colored servant who claimed to be more than one hundred years old and who grew remarkably reminiscent as we listened,[1] Mary and Miss Menard came to inform us that they were ready, and asked if we would be on our way as it began to grow late.

We took leave of Mrs. Menard and found our Indian escort, who had waited patiently for us at the door and who resumed their position near us at some distance in front, to guide and protect our march, as if we had been crossing an enemy's country. The night was quite dark, but the temperature was mild, and the fireflies illuminated the atmosphere around us. M. De Syon conducted Miss Menard, and I gave my arm to Mary, who, notwithstanding the darkness, walked with a confidence and lightness which only a forest life could produce. The fireflies attracted and interested me much; for, although this was not the first time I had observed them, I had never before seen them in such numbers. I asked Mary if these insects, which from their appearance seem so likely to astonish the imagination, had never given place among the Indians to popular beliefs or tales. "Not among the nations of these countries, where every year we are familiarized with their great numbers," said she to me, "but I have heard that, among the tribes of the north, they commonly believe that they are the souls of departed friends who return to console them or demand the performance of some promise. I even know several ballads on this

[1] Adapted by omitting the "reminiscences."

subject. One of them appears to have been made a long time since, in a nation
which lived farther north and no longer exists. It is by songs that great events
and popular traditions are ordinarily preserved among us, and this ballad, which
I have often heard sung by the young girls of our tribe, leaves no doubt as
to the belief of some Indians concerning the firefly.'' I asked her to sing me
this song, which she did with much grace. Although I did not comprehend the
words, which were Indian, I observed a great harmony in their arrangement,
and, in the very simple music in which they were sung, an expression of deep
melancholy.

When she had finished the ballad, I asked her if she could not translate it
for me into French, so that I might comprehend the sense. ''With difficulty,''
she said, ''for I have always found great obstacles to translating exactly the
expressions of our Indians into French, when I have served them as interpreter
with the whites; but I will try.'' And she translated nearly as follows:

LEGEND OF THE FIREFLY

''The rude season of the chase was over. Antakaya, the handsomest, the
most skilful, and bravest of the Cherokee warriors, came to the banks of the
Avolachy, where he was expected by Manahella, the young virgin promised to
his love and bravery.

''The first day of the moon of flowers was to witness their union. Already
had the two families, assembled round the same fire, given their assent: already
had the young men and women prepared and ornamented the new cabin, which
was to receive the happy couple, when, at the rising of the sun, a terrible cry,
the cry of war, sent forth by the scout who always watches at the summit of
the hill, called the old men to the council, and the warriors to arms.

''The whites appeared on the frontier. Murder and robbery accompanied
them. The star of fertility had not reached its noontide height, and already
Antakaya had departed at the head of his warriors to repel robbery, murder
and the whites.

''Go, said Manahella to him, endeavoring to stifle her grief, go fight the
cruel whites, and I will pray to the Great Spirit to wrap thee with a cloud,
proof against their blows. I will pray him to bring thee back to the banks
of the Avolachy, there to be loved by Manahella.

''I will return to thee, replied Antakaya, I will return to thee. My arrows
have never disappointed my aim, my tomahawk shall be bathed in the blood
of the whites; I will bring back their scalps to ornament the door of thy cabin;
then I shall be worthy of Manahella; then shall we love in peace, then shall
we be happy.

''The first day of the moon of flowers had brightly dawned, and many
more had passed away, and none had heard from Antakaya and his warriors.
Stooping on the shores of the Avolachy, the mournful Manahella every evening
raised to the evil spirits little pyramids of polished pebbles, to appease their
anger and avert their resistance to her well beloved; but the evil spirits were
inflexible, and their violent blasts overthrew the little pyramids.

''On evening of the last moon of flowers, Manahella met on the banks of
the river a pale and bloody warrior. 'Die, poor ivy,' said he to Manahella;
'die! the noblest oak of the forest, that proud oak under whose shade thou
hopest to enjoy repose and happiness, is fallen! It has fallen under the re-
doubled strokes of the whites. In its fall it has crushed those who felled it,

his defeat and meditate vengeance with Manahella. When he arrived, she was no more. Agitated by the most violent despair, he ran in the evening to the banks of Avolachy, calling Manahella, but echo alone replied to the accents of his grief. .

"O Manahella! he exclaimed, if my arrows have disappointed my skill, if my tomahawk has not spilt the blood of the whites, if I have not brought thee their scalps to ornament the door of thy cabin, forgive me! It is not the fault of my courage, the evil spirits have fought against me. And yet I have suffered no complaint to escape me, not a sigh, when the iron of my enemies tore my breast: I have not abased myself by asking my life! They preserved it against my will, and I am only consoled by the hope of one day avenging myself, and offering thee many of their scalps. O Manahella! come, if but to tell me that thou pardonest me, and that thou permittest me to follow thee into the world of the Great Spirit.

"At the same instant a vivid light, pure and lambent, appeared to the eyes of the unforunate Antakaya. He saw in it the soul of his beloved, and followed it through the valley during the night, supplicating it to stay and to pardon him. At the dawn of the day he found himself on the border of a great lake; the light had disappeared, and he believed that it had passed over the water. Immediately, although feeble and fatigued, he made a canoe of the trunk of a tree which he hollowed, and with a branch he made a paddle. At the end of the day his work was achieved. With the darkness the deceptive light returned; and during all the night Antakaya pursued the delusion on the face of the unsteady waters. But it again disappeared before the light of the sun, and with it vanished the slight breath of hope and the life of Antakaya.''

. Mary ended her ballad, and I expressed to her my thanks as we arrived at the bridge of Kaskaskia. There, Sciakape collected his escort, said a few words to his wife, and left us to enter the village alone. We approached the house of Mr. Morrison, at which the ball was given to General Lafayette. I then felt that Mary trembled; her agitation was so great that she could not conceal it from me. I asked her the cause. "If you would spare me a great mortification," she said, "you will not conduct me among the ladies of Kaskaskia. They are now without doubt in their most brilliant dresses, and the coarseness of my clothes will inspire them with contempt and pity, two sentiments which will equally affect me. Besides I know that they blame me for having renounced the life of the whites, and I feel little at ease in their presence." I promised what she desired, and she became reassured. Arrived at Mr. Morrison's, I conducted her into a lower chamber and went to the hall to inform General Lafayette that the young Indian girl awaited him below. He hastened down and several of the committee with him. . He saw and heard Mary with pleasure and could not conceal his emotion on recognizing his letter and observing with what holy veneration it had been preserved during nearly half a century in a savage nation, among whom he had not even supposed his name had ever penetrated. On her part, the daughter of Panisciowa expressed

with vivacity the happiness she enjoyed in seeing him, along with whom her
father had the honour to. fight for the *good American cause.*

After a half hour's conversation, in which General Lafayette was pleased
to relate the evidences of the fidelity and courageous conduct of some Indian
nations towaids the Americans, during the Revolutionary War, Mary manifested
a wish to retire, and I accompanied her to the bridge, where I replaced her
under the care of Sciakape and his escort and bade them farewell.

Bids Farewell to Kaskaskia

Shortly before midnight Lafayette bade farewell to the citizens
of Kaskaskia and accompanied by his party and Governor Coles
embarked for Nashville, Tennessee. Levasseur was very favorably
impressed with the Governor as may be gathered from his journal
where he recorded the following tribute:

All persons agree in saying that he fulfills his duties as Governor with
as much philanthropy as justice. He owes his elevation to the office of governor
to his opinions on the abolition of the slavery of the blacks. He was originally
a proprietor in Virginia, where, according to the custom of the country, he
cultivated his lands by negro slaves. After having for a long time strongly
expressed his aversion for this kind of culture, he thought it his duty to put into
practice the principles he had professed, and he decided to give liberty to all
his slaves; but knowing that their emancipation in Virginia would be more injurious than useful to them. he took them all with him into the state of Illinois,
where he not only gave them their liberty, but also established them at his own
expense, in such a manner that they should be able to procure for themselves
a happy existence by their labor. This act of justice and humanity considerably
diminished his fortune, but occasioned him no regret. At this period, some men,
led astray by ancient prejudices, endeavored to amend that article of the constitution of the state of Illinois, which prohibits slavery. Mr. Coles opposed
these men with all the ardor of his philanthropic soul, and with all the superi-
ority of his enlightened mind. In this honorable struggle he was sustained by
the people of Illinois. Justice and humanity triumphed, and soon after Mr.
Coles was elected Governor, by an immense majority.[*] This was an honorable
recompense,and to this there is now joined another which must be very grateful
to him; his liberated negroes are perfectly successful, and afford a conclusive
argument against the adversaries of emancipation.

Visits Tennessee

The boat steamed down the Mississippi to the Ohio, and ascending
this, reached the mouth of the Cumberland the following evening.

---

[*] While the above statements in regard to Governor Coles and his attitude
toward slavery are correct, he was not elected by an "immense majority," but
by a very small plurality. The vote was as follows: Coles, 2,810; Phillips, 2,760;
Brown, 2,543; Moore 522. Coles was therefore elected by a plurality of only fifty
votes. By these votes Illinois was saved to freedom.

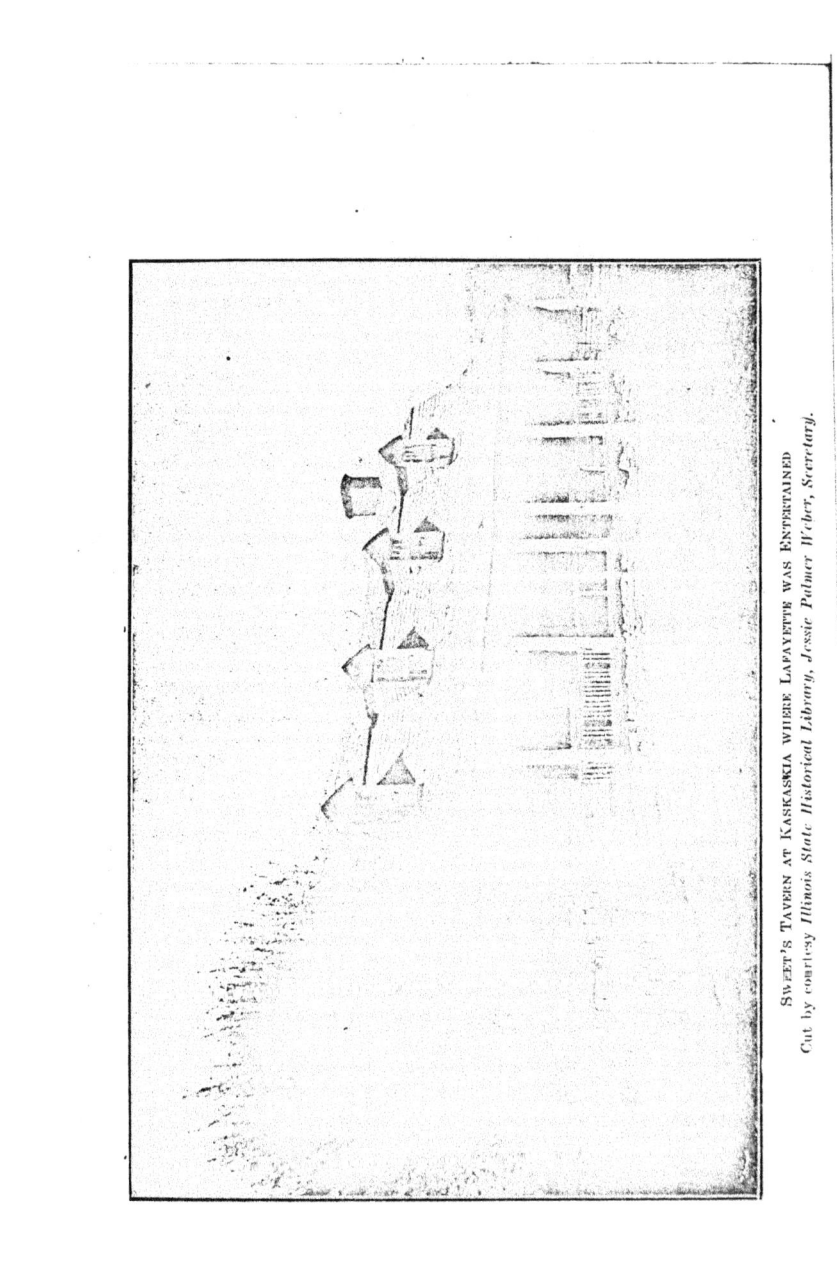

SWEET'S TAVERN AT KASKASKIA WHERE LAFAYETTE WAS ENTERTAINED

Cut by courtesy Illinois State Historical Library, Jessie Palmer Weber, Secretary.

Soon after the arrival, the steamboat *Artisan* came down the river: To this Lafayette and his companions, after bidding an affectionate farewell to their friends from Louisiana and Mississippi, were transferred, and the journey was continued up the river to the capital of Tennessee. On the 4th of May they reached Nashville where a great ovation was tendered the illustrious guest. At the landing he was met by General Andrew Jackson with whom he rode in a carriage at the head of a long procession under a triumphal arch and through streets strewn with flowers. Here forty officers and soldiers of the Revolution greeted Lafayette, among them a German veteran by the name of Hagy who had come with the General on his first voyage to America and had served under him through the Revolution. The white haired old soldier who had walked many miles to see his General, threw himself into Lafayette's arms exclaiming: ''I have enjoyed two happy days in my life; one when I landed with you at Charleston, and the present. Now that I have seen you once again, I have nothing more to wish for; I have lived long enough.''

Lafayette was welcomed by the Governor of Tennessee and the mayor of the city. He visited the camp of the militia, Cumberland College, and the home of General Jackson. The ceremonies in his honor closed with a ball, after which he started down the river to resume his journey toward the east.

ILLINOIS — SHAWNEETOWN

On the 7th of May the boat again entered the Ohio, and on the day following the party with Governor Coles and other members of the committeee from the state of Illinois, landed at Shawneetown. Here the greeting of the people was most cordial. As the boat approached the landing, a salute of twenty-four rounds was fired. The people were out in great numbers to welcome the hero. Two lines were formed extending from Rawling's Hotel to the river. Down this passed the committee of reception, town officials and other dignitaries, and received the nation's guest, who with the distinguished party accompanying him passed up the line, the citizens standing uncovered in perfect silence, until he arrived at the hotel where many ladies were assembled. Here James Hall, one of the judges of the state and a literary man of note in his day, delivered the following address of welcome:

JUDGE HALL'S ADDRESS

Sir:—The citizens of Shawneetown, and its vicinity, avail themselves with infinite pleasure of the opportunity which is this day presented to them, to

discharge a small portion of the national debt of gratitude. The American people are under peculiar obligations to their early benefactors. In the history of governments, revolutions have not been unfrequent, nor have the struggles for liberty been few; but they have too often been incited by ambition, conducted with violence, and consummated by the sacrifice of the noblest feelings and the dearest rights. The separation of the American colonies from the mother country was impelled by the purest motives, it was effected by the most virtuous means, and its results have been enjoyed with wisdom and moderation. A noble magnanimity of purpose and of action adorned our conflict for independence;— no heartless cruelty marked the footsteps of our patriot warriors, no selfish ambition mingles in the councils of our patriot sages. To those great and good men we owe, as citizens, all that we are, and all that we possess; to them we are indebted for our liberty—for the unsullied honor of our country— for the bright example which they have given to an admiring world!

Years have rolled away since the accomplishment of those glorious events, and few of the illustrious actors remain to partake of our affection. We mourn our Hamilton—we have wept at the grave of our Washington—but Heaven has spared us LAFAYETTE, to the prayers of a grateful people.

In you, sir, we have the happiness of recognizing one of those whom we venerate—the companion of those whom we deplore. We greet you as the benefactor of the living, we greet you as the compatriot of the dead. We receive you with filial affection as one of the fathers of the Republic. We embrace with eager delight an opportunity of speaking our sentiments to the early champion of our rights—but we want language to express all we feel. How shall we thank you, who have so many claims upon our gratitude? What shall we call you, who have so many titles to our affection? Bound to us by a thousand fond recollections—connected with us by many endearing ties—we hail you by every name which is dear to freemen. Lafayette—friend—father— fellow citzen—patriot—soldier—philanthropist! We bid you welcome! You were welcome, illustrious sir, when you came as our champion; you are thrice welcome as our honored guest. Welcome to our country and to our hearts—to our firesides and altars.

In your extensive tour through our territories, you have doubtless beheld many proofs that he who shared the storms of our infancy has not been forgotten amid the genial beams of a more prosperous fortune. In every section of the Union, our people have been proud to affix the name of Lafayette to the soil, in fighting for which that name was rendered illustrious. This fact, we hope, affords some testimony that although the philosophic retirement in which you were secluded might shelter you from the political storms which assailed your natal soil, it could not conceal you from the affectionate solicitude of your adopted countrymen. Your visit to America has disseminated gladness throughout the continent, but it has not increased our veneration for your character, nor brightened the remembrance of those services, which were already deeply engraven in our memories.

The little community which has the honor, today, of paying a tribute to republican virtue, was not in existence at the period when that virtue was displayed in behalf of our country. You find us dwelling upon a spot which was then untrodden by the foot of civilized man; in the midst of forests whose silent echoes were not awakened by the tumults of that day. Around us are

none of the monuments of departed patriotism, nor any of the trophies of that valor which wrought the deliverance of our country. There is no sensible object here to recall your deeds to memory—but they dwell in our bosoms—they are imprinted upon monuments more durable than brass. We enjoy the fruits of your courage, the lesson of your example. We are the descendants of those who fought by your side—we have imbibed their love of freedom—we inherit their affection for Lafayette.

You find our state in its infancy, our country thinly populated, our people destitute of the luxuries and elegancies of life. In your reception we depart not from the domestic simplicity of a sequestered people. We erect no triumphal arches, we offer no exotic delicacies. We receive you to our humble dwelling and our homely fare—we take you to our arms and our hearts.

The affections of the American people have followed you for a long series of years—they were with you at Brandywine, at York, at Olmutz, and at La Grange—they have adhered to you through every vicissitude of fortune which has marked your virtuous career. Be assured, sir, that you still carry with you our best wishes—we firmly desire you all the happiness which the recollection of a well spent life and the enjoyment of venerable age, full of honor, can bestow—we pray that health and prosperity may be your companions, when you shall be again separated from our embraces, to exchange the endearments of a people's love for the softer joys of domestic affection, and that it may please heaven to preserve you many years to us, to your family, and to the world.

The reply of Lafayette was short and extempore. His voice was tremulous with emotion. He said, in substance: :

I thank the citizens of Shawneetown for their kind attention. I am under many obligations to the people of the United States for their manifestations of affectionate regard since I landed on their shore. I long wished to visit America, but was prevented by circumstances over which I had no control. This visit has afforded me unspeakable gratification. I trust that every blessing may attend the people of this town and the state of Illinois.

A collation prepared by the citizens was then served, at which General Joseph M. Street presided, assisted by Judge Hall. A number of toasts followed, appropriate to the occasion. After spending a few hours in pleasant converse and greeting many citizens, the General was conducted back to the steeamer. Here Governor Coles bade him adieu and proceeded by land to Vandalia. A salute was fired as the vessel bearing the guest ascended the river and vanished from the sight of loving eyes.

C. B. GALBREATH.

Columbus, Ohio.

CATHOLIC STATESMEN OF ILLINOIS[1]

This subject invites some discussion as to the meaning of the word statesman and as to just what qualities must be possessed by a man to be classed as a statesman. Some affect to draw a distinction between politicians and statesmen, but there is a tendency to call the public man you do not like a politician and the one you do like a statesman.

MARQUETTE AND JOLLIET

Our history begins in Illinois in 1673 when Marquette and Jolliet discovered and to some extent explored the State. Each of them had the qualities of statesmen and exercised some acts of statecraft, but their stay was so brief, and they have been so well otherwise classified that we do not need here to dwell upon their records in the light of statesmen.

CLAUDE JEAN ALLOUEZ, S. J.

No one can read what is known of the life of Father Claude Jean Allouez, S. J., without judging him to be a statesman. Allouez was not only a great divine but an able civilian. It was he that pronounced the great oration at the pageant of the Sault when St. Lusson with a commission from Louis XIV of France took possession of:

St. Marie of the Falls as well as of Lakes Huron and Superior, the Island of Manitoulin and all other countries, rivers, lakes and tributaries contingent and adjacent thereunto as well discovered as to be discovered, which are bounded on the one side by the northern and western seas and the other side by the South sea including all its length and breadth.

In the course of the eloquent oration which followed, pronounced for the benefit of the Indian Tribes assembled from all the surrounding country, Father Allouez raising his eyes to the Cross which had been erected and the Standard of France by its side, said:

Cast your eyes upon the Cross raised so high above your heads. There it was that Jesus Christ the son of God making Himself man for the love of men was pleased to be fastened and to die in atonement to His Eternal Father for our sins. He is the master of our lives, of heaven, of earth and of hell. Of Him I have always spoken to you, and His name and word I have borne into all these countries; but look likewise at that other post to which are affixed

---

[1] An address before the Sacred Heart Alumni, Chicago.

196

the armorial bearing of the great Captain of France whom we call King. He lives beyond the sea; He is the captain of the greatest captains and has not His equal in the world. All the captains you have ever seen or whom you have ever heard are mere children compared with him. He is like a great tree and they only like little plants that we tread under foot in walking.

He then exhorted the Indian tribes to friendship and fealty to the King, and urged upon them the treaty they then and there entered into with the representative of the Canadian Government.[2] This was by no means his last act of statesmanship. It was he that civilized the Indian tribes around Peoria Lake, the Great Rock now known as Starved Rock and the Miami country in the neighborhood of the St. Joseph and Notre Dame.

He was in the Illinois country some fifteen years, and besides the services of a civil nature which he rendered the Indian Tribes and the few Frenchmen of his time, he is credited with having instructed during his apostolic career in Canada and the Illinois country one hundred thousand natives and having baptized ten thousand native converts.[3]

HENRI DE TONTY

The next commanding figure is that of Henri de Tonty. I at once hear objections and the call for Robert Cavalier Sieur de La Salle, but despite the volumes that have been written about this great explorer and the acclaim which has accompanied his name down through the generations, I am convinced La Salle played a less important part in our immediate affairs than did his unostentatious but most efficient lieutenant, Tonty.

As we read the history of those early days and note the fact that Tonty took, and to all appearances maintained an inferior position in the La Salle regime, we must, unless we discriminate carefully, be convinced that he was but a secondary figure. If, however, we consider that when de La Salle's plans, sometimes very extravagant, went awry, it was always Tonty that bridged over the difficulties, if such a performance were possible. When La Salle with the bitterness of his invective and in the apparent sourness of his spirit, disagreed and quarreled with his confreres, his servants or assistants or with the clergy of any or of no order, it was Tonty that ironed out

---

[2] Thwaite, *Jesuit Relations* IV, 105-115. See also Kellogg, *Early Narratives of the Northwest*, p. 213 et seq.

[3] Campbell, *Pioneer Priests of North America* III, 164.

the difficulties if it were possible, and that in fact made any progress in the La Salle undertaking possible.

It was Tonty too, and not La Salle that organized and established the great Indian confederacy, the only peaceful, progressive and law abiding combination of Indian tribes that ever existed on the American continent, and for twenty years from his castle-fort on Starved Rock, ruled his Indian nation of from ten to twenty thousand souls, the first and in many respects the greatest of the ⸗Governors of Illinois.

Tonty had an iron hand, and in courage, perseverance and endurance was an iron man—the "Man-de-fer" of Indian story and legend. Nobody ever spoke of Henry de Tonty except in praise. He inherited from his Italian father a love of liberty and he exhibited his courage in his relations wth the savage Indian tribes as no other man before or since had demonstrated that quality.

Tonty in a large sense was omnipresent. From the snows of Quebec to the tropics was but a usual and customary undertaking for the intrepid explorer and administrator. When war demanded the presence of strong men, he was at the front; when religion required an earnest votary, none was more sincere than Tonty; when the oppressed needed a defender, they could turn to none so confidently as Tonty; when the missionary needed a guide, and guard, a counsellor, a friend, he found all in Henry de Tonty.

Not half has ever been told of the merit of this humble Italian. History has done him slight credit in comparison with the signal commendation he deserves. Simple justice demands that his name be placed amongst the list of the most notable men of our State.[4]

La Salle should not be overlooked as a statesman of the Illinois country, however. His conceptions partially executed by Tonty were most statesmanlike, and he is unquestionably entitled to such a rank—rather however as a world figure.

Gabriel Marest, S. J.

The inexorable hand of time has changes wrought. Tonty's government on the rock has fallen. His empire has scattered and the inhabitants of Illinois have migrated to and settled in the lower valleys of the Mississippi along the now romantic region of the Kaskaskia. Men of savage and men of gentle birth gathered from year to year in this new community. A strange transformation is

---

[4] For good sketch see the booklet on Tonty by the late Henry Ligher.

Tonty's glorious administration, Father Gabriel Marest came, and partly because Tonty had been deposed and was leaving the Fort and partly because the Iroquois Indians were still savage and unmerciful and were wont to attack and destroy the Illinois, Father Marest in the exercise of his best judgment removed the mission and its Indian congregation farther south and nearer to the civilized communities established by his countrymen near the Gulf of Mexico, and though Father Gravier was somewhat disappointed, and in fact remained behind with the Peorias, nevertheless the stalwart men of the Kaskaskia and other tribes closely associated with them around Starved Rock, as well as the French inhabitants accompanied Father Marest and gladly followed his guidance in the succeeding years.

. As we consider the relations between Father Marest and of all the inhabitants of the lower Mississippi country in the new habitation, we are reminded of what Southey, in his beautiful Tale of Paraguay, said of the Paraguay Indians:

> They on the Jesuit, who nothing loath,
> Reposed alike their conscience and their cares;
> And he, with equal faith, the trust of both
> Acceptted and discharged. The bliss is theirs
> Of that entire dependence that prepares
> Entire submission, let what may befall;
> And his whole careful course of life declares
> That for their good he holds them thus in thrall,
> Their Father and their Friend, Priest, Ruler, all in all.

During all the years that Father Marest was in the Missions of Illinois, he was not only the spiritual but also the temporal leader of all its inhabitants, and therefore eminently entitled to a place on its highest roll of honor, and amongst the greatest statesmen of Illinois. It was he and the worthy Jesuits who were his contemporaries and successors, that Judge Sydney Breese had in mind when he said:

No evidence is to be found among our early records of the exercise of any controlling power save the Jesuits up to the time of the grant to Crozat in 1712, and I have no idea that any such existed in the shape of Government or that there was any other social organization than that effected by them, and of which they were the head.[5]

And the same author further argues that even after Crozat and the succeeding Company of the West came on the scene:

Their sway was more in name than in fact, for aside from their power to grant land, the real control over the minds and will of the people was with the Jesuits.[6]

The law and the government during the early days of the permanent settlement of Illinois is described by Blanchard, who says:

French villages in the Illinois country, as well as at most other places, were each under the government of a priest, who, besides attending to their spiritual wants, dispensed justice to them, and from this decision there was no appeal. Though this authority was absolute, the records of the time disclose no abuse of it, but on the contrary, prove that it was always used with paternal care.[7]

Father Marest and Fathers Mermet and Deville who were associated with him there taught the natives how to plow and cultivate the land, introduced the culture of wheat, taught domestic economy and home hatbits to such an extent that the Indians ceased to go upon their hunts, but remained in their own dwellings, married and reared up God-fearing families, and as was told in a contemporary letter, out of the more than two thousand two hundred Indians in the immediate vicinity, there were not to exceed forty that did not become christianized and civilized.

Father Marest was succeeded in his great work by Fathers Guymonneau, Le Boullenger, De Beaubois, Watrin, Guyene and Vivier, all of whom possessed qualities of statesmanship and exercised the control of which Breese, Blanchard and other historians have spoken.

[5] *Early History of Illinois*, p. 146.
[6] *Ibid.*, p. 180.
[7] *Discovery and Conquest of the Northwest*, p. 63.

REV. JAMES MARQUETTE, S. J.
First white man to deal with the natives
of Illinois

LOUIS JOLLIET
Fellow voyager and discoverer with
Marquette

ROBERT CAVALIER SIEUR DE LASALLE
First Commandant of the Illinois
Country.

HENRI DE TONTI
Twenty years governor of the Illinois.
Headquarters Fort St. Louis

In time, however, laymen of ability and capacity came into or arose in the country, and it is gratifying to know that one of the results of the splendid teaching and statecraft of Father Marest and his immediate successors was the development of Chikagou and Mamantouensa, chiefs respectively of the Metchagami and Kaskaskia, perhaps the ablest men of the American Indian race. It was Chief Chikagou and three of his associates that in 1825 went with Father De Beaubois to France, was received in audience by the King and feted and courted as a man of distinction as he really was. From the transcript of the addresses of these two Indian Chiefs made to the French Governor, Perrier, at New Orleans, we can judge of their civil ability and their sincere Catholicity. They showed that while they cherished their civil rights, they thought then best assured to them by the influence of religion.

'When I went over to France', said Chikagou, 'the King promised me his protection for the prayer and recommended me never to abandon it. I always remember it. Grant then your protection to us and to our Black Robes.'[8]

And Mamantouensa in the course of his address to the Governor, said:

All that I ask of you is your heart and your protection. I am much more desirous of that than of the merchandise of the world, and when I ask this of you, it is solely for the prayer.[9]

These two chiefs who were visiting the Governor to urge his protection against the savage Choctaws and Chickasaws who were making war upon them largely on account of their religion, were accompanied by another old chief who is described as an ancient patriarch but whose name is not preserved. At this meeting he arose last and said:

The last words which our fathers have spoken to us when they were on the point of yielding up their last breath were to be always attached to the prayer and that there is no other way of being happy in this life and much less in the next, which is after death.[10]

THE FRENCH GOVERNORS

Though the records are meagre, yet they furnish an indication of the highest civilization attained by the Indians in their free state.

---

[8] Thwaite, *Jesuit Relations*, LXVII, p. 341.
[9] *Ibid.*
[10] *Ibid.*

While the French company that secured proprietary rights in the Illinois country did not attain any very great results, some of the men who came to govern the territory were men of ability. The first Governor, Pierre Dugue de Boisbriant, was undoubtedly a man of capacity, and his administration of the affairs of the country, if not more able than that of the Jesuit Fathers, was at any rate most brilliant and introduced the period of gayety and romance.

Amongst his successors worthy of special mention were D'Arta-St. Clair Makarty and St. Ange.[11]

The mention of D'Artaguette calls to mind one of the most moving incidents connected with the early history of Illinois. As before noted, the Choctow and Chickasaw Indians in 1735 and 1736 were committing depredations upon civilized Illinois tribes and French settlements to such an extent that it became necessary to organize a campaign against them, and it was arranged that Bienville would march with a force from New Orleans, D'Artaguette with another from Kaskaskia or Fort Cartres and Francis Morgan, known as Vincennes, with another from the post on the Wabash which later became the town and city of Vincennes. But the rest of the story concerning the brilliant young Governor, Pierre D'Artaguette, his charming and romantic friend, Vincennes, who, according to the parish records at Kaskaskia was a frequent visitor at the old Church of the Immaculate Conception as witness in brilliant weddings and other social functions and of the intrepid Jesuit, Father Antoine Senat, is best told in the words of Monette in his History of the Mississippi Valley:

D'Artaguette, the pride and flower of Canada, had convened the tribes of the Illinois at Fort Chartres; he had unfolded to them the plans and designs of the great French captain against the Chickasaws, and invoked their friendly aid. At his summons, the friendly chiefs, the tawny envoys of the North, with "Chicago" at their head, had descended the Mississippi to New Orleans, and there had presented the pipe of peace and friendship to the governor. 'This', said Chicago to M. Perrier, as he concluded an alliance offensive and defensive, 'this is the pipe of peace or war. You have but to speak, and our braves will strike the nations that are your foes'. They had made haste to return, and had punctually convened their braves under D'Artaguette. Chicago was the Illinois chief from the shore of Lake Michigan, whose monument was reared, a century afterwards, upon the site of the village, and whose name is perpetuated in the most flourishing city of Illinois.

In due time, D'Artaguette and his lieutenant, the gallant Vincennes, from the Wabash, with their respective forces and Indian allies, had descended the Mississippi to the last Chickasaw bluff, and, agreeably to his orders, had pene-

---

[11] The most satisfactory connected account of the French governors will be found in Alvord's, *The Illinois Country*, Vol. I, Centenial History of Illinois.

trated the Chickasaw country, and, on the evening before the appointed 10th of May, had encamped among the sources of Yalobusha, probably not six miles east of the present town of Pontotoc, near the appointed place of rendezvous, and not more than thirty miles from the point of Bienville's debarkation. Here, ready for co-operation with the commander-in-chief, D'Artaguette and his brave troops were prepared to maintain the arms and the honor of France.

With his lieutenant Vincennes, the youthful Voison, and his spiritual guide and friend, the Jesuit Senat, D'Artaguette sought in vain for intelligence of his commander. But he maintained his post, and from the 9th until the 20th of May he encamped in sight of the enemy, until his Indian auxiliaries, becoming impatient for war and plunder, refused all further restraint. D'Artaguette then consented to lead then to the attack. His plans were wisely devised and vigorously executed; but, unsupported by the main army, what could he effect against a powerful enemy?

The attack was made with great fury against a fortified village; the Chickasaws were driven from their town and the fort which defended it; at the second town, the intrepid youth was equally successful. A third fort was attacked, and, in the moment of victory, he received a severe wound, and soon after another, by which he fell disabled. He distinguished himself, as he had done before in the Natchez War, by acts of great valor and deeds of noble daring. 'The red men of Illinois, dismayed at the check, fled precipitately. Voisin, a lad but sixteen years old, conducted the retreat, having the enemy at his heels for five-and-twenty leagues, and marching forty-five leagues without food, while his men carried with them such of the wounded as could bear the fatigue.' But the unhappy D'Artaguette was left weltering in his blood, and around him lay others of his bravest troops. The Jesuit Senat might have fled; but he remained to receive the last sigh of the wounded, regardless of danger, and mindful only of duty. 'Vincennes, too, the Canadian, refused to fly, and shared the captivity of his gallant leader'.

D'Artaguette and his valiant companions who fell into the hands of the Chickasaws were treated with great kindness and attention; their wounds dressed by the Indians, who watched over them with fraternal tenderness, and they were received into the cabins of the victors in hopes of a great ransom from Bienville, who was known to be advancing by way of the Tombigby with a powerful army. But the same day brought the intelligence of the advance and the discomfiture of the commander-in-chief. His retreat and final departure soon followed, and the Chickasaws, elated with the success, and despairing of the expected ransom, resolved to sacrifice the victims to savage triumph and revenge. The prisoners were taken to a neighboring field, and while one was left to relate their fate to their countrymen, the young and intrepid D'Artaguette, and the heroic Vincennes, whose name is borne by the oldest town in Indiana, and will be perpetuated as long as the Wabash shall flow by the dwellings of civilized men, and the faithful Senat, true to his mission, were, with their companions, each tied to a stake. Here they were tortured before slow and intermitting fires, until death mercifully released them from their protracted torments.[13]

[13] PP. 268-288.

As before indicated, D'Artaguette was succeeded by other governors, amongst whom Makarty and St. Ange were especially distinguished. Makarty was the great fort builder, the logical successor of La Salle who erected the new Fort Chartres, the strongest fortification on the western continent at the time, remains of which may still be viewed on the Mississippi twelve miles North of the island of Kaskaskia. He also built a fortification at the State Park now known as Fort Massac, in his day known as Fort Ascension, near the present city of Cairo.

St. Ange was the last and perhaps the noblest of the French governors and one of the most pleasing characters of the French regime.

PIERRE GIBAULT

In the year 1768 a towering figure arose in Illinois in the person of the just ordained French secular priest Pierre Gibault.

The population now was greatly different in character from that which Father Marest found. The majority of the inhabitants in the immediate vicinity of the settled parts at least were white, the Indians constituting a constantly diminishing element, and the problems which confronted Father Gibault were of a vastly different nature, if not more difficult.

Despite all these adverse conditions, however, the young priest seems immediately to have by common consent become the leading and foremost resident of the whole territory then known as the Illinois Country.

The good old Jesuit, Father Sebastian Louis Meurin, the last of that illustrious band of missionaries that tamed the Illinois wilderness and who, upon his own entreaties and those of the residents of Illinois, was permitted by the lawless coterie that ravished the Illinois Missions to remain, was located at Kaskaskia when Father Gibault came. In consideration of the necessity for a younger and more active man at that point, it was agreed between the two priests that Father Gibault should make Kaskaskia his headquarters, and that Father Meurin should go to Cahokia where the priests of the foreign missions had been located prior to their departure.

The ten years of unremitting toil and sacrifice on the part of Father Gibault had by 1778 made him beloved of every one with whom he came in contact. The fortunes of international warfare had wrested the territory from the French and vested it in the English but a few years before Father Gibault's advent, thus introducing

another element of difficulty; but the priest, the diplomat, the able administrator was able to cope with each problem as it arose, and when the Revolutionary War broke out and the contest was between Great Britain and America, there was never any doubt upon which side this leader of the people in Illinois stood. If there ever had been such doubt, his position was made evident on the Fourth of July, 1778, when he made possible George Rogers Clark's peaceable conquest of the Illinois country, and delivered this territory from the domination of Great Britain.

It is entirely permissible to give to many others much credit for the gaining of the Illinois country to the American cause, but there can no longer be any question that the dominant figure in the actual transfer of allegiance from British domination to American sovereignty was the work of Father Gibault. In justice it ought to be conceded that he was the most commanding personage connected with the conquest of the Northwest. Up to his time, there was no man of as great intelligence, of broader education, of more powerful address and indeed of more deserving popularity than Father Gibault. Not in religious matters alone, but in everything that pertained to the progress of the country; Clark was an intellectual child as compared with him. There were a number of Frenchmen and some Englishmen of considerable ability in the district during his time, but nobody that was at all within reach of his ability and capacity, and he was a patriot *par excellence*.

POLLOCK, VIGO, THE MURRAYS AND KENNEDY

Associated directly with Father Gibault in these stirring times was a man of Italian nativity and to that time of Spanish adoption named Francois Vigo and three Irishmen—Daniel and William Murray and Patrick Kennedy. And embarked in the same cause, though located at New Orleans, an Irishman named Oliver Pollock, all of whom rank deservedly as great benefactors of Illinois and are entitled to be classed as statesmen.

After the Illinois settlements were secured to Clark, Father Gibault volunteered to go to Vincennes and secure the allegiance of the French located there. His proffer was gratefully accepted by Georg Rogers Clark, and upon the successful culmination of his mission he was highly complimented by the Virginia Assembly and the Governor of Virginia, Patrick Henry.

Within a short time, however, Lieutenant-Governor Hamilton, the Commanding General of the British forces, attacked Vincennes

and regained possession. It is here that we first become acquainted
with Colonel Vigo. Pursuing his trade as a merchant he went to Vincennes and was arrested as a suspect by Lieutenant Governor Hamilton and held a prisoner. Learning of this incident, Father Gibault,
who was again in Vincennes in the discharge of his spiritual duties,
went at the head of his congregation after Mass and demanded Vigo's
release under penalty of the denial of any further supplies for the
troops. Hamilton released Vigo, who, at the instance of Father
Gibault, at once repaired to George Rogers Clark at Kaskaskia, gave
him complete information of conditions at Vincennes and tendered
his assistance. On account of the information thus obtained, Clark
was able with the assistance of two companies raised in the Illinois
settlements to regain Vincennes, thus subjecting the whole of the
Illinois and the Wabash country to the American cause.[13]

The gaining of the territory was not the most serious problem
for George Rogers Clark. The financing of the enterprise was the
most difficult, and it was here that Father Gibault, Francis Vigo
and Oliver Pollock demonstrated their loyalty clearly. Father Gibault,
of course, had but little means, but what little he had, including his
personal belongings and even his servants he sacrificed to the new
government, altogether advancing the sum of 7,500 French livres.
Francis Vigo in one way and another advanced more than $20,000
and suffered a total loss of $12,000 besides the incalculable cost and
annoyance from insistent creditors whose accounts for furnishing
supplies to the government he had guaranteed. Oliver Pollock as
agent for Virginia and the Federal Government, raised for the Clark
Campaign, over $80,000, sacrificing his entire personal fortune and
being cast into prison by reason of his inability to make good engagements which he had made for the American government by
authority of the American and Virginia Councils of Defense. It does
not appear how much money the Murray's and Patrick Kennedy
lost in the transaction, but it does appear that the Murray's fed
the troops and assisted in the recruiting and that Patrick Kennedy
at once became the Quartermaster of the army and was for some
years burdened with supplying the troops.[14]

In the midst of these trying times, but a few months after the
famous Fourth of July, 1778, when Kaskaskia re-enacted the Declara-

---

[13] For a detailed account of these activities see ILLINOIS CATHOLIC HISTORICAL
REVIEW, for October, 1918 and January 1919.

[14] Ibid.

tion of Independence, a pleasant little incident occurred in the Church of the Immaculate Conception, the same mission and church founded by Father Marquette and now under the guidance of Father Gibault. It appears from the entry on the parish records that on the 29th day of November, 1778, Heleine Murray was baptized, the daughter of Daniel Murray and Sarah Gerrault Murray, his wife, and that amongst the signatories of the record were Daniel Murray, the father, Sarah Gerrault Murray, the mother, Colonel George Rogers Clark, Commandant-in-Chief of the forces of Virginia in the Illinois country and other distinguished men of the locality.[15]

What was the reward of these distinguished patriots and statesmen? Father Gibault, the most distinguished of the group, was disowned by the Canadian Bishop who espoused the British cause. He was looked upon with suspicion by Prefect Apostolic Carroll, later Bishop and Archbishop, on account of slanders spread by British enemies against him, of the falsity of which Bishop Carroll was not apprized. He was never repaid a farthing of the money advanced by him; was deprived of his spiritual charge, compelled to leave his adopted country and go into the Spanish dominion where he dragged out an existence of poverty and died in obscurity. So completely effaced was he in his later years that no man knows his grave. A distinguished non-Catholic writer, William H. English in his Conquest of the Northwest says:

There was no reason, however, why his great services should not have been properly recognized, but they never were. As far as the author is advised, no county, town or post office bears his name; no monument has been erected to his memory, and no headstone marks his grave, as its location is entirely unknown. It is well for him that he could turn to the religion of which he had been so faithful a servant and find consolation in the trust that there was a heaven where meritorious deeds, such as his, find reward since they were so poorly appreciated and requited on earth.[16]

Colonel Vigo spent many years thereafter in the service of his country, was the trusted advisor of General (Mad Antony) Wayne and of General, afterwards President, William Henry Harrison, but was so harassed and burdened by his creditors on account of the advances and guarantees he had made for the benefit of the Government, that he was ruined and bankrupted and died in abject poverty when the Government owed him many thousands of dollars. So impoverished was he that his funeral expenses remained unpaid

---

[15] Kaskaskia *Parish Records* in the Archives of the St. Louis University.
[16] PP. 189-90. See also Thompson, *Penalties of Patriotism*.

for forty years and until heirs secured a judgment against the United States Government for the payment of $40,000 the principal and interest of the debt due Francis Vigo.[17]

As for Oliver Pollock after having at the instance of the United States and the State of Virginia obligated himself to the Spanish authorities for large loans with which to finance the American cause he was on default of repayment cast into a Spanish prison.

MADAM LE COMPT

The next statesman to which it is desired to direct attention was a woman—a cosmopolitan character, a traveler and resident of several of the chief settlements of the early days—known as Madam La Compt, born of French parents of the name of La Flamme at St. Joseph on Lake Michigan in 1734. From there she went to Mackinack where she lived for some time, but later and about 1756 she was a resident of this immediate neighborhood nearly fifty years before Chicago was founded. Later she removed to Cahokia where she remained until death. Governor John Reynolds knew Madame La Compt for thirty years and has left us a comprehensive description of her. In his Pioneer History of Illinois Governor Reynolds says:

This female pioneer possessed a strong mind, with the courage and energies of a heroine. She was also blessed with an extraordinary constitution. She was scarcely ever sick, although exposed often in traveling and otherwise to the inclemency of the weather and other hardships.

The Indians were her neighbors and friends from her infancy to nearly her death. By a wise and proper course with these wild men, and by sage councils to promote their interests, she acquired a great influence over the Pottawatomies, Kickapoos and other nations bordering on the lakes.

She was familiar not only with the language of the Indians, but also with their character. In the early American settlements of the country, from 1781 down to the peace in 1795, this lady prevented many an Indian attack on the white population. The Indians often became hostile to the French during the American Revolution, by the intrigues of the British, as the French had joined Clark in the capture of the British garrisons in the West.

On many occasions this lady was awakened in the dead hours of the night by her Indian friends, from the hostile warriors, informing her of the intended attacks, that she might leave Cahokia. Her friends among the Indians could not think of permitting her to be killed. She has started often to meet some hundreds of warriors who were camped near the Quentine Mound, at the foot of the bluff near the present French Village, or at some other place in the neighborhood. She would cause herself to be conveyed near the Indian camp, perhaps, in the night, and then dismiss her company and proceed on foot to the camp of the

---

[17] *Ibid.*

U. S. Senator Elias Kent Kane
"Father of the Constitution"

Stephen A. Douglas
The "Little Giant," Leading Statesman
of his day.

Maj. General James Shields
Hero of two wars and United States
Senator from three states.

Governor William H. Bissell
First Republican Governor of Illinois.
Mexican and Civil War Hero.

Indians. No one knew the Indian character better than she did. A female on foot approaching several hundred armed warriors would produce a sympathy that she followed up with wise councils to the Indians that were irresistible. She often remained with them for days and nights, appeasing their anger. She never failed to avert the storm and prevent bloodshed. The inhabitants of the village were often waiting with ttheir arms in their hands, ready for defence, when they would see this extraordinary woman escorting to the village a great band of warriors, changed from war to peace. The Indians were painted black, indicating the sorrow they entertained for their hostile movements against their friends. The Indians were feasted for days in the village. They would remain in peace for some time after these reconciliations.[18]

I submit that Madame La Compt displayed many of the highest qualities of statesmanship.

In her long career she was the dutiful wife of four husbands, all of whom according to all records were men of parts and were aided by her.

Her last husband and by no means the least apparently, was an Irishman named Thomas Brady, who himself exhibited many statesmanlike qualities. He was the hero of an attack on Fort St. Joseph which he captured with a large amount of supplies during the Revolutionary War. Being later taken prisoner, he managed to elude his jailer, escaped and returned to Cahokia where he became the first sheriff of St. Clair County, then the highest office within the gift of the people, was later Judge and Indian Commissioner and appears in the land records as owner of a large part of the site upon which East St. Louis is built.

UNITED STATES SENATOR ELIAS KENT KANE

We are now approaching the more modern period and the time when non-Catholic influences were becoming stronger, yet it is gratifying to know that at no period in our history and in no important juncture have we been without distinguished Catholics who would rank as statesmen. In the twenty-five or thirty years succeeding the Revolutionary War there was a great influx of settlers who of course differed widely from what might be called the native French, and public affairs came largely into the hands of these newcomers. Amongst them were many able men, but no man of his time excelled in merit the young Elias Kent Kane who arrived here shortly after the year 1800. He was a brilliant young lawyer from the East, a graduate of Yale and had crossed intellectual swords in the legal

18 PP. 168-9.

arena with Webster, Clay and Calhoun; early held a commission from the President of the United States as Judge of the Territorial Court and at once became a leading lawyer and citizen. Judge Sydney Breese the nestor of the Illinois Bench and Bar studied law in his office. During the territorial period he was the most prominent man and leader in the Territory, and when the Constitutional Convention of 1818 was called, he at once became the dominating figure. Judge Breese.has stated that the Constitution was written in Kane's office before the Convention met. However, every clause of our organic law was thoroughly considered in the Convention, and Elias Kent Kane is shown by the records to have been the most influential man amongst all the delegates. He has been called the Father of the Constitution, and is conceded to have had more to do with its framing and adoption than any other man.[19]

When the State government was formed, his friend and protege Shadrack Bond became Governor and he himself became the first Secretary of State and is conceded to have launched the State government. He was afterwards elected Senator and died while serving his second term at the age of twenty-eight.

Elias Kent Kane was undoubtedly one of the most brilliant figures that ever arose in Illinois.[20]

Here and there some interesting side lights have been thrown upon his career which in the main has remained obscure for all these years. When a son was born to him during the time that he was United States Senator, the great Lazarist Bishop Joseph Rosati of St. Louis came to Kaskaskia for the baptismal ceremony an extended record of which appears on the old parish records.

When Father Stephen Theodore Baden, the noted Sulpitian apostle of Kentucky and Indiana, the first priest ordained in the United States, was seeking a grant from the Indians of the ground upon which Notre Dame University now stands, the favorable and powerful interest of Senator Kane was enlisted.

By mere chance reference we learn that his charming widow and beautiful daughters were for many years the leading and most admired people of Kaskaskia. Elizabeth, the younger daughter is described as "an almost ethereal beauty" and it was this charming

---

[19] Buck, *Illinois in 1818*, Introductory Volume, Centennial History of Illinois, p. 166.
[20] For good sketch of Senator Kane see paper by Henry Barrett Chamberlin in Transactions of the Illinois State Historical Society, 1908, pp. 162-170.

girl that became the wife of William H. Bissell and had the happiness to see him received into the Church several years before his death.[21]

PIERRE MENARD

Amongst the very early population during the period when we gained the honors and benefits of statehood, Pierre Menard, a distinguished Frenchman possessed the universal public confidence. He was the chief representative of the Illinois division of the Indiana territory in the Indiana Territorial Legislature. The Constitution of Illinois of 1818 was modified expressly with the view to qualifying him for the office of Lieutenant-Governor to which office he was immediately elected upon the adoption of the Constitution. Pierre Menard was a composite of the Frenchmen of Illinois, a splendid example of the French-American; and, not perhaps because he towered above all his contemporaries, but because he was a most worthy representative of a large contingent of the population, and at the same time a true American citizen who displayed in a remarkable degree a helpful public spirit, he is entitled to have his name inscribed with the greatest men of Illinois.

Pierre Menard was a man of wealth, but recognized the doctrine of trusteeship of gifts bestowed upon him and used his wealth accordingly. Judge Caton, perhaps the foremost man of his day in Illinois said: "Pierre Menard was the best man I ever knew." He was universally and justly known as a devout Catholic.[22]

MAJOR.-GEN. JAMES SHIELDS

At one period the State of Illinois through its legislature, declared James Shields its most distinguished citizen by making him the subject of the statue to be placed in Statuary Hall in Washington. He has not been otherwise commemorated through any monument or tablet publicly erected in the State, however. That he deserved well at the hands of his contemporaries and of posterity, cannot be questioned. Among all the distinguished men of Illinois none was his superior intellectually. None lead a cleaner life. None served his country with greater distinction either in peace or war. None presented a better model of the ideal public man, the ideal neighbor,

---

[21] *Memoirs of Gustave Koerner*, pp. 333-4.

[2] For much of interest respecting Pierre Menard see Mason, *Pierre Menard and Pierre Menard papers*, in Early Chicago and Illinois, Volume IV, Chicago Historical Society Collection, pp. 142-180.

the ideal husband and father. He was accorded public distinctions unique in the history of these United States, when he was chosen United States Senator successively by the states of Illinois, Minnesota and California.

Several men served in both the Mexican and the Civil War, but no officer served with greater distinction in both these wars than did General James Shields. If there is a single blot upon his escutcheon, nobody as yet has revealed it. Through life and since his death, there has been but the best report of his career. There is every reason to believe that had James Shields been called upon to serve in any capacity that any other great man served his country, he would have discharged the obligations of such service fully as well as any of the others did. To omit James Shields from the list of most distinguished men in Illinois would be as grave an error as to omit Stephen A. Douglas, Ulysses S. Grant, John A. Logan or Abraham Lincoln.[23]

STEPHEN A. DOUGLAS AND WILLIAM H. BISSELL

Through many years of their public careers, Stephen A. Douglas and Abraham Lincoln were each the counterpoise of the other. They were the leaders of the opposing schools of opinion in their day, and the contestants for the chief distinctions available to American citizens. Generally speaking, Abraham Lincoln won, but at this distance the loss suffered by Douglas has not dimmed the glory of his career. He was great in life, and his memory has grown greater as the generations have progressed.

The lives of the men of whom we are now speaking are of intense interest in every detail, and their more public acts are so well known as to need no repetition, but there are a number of side lights that have been cast upon their records, revealing characteristics and circumstances that lend an additional interest and show cause for increased admiration. In the life of Douglas for example, the circumstance of religious prejudice in his day caused some interesting incidents. During the 50's the "Know Nothing" party came into existence and undertook to exert an influence in politics. Generally speaking, persons who took an interest in Anti-Catholic agitation or propaganda were not Democrats. There were too many Catholics in

---

[23] William H. Condon in his life time rendered his fellow men a distinct service when he wrote and published his *Life of Major General James Shields*, to which the reader is referred for many interesting details of this distinguished American Irishman's career.

the Democratic Party for such sentiments to thrive very well there, and so the "Know Nothing" movement was not only Anti-Catholic, but in its results, Anti-Democratic. Douglas being the leader of his party, was called upon more or less to deal with the "Know Nothing" movement, and it has been said that he had some connection with a wing or branch of the "Know Nothings" the members of which were favorable to the Missouri Compromise style of slavery legislation, or in other words, against the Kansas-Nebraska plan. Statements have also been made that his connection with this organization was for the purpose of check-mating or keeping "tab" on the "Know Nothings" learning their secrets and counteracting their efforts. At any rate Douglas was made fully acquainted with the ends and aims of the "Know Nothings" and no doubt heard all and the worst that they had to say about Catholics and about the Catholic Church, and in the oversight he had of the selection of candidates for state offices, he became acquainted with its secret workings.

In 1852 David L. Gregg and Joel A. Matteson were candidates for the Democratic nomination for Governor, and though as above stated, the "Know Nothings" were usually anti-Democratic, nevertheless, Matteson won the nomination, and his victory was at the time attributed to the fact that Gregg was a Catholic. In 1854 Buckner S. Morris became the candidate of the "Know Nothings" for Governor, and was opposed by William H. Bissell who was elected.

Here then were several distinguished men who were closely connected with the "Know Nothing" movement and whose political destinies were more or less effected by it. It is most interesting to reflect that Buckner S. Morris, the chosen candidate for Governor of the "Know Nothing" organization, william H. Bissell the man who was elected Governor as one of the opponents of Buckner and Stephen A. Douglas the Democratic party leader so gravely disturbed in his leadership by the "Know Nothing" movement, all, during their lives embraced the Catholic Church. It would perhaps be going too far to say that what they learned of the Church, perhaps from its opponents, possibly from its friends, during this time, caused them to adhere to it. It is undoubtedly true at any rate that they were all men of the very highest order of intelligence, which is some evidence in contradiction of the frequently repeated charges of ignorance against members of the Catholic Church.[24]

_____

[24] For a very interesting paper on the Know-Nothings, see *The Know-*

AS TO ABRAHAM LINCOLN

Almost every incident of Abraham Lincoln's life is very familiar, by reason of his great popularity, but there are some circumstances in reference to his knowledge of Catholicity that undoubtedly had an influence upon his whole life which are not so well known.

Occasionally an item is seen in some of the anti-Catholic publications to the effect that Lincoln expressed this or that unfavorable opinion of Catholics or of the Catholic Church. It is sufficient here to say that every such statement has been run down and proven false.

On the other hand, reports have gotten into circulation of Lincoln's more or less close connection with the Church, and some years ago Archbishop Ireland of St. Paul communicated to the *American Catholic Historical Researches* the following statement:

I happen to be able to furnish a slight contribution to the discussion by repeating, beyond peril of mistake, what the old missionary, Father St. Cyr, was wont actually to say touching Catholicity in the Lincoln household. Father St. Cyr was a priest of the Diocese of St. Louis, from which in early days the scattered Catholics of Southern Illinois received ministerial attention. He was a remarkable man, intelligent to a very high degree, most zealous in work, most holy in life. I knew him when in his later years he was chaplain to the Sisters of St. Joseph, of Caronielet. He held in vivid recollection the story of the Church in olden times through Missouri and Illinois. It was a delight and a means of most valuable information to sit by and converse with him. In 1866 he spent a month visiting me in St. Paul. Here is his statement, as I then took it down in writing, regarding the Lincoln family: 'I visited several times the Lincolns in their home in Southern Illinois. The father and the stepmother of Abraham both were Catholics. How they had become Catholics I do not know. They were not well instructed in their religion; but they were strong and sincere in their profession of it. I said Mass repeatedly in their house. Abraham was not a Catholic; he never had been one, and he never led me to believe that he would become one. At the time, Abraham was twenty years old or thereabouts, a thin, tall young fellow, kind and good natured. He used to assist me in preparing the altar for Mass. Once he made me a present of a half dozen chairs. He had made those chairs with his own hands, expressly for me; they were simple in form and fashion as chairs used in country places then would be.'[725]

Even before Lincoln came to Illinois he was surrounded by Catholic influence. The little education he did receive was given by an

Nothing Movement in Illinois by John P. Senning, in Journal of the Illinois Historical Society, V. 7, No. 1, p. 7, et seq.

[725] See paper by Rev. Gilbert J. Garraghan, S. J., in ILLINOIS CATHOLIC HISTORICAL REVIEW, Vol. 1, p. 162.

Irish schoolmaster named Sweeney and another Catholic teacher named Zacariah Riney. A history of Lincoln written in 1860 says that:

> Riney was probably in some way connected with the Trappists who came to Kentucky in the autumn of 1805 and founded an establishment under Urban Guillet as superior at Pottinger's Creek. They were active in promoting education especially among the poorer classes and had a school for boys under their immediate supervision.[24]

It is worthy of note that the Trappists under this same Father Urban Guillet re-established themselves at the Cahokia Mound a few miles from East St. Louis in 1810.

In after years when speaking of Riney, Lincoln loved to dwell on his many pecularities, but always bore witness to the fact that that though the schoolmaster was an ardent Catholic himself, he never made any proselyting efforts among his pupils most of whom belonged to a different faith. When any religious exercises or teachings were in progress, Protestant children were always permitted to leave the room.

Lincoln's breadth of character was perhaps better illustrated in what he said about and did for the Sisters of Charity than otherwise. During the Civil War the sufferings of which called out the strongest sympathies of his great heart, he visited the wounded in the hospitals and speaking of one of these visits he said:

> Of all the forms of charity and benevolence seen in the crowded wards of the hospitals, those of some Catholic sisters were among the most efficient. I never knew whence they came or what was the name of their order. More lovely than anything I have ever seen in art, so long devoted to illustrations of love, mercy, and charity, are the pictures that remain of those modest sisters going on their errands of mercy among the suffering and dying. Gentle and womanly, yet with the courage of soldiers leading a forlorn hope, to sustain them in contact with such horrors. As they went from cot to cot, distributing the medicines prescribed or administering the cooling, strengthening draughts as directed, they were veritable angels of mercy. Their words were suited to every sufferer. One they incited and encouraged, another they calmed and soothed. With every soldier they conversed about his home, his wife, his children, all the loved ones he was soon to see again if he was obedient and patient. How many times have I seen them exorcise pain by their presence or their words. How often has the forehead of the soldier grown cool as one of these sisters bathed it! How often has he been refreshed, encouraged, and assisted along the road to convalescence,

---

[24] See as to the Trappist foundation, Rev. John Rothensteiner in ILLINOIS CATHOLIC HISTORICAL REVIEW, Vol. II, p. 269.

when he would otherwise have fallen by the way, by the home memories with which these unpaid nurses filled his heart."

A single act of Lincoln's during the trying times of the War illustrates his confidence in the Sisters. It was the unlimited authorization to buy supplies evidenced by a letter which reads as follows:

On application of the Sisters of Mercy of Chicago of the Military Hospital in Washington furnish such provisions as they desire to purchase and charge the same to the department.[28]

(Signed)   ABRAHAM LINCOLN.

Naturally I refrain from speaking of living Catholic statesmen, and have thought it best not to mention more recent public men even though they be dead, but I would not wish to give the impression that we have had no great Catholic men or women in recent years. There were and are many others who of course can be more accurately valued later, but who nevertheless have merited our confidence and the preservation of their memory, and who, if still living, are entitled to our earnest support.

Nor does this paper purport to be exhaustive. There are many other names deserving of record on the pages of Illinois history as promoters of the best interests of their state or country. Only such are named here as shine out with special radiance.

JOSEPH J. THOMPSON.

Chicago.

---

[27] See Address of Hon. Ambrose Kennedy in House of Representatives. Monday, March 18, 1918.
[28] *Ibid.*

CHICAGOU
Great Catholic Indian Chief, leader of
the natives.

REV. PIERRE GIBAULT
Patriot Priest, Revolutionary Leader.

COL. FRANCIS VIGO
Financial Sponsor of the American
Government in the Illinois Country.

PIERRE MENARD
Most conspicuous Territorial Leader and
First Lieutenant Governor of Illinois.

Illinois Catholic Historical Review

Journal of the Illinois Catholic Historical Society

617 Ashland Block, Chicago

EDITOR IN CHIEF

Joseph J. Thompson.........Chicago

ASSOCIATE EDITORS

Rev. Frederick Beuckman.......Belleville   Kate Meade ....Chicago
Rev. J. B. Culemans.............Moline   Rev. Francis J. Epstein..........Chicago
William Stetson Merrill .... Chicago

COMMENDATION OF MOST REVEREND ARCHBISHOP
GEORGE W. MUNDELEIN

This publication is one we can be proud of. It is gotten up in an attractive form and its contents are interesting and instructive. I have been complimented on it and have heard it praised in many quarters. * * * The Society should receive encouragement from every source, and all who possibly can should enroll in its membership. * * * I need not add that your work has not only my blessing, it has my encouragement. It has every aid I can give it.

EDITORIAL COMMENT

Don't Miss Anything. Every article appearing in the ILLINOIS CATHOLIC HISTORICAL REVIEW is prepared or selected because it has an especial bearing, and should have a special appeal to the people living in or near Illinois. The headings or introductory remarks cannot always be relied upon as a criterion for the contents of the article, but we undertake to say that no one who lives or has lived in this particular part of the world can read any article appearing in the REVIEW without finding something of especial interest.

For illustration of this point, attention is directed to the very attractive article of Rev. Laurence J. Kenny, S. J., of the St. Louis University, treating of "Some First Ladies of Illinois," meaning wives of certain Governors. Unless we are greatly mistaken everyone who has the opportunity will be not only deeply interested, but charmed by this article. Almost the same may be said of the present installment of Father Rothensteiner's most valuable articles. Since the earliest Jesuit Missionaries hardly another Priest has had such a wonderful missionary career as Father Samuel Mazzuchelli, of whom Father Rothensteiner writes.

And who is there in this part of the country that is not anxious for information about the visit of Lafayette to Illinois. That story has not before been so satisfactorily told as Mr. C. B. Galbreath, Secretary of the Ohio Archaeological and Historical Society, tells it in this number.

Those who have been following Father Barth's articles on the Franciscans will be pleased too with the current installment.

The book review columns may always be counted upon too to contain much

217

of interest. Here the names of the reviewers are not always given, but Miss Gertrude Corrigan, whose initials have appeared from time to time, has in this number sustained her reputation as a reviewer in her sketch of Miss Russell's timely work.

As for our own humble efforts, we claim for them only their informative quality. In all of them we deal with facts and personages that we think all Catholics ought to know, and if we are found guilty of occasional repetition, we may justify it as by way of emphasis.

The reader has three full months between issues of the REVIEW, and it is respectfully suggested that even though your time be closely occupied you endeavor to find time in that period to read every article.

The Illinois Centennial History Series Complete. The six volumes setting forth the history of Illinois, prepared under the direction of the Illinois Centennial Commission, are now all published, and the last volumes from the press are being distributed as directed by law.

These valuable books, with the exception of the first issue, viz., "Illinois in 1818," treat severally of different periods of our history. As to the volume named, it is introductory in character, and gives a general view of the condition of the state at the time it was admitted into the Union. Volume I, under the title "The Illinois Country" treats of the province and territory 1673-1818. Volume II "The Frontier State 1818-1848." Volume III "The Era of Transition 1848-1870. Volume IV "The Industrial State 1870-1893. Volume V "The Modern Commonwealth 1903-1918.

These several volumes were prepared by different authors, but all were under the supervision of Clarence Walworth Alvord, late Professor of History in the University of Illinois, and now with the Historical Department of Minnesota.

As these volumes have been issued, we have reviewed them in the columns of the ILLINOIS CATHOLIC HISTORICAL REVIEW, and have had occasion to express some criticism. Some of the volumes, while scholarly and able from a historical standpoint, nevertheless contained passages and references which, by omission or commission, did injustice to Catholics and things Catholic, and in some instances to representative racial strains in the state. In reference to each volume, however, we have fully recognized the merit of the work, and desire only to add, after a careful perusal of the entire series, that the Centennial History is a notable achievement.

Not in all the years that have sped since the planting of our American civilization, and in no state of the union we believe has such a satisfactory result with reference to the collection and publication of the historical record been achieved.

Volume I not alone because of the masterly grasp of history of its author, but as well by reason of the romance of the period of which it treats, will perhaps be conceded on all sides the best of the series, but every volume and almost every part of each volume is ably and brilliantly done, and the authors who wrote the books, the publishers who issued them in a most attractive form, and the Centennial Commission that supervised their production, are all entitled to the lasting gratitude of the people of Illinois, and indeed of posterity in general.

Guarantees Needed. In the absence of a specially trained and efficient force for the purpose of procuring members or subscribers, a serious periodical like the ILLINOIS CATHOLIC HISTORICAL REVIEW always comes upon anxious moments. The expenses incident to the conduct of such a work have an ugly habit of going right on regardless of how the income may halt.

The ILLINOIS CATHOLIC HISTORICAL REVIEW was launched at a most difficult time, and so far as a periodical of that character is concerned conditions have not materially changed or improved. We started when the war was at its height, and when one form of drive followed another, thus absorbing every inactive dollar; and the indications are so plain that drives have lost their power, that it has not seemed advisable for the ILLINOIS CATHOLIC HISTORICAL SOCIETY to inaugurate a money campaign.

As the promoters of the work view it, it ought not to be necessary to take such steps. If a small fraction of the Catholics of the Mississippi Valley, who are abundantly able to do so, would subscribe for the ILLINOIS CATHOLIC HISTORICAL REVIEW, we would never have any difficulty in meeting our expenses; and since a large subscription list cannot be obtained without personal solicitation, involving of course heavy expenditures, the organization is put to the necessity, either of setting up subscription machinery, or of finding some other means.

We have on occasion suggested different means by which the permanence of this work could be assured, some of the suggestions involving rather large individual contributions. To such suggestions there have been some generous responses, but not sufficiently general to meet the difficulty.

If even 1,000 men or women would obligate themselves to the payment of $10.00 a year, for a limited number of years, for the furtherance of the work we are doing, every item of our expenses would be assured.

With such a dependable income we would be enabled to provide for some personal solicitation for subscribers, and would be placed beyond the anxieties that tend to depreciate the quality of such works as we are engaged in.

Are there not amongst the more than one million adult Catholics of the Mississippi Valley at least 1,000 who are willing to give this work their approval, to the extent of $10.00 a year for at least a limited period?

BOOK REVIEWS

What's the Matter With Ireland? By Ruth Russell. Devin-Adair Co., New York.

This brilliant young writer has given a close-up picture of conditions in Ireland which no one interested in knowing the truth about the Irish question can afford to miss.

. The foreword by Eamon de Valera contains the lines, "I hope we shall have many more impartial investigators such as you, who will take the trouble to see things for themselves at first hand," and "You succeeded in understanding Irish conditions and grasped the Irish view-point."

. Miss Russell went to Ireland as a newspaper correspondent and while there to gain information for her paper, became as impressed with the situation that she has written a powerful book, in language simple and direct, and yet at times dramatic or poetic, as events transpired so far beyond the commonplace that they seemed to demand more than the usual calm and dispassionate statement of facts to which she confines herself for the most part. Indeed, the most valuable contribution the author makes to the cause is the mass of statistical information and the ready references, for proof of any assertion made. Most of these references are from British sources and thus furnish indubitable evidence of the fairness of the text.

Miss Russell donned the garb of the working girl so as to be in close touch with the class to which seven-eighths of the Irish people belong, and as a working girl, lived and struggled for employment. Thus as worker and as newspaper woman, she has been able to give the answer to the title of the book.

The first chapter of the book deals with the grim struggle with the poverty which is so speciously denied by British propaganda, one of the most painful features of which is the search for employment that so often ends in forced emigration to England, Scotland, or America, from this land which could well support its population in comfort at home under good administration. The accompanying diseases of semi-starvation are touched upon, each in turn, with data and figures to prove the statements to any doubters, and over the signatures of such names as the Countess of Aberdeen and Sir Charles Cameron, Health Officer for Dublin; it is a story which includes a lowering of the birth rate, insanity, tuberculosis, unemployment, unsanitary housing, neglect of education, child labor, and all

220

the evils of hopeless and widespread poverty except crime. The extraordinary freedom from vices and crimes which are the usual accompaniments of such frightful conditions elsewhere is the most convincing evidence of the worthiness of this oppressed people to have self-determination according to the writer's opinion.

A chapter of great interest to American readers on Sinn Fein and the Revolution includes an account of the reception to Governor Dunne, Frank Walsh and Michael Ryan, at the Mansion House, Dublin. Here in all its sinister ugliness, the monster bogie of the British army of occupation, the Mailed Fist, is portrayed against the shining background of the heroism of a people ready to make the supreme sacrifice for their vision of freedom.

As in all the countries of the world at the present day, so in Ireland, the unsettled question of labor is adding its bit to the problems confronting the New Republic as it is trying to function. Miss Russell places before the reader in a clear and interesting manner outlines of the different plans that are presented by various parties as solutions of the questions that are raised between classes.

George Russell's Co-operative Commonwealth has a whole chapter devoted to its splendid history, a story which is worth an entire book in itself; there is the Worker's Republic with its counter current of agrarian interests; there is the idea of Communism which was successfully worked out under the Church as far back as the fifth century. Reverend Michael Fogarty of Killaloe is quoted as saying that the reason England has found it difficult to rule Ireland, was that she had attempted to force a feudal government on a socialistic people.

Sinn Fein is trying to harmonize all the factions so as to conserve all the constructive forces of the land toward the first great goal, the right to self-determination. Sinn Fein with its parliament duly elected by a large majority is in a position to take this stand in regard to all parties.

The closing chapter of the book deals with the situation in Ulster and should be illuminating to those who are reading the British reports on Carsonism.

What is the Matter With Ireland? is a book that will repay the reader to read more than once, for every page deals with the largest movements and the last word on the difficulties of the unhappy country. On sale in best book shops, $1.75.

G. C.

Franciscans and the Protestant Revolution in England. By FRANCIS BORGIA STECK, O. F. M. Published by Franciscan Herald Press, Chicago. Price, $2.00.

Until comparatively recent years it has been the custom for the credulous public to accept as true many of the gross misstatements given by Protestant writers as the causes of the religious revolt of the 16th Century. Among the reasons assigned for the rapid growth of Protestantism in Europe is "the inactivity and degeneracy of the so-called old Orders at the time when the conflict began."

This false accusation is ably refuted by Rev. F. B. Steck in his recently published work, *Franciscans and the Protestant Revolution in England* and here the reader will find a true record of the activity and courage of the Friars Minor during the troubled times of the Tudors in England.

The author gives an interesting account of the Franciscan foundations in the early part of the 13th Century, and then traces briefly the rapid growth of the Order until 1527 when the question of "the Divorce" became the all-absorbing topic of interest to Englishmen. Henry VIII, like all the Tudors, could brook no contradiction, and when the Franciscans opposed his imperious wishes, the expected result followed persecution and death for many members of the Order. The unfair trials are graphically described by Father Steck, and the reader cannot fail to recognize that these martyrs belonged to a body of men ready, nay glad, to give their lives for the truth.

Under the Stuarts, too, the Franciscans endured many sufferings, and the writer traces the fortunes of his brethren through later times when persecution took the form of laws against religious communities, until finally in 1841 the English Friars ceased to exist as a province.

From beginning to end the work is scholarly and will prove a valuable addition to every historical library.

THE DOUBLE JUBILEE—CORRECTIONS

The fallibility of hearsay evidence is well illustrated in the following observations and communications. Not possessing a trained repertorial force we were compelled to depend upon such agencies as seemed most reliable for details of the great double jubilee of June, 1920. In so doing we seem to have adopted some errors that did injustice to some of the participants. Needless to say we regret exceedingly that these errors occurred, and both on account of the injustice done and the earnest wish that our columns speak the truth —that history be kept straight—we are publishing the corrections:

CONCERNING THE CELEBRATION AT JOLIET

"The procession filed through the loop at eight-thirty o'clock," should read thus: "The procession filed through the loop at one-thirty o'clock in the afternoon."

In the next paragraph—the Louis Joliet statue is not in the courthouse yard, but before the Public Library, a distance of about three blocks from the courthouse.

At the bottom of the page the account records "St. Francis Academy float, instead of floats." The four boys who carried banners did not walk but rode ponies.

Page thirty-four, paragraph two should read: "The Guardian Angel Home one float," this is our Institution.

Paragraph seven on this page readds: "On the St. Mary's float, etc.," it should be: "On the St. Francis float was a tableau of Cardinal Gibbons blessing Columbia." Since this float received the first prize we ask you most kindly to make a correction of this error in particular.

St. Francis Academy had two units. The first unit contained two floats—one represented "The Pope commissioning the Franciscans to come to America;" the other, "Father Serra baptizing the Indians." The second unit represented Cardinal Gibbons blessing Columbia. The senior students of St. Francis Academy posed on this float.

In the parade was a pretty banner of His Grace, The Most Reverend Archbishop. This commemorated the twenty-fifth anniversary of His Grace's ordination. The banner was carried by one of the graduates. Four of the younger students carried the silver tassels which were suspended from the banner.

223

August 20, 1920
Joseph J. Thompson,
Editor-in-Chief,
Illinois Catholic Historical Review,
Chicago, Illinois.
Dear Sir:
    As Secretary of the Will-Grundy Counties Diamond Jubilee
Celebration Pageant Committee, I have been asked to call your
attention, to an incorrect statement in your account of the Joliet
celebration on June 12, which appears in your July issue. On page
34, you credit St. Mary's Academy with having in the Pageant the
float which represents Cardinal Gibbons blessing Columbia, whereas
it was St. Francis' Academy which put forth the float under that
idea. St. Mary's through unforeseen mishaps was unable to participate.
    The Guardian Angels' Home had only one float, representing the
two ideas you credit them with.
    On page 33 you start the pageant at eight o'clock, on page 36
your account starts it at two, the latter hour being the correct statement of fact.
    Outside of that, I may state frankly and sincerely that the Pageant
Committee is grateful to you for the splendid write-up, and in no
way wishes you to think that it attaches any blame to you. However,
we should be indeed grateful were it possible for you to make some
correction concerning the mistake about the float credited to St.
Mary's.
    With sentiments of highest personal regard for you and best wishes
for the continued success of your work, I remain,
                                     Sincerely yours,
                                         REV. J. P. MORRISON.

                            IN CHICAGO

                                         Chicago, Ill., Aug. 4, 1029.
Mr. Joseph J. Thompson,
    City.
Dear Sir:
    In looking over Vol. III of the ILLINOIS CATHOLIC HISTORICAL RE-
VIEW I find that on page 26, etc., you give a "complete list" of floats
that took part in the Diamond Jubilee Pageant. In this list our float,
"St. Benedict and His Order" is omitted on account of which it
looks as though the Benedictines had done nothing for this occasion.
The same holds good for the "Notable Jubilee Visitors" where the
three Benedictine Abbots were entirely overlooked.
    *Errare humanum est, sed perseverare in errore condemnandum
est.*
                                     Sincerely yours,
                                         REV. JUSTUS WIRTH, O. S. B.

ILLINOIS

OLIC HISTORICAL

REVIEW

JANUARY, 1921   Number 3

PUBLISHED BY

ILLINOIS CATHOLIC HISTORICAL SOCIETY

CHICAGO, ILL.

225

CONTENTS

LOYOLA UNIVERSITY PRESS

CHICAGO, ILLINOIS

Illinois
Catholic Historical Review

VOLUME III   JANUARY, 1921   NUMBER 3

THE FIRST CATHOLICS IN AND ABOUT CHICAGO

A REMARKABLE DOCUMENT

It is always a matter of interest to be able to determine who first visited or settled in an afterwards prosperous and progressive locality.

Although facts of this nature frequently go unnoticed and by the mutations of time are often lost, yet careful research by many investigators has enabled us to tell with quite a degree of certitude who first visited and dwelt within the borders of our great metropolitan city,—Chicago.

Leaving out of consideration the red men who, for perhaps many centuries prior to recorded history, roamed about the region, or from time to time fixed their habitation within its present confines, we can quite definitely state who were the first white visitors.

In this connection the investigations of historians leave no doubt that Rev. James Marquette, S. J., and Louis Jolliet, together with five Frenchmen, passed through the territory now known as Chicago in late August or early September of the year 1673, as they returned from their journey from what is now known as Mackinac to the Red River of Arkansas.[1]

We have no record to indicate that they stopped at Chicago, but the record is clear that on the 4th of December, 1675,[2] Father Marquette, accompanied by two Frenchmen, landed at the mouth of the Chicago River, then located where the present Madison Street, if pro-

---

[1] Marquette's report of his first trip and his journal of the second trip are the best authorities for these earliest days. Both are printed in Vol. 59 Thwaites *Jesuit Relations*. Also in Kellog *Early Narratives*.

[2] Marquette's Jouurnal, *op. cit.*

jected, would intersect the lake. It is quite definitely settled too that the trio remained at the mouth of the River from the 4th to the 11th of December;[3] that they then lifted their canoe to the ice of the Chicago River, and dragged it up the river to the junction of the branches and thence southwest up the southern branch to a point two leagues from the entrance,[4] which would bring them about where Robey Street intersects the present drainage channel.[5]

They lived there in a cabin which they erected from at least the 14th of December, 1674, to the 29th of March, 1675.[6]

These were then the first Catholics in Chicago, and the first white men ever known to have inhabited the present territory now within the boundaries of Chicago.

The next white dwellers of Chicago, of which we have a definite account, were Rev. Pierre François Pinet, S. J., and Rev. Julius Bineteau, S. J., who established the Mission of the Guardian Angel in 1696.[7] Between the visit of Father Marquette and the establishment of the Guardian Angel Mission Robert Cavalier Sieur de La Salle had no doubt passed through what is now Chicago, perhaps in 1679, 1680 or 1682. There is some dispute as to which route La Salle took on some of his journeys. There is no dispute, however, that the Mission of the Angel Guardian existed in this region. Various locations have been assigned to it, but there seems little reason for doubting that it was very near the mouth of the Chicago River. This Mission existed from 1696 to 1699.[8] For a short interval it was suppressed, but was re-established again.

Because no definite record has been discovered proving the contrary, it has been assumed by many writers that no white men lived in Chicago for the next century and a quarter or more. When the circumstances are considered, however, this is a most unreasonable assumption. Both missionaries and traders were passing from Canada to the interior of Illinois, and both the mouth of the river and what was known as the portage (the land passage between the Chicago

---

[3] *Ib.*

[4] *Ib.*

[5] The Crilly Lumber Company, at the instance of Mr. G. A. O'Shaughnessy, has planted a mahogany cross at the point, as nearly as can be ascertained, where Father Marquette's cabin was located.

[6] *Marquette's Journal, op. cit.*

[7] The best authority on this mission is a letter of Father Francis Buisson de Saint Cosme, a priest of the Seminary of Foreign Missions, who, with two other priests, came through Chicago in 1699. The letter is published in Shea's *Up and Down the Mississippi*, and also in Kellog's *Early Narratives*.

[8] See letter of Rev. James Gravier Thwaites *Jesuit Relations*, Vol. 65, p. 53.

River and the Calumet River) were good trading points, and it is more than probable that both missionaries and traders were located in what is now Chicago during the most of that period.

Whatever the facts in this regard may be, the earliest records we have show that in 1765 a woman named LaCompt, formerly named LaFlamme, who was born at St. Joseph, on Lake Michigan, and afterwards became a woman of considerable note, lived in Chicago.[9] Madame LaCompt was a devout Catholic, and became quite a figure in history as a resident of Cahokia.[10]

There is a tradition that has persisted of a trader by the name of Guarie, who lived on the north branch of the river in 1778.[11]

In 1790, a mulatto, Jean Baptiste Pointe de Saible, from San Domingo, lived on the north side of the main branch of the River, in what afterwards became better known as the John Kinzie House. De Saible was a colored man, and is described as a "well educated and handsome negro, very much in the French interest."[12] He cultivated the Pottowatomi Indians, and the baptismal records of St. Louis bear some indication that some of his family was Catholic. He remained in Chicago until 1796, when he removed to Peoria or St. Louis.

There is evidence that Antoine Ouilmette lived in the vicinity of Chicago,—possibly farther to the north at the time,—in 1790.[13] Ouilmette was a Frenchman, and a Catholic, and a signer of the first petition for a priest sent to Bishop Rosati at St. Louis in 1833.

When de Saible left the region he sold his cabin to Francis LeMai, a French Canadian trader, who remained here until after 1800.[14]

To these names of the very earliest Catholic settlers must be added that of Louis Pettel, who lived here at least prior to 1805.

Rev. Gilbert J. Garraghan has called attention to a church record which throws some light upon the earliest residents of Chicago:

"On October 7, 1799, a party of Chicago residents (habitans Chicagou) were in St. Louis enlisting the services of the acting pastor of the place, the Recollect Father Lusson for the baptism of their children. The party included Francis LeMay (Mai) and his wife, Marie Theresa, Roy and Jean Baptiste Peltier and the latter's wife, Susanne

---

[9] See Quaife, *Chicago and the Old Northwest*, p. 137.
[10] *Ib.*
[11] *Ib.* p. 138.
[12] *Ib.* p. 139.
[13] See letter in *fac simile* in *New World*, April 14, 1900.
[14] Quaife, *op. cit.*, 141.

Pointe de Saible. Joseph and Marie Theresa LeMay (Mai) and Eulalia Peltier were the names of the children baptized."[15]

We are without definite records concerning the faith of the residents of what is now Chicago for a few years running from 1800 to about 1813. There were several French families[16] and several Irish settlers or soldiers,[17] all of whom were perhaps Catholics, but there is no means of establishing what their religion was. It is known that at the time of the Fort Dearborn massacre, August 15, 1812, or at least the day after, Alexander Robinson, a half-breed Pottawatomi chief, came to Chicago, and that he was a Catholic.[18]

On the day after the massacre William Caldwell, another half-blood Indian chief, half Irish and half Indian, arrived, who was a Catholic, and either remained or came again later and remained.[19]

Jean Baptist Beaubien came in 1805 (?), 1814 (?), or 1817, and was the forerunner of the big family he represented, as well as of the French Canadian influx.[20]

PETITION FOR A PRIEST

From this time on the little settlement grew, and the accessions for some time were largely Catholic. The best record we have of these early Catholics is contained in a petition which was sent to Bishop Rosati in 1833, requesting that prelate that he send a priest to Chicago. On this petition is found the following names of heads of families and the number of persons connected with the family. The petition reads as follows:

PETITIONERS FOR FIRST PRIEST IN CHICAGO

To the Right Rev. Catholic Bishop of the Diocese of Missouri, of St. Louis, etc., etc.

"We, the Catholics of Chicago, Cook Co., Ill., lay before you the necessity there exists to have a pastor in this new and flourishing city. There are here sev-

---

[15] Garraghan, ILLINOIS CATHOLIC HISTORICAL REVIEW, Vol. I, p. 19.

[16] The Beaubiens, Pettel, LeMai, LaLime and LaFrambois.

[17] Matthew Irwin, U. S. factor, lived here in 1810 and was no doubt a Catholic. John Burns lived here before 1812. In the garrison at Fort Dearborn in 1812 were the Whistlers, Ensign George Rowan, Sergeant Otho Hays, Sergeant McPherson and John Hamilton, Privates James Corbin, Phelim Corbin, Dyson Dyer, Daniel Dougherty, John Furey, Samuel Kilpatrick, James Latta, Michael Lynch, Hugh Logan, Duncan McCarthy, John Simmons, Walter Jordan, John Smith, Sr., and John Smith, Jr.

[18] Garraghan, ILLINOIS CATHOLIC HISTORICAL REVIEW, Vol. I, p. 27.

[19] Ib.

[20] See Quaife, *Chicago and the Old Northwest*, p. 278.

eral families of French descent, born and brought up in the Roman Catholic faith, and others quite willing to aid us in supporting a pastor, who ought to be sent here before other sects obtain the upper hand, which very likely they will to do. We have heard several persons say were there a priest here they would join our religion in preference to any other. We count about one hundred Catholics in this town. We will not cease to pray until you have taken our important request in consideration.'"

The following names appear on the petition and the number of members of the family or persons represented was added after each name. The names are here given in alphabetical order:

Assgood, Dexter 1
Beaubien, Jean Baptiste 14
Beaubien, Mark 12
Bourassa, Leon 3
Broudeur, Jean Baptiste......................... 1
Caldwell, Billy 1
Caldwell, J. 1
Chassut, Jacques 5
Chevalier, Louis 3
Deplat, Bazile 1
Duvocher, Jean Baptiste......................... 1
Falevy, I. B...................................... 1
Francherez, Louis 1
Hogan, John Stephen Coates..................... 1
Hondorf, John 1
LaFramboise, Alexis 4
LaFramboise, Claude 4
LaFramboise, Joseph 7
LaFramboise, R. 4
Leclerc, Pierre 3
Mann, John....................................... 4
Miranda, Jean Baptiste 3
Monselle, Charles 1
Ouilmette, Antoine 10
Owen, Thomas Joseph Vincent 10
Perry, Nelson Peter.............................. 1
Pothier, Jean 5
Proulx, Jean Baptiste............................ 1
Rabbie, Jean Baptiste............................ 1
Robinson, Alexander 8

The foregoing petition was written by some individual then in Chicago, but by whom this writer would not hazard a guess, especially in view of the fact that he has not seen this particular document. A likely person to have written the petition was John Stephen Coates Hogan, who was then postmaster of Chicago, an alderman, or rather, a member of the town council, because the settlement had not yet been organized as a city, and was in 1830 elected a justice of the peace. He was too, during his entire residence here, prominently associated with the existing military organizations, and an active officer. It was said of him that he was the best educated man in Chicago during his residence here.[22]

It has been stated that a meeting was called at the hotel kept by Jean Baptiste Beaubien, which became known as the Sauganash, the popular Indian name given William, familiarly known as "Billy" Caldwell, and meaning Englishman, or, generally speaking, whiteman. Beaubien named his hotel, the first in Chicago, in honor of Billy Caldwell.[23] At this meeting it was agreed to ask Bishop Rosati to send a priest to Chicago, and someone wrote the foregoing petition, and in the same handwriting affixed the name and number of Catholics in the locality.[24]

This petition may, therefore, be regarded as containing the first official list of members of the Catholic Church of Chicago.

Immediately upon receipt of the petition Bishop Rosati assigned Rev. John Mary Irenaeus St. Cyr, whom he had ordained to the priesthood a few days before, to Chicago, and by the first of May of the same year (1833), Father St. Cyr had arrived in the town and cele-

---

[22] Kirkland, The Story of Chicago, p. 129.
[23] Andreas, History of Chicago, Vol. I, p. 106.
[24] Garraghan, ILLINOIS CATHOLIC HISTORICAL REVIEW, Vol. I, p. 147.

brated his first Mass in a little building belonging to Jean Baptiste Beaubien, on Sunday, May 5, 1833.[25]

Father St. Cyr soon began keeping a parish record, the entries upon which for some years, having escaped the great fire of 1871, have been preserved. These records help to identify the early Catholics, and will be further alluded to.[26]

PETITION TO RETAIN FATHER ST. CYR

The most important document concerning the establishment of the Church in modern Chicago has recently come to light, and the writer has been most fortunate in being able to inspect the original. It is another petition by the Catholics of Chicago begging Bishop Rosati to permit Father St. Cyr to remain. The new diocese of Vincennes had been created in 1834, and when the new Bishop, Right Rev. Simon William Gabriel Bruté assumed jurisdiction, Bishop Rosati wrote Father St. Cyr to return to St. Louis, as the Bishop of Vincennes was under the obligation of providing clergy for Chicago.

In the few years that had passed since Father St. Cyr established the Church (St. Mary's,—now the Paulist Church), the people had grown to like the sincere young French priest, and accordingly petitioned the Bishop that he might remain.

This remarkable document reads as follows:

TO THE RT. REV'D DOCT'R ROSATI—ST. LOUIS

The undersigned Roman Catholic inhabitants of the town of Chicago have heard with the deepest regret that you have recalled the Rev'd Mr. St. Cyr from this mission and as such an event would in their opinion be productive of injurious consequences to the cause of Catholic truth in this place they humbly beg leave to call your attention to the actual situation of our people in this mission and request that you will carefully consider all the circumstances previous to such removal.

They would in the first place inform your Grace that the Rev'd Mr. St. Cyr by his exemplary conduct great zeal in the cause of religion and incessant perseverance has endeared himself to every member of our congregation and is highly esteemed by the members of other denominations. And having acquired a sufficient knowledge of the English language to enable him to preach and instruct with fluency and elegance they conceive that his removal would be a subject of bereavement to the whole congregation.

---

[25] Ib.

[26] A future number of the ILLINOIS CATHOLIC HISTORICAL REVIEW will contain a study of these records, a copy of which was found amongst the effects of the late William J. Onahan.

That his associate the Rev'd Mr. Shaffer although equally distinguished for piety and zeal has but an imperfect knowledge of the English language and is consequently unfitted for discharging the spiritual duty of a pastor among an English population.

That as we have in this town two thousand and perhaps more Catholics as there are a large number of Catholic families in the adjacent country particularly on the line of the Chicago and Illinois Canal the great body of the laborers on which are Catholics to all of whom the clergy here must render spiritual assistance, the attention therefore of a clergyman speaking the English language will be indispensably necessary and they would humbly represent that nothing but the most imperious necessity should induce the removal of a man from such a vast field of labour who is so beloved and revered by his congregation.

That as our church is totally inadequate to contain the fourth part of the attending congregation we have taken the preliminary steps to erect a new chapel for accommodating our large and increasing society. The removal of the Rev'd Mr. St. Cyr will operate to retard and delay that work so much desired not only by Catholics but by various members of other denominations.

That as this is the most important place in this State as the population is so rapidly increasing that we can in a few years justly expect a Catholic population of several thousand. And as one clergyman cannot possibly discharge the duties annexed to it good policy as well as duty requires that we should have clergymen stationed here capable by their example of improving respect—by their talents of dissipating ignorance and prejudice and by their zeal and perseverance of building up in this new region the imperishable monuments of our holy religion.

We therefore humbly entreat Your Grace not to deprive us of a dearly beloved pastor at the commencement of his usefulness but to leave him where his zeal and virtue are so well appreciated and so likely to redound to the best interests of the Church.

This remarkable document was signed by the following:

SIGNATURES TO PETITION TO RETAIN FATHER ST. CYR

Ahearne, James	Butler, Peter	Cummins, Thomas E.
Allen, John	Cahill, John	Cunningham, Patrick
Allen, William	Canavan, Dennis	
	Canavan, Martin	Dalton, David
Barron, William	Carel, Thomas	Di Fortz, Emanuel
Bartly, James	Carpenter, Samuel	Dillon, John
Beaubien, Jean B.	Carroll, J. W.	Dimmen, Francis M.
Beaubien, M.	Cassidy, Thomas	Donovan, Michael
Beaubien, Mark, Sr.	Chaffe, Peter	Donovan, Simon
Beaubien, Mark, Jr.	Clark, Henry	Donovan, Simon, Jr.
Bolland, William	Clark, Lawrence	Dowd, James
Brannen, James	Connelly, Dennis	Doyle, Joe
Breen, Thomas A.	Cody, Thomas	Doyle, Sam O. C.
Brennan, Joseph	Conroy, James	Doyle, Thos.
Burke, Edmund	Conroy, William	Duffy, Hugh
Burk, Henry	Creamen, Daniel	Dunn, Charles
Burke, Michael	Cremin, Daniel	Dunn, John

Dwyer, James	Hurle, William	O'Donnell, John
Dwyer, James		
Dwyer, William	Kelliher, Edmund	Powers, Jefferry
	Kelly, John	Powers, Patrick
Early, Bryan	Keenan, John J.	
	Keenan, Patrick	Ranney, William S.
Falvey, Dennis	Killeen, Patrick	Rattol, H.
Farrell, Thomas		Rea, William
Fenton, Dennis	Lally, A. M.	Reid, Henry Herm
Fernel, Patrick	Levy, S.	Ring, Thomas
Filler, George L.	Ludlong, James	Rustre, Edmund
Flavin, John V.		Rogers, James
Floethary, James	Madigan, Mathew	Ryan, Edward
Forrester, Michael	Markey, Pretor	
Fox, Thomas	Manhal, Richard	Sautryn, I. H.
	McDonnell, Charles	Schrage, John
Gainor, Henry	McFail John	Scot, John
Geary, Dennis	McGrath, Daniel	Shill, Thos. A.
Gehen, Thomas	McGrath, James	Sullivan, John
Glynn, Michael	McGuire, John	Sullivan, Owen
Gorman, Patrick	McNamara, James	Struell, Edward
Grady, Patrick	McNamara, Patrick	
	Meagher, Michael	Talbot, James
Hainey, John	Molloney, James	Taylor, Augustin D.
Hanacy, Cornelius	Mooney, James	Taylor, Charles
Hanrahan, Thomas S.	Mun, Jeremiah	Taylor, Haran
Harney, Richard	Murphy, Edward	Taylor, Solomon
Higgins, John	Murphy, Patrick	Tobin, John P.
Higgins, Michael	Murphy, Richard	Tobin, Thomas
Higgins, Patrick		
Higgins, Timothy	O'Brien, James	Walsh, Patrick
Howe, Joseph	O'Brien, Patrick	Ward, Bernard
Hurley, John	O'Brien, James	Ward, Thos.
Hurley, John	O'Bryen, Michael	Watkins, Thos.
Hurly, Thomas	O'Connor, Timothy	White, Patrick

The following *facsimile* must prove most interesting:

JOSEPH J. THOMPSON

FAC SIMILE OF PETITION TO RETAIN FATHER ST. CYR

1837 — Petition of the Catholics of Chicago

To the Rt. Revd. Doct. Rosate St. Louis.

The undersigned Roman Catholic inhabitants of the town of Chicago have heard with the deepest regret that you have recalled the Revd. Mr. St. Cyr from this mission and as such an event would in their opinion be productive of injurious consequences to the cause of Catholic truth in this place they humbly beg leave to call Your attention to the actual situation of our people in this mission and request that you will carefully consider all the circumstances previous to such removal

They would in the first place inform your Grace that the Revd. Mr. St. Cyr by his exemplary conduct great zeal in the cause of religion and unassuming perseverance has endeared himself to every member of our congregation and is highly esteemed by the members of other denominations. And having acquired a sufficient knowledge of the English language to enable him to preach and instruct with fluency and elegance they concur that his removal would be a subject of bereavement to the whole congregation

That his associate the Revd. Mr. Pfeiffer although equally distinguished for piety and zeal has but an imperfect knowledge of the English language and is consequently unfitted for discharging the spiritual duty of a pastor among an English population

That as we have in this town two thousands and perhaps more Catholics As there are a large number of Catholic families in the adjacent country particularly on the line of the Chicago and Illinois Canal the great body of the laborers on which are Catholics to all of whom the clergy here must render spiritual assistance, the attention therefore of a clergyman speaking the English language will be indispensably necessary and they would humbly represent that nothing but

the most imperious necessity should induce the removal of a man from such a vast field of labour who is so beloved and revered by his congregation

That As our church is totally inadequate to contain the fourth part of the attending congregation we have taken the preliminary steps to erect a new Chapel capable of accommodating our large and increasing society. The removal of the Rev'd Mr St Cyr will operate to retard and delay that work so much desired not only by Catholics but by various members of other denominations

That As this is the most important place in this State as its population is so rapidly increasing that we can in a few years justly expect a Catholic population of several thousands. And as one Clergyman can not possibly discharge the duties attached to it good policy as well as duty requires that we should have Clergymen stationed here capable by their example of inspiring respect — by their talents of dissipating ignorance and prejudice and by their zeal and perseverance of building up in this new region the imperishable monuments of our holy religion

We therefore humbly entreat your grace not to deprive us of a dearly beloved pastor at the commencement of his usefulness but to leave him where his zeal and virtues are so well appreciated and so likely to redound to the best interests of the church —

Bernard Ward
Thos Watkins
Jean B. Beaubien   Parnee Rogers
M. B. Beaubien   Henry Gainor
Sirique Decovan   Patrick Walsh
Richard Murphy   Patrick White
Charles McDonnell   Samuel Carpenter
Peter Dillon   Henry Hawkins
Hugh Duffy   Solomon Taylor
William Read   Charles Taylor
James Carney   Mark Beaubien Sr
Henry Beery   Marke Beaubien Jr
Jeffries Powell   O. H. Lacken

JOSEPH J. THOMPSON

James Owen
Thos. Doyle
James McGrath
Dennis Trister
George J. Fill
William Kinney
Dennis Geary
Dennis Lalley
James Brown
Thos. Ward

There are several remarkable features about this document. To begin with, one is struck not only by the pen artistry of the writer of the petition, but as well by the choice English employed.

As one reads this petition he is consumed with curiosity to know who it was in the early uncultivated day that not only possessed such expertness in handwriting, but displayed such scholarship and lofty expression in composition. Who wrote this remarkable petition? After long study by the writer of this article and consultation with others, it was determined to submit the petition to a handwriting expert, and accordingly Mr. James I. Ennis, of Chicago, who enjoys a national reputation as a competent handwriting expert, was consulted. After careful study and upon the authority of Mr. Ennis, the conclusion is arrived at that the fourth signer, Richard Murphy, drafted the petition. The reader may for his own satisfaction examine the several letters in Mr. Murphy's name in comparison with the same letters where they appear in the petition, and may or may not arrive at the same conclusion.

Assuming that we have made the right surmise as to the writer of the petition, the question naturally arises, who was Richard Murphy; and it is a matter of keen regret that such study as we have been able to give the matter has not enabled us to trace this scholarly gentleman.

If the petition itself is notable in its diction and penmanship, the signatures of the petitioners are scarcely less so. The *facsimile* pre-

sented herewith enables a study of these signatures by the reader, and it seems entirely safe to predict that should a similar number of signatures be collected promiscuously in any part of the City of Chicago today, they would not excel in merit of execution and in the display of sterling characteristics, that handwriting is supposed to indicate, the signatures attached to this petition, made long ere schools were a universal blessing, and made too, by a class of men, mainly Irish, and altogether of what used to be slightingly alluded to as "foreigners" and who have received very little credit in general for education and culture.

Another interesting feature of this petition illustrates a distinct metamorphosés in the resident population of Chicago. Whereas the petition of 1833, containing thirty-nine family names, and totalling one hundred and twenty-nine persons, clearly shows twenty-three of the families, and a larger proportion of the individuals to be French, with only seven Irish family names, the new petition shows one hundred and seventeen Irish, and not to exceed a dozen Frenchmen. This indicates the advance tide of the Irish influx that brought so many of that nationality to Chicago and other parts of the State of Illinois and the West.

How interesting it would be to be able to go into the details of the lives of the men represented in these petitions: How and when they came to this remote station on civilization's frontier. What was their business or profession? What of the family and home ties, which it is safe to say they highly prized, else they would not be so solicitious regarding their religious welfare. These are in the truest sense the first families of Chicago, and proud indeed should be all those who can trace their lineage thereto.

JOSEPH J. THOMPSON.

Chicago.

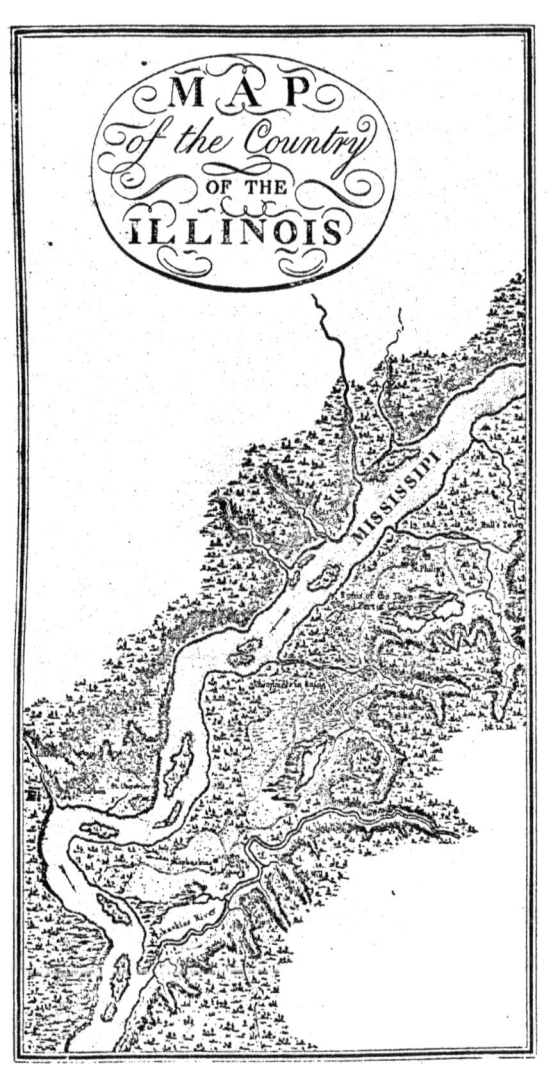

Courtesy of *Illinois State Historical Library.*

MAP OF THE ILLINOIS COUNTRY
FROM COLLET'S VOYAGE, 1796

SEBASTIEN LOUIS MEURIN

I.

The Last of the Illinois Jesuit Indian Missionaries

Heroism and deeds of valor will ever command the respect and admiration of men. Although heroism has been displayed by many men and women it may be questioned whether a series of heroic deeds equal to that of the Catholic missionaries in foreign and pagan lands was ever chronicled by the historian. It is no exaggeration to say that the records of her missions are some of the brightest pages in the history of the Church, who has ever sent her sons and daughters to foreign fields to preach the word of God and win souls to Christ.

Three centuries ago Canada was a mission field, sanctified by the labors and blood of the French missionaries and martyrs who sacrificed talents, wealth, position, home, country, all, to labor for Christ in the wilds of America. Indeed, so striking is the heroism, so great the devotion and constancy of these champions of Christ that they elicit the eulogy of some and the admiration of all. ''The physical vigor, the moral heroism, and the unquenchable religious zeal of these missionaries were qualities exemplified in a measure and to a degree which are beyond the power of pen to describe. Historians of all creeds have tendered homage to their self-sacrifice and zeal, and never has work of human hand or spirit been more worthy of tribute. The Jesuit went, often alone, where no others dared to go, and faced unknown dangers which had all the possibility of torture and martyrdom. Nor did this energy waste itself in flashes of isolated triumph. . . . . The great services which the Jesuit missionary rendered in the New World, both to his country and to his creed, were due not less to the matchless organization of the Order to which he belonged than to the qualities of courage, patience, and fortitude which he himself showed as a missionary.[1]

Even those who misunderstand the missionaries or are unable to appreciate the motives which actuated them are loud in their praise. Bancroft, however, would have us believe that ''the missionaries encountered with dismay the horror of life in the vast, uninhabited regions where in a journey of twelve days not a soul was met.''[2] We

[1] Munro, William B., *Chronicles of New France*, pp. 117,118.
[2] Bancroft, George, *History of the United States of America*, Vol. II, p. 186, edition of 1883.

have serious doubts as to the objective truth of this statement, but if dismay ever entered the soul of the missionary it was soon dispelled by the courage born of a love of Christ and the souls He redeemed. No one familiar with Parkman's works on early Canadian history will insinuate that he was partial to the Catholic Church or her priests, and yet he says: "The lives of these early Canadian Jesuits attest the earnestness of their faith and the intensity of their zeal. . . . . One great aim engrossed their lives. 'For the greater glory of God'— *ad-majorem Dei gloriam*—they would act or wait, dare, suffer, or die. . . . ."[3] "Far from shrinking, the priest's zeal rose to tenfold ardor."[4]

In the ranks of this army of heroes, Jogues the martyr and Marquette the explorer and missionary are most familiar to students of American history—their lives, their achievements, their sufferings are known, but after all they were only two, the most conspicuous indeed, yet only two of a host of brave hearts. That their devotion, their intrepidity and zeal were not singular, but typical rather of a large class, is brought home to us by the study of the lives of their fellow-laborers. Peculiar interest to the citizens of the states of the Mississippi Valley attaches to the person and career of Father Sebastien Louis Meurin, missionary for many years at Kaskaskia, Ste. Genevieve, Cahokia and Ft. Chartres, pioneer priest of Saint Louis, and the last Jesuit of the old Society to die in the Mississippi Valley.

Sebastien Louis Meurin was born at Charleville, northeastern France, December 26, 1707. Although his early life is shrouded in obscurity and we know nothing of his childhood and boyhood days we have reason to conjecture that his education included a good primary schooling, supplemented by attendance at a Jesuit college. At the age of twenty-two he entered the Society of Jesus, at Nancy, becoming a member of the province of Champagne. When he had completed the studies pursued by members of his order, he was ordained priest and assigned to the mission of Canada. Canada, at the time of which we speak, was but a vague geographical term, including nearly all the immense French territory in North America, large portions of which were not only not colonized but even unexplored. That the young priest had volunteered for this arduous mission scarcely admits of a doubt when we recall to mind that throughout the previous half century the French Jesuits had signalized themselves by zeal for the mission of Canada. To labor in Canada, sanctified by the

³ Parkman, Francis, *The Jesuits in North America*, p. 43.
⁴ Parkman, Francis, *op. cit.*, p. 43.

labors and blood of their countrymen, Jogues, Brebeuf and others,
was the ambition of many noble young souls. The achievements of
their countrymen were an inspiration to them, arousing them to like
effort. Father Meurin arrived in Canada some time in November,
1741; early the next February he began his apostolic career among
the Illinois Indians..

The Illinois Indians,[5] members of the Algonquin family of aborig-
ines, included the Kaskaskias, Cahokias, Tamaroas, Peorias and Mitch-
igamias; they occupied the territory south and west of the river to
which they eventually gave their name, and the land between the Illinois and Sangamon rivers. Of these tribes "the Tamaroas had settled
the country about the mouth of the Illinois and Missouri rivers as
early as 1680,[6] while at Cahokia "as early as 1699, an Indian and a
French Mission of the Holy Family were established, the former by
the Jesuits, Julien Binneteau and Francis Pinet, and the latter by
Father St. Cosme of the Seminary of Foreign Missions."[7]

When Father Marquette entered the Illinois river on the last stage
of his epoch-making exploration of the Mississippi he discovered a
thriving village of the Kaskaskias, opposite the present Starved Rock,
Illinois, a tribe so friendly and well disposed towards the black robe
and his message of Christianity that they entreated him to return.[8]
This he did in 1675 and established in their village the mission of "the
Immaculate Conception of the Blessed Virgin," just as he had named
the great river in honor of the sinless Mother of Christ.[9] At first the
mission flourished. Father Claude Jean Allouez, S. J., who succeeded Father Marquette, writes: "I found this village largely in-

---

[5] The following spellings of this name are found: Ilinois, Illenois, Illi-
noies, Illinoise, Ilonois, Islinois.
[6] Alvord and Carter, *The New Regime*, p. 216.
[7] Beuckman, Rev. Frederick, *Civil and Ecclesiastical Juurisdiction in Illinois*.
ILLINOIS CATHOLIC HISTORICAL REVIEW, July, 1918, p. 65.
[8] *Jesuit Relations*, 59:161. "We have seen nothing like this river which
we enter, as regards its fertility of soil, its prairies and woods; its cattle, elk,
deer, wildcats, bustards, swans, ducks, parroquets, and even beaver. There are
many small lakes and rivers. That on which we sailed is wide, deep, and still, for
65 leagues. In the spring and during part of the summer there is only one portage
of half a league. We found on it a village of Illinois, called Kaskaskia, consisting of 74 cabins. They received us very well, and obliged me to promise that I
would return to instruct them. One of the chiefs of this nation, with his young
men, escorted me to the Lake of the Ilinois, whence, at last, at the end of September, we reached the bay des puants, from which we started at the beginning
of June."
[9] Brown, Stuart, *Old Kaskaskia Days and Ways,*—ILLINOIS CATHOLIC HIS-
TORICAL REVIEW, April, 1919, p. 414.

creased since a year ago. Formerly, it was Composed of but one
nation, that of the Kachkachkia; at the present time there are eight
tribes in it, the first having summoned the others, who inhabited the
neighborhood of the river Mississippi. One cannot well satisfy himself as to the number of people who Compose this village. They are
housed in 351 cabins, which are easily counted, as most of them are
situated upon the bank of the river.''[10] Prosperity did not abide
with this Indian village, for during the last decade or two of the
century the Illinois suffered so severely at the hands of the Pota-
watomi and Iroquois that hundreds of their men, women and children
were killed or reduced to slavery. As continuation in this locality
could not but result in the utter destruction of the Kaskaskia tribe[11]
the remnant of the tribe resolved to migrate to new fields. They set out
under Father Gabriel Marest, S. J., and it seems that they intended
to go to the vicinity of New Orleans. Considerable obscurity involves
both the time and immediate objective of this migration. Investigators agree that it must have occurred about the year 1700; they
likewise agree that eventually the Kaskaskia founded the village
which perpetuates their name, but while some are of the opinion that
the Indians proceeded directly to Kaskaskia and founded their village
in 1700 or 1701,[12] one authority has recently proved that the village
was founded later after the Indians had spent the intervening years
at the mouth of the Des Peres river in Missouri.[13] According to the

---

[10] *Jesuit Relations*, 60:159.

[11] This name occurs in the following forms: Kaskaskias, Cascakias, Cascaskias, Caskakias, Kachkachkia, Kakachkiouek, Kaskasia, Kaskaskia, Kaskias. To
these must be added the abbreviated form of ''Kats.'' ''Kaskia'' is in common
use today among the people in the vicinity of Kaskaskia.

[12] *Jesuit Relations*, 65:101-103. On the 16th of February, 1701, Father James
Gravier writes: ''I received on my return from Michilimachinack the letter that
you did me the honor of writing to me by way of the Mississippy, Addressed to
Father Aveneau, who sent it to me at Chikagoua—whence I started in 1700, on
the 8th of September, to come here. I arrived too late among the Illinois of the
strait—of whom Father Marest has charge—to prevent the migration of the Village of the Kaskaskia, which has been too precipitately made, in consequence of
uncertain news respecting the Mississippi settlement. I do not think that the
Kaskaskia would have thus separated from the Peourooua and from the other Illinois of the strait, if I could have arrived sooner. I reached them at least soon
enough to conciliate their minds to some extent, and to prevent the insult that the
Peouroua and the Mouingouena were resolved to offer the Kaskaskia and the
French when they embarked. . . . . After journeying four days with the Kaskaskia, I went on ahead with Father Marest, whom I left ill among the Tama-
rouha, where Father Pinet performs in peace all the Duties of a Missionary.''

[13] Kenny, Rev. Lawrence, S. J., *Missouri's Earliest Settlement and Its Name*,
St. Louis Catholic Historical Review, Vol. I, No. 3, April, 1919, pp. 151-157.

traditional, and, hitherto more generally accepted interpretation, "this removal of the Kaskaskia tribe from their old home was to the site of the modern village of Kaskaskia. These savages at first intended to migrate to the vicinity of Iberville's new post in Louisiana; but Gravier induced them to remain at the above place. The village was called by them Rouensac, after their chief Rouensa; the Jesuit mission therein was named for the Immaculate Conception."[14]

Kaskaskia, the new settlement, was "on the right bank of the Kaskaskia river about six miles above its entry into the Mississippi river and about two miles from the latter. Here the Kaskaskia river was about three hundred and fifty feet wide, and the bluffs on the opposite side were about two hundred feet high. The village was named by the Jesuits "Le Village de l'Immaculée Conception de Cascasquias," and was not laid out in any regular form, but like most Indian villages consisted of a row of lodges or huts scattered along the river.[15] To this oasis of civilization in the heart of America came traders, trappers and voyageurs from Quebec and Detroit, who in due time formed marriage alliances with the daughters of Indian chiefs and warriors. At first a mission, Kaskaskia developed into a trading, and eventually into a military post. Among the natural advantages which induced people to settle at Kaskaskia must be numbered the extraordinary fertility of the soil and the mineral resources. "The Country is extremely Fertile," says Aubry. "Wheat and Indian Corn grow very well, and all the European Fruits succeed to a Wonder. They make very passable Wine from the wild Grapes, and their Beer is very good, they make Indian Sugar. There is Mines of Lead, Quarrys of Stone, and plenty of Salt."[16] That he did not exaggerate is proved

---

"The Kats to the extent of about thirty cabins have established their new village two league below this one on the other side of the Mississippi. They have built a fort there and nearly all the French hastened there.

"The chief of the Tamarois followed by some cabins joined the Kats, attracted by Rouensae who promises them much and makes them believe him saying that he is called by the great chief of the French, Mr. d'Iberville, as Father Marest has told him.

"The remainder of the Tamarois numbering about twenty cabins are shortly going to join their chief, already settled at the Kats. So there will remain only the Cahokias numbering 60 or 70 cabins. They are now cutting stakes to build a fort." Extracts from a letter of Rev. Mr. Bergier, of April 13, 1701. Transactions of the Illinois State Historical Society, 1908, No. 13, p. 238.

[14] *Jesuit Relations*, 65:263.

[15] Brown, Stuart, *Old Kaskaskia Days and Ways*, ILLINOIS CATHOLIC HISTORICAL REVIEW, April, 1919, p. 415.

[16] Alvord and Carter, *The Critical Period*, p. 5.

by the words of another writer, who affirms that the land is suited to the growth of Indian corn, wheat, rye, oats, barley, hemp, tobacco, etc. He even asserts that no land could be more fertile than these bottom lands, of which the Kaskaskia Indians had taken possession.[17]

Father Meurin began his labors at Kaskaskia in the spring of 1742. The other Jesuit missionaries, succeeding Father James Marquette, the founder of the mission, in their order were: Claude Jean Allouez, Sebastien Rale, Jacques Gravier, Pierre François Pinet, Julien Bineteau, Pierre Marest, Louis Marie de Ville, Jean Charles Guymonneau, Joseph François de Kereben, Jean Antoine le Boullenger, Nicholas Ignace de Beaubois, Jean Dumas, Réné Tartarin. Philibert Watrin, Étienne Doutreleau, Alexis Xavier Guyenne, Louis Vivier, Julian Joseph Fourre and Jean Baptist Aubert. In Father Meurin's day there were two missions, one for the French in charge of Father Jean Baptiste Aubert, S. J., and one for the Illinois Indians; for two decades and more—til 1763—this Indian Mission was the chief scene of his ministry. In all probability he would have spent many more happy years in this retreat had not disaster overwhelmed the mission and all but terminated his own efforts to spread Christ's kingdom in the hearts of these wild children of forest and prairie. Here at Kaskaskia his duties were identical with those of missionaries at other missions; there was no variety in essentials, but details of course differed according to the disposition and customs of the Indians.

A beautiful picture of the daily life at Kaskaskia has been left us by one of the missionaries:

"At sunrise, the bell rang for prayer and mass; the savages said prayers in their own language, and during mass they chanted, to the air of the Roman chant, hymns and canticles, also translated into their language, with the suitable prayers; at the end of the mass the missionary catechized the children. Having returned to his house he was occupied in instructing the adult neophytes and catechumens, to prepare them for baptism or for penitence, for communion or for marriage; as soon as he was free, he went through the village to arouse the believers to fervor, and to exhort unbelievers to embrace Christianity. The rest of the day was needed for reciting the divine office, studying the language of the savages, and preparing the instructions for Sundays and feast-days. . . . . ."[18]

So much for the life of the missionary. The life of the Indians has been detailed by Bancroft in his great work:

[17] Brown, Samuel R., The Western Gazeteer or Emigrant's Directory, 1817. Transactions of the Illinois State Historical Society, 1908, p. 301.

[18] Jesuit Relations, 70:227-229.

[19] Bancroft, George, op. cit., Vol. II, p. 187.

"At the mission of Kaskaskia at early dawn, the pupils came to church, dressed neatly and modestly . . . . after receiving lessons, they chanted canticles; mass was then said in presence of all the Christians in the place, the French and the converts,—the women on one side, the men on the other. . . . . In the afternoon the catechism was taught in the presence of the young and the old, and every one, without distinction of rank or age, answered the questions of the missionary. . . . . At evening, all would assemble at the chapel for instruction, prayer, and to chant the hymns of the church . . . . at the close of the day, parties would meet in the cabins to recite the chaplet in alternate choirs. . . . . Saturday and Sunday were the days for confession and communion, and every convert confessed once in a fortnight.'"[19]

How like the reductions of Paraguay these missions among the Illinois! How different the Indian portrayed in these lines from the blood-thirsty savage, gloating over the bloody scalps which dangle from his girdle!

The first documentary proof of Father Meurin's pastoral duties at Kaskaskia is to be found under date of September 19, 1746, when he baptized Madeleine and Pierre Pani, Chicasaw slaves of Jacque Michel, who had previously contracted a natural marriage.[20] Two years later on May 19, 1748, he united in marriage Nicolas Boyer and Dorothy Olivier,[21] both of whom were parishoners of Kaskaskia. As neither bride nor groom had acquired the art of writing they had to content themselves with a mere cross affixed to the official entry. Father Meurin's entries and signature are read with ease, but his script is not as legible as that of Father Watrin, who made and signed most of the records for this period.

Though Kaskaskia was the chief scene of Father Meurin's labors it was not the only place where he labored, for at the distant post of Vincennes he likewise discharged the duties of parish priest.[22] The parish records of this place begin under date of April 21, 1749, with

[19] Registre des Marriages dans l'Eglise de Notre Dame de l'Immaculee Conception aux Cascaskias, Nov. 20, 1741-Feb. 10, 1884, p. 12.

"1746. Le 19 de Septembre le Pere Meurin a baptisé Marie Madeleine de la nation des Tchicachas appertenant a Jaque Michel dit Dufrene et a supplié le meme jour les ceremonies du bapteme a Pierre Pani de nation appartenant au meme: Ils etoient auparavant mariés de mariage naturel, et par leur bapteme leur mariage est devenu chretien. Les temoins du bapteme de Madeleine ont eté Jean Jeantry, et Marie Francoise Michel fille de Dufrene l'un parrain l'autre marraine de Madeleine qui ont signé au registre des baptemes avec le F. Meurin.

P. F. Watrin, J.

[21] Registre des Marriages, etc., p. 19. This entry is the first made and signed by Father Meurin. The Parish records of Kaskaskia are in an excellent state of preservation; at present they are kept in the archives of Saint Louis University, Saint Louis, Missouri.

[22] Shea, *History of the Catholic Church in the United States*, I:578.

an entry of the marriage of Julian Trottier des Rivières and Josette Marie[23]—a marriage performed by Father Meurin himself after he had proclaimed the banns according to custom.   On June 25th of this same year he also begins the baptismal register by recording the baptism of an Indian child, christened not inappropriately Jean Baptiste.[24]   The following day he baptized the boy's mother and then conferred the nuptial blessings on his parents, who had been united in a natural marriage for a long time.[25]   In 1750, Father Louis Vivier, one of Meurin's four colaborers, writing to another Father, gives us a passing glimpse of our hero:

[23] Records of the American Catholic Historical Society, Vol. XII, p. 209.
"In the year one thousand seven hundred and forty nine the 27 day of the month of april ,after having published three bans between julien trottier du rivieres son of julien trottier des rivieres of the parish of Mont real and josette marié daughter of antoine marié and marie anne chicamicge the parents ("les peres et meres") living in this parish without their being any impediment, I the undersigned missionary of the company of jesus performing the functions of pastor have received their mutual consent of marriage and have given them the nuptial benediction, with the ceremonies prescribed by Holy Church in the presence of monsieur de St. Ange. Lieutenant of a company of detached marines Commandant at poste Vincennes, of jean Baptiste Guilbert, Toussaint Guilbert, antoine Bouchard, jean B. Ridet, Louis Gervais witnesses who have signed with me. S. L. Meurin jesuite.

    St. Ange Commandant   Boucher
      at poste vincén   J. B. Ridday
       filliatro   ·   Louis Gervais
This sheet has been transferred by me the undersigned.
                                          S. L. Meurin Jes.
This happy family was soon broken up by death. On page 56 of the Records we read:
"27 December 1750 died in this parish Josétte Marie Wife of julien trottier Desrivieres, trading in this poste, 18 years of age, after having confessed and received the Holy Viaticum and the sacrament of extreme unction. Her body was buried with the usual ceremonics in the church of the parish under her bench on the gospel side the 28th of said month and year. S. L. Meurin Jes.
Two months later occurred the death of the infant son, whose birth had most probably occasioned the death of the youthful mother.
"15 February, 1751, died in this parish Julien desriviers son of julien des rivieres & josette marie two months old. Buried with the usual ceremonics in the church of this parish near the body of his mother. S. L. Meurin S. J.''
[24] Records of the American Catholic Historical Society, Vol. XII, p. 42.
[25] Records of the American Catholic Historical Society, Vol. XII, p. 42.
"Conferred nuptial benediction on pierre giapichagane called let petit chis & Catharine mgkicge (already united in a natural marriage for a long time) the 26th of June, 1749.''
The missionaries evidently found difficulty in spelling the names of the Indians.

At this date Father Meurin's name begins to appear frequently in the parish records, but always in the hand of Father Watrin, who records marriages of Indians and negro slaves performed by Father Meurin.[27] However, nothing out of the ordinary occurred to feature his missionary life among white men and red. In the catalogue of the Province of France of the Society of Jesus, at the end of the year 1756, he is recorded as ''among the Illinois'';[28] he is still assisted by four other fathers, of whom Father Alexander de Guyenne is superior. These few references spread over a period of fourteen years must convince us that Meurin's life in the missions was a life of toil and obscurity, a life hidden in Christ and devoted solely to God; vainglory and worldly praise had no place in such an existence. Someone has said that the nation without a history is the happiest of nations. If this be true and if it apply equally well to individuals we must infer that these long periods which have nothing special to chronicle in the life of Father Meurin must have been happy years, and if we contrast the years which succeeded this period with those happy days, we must admit, that in Father Meurin's case at least, the adage is indeed verified.

The peace of the missions was not to endure; the sweet calm was to give place to storms; disaster loomed close at hand. God's

[26] *Jesuit Relations*, 69:201-203.
[27] Among the marriages are the following:
    April 7, 1755, Francis and Mary Anne, slaves of J. B. Bauvais.
    March 27, 1757, Joseph and Marie Louise, negro slaves.
    December 10, 1757, Jean Louis and Genevieve, negro slaves.
    December 11, 1757, Alexander and Marguerite, slaves.
    January 17, 1758, Nicholas and Angelique, negro slaves.
    January 28, 1758, Joseph and Susan, Christian Indian slaves.
[28] *Jesuit Relations*, 70:89.

enemies became active in America even as they were active in Europe, and they purposed to bring the missions to ruin by sacrificing the devoted men who conducted them. The Superior Council of Louisiana, in servile imitation of similar proceedings by the Parliament of Paris and other French Parliaments, arrogated to itself the role of reformer, as evil men are prone to do, and resolved upon examining the Institute of the Society of Jesus with a view to its ultimate suppression. It is self-evident that a secular council such as this enjoyed no ecclesiastical authority or jurisdiction; it is more than probable that its members were ignorant of theology and canon law, upon which any just sentence must necessarily be based; finally, it is known that the majority of them at least could even be reproached for ignorance of the very language of the document upon which they were about to pass judgment.[29] But such considerations were too trifling to deter the Council from action! Could fairness or justice be expected in the findings of such a tribunal inspired by such motives? Assuredly not, and hence we are not startled by the verdict, but we are pleased to learn that there was at least one gentleman who refused to sacrifice his conscience. Monsieur de Chatillon cast the one dissenting vote in favor of the Jesuits.[30] History has passed verdict on the action of this Council, and in the words of Judge Edward O. Brown, she acquits the devoted missionaries of the charges lodged against them. After examining the evidence upon which the decision was based, he says: "By virtue of an infamous decree the Superior Council of Louisiana, an insignificant body of provincial officers who undertook in 1763 to condemn the Society of Jesus, and to suppress the order within Louisiana,"[31] the Jesuits were seized, taken to New Orleans and sent from there to France.

As the people in the colonies and missions were not bereft of all sense of justice, injustice such as that premeditated must needs be disguised, the real motives for action must not be divulged, but some reasons must be advanced. The decree was issued July 9, 1763. With rare effrontery, it asserted "that the Institute of the Jesuits was hostile to royal authority, the rights of bishops, and the public peace and safety; and that the vows taken according to the Institute were null."[32] Evidence to substantiate these charges was not forthcoming —the honorable council overlooked minutiae. Did this deluded Coun-

---

[29] *Jesuit Relations*, 70:217.
[30] *Jesuit Relations*, 70:219.
[31] Brown, Edward Osgood, *The Parish Records of Michilimackinac*, p. 47.
[32] *Jesuit Relations*, 70:219.

any province in France where there is not some prominent person who has lived in Louisiana; of these persons, there is not one who has not known Jesuits there, and most of them have been able to scrutinize these Jesuits very closely. Now, the Jesuits await with confidence the testimony that can be rendered concerning them, upon the points in question here, still more, they dare to cite, as witnesses of their conduct, three governors of Louisiana, and a vicar-general of the episcopate of Quebec for this same colony. All were still living in the month of June, 1764; no one has begged for their suffrages; no one has even informed these gentlemen of what is about to be cited from them.''[37] The witnesses referred to are Monsieur de Bienville, Monsieur the Marquis de Vaudreuil, Monsieur de Kelerec, and Monsieur the abbé de L'Isle Dieu, all of whom concurred in denying the charges of the council.

The utter baselessness of these charges when Kaskaskia is considered is apparent when we reflect upon the detailed account of Father Watrin, who writes:

''At one and one-fourth leagues from the Illinois savages, there was a French village also named Cascaskias; for 44 years there has been in this village a parish, which has always been governed by the Jesuits. Now, we dare to repeat here, regarding those who were charged with this employ, what has been said above of their associates in general [he has already given an account of Fther Meurin's work among the Indians] that there is hardly any province in France where there are not still witnesses of the exactness of these curés in discharging their functions, that is, in visiting the sick and relieving the poor. These too are witnesses of their assiduity at the tribunal of penance, and at the almost daily instruction of the children,—to which must be still added the instruction of the negroes and savages, slaves of the French, to prepare them for baptism and for the reception of the other sacraments. Besides, every evening, a public prayer was said in the church, and some pious book was read; finally, on Sundays and feast-days, two instructions in the catechism were given, one for the French children and the other for the black slaves and the savages,—without counting the solemn mass, and the vespers that were sung punctually with the benediction (of the Blessed

---

[37] *Jesuit Relations,* 70:223.

Sacrament). But here is something which is more than care; since the year 1753, there has been in the French village of Cascaskias a newly built parochial church; this church is 104 feet long and 44 wide. Now, it never could have been finished if the expense of the building had not been drawn from the building fund and from the contributions of the parishioners. Three Jesuits, successively curés of this parish,—Father Tartarin, Father Watrin, and Father Aubert,—have employed for this purpose the greater part of what they obtained from their surplice and their mass-fees. When the curés have the construction and ornamentation of their church so much at heart, it is also probable that they did not fail in their other duties.

"But here is yet another proof of the care that the Jesuits have taken of this parish; fifteen years ago, at a league from the old village, on the other bank of the Mississippi, there was established a new village under the name of Sainte Geneviève. Then the curé of Cascaskias found himself obliged to go there to administer the sacraments, at least to the sick; and when the new inhabitants saw their houses multiplying, they asked to have a church built there. This being granted them the journeys of the missionary became still more frequent, because he thought that he ought then to yield himself still more to the willingness of his new parishioners, and to their needs. However, in order to go to this new church he must cross the Mississippi, which, in this place, is three-eighths of a league wide; he sometimes had to trust himself to a slave, who alone guided the canoe; it was necessary, in fine, to expose himself to the danger of perishing, if in the middle of the river they had been overtaken by a violent storm. None of these inconveniences ever prevented the curé of Cascaskias from going to Sainte Geneviève when charity called him thither, and he was always charged with this care until means were found to place at Sainte Geneviève a special curé,—which occurred only a few years ago, when the inhabitants of the place built a house for the pastor. These two villages, that of Cascaskias and that of Sainte Geneviève, made the second and third establishment of the Jesuits in the Illinois country. There is no need to call attention to the fact that, to accomplish only a part of the work that had just been indicated care, courage and constancy are necessary."

Nevertheless, in the face of the evidence in favor of the persecuted priests, the council ruled that the Jesuits, hitherto so styled, were not to take that name hereafter, and that they were to adopt the garb of the secular clergy. Furthermore, all their property, their books and necessary wearing apparel alone excepted, was to be seized and sold at auction, the chapel ornaments and sacred vessels were to be delivered to the royal procurator, the chapels themselves were to be demolished; finally, the Fathers were to embark for France without delay, but meanwhile they were prohibited from living together. Six months after their arrival in France each one was to present himself to the Duc de Choiseül to petition him for a suitable pension. To cover the expense of the voyage and afford means of subsistence for six months some $420 was assigned each of the exiles. This decree was

---

carried out to the letter, first in New Orleans, then in the missions among the Indians.[35]

Father Meurin was at Kaskaskia when the 24th of September, 1763, a day memorable in the history of the Kaskaskia mission, dawned. The night previous the courier from the Council of New Orleans, bearer of the decree of suppression, arrived at Ft. Chartres, six leagues distant from the residence of the missionaries. Accompanied by the registrar and the bailiff this messenger of evil presented himself at the residence of the missionaries about eight or nine o'clock on the morning of the 24th. He addressed himself to the superior, Father Watrin, read the decree of condemnation, handed a duplicate copy to him, and, forcing him to leave the room at once, he put the official seal on the door. Then the other missionaries were likewise ordered from their rooms. As the procurator of the king feared to displease the soldiery detailed to guard the confiscated property he "would not even permit the Jesuits to remain at the house of one of their confrères, who, being pastor of the place, had his private lodging near the parish church."[36] But in this case the utter poverty of the place made it unnecessary to affix the seal.

Expelled thus summarily from their own house, the missionaries found shelter as best they could. The aged superior—he was sixty-seven years old—accompanied by Father Meurin, departed on foot to find a lodging a long league away, much to the sorrow and regret of all who witnessed the expulsion. No sooner had they arrived at their destination than the astonished savages gathered about them in great excitement. They made no effort to conceal their grief; they had already heard of the suppression, but their simple minds could not fathom such proceedings. "Why have you been treated thus," they asked again and again with true Indian persistence. Despite the accusation of the decree that the missionaries had been neglectful of the missions, the artless savages were convinced that the Jesuits had taken care of them and had sacrificed themselves in behalf of their flocks. In their unwillingness to part with their blackrobes these devoted Indians hit upon the scheme of dispatching a delegation to the civil authorities to plead that Father Meurin at least be allowed to remain with them. Such devotion must have touched the hearts of the persecuted priests and proved a solace to them amid their sorrows, but since they knew well that this worthy petition would receive scant consideration from the Council, they dissuaded the Indians from this

[35] *Jesuit Relations*, 70:263.
[36] Alvord and Carter, *The Critical Period*, p. 102-103.

course of action. One request, however, the Indians did make, namely, "that at least the chapel and the house of the missionary be preserved, in order that the best instructed person among them might assemble the children and repeat the prayers to them; and that every Sunday and feast-day he might summon those who prayed, that is to say, the Christians, by the ringing of the bell, to fulfill as well as possible the duties of religion."[37] The request, though granted at the time, was shortly after ignored.

At this juncture the procurator of the king was induced to curb his ardor by four letters of protest received in a single day from M. Bobe, the commissary, who intervened in behalf of the missionaries, requesting that those who had labored among the Indians be allowed to live together with those who had administered to the French. A slight mitigation of the severity of the decree resulted, for each of the Fathers was allowed to secure his mattress and blankets and spread them on the floor in the house of the pastor of the French village. The French inhabitants, who were sincerly devoted to their pastors, presented without delay "in the name of nearly all the inhabitants a petition addressed to the commandant and commissary of the country, in order to secure the retention of at least Father Aubert, the pastor of French Kaskaskia; and as the answer seemed to be deferred too long a time, a little while afterward a second petition was sent. While waiting for an answer, the more intelligent of the inhabitants asked by what right the government had taken possession of the property of the Jesuits, and what power it had over their persons in a couuntry ceded by the treaty of peace to the crown of England. They also asked why the Jesuits were excepted from the privilege granted without distinction to all the inhabitants of the Illinois of having eighteen months to choose either to remain in this country or to go elsewhere."[38]

The request was granted temporarily till the Council could take cognizance of the case, more because of fear that a refusal would result in serious disturbance at Kaskaskia than from any more noble motive. Hence we find Father Aubert recording marriages performed by him at Kaskaskia on November 6th, December 6th and 26th, 1763, and January 17th, 24th and 31st, 1764; during the same period he conferred thirty-seven baptisms, the last being June 16th. With the return of Father Meurin to Sainte Genevieve Father Aubert's name disappears from the records.

[37] Alvord and Carter, *op. cit.*, p. 104.
[38] Alvord and Carter, *op. cit.*, pp. 106-107.

A public auction was held in conformity with the decree of suppression, and house, furiture, cattle, lands, everything was sold. "The Jesuits' plantation consisted of two hundred and forty arpents of cultivated land, a very good stock of cattle, and a brewery;"[39] Jean Baptiste Beauvais purchased the Kaskaskia chapel and Cahokia cemetery. A full account of the auction, signed by the notary Labuxierre, and preserved to us, runs as follows:

Before noon of November 6, 1763, in pursuance of the decree of the superior council of Louisiana, dated July 9 last, issued in favor of his majesty against the late self-styled Jesuits, bearing permission to seize and sell the property belonging to their mission, I, at the request of M. Etienne Marafret Laissard, deputy of the king's attorney-general of the superior council of New Orleans living at Nouvelle Chartres, where he has chosen his home, I, Jean Robinet, undersigned royal huissier in the district of the Illinois, living at Nouvelle Chartres, went purposely with my two witnesses, who were for this purpose brought, to the principal door, entrance, and exit of the parish church of Kaskaskia, at the close of high mass, when many people were coming out of the said church; I read, published, posted, and cried out in an intelligible voice and publicly, and made known to the public that I was presently going to proceed, for the third and last auction, to the sale of property consisting of a house covered with boards and divided into different rooms and apartments, a garret and a cellar, and another building of posts, covered with boards and divided into many low apartments, and a Negro cabin, many other buildings, cow sheds, Negro cabins, a barn, a stable, a weaving room, a horse mill, a dovecote, and, generally, all the buildings belonging to the late self-styled Jesuits in the borough of Kaskaskia, seized in pursuance of the aforesaid decree for the benefit of his majesty. At the auction everyone will be welcome to bid according to the following charges, stipulations, and conditions, to-wit: The purchaser must pay the price of his purchase in cash in the king's bonds; he must pay in cash also, the expense of the public sale and the recording. In case of failure to do this, the aforesaid property will be cried at auction at the price bid and the original purchaser will pay for the delay of the sale and the expense of the same. Consequently, the said house, building and land were bid for by Jean Baptiste Beauvais at 8,000 livres, by Raphael Beauvais at 20,000 livres, by M. de Rocheblave at 25,000 livres, by M. Laclede at 30,000 livres, by Jussiame at 32,000 livres, by Jean Baptiste Beauvais at 35,000 livres, by M. Laclede at 39,000 livres, by Jussiame at 40,000 livres, and by Jean Baptiste Beauvais at 40,100 livres. And having waited until noon struck and not finding anyone to bid higher, and as everyone was leaving, the said Jean Baptiste Beauvais demanded a deed of his bid, which was given to hint as the last bidder, and to him was knocked down the said house, buildings, land and dependancies which were accorded and adjudged him by M. Laissard, deputy of the king's attorney-general, in the presence of M. Labuxierre, clerk in this province, and in the

[39] Pittman, Captain Philip, *European Settlements on the Mississippi*, p. 43. Quoted in *Jesuit Relations*, 70:317. It should be noted that the official inventory of Jesuit property cited below does not mention "a brewery." M. LaGrange is reported to have purchased a "brewing-caldron" not "a brewery."

[40] Alvord and Carter, *op. cit.*, pp. 125-129.

presence of Jean Baptiste Hervieux, armorer of the king in the Illinois, for the said sum of 40,100 livres, which the said Jean Baptiste Beauvais then delivered and paid in cash to M. Laissard, who acknowledges it, and is satisfied with it. M. Jean Baptiste Beauvais is released of it and all other for which this is a receipt. We have signed the said day and year, and we have signed in the records of these presents: Hervieux, Labuxierre, Laissard, and Robinet, huissier. Signed, Labuxierre, notary. Endorsed February 2, 1767.''⁴¹

That the financial resources of the gentleman who purchased the property stolen thus publicly from the missionaries were unusually great is brought home to us when we learn that ''he furnished to the King's magazines as much as 86,000 weight of flour in a single year, which was only a part of one year's harvest.''⁴¹ Again we are informed that he ''is the richest of the English subjects in this country; he keeps eighty slaves.''⁴²

The chapel was to be destroyed, but not until after some interval of time, because the authorities feared the wrath of the Indians if they should presently disregard their promise to spare the house of God. But Beauvais, perhaps because he was suspicious of the legality of the sale and purchase, leased the chapel for a warehouse to the English, and he likewise leased the cemetery for a garden; whilst he made personal use of the altar cruets, the presses for the vestments, and sacred vessels.⁴³ We are not surprised to discover that his conduct soon involved Beauvais in such serious difficulty with the ecclesiastical authorities that he kept away from the Sacraments for three years.⁴⁴ The altar was saved in some way, so too the ''bell cast at Rochelle in 1741 for the parish, the first that rang between the Alleghanies and Mississippi,'' but the chapel ornaments were dispersed and profaned, and, as happens not infrequently, soon became the wages of sin as the *Relations* themselves testify. How great must have been the sorrow of the missionary who recorded that ''the linings of the ornaments had been given to negresses decried for their evil lives, and a large crucifix which had stood above the altar, and the chandeliers, were found placed above the cupboard in a house whose reputation was not good.''⁴⁵ The negro slaves, for the most part blacksmiths, carpenters, joiners, brewers, masons, who with their wives and children numbered sixty-eight⁴⁶ were to be taken to New Orleans and sold there, the pro-

---

⁴¹ Mason, Edward G., *Kaskaskia and Its Parish Records*, p. 17. *Fergus Historical Series*, No. 12.
⁴² Pittman, Captain Philip, op. cit., p. 43. Cf. *Jesuit Relations*, 70:317-318.
⁴³ *Jesuit Relations*, 71:39.
⁴⁴ *Jesuit Relations*, 71:39.
⁴⁵ *Jesuit Relations*, 70:281.
⁴⁶ Alvord and Carter, *The New Regime*, p. 327.

ceeds of the sale to be added to the royal portion of the booty. Finally
the forge and brewing caldron were purchased by Σ. Lagrange,[47] who
also secured "the property of the ' Mission of the Holy Family among
the Cahokias.' "[48] In distant Vincennes similar scenes of violence
and profanation occurred.

Thus with one fell stroke the missions were wiped out, the rights
of the missionaries ignored and disregarded, the missionaries themselves forced away, the fruits of many years of patient toil and suffering all but obliterated. To this work of destruction Jean Baptiste
Beauvais, Catholic though he was, contributed in part. The Indians
were left destitute and the work of civilizing them interrupted and
made more difficult. Nor were the evil results confined to the swarthy
children of the forest; the French suffered as well. Need we wonder,
that, cut off thus suddenly from the guidance and example of their
pastors and the spiritual helps of which they stood in need, they re-
lapsed into vicious habits and evil living. Old evils again made their
appearance, the passion for fire-water was indulged so freely that
three years later Lieutenant Alexander Fraser could write to Sir
Frederic Haldimand: "The Illinois Indians are about Six hundred
& fifty able to bear Arms, Nothing can equal their passion for drunkeness, but that of the French Inhabitants, who are for the greatest
part drunk every day while they can get Drink to buy in the Colony,
they import more of this Article from New Orleans than they do of
any other & they never fail to meet a Speedy & good Market for it."[49]
Colonel Robertson in like manner bears testimony to the prevalence
of drunkeness among the Illinois Indians.[50]

The war known in American history as the French and Indian
war had already terminated. From the French point of view it was
a distinct disaster; the conflict had dealt so terrible a blow to the military prestige of France that it did not revive till the days of the great
Bonaparte; it deprived her of her colonies in America and India and
thus negatived her pretensions to a colonial empire. By the secret
treaty of Fontainebleau, November 13, 1762, France ceded to Spain
all her possessions west of the Mississippi, together with New Orleans
and that portion of Louisiana south of the Iberville, while by the
public treaty of Paris, February 10, 1763, England secured Canada,
Nova Scotia, and all the land east of the Mississippi and north of the

[47] Alvord and Carter, op. cit., p. 38.
[48] Houck, Louis, History of Missouri, Vol. II, p. 295.
[49] Alvord and Carter, op. cit., p. 228.
[50] Alvord and Carter, The Critical Period, p. 218.

Iberville. Thus the Illinois missions had become English territory seven months before the enforcement of the Louisiana decree at Kaskaskia. The fact that "it was not till the tenth of October, 1765, that Captain Thomas Sterling came from Fort Pitt with 100 Highlanders of the 42nd to take possession of Kaskaskia and Fort Chartres"[51] did not alter the case so substantially as to justify the destruction of the missions or spoilation of the defenceless Jesuit missionaries by the French authorities. French power and authority ceased with the signing of peace. The most that can be said for the New Orleans authorities is that they were the representatives of the British authorities and could only act in so far as they were commissioned by the latter; but they acted without the knowledge of the British.

We have seen how the French citizens at Kaskaskia questioned the legality of the action of the king's procurator. Let us now turn to an authority of greater experience and weight—General Thomas Gage. To his mind there could be no doubt about the illegality of the procedure of the Louisiana officials; they had clearly exceeded their powers; they had infringed upon the rights of his majesty, King George III. Writing from New York to General Conway, June 24, 1766, he says:

"I have the honor to transmit to you a Paper relative to the Effects of the Jesuits in the Ilinois Country; from whence it appears, that their Effects were confiscated for the use of the French King, by a Decree of the Superior Council of New Orleans, after the Treaty was concluded, which ceded that Country to the Crown of Great Britain; and which I think must have been known by the said Council at the Time the Decree was issued. I am informed, that the French Governor alleged, he had a Right to seize their Effects, because the Society was considerably indebted to the King His Master who would on that Account demand also an Attachment upon the Effects of the said Society, in the Province of Quebec. The French King may have a Right to demand Payment for a just Debt from the subjects of another Prince, and Sue for the Same; but I don't conceive that it is consistent with the Law of Nations that he should confiscate the Effects belonging to the Subjects of another Prince, out of his own Dominions, on any Pretence. The Negroes and Moveables sold and carried away are not easily recovered; but I presume that the Lands, Buildings and other Immoveables, as the Jesuits are gone, must fall to the King, and I have ordered them to be claimed in His Majesty's Name.'"[52]

The missionaries were transported under guard to New Orleans. where they enjoyed every mark of friendship and hospitality at the hands of the Capuchin fathers. In gratitude they pressed their hosts

[51] Brown, Stuart, *Old Kaskaskia Days and Ways,* ILLINOIS CATHOLIC HISTORICAL REVIEW, *July,* 1919, p. 65.
[52] Alvord and Carter, *The New Regime,* p. 323.

to accept the small library which alone had been spared to them from the wreckage of their missions. In New Orleans Father Neurin pleaded so earnestly for permission to remain and labor among the Indians that his request was granted. Father de Baudoin, a man seventy-two years of age and an American by birth, was also suffered to remain because influential men interfered in his behalf, but the others were packed aboard the Minerve, the first ship sailing for France. A narrow escape from shipwreck in the Bahama Channel was followed by a stormy passage of three months' duration, during which the ship was so badly battered that it was compelled to put into San Sebastian, Spain, instead of proceeding to Bayonne as originally intended.

(To be continued)

CHARLES H. METZGER, S. J.
Saint Louis University,
St. Louis, Mo.

THE FRANCISCANS IN SOUTHERN
· ILLINOIS

(Continued from October, 1920)

The second institution of learning founded in Illinois by the Franciscans, is St. Joseph's Seminary and College at Teutopolis. · It owes
its beginning to the zeal of the Rt. Rev. Bishop Damian H. Juncker,
who strove in every way to increase the number of priests in his diocese and who, therefore, was anxious to possess an institution which
would foster vocations and prepare aspirants to the priesthood for
their sacred calling. It was this desire which caused him, in the very
first year after his consecration, to undertake a voyage to Europe in
order to obtain recruits for his diocese. The episcopal residence, moreover, erected after his return from Europe in July, 1858, was designed to serve as his ecclesiastical seminary.[1] For various reasons,
the latter never fully served its purpose. Most of the seminarians continued to pursue their studies at other institutions in this country and
abroad.[2] A few, however, completed their studies in the episcopal
residence at Alton. A letter of Rev. Herbert Hoffmanns, O. F. M., to
the Very Rev. Provincial in Germany, informs us that he taught theology there for about one year. Under date of January 27, 1862, Fr.
Herbert writes from Teutopolis:

"Allow me to offer you my heartiest good wishes for the new year,
and to inform you that I have at last returned from Alton to the convent at Teutopolis. When I answered the call of the Rt. Rev. Bishop
in October, 1860, I hoped to finish my work at Alton in three or four
months, but I was greatly disappointed. The circumstance that Rev.
(John J.) Menge was in Europe, and that almost all the theologians
were called from the seminaries to Alton, detained me there over a
year and three months, since the last three seminarians were ordained
priests as late as November 24, 1861."[3]

[1] Cf. Clarke: *Lives of the Deceased Bishops of the Catholic Church in the
United States*," p. 535; Zurbonsen: *Clerical Bead Roll of the Diocese of Alton*,"
p. 13, sq.
[2] In 1860, there were students of the diocese of Alton at All Hallows, Ireland; Mt. St. Mary's of the West, Cincinnati, O.; Cape Girardeau, Mo.; St. Francis de Sales, Milwaukee, Wis.; St. Thomas, Ky. The total number of students
was twelve. Cf. *The Metropolitan Catholic Almanac*, for the year 1860.
[3] A copy of this letter is in the Seminary archives. According to information
kindly furnished the writer by Rev. Michael A. Tarrent, Secretary to the Rt. Rev.

260

A short time after the arrival of the Franciscans in his diocese, in 1858, Bishop Juncker conceived the idea of entrusting to them the building and management of an institution such as he had in view. He broached the matter to the Rev. Damian Hennewig, pastor at Teutopolis, and met with a hearty response; for the latter was very desirous of offering to the boys and young men of his parish and of the surrounding territory an opportunity to obtain a higher education. The matter was thoroughly discussed and, as there could be no question of two institutions, it was decided that the projected institution should serve both as a high school and as the diocesan seminary.

The consent of the Rev. Provincial was obtained, in 1860, on the occasion of his visit to this country, in order to perform the canonical visitation of the missions at Teutopolis and Quincy. The chronicle of the Province *ad annum* refers to these facts in the words: "Even before this time (the visit of the Rev. Provincial), the erection of a college had long been desired by the parish, strongly urged by Father Damian, and advocated by the Rt. Rev. Bishop; hence the Very Rev. Father Provincial felt constrained to give his consent. He also promised to provide competent teachers."

The energetic Father Damian at once took steps to carry out the project. He called a meeting of the townspeople, and at this meeting, held on October 19, 1860, a committee was chosen to select a suitable site for the institution and to collect the necessary funds. The "Program," drawn up at the meeting, reads as follows:

"Since the town of Teutopolis, on account of its healthful climate and retired location, appears to afford a suitable site for an institution of learning; and since the Rt. Rev. Bishop Damian H. Juncker desires to possess in his diocese a Seminary, equipped according to the canonical regulations, in which pious and gifted young men who feel called to the priesthood can be properly trained for the holy ministry, for the honor of God, their own salvation, and that of their fellowmen; and since his Lordship has graciously accepted the offer of the town to erect a seminary building, with the assurance that, if the local and the surrounding parishes successfully carry out this undertaking, they, as the first, should exclusively possess an institution of this kind, until others be considered necessary; and since the Rev. Father Provincial of the Rheno-Westphalian Province of the Franciscan Order has promised to provide that, as far as possible, competent teachers be sent by said Province; hence, the inhabitants of this town and of the surrounding territory have agreed to contribute, according to their means, toward this useful purpose.

Bishop of Alton, two ordinations took place at Alton during the year 1861: one on April 21, the other on November 24. On the occasion of the former, the following theologians were ordained: Rev. Theodore Elshoff, Rev. William Busch, Rev. Peter Peters, and Rev. Peter McGirr; on the occasion of the latter: Rev. John F. Mohr, Rev. Henry J. Hoven, and Rev. John Larmer.

"And in order that this institution be of more general benefit to the people of this part of the state, it shall have a department in which boys who have completed the course in the elementary school, and who have received their first Holy Communion, shall have an opportunity to pursue advanced studies and to prepare themselves for life.

"The building committee chosen by the majority of the members of the parish, and consisting of Messrs. Clement Uptmor, John Henry Wernsing, Diederich Eggermann, Gerard Bergfeld, Henry Schumacher, and John F. Waschefort, after mature deliberation, has selected as the most healthful, retired, and suitable site for the projected institution, the former site of the windmill;[4] and the committee has received assurances from the present owners, that they would be willing to dispose of the property for the intended purpose.

"Hence, to carry out the project which redounds to the common good, the undersigned have promised, on their honor and good faith, to pay to said building committee the following sum in installments, as follows: the first third, on February 1, 1861; the second third, on July 1, 1861; the last third, on January 1, 1862.

"Thus done at Teutopolis, on October 19, 1860, with the approbation of the Superiors, as testifies the President of the Building Committee,

DAMIAN HENNEWIG, Praeses.

By order of the Rt. Rev. Bishop H. Damian Juncker."[5]

The land described in the "Program," comprising eleven lots in blocks 18 and 34, was acquired partly by purchase, partly by donation. Other lots were bought in 1871 and 1872, so that the entire property of the College comprises almost two blocks. The building committee took up subscriptions according to the agreement made at the meeting. One of the books used by them is still extant and shows the names of thirty-five families well known in Effingham County.

BUILDING OPERATIONS

Excavations were begun early in the spring of 1861, and on July 2, Father Damian, in the name of the Bishop, solemnly blessed the

---

[4] During the first years after the founding of Teutopolis, the people had to bring their grain to Newton, twenty-one miles distant, to have it ground. "Often the road was so bad that the people could not get to the mill by wagons (such as they had) and would go on foot and carry their grist on their back. When out of meal, they would crack corn with a hammer and make bread of it. But in the year 1842, Mr. Clement Uptmor and his brother, Henry Uptmor, built a four-arm windmill. This mill had only one pair of buhrs. It had a bolt which had to be turned by hand." It was a clumsy structure, as the timber, felled in the woods near-by, had to be prepared by hand, there being no sawmill far and wide. A strong wind was required to set it in motion. "In its day it was a tremendous event. More curious and glad people visited this wonder of the day, by far, than do now go to see the magnificent four-story grist mill." In 1857, Mr. John F. Waschefort built a steam mill with a capacity of fifty barrels a day. The windmill was torn down about the month of May, 1860. Cf. History of Effingham County, Part I, p. 252, sq., and Part II, p. 145.

[5] Original, in German, in the Seminary archives.

cornerstone of the new building. About Christmas of the same year, Father Damian wrote to the Very Rev. Provincial:

"Our Seminary building is finished to the roof, by dint of the greatest exertion and amid prospects far from promising." If I had not pushed the work with all my might, we should not have got beyond the foundation walls, and the congregation' would perhaps have lost confidence in the undertaking. The building now stands a stately structure and, they say, an ornament to Teutopolis, 80 feet long by 50 feet wide, a four-story building, offering accommodations for 50-80 students. All now depends on the support we find; in case we find support, we shall, with the help of God, continue the work this coming year until it is completed."⁸

On February 10, 1862, he again wrote:

"The Seminary building is now under roof, but the treasury, owing to these sad war times, is exhausted, so that, unless we obtain aid from elsewhere, we are at a loss how to continue. I was appointed president of the Building Committee by the Bishop, and in consequence have had many cares and anxieties. To be able to continue building operations, I saw myself compelled to go to Cincinnati.⁹ I have just returned from that city."

Meanwhile Bishop Juncker and the clergy did not fail to show active interest in the coming Seminary and College. In the letter of January 27, 1862, quoted above, Father Herbert, who was appointed first President of the institution, wrote to the Very Rev. Provincial Othmar Maasmann, the successor of Father Gregory Janknecht:

"At the retreat of the clergy of Alton (preached by the Rev. Francis X. Weninger, S. J.), which I attended, his Lordship spoke of the Seminary and exhorted all to support it, declaring that it would be opened this fall. His words were received with great satisfaction, and all priests promised to co-operate in promoting the undertaking. Ever since, all eyes in the diocese are directed to Teutopolis; yes, even Missouri is interested; for, as the Rt. Rev. Joseph Melcher, Vicar-General, and other priests say, his Grace, the Archbishop of St. Louis, will undoubtedly send hither his seminarians, as soon as the institution is ready to receive them. The Bishop will probably send the seminarians who are now studying at other institutions in this country or abroad, because, as he says, he is not able to meet the expenses which their education elsewhere entails."

OPENING OF THE SEMINARY

In spite of all difficulties, building operations continued without interruption, and in August, 1862, the structure was finished and

---

*It was during the first year of the Civil War, and the treasury was soon empty.

⁷ The Catholics of Teutopolis, Effingham, and Green Creek.

⁸ Copy of original, in German, in the Seminary archives.

⁹ To collect or borrow money.

ready for occupancy. The solemn dedication took place on Sunday,
September 15th. At 7 o'clock, Father Nazarius Kommerscheid, who
had been ordained by Bishop Juncker in the parish church the day
before, said his first Holy Mass, in the presence of the Bishop. Services over, a procession was formed, consisting of the students, seminarians, the community of the friary, the invited guests, and the
officiating clergy, which marched to the new building. The ceremonies took place in a large apartment in the second floor, subsequently used as a chapel. The Rt. Rev. Bishop delivered English and
German addresses, in which he emphasized the importance of the
institution for the diocese, praised the zeal of the Franciscans and of
the people, and expressed the heartiest good wishes for a successful
future. On the next day, September 16th, the first scholastic year was
opened. The faculty consisted of:

Rev. Herbert Hoffmanns—President, Professor of Dogmatic Theology.

Rev. Damian Hennewig—Professor of Moral Theology.

Rev. Anselm Mueller.[10]

Mr. Lawrence Holmes—Teacher of Music.

Rev. Eugene Puers joined the faculty in December of the same
year.

The seminarians present at the opening of the school year numbered six, the students of the high school department twenty-five.
These numbers increased during the year to eight and fifty, respectively. Of the latter, thirty hailed from Effingham County. The
seminarians were: James Harty, —— Krocker, William Kuchenbuch,
Maria Mueller, Ferdinand Stick, Joseph Stumpe, Henry Vogt, and
Sylvester Wegener.[11]

During the second school year, 1863-1864, there were eleven seminarians, and fifty-two students in the high school department; during
the following year, the seminarians numbered sixteen, while forty-
eight students pursued the high school course. Most of the latter
came from towns in Illinois; several are recorded, during these first
years, as hailing from Missouri; one each from Ohio, New York,
and Louisiana.

---

[10] Cf. ILLINOIS CATHOLIC HISTORICAL REVIEW, October, 1920, p. 172, note.

[11] *Jubilee Catalogue for the Twenty-Fifth Anniversary of St. Joseph's Diocesan College*, 1887.

Quincy Parish Church and Convent, 1875

By courtesy of *The Teutopolis Press.*

Franciscan Seminary, Quincy, 1875

THE SEMINARY DEPARTMENT DISCONTINUED

Thus, the Fathers had reasons to hope that the institution would continue to expand and to fulfill the expectations of it founders. But difficulties arose which, for a time, threatened to put an end to the work of education so propitiously begun. The maintenance of the Seminary and College demanded many sacrifices of the Fathers, for they were few in number. Besides this, owing to the circumstances of the time, they had to attend missions and engage in other pastoral duties. It was but natural that this worked to the detriment of the institution. The Rev. Provincial, moreover, declared that the needs of the Province in Germany were such that he found it impossible to send more teachers;[12] hence the Fathers seriously thought of closing the institution. After long and earnest deliberations, it was decided to discontinue only the seminary department. This was done in the summer of 1865. The greater number of the seminarians continued their studies at the seminary at Montreal.

The number of seminarians during the three years, 1862-1865, was twenty-five. Their names, besides those mentioned above, are: Joseph Beineke, Frank Fokele, Bernard Hillebrand, Theodore Kamann, Stanislas Kane, Charles Klocke, Francis Lohmann, G. Luecken, O'Brien, Longinus Quitter, Anthony Rustige, William Schamoni, Jeremiah Sullivan, Michael Weis, Adolph Wibbert, Herman Wigger, Blase Winterhalter.

---

[12] To understand the difficulties with which the Rev. Provincial had to cope, it may not be out of place to refer to the condition of the Province in Germany during the first half of the nineteenth century. At the beginning of the century the Province had eighteen large convents and two residences in the Rhineland, and several missions in Protestant districts. All these houses were seized by the French and later on by the Prussians during the period of secularization, beginning with 1802. The religious were permitted to remain in a number of convents, but they were forbidden to receive novices. As a result, the number of the religious gradually dwindled, and the Province was threatened with extinction. In the year 1828, the king of Prussia, as a special favor, permitted twelve young men to be received as clerics, and a few as brothers. Thus, the condition of the Province continued to be a precarious one, until King Frederick William IV, in 1843, among other concessions, permitted the reception of novices under certain conditions. After some time, the friars were gradually enabled to reoccupy their former convents and to devote themselves to their accustomed labors. It was, therefore, a sacrifice for the Province to send men to the United States in 1858, at a time when it was as yet on the way of recovery from its sad and weakened condition; and at this critical time, the illness and death of a number of Fathers and urgent needs of the Province, made it impossible for the Rev. Provincial to live up to his promise to provide more teachers for the Seminary at Teutopolis.

St. Joseph's Ecclesiastical College

Meanwhile Father Herbert had resigned his position as President of the institution and had been appointed to teach theology to the clerics of the Order. His successor was Father Maurice Klostermann, who guided the destinies of the College from the summer of 1864 till the summer of 1882.[13] The aim of the institution, henceforth known as "St. Joseph's Ecclesiastical College," now was to impart to its students a thorough classical education. The course of studies was arranged to extend over six years; subsequently a commercial course was added. About this time, or during the last years of Bishop Juncker's administration, an agreement was reached, by which the College became the property of the diocese of Alton and stood under the supervision of the bishop. Though it was open to all who wished to take advantage of its course of studies, it was "intended principally for youths who wished to prepare themselves for the holy ministry."[14] In spite of many difficulties, which at one time again almost caused it to close its doors, the College successfully continued its educational work. The number of students increased from year to year, so that it was found necessary in the course of time to build several additions to the original structure. In 1877 an addition was erected on the east side of the building. In 1884, during the administration of Father Michael Richardt, President of the College from 1882 till 1891,[15] a wing was built on the west side. A further enlargement was made in the year 1889, when the present study hall, auditorium, and gymnasium were erected. The beautiful Romanesque chapel, together with an extension of the western wing, was built in 1895-1896, during the administration of Father Hugoline Storff, President from 1893 till 1900, and again from 1906 till 1912.

The College was incorporated by Rt. Rev. Bishop Peter Joseph Baltes in 1881, as "St. Joseph's Diocesan College." It bore this title until 1898, when, by an agreement with the Rt. Rev. Bishop James Ryan, it passed entirely under the control of the Franciscans and was made a preparatory seminary exclusively for boys and young men who wish to become priests of the Order of St. Francis. It is now called "St. Joseph's Seminary."

That the institution has lived up to the intention of its founders is evident from the fact that, since 1862, no less than 482 of its students have become priests. Of this number, 289 are members of

---

[13] For sketch of Father Maurice, see Zurbonsen: *Bead Roll*, etc., p. 70, sq.

[14] Official document signed by Bishop Baltes, in the Seminary archives.

[15] For sketch of Fr. Michael, see Zurbonsen: *Bead Roll*, etc., p. 117.

religious Orders, principally of the Franciscan Order. Fifteen died as Franciscan clerics. At present forty-six are pursuing the studies of philosophy and theology as Franciscan clerics, and seventeen are novices of the Order. Besides, a large number of teachers, physicians, lawyers, and of men successful in various callings, also point to St. Joseph's Seminary and College as their *Alma Mater*. This is a record of which, we think, the institution may be justly proud.

SILAS BARTH, O. F. M.

Teutopolis, Illinois.

THE KNIGHTS OF COLUMBUS IN THE WAR AND AFTER

CASEY

"High be the mission and honored the name of her,
Wherever her course o'er the waters may be,
Brave the behavior and glowing the fame of her
Worthy to carry the emblem—K. C.
Safe be each journey and swift each return of her,
Smooth be the seas she is destined to plow,
With the Red, White and Blue streaming out from the stern of her,
And her good Irish name on her bluff, honest bow."[1]

Thus versified the popular poet, James J. Montague in the columns of the *New York World* when the United States Shipping Board was about to launch a great vessel named "Casey" in honor of the splendid war welfare service of the Knights of Columbus. *Qu'est — ce que C'est*[1] tells how the Knights of Columbus acquired the name of "Casey."

"It was in the Argonne drive that some one dubbed them 'Casey'—those chaps who wore the K. of C. brassard; and because they were generally around when one was 'smoke hungry'—the call was taken up by all ranks, "Keep coming, Casey,' and if we remember rightly—and we do—they did keep coming."

Yes, K. C. was in evidence and he kept coming. There were over 100,000 of him in the actual service, on land, on water and in the air.[2] In the ranks of the officers he gave an excellent account of himself and amongst the privates his services were unsurpassed. More than twenty-five thousand young fellows who associated with K. C., in the service or contemplated his creditable conduct have since fraternized with him through membership in the same Order.[3] This is not the place, however, to detail the war record of Knights of Columbus. Not sufficient space is here available.[4] A brief reference to the welfare work of the Knights of Columbus may, however, be made.

---

[1] A paper published by the American students in the University of Toulouse.
[2] *Knights of Columbus in Peace and War*, Egan and Kennedy, lists 87,300 names of Knights of Columbus in the service from 1,645 Councils, 396 Councils are not included in this list.
[3] Since the demobilization of the forces 250,000 men have joined the Knights of Columbus, two-thirds of whom are estimated to have been former servicemen.
[4] An official work of two substantial volumes entitled *Knights of Columbus in Peace and War*, edited by the able Catholic author, Maurice Francis Egan, and

TIMELY MOVEMENT

Timeliness is frequently the best quality of action. There is really more merit in the familiar expression "the psychical moment" than is sometimes supposed. Promptitude has in a sense at least been a virtue of the Knights of Columbus. Glancing back a few years it is easy to recall the distress of the residents of San Francisco as the result of the calamitious earthquake. Ere the echoes of that catastrophe had died away, telegraph wires were vibrating with messages of succor and condolence from the Knights of Columbus, and almost before any other outside aid reached San Francisco $100,000 was placed at the disposal of the earthquake sufferers.

In like manner, flood sufferers in Pennsylvania, Ohio, and Kansas, the storm-wrecked in Illinois and sufferers from an explosion in Halifax, Nova Scotia were promptly aided.[5]

INTRODUCTION TO WAR WORK

The Knights of Columbus have apparently felt it a duty incumbent upon them to follow the fortunes of their countrymen into war. Although little necessity existed, the Order nevertheless offered and indeed furnished some help at the time of the Spanish-American War.[6] When there was a prospect of disturbance with Mexico, and our boys were stationed along the border, the Order entered wholeheartedly into the work of making the service less distasteful and of carrying a ray of cheer and comfort to the men on duty.[7] Knights of Columbus were not therefore, strangers to the character of effort that would be helpful in the contingency of a serious war such as appalled the world in 1914, and involved the United States in 1917.

EXPEDITION THE WATCHWORD

Scarcely had congress, at the call of the President, declared a state of war to exist between Germany and the United States, and

---

Mr. John B. Kennedy, the able Director of Publicity for the Knights of Columbus during the war, has been published, which tells the war story in general terms, and lists in Volume II a large number of the members that were in the service. A *History of the Knights of Columbus in Illinois* is in preparation, in which the record for Illinois Knights of Columbus will be given in greater detail.

[5] *Knights of Columbus in Peace and War*, Egan and Kennedy, ch. XII.

[6] An appropriation was made to aid returning soldiers at Montauck Point.

[7] A chain of recreation buildings were erected along the border in New Mexico, Arizona and Texas similar to the welfare buildings at the cantonments in the late war. See for full account of Mexican border work, *Knights of Columbus in Peace and War*, Egan and Kennedy, ch. XV.

war preparations begun, than the Supreme Officers tendered the services of the Order to assist at home and abroad, in camp and field, and wherever American men went, or wherever faithful service was needed. The generous offer was accepted, and without losing a moment the great camp program of the Knights of Columbus was begun. As fast as mobilization camps were located in this country the Knights of Columbus began and completed buildings at such camps, until a total of 461 buuildings were erected at the camps, and in addition 32 great tents were brought into service. There were also eleven buildings constructed at permanent army posts.[8]

These Knights of Columbus buildings were the clubs of the army men. Within their walls was brought to the service man as much of home as it was possible to translate. The rigid discipline of the service was here relaxed, and the naturally lonesome boy was provided with comforts and conveniences, including books, periodicals, writing paper and other adjuncts of convenience.[9] In these buildings also were the recreational facilities and the entertainments which helped to make this new strange life, away from home and friends, tolerable.[10] And,

---

[8] *Report of the Supreme Board of Directors, Knights of Columbus, for Fiscal Year ending Jan. 30, 1919,* summary p. 24.

[9] The following description of the Knights of Columbus buildings at the camps is taken from the *Literary Digest:*

"At one end of the building there is an alcove in which the altar is placed. After Mass is celebrated, the alcove is closed, shutting off the altar from view. There is also a small room used as a sacristy. Two small rooms are in the rear. One is used by those in charge, the other for a library. Around the inside of the building desks are made fast to the walls for the men to write on. The room also contains a piano, billiard table and other means of amusement."

[10] The following communication from a very competent Knights of Columbus Secretary, Mr. T. J. Leanord, gives a very good idea of the welfare work in the camps. In speaking of the completion of the three Knights of Columbus buildings at Camp Grant Mr. Leanord says:

"The halls are now fully equipped, being replete with player-pianos, victrolas, and games of all kinds. They are regular hives of activity in the evenings when the boys are dismissed from their arduous duties of the day. The supply of magazines is plentiful, but there is an insistent demand for 'up-to-date stuff.' Many of the good people of Rockford have been kind enough to donate some splendid framed pictures which give the place a homelike atmosphere, besides being very ornamental. There are now four secretaries on the ground, and by close coöperation they are accomplishing wonderful results. Every other evening an entertainment is provided in all of the halls and the boys 'pack the house.' Friends at home have noticed that stationery bearing the emblem has been provided and is being used extensively. Cards of invitation have been received from the various Catholic societies in Rockford, inviting the boys to their doings, and they have been distributed to the boys. Three Masses are celebrated on Sunday

true to its purpose and mission, in these same buildings were, on the proper occasions, Sundays and Holy days, held the consoling and inspiritional divine services that brought so much comfort into the very shadow of war.[11]

"EVERYBODY WELCOME AND EVERYTHING FREE"

In these Knights of Columbus buildings as well as in all the huts and dugouts abroad, the policy which crystallized into a slogan was "everybody welcome and everything free." It is one of the glories of the Knights of Columbus welfare work that from the beginning to the end absolutely no distinction was ever made or recognized on account of race or creed. The one badge to full recognition and fellowship in the Knights of Columbus welfare work and its benefits and advantages was the colors of the United States.[12]

---

morning in each hall, at 6:30, 8:30 and 9:30 a. m., the halls being taxed to their capacity. A most gratifying feature of the work is the large and increasing number of communionists. Confessions are heard every Saturday at all the halls in the afternoon and evening."

[11] How universally these agencies were employed is well illustrated by an extract from the *Monitor*, quoted in the *Literary Digest* of January 19, 1918: "Ten Masses are said every Sunday in the Y. M. C. A. and K. of C. buildings (the Y. M. C. A. permit the use of their building). The buildings are overfilled at each Mass. The men kneel in the aisle, on the doorsteps and even outside on the grounds. Protestants marvel at this. They can't understand it. A lasting impression is being made on them. One of the chaplains told us of a wealthy man who gave up his business in order to take up the Y. M. C. A. work in the camp. For several Sundays he had watched these great gatherings of Catholics at the Masses. One Sunday he came to the priest and said: 'Father, every Sunday you have thousands at the Mass, while we get only a handful at our services. Every Sunday you have the same thing; you never change, and the buildings won't hold the men. We change, we bring in new speakers, men of national reputation; we do everything to attract the men without avail. Father, how do you do it? Why do they come to the Mass?' "

[12] "They do not ask the faith or creed
Of him that comes into their hut;
True Knighthood's door is never shut
Against a pilgrim warrior's need.
They question only: 'Would you rest
And are you weary and oppressed?
Then, brother, lay aside your care,
And come, this sheltering roof to share.' "
EDWARD A. GUEST, *Detroit Free Press.*

"CREATURE COMFORTS"

The Sun of Baltimore has given us the most expressive statement of this comparatively new term for a really ancient desire:

"'Creature Comforts!' What a phrase to conjure with. Like the dough-nuts and flapjacks of the Salvation Army lassies, 'creature comforts' will stick in the memory of the average soldier when many other things have been for-gotten. 'Creature comforts' is what we are all after, and the boys in the army, cut off from home and friends, prized them probably as never before. Not so elevating or idealistic, perhaps, as sermons or tracts, but these "creature com-forts' went straight to the right spot.

"We congratulate the Knights of Columbus on the sagacity of their human psychology. Man does not live by 'creature comforts' alone, but he cannot live happily without them if he has once enjoyed them. The wisdom of the Knights of Columbus, as of the Salvation Army, was shown in dealing with these soldier boys as a mother would in remembering their bodies and their stomachs, as well as their minds and souls.

"'Creature comforts' are two great words. May they never be forgot."

For "Creature Comforts" thus so highly commended $7,000,000 of the funds secured and expended by the Knights of Columbus were used, and the Brooklyn Eagle said:

"The amount expended on free creature comforts for the soldiers was larger than that spent for a similar purpose by all of the other organizations partici-pating in the United States War Drive Fund combined."

"Creature Comforts," to be explicit, included cigarettes, tobacco, chewing gum, chocolate, candy, soap, handkerchiefs and similar articles.[13]

---

[13] A letter written by Lieutenant John E. O'Brien of the 147th Infantry to the State Deputy of Illinois, Edward Houlihan, furnishes some evidence on this point. From the battle front Mr. O'Brien wrote:

"I do not know whether this letter is going to interest you or not—you are doubtless flooded with notes of a like nature,—but I cannot forbear adding my little testimonial of appreciation of the work the Knights are doing for the fel-lows in the line. To the man back home it seems a little, trivial thing—a piece of chocolate, a newspaper, a magazine, a cigarette. You could stop any man and ask for those things and he would accommodate you—unthinkingly. But up here in the first of the front lines, with every meal the same—canned Willie and alfalfa soup—those little things assume a magnitude, an importance, in our minds, that is almost unbelievable. To come in at two or three in the morning after working all night on the wire, and in it; your nerves taut and barbed; your eyes strained and weary; tired to the very soul of you, to come in and close your dugout door and take a long deep drag of a cigarette—well, he who has not done it does not know what a boon tobacco is. And you are hungry, too; but there is a small bit of chocolate to stay your pangs till daylight comes, and you may have a fire and cook your breakfast—your delicate breakfast of Willie and soup. And

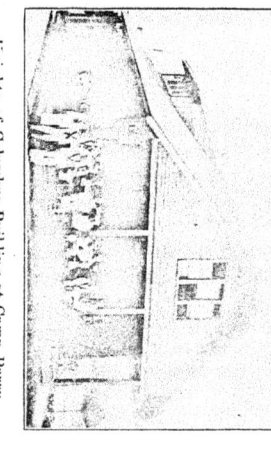

Knights of Columbus Building at Camp Perry

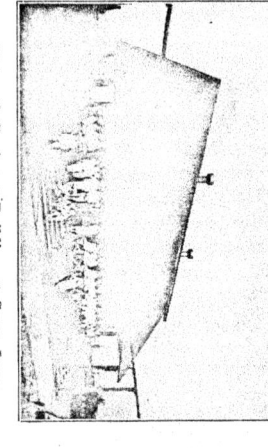

Sixteenth Regiment Building at Camp Luce
By courtesy of *Columbian.*

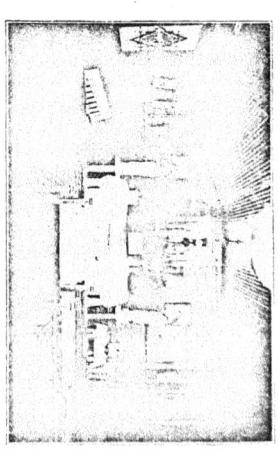

Our Lady of the Lake's Chapel, Camp Perry

K. of C. Building at Camp Luce

TYPES OF KNIGHTS OF COLUMBUS BUILDINGS

Besides these various items other articles were supplied free, such as writing materials, musical instruments and athletic supplies and equipment.

FOLLOWING THE FLAG

As soon as leave could be obtained to do so, the Knights of Columbus set out to follow the flag across the sea, and very soon after the first soldiers landed in France they found K. C. there ready to serve them. The first care of the Order was to get supplies across the ocean, and from established supply stations goods were sent out to the servicemen, at first by any possible means that could be secured, and later by automobile trucks.[14] During the engagement at Mihiel 20,000

then in the afternoon, after you get up, and sit around waiting the order, knowing that when it comes you must go out and throw the dice with death again, and your nerves get run and you get restless and uneasy—there is a newspaper or a magazine to take your mind off your beastly task, to remind you of the living, breathing world across the sea; to tell again that the millions back there are with you—well, it helps, Mister, it helps.

"Little things like, trivial, inconsequential things, plenty of them in France. Back of the lines you can buy them—*buy* them—*buy* them at retail prices; back of the lines—where you don't really need them. But on the front you get them and you get them *free*. I have a detail of men whose task is repairing the front line wire. While the division is in, we never get back of the first line of defense. Every night we spend in No Man's Land, and it is not pleasant. But when we get in, it is waiting for us—our candy, cigarettes and papers—awaiting us with the K. of C. stamp on it all. Doesn't matter if Jerry is shelling the roads; doesn't matter if it's raining, that dirty, beastly French rain; doesn't matter if it's dark and gruesome and weird up here—always we can look for and expect that old one-lunged motorcycle of Brother Thomas—and we never yet waited in vain."

[14] The story told by Father Thomas F. Coakley, chaplain of the 147th Infantry, A. P. O. 746, indicates some of the difficulties connected with this part of the Knights of Columbus program. In writing to Mr. Lawrence O. Murray, in charge of the Knights of Columbus Headquarters in Paris, Father Coakley said: "My Dear Mr. Murray:

"I wish to thank you most heartily in my own name, and in the name of the officers and men of this Forty-Seventh Regiment of Infantry, for the large supply of candy, chocolate, cigarettes, smoking and chewing tobacco, cigars, chewing gum, writing paper, envelopes and postcards that reached me today from Paris by truck in spite of the roads that could not in the wildest flight of fancy be imagined worse than they are.

"After strenuous efforts we managed to transport these K. of C. supplies by auto truck—which soon stuck in the mud; then by ambulances, which stuck in turn; then in machine gun limbers; then on stretchers and on the backs of the grateful and appreciative men, clean up to the front line trenches and dugouts, right under German fire; and there was plenty for each man, distributed free,

packages of cigarettes were delivered to the boys at the front by the K. of C. Secretary by means of an aeroplane. In the most active stage of American participation the Knights of Columbus Secretary was about as well known by his overworked wheezy automobile as by the uniform in which the government permitted him to be clothed. K. C.'s place was with the servicemen, and wherever the servicemen went he followed, consequently his place of abode was temporary, but when the batallion or division settled down, K. C. settled down with him, and constructed a hut from any refuse obtainable; and if nothing better could be devised he dug a hole in the ground and established himself in this dugout. Here he brought up the "creature comforts" especially, and here the weary serviceman found an opportunity to while away a pleasant hour in the midst of his discomforts and desolation.

ENTERTAINING THE SERVICEMEN

K. C. will perhaps be best remembered by the servicemen on account of the altogether pleasing manner in which these "creature comforts" were distributed, but next after this feature of the work came the really meritorious entertainment program. The big features of K. C. entertainment abroad were "The A. E. F. Circus," the "Wild West Show," several Minstrel Shows, and the Motion Pictures. Numerous entertainments were staged and almost an army of bands and orchestras equipped, there being more than 50,000 musical instruments supplied. Several hundred motion picture machines were placed in clubhouses and huts. It is estimated that more than half a million of servicemen were entertained each night during the active period of the war by the Knights of Columbus moving picture service alone. Besides this, 5,000 games of baseball were daily played by servicemen, outfits for which were supplied by the Knights of Columbus.

The great marathon race from Chateau Thierry to Paris that

and the praise and appreciation for the K. of C. initiative and anxiety for the welfare of the fighting men are on every lip.

"Rarely, even in the commissary, has such a quantity of good things been given to the men who are bearing the real burden of the war in this inclement weather, and I am sending you this word of gratitude so that you may convey it to the K. of C. officials back home as an evidence of my being alive to their efforts to handle their immense and complicated problem in a big and generous way, without thought of themselves."

attracted so much attention the world over was entirely under the auspices of the Knights of Columbus.[15]

The ingenuity of the best managers available was drawn upon for these entertainments, and much of the entertainment was of a character equal to the best that has been produced in the amusement and theatrical world.

THE FRIEND IN NEED

It should not be supposed, however, that the activities of the Knights of Columbus were limited to furnishing ''creature comforts'' and entertainment—indeed they engaged in much more serious, if not more helpful work. The heralds of the Knights of Columbus were the Knights of Columbus Chaplains[16] and the Knights of Columbus Secretaries. It was desirable to make provision for these functionaries to live in some comfort amongst the soldiers, but they were not of a character to wait until comforts had been provided.

''Often the only shelter a chaplain or secretary had was the hat on his head. .... Before huts could be erected men had to be served, and the Knights of

[15] *Report of the Supreme Board of Directors, Knights of Columbus, Jan. 30, 1919*, p. 50.

[16] The popularity of the chaplains is illustrated by a communication of Charles N. Wheeler, the noted war correspondent, in the *Chicago Tribune* of Sunday, December 15, 1918. Mr. Wheeler, in speaking about the assignment of chaplains upon reports from the different regiments and divisions, says:

''In this work there developed the need of a sort of religious census of the units in order to determine what sort of a chaplain would be sent to the respective unit, always having in mind the advisability of sending a Protestant to a Protestant regiment and a Catholic to a regiment in which the Catholics predominate.

''The reports came in from several regiments the other day and the senior chaplain of the division read one over very carefully, a couple of times. Then he wondered if a mistake had been made, for this regiment was listed as 100 per cent Catholic. He thought a new record had been made and that if such a regiment was serving it was worth while to emphasize the point. He ordered an investigation made to be sure that no mistake had been committed. When the second report came in it was disclosed that the regiment was only 50 per cent, or a little less, perhaps, Catholic. Then the real story was divulged. The report had been circulated among the boys that their chaplain, who was a Catholic, might be assigned to another regiment, where there was a greater percentage of Catholics. This particular chaplain was a great favorite in the regiment, with the Protestant boys as with the Catholics. Soon after this report was started the census was taken—and the regiment to a man went down on the record as a Catholic 'for the duration of the war.'

''It is needless to state that this chaplain is still on active service with this regiment.''

Columbus worker with his motorcycle, or his car, or on foot, went through the camps as his co-workers were going to the front, their bags on their backs, just as the fighting man carried his, and distributed the little things that help to make life comfortable.''

These secretaries, of whom there were over one thousand in the service abroad before the conclusion of the war, were veritably all things to all men. They knelt by the side of the wounded soldier, and took his dying message to the loved ones at home. They were at once the counsellor and guide to the wavering and lonesome soldier boy, and his messenger and servant. With equal propriety they could, if occasion demanded, admonish the wayward youngster, or, when necessity pressed upon them, become the camp barbers. The secretary or chaplain was the intermediary between the sometimes derelict serviceman and his sometimes too exacting superior officer. No intercession was more potent in obtaining desired advantages so valuable to the serviceman than that of a K. C. Secretary or Chaplain, and by all accounts the especially luminous service of K. C. was rendered in the hospitals and hospital ships. Back of the lines in all the hospitals the Knights of Columbus Secretaries and Chaplains were always to be found, and no part of the K. C. work has been more feelingly described than that which had to do with the sick and wounded and dying.[17] On the hospital ships generous supplies were provided for

---

[17] The noted war correspondent, Floyd Gibbons, relates a touching incident of the hospital where he was himself confined after he had lost an eye and almost his life on No Man's Land, in his determination to be with the men nearest the front. When convalescing in the hospital, Gibbons said:

''Two beds on my right was a young American soldier. A German high explosive shell had shattered his leg at the battle of Cantigny and it had been necessary to amputate the limb. The amputation had been made above the knee. Without introducing himself—without saying a word—Pallen (a K. of C. Secretary) proceeded to this man's bedside and began to walk up and down nervously in front of it. He soon attracted the attention of the sufferer, whose curiosity was aroused immediately by Pallen's peculiar actions.

'' 'How does that look?' Pallen stopped in his floor pacing and directed the question to the man on the bed. 'Do I walk all right?' 'Looks all right to me,' replied the man on the bed. Then Pallen hopped across the ward on one foot and hopped back to the bed on the other foot. Then he jumped and skipped at the bedside and danced an impromptu jig. He turned again to the man on the bed.

'' 'Do you see anything the matter with me?' he demanded in almost a challenging tone.

'' 'I don't see anything the matter with you, Mister,' replied the man on the bed; and then he added, 'unless it is they've got you in the wrong ward.'

''Pallen walked close to the bedside and took a position where the man in the bed could closely watch him. Pallen took his cane and brought it down with

the wounded. It was found that cold drinks were more appreciated than any other thing by the wounded and seasick soldier, and accord-' ingly tons of fruit syrups were distributed by the Knights of Columbus amongst both the hospitals and troop ships for the benefit of the men on board. Delicacies, like jam and crackers, were also provided in abundance.[18]

THE SERVICE HOUSES

One of the special lines of service that proved of great value was rendered in the service houses which the Knights operated entirely free of charge in Boston, New York, Philadelphia, Chicago, Detroit and other cities. The handsome house on Berkeley Street, Boston, was typical. Here the Knights provided nightly over 700 free beds for men of the Army and Navy, with free baths, free breakfasts, consisting of doughnuts and coffee, free barber service, free laundry and free tailoring. It was altogether the most popular hotel on the Atlantic seaboard, for not a night passed without its being packed to the doors. Its spacious dormitories were always lined with cots, while, when necessary, the billiard and other rooms were made to accommodate the overflow. The reputation of this hotel, which had provided everything from shower baths to shoe shining, and all free of cost, became established in the navy from ocean to ocean. Upwards of 250,-

a sharp rap against his leg. The sound was unmistakably wooden. Everyone in the ward knew that Pallen's leg was artificial.

"This was the keen, big meaning thing that had been done for that American soldier who lay there with one leg off. Many black misgivings for the future had been removed from his mind. He now knew that he could go through life with an artificial leg almost as conveniently as he had before the amputation. This was one thing, bigger than anything that money could buy, that McDougal Pallen performed in our ward in the name of the Knights of Columbus."

Incidentally, Gibbons tells us who Pallen was:

"When I had known him," says Gibbons, "he had been a fellow-student at Georgetown University. Our football team never had a faster end than Pallen. He was a vigorous, hard-fighting, sport-loving student. As he stood there that day by my bed, I saw on the sleeve of his service uniform the red shield of the Knights of Columbus. Knowing Pallen as I did, I wondered why he was engaged in this work. He must have noticed my silence, for he said: 'Gig, do you remember that Thanksgiving game with the Indians?' 'Yes,' I replied, 'your leg was hurt pretty badly that day.' 'Well,' said Pallen, 'I lost that same leg three years afterwards.' Then I knew why Pallen was engaged in the noble work of the Knights of Columbus in France, and I wondered what it was that he could do in our ward that might possibly be different from the letter writing and distribution of tobacco and chocolate usually expected. I soon found out."

[18] *Knights of Columbus in Peace and War*, Vol. I, p. 275.

000 men in service enjoyed its hospitality during the war, and its
success was in a large measure due, as was the success of all other
Knights of Columbus service stations, to the noble and indefatigable
coöperation of Catholic women of the neighborhood.[19]

It is worth while repeating that the Knights of Columbus had to
fight to provide these services and most of their "creature comforts"
free. The reasons need not here be stated. It is sufficient to say that
pressure enough had been brought to bear upon the War Department
to induce that agency of the government to forbid this free service
and distribution, but after a firm contest on the part of the Knights
of Columbus they were permitted to pursue their liberal policy.[20]

WELFARE WORK DEFINED

Chaplain McCarthy, so well known to the Knights of Columbus,
in his charming book, "The Greater Love," just issued by Extension
Press, thus speaks of the war welfare work:

"A distinct contribution to modern civilization, and a form of national and
international altruism making for the betterment, not only of him who receives,
but as well of him who gives, was organized welfare work. The need of such
work always existed; and the organization of trained and equipped auxiliary
forces intelligently to perform it must have ever been apparent. It remained for
the World War, conceived, at least in the American mind in unselfish motive, to
create and give flesh and blood expression to so Divine a vocation; and assign it
honored rank among National institutions eminently to be desired, and, without
invidious comparison, devotedly to be maintained."

GETTING THE MONEY

Needless to say it required a large amount of funds to conduct the
work carried on by the Knights of Columbus. At the outset a modest
fund of $1,000,000 was asked for by the Supreme Officers, and when
the Supreme Council met in August a call for a voluntary contribution of $3,000,000 was sent out. The story of the splendid success of
these appeals, in which every jurisdiction of the Order far exceeded
its quota is a most interesting one. The independent campaign of the
Knights of Columbus, later joined in by the National Catholic War
Council, resulted in raising a fund of $14,000,000, thus more than
quadrupling the modest sum for which the Order had asked. It is
true that the great needs were not fully appreciated in advance, and
it has been seen that even a much larger sum than that actually

---

[19] Ib. pp. 275-6.
[20] See *Knights of Columbus in Peace and War*, op. cit. Ch. XXVII.

realized was needed, and, when the time came, it was provided. From the joint drive in which the Knights of Columbus participated with . the Y.). C. A., the Salvation Army and some other welfare organizations, some $20,000,000 more was realized. The public treated the Knights of Columbus generously, and supplied them with an abundance of funds. It is to the everlasting credit of the Knights of Columbuus that they proved faithful to their trust. Although the peculiar circumstances tended to increase the cost of administration, as well as of supplies, the Knights of Columbus made an enviable record by holding administration costs down to the insignificant figure of 2.68 per cent, and by prompt payment of bills saved in cash discounts more than the operating cost.[21]

THE PART OF RELIGION

In no single instance has the Knights of Columbus been charged with a neglect of religion in connection with its war service, nor to date has there been any single complaint that the Order or any of its representatives unduly urged religion upon anyone. Quoting from *"Qu' est-ce que C'est"* again:

"They have never crowded religion down our throats—though religious consolation was theirs to give for the asking."

There were scenes and events that will live long in the minds of servicemen, some of which involved hours of waiting in long lines for an opportunity to kneel in the mud and go to confession. There were like scenes on disagreeable mornings when thousands knelt before the temporary altar constructed by the K. C. Chaplain to receive Holy Communion.[22] There were great gatherings in the community build-

---

[21] *Report of Supreme Board, op. cit.* p. 23.

[22] Lieutenant Leo D. Sheridan, Company E, 327th Infantry, in a letter to his brother of Macon, Ga., helps us to realize what the religious consolations which the secretaries were so efficient in arranging, meant to the boys entering upon battle:

"I want to tell you what happened the day before we went into the front lines," says Lieutenant Sheridan. "Our battalion was located in a dense woods and we were living in shelter tents; the officers had little shacks with hardly room to turn around in. The K. of C. Secretary also had a small shack about as big as your bathroom, and in this he had a victrola, cigarettes, candy, etc.; needless to say, this was the most popular place in the woods. No doubt you know that the K. of C.'s give away everything and won't take money for anything.

"The morning of the same night we went to the first line the K. of C. Secretary sent down word that Mass would be celebrated at the K. of C. shack at 9:30. I immediately formed our company, and read this notice and gave all permission to attend. This was also done in the three companies.

ing when thousands reverently knelt during the Sunday Masses, and above all there were the dying consolations behind the battle lines. Yet no non-Catholic serviceman retired to private life with the feeling that his conscience had been outraged by Catholic proselytism. The Knights of Columbus must be given credit for a very reasonable and sensible administration of the religious features of the welfare work.

EMPLOYMENT SERVICE

When the actual war welfare work was over, the Knights of Columbus found themselves with an available balance of more than $10,000,000. The record of the use of this balance is a most interesting one.

That there would be considerable difficulty in readjusting the employment situation was early anticipated by the Knights of Columbus, and, accordingly, as soon as the men begun to return after the armistice, steps were taken to assist the servicemen and employers. To begin with, every Council of the Order was transformed into an employment agency and, as circumstances required, employment quarters were opened in the principal cities. The Knights of Columbus Employment Service has become familiar, located as it quite generally is in the most prominent square or thoroughfare in the various cities, with its flaming posters announcing "A Free Employment Service for Soldiers, Sailors and Marines."[23] The details of this employment service are of extreme interest, and the story told in the records of the various offices is startling. In general it has been stated that 55 per cent of the men who applied for employment at the free Knights

"There is another lieutenant in my company named Nickelson, who is also a Catholic; he is from New York and is a mighty fine fellow; has been with our company about one month. We at once decided to attend Mass, and beat it through the woods to the K. of C. hut. Upon arriving there we found about 300 or more soldiers gathered around. It was raining, but this did not keep the men from kneeling in the mud. Finally, the priest arrived and the men began going to confession. After hearing confessions, Mass began, and I honestly believe every soldier, including myself, went to communion.

"I never will forget this sight as long as I live, and am sorry I can't give a better description. There we were in the thick woods, with rain falling, and men on their knees in mud. Overhead and sometimes striking near, were artillery shells. Overhead aeroplanes would buzz and we could hear them signaling to each other; you could hear shells whistling by, bound for the German trenches, and I am sure God was looking down on these devout soldiers. I would have given anything in the world to have had a camera and to have taken a picture of this wonderful assembly, but, anyhow, it is imprinted indelibly on my mind and I never will forget the scene."

[23] *Knights of Columbus in Peace and War, op. cit.* Ch. XXIX.

of Columbus employment offices have been satisfactorily placed.[24] Figures have been published illustrating the work of the Eastern offices. Those for the Chicago office are of extreme interest. In Chicago the general employment service was opened on January 5, 1920. Up to and including November 22, 1920, 55,138 men made application for employment. During the same period the employment service had found 45,867 opportunities, that is, places in which men were wanted. The office actually placed 32,571 men. During the same period the service sent 38,026 men out to take places that were available, but with which the applicants were not quite satisfied. Some of these of course tried again and secured places more to their liking. It is to be remembered that this service was furnished absolutely free, neither applicant nor employer being required to pay any fee. Casting up the total expenditures of the Chicago office, it appears that it cost the Order—the expenses being paid out of the war welfare fund—in the neighborhood of $2.00 per man placed in employment. Thus has been used a portion of the balance remaining of the welfare fund.[25]

EDUCATION FOR SERVICEMEN

Even during the war the Knights of Columbus established, wherever they could obtain permission, in the camps and cantonments, free schools for servicemen. Several of those reached a high state of efficiency before the close of the conflict.[26] Immediately after the war the Order offered one hundred scholarships in the leading technical and academic institutions of the country to former servicemen, with free scholarships and tuition, books and maintenance. The applicants were so numerous that the offer was afterwards extended to include such number of applicants as might, upon examination, prove to be qualified. These scholarships were awarded independent of race or religion, and were secured by the Order in various colleges without respect to religious affiliations. That no favoritism was shown is evidenced by the fact that the Catholic University of America secured twenty-three of those scholarships, while the State University of Illinois secured forty-nine, and the Massachusetts Institute of Technology fifty-eight. As the first award stood the scholarships were divided be-

---

[24] "The average record of jobs found throughout the entire country by the Knights of Columbus was over 5,000 per week," *Knights of Columbus in Peace and War, op .cit.* p. 390.
[25] Books of Chicago K. of C. Employment Service office. At the close of the service December 31, 1920, there had been placed 39,872 men.
[26] See *Report of Supreme Board of Directors, Jan. 30, 1919,* p. 38 et seq.

tween thirty-three colleges. The total expense of these scholarships is estimated at above one million and a quarter dollars for the four-year period. In addition to what goes with the scholarship the Knights of Columbus supply $12.00 per week during the scholastic year for maintenance to men who do not secure board and lodging at the colleges or schools.[27]

But the Knights of Columbus were not satisfied with merely providing a limited number of men with a college education. They sought a wider field and found it in the popular free schools established in the principal cities throughout the country. Not all of the figures with reference to these schools are available yet. Those of New York, Boston and Philadelphia, earliest established, have proven extremely popular. The schools of Chicago, however, will suffice for illustration of the stupendous work being accomplished.

The Knights of Columbus free schools for servicemen opened in Chicago February 9, 1920. From that date to July 31, 1920, when the schools closed for vacation, 4,333 students enrolled and attended the classes. After the summer vacation the schools opened again on September 13th, and to November 12th, 4,100 men had enrolled and were attending the various classes.

At the present time there are one or more classes in accounting, advertising, bookkeeping, commercial art, commercial law, English for foreigners, grammar school course, automobile mechanics, mechanical drafting, typewriting, public speaking, reinforced concrete work, electricity, machine shop practice, woodworking, oxy-acetylene welding, salesmanship, French, Spanish, traffic management, mathematics, English, radio telegraphy, engineering, stenography and a high school course.

Besides free tuition, the books, tools, drawing instruments and supplies are furnished free to ex-servicemen and women of these schools.[28]

---

[27] The official report for 1920 of the Knights of Columbus committee on education concerning K. of C. college scholarships for former servicemen has just been made public. It shows that where last year the Knights maintained 415 former servicemen in colleges and universities in all courses but law and medicine, that this year the number has been reduced to 322 through resignations and failure to meet standards, as well as through transference on the part of many scholars to K. of C. free night technical courses. Apart from these specifically limited scholarships the K. of C., through state and national boards, are maintaining scores of veterans in colleges in law and other courses.

[28] Taken from records of Free K. of C. School of Chicago.

A ·VICTORY MEMORIAL

Calculating the cost of its program of education, based upon the economies observed in all its work, it was considered that a balance of the trust fund donated by the American people would remain, and with a view to conferring a lasting benefit, both upon the loyal men who followed the flag, and upon their country, the Knights of Columbus have offered to the American Legion, the official organization of the United States Servicemen, $5,000,000 with which to erect a memorial building in Washington, D. C., for the perpetual use of veterans of all wars.

Thus will the Knights of Columbus have administered the trust reposed in them by their fellow countrymen. But it is not contemplated that this brilliant conclusion of their war activities shall bring to an end their private benevolences or their public usefulness. There are the best of reasons for believing that the future of the Order may safely be forecast by the character of its past accomplishments.

JOSEPH J. THOMPSON.

Chicago.

THE NORTHEASTERN PART OF THE DIOCESE OF ST. LOUIS UNDER BISHOP ROSATI

VIII. QUINCY AND ITS ENVIRONS

With the recall of Father St. Cyr from Chicago in 1837, Bishop Rosati, indeed, severed the connection that had subsisted since 1833 between himself and his representative in that city on the one hand, and the chief city of Illinois itself on the other, but not his connections with the church in the western part of that state as delimited in Bull of Pope Gregory XVI in 1834. Father St. Cyr at once received the appointment to the congregation at Quincy and on Crooked Creek Mission, that had been founded, as we have seen, by Peter Paul Lefevere. In 1837 the church had been firmly rooted on the banks of the Mississippi from St. Louis upwards to Galena, Dubuque and Prairie du Chien, and now began to branch out east and west, but naturally with greater vigor along the chief tributary of the Mississippi above its confluence with the Missouri the haunted stream of Indian legend and Christian tradition, the far famed Illinois of Father Marquette's eulogy: "We had seen nothing like this view for fertility of the land, its prairies, woods, wild cattle, stag, deer, wild cats, swans, ducks, parrots, and even beaver; its many lakes and rivers. That on which we sailed is broad and deep and gentle for sixty-five leagues."[1]

This beautiful and diversified country running diagonally through the heart of Illinois, from the neighborhood of St. Louis towards Chicago, was being rapidly reclaimed from the state of wild nature. From 1833 on Father Lefevere had visited the scattered settlements as far east as Sangamon County. But now the increase in population required a concerted movement of numerous soldiers of the cross to do battle with the enemy, and to conquer the land for Christ. In 1837 Father Lefevere is succeeded in Quincy by Father August F. Brickwedde; in Fountain Green, and in the stations around the headwaters of Crooked Creek by Father St. Cyr; in Springfield, a year and a half later, by George A. Hamilton, whilst the English-speaking people of Quincy receive their own pastor in the person of

---

[1] Shea, *Discovery and Exploration of the Mississippi Valley*, 2nd edition, p. 54.

284

Father Hilary Tucker. In 1838 the Vincentian Fathers J. B. Raho and Aloysius Parodi entered upon their most fruitful labors in and around La Salle County, whilst Alton, having been visited by Father E. DeBryn, S. J., since 1836, received its first resident priest, Father James Flynn, in February, 1838.

Father Lefevere had made a special plea to the bishop for Quincy, his first mission in Illinois and had been promised an assistant, Father St. Cyr of Chicago. Father Lefevere expressed his great joy and gratitude, especially as Father St. Cyr was reported to be a fair German scholar. For more than half of the Catholics of Quincy were German. In fact, Bishop Rosati had been asked to send the only German priests he then had, Father Lutz or Father Helias, S. J., to Quincy at least two or three times a year. Father St. Cyr received his appointment to Quincy June 12, 1837, and was about to start for his new and promising field, when something unforeseen occurred that changed Bishop Rosati's plans. A large congregation of German Catholic immigrants, accompanied by their priest, August Florentius Brickwedde arrived in St. Louis, intent upon a settlement somewhere in the wilds of Missouri or Illinois. Father Brickwedde was born June 24, 1805 in Fürstenau, in the Kingdom of Hanover. He was descended from a prominent family of jurists. Having completed his classical course at Osnabrück, and his philosophical and theological studies at the universities of Munich and Bonn, he was ordained priest in the Cathedral of Hildesheim, September 20, 1830. The young curate of five years' experience in the ministery casually heard of the great need of missionaries in far away America, especially among the German colonists that were just then beginning to make their numerous settlements in the new world, and decided to devote his life and talent to their service. The Bishop of Osnabrück, Dr. Lüpke, gave him his dimissorials and his paternal blessing, and the young enthusiast set out for America in company of a band of German emigrants in May 1837, arriving in New York July 4th of the same year.

When Father Brickwedde arrived in St. Louis, Bishop Rosati was absent from home. Father Lutz received the stranger as a guest, until the bishop could dispose of him, and wrote a letter at once communicating the news. Father Lutz seems to have been in constant fear of displeasing the bishop: and the letter of July 24 bears witness to the fact:

It appears rather singular that just at the time of your absence from home German priests should happen to arrive. However, though this incident may have proved disagreeable to your Reverence sometimes, it will not, I hope prove so at present. Perhaps you say, that I have suffered myself to be imposed

upon once more. To this I answer: That I shall always invariably follow and have followed in the present case your precepts, as far as the personal circum-. stances of the individuals require it. Being aware of. your just severity on this point, I was at first inclined not to receive the German Priest at your house, but having examined his papers, especially his Dimissorial letters from his Bishop, the Revd. Dr. Lüpke of Osnabruck, and moreover became acquainted with the particulars, relating to his mission hither, I thought it more proper to receive him, than to let him stay out of the house, whilst he has no acquaintances. He appears to be a worthy Ecclesiastic, and well disposed to consecrate his labours to the salavtion of so many hundreds of his country-people that are scattered all over your diocese. I told him to wait, till you would return and to abstain from celebrating Mass; in short he approved with his whole heart without the least displeasure, of your measures in relation to admittance of German priests. You remember, that, a few years ago, I had written a letter to a worthy German priest of the name of Beckmann in Osnabruck, to which letter you deigned to add a few lines. The answer received from the said Revd. gentleman expressed his own wish, yet actual impossibility of doing as he wished, to join your clergy. This priest therefore, the Rev. August Brickwedde, came, as it were, in the place of the former. He is 32 years and apparently of a strong constitution. I have to observe, that with regard to the censuras ecclesiasticas, nothing at all is said in his dimissorial letters. The latter amongst others state, *Dictum Vicarium Augustum Brickwedde per plures jam annos in animarum cura subsidaria versatum optimè Nobis commendatum existere, proindeque eundum Reverendissimis Dnis in Reg. Americae Episcopis enixe a Nobis commendari.*

I trust therefore, that under the like circumstances I have not done wrong in giving hospitality to a priest for a few days, till you yourself will in a conclusive manner settle the whole affair. From what I understood, the name of the priest has been stated to you in a former letter, which you must have received from the Revd. Bishop of Osnabruck.[1]

Indeed, Bishop Rosati had received a letter from Bishop Lüpke in regard to the mission and personality of Father Brickwedde, and was well pleased to secure such a helper in his greatest need. For did not Father Lefevere insist that a good part of the congregation of Quincy consisted of Germans, who required the ministry of a German priest. Father Brickwedde was immediately adopted and sent to Quincy for the purpose of founding a German parish, the first national parish in the Mississippi Valley, whilst the English-speaking Catholics of Quincy were to be under the pastoral care of Father St. Cyr, who however was to reside at Fountain Green. It is not known whether Father St. Cyr ever came to Quincy. In his report for 1837 he writes: "I did not include in the number of my parishioners the English Catholics of Quincy, because I thought that Rev. Brickwedde will give their number in his report."

[1] Archives of the Catholic Historical Society of St. Louis.

Father Brickwedde held his first service in the new parish on the
Feast of the Assumption of our Blessed Lady. One of the upper   ·
rooms of the dwelling of Adam Schmitt formed the chapel, and the
adjoining porch was enclosed to serve as the priest's sitting- and
sleeping-room. The Parish was dedicated in honor of the Ascension of
Our Lord. At the first Mass there were only thirteen persons in
attendance, although the congregation numbered more than 170 souls.
There were only two baptisms and four burials in all Adams County
from August 15 to December 31, 1837. In January, 1838, Father
Brickwedde notified Bishop Rosati that a non-Catholic, a Mrs. Wats,
had donated a lot in Quincy for the purpose of a Church, and that
a committee had been appointed to arrange for the construction of
a suitable building, which should be finished before the Feast of the
Ascension. In January, 1839, he writes that since Pentecost the
services have been held in his own house. On account of the dull
times the people could not build the church, but they are hopeful
of building one within the year. As to the spiritual progress of his
people, Father Brickwedde has only words of praise. In regard to
his out missions he states that at West Point in Iowa Mass is said
in the house of Mrs. Kempker, and that the people of the place wish
to have a resident priest, as they already possess a lot of about four
acres for church, parish house and graveyard.

It is greatly to the credit of this German pastor of souls that
one of his first undertakings at Quincy was to establish a school
for the lambs of his flock. School was held in Father Brickwedde's
own building, which also contained the church and priest's residence.
There were 14 boys and 10 girls in attendance the first year. A few
weeks after his coming to Quincy the zealous missionary visited the
German settlements at Fort Madison and West Point on Sugar Creek
in the southeast corner of Iowa. At Fort Madison High Mass was
sung in the log house of J. H. Dingmann, and at Sugar Creek
in the barn of J. H. Kempker. At Sugar Creek Father Brickwedde
built a church in 1839 under the title of St. Paul's, the first church
erected in that part of the diocese of Davenport.

Father Brickwedde's report, dated April 22, 1839, contains a
few more items of interest: Mass is still celebrated in the private
house of the pastor, but the place (a room 28x18 feet) cannot contain the multitude. There is no farm attached to the parish, as the
good Father had been accustomed to find in his native land; there
are no resources, the pastor lives on his own private fortune. Lately
a Mr. Whitney donated to the bishop a lot of ground on Main and
Eighth Streets, suitable for the erection of a church, a hundred feet

long and forty wide. For the building of the church about $900 have been subscribed either in money or in labor. There are now 241 German Catholics in the county, and about 50 speaking the English language, forming a rather floating population. Every Sunday there is High Mass and a sermon in the German language, at 2 o'clock in the afternoon Catechism instruction for the children, after that Vespers, and the Rosary or some other popular devotion. As Father St. Cyr failed to visit the English speaking people of Quincy, they were obliged to attend High Mass at Father Brickwedde's church. But as the good German priest was far from proficient in this language, they naturally desired a priest of their own.[3]

But what had become of their English speaking pastor, Father St. Cyr? As we have seen his destination was suddenly changed from Quincy to Fountain Green. It is from this latter place Bishop Rosati received the following, rather plaintive letter:

McDonough County, March 4, 1838.

Most Reverend Bishop:

I ought to have written to you a long time ago. But for one thing or other I put it off till today. However, Most Reverend Bishop, I thought I had always time enough to write to you, when I had nothing to inform you of but bad news, which certainly afflicts your sensitive heart.

When I left St. Louis in November last I was very unwell, and I have been so ever since. However, I tried to visit several of my congregations before the cold weather set in, which I did, as I had promised. I rode there, I went, I came back and fell; when I shall rise again, I do not know. Since the 28th of January I did not leave my bed. I have almost lost the use of my right leg by pains, first in the hip, then between the knee and the ankle, in which they are now most horribly felt, which rendered me incapable of setting out and doing anything.

A hundred things have been applied to it; but nothing seems to do me any good. I leave it to the hand of God to chastise me as long as He pleases, *modo*

[3] As a sample of Father Brickwedde's English, we will transcribe a letter sent to Bishop Rosati from, ''Quincy 4 Januar, 1839: These tables I send you for you to see the statement of my missions. Sense last Pentecost the meeting has been kept in my house. By the cause of dull times we could not built a new curch. But we are in hopes that we shall have one this year. I am very happy to tell you that the christians improve in ther works and keep ther meeting regular. We all emplor to see you next summer, mot reverend father! in consequence of consecration of the curch and graveyard and at the same time meny people would like to keep the holy sacrament of confirmation. The congregation near Westpoint keep meeting in private lady haus, that belongs to Mrs. Kampker. . . . . To for right Reverend Bishop my best respects.

AUGUST BRICKWEDDE.''

In our next paper we shall hear more about Father Brickwedde in Quincy.

in aeternum parcat, or to His holy will to cure me: *in patientia vestra possidebitis animas vestras.*

I received your last letter last Friday, a little too late to give me time to write to the different congregations to inform them of the rules of Lent.

The church building in Fountain Green is going on very slowly on account of the weather. Mr. Henry Riley, who contracted for the building, is to go down to St. Louis at the opening of the river for to buy different things for the church. If it should be then in your power to pay him what you promised to give towards *St. Simon's* Church, I would be very thankful to you.

Report of 1837 is all ready since the last of December; I will send it to you by Mr. Henry Riley.

My best respects to Messrs. Lutz, Jamison, and Fontbonne.

I am, Most Reverend Bishop your,

Humble Servant,

I. M. I. ST. CYR, *Cath. P.*

Within three weeks another letter was sent with the same complaint of bodily ills, but showing a little more hope. It was dated:

McDonough County a few miles from Macomb, March 30, 1838.

Very Reverend Bishop:

The spirit is willing but the flesh is weak.

I wrote to you some time ago a letter in which I informed you of my bad situation, not being able to walk at all. Well, I am still in the same situation, with that difference however, that, the weather being warmer, I can step out of my room with the help of two sticks. But the pains keep on the same train, and many a time worse than in the cold weather. We did all we could, but nothing had done me any good. Wherefore, Reverend Bishop, if by next week I feel no better or perceive no mending, I will venture myself on a horse or wagon to cross that long, long prairie. But whether I will be able to do it is a matter of doubt. However, I will try my best; so that if you do not see me in St. Louis before long, you may conclude that I got better or worse.

My best respect to Father Lutz, Jamison, etc. I am very Reverend Sir,

Your most obedient servant,

ST. CYR.

As the summer came on the bodily troubles of the missionary must have been relieved considerably, as we find him on a still hunt for souls in the various counties of his vast parish. It seems to have been his farewell visit. It may strike many as singular to note the importance attached by these pioneers of the faith to any church or chapel, however poor and homely, as a means of developing the country round about, yet they had the experience. The little church becomes the center to which all the roads converge, since its presence in the locality is the means of determining the Catholic people to settle in the neighborhood. And what a fine instinctive feeling these pioneers had in discovering the signs of coming greater things. In illustration of this let us proceed to Father St. Cyr's last

letter from the missions in McDonough, Fulton, Peoria and Tazewell Counties:

Fountain Green, August 6th, 1838.

Very Reverend Bishop:

I have fulfilled my promise concerning my going on a mission to Peoria. I also visited the Catholics in Tazewell County. They are very numerous, some Americans, some French, German and Irish. The 15th of July I said Mass at Mr. Tuckers' (Tazewell). Mr. Menard and his wife attended. And I baptized several children. The week after I visited likewise several wealthy Irish families in Lotall Prairie, forty miles from Peru (Peoria County). Amongst which families is Mr. Mooney, a rich and zealous Catholic; all from the city of New York. A great many more families would have come to this part of the country, they told me, had it not been for the scarcity of money. Many again have been prevented from moving for not hearing of any Catholic church being established, or of any prospect of establishing one. Let therefore a Catholic church be established with a priest stationed at Peoria, and the Catholics will flock into that part of the country.

Peoria is already and will be more so, one of the most important points on the Illinois river for Catholicity, if nothing be neglected on our part. It is therefore high time to take the matter into consideration; it is now the very season to plant.

It has not been in my power to do anything respecting the church and the lot that had been promised. Being a perfect stranger to the Catholics, they not having received the letter you promised me to write to them as an introduction, and myself not having the list of the Catholics which M. Timon made. Mr. Peter Menard, who alone could give me all the information I wanted, was not then in Peoria; he has moved on his farm with his family, 12 miles south of Peoria (Tazewell County). However, I requested Mr. Mooney, a zealous member of our church and a great friend to that Mr. Nolone (Nolan), who promised Mr. Timon to give a lot for the church, and who since retracted, that, in case he would make his first words good, to have the lot deeded. So far the whole matter is hanging on promises. I found in Peoria and its environs 32 Catholic families, whose names I took on a list; there are some more, but I could not see them for want of time. I promised to visit them again in October if nothing should prevent me; this will be the last time, for I do not propose to visit them any more, as my health does not permit me to undertake such long trips, and my finances are not much better. I hope you will send them a priest, but a priest who must speak French, English and German; that he should speak French and English is absolutely necessary.

I expect to start Thursday for Quincy, thence to Commerce, then home again. I am very sorry, Very Reverend Bishop, not to be able to comply with the great obligations which charity towards one another imposes upon each one of us, and even more so to be deprived of the blessings attached to their fulfillment. They are, I see by the letter which I received last week with your name affixed to it, humbly begging money to rebuild churches amongst the rich and wealthy people of South Carolina,[4] whilst we are here in the state of Illinois,

---

[4] The terrible conflagration in 1838, which swept away the better part of Charleston, S. C., Bishop England's Cathedral City, caused Bishop Rosati to

not rebuilding, but creating what we euphemistically name churches, not among the rich, but among the poorest of the poor. Yes, Dear Bishop, take notice, that all my congregations are so very poor that, in spite of their good will, they cannot afford enough to put up a very humble house of worship for themselves. Therefore, Bishop, do not expect anything from me.

Our church at Fountain Green is very slowly building; we having been disappointed in the sawing of the lumber.

My leg is plaguing me yet, and some time very much so; I fear I will not be able to spend the winter here.

I did not hear of Mr. Jamison since I left St. Louis; how is he? how does the large organ sound?

If you would keep some intentions of Mass for me, Bishop, I would be very much obliged to you.

My best regards to Mr. Lutz and to all,

I am Sir, you very obedient Servant,

I. M. I. ST. CYR, Cath. P.

With this letter we take leave of good Father St. Cyr. Broken in health, as he was, and unfit to cope with the hardships and privations of missionary life in the backwoods, he was appointed in 1838 pastor of the ancient parish of Kaskaskia in succession to Father Benedict Roux. Here within a comparatively small compass he ministered to 815 souls, had 61 baptisms in the first year, 22 marriages, 19 funerals and 4 converts. He also acted as confessor and chaplain to the Sisters of the Visitation until July 19, 1843, when Father Heim took his place as confessor of the Sisters, but not as pastor of the parish. The diocese of Chicago being erected in 1844 with all Illinois as its territory, Father St. Cyr declined to sever his connection with St. Louis; and on the 11th of September, 1844 left Kaskaskia in charge of Father Vital Van Cloostere. On the 23rd of September of the same year, he was appointed chaplain of the Sisters of the Visitation⁵ on Sixth Street in St. Louis at a salary of $100.00 a year, as Father St. Cyr himself states. Of his first year's salary the chaplain devoted $10.00 to help pay St. Patrick's church debt; the whole amount received from the Sisters on Sixth Street for the services as chaplain during 21 months came to $150.00.

send an appeal for help to his priests. A good number of them responded quite liberally, so that the sum of about $200.00 could be sent to help build up the churches of the devastated city. Missionaries like Father St. Cyr belonged to the poorest of the poor, and might well have been spared the necessity of a refusal.

⁵ The great flood of 1844 destroyed the Visitation Convent at Kaskaskia, and the foundation was transferred to St. Louis, at first to a temporary location on Sixth Street, then to more commodious home on Broadway. At both places Father St. Cyr acted as chaplain.

On the 19th day of June, 1846, Father St. Cyr was sent as
chaplain to the Sisters of the Visitation on Broadway: but on July
20, 1847 he was appointed one of the priests at the Cathedral.
With the year 1848 Father St. Cyr reverted to missionary life,
attending the old parish of Potosi, and the following year the oldest
parish in the state, St. Genevieve. Here he had an assistant in the
person of Father Anselm. In 1851 he was left without regular
assistance in St. Genevieve with a congregation of 900 souls, and
remained as pastor until 1862. During this period of quiet content
and faithful labor among his countrymen, Father St. Cyr did what
was perhaps his best work, not of outward brilliancy, but of deeper
faith and spirituality. But even here his strength gave way, and
he was forced to resign the charge, where his kindness of heart, and
his gentle ways had endeared him to all.

On the 1st of April, 1862, Father St. Cyr took his residence at
the Brothers of the Christian Doctrine, to be chaplain of the Sisters
of St. Joseph Carondelet, Missouri. On the 3rd of November, 1864,
he moved from the Christian Brothers' de La Salle Institute to a
house of the Sisters of St. Joseph, nearer the convent, to be their
chaplain exclusively. On July 20th Father St. Cyr marks in his
note-book: "My trip to Notre Dame, Indiana, going and coming
amounted to $30.00." On June 10, 1872 he moved from Carondelet to
Nazareth, the Novitiate of the Sisters of St. Joseph to be their chaplain, and there witnessed the blessing of the chapel and its bell by
Archbishop Kenrick.[6] At Nazareth, he received, as we have already
stated in a former article, the visit of the great Archbishop of St.
Paul, who liked to talk with this living monument of heroic days,
about the men and affairs long past. Among other statements of
Father St. Cyr treasured up by Archbishop Ireland was that concerning the Lincoln family. It had been asserted on the supposed
authority of Father LeFevere and St. Cyr that Lincoln, the great
President, was a Catholic: "I visited several times the Lincolns in
their home in Southern Illinois. The father and the stepmother of
Abraham Lincoln were Catholics. How they had become Catholics I
do not know. They were not well instructed in their religion; but
they were strong and sincere in their profession of it. I said Mass
repeatedly in their house. Abraham was not a Catholic; he never
had been one, and he never led me to believe that he would become

_____

* These items are taken from a Diary kept by Father St. Cyr from 1836-1876.
It contains 254 pages of very small writing. The book is preserved in the
Museum of Quincy College and Seminary. Father Justinian Kugler, O. F. M.,
kindly made the extracts for me.

one. At the time Abraham was twenty years old or thereabouts, a thin, tall young fellow, kind and good-natured. He used to assist me in preparing the altar for Mass. Once he made me a present of a half-dozen chairs. He had made these chairs with his own hands, expressly for me; they were simple in form and fashion, as chairs used in country-places then would be."[7]

Father St. Cyr died February 21, 1883. His remains were laid to rest in the little cemetery of Nazareth Convent of the Sisters of St. Joseph.

IX. FROM SANGAMON COUNTY TO ALTON.

The priests chosen by Bishop Rosati to continue the work inaugurated by Father Lefevere and Father St. Cyr in the heart of the Illinois country were the two Missourians that had the privilege, as the advance guard of a multitude of others, to receive their theological training in the Eternal City, George Alexander Hamilton and Hilary Tucker, 1831-1838. Father George A. Hamilton was born in Marion County, Kentucky, had come to Perry County about 1825. He entered the Seminary of St. Mary's, accompanied Hilary Tucker to Rome, was attacked by the smallpox, which put him back in his studies so that he could not be ordained at the time of his companion's ordination, returned with Rev. Fr. Tucker in 1838, and was immediately sent to the missions in Springfield and Sangamon County, Illinois. There is a large collection of letters from Rome written by these young propaganda students to their beloved Bishop and friend, Rosati. These letters are, of course, of no great historical value, but what must strike every reader as something singular is the easy familiarity of these young men in their intercourse with a man of the highest station and influence in the Church.

On Christmas Day, 1833, young Hamilton writes to Bishop Rosati:

When I consider the extreme necessity in our Diocese of zealous priests, I long to be ready to carry the word of life to those desolate people who still walk in darkness and in the shadow of death; but again when I consider my extreme want of the virtues and learning requisite to the due fulfillment of so sublime a ministry, my heart shrinks in dismay from the arduous undertaking. And with this thought always before me, I should be induced to abandon the hope of even doing any good, were I not assured by the Eternal Truth Himself that He does not choose the great and learned of this world for His Apostles, but the lowly and ignorant to confound the pride and vain knowledge of the worldly wise. Confiding entirely in the promises of Eternal Truth, I am again assured that, if I use my best exertions to fit myself well for the office to which I am

---

[7] Cf. Griffin, *The American Catholic Historical Researches*, XXII, 3.

destined, though of myself I can do nothing, Almighty God will supply from His inexhaustible treasures every deficiency. I must then endeavor to prepare myself for the sublime dignity to which I hope one day to be raised; and nowhere could I better do it than in the college where I now am."

The deep interest George Hamilton felt in all things that con-cerned Bishop Rosati, as well as the great desire of the zealous prelate himself to obtain German priests for the numerous German settlements rising as if by magic in every part of his extensive diocese, especially Illinois and Northern Missouri, gives more than a passing interest to a passage from a letter of George Hamilton dated Mont Alto, near Frascati, September 28, 1836:

> I had hoped you would be assisted very soon by a young student of this college, who had expressed a determination to go to St. Louis; he would have been of great service among the Germans. But the secretary has thought fit to send him to Calcutta. There is a young gentleman in the Greek College in Rome, who has expressed a strong desire to consecrate himself to the American missions. He is determined, if possible, to go to America. He is not of the Greek rite. His superiors seem favorable to his inclination, as he is a young man of great abilities, and likely to do a great deal of good, and as they see he is not likely to do much at home, on account of the oppressive laws which cloy the zeal of the missionary. He has already acquired a pretty competent knowledge of the English language, which he begins to speak with fluency; he also understands French. He is a very accomplished Greek and Latin scholar. His health and strength, and above all, his zeal, admirably fit him for the American missions. He has often expressed to me an ardent wish to go to St. Louis. He would, under many respects, be a very valuable acquisition to the diocese. With one word, I am persuaded, you can prevail on Mgr. Mai to send him to St. Louis. You will not, I know, let slip so favorable an opportunity to enrich your diocese with such a learned and valuable missionary. He had wished to disclose his designs to other Americans who would immediately have written on to their Bishops to ask him; but I prevailed on him to wait till I got an answer from you. It is seldom, Sir, that you or any other Bishop can have so advantageous an offer. As you are coming to Rome next year, you will, I hope, secure the services of this young gentleman, or if Providence so dispose it that you cannot come, you can write to the Prefect of Propaganda to send him. He will have completed Theology with me. His name is Nicholas Perpignan.

In another letter student George gives his views on a topic that was then as now, a burning one:

> I must tell you that I am no friend to such begging, although I wish well to Mr. Odin, and I should show great ingratitude were I to act otherwise. Still I maintain that it does not look well here to see a priest of our missions making such collections. I have heard many, and very respectable persons, too, say that there appears to be too great a solicitude, or rather too much confidence placed

---

*Cf. "First native Missourians to go to Rome for studies and to be ordained there," in the *Church Progress of St. Louis*, December 19, 1915.

in human means. For, say they, if it be for the honor and glory of God, God will find means, to carry into execution what is for His greater glory. Be that as it may, I am of the opinion that too much begging does not suit well for a priest of our missions, and I think I could do as much without coming to Europe. For I think it is only underestimating our own people to expect to be supported by the contributions made by the faithful of foreign countries. No, I say the faithful of our country are far more able to support their clergy, than those of Europe are to support their own, and we only need to take them in the right way to succeed.

I am very sorry to learn that no natives of the country seem disposed to embrace the ecclesiastical state, for I am convinced of the necessity of a national clergy. The reasons are obvious and need no elucidation, but in a country like ours, I fear it will be long before a clergy can be had, for there are so many employments open to the youth that few think of the priesthood. Nevertheless, I hope with the help of God's grace, we shall yet have a flourishing clergy before many years.

But the peaceful happy days of George Hamilton's stay in Rome came to an end in 1837. Arriving in New York on the 24th of September, 1838, both Hilary and George, as Bishop Rosati affectionately called our noble pair of Roman students, slowly travelled to St. Louis, when on their arrival in November, they received their faculties and were sent to their missions, Hilary Tucker to Quincy, George Hamilton to Springfield and the Sangamon country.

But alas, Father Hamilton's first letter from Springfield is a sad commentary on his light-hearted hopes. He would borrow money for his church, because he failed "to take his people in the right way" to "succeed" in raising the necessary funds among them. Indeed, good Bishop Odin was wiser, as he well might be, than the young student, in placing the facuulty of begging above the helplessness of borrowing. Interest was indeed exorbitant in those early days of Illinois, fluctuating between 12 to 25 per cent, according to the needs of the borrower. Father Hamilton, however, was not disposed to wait for something to turn up. The calls of his missions fully occupied his time. The country was growing rapidly. Again we meet the old saying: "All we require to attract Catholic immigration is a church." But let us see what Father Hamilton has to say on the subject:

Springfield, Ill., July 7, 1839.

Rt. Revd. Sir:
I would request you let me know whether I can borrow one or two thousand dollars, and upon what terms, in St. Louis. For as I am compelled to borrow, I desire to make my bargain to the best advantage. Here I cannot think of borrowing money, the interest is so exorbitant. The least they think of asking is 12 per cent. Will you please write me immediately upon what terms I can expect to get the desired loan.

I have just returned from an excursion in the country, where I have been pretty successful in finding out new Catholics. I discovered a new settlement of Irish Catholics near Mount Sterling,* Brown County, Ills. There are 6 families already there, and twelve or fourteen others have entered land in that neighborhood and are expected this fall and next spring. There is a fair prospect of there being a large congregation in a few years in and about Mount Sterling. The distance thence to Springfield is about 60 miles and to Quincy about 45 or 50. Several others about Jacksonville,[10] New Lexington and Virginia have made themselves known. They are rapidly increasing in Springfield.[11] When I first arrived here, there were only 5 families known to be Catholics, besides seven or eight single individuals. Now there are 13 or 14 families, besides 40 or 45 single persons residing in town. I doubt not that Catholicity will rapidly increase in this part of the country. All we require to attract Catholic immigration is a church. We have been greatly disappointed in getting the lot. Persons owning property in that quarter of town were anxious we should get that lot, which was better situated than any other for a church, and the owner was willing to let us have it, but he wanted to speculate and asked an enormous price. We declined, and he came down a little in his demands. He offered it for $300.00. We accepted it and requested a deed, and if he could not give that, a bond to make a deed when he should get out an order of court to sell the property (it being the property of minors), binding himself to secure us against any damage we might sustain in case he failed to make the deed by the 1st of January, 1840. When he saw the condition, he hesitated, consulted for days, shuffled and finally backed out. And now, after causing us to lose so much time, we are compelled to seek somewhere else for a suitable lot. I hope, however, we shall be able to commence this work. We have partly engaged with a gentleman who will not, it is thought, deceive us, for two lots 53½ by 157, in a very eligible situation in the town. If you could make it convenient to lay the corner stone, I should be happy to wait. Please let me know as soon as possible.

Your Obedient Servant,

G. A. HAMILTON.

Bishop Rosati was a great borrower himself for church purposes, and very probably knew no advantageous opening for Father Hamilton. But he returns to the charge.

Springfield, Ills., August 17, 1839.

Rt. Rev. Sir:
I deem it my duty to apprise you of everything I do here. I have used every effort in my power to build a church this season in Springfield, but all

---

*Mount Sterling, County Seat of Brown County, was laid out in 1833. Originally Brown County was a part of Schuyler until 1839. Mount Sterling now has two flourishing parishes.

10 Jacksonville in Morgan County is the seat of Routt College, under the direction of the Pastor of Our Savior's Church. Virginia, County Seat of Cass County, has a Parish of its own, with a number of missions.

11 Springfield, in Sangamon County, was selected to be the Capitol of the State after 1840, in succession to Vandalia in Fayette County. There are now nine churches and two chapels in Springfield. All these places are in the diocese of Alton.

my efforts have failed of success. I had indeed obtained subscriptions to the the amount of $2,000 or $2,300, and this created a hope of being able to proceed immediately with the building; but, Sir, I perceive, there is a wide difference between subscribing one's name for money and paying down the money. About the time we wished to commence, *hard times* began and many subscribers felt it inconvenient to pay and, as they were not Catholics, we did not like to urge the matter on them. Many of the Catholics paid their subscriptions and, if we had pressed them, would have paid up every thing, but when we saw we could not get money from our other subscribers, we told them not to put themselves to any inconvenience for the present. I think, however, there is no danger of not getting the amount subscribed this Fall and next Winter. And in considera- tion of this, I determined to effect a loan, if I could get it on fair and reason- able terms. The exorbitant interest required here deterred me from borrowing and, in the hope of getting it on more advantageous terms, brought me to St. Louis. But my inquiries soon satisfied me of my mistake. So I resolved to return to Springfield and wait till I could procure from some source or other the means to build my church. In the meantime I have tried to obtain a room which might be set apart for the purpose of Divine Worship, but as yet I have been unable to find one large enough, every room more than ten feet square being occupied, except one which was built for a theater and which will again probably be applied to the same use. I have refused to take it, thinking that it was not becoming for a house, that has once been appropriated to Divine worship, to be turned into a theatre. I know not whether I shall be able to get a room this season or not.

As I am situated, I assure you, I feel very uncomfortable, being compelled to celebrate Mass in a private house and perform all my functions exposed to the danger of being interrupted by every one who may wish to come into the room. I have not even a private apartment where I can hear confessions. My situation is so unpleasant that, if it was not for the kindness of the family I live with, I could not reconcile myself to remain. This family talks of moving and, if they do, "actum est de me," I am undone. For it will be utterly impossible for me, with my present salary, to pay my board at any house in town and there is no other Catholic family in town. There are, to be sure, several Catholic ladies, but their husbands are Protestants and I could not expect to board at their houses without paying the usual fare.

Owing to the scattered condition of the Catholics in this section of country I am compelled to be always on the move, in order to visit them once or twice a year. I most always find some, that I never heard of before. My opinion is that, instead of one, there ought to be two priests here in order properly to attend the Catholics and to enable themselves to derive advantage from their own labors. A priest wandering over these woods without ever seeing another priest, with whom he may advise and to whom he may unbosom his thoughts, is very apt to grow cold. If there were two, it might render their situation somewhat more pleasant. But these Catholics are too few and generally too poor, to afford a competent support even to one clergyman and I am persuaded, I could not live here, were it not for the good family I reside with.

It will require, in my opinion, a Society of men, who have funds of their own to start with, to effect a permanent and extensively useful establishment: once that is done everything will go on prosperously.

I informed you in my last letter of a new Catholic settlement I had discovered north of the Illinois River. I have been told since that there are several Catholic families south of Meredosia.[12] These I have never visited nor do I know how many there are. There are some too about Vandalia,[13] and south of that. I intended to visit them next month; I thought I would take them in on my way home, whither I have to go in order to settle my affairs, which if I do not then, I might not be able to do for a year; as some of those, who owe me, are going down the river, and may not return for twelve or eighteen months. I request your permission to do it.

I have now given you all the information I think worth your attention. If you desire any further particulars, I shall make it my pleasure to afford them, especially the names of the Catholics and the places of their residences.

Your obedient Servant,

GEORGE A. HAMILTON.

The hint as to a society of men who have funds of their own to start with, was perhaps suggested by the establishment of the LaSalle Mission under the Vincentian Fathers Raho and Parodi, an undertaking that certainly did wonders in central Illinois.[14] But we will turn from speculations to facts, pleasant and unpleasant, as contained in Father Hamilton's report for 1839:

Rt. Revd. Sir:

As I have been unavoidably compelled to omit many things in the printed account relating to this mission, I herewith transmit them to you. There are in this mission, as you may see by reference to the printed account 15 stations of which I consider Springfield as the centre. They lie at every point of the compass from twelve to sixty miles from Springfield. A brief description of each one I here subjoin. Sugar Creek, a small settlement 12 miles south of Springfield, in Sangamon County, comprising 8 families, averaging 7 members or 56 (souls) in all. Bear Creek, a large settlement 35 miles southeast of Springfield in Macon County, containing 23 families average about 6, or 136 (souls). Flat Branch, Macon County, 40 miles east of Springfield, 3 families, averaging about 7, or 21 (souls). Shelbyville, seat of justice of Shelby County, 56 miles a little south of east of Springfield containing 6 families. It has been nearly a year since I visited them. Lick Creek, 16 miles southwest of Springfield, count-ing but one family. Jacksonville, 35 miles west of Springfield, has but one resident Catholic though there are several transient ones laboring there. Jersey Prairie, north west corner of Morgan County, 3 Catholic families, 34 miles from Springfield; Virginia,[14] Cass County, 3 or 4 families comprising about 10 (souls), 34 miles north of west of Springfield. Meredosia, Morgan County, 55 miles from Springfield, some few transient Catholics. Naples,[15] Scott County, 58 miles west

---

[12] Meredosia in Morgan County, had 300 inhabitants in 1837. Morgan County has a number of parishes at present, but Meredosia is not mentioned in the list.

[13] Vandalia has but one church and one priest.

[14] Cf. Father Shaw, C. M., The LaSalle Missions, 2 vol.

[15] Naples is another one of the early towns that are not mentioned as centers of Catholic life.

next:

Springfield, February 10, 1840.

Rt. Rev. Sir:

Your letter of the 5th of January came to hand during my absence on a mission to Jacksonville and Mt. Sterling, and I have been prevented from answering it by visits which I was obliged to make several different places. I have already published the regulations to some of my widely scattered Congregations, to some others I shall promulgate them this and the ensuing weeks. I have received the "Ordo" and said two Masses for the same.

I have now been in the mission for one year. When I arrived, there was, I believed, a fairer prospect of erecting a church than there is at present. Whether the failure proceeds from my inability or mismanagement, from coolness of zeal on the part of subscribers, or from the pressure of the times, I am unable to ascertain. Sir, I believe, I have done all that I could to effect the erection of a church. I have traversed large portions of the state, begging at every house where I thought there was a hope of obtaining assistance, and preaching in every congregation for the same purpose, and I have failed. I have reflected much upon the subject, and I have come to the conclusion, that it is useless for me to try to build a church with the means I at present can command. The Catholics are, as I said before, too few and too poor to build one themselves, and their members do not appear to augment. There are nine entire Catholic families, and two, of which the females are Catholics, in town.

---

[16] Excluding the Archdiocese of Chicago, which was never strictly speaking, a part of Rosati's diocese of St. Louis, as the rest of Illinois was, the territory of Illinois once covered by the ministrations of Father Lefevere, Mazzuchelli, Brickwedde, St. Cyr, Hamilton, Tucker and the rest, now comprises four dioceses, with four bishops, 675 priests, 449 churches with resident priests, and 182 missions and a Catholic population of 332,945.

There are other transient families, that remain here while they can get employment. In these circumstances, Sir, I confess I am at a loss to know how to
proceed. I would write you a full account of my situation, but believing that
I can do it more to my satisfaction by oral communication, I have deferred to
do so until the first of March, when I hope to see you in St. Louis whither I
desire to go about that time, as it has been some months since I was at Confession.

> Your obedient Servant,
>
> GEORGE A. HAMILTON.

On April 18, 1840, Bishop Rosati appointed Rev. George A.
Hamilton pastor of Alton, remarking in his letter of appointment
that the missions of Springfield will be visited by the Rev. Raho and
assistant. On February 20, 1842, the Coadjutor, Bishop Peter Richard
Kenrick transferred Father Hamilton from Alton to the St. Louis
Cathedral.[17] In 1846 his name is mentioned for the last time in the
records of St. Louis diocese as assistant rector at St. Patrick's
Church in St. Louis, with Rev. W. Wheeler as rector. When and
why Father Hamilton left his native diocese we cannot say, but
in 1865 we find him as pastor of St. Francis de Sales' parish in
Charlestown, Mass.; and as a member of the Bishop's Council of
the Diocese of Boston. His death occurred on July 21, 1874, in
Charlestown, Mass.

Among the pioneer settlers of Alton on the Mississippi there were
but few Catholics. Yet one by one Irish and German families built
their homes on the hills, the site of the present city. They were
visited at regular intervals from Portage des Sioux beyond the river
by the Jesuit Fathers, Peter Kenny and Jodocus Van Asche. The
report for 1836 gives Alton 150 souls and the neighboring village
of Grafton 15. At Bishop Rosati's suggestion two Irish Catholics,
J. P. B. McCabe and Richard McDonnell, made the first church
census on June 26, 1836, and sent the list to St. Louis with the
request for a resident priest.

NAMES OF MEMBERS OF THE CATHOLIC CHURCH, RESIDING IN ALTON AND
ITS ENVIRONS

Taken by Julius P. B. MacCabe and Richard MacDonnell, Sunday, June 26, 1836:

Julius P. B. MacCabe, Lower Alton;
Richard MacDonnell, dto;
Matheus Schaub, die Frau und zwei Kinder;
Friederich Hermann, Frau, drei Kinder;

---

[17] Bishop Kenrick is reported to have said that Father Hamilton was the
first priest stationed at the Cathedral that could preach an English sermon.

Theresia Kuni und Schwester, drei Kinder;
Frantz Walter, Frau, drei Kinder;

Urbanus Langenberger, Frau und 2 Kinder;
Christian Heitzig und Frau;
Antoni Ulrich, Upper Alton;
John Wiedfield, Upper Alton;
Casper Heitzig, 3 Kinder, Upper Alton;
Christoph Heitzig, Upper Alton;
Elizabeth Heitzig, Upper Alton;
Anton Teipel, Frau und 2 Kinder;
Arnold Weigler;
Theod. Mueller, Frau, 2 Kinder, Lower Alton;
Franz Pottger, Frau und Schwager, Lower Alton;
Heinr. Hohoff, Frau und 2 Kinder, Upper Alton;
Anton Wrede, Upper Alton;
John Glandgy & wife and family, Middletown;
Francis Tissney (E) wife & 2 children;
Lewis Cayn (F) wife & 2 children;
Lewis Pellan (F) & wife;
Patrick Monaghan, wife & 4 children;
Timothy O'Brien at Mr. Clare's;
Thos. Howley at Mr. Monaghan's;
John Carrolin at dto;
Patrick MacDonnell at dto;
John Doyle at dto;
Wm. Ryan at dto;
Martin Kelly at dto;
Anthony Dwyer at dto;
Peter Cantwell dto;
Wm. Moore dto;
James Sweeny dto;
Lawrence Lawler dto;
Michael Daly;
Andrew Daly dto;
Stephen Higgins dto;
J. C. Bruner;
Joseph (the rest is illegible);
Josias Hercules, Lower Alton;
Ninela (?) Diaz (?);
James Shannon;
Charles Ubert, Lower Alton;
Thomas Clare, wife and child;
Paulin Walter, Lower Alton;
Peter Ryan, Lower Alton;
Isidor Baur;
John Faller, wife and one child;
Thomas Holden, Lower Alton;
Francis Antwein Stùwer, Frau und zwei Kinder;
Henry Sailor, Lower Alton;
Thomas Farrell, dto;
Michael Farrell, Lower Alton.

Together with the list Mr. McCabe sent a long letter explaining the conditions in Alton:

The people received us very kindly and rejoiced at the prospect of having this means afforded them of attending to their religious duties and bringing up their children in the faith of their fathers. One German farmer, a Mr. Scharf, escorted us to the dwellings of five or six of his neighbors, and then we were joined by two young men, who with pleasure conducted us to Upper Alton, calling at every house where they knew a member of the church could be found. At Upper Alton I met with a Frenchman (Mr. Fecht) who put me in possession of a subscription list, which contained the names of nine individuals, with the sum of $71.00. Among the many promises of aid which I have received here is Mr. Lane's of a lot in any part of his property in Lower Alton and the sum of $500.00. Col. Snowden, who resides on the Prairie a few miles from town has, I understand, stated, that he will give $500.00. I have seen two Irish protestants here, men of property, who signified their intention of subscribing liberally towards the building. I fear that the want of a pastor has been the means of making some of the weak-minded or uneducated to join the sectarians, or become quite indifferent about religion in any shape.

I am informed that several respectable families, who emigrated this season with the intention of settling in this neighborhood, declined doing so upon learning that there was no church nor priest here.

I have no doubt that with the blessing of God, I shall see a substantial edifice erected in Lower Alton and attended by a congregation of 500 to 600 before two years have elapsed. If the bishop will send a priest here I am instructed by the Catholic inhabitants to give them notice so that a meeting may take place, to make arrangements for having the lot laid out and the foundation sunk, and the building commenced. Stone is plentiful here, and a Dutchman in Upper Alton holds out a promise of a donation of the brick. I trust I shall have the pleasure of drawing the deed.[13]

Bishop Rosati gladly acquiesced and in February, 1837, appointed the Rev. James O'Flynn as Alton's first resident pastor. But Father O'Flynn soon found himself at odds with a substantial part of his congregation and on February 25, 1838, asked for his recall. Among the reasons given for this resolve, is this:

The Germans are more numerous here than the Catholics from any other country. They are complaining that they derive no benefit from my instruction and consequently are not very willing to contribute to my support, except three or four families in the country and about the same number in Upper Alton, who have attended Mass very regularly.

Father O'Flynn left Alton and the diocese soon after this. The Jesuit Father Van Assche once more took charge of the place until the arrival of Father George A. Hamilton from Springfield, April, 1840.

REV. JOHN ROTHENSTEINER.

St. Louis.

Archives of Catholic Historical Society of St. Louis.

RICHARD C. GANNON

Richard Camillus Gannon who died December 24, 1920, was born in the city of Dublin, Ireland, December 19, 1842 and was brought by his parents, Patrick Gannon and Elizabeth Lowe Gannon, to Chicago in 1853. The families of both his parents were devotedly attached to the Catholic religion. His father was one of the organizers and President of the St. Andrew Benevolent Society, Dublin. He took an active interest in Irish National affairs and was a strong supporter of the Young Ireland Party in 1848. Mr. Gannon was the second eldest son, there being eleven children in the family. Among his school mates in Dublin was William Walsh who is now the Archbishop of that See.

Mr. Gannon attended St. Patrick's School, the University of St. Mary of the Lake which was then located where the Holy Name Cathedral now stands, and subsequently took a course in the University of Notre Dame, Notre Dame. Indiana. He taught school in Nashville, Tennessee for Bishop James Whelan of that diocese in 1860, returning to Chicago on the last train coming north after the State Legislature had passed the ordinance of withdrawal from the Union in 1861. Afterwards he accepted employment as an express messenger on the Pennsylvania Railroad and worked in this capacity for nearly five years. He then gave his attention to the wholesale grocery business and identified himself with the firm of Franklin MacVeagh & Company. He traveled for this firm for forty years, retiring five years ago. His travels as representative of his Company took him to nearly all the towns and cities of Northern and Central Illinois. Due to his ability, enthusiasm and tact he was most successful in extending the firm's business and soon became one of its most valued advisers.

Mr. Gannon was so solicitous about the welfare of traveling salesmen that he took an active part in the formation of the Illinois Commercial Men's Association in 1900, which now has a membership of over 150,000. He had been its Vice-President from 1910. In addition he was one of the organizers of the Illinois Commercial Men's Health Association about eight years ago, which now has a membership of 55,000, and held the position of President from its organization. Mr. Gannon's attendance at the annual Conventions of the Commercial Men's Insurance Association brought him in contact with the leaders of nearly all these associations in the United States, and among whom he had many warm personal friends.

He was one of the charter members of the Union Catholic Library Association organized in 1869. He aided in forming the Irish American Club in 1880 and the Columbus Club of Chicago in 1892. On different occasions the members of these associations elected him to their Board of Directors. He was a member of Chicago Council, Knights of Columbus, and, in 1906, aided in the formation of Americus Council. He was its first Grand Knight. In 1917 he was appointed by Mayor Thompson a member of the School Board of Chicago.

Mr. Gannon from his youth manifested a keen interest in Catholic education and charity work. He became a member of St. Patrick

Conference, Society of St. Vincent de Paul of Chicago, February, 1868. His zeal in the Society's work soon attracted the attention of his brother members and before the end of the year he became the Conference Secretary. At the time of the great Chicago fire in 1871 he was its President. During this trying period he and the members of St. Patrick and sister Conferences of Chicago made many sacrifices and did heroic work in providing sustenance and shelter for the fire sufferers. In 1878 he was chosen one of the Vice-Presidents of the Particular Council of Chicago, retaining this position until he succeeded to the office of President, May, 1888, holding the latter post until January, 1910.

Mr. Gannon was actively attached to the work of the Society of St. Vincent de Paul. However, his enthusiasm and zeal extended to other phases of charity work besides the visitation and relief of needy families in their homes. As a member and officer of the Particular Council of Chicago he was active in safe-guarding the welfare of dependent and neglected children. During the seventies and early eighties the Particular Council was one of the Principal aids and supports of the Industrial School for Boys at Bridgeport and conducted lectures for the raising of funds for its financial support. Later its members selected the land and promoted the up-building of St. Mary's Training School for Boys at Desplaines. The records of the Council show that Mr. Gannon took an active part in this work. After the great fire the aged poor became a problem in Chicago and Mr. Gannon with James McMullen John Adams, Frank W. Young, I. C. Hildreth, Daniel Scully and other officers and members of the Particular Council, besought Bishop Foley to invite the Little Sisters of the Poor to come to Chicago to establish a Home for the care of the aged. As a member of the special work committee of the Council he also contributed to the well-being of the inmates of the County Infirmary at Dunning.

In 1902 Mr. Gannon took steps to obtain financial aid from the State for the support of the Catholic Chaplain of the Illinois State Prison, at Joliet. He became conversant with the hardships endured by the Rev. Fideles Kaercher, O. F. M., the Catholic Chaplain devoting his life to the spiritual welfare of the inmates of the Catholic faith. No compensation was provided for the Chaplain except ten dollars monthly for carfare. Through the efforts of Mr. Gannon this unjust state of affairs was brought to the attention of the members of the Legislature of the State of Illinois in 1911 a just compensation was granted by this body for the maintainance of the Catholic Chaplain of the State Prison. Pending this period Mr. Gannon was untiring in his efforts to assist the Chaplain.

During his membership in the Society he was a commanding figure, not only locally but in its National Conferences. He presided as Chairman of the International Congress of the Society which convened in Chicago September 1893, during the time of the World's Fair. He acted in a similar capacity at the National Convention of the Society in Louisville, Kentucky in 1898 and participated in the International Congress of the Society in St. Louis September, 1904.

Upon the foundation of the Central Council of the Society of

RICHARD C. GANNON

DISTINGUISHED CATHOLIC LAYMAN

Born December 19, 1842, Died December 24, 1920

St. Vincent de Paul of Chicago in 1894 he was elected its first President. He continued in this position until the institution of the Superior Council, January, 1909 with jurisdiction for the Ecclesiastical Province of Illinois, when he became its first President. He occupied this responsible position until the unification, November. 1913, of the Superior Councils of Chicago, New York, New Orleans, St. Louis and the Council of Brooklyn under the Superior Council of the United States. Mr. Gannon then became one of the Vice-Presidents of the Superior Council and continued in the Presidency of the Metropolitan Central Council of Chicago until his death.

Mr. Gannon was recognized as one of the most prominent Catholic laymen of our country. In March, 1903 he was selected by the clergy of the diocese of Chicago to present the address of welcome for the laity on the occasion of the enthronement of the late Archbishop Quigley. He read a paper at the First American Missionary Congress held in Chicago, November, 1908, in which he embodied an outline of the work of the Society of St. Vincent de Paul and held it up as a type of organization adapted for charitable and missionary work.

President Roosevelt invited Mr. Gannon with a representative group of two hundred men and women interested in charitable and welfare work in the United States to attend a Conference called by him to discuss the problems of caring for the dependent children of our country, which held its opening session January 25, 1909 in the White House, Washington, D. C.

Mr. Gannon took an active interest in the National Conference of Catholic Charities, attending the first general session, September, 1910, at the Catholic University of America, Washington. He was chosen one of the Vice-Presidents of the National Conference of Charities and Corrections at its 38th Annual Session, June, 1911, at Boston and was honored with the Vice-Presidency of the National Conference of Catholic Charities of the 4th Biennial Meeting September, 1916, at the Catholic University of America.

The Committee appointed by the clergy to welcome Archbishop Mundelein upon his coming to Chicago as Archbishop, chose Mr. Gannon as its Chairman. Accompanied by the members of the Committee he proceeded to LaPorte, Indiana, February 8, 1916. and awaited the special train bringing the new Shepherd to his flock. Upon the arrival of the train the entire party alighted and Mr. Gannon, in the name of the Catholic laity of Chicago in a few well chosen words, welcomed His Grace and pledged their loyalty.

Mr. Gannon was the backbone and main-stay of every Vincentian work undertaken by the Society in Chicago during his career. In his administration as President of the different Councils he achieved great success in advancing the Society which he loved and served so devotedly. He had the satisfaction of seeing the five parish Conferences existing in Chicago at the time he became a member, increase, largely through his self-sacrificing efforts, to 125. besides branches formed in Rockford. Alton, East St. Louis and Peoria. His example was an inspiration to all the Vincentians with whom he came in contact. His cheerful and sunny disposition encouraged and heart-

ened them in their labor. His implicit faith in the goodness and
mercy of Almighty God inspired them to persevere in their efforts in
behalf of the poor and needy. He had reverence for the poor and
unfortunate and saw in them, as in all men, the image of his Maker.
He often recalled the spiritual benefits that may be gained by all
members who imbibe the spirit of the Society and persevere in its
membership. He possessed qualities of leadership that inspired confidence in all. He followed closely the ideal set by the saintly Ozanam
who founded the Society which seeks to perform its works efficiently
and consolingly, without ostentation and without any ulterior motive,
than the glory of God and the welfare of His poor.   .
    As an active member of St. Patrick Conference he never tired of
his weekly visits to the homes of the needy families. He had a relish
and talent for the work and, in addition to the required assistance,
he gave in his kindly manner; the alms of good advice. The personal
sacrifices made by him in the reconstruction and rehabilitation of
families, thus placing them in a self-supporting position in society,
earned for him their lasting gratitude and prayers. One may form
some idea of the vastness of the personal service rendered by Mr.
Gannon in the cause of the spiritual and temporal welfare of the
poor by calculating the number of times he attended weekly Conference meetings, the weekly visits made to the homes of needy
families and the monthly Council meetings attended during his membership of nearly fifty-three years.
    Mr. Gannon numbered among his friends, nearly all the pioneer
Catholic clergymen of the diocese of Chicago. They cherished him
as a staunch friend ever ready to advance the cause of religion and
charity. He saw the Catholic Church in Chicago from its infancy
having lived under the rule of all the Archbishops and Bishops, save
the first. He was an intimate friend of each, having been married in
St. Patrick's Church by the Rt. Rev. Bishop Thomas Foley, D. D.,
and in this same church December 27, 1920, the Most Rev. George
W. Mundelein, presided at his funeral Mass and gave the final
absolution.
    As a friend, Mr. Gannon was unselfish and helpful. As a citizen
he was public spirited and always interested in civic betterment. In
business matters he was the soul of honor. As a leader he won men
to his aid by force of his example and was ever ready to give recognition for services. As a man his strong convictions and clear sense
of duty based upon principles of justice and charity and his generous
attitude toward all men, irrespective of race or creed, made him a
tower of strength in the community and earned for him the highest
esteem.
    On February 8, 1877, Mr. Gannon was united in marriage to
Miss Mary Ann Hildreth of Chicago. His home life was a happy one.
He was devotedly attached to his family, and he had the sympathy
and encouragement of Mrs. Gannon in all his plans. She took a special
interest in the efforts in the furtherance of the work of the Society
of St. Vincent de Paul. Mr. Gannon is survived by his widow, Mrs.
Anna Gannon, and their two sons, Richard C. Gannon, Jr., and Edward A. Gannon.
                                            JAMES F. KENNEDY.

Illinois Catholic Historical Society

617 ASHLAND BLOCK, CHICAGO

Illinois Catholic Historical Review

Journal of the Illinois Catholic Historical Society
917 ASHLAND BLOCK, CHICAGO

EDITOR-IN-CHIEF
Joseph J. Thompson...............*Chicago*

ASSOCIATE EDITORS

Rev. Frederick Beuckman........*Belleville* Kate Meade ....*Chicago*
Rev. J. B. Culemans.............*Moline* Rev. Francis J. Epstein..........*Chicago*
William Stetson Merrill.............*Chicago*

EDITORIAL COMMENT

Gathering Historical Data.—It is important for coming generations that a movement to gather and preserve historical data has been advantageously launched in nearly every state in the union. It is more important still that the movement is not confined to the gathering of ancient data, but takes into account even the most recent happenings, the best example of this feature of the movement being the efforts being put forth to get together such materials as shall in the future constitute historical sources of the recent war. Nearly every state in the union, to say nothing of national movements, has engaged in this undertaking.

Historical data consists of a mass of written and printed information of various kinds. The newspapers and other periodicals constitute one important source of history, their value of course being influenced by their character. Current literature is another source. The government reports of every kind furnish still another, and every kind of document, public and private, is a more or less valuable source of history.

It is of course natural that the collection of data should be and will be influenced by the purposes and desires of those who make or supervise them, and it is wholly unnecessary to suggest that a collection of data made by a Catholic organization would be more interesting and more valuable to Catholics than one made by an organization antagonistic or indifferent to Catholicity. If any doubt should

exist upon such a proposition, it may easily be solved by the examination of almost any collection of data now in existence.

It is very well to assert that historical data is historical data, and that the same conditions should result from its collection, regardless of the responsible agency. The best answer to such an assertion is that it isn't true; and it is entirely appropriate to observe that it is useless to expect results satisfactory from the Catholic standpoint, where Catholics have no voice or influence. In making such an assertion no special reflection is intended, but simply that under conditions which have obtained almost since the beginning of the so-called reformation, it has been considered permissible, and indeed quite commendable, to ignore what is creditable in the history of the church, and misrepresent the true teachings and activities of the church.

What is the one unfailing remedy for this condition? Appeals and even threats have been tried, but without results. The remedy is best found in the old fable of the "Lark and her Young Ones." A lark, who had young ones in a field of corn which was almost ripe, was afraid lest the reapers should come before her young brood was fledged. Every day, therefore, when she flew away to look for food, she charged them to take notice of what they heard in her absence, and to tell her of it when she returned. One day when she was gone they heard the master of the field say to his son that the corn seemed ripe enough to be cut, and tell him to go early tomorrow and desire their friends and neighbors to come and help to reap it. When the old lark came home, the little ones fell quivering and chirping around her, and told her what had happened, begging her to remove them as fast as she could. The mother bade them to be easy, "for," said she, "if he depends upon his friends and his neighbors, I am sure the corn will not be reaped tomorrow." Next day she went out again, and left the same orders as before. The owner came, and waited. The sun grew hot, but nothing was done, for not a soul came. "You see," said he to his son, "these friends of ours are not to be depended upon, so run off at once to your uncles and cousins, and say I wish them to come betimes tomorrow morning and help us to reap." This the young ones, in a great fright, reported to their mother. "Do not be frightened, children," said she; "kindred and relations are not always very forward in helping one another; but keep your ears open, and let me know what you hear tomorrow." The owner came the next day, and, finding his relations as backward as his neighbors, said to his son, "Now, George, listen to me. Get a couple of good sickles ready against tomorrow morning, for it seems we must reap the corn by ourselves." The young ones told this to their mother. "Then, my dears," said she, "it is time for us to go indeed, for when a man undertakes to do his business himself, it is not so likely that he will be disappointed." She removed her young ones immediately, and the corn was reaped the next day by the old man and his son.

The parable applies in a special manner to American Catholics. The historical harvest for them is abundant. For centuries the Catholics have left the burden of garnering the harvest to others, with most disappointing results. The true course lies in a prompt and vigorous execution of the work by the Catholics themselves.

BOOK REVIEWS

The Right Reverend Edward D. Fenwick, O. P., Founder of the Dominicans of the United States, by Very Reverend V. F. O'Daniel, O. P., S. T. M. Frederick Pustet Co., Inc. The Dominica, 487 Michigan Avenue, N. E., Washington D. C. Net, $3.50.

Father O'Daniel's latest publication as above entitled, is, in our opinion, the best of the many excellent works of that erudite and painstaking author.

To begin with, Father O'Daniel treats of one of the most interesting characters in all the history of the Church in America.

In the next place, the life of Bishop Fenwick is highly interesting to the readers of the ILLINOIS CATHOLIC HISTORICAL REVIEW, because his field of labor was located in the West, and his connection with the Illinois country was most intimate.

There are somewhat more than 400 pages in Father O'Daniel's book, and the type and general make-up is very satisfactory.

In his treatment of the subject the author applies purely scientific methods, never leaving the reader in doubt of assertions made by him. Copious foot-notes direct attention to authoritative sources of information upon which he has drawn, and the greatest merit of the work lies in the directness with which the facts are set forth.

Those who have read Father O'Daniel's previous works, like "The Life of Reverend Charles Hyacinth McKenna, O. P., P. G., Missionary and Apostle of the Holy Name Society," and have followed his work in the *Catholic Historical Review* and other periodicals, were prepared for the reception of such a splendid work as his "Life of Bishop Fenwick."

For the first time almost the introduction of Catholicity and the record of the early years of the Church in Ohio have been set forth connectedly; and in so doing Father O'Daniel has rendered a distinct service.

The Illinois Country—1673-1818. Alvord, Volume I—Centennial History of Illinois.

"The Illinois Country," Volume I, of the Centennial History of Illinois, by Clarence Walworth Alvord, may justly be termed a model history.

A model history would approach perfection, both in form and substance. "The Illinois Country," fills that specification.

The expectation that the Centennial volume being prepared by
Dr. Alvord personally would be a work of the highest merit, has
been fully realized.

In writing this his latest and in our judgment his greatest work,
Dr. Alvord has disproven his own assertion, sometime made, as to
the prosiness of historians in general, and including himself specifically. His suggestion that he and most historians could not hope to
reach the beauty of expression, for which Francis Parkman and a
. few other great historians were noted, must be discounted, since the
production of "The Illinois Country."

This volume covers the Catholic period of Illinois. Though the
so-called "Reformation" had been under way for more than a century
before the Illinois country found a place in history, yet there is no
record indicating that any man of other than the Catholic faith ever
set foot on Illinois soil during the first three-quarters of a century
after the discovery of the country. Beginning with Father Marquette
and his associate explorer, Joliet, all explorers, travelers, traders and
white men of every description who came to the region were Catholics. Every course of travel was marked out and every trail blazed
throughout the region by sturdy Catholic pioneers.

Dr. Alvord does not chant a pean of praise to the Catholics,
much as they deserve the best that could be said of them, but more
than any non-Catholic writer to the present time has he eliminated
the indications of inborn bias that have disfigured other historical
works, making even such notable efforts as Francis Parkman's re-
volting to a discriminating sense of justice.

A few features chosen here and there sustained by the general
tenor of the text will illustrate the fairness with which Dr. Alvord
approaches and discusses his subject:

To begin with he uses a reproduction of the painting of Marquette,
rescued from destruction, as a frontispiece. The most exacting Catholic could find no fault with the character Dr. Alvord gives Father
Marquette and the other great missionaries, and in summing up this
early civilization he says:

> The early history of this region is identified no more completely with the
> enterprising traders than with the Order of the Jesuits who for almost a
> century maintained a long succession of zealous missionaries in this distant field.
> From the first one, Father Marquette, to the last, Father Meurin, these learned
> men of religion, with little thought of worldly wealth or desire of self-advance-
> ment, gave the best of their lives to the conversion of the Illinois Indians.
> Marquette's successor in the Illinois mission, Father Claude Jean Allouez, S. J.,
> played an important role in the establishment of the white man in the West. For

twenty-four years his figure was a familiar one wherever new missions were to be established or maintained.—(pp. 102-103).

And he quotes a modern writer to the following effect:

Heedless of fatigue or hunger, cold or heat, he traveled over snow and ice, swollen streams or dangerous rapids seeking distant Indian villages, counting it all joy if by any means he could win a few savages for a heavenly future.— (p. 103).

As time went on and missions grew into parishes, Dr. Alvord gives this tribute to the missionaries:

In all accounts that have been preserved the praise of the Jesuits in the performance of their duties to their parishioners is almost universal, only an occasional voice being raised against their strictness. . Besides the regularly recurring functions of their calling the Fathers gave daily instruction, for the most part religious, to the French children, thus becoming the first school teachers in the Illinois country.—(p. 198).

Not the missions alone, but the French pioneers themselves are, contrary to the usual course, treated sympathetically, even admiringly, and so late as the territorial period Dr. Alvord feels justified in this passage:

To the French inhabitants migration into the wilderness had brought only a slight relaxing of the bonds of civilization. In the early days both Church and State had made every effort to follow them into their new abode and to maintain a firm hold over them, with the result that even at this time the Illinois French were described as an orderly, peace-loving people. With the Americans matters were far different.—(p. 455).

In a general way these passages indicate the author's style. The habit of belittling or reflecting upon the missionaries and the French so usual in historical works by non-Catholics dealing with such subjects is entirely absent from this volume.

In addition Dr. Alvord has told the story of Illinois covering this earliest and most interesting period much better than the early story of any state of the union has ever been detailed. It is a story of fact and not of incidents recited for the purpose of drawing a conclusion. When the author does indulge in conclusions they are so obvious from the facts as not to be questionable. .

Just as a ray of hope thrown out to aspiring historians to prove that even the greatest of the cult may occasionally slip, attention may be drawn to an error or inaccuracy here and there. For example: In describing the great ceremony on the occasion of the establishment of the mission of the Immaculate Conception of the Blessed Virgin among the Illinois, near the modern city of Utica in LaSalle County,

312 BOOK REVIEWS

Dr. Alvord says "This service occurred on Good Friday." (p. 67). As a matter of fact the service occurred on Holy Thursday, the day before Good Friday. In speaking of the fur trade, while the author commends the enterprise of the French in this regard, but is like all writers averse to the principle of monopoly so prevalent in that day, he perhaps inadvertently falls into another little error:

There can be no doubt that the religious order (that is the Jesuits) drew a profit from the partnership, since the Jesuits have always proved themselves thrifty and shrewd in the handling of their business.—(p. 69).

That the missionaries handled their business efficiently and made it help to sustain their missionary work is beyond question, but that they "drew a profit from" any partnership with government agents or traders is not sustained by any record.

The best historians, to say nothing of the army of near historians, would, however, be delighted if the errors to be found in their books were as few as those discoverable in "The Illinois Country."

Volume I of the Illinois Centennial History is worth all the money and effort expended for the series, and the author, the publishers, and the Centennial commission are to be congratulated upon its issue.

J. J. T.

The Modern Commonwealth, Vol. 5, of the Centennial History of Illinois, by Ernest Ludow Bogart and John Mabry Matthews. Published by Illinois Centennial Commission, Springfield, Ill.

Another volume, Vol. V, of the Illinois Centennial History has been added to our collection. It is entitled "The Modern Commonwealth" and covers the period from 1893 to 1918. The authors have given a very interesting, well organized and clear account of the economic, political and social development of the state during the period designated. The book, besides being very readable for the average man, should prove a convenient and valuable reference for students of Illinois history. The array of facts is very impressive, as might be expected from the authors' acknowledgments to the research assistants who had made preliminary reports on agriculture, manufacturing, labor organizations, etc. By special arrangement the chapter on Education Art and Letters was written by H. B. Fuller and the supplementary chapter on "Illinois and the Great War" by Arthur C. Cole. There is an appendix of especial value to those interested in the study of agriculture, the growth of manufacturing and of transportation. The bibliography, too, is excellent.

The account of Illinois' part in the World War is a very complete story of an interesting and critical period in our history. The writer takes a broad view, free from hysteria, giving due credit to the participation of labor, the schools, women, and to the loyalty of German-Americans in Illinois. He concludes his account of the attitude of the latter with the following words:

"It is in many ways remarkable that, with the army of officials and volunteers bent upon detecting treachery, so few German-American citizens were convicted of or even charged with acts of treason or disloyolty."

Space does not permit even a brief review of each chapter of the book, but the two chapters which are likely to be of universal interest are Chapter XXI, to which reference has just been made, and Chapter II, "The Growth of Education, Art and Letters." This chapter should not be overlooked in a review appearing in the ILLINOIS CATHOLIC HISTORICAL REVIEW.

Thre are two methods of minimizing the part which Catholics have played in history—one is the old and rather crude method of attack; the other the newer, more refined and undoubtedly more effective method of silence; of omitting any reference to Catholic activity or excellence. To ignore the share of so important an institution as the Catholic Church in educational and civic advancement, is to leave the impression that that share is insignificant, that it really does not count for much, that it is an historical fact of which one may be ignorant and yet be considered a well informed historian. Consequently histories are made omitting reference to things Catholic; ignorant and yet be considered a well informed. Consequently histories are written omitting reference to things Catholic; these histories are used as reference books for students who will write later histories and the searcher after truth is amazed, when he consults such works, to find that a force to which he can find no reference, has been a powerful factor in the history of the period he is studying.

It was the realization of this situation that brought about the organization of the ILLINOIS CATHOLIC HISTORICAL SOCIETY, which is doing a service in making available facts and material apparently unknown to some compilers of the Centennial History of Illinois, a work published at state expense under the authority of the State Legislature. We trust that we may suppose that if the author of the chapter on education in the volume under consideration had taken a comprehensive view of the subject he would not have confined his account of Catholic activity to the single statement:

"In 1898 Archbishop Spalding of Peoria established there the

Spalding Institute, a high school with some technical features for young Catholics."

The author gives an excellent account of the building activities and general expansion of the University of Chicago, University of Illinois, Northwestern University, Rockford College, and Knox College, but he makes no mention of the great expansion of St. Viator's College, De Paul University or of Loyola University with its departments of law, medicine and sociology, the last a distinctly new departure, worth at least a paragraph in itself. Would it not be interesting for the average non-Catholic to learn that these activities are actually under the direction of the Jesuits who, he has been taught, are people of the past, out of touch with modern life, "learning nothing and forgetting nothing," reactionaries among reactionaries? The writer evidently does not know of the excellent scientific laboratories and library of forty-six thousand volumes at Loyola University, containing many original manuscripts and old publications, valued beyond price. If he had known of this remarkable collection, we hope he would have considered it at least worthy of mention equally with the library which Knox College has collected from the authors among its faculty and alumni.

Catholics will miss also a mention of the great progress made in the growth of Catholic elementary and high schools of the state. Illinois is justly proud of the splendid advance in the number and progress of her public schools. She may also be proud of the development of the parochial schools, academies and colleges of the Catholic Church, which are making capable and loyal citizens, a development whose extent and import would almost be a revelation, to our learned authors; to know that in 1918 the term of their educational survey, there were 166,000 pupils in the parochial schools of the five dioceses of Illinois. There were besides the academies and colleges for both sexes and the seminaries for the education of the clergy none of which is noticed by the author.

J. J.

SOURCE BOOKS OF HISTORY

The *Annals of the Society for the Propagation of the Faith* are among the most valuable sources of early American History, especially such as is of interest to the Church. The numerous letters of the early missionary clergy are of the highest degree of interest and especially valuable because of the learning and ability of the writers. We have had several of these letters translated from the French in which they were originally published and present our readers in this number a typical example:

LETTERS FROM FATHER RONDOT, APOSTOLIC MISSIONARY, TO FATHER CHOLLETON, VICAR-GENERAL OF LYONS

J. M. J.

St. Louis, May 21, 1831.

Sir:—

It surely is time to keep the promise which I made you to give some details of my trip and the state in which I found the Catholic churches in America which we have visited.

I will add, if you permit it, a short description of the country and villages also, particularly that of the diocese of St. Louis. Mgr. Rosati, would have preferred to give you a picture of the situation himself, and the progress which the Catholic Religion is making in Missouri, but as his numerous occupations will not permit him to do so, I will try to replace him, conforming to the notes which he gave me, with a scrupulous exactitude.

Our boat entered the harbor of New York the 3rd of April, Holy Saturday, after fifty days of navigation; contrary winds and furious storms kept us back a great deal. We saw land for two days before landing, a wonderful island about seventy-five miles (twenty-five leagues) long, which the Americans call Long Island. There is nothing more imposing and beautiful than the spectacle which is offered to travellers entering the harbor of New York. The sky was pure, the sea smooth as a mirror, and a slight breeze pushed us towards land. The scene was complete as it presented itself to us in all its unequalled beauty. The enormous island just mentioned stretched out to the right of us, with vast forests which rose above the farms and villages. On the left, was a lower hill, covered with green trees and houses, in the middle of which rose a great edifice, a bath house. Before us, on a small island covered with verdure, were two high towers, which served as Light Houses. Another one seemed to emerge little by little from the bay in which we were entering and a number of towers farther off, drew our attention by their startling whiteness. A multitude of sails, illumined by the rising sun, sailed through the bay in all directions and gave a new charm to the picture in animating it. Behind us was the ocean, the sky brightened by the sun, and the two extremities of land, which, as they melted into the distance became one with the horizon. We soon passed the bar, the only passage open to vessels, and found ourselves in a vast bay surrounded with wonderful scenery. A little to the right, one could see a large opening dominated

315

by the fortifications. It was the route which we would take to enter the Hudson. This natural canal is bordered with public buildings, and beautiful little homes and farms. It widens in a short time and there is a second bay, after which comes the city. It is built on an island, between the two arms of the Hudson River, a large and majestic river. One can see the numerous elegant towers from afar, and the forest of masts on the water seems to build a wall around the city. A number of little islands, covered with trees or batteries, make the bay even more picturesque. As to the river, I have never seen one in France which could compare to it in width, for it is over a mile wide, (a third of a league) or in beauty. But, to the emotions which naturally fill the heart of a European who sees these beauties for the first time there are added the supernatural sentiments present in the heart of a Minister of God at sight of this land which seems destined by the Divine Providence to the most startling triumphs for the true Faith. These towers and domes which are not surmounted by a Cross, announce only too clearly how many triumphs the Catholic Religion still has to make in this great city, whose beauty, commerce and opulence place it in the first rank among the flourishing cities of the two Americas. New York is regarded as the most important city on the American continent. There are about two hundred thousand persons living there at this time. The port of New York si the meeting place of all nations. You can see, at one time, vessels from different parts of Europe, from South America, China and India. You can see merchandise arriving at New York from Liverpool, Havre, Calcutta, Canton and Mexico at the same time. The docks are covered with merchandise from thousands of boats and are animated by the movements of the thousands of sailors and men whose language is as varied as their costume.

The aspect of the cities in the United States is very different from that of European cities. Wide streets, laid out by means of string drawn in a straight line stretched out as far as you can see them; magnificent sidewalks, lighted by lanterns supported on iron posts; beautiful trees planted symmetrically; the fronts of the houses almost exactly alike with an outside staircase of marble, trimmed with rich iron fences; houses built of brick, most of them simple but very elegant; a look of cleanliness everywhere and an air of easy prosperity rather than grandeur; these are the things which strike a stranger at the first glance. There are a great number of temples, which are recognized by their marble fronts and by the towers which surmount them. The cemetery is close at hand, directly off the street and surrounded by magnificent fences. These temples are not of the same size as ours in Europe; there are a great number of them; for instance, in New York alone there are about one hundred. The Catholic Cathedral is, without any doubt the most beautiful religious edifice in New York. The tower is not yet finished. It is in the Gothic style, built with a pure and noble taste, but it cannot be compared, neither in size or in beauty of its interior ornaments, to our beautiful French churches. Besides the Cathedral, there are four other Catholic churches. They are too far apart to be convenient for the great number of faithful, of whom there are at least forty thousand. There are at least fifteen thousand French, and unfortunately, there is not a single priest here who can preach to them in their own language.

There is only one really remarkable public edifice in New York, and this is the court house. It is built of white marble which, from a distance resembles that of Carrara, but the grain is not as fine or as beautiful. A number of banks and private houses are built of this marble.

The most popular walks are the Battery, a vast place at the extremity of the town, where the two branches of the river meet and from which one can see the bay and the other sides of the river; also the City Hall, beautiful square which is in front of the City Hall building. These two walks are planted with beautiful trees and grass, and have high iron fences around them. The port of New York is not entirely protected from the wind, especially from the East. During our stay in this town, a terrible tempest, which was felt even in the bay, ruined several buildings and upset a few boats. We should thank Divine Providence that we were not on sea that day.

It takes one day to go from New York to Philadelphia, although it is about one hundred miles away, after having crossed over the bay on a steam boat as far as New Brunswick. There, twenty stages take the travellers and conduct them as far as a little town called Trenton, which is celebrated on account of the victory over the English by Washington in 1776. They then embark again on the Delaware, a charming river a little wider than the Saone, which passes Philadelphia and finally joins the Delaware River. The banks of the river are under complete cultivation, and one can see, on both sides elegant habitations, which, with their gardens which are beautiful, make a most delightful picture.

Philadelphia is the most regular and beautiful city in the United States. One of the streets, which are all perfectly straight, runs directly through the city and is two miles long. By standing in the middle of this street, which is imperceptibly inclined to right and left, one can see, at each extremity of the river, at one end, the Delaware River, and at the other end, the Schuylkill River. The city extends from one of these rivers to the other. The Delaware River is navigable, above the city of Philadelphia, for the largest war vessels. In the harbor, there is a war vessel which has one hundred and sixty cannons mounted on its decks. It do not think there is anything to compare with this in all Europe.

Philadelphia is remarkable for the politeness of its inhabitants, the regularity of its streets, which are all running at right angles to one another; the elegance and cleanliness of its private residences; and lastly, for the number, size and, in some instances, beauty of its public edifices and monuments.

Among the most important of these public edifices, the United States Bank, which is a vast and beautiful building, constructed of pure white marble, is worthy of first mention. The Girard Bank, which is also built of white marble in the Corinthian style of architecture, and which has a beautiful peristyle, is remarkable because of its richness of style and finish of its work. The Pennsylvania Bank, the Academy and the Museum, etc., especially the Museum, are all worthy of more than a passing visit of curiosity, even when one has seen the Museum of Paris. Outside of an interesting collection of objects of natural history, it contains a picture gallery, where one may see the portraits of all the statesmen who have made a name for themselves in the United States. Among these, and it holds a position of much importance is the portrait of Mgr. O. Karoll [sic], the first Catholic Archbishop of Baltimore, a prelate whose name merits all the veneration and respect which can be given, whose virtues were so many and so brilliant that even the Protestants themselves were obliged to render homage to him. The skeleton of a Mammoth or Mastodon is strange enough to attract the attention of any curious sightseer. The gigantic bones of this fossil were mostly discovered between 1799 and 1801, in Newburg, which is situated in the State of New York; these bones were united to those found in

different other parts of the United States, and which were of different parts of
the body, and the whole thing was mounted on heavy wires and form an almost
complete skeleton of this extinct animal, which Mr. Cuvier has vividly described
and which he declares to be without doubt, antediluvian. This enormous skeleton
has been placed alongside of the skeleton of an elephant from India,—and the
latter appears small and insignificant beside the mammoth's awe-inspiring carcass.
    The Water Works, which is situated at a distance of about one mile from
the City, is the most curious as well as the most intricate and largest construction of its kind that I have ever had the good fortune of examining.
Enormous wheels are set in movement by a current, which puts the pumps in
motion and throws the water up to a height of about one hundred and fifty
feet. Three enormous reservoirs distribute the water all over the city, and it
is conducted through canals which run under all the streets up to the highest
floor of every private house.
    There are about one hundred and sixty thousand people now living in
Philadelphia. There are notably a great number of Quakers. The Catholics
have but three Churches there.
    I will interrupt my narration here, as the time which I was able to devote
to it, will not permit me to linger for a longer space of time. I will take
it up at another moment, however, when the occasion will be more propitious,
for in the few short pages which I felt able to devote to Philadelphia at
this time, I was naturally not able to do this beautiful and gracious city the
justice which it merits.
    Therefore, I will pass on to St. Louis, which is situated at about five
hundred leagues to the west of New York, a trifle to the South as well.
    You can travel to St. Louis from Philadelphia in a number of ways, the
most convenient and most widely travelled routes being to pass through Baltimore
and Wheeling, or, if you prefer by way of the Pittsburg road. It is this last
route which I followed. There are about four thousand Catholics in the city
of Pittsburg. There are three Catholic churches there. The entire population
comprises more than twenty thousand souls, and the city might be called the
St. Etienne of the United States, as it is the most important manufacturing
center of the United States. One can embark at Pittsburg, on the Ohio River,
and after having stopped at Cincinnati and Louisville, you enter into the Mississippi which you go up until you reach St. Louis. St. Louis has at the present
time about seven thousand persons living there. There are at least four
thousand Catholics among this number, and three thousand of these are French.
Almost all of the surrounding villages are French also.
    I will not take the time today to tell you about the site or the climate,
the productions of St. Louis, the characteristics of its inhabitants, or the
natural curiosities of Missouri, for I will tell you all this at a later date when
I can enter into all the minute but so interesting details which the subject
inspires and, indeed, merits of my pen. I will tell you now, however, in a short
and concise form, what I can about these details which I judge you would be
most interested in as to the present state of the diocese.
    St. Louis.—In this city, there are, as I already mentioned to you, about
four thousand Catholics, who are watched over spiritually, by four priests, including Father Roux. The Hospital, which is under the care of the Nuns, of
time. There is also the convent of the Ladies of the Sacred Heart. At the
whom there are at present eight, is able to take care of eighty patients at a

present time, they have ten boarding pupils, about eighty day scholars, as well as twelve orphans whom they are raising. There is also a Jesuit College, which is directed by five priests. They have thirty boarding pupils, and about one hundred day scholars.

St. Ferdinand. — This beautiful little city is situated about sixteen miles from St. Louis. There are about four hundred and eighty Catholics in the town, and two priests who oversee their spiritual welfare. The Ladies of the Sacred Heart have their Novitiate there, and have besides, a boarding school as well as a free parish school.

St. Charles and Suburbs.—This city is at a distance of approximately eighteen miles from St. Louis. There are about one thousand Catholics living there at the present time, but there is only one priest with them now. They have a free school for the boys, as well as one for the girls. This latter is under the direction of the Ladies of the Sacred Heart.

Besides that, there is always a Missionary who is traveling and who stops there. The limits of the diocese to the west is the Pacific Ocean. The number of Catholics, scattered within seven hundred miles of St. Louis, is about two hundred and twenty-seven.

Saint Genevieve.—There are about two thousand Catholics living here, with one priest.

Les Mines.—This city also has about two thousand Catholics living there and has one priest.

Saint Marie.—There is a seminary as well as a college here. About sixteen hundred Catholics living here are under the supervision of the priests who direct the two establishments. There are about one hundred boarding scholars at the present time at the college, and twenty-five seminarists, although there is every reason to hope that in the near future, the number of the latter will be most agreeably augmented. Nine of the students now at the seminary, among the twenty-five are taking the theological course.

In the State of Illinois, which extends over an area of approximately three hundred leagues, there are at the present time, four thousand, one hundred and sixty-eight Catholics residing in this state, that is, this is as close to the true number as can by the means at our disposal, be ascertained. There are only three priests, however, in the whole territory.

New Madrid.—This little town is situated at a distance of about one hundred and fifty miles from St. Louis. There are about six hundred and forty Catholics living here, but they have no priest unfortunately, although there is doubtless sore need of one.

Arkansas.—In this State there are about eight hundred Catholics, who also are without the care of a priest.

We have just received a long and very interesting letter from Father Lutz, who at the present time is staying at the Prairie du Chien. The Indians of four different nations, or tribes, caused him a very great amount of worry about two months ago, but he writes that at the present time, peace has been declared between them, and he has every reason to hope that it will be a lasting one. Suddenly, one day, without the least warning, one of the tribes, the Foxes, a very savage nation of Indians, descended the course of the Mississippi River in canoes secretly. The Missionary Father, who had gone for a stroll by the river banks that evening, surely by Divine intervention, heard the sound of oars being softly used and tried to determine who was on the river at that time,

without being able to do so, as almost complete obscurity had already fallen over the land. However, the good Father, was far from guessing that anything of this kind was going on, and continued his walk quietly, returning after half an hour's promenade, to his home, which was situated at about a half a mile from the camp of the Memonis, a nation of savages who are more or less civilized and who are allied to the United States.

He had scarcely reached his house, when he was horrified and startled to hear rifle shots and the most terrifying cries. The Memonis had been surprised in their sleep, and indeed, it must be admitted that a great number of them were drunk.[1] There were thirty unhappy victimes of this cowardly attack, men, women and children having been killed indiscriminately. The Fox tribe on account of the suddenness of their attack and the darkness which covered their retreat, were able to escape without reprisals, as word could not be taken to the Fort in time to cut off their retreat. War between them now is inevitable. We fear greatly that this will bring new obstacles in the progress of our Church.

Father Paillasson leads an altogether saintly life in every sense of the word. He is obliged to be almost continually travelling from one place to another on horseback, and frequently he has barely the necessaries of life to sustain his efforts, which necessaries means a small piece of bacon and slice or two of corn bread. His zeal is above all question or even belief and nothing can daunt or discourage him. He is the kind of missionary of whom we should have many in this country, but, alas, his kind is more than rare.

The Americans who have been converted, are admirable in the faith which they display. A short time ago, one of these converts came over eighty miles to get the priest to visit a sick man who was dying with a fever. When the priest visits any of them who are sick, they almost invariably partake of all of the Sacraments.

Mgr. received Father Roux and Father St. Cyr with the greatest possible joy. His diocese has the most pressing need of a number of other priests. For instance, the whole great state of Arkansas is without the service of a single priest. It is the same state of affairs at New Madrid, where they are also without a priest, at Kaskaskia also, where it is of the utmost importance that one should be placed permanently. As to the State of Illinois and the whole Northwest, in the whole length of the country which stretches out some three hundred leagues in length and twenty leagues in width, there are but three priests in all.

Yesterday, Mgr. himself, was obliged to make a trip of more than fifteen miles from here to see a dangerously sick person, as there was no one else to send, and the need of a priest was urgent. When I tell you that he is suffering himself from an infirmity which absolutely forbids him from riding on a horse, and when you realize that horseback was the only possible way in which to make the trip you will be able to have some idea of the suffering which he was obliged to undergo, and you can judge of his condition when he returned the same day. His suffering was truly pitiable.

Mgr. never spends the smallest sum which is not absolutely necessary, consequently his Missionaries sometime lack the necessities of life, as the amount of money at the disposal of each priest in the diocese of St. Louis is so small that in spite of everything being of a most modest price here, and the priests

---

[1] Of course, they are not yet Christians.

drink water only, it is still often impossible to meet all the necessary expenses. The priests in this diocese have no other resource than the pittance they each receive, and outside the diocese of St. Louis, the other priests do not even receive this. The people here are so very poor that they have not even any prayer books with which to follow the Mass. You once had the great kindness to offer me some, and if you could send me five or six hundred, Father Condamine and myself would be more than grateful and they would surely serve a good cause.

You cannot imagine what poverty really is until you have seen it here, where there are practically no resources of any kind, and where hunger and want are ordinary bed fellows in your every day life.

The resignation and zeal of our good missionaries who, many of them left lives filled with every necessity if not luxury, is to say the least, most satisfying.

I am, dear Sir, etc.,

RONDOT, *Missionary.*

P. S.—I forgot to mention in my letter, that when I spoke of the population of St. Louis, I did not include the population of the territory, which includes at the very least, two thousand Catholics, served by the priests who live there. I also omitted a number of other places less important, which I imagined to be of little interest to you.

Annals of the Association for the Propagation of the Faith,
Vol. XXV, p. 577, *et. seq.*

THIRD ANNUAL MEETING OF THE ILLINOIS CATHOLIC HISTORICAL SOCIETY

December 3, 1920

In accordance with the established custom, the third annual meeting of the ILLINOIS CATHOLIC HISTORICAL SOCIETY was held on Illinois Day, December 3, 1920, at Loyola School of Sociology. The meeting was called to order by the Reverend President, Father Frederic Siedenburg, S. J.

After the minutes of the previous meeting of the Executive Council were read and approved, the following financial report was read by Miss Marie Sheahan:

APRIL 1918 TO DECEMBER 3, 1920

RECEIPTS—

Membership	$ 7,262.30
Advertising	2,757.23
Cash Copies	77.80
Donations	956.20
Rebate on postage	50.00
Interest	26.33

$11,129.86

EXPENDITURES—

Editor and office	$ 1,755.00
Advertising and commissions	2,172.15
Printing and half tones	5,406.19
Stationery	183.80
Binding	58.00
Packing, mailing, etc.	364.97
Postage	311.40
Fixtures	62.50
Refund on membership	2.00

$10,366.01

$11,129.86

The Treasurer's report was then submitted:

First National Bank—Certificates of balance........$ 29.84
$100.00 U. S. Liberty Bond—4¾%............... 100.00
$500.00 U. S. Liberty Bond—4¼%............... 464.49
Total with Mr. Lawlor.:........................... $594.33
Miss Sheahan submitted the office report as follows:
Cash on hand..................................... 169.52

Total surplus $763.85

On motion of Miss Sheahan, seconded by Miss Margaret Madden, the President was authorized to appoint a committee to examine the books of the Society. The Chair named Judge Michael F. Girten, Dr. Alexander Pope, and the Treasurer.

Upon motion of Judge Michael F. Girten the name of the corresponding secretary was changed to corresponding and financial secretary.

The Chair, Father Siedenburg then stated that the election of officers was in order and announced that the treasurer, Mr. William J. Lawlor had asked that his name be not proposed for re-election. Miss Jennie Dignan moved that the secretary be instructed to cast one ballot re-electing the present officers, with the exception of the Treasurer. Miss Gertrude Corrigan seconded the motion. It was carried.

The President, on motion of Monsignor Riordan and seconded by Father Furay, was authorized to propose a candidate for treasurer at the next meeting of the Executive Council. The Council was empowered to act for the Society in the election of the proposed candidate.

The following amendments, which, in accordance with the by-laws, had been duly approved by the Executive Council were then voted upon and adopted:

AMENDMENTS TO ARTICLE THREE

Amend Paragraph (b) Article Three to read as follows:

Regular members hereafter joining and until otherwise provided by law shall pay an annual fee of $3.00 and shall be entitled to receive the ILLINOIS CATHOLIC HISTORICAL REVIEW for every year for which said annual fee shall be paid.

Amend Paragraph (c) to read as follows:

Life members shall hereafter and until otherwise provided by law pay $100.00, and shall be entitled to receive the Illinois CATHOLIC HISTORICAL REVIEW during the remainder of their lives.

Add the following paragraphs:

(cc) Members who pay $10.00 or more per year shall be known as guarantors, and when such members shall have paid $100.00 in any kind of partial payments, not less than $10.00 per year, they shall become life members, and enjoy all the privileges of life membership.

(ccc) Any institution or corporation, other than colleges and schools which may become perpetual members upon payment of $100.00 may become a perpetual member and entitled to receive the official publication of the Society upon payment of $200.00 in cash or in installments of not less than $20.00 per year. Institutions or corporations having heretofore contributed to the Treasury of the Society, shall be entitled to the official publication for a period equal to the time for which their contribution would pay at the regular subscription price during the whole of the period.

Monsignor Riordan moved that in the future the REVIEW be not sent to those who are a year or more in arrears. The motion was seconded by Mr. Haub and carried.

Reverend A. Zurbonsen, Springfield, suggested that every Illinois bishop be requested to sign a letter urging each priest in his diocese to become a member of the ILLINOIS CATHOLIC HISTORICAL SOCIETY. Father Zurbonsen expressed the belief that nearly every priest of Illinois would become a member and that many would become life members if an active campaign were inaugurated. The suggestion was referred to the Executive Council. The Chair urged all of the members to obtain new members since there was only a surplus of about $800.00 in the treasury and funds were essential to the work of the Society.

The Editor, Joseph J. Thompson, read a paper on "The Past, Present and Future of the ILLINOIS CATHOLIC HISTORICAL REVIEW. A vote of thanks was given Mr. Thompson for his interesting paper.

At the request of the Editor, letters of appreciation were read by the Secretary. They are as follows:

GREETINGS AND FELICITATIONS

THE STATE HISTORICAL SOCIETY OF WISCONSIN
Madison, Nov. 11, 1920.

Joseph J. Thompson,
    Editor, ILLINOIS CATHOLIC HISTORIC REVIEW.
My dear Mr. Thompson:

The task of preserving the sources of our history and of disseminating a knowledge thereof is an enormous one. Since it offers no adequate financial return for the labor involved it must either be subsidized by the State or be performed as a labor of love, unless it is to be permitted to go undone. Since it is not to be supposed that the State will ever be able to subsidize all the historical work, which should be carried on, we must conclude that a great

and pressing field remains open for cultivation by voluntary organizations. If so, who should perform this work if not those who are most directly interested in the results to be achieved? More concretely, who shall look after the Catholic contribution to Illinois history if not the Catholics themselves? Your REVIEW is performing a worthy work in this connection which should not be allowed to lapse for lack of adequate support. In my opinion the other religious organizations of the State might well afford to imitate the excellent example you are setting.

Sincerely yours,
(Signed) M. M. QUAIFE,
Editor, Wisconsin Historical Society.

THE CATHOLIC HISTORICAL REVIEW
Catholic University of America, Washington, D. C.
Rev. Peter Guilday, Managing Editor.
November 15, 1920.

Mr. Joseph J. Thompson,
917 Ashland Block, Chicago, Ill.
My dear Mr. Thompson:

If any word of mine would encourage the members of the ILLINOIS CATHOLIC HISTORICAL SOCIETY and in particular the editorial board of your excellent quarterly historical REVIEW, then you certainly may have them *ex intimo corde*. The REVIEW has been a delight to all who are interested not only in historical study, but especially in accurate, painstaking, and attractive historical study. I have never missed reading each number from cover to cover, and on more than one occasion its scholarly articles have been of assistance to my students and myself in our study of American Church history. I hope and pray that it may prosper and that it may meet with the welcome it undoubtedly deserves from all Catholics in the old Illinois Country.

Yours very truly,
PETER GUILDAY.

THE OHIO ARCHEOLOGICAL AND HISTORICAL SOCIETY
Columbus, Ohio
November 9, 1920.

Mr. Joseph J. Thompson, Editor,
ILLINOIS CATHOLIC HISTORICAL REVIEW,
617 Ashland Block, Chicago, Ill.
My dear Mr. Thompson:

I have just received two copies of the October number of your REVIEW. I am very much pleased with your reproduction of that part of my contribution relating to the visit of Lafayette to Illinois. Your complimentary introductory notice is especially gratifying to me.

In the next issue of our Quarterly I am reproducing Father Lambing's "Journal of Celoron." He published this in Volume 2 of his Historical Researches. This is now so very rare that I have thought it worth while to reproduce it along with Father Bonnecamp's Journal and other matter relating to this expedition. As I contemplate publishing this in separate form I have been wondering whether you could furnish me a brief biographical sketch of Father Lambing, or refer me to someone who could do so.

In this connection permit me to congratulate you upon the attractive form in which the ILLINOIS CATHOLIC HISTORICAL REVIEW is published. It is very satisfactory in every way. We are thinking of changing the form of our Quarterly with the beginning of the new volume and are taking note of the appearance of other historical periodicals that come to us in exchange.

Sincerely yours,

C. B. GALBREATH,
Secretary.

UNITED STATES CATHOLIC HISTORICAL SOCIETY

346 Convent Avenue, New York City

November 24, 1920.

Mr. Joseph J. Thompson,
917 Ashland Block, Chicago, Ill.

My dear Mr. Thompson:

I have read with much pleasure and profit the successive numbers of the ILLINOIS CATHOLIC HISTORICAL REVIEW. Its contents certainly make up a very valuable addition to the material available for the student of our past records. The REVIEW has shown in the most practical manner that it merits the generous patronage of all who are interested in the preservation of the annals of the progress of the Church in the United States.

Yours very truly,

THOS. F. MEEHAN.

ST. LOUIS UNIVERSITY

Grand Avenue and West Pine Boulevard

St. Louis, Armistice Day, 1920.

Mr. Joseph J. Thompson,
The ILLINOIS CATHOLIC HISTORICAL REVIEW,
917 Ashland Block, Chicago, Ill.

My dear Mr. Thompson:

I believe we ought at times to tell our friends that they are doing well; we should at least be as willing to do this as to inform them of their failings. We, historians in particular, should not always wait till men are dead before we say a word of commendation. The word to the living may be as rain to the wilting plant; it may not only sustain but be itself transformed into sweet fruit.

After so abject an apology on my part, I believe your humility will permit me to say now what I have been thinking about your work and that of your associates on the ILLINOIS CATHOLIC HISTORICAL REVIEW. And that is that it is typical of the best things of Chicago, which have made the world wonder at that marvellous city. It is young; it is always fresh; it throbs with life; in a day it jumped into the size of its compeers of a hundred years; it has always something new and unexpected; it wears its Sunday clothes, but lets us know that it has other garments in which it can dig canals, in-takes, or aught good for

human existence; in a word, it is what it ought to be and always just a little more.

With blessings on you and all who are abiding in this good work,
I am your servant in Christ,

LAURENCE J. KENNY, S. J.

At 6:00 P. M. the meeting adjourned.

MARGARET MADDEN, Secretary.

LIFE MEMBERS

Most Rev. G. W. Mundelein, D. D.
Most Rev. S. F. Messmer, D. D.
Rt. Rev. Henry Althoff, D. D.
Rt. Rev. James Ryan, D. D.
Rt. Rev. P. J. Muldoon, D. D.
Rev. Frederic Siedenburg, S. J.
Very Rev. F. A. Purcell
Mr. William A. Amberg (Deceased)
Mr. Edward Osgood Brown
Mr. William J. Onahan (Deceased)
Loyola University
De Paul University
Sisters of Christian Charity
School Sisters of Notre Dame
Academy of Our Lady
Mr. Frank J. Seng
Mr. Simon J. Morand
Miss Harriet McDonnell
Rev. Edward J. Fox
Mrs. Leonora Z. Meder
Miss Kate Meade
Mr. Edward A. Cudahy
Miss Mary T. Cudahy
Msgr. M. J. Fitzsimmons
Rev. Wm. M. Foley
Mr. Charles J. Trainor
Mr. Patrick J. Lucey
Mr. J. P. Harding
Mr. L. J. Behan
Msgr. E. F. Hoban
Rev. D. J. Dunne, D. D.
Rev. John J. Dennison
Msgr. E. A. Kelly
Rev. T. F. O'Gara
Mr. William F. Ryan
Mrs. Catherine Murray Warnock
Rev. W. J. McNamee
Rev. Thos. V. Shannon

Mr. Joseph Joyce
DaPrato Statuary Co.
Rev. Joseph McNamee
Rev. J. J. Flaherty
Mr. D. F. Bremmer, Jr.
Rev. A. Croke
Rev. William M. Dettmer
Servite Fathers
Rev. D. D. Hishen
Mr. Joseph M. Cudahy
Mr. Edward A. Cudahy
Miss Mary A. McLaughlin
Mr. B. G. Brennan
Mr. Peter T. White
Mr. Edward Kirchberg
Rev. P. T. Gelinas
Msgr. D. J. Riordan
Mr. Napoleon Picard
Mr. Anthony Matre
Mr. M. J. Gallery
Mr. Thomas O'Connor
Mr. Thomas A. Smyth
Mr. George E. Brennan
Rev. John M. Lange
Rev. George Blatter
Msgr. P. J. McDonnell
Mr. John P. Daleiden
Mr. W. J. Cummings
Mr. John J. O'Brien
Rev. George Eisenbacker
Mr. O. M. Carry
Mr. Frank Baackes
Mr. Charles E. Schick
Mr. Robert M. Sweitzer
Mr. Dennis J. Egan
Rev. H. P. Smyth
Rev. Edmund Byrnes
Mr. John A. Schmidt

St. Procopius Abbey
R. Philip Gormally
Edward Hines
F. G. Nelson
Edgar H. Walker
Thomas M. McHale
Mrs. George H. Simpson
Sisters of St. Francis
Mrs. Bedelia Kehoe Garraghan
W. A. Magner, M. D.
Mr. James Quinn

Miss Rose Turk
Quincy College
F. J. Lewis
Rev. Anthony Kiefer
James M. Bray
M. W. Murphy
Rev. A. Zurbonsen
Miss Marie Thumser
Mr. Hugo J. Haub
Mr. John P. McGoorty

CONTRIBUTORS

Mr. Edward A. Cudahy..$100.00
Mr. Thomas M. McHale... 100.00
Mr. Edward Hines... 100.00
Miss Harriet McDonnell.. 50.00
Miss Mollie Scanlon... 5.00
Illinois State Court, Illinois Catholic Order of Foresters............... 100.00
State Council, Knights of Columbus (J. J. Thompson)............... 50.00
State Council, Knights of Columbus (J. J. Thompson)............... 50.00
Englewood Council, Knights of Columbus......................... 24.35
Alleman Council, Knights of Columbus, Nauvoo.................... 7.50
Dwight Council, Knights of Columbus............................. 6.00
St. Cyr Day Council, Knights of Columbus........................ 10.00
St. Rita Council, Knights of Columbus............................ 15.00
McHenry Council, Knights of Columbus, McHenry, Illinois.......... 12.50
Commercial Council, Knights of Columbus........................ 15.00
Leo Council, Knights of Columbus................................ 11.50
Lemont Council, Knights of Columbus............................ 16.00
Ft. Dearborn Council, Knights of Columbus....................... 25.00
La Fayette Council, Knights of Columbus......................... 109.35
Spalding Council, Knights of Columbus, Peoria, Illinois............ 50.00
Catholic Order of Foresters...................................... 100.00
Galena Council, Knights of Columbus, Galena, Illinois............. 24.00
Ravenswood Council, Knights of Columbus....................... 21.50

MARIE SHEAHAN, Financial Secretary.

THE PAST, PRESENT AND FUTURE OF THE ILLINOIS CATHOLIC HISTORICAL REVIEW

A paper read at the Annual Meeting of the ILLINOIS CATHOLIC HISTORICAL SOCIETY, December 3, 1920.

The legislature of Illinois, upon being urged by several historical organizations, including the Illinois State Historical Society, the State Historical Library, and many individuals, passed resolutions and laws providing for the observance of the Hundredth Anniversary of the admission of the State of Illinois into the Union, and providing for the appointment of a commission, known as the Illinois Centennial Commission, to have general charge of the observance.

As the commission was finally constituted it contained amongst its membership Rev. Frederic Siedenburg, S. J.

Taking up the work of the commission it was determined amongst other activities to have prepared a complete history of the State, and an arrangement was entered into with certain historians, chiefly of the State University of Illinois, for the preparation of the materials and manuscripts.

As time passed and the history was taking shape, the attention of some of the commissioners, and of Father Siedenburg especially, was drawn to the scant mention in the manuscripts of the part played by Catholics in the State's history, and as the work proceeded some very objectionable references were found in the manuscripts. Needless to say that these objections were vigorously drawn to the notice of the commission in session, and it may also be said that the gravest of them were corrected.

It transpired, however, that despite objections and appeals for fuller treatment, the Catholic aspect of the State's history was not being, and would not be, fully, and, to the minds of conservative Catholics, justly developed.

There were of course some reasons for this state of circumstances. To begin with, there was the age-long prejudice against Catholics and things Catholic that has existed since the so-called reformation got under way. There was too a seeming dearth of reliable Catholic data or source material, and, finally, the writers of the manuscripts were non-Catholic, and with one or two possible exceptions wholly unacquainted with anything concerning the Catholic Church or Catholics.

LAUNCHING THE ENTERPRISE

During the years in which the preliminary steps for the observance of the Illinois Centennial were being taken, the editor of the ILLINOIS CATHOLIC HISTORICAL REVIEW was engaged in legislative work in Springfield, and kept in close touch with all that was being done in relation to the Centennial observance, and the preparation of a state history. He had endeavored to secure connection with the preparation of the manuscripts, but did not succeed. As the work proceeded he became convinced that very little of what Catholics might hope for would be recorded in the history which was being prepared.

In this state of circumstances the actual occurrences which were the determining factors in the movement which resulted in the forming of the ILLINOIS

329

CATHOLIC HISTORICAL SOCIETY were most likely the following: One day in June, 1917, the writer met Father Siedenburg, S. J., in the rotunda of the capitol at Springfield. Father Siedenburg was attending a meeting of the Illinois Centennial Commission and the writer inquired about the progress of the Centennial State History. He was told that it was useless to hope for an adequate representation of Catholic history in the volumes until Catholics themselves made their history as available as an open book. The writer then told of a History of the Church in Illinois which he had almost finished and which he hoped to publish for the centenary. Father Siedenburg was much interested and later in Chicago talked the matter over with the writer. When shown the contents and scope of the volume, Father Siedenburg offered to dispose of one hundred copies of the work, but suggested that the history would do more good if published serially in a review, where it could invite criticism, correction and especially imitation. Thus the matter rested for several weeks. The next occurrence of consequence was a pictorial lecture on Father Marquette, given by Mr. James Fitzgerald from data prepared by Rev. F. G. Dinneen, S. J., of St. Ignatius College. Being present at the lecture and pleased with the presentation of the subject, the writer communicated with Father Dinneen, suggesting that some means should be provided for publishing such matter as had been presented in the lecture.

In due course of mail a reply was received from Father Dinneen, in which he stated that he had talked with Rev. Frederic Siedenburg, S. J., who, he said, had expressed the opinion, gathered from his experience with the State Centennial Commission that an Illinois Catholic Historical Society should be organized to publish a periodical containing articles relating to Catholic history, and suggesting a conference with Father Siedenburg.

Such conference was quickly arranged, and after an exchange of ideas Father Siedenburg conferred with his Grace the Most Reverend Archbishop and secured his hearty approval. Within a few weeks thereafter preliminary details were settled at several conferences between Father Siedenburg and the present Editor of the ILLINOIS CATHOLIC HISTORICAL REVIEW.

The records as printed in the first number of the REVIEW disclose the call for the meeting to organize, the holding of the meeting, the name of the society, the appointment of a committee on constitution and by-laws, and the provision for the publication of a quarterly magazine to be known as the ILLINOIS CATHOLIC HISTORICAL REVIEW; also the selection of an Editor-in-Chief.

This memorable meeting occurred on the 25th of February, 1918. At the moment our country was plunged into war, the minds of all patriotic men and women were filled with the considerations of the world's present predicament. It seemed a most inauspicious moment for a new and largely cultural enterprise. It was kept in mind, however, that anniversaries and centenaries do not wait upon convenience. As the centenary of the state was upon us—the actual hundredth anniversary only a few months ahead—and as the state was obliged to go on with the observance of the Centennial in spite of the war, so it was incumbent upon us to proceed with the organization..

BEGINNING AT THE BOTTOM

Nearly two hundred and fifty years have passed since Father Marquette, on April 11, 1675, established the Catholic Church in the heart of what is now Illinois, and although this particular part has been almost the most active Catholic center during the entire period of all America, yet there has never been

an attempt to set down the Catholic history of the region. Books have been written, and periodicals published by tons, detailing more or less of the record of Illinois, but not one of them, even in a summary fashion, ever pretended to tell the Catholic story of Illinois.

Prior to July 1, 1918, should one wish information with respect to the work, or even the names, of the Jesuit Missionaries who were in Illinois prior to 1800, it would be necessary to search through not less than fifty different works, in which mention of one or more of the missionaries was more or less incidental.

Prior to that time if it were desired to know anything of any event or incident of our early history that concerned Catholics, one must go to the most out of the way and unexpected publications, and then find only stray and disconnected items here and there.

And for even a later period there were in existence at that time just two published works that would assist the diligent student in his research. These were the Souvenir Publication issued as a memorial of the Silver Jubilee of the Most Reverend Archbishop Patrick A. Feehan, D. D., and a large edition of the *New World*, dated April 14, 1900. Both of these publications were prepared by the same author, Rev. James J. McGovern, D. D.; and though they reflect undying credit upon the erudite and scholarly priest, they were but meagre outlines of the great Catholic story.

We have waited long, it is seen, before giving the subject of history the attention it deserves; and on occasion we were grieved and betimes offended that some of the subdivisions of history in which we were particularly interested were either overlooked or inadequately or falsely treated.

At last fully realizing that if we desire adequate historical recognition, we must ourselves move to secure it, and understanding the difficulty of rousing attention, in the face of the multiplicity of interests and occupations that enchain the human mind in the present state of society, we realized that our action must be, to an extent, striking. No mere everyday pamphlet or unadorned brochure made up in solid columns of dry narrative or close reasoning would arrest the headlong rush of human thought sufficiently to impress itself.

Accordingly, the ILLINOIS CATHOLIC HISTORICAL REVIEW from its initial number was made in appearance and content comparable with the best specimens of the publisher's art, combined with the best compositions of scholars and writers.

PLANNING THE WORK

One requisite of success in any measure is an objective. In undertaking a journey one of the first essentials is more or less definiteness of destination. It would be a poor house indeed that were built without a plan. The plan is of great value in any venture, whether it be strictly adhered to or not. Naturally, therefore, we have planned for the ILLINOIS CATHOLIC HISTORICAL REVIEW, and our plans contemplated first of all something of an outline of the relation of the Catholic Church and its votaries to the discovery, development and progress of the state.

Following that idea, we briefly and almost in bare outline sketched the history of the Church in the state in the first four numbers of the ILLINOIS CATHOLIC HISTORICAL REVIEW.

Succeeding this and of course secondary to it, we entered upon a study of the racial elements in the state which were in general more or less Catholic.

These have been supplemented by intensive studies of particular events or distinguished personages that cast special light upon the general theme.

EXCELLENT STAFF OF CONTRIBUTORS

It seems entirely safe to assert that no new publication has ever been more fortunate in attracting to itself the aid of a better corps of contributors than has the ILLINOIS CATHOLIC HISTORICAL REVIEW. If this publication should by any misfortune suspend, it will have attained a notable achievement in inspiring and putting in a state to be preserved the studies of the scholars that have contributed to the volumes already published. The work of Fathers Garraghan, Rothensteiner, Holweck, Souvay, Barth and Kenny, and, indeed of all of our contributors, has been marked by scholarly excellence and historical discernment.

IDEAL PUBLISHER

We have been peculiarly fortunate too in our publisher. It is just possible that had Father William Lyons, in charge of the Loyola University Press, fully realized the magnitude of his task, he might not have consented to undertake the publication of the ILLINOIS CATHOLIC HISTORICAL REVIEW. Having attempted it, however, he has made it a prime consideration. It has been the subject of remark wherever the REVIEW has been introduced that the makeup and execution is of the highest character. For these excellences we are largely indebted to Father Lyons.' Himself a classical scholar, and a man of the broadest information, he possesses the qualifications so essential in the superintendence of a high-class publication. Add to this his personal interest which, by his voluntary corrections and proofreading, we have learned is not second to that of any other individual interested in the REVIEW, and you have an ideal publisher.

It is worth while, too, to note that Father Lyons' interest has been of great advantage to us from a financial standpoint. The Loyola University Press has no dividends to pay, and in order to help the cause, the ILLINOIS CATHOLIC HISTORICAL REVIEW has been published at cost.

GENEROUS PATRONS

The Most Reverend Archbishop and the several Bishops of the Province have given a continuous approval and support that has been of the highest value.

It is due the reverend clergy and the religious to state that they have rallied to the support of this movement in large numbers throughout the state. Their assistance is doubly appreciated, since it not only materially aids in making the work possible, but is a much prized expression of confidence.

The generosity of a number of Catholic laymen and women who have made liberal contributions is also deserving of our recognition and appreciation.

AN INVENTORY

At the end of three years from the organization of the ILLINOIS CATHOLIC HISTORICAL SOCIETY, and more than two and one-half years from the issuance of the first number of its REVIEW we can take stock of our accomplishments. In a wholly unoccupied and uncultivated field, we have planted a sturdy enterprise,

and, relying upon the word of competent critics, as well as the evidences of our own senses, have brought it to a gratifying state of fruition.

No longer need the seeker after information concerning the relation of the Catholic Church and of Catholics to the progress and development of the Illinois country waste time and effort in a vain search for reliable information. In the principal libraries throughout the country, and in the homes of some thousands of our people, may be found today the volumes of the ILLINOIS CATHOLIC HIS-TORICAL REVIEW, containing more of the record of the Catholic Church and its association with the facts of history, especially in the Mississippi Valley, than has ever been collected and put in a state for preservation.

In the work in which we have been engaged we have never for a moment lost sight of the exalted character of our undertaking. Controversy is never courted, but we have effectively served notice upon all concerned that records in which the Church is concerned cannot be falsified, nor can Catholics be outraged with impunity. Whenever writers or speakers within our sphere have essayed to mis-state history, or misrepresent the part the Church has played in history, we have promptly and without apology called them to account.

So much for the past and present of the ILLINOIS CATHOLIC HISTORICAL REVIEW. What of the future?

THE FUTURE OF THE WORK

There have been some valuable by-products, so to speak, of the ILLINOIS CATHOLIC HISTORICAL SOCIETY; for instance, the aims of the Society are laid before some organizations of Catholic men and women, and these fortified by the work already accomplished have made such an appeal, that several such organizations, including the State Council of the Knights of Columbus, and several subordinate councils, and the State Court of the Catholic Order of Foresters, as well as other Catholic societies, have pledged co-operation and made substantial contributions of funds.

Observing the success attained thrugh the ILLINOIS CATHOLIC HISTORICAL REVIEW, the editor has been entrusted with the preparation of the general history, contained in the massive volume ''Archdiocese of Chicago,'' published in June, 1920, at the conclusion of the notable Diamond Jubilee observances. He has also been entrusted with the preparation of the manuscript of a history suitable for use in the schools, and with the preparation, in conjunction with a commission representing each diocese in the state, of a comprehensive history of the Church in Mid-America, to be completed by 1925, as a memorial of the 250th anniversary of the Church in the Illinois country. In somewhat the same connection a record is to be made of the activities of the Knights of Columbus in the State of Illinois, covering the quarter of a century since its introduction.

These activities are to proceed side by side with the work of the ILLINOIS CATHOLIC HISTORICAL SOCIETY, and it should be sufficient for our purpose if we project the future of the ILLINOIS CATHOLIC HISTORICAL REVIEW for at least five years, or until this notable 250th anniversary.

The writer hereof has set himself the task of knowing intimately all that there is to be known that is of interest in connection with the history of this part of the world, and especially wherein it relates to the Catholic Church or things Catholic, and to put such knowledge in a condition to be preserved and made available to all who will read it. To that end, not only is it proposed

to study with care everything that any one else has written, but as far as possible to examine every document, every historic object and place within the scope of our projected work.

SACRED PLACES AND RELICS

Already I have afforded myself the pleasure of a visit to a few of the historic spots in the state, and an examination of a few of the notable relics of the earliest days of the Church still in existence. I have stood upon the summit of Starved Rock, and pictured to myself the passage of Father Marquette's lonely canoe, when he, on the 8th of April, 1675, with his two lay companions, landed almost in the shadow of that natural monument, and after three days' preparation planted the Catholic Church. In imagination I saw his successor Father Claude Jean Alloucz, S. J., superintend the erection of a chapel on the rock, and in succession saw Father Rale, Father Gravier, Father Pinet, Father Bineteau and Father Marest celebrate the august Sacrifice, and minister to the spiritual needs of native Indians and pioneer Frenchmen.

In St. Louis, through the fine courtesies of Father Kenny and Father Garraghan, I held in my own hands and examined with my own eyes, the records, nearly two and one-half centuries old, of the baptisms, marriages and deaths, and other important events, as they occurred among the earliest white people to come to Illinois and their Indian neighbors.

A few miles out from St. Louis, on the Illinois side of the river, I visited the church established at Cahokia in 1699 by Father Pinet, and held in my hands the beautiful missal used there for many years in the celebration of the Holy Sacrifice, published in the year, 1667. At the same point I beheld a monstrance used in the earliest days of the mission, with the date of its manufacture, 1717, stamped upon it. I visited the little church, erected near the site of the first church, built there in the year, 1797, still standing, as trim and trig and strong as though it were but recently built, and still in use by the congregation as a parish hall and meeting place,—undoubtedly the oldest building now standing in the Mississippi Valley. Just outside its walls I knelt silently for a moment at the grave of two of the 18th century missionaries whose work ended there and who there found repose from the hardships of missionary lives.

These are but a few of the historic spots and relics of which the Catholics, and, indeed the whole public, know too little.

THE VIA CRUCIS OF THE NEW WORLD

It was the invariable custom of the missionaries upon the establishment of a mission to set up a cross, rudely made, generally from a felled tree of the native forest. Beginning with the first landing of French pilgrims, the latter part of the 16th Century, at the mouth of the St. Lawrence, mission crosses were raised as exploration and settlement progressed, until at a date prior to the middle of the 18th century, there stood a row of crosses dotted all the way along the St. Lawrence, winding about the Great Lakes, and extending from Chicago up the Chicago River, down the Calumet to the Mississippi, and thence to the Gulf of Mexico. This *via crucis*, traversed by the martyr missionary, would be, if it were known, one of the marvels of American history.

We shall be able to find interesting employment in tracing out the spots where these crosses were raised, and reclaiming the record of their planting.

While doing so we shall all the time be drawing upon the hitherto hermetically sealed archives of Church, state, city and county, hidden at least, if not sealed, and coming to light now under the inspiration of a renewed interest in Catholic history, for which the ILLINOIS CATHOLIC HISTORICAL SOCIETY and its mouthpiece, the REVIEW, can modestly claim some credit.

GRATIFYING SUCCESS

Without boasting, it may truthfully be said that our movement has succeeded. In the face of adverse conditions we have so far accomplished what we set out to do. If there was an obligation upon us to succeed in the past, that obligation has been multiplied by our success. Had we made a brave attempt and, under the difficult circumstances surrounding our beginning, failed, we could easily have been forgiven. The case is now different. We have passed the experimental stage,—the ILLINOIS CATHOLIC HISTORICAL SOCIETY and its REVIEW are institutions,—institutions of the archdiocese of Chicago, and of the State of Illinois. We are not only interested in maintaining these institutions for our own sakes, but as well for the good name of the archdiocese and the ecclesiastical province that have approved them. We must succeed. To fail would now be a calamity; and to succeed we must at least maintain the standards we have set up.

It is gratifying to be able to give the assurance that there is only one thing that could stand in the way of success, and that is, means. Understand, we have had the means to carry on the work so far and are in a solvent financial condition. Financial difficulties are not apprehended, but we do stand in need of a financial guarantee that we have not yet attained. It is essential to the continued success of this enterprise that we shall be able, not only to discharge our financial obligations, but to count reliably upon being able to do so. If the time should come, and I do not apprehend such a time, when it is no longer practical to continue our work in at least as creditable a manner as it has been done in the past, it is my hope that the members will snuff out the enterprise at one thrust, and never, as has sometimes been the experience, permit our publication to dwindle away piece by piece, or depreciate in appearance or quality.

Let it be understood by all who shall take even a remote interest in this work, that those in active charge of the work propose to match their energies and their ability against the means of all those who believe in the project; and while the workers will be called upon for the heavier individual contributions, yet the effort of the others is in a sense more essential, for without it the work cannot continue.

PLANS OF FINANCE

It is the sincere hope that this meeting will devise ways and means by which the work of the Society can be made secure and permanent.

From the financial reports it is seen that we have had an average of less than $3,500.00 a year. With this sum, due to the financial management of our Rev. President, Father Siedenburg, we have made a creditable beginning. We have paid all bills and have a small balance, but we have largely begged our way; have been continually receiving favors, and always unable to give. Aside from a nominal salary of the Editor-in-Chief and of the Secretary, our officers

receive no compensation. We pay no office rents or expenses. Contributors are paid nothing and, in general, everything done for us, except that to which there is attached a fixed charge, is on the thank-you basis. Had we a certain income of $5,000 a year, it would give us some leeway, and enable us to put something into promotion expenses. Had we a fixed income of $10,000 a year, we could undertake anything appropriate to our work. That would enable us to compensate reasonably and decently those who work for us; to employ one or more field secretaries, a crying necessity, and to take steps for the extension of our circulation.

To secure a substantial income of this sort looks easy. If out of the two million people in the Mississippi Valley who must be interested in our work, and who are abundantly able to do so, only five hundred could be induced to contribute $10.00 a year, for a limited period, that would assure us an income of $5,000 a year, and if we could find one thousand such contributors, that would give us an income of $10,000 a year.

On this Third Annual Conclave of the ILLINOIS CATHOLIC HISTORICAL SOCIETY, and the 102nd Anniversary of the admission of our great State into the Union of States, let us reconsecrate ourselves to the task of putting in its true light the beneficent relationship between the great work of the Church and the discovery, development and progress of our beloved state.

JOSEPH J. THOMPSON.

ILLINOIS
CATHOLIC HISTORICA
REVIEW

Volume III   APRIL, 1921   Numb

PUBLISHED BY

THE ILLINOIS CATHOLIC HISTORICAL SOCIETY

CHICAGO, ILL.

337

CONTENTS

LOYOLA UNIVERSITY PRESS
CHICAGO, ILLINOIS

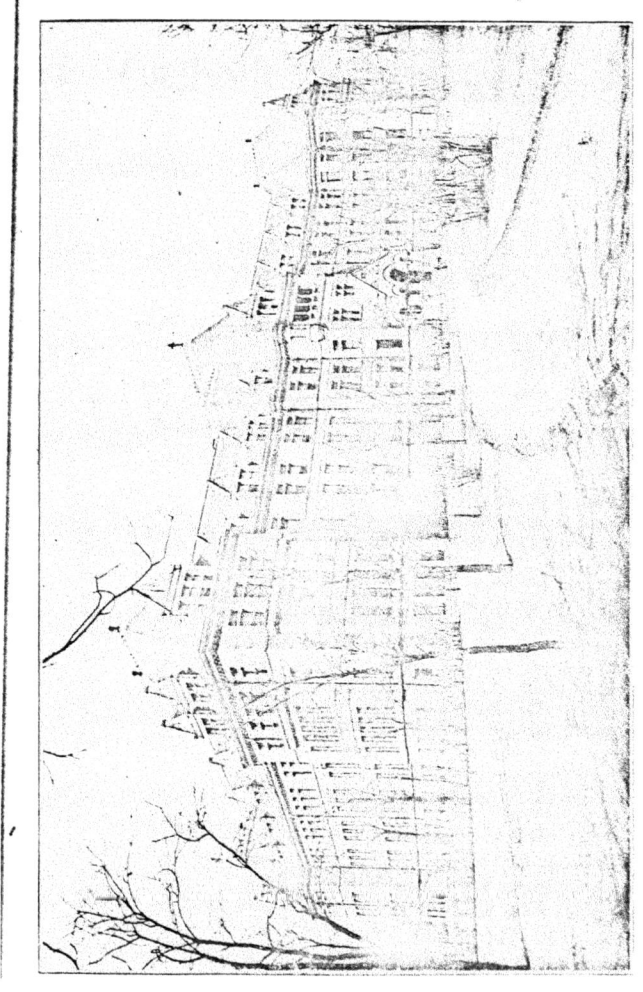

St. Xavier's Mother House of the Sisters of Mercy, 49th Street and Cottage Grove Avenue, Chicago.

Illinois

Catholic Historical Review

VOLUME III APRIL, 1921 NUMBER 4

THE SISTERS OF MERCY

CHICAGO'S PIONEER NURSES AND TEACHERS — 1846 - 1921

SOURCES

Records of the Sisters of Mercy, St. Xavier's Convent of Mercy, and of Mercy Hospital, Chicago, Illinois: Personal memoranda of historical reminiscences; Diocesan and parish records; ILLINOIS CATHOLIC HISTORICAL REVIEW, Chicago.

WORKS

The Catholic Encyclopedia, N. Y.; Richard H. Clarke, The Deceased Bishops of the Church in the U. S., N. Y., 1872; John E. McGirr, Life of Bishop Quarter, N. Y., 1850; Rev. J. J. McGovern, Life of Bishop McMullen, Chicago, 1888; McGovern, The Catholic Church in Chicago, Chicago, 1891; H. de Courcy, The Catholic Church in the United States, New York, 1857; The Life of Catherine McAuley, Foundress and First Superior of the Religious Sisters of Mercy, by a Sister of Mercy, N. Y., 1874; Leaves from the Annals of the Sisters of Mercy in Four Volumes, by a member of the Order of Mercy, 1888-1895; Reverend Mother M. Xavier Warde, Foundress of the Order of Mercy in the United States, by the Sisters of Mercy of Manchester, N. H., Boston, 1902; Life of Mary Monholland by a member of the Order, Chicago, 1894; Reminiscences of Seventy Years, Sisters of Mercy, Chicago, 1916; Historic Nuns, Bessie R. Belloc, London, 1911.

FOUNDING OF THE ORDER

In her introduction to *Historic Nuns*, Bessie Belloc says that "it would be all too easy to wrap a veil of poetic mist round any story which begins in Ireland;"[1] but in tracing the spiritual ancestry of Chicago's pioneer Sisters back to the "land of faith and romance" one finds at every turn only stern realities. The faith is there—steadfast and penetrating—of the sort that moves mountains, but the

---

[1] In treating of the origin of the Congregation of the Sisters of Mercy and of the foundress the facts have been freely taken from Mother Austin Carroll's *Annals of the Sisters of Mercy* and from the biography mentioned in the *Works*.

romance exists only in the great vision of those who were destined to come together in Chicago as fellow workers in Christ's service. When in 1822 Catherine McAuley, who had always loved the poor, found herself at the age of thirty-five with "thirty thousand pounds in the Bank of Ireland, six hundred a year in perpetuity, Coolock House, with its appendages, jewels, plate,"[2] and several life insurance policies she had no notion of founding a religious Community; God made use of her and gave to the world the Sisters of Mercy. The same year marked a visit to Ireland by a Reverend Mr. McAuley from the American Missions in the United States. This missioner, by his stories of missionary work in America, so fired the zeal of a young candidate for Maynooth, William Quarter, that the boy sought and obtained his exodus to labor in a far-away land.[3] It was also in 1822 that Margaret O'Brien, the most important character for this record was born in Queen's County, Ireland.[4] It was the actual poverty of Dublin's poor that brought out the heroism of Mother McAuley and prompted her to separate herself from the world, and it was the spiritual needs of his fellow countrymen in a strange land that touched the heroic in the boy destined to be the first bishop of Chicago. But it was a call clear and distinct to minister to the soul and body of the Catholic immigrant in the United States which prompted the future Mother Agatha O'Brien to leave home and country when the first band of Sisters of Mercy set out from Carlow with Pittsburgh as an objective.

In order to dispense aid to Dublin's poor, Catherine McAuley decided to build a sort of settlement house in what was then a fashionable part of Ireland's Capitol. Her architect was directed to plan three or four large rooms for school purposes; four large dormitories for young women; one room loftier than the others, which might serve for an Oratory and a few small rooms for ladies who might wish to help her. On inspecting the premises Miss McAuley was surprised to find that the architect had built a convent.[5] Like so many founders of religious orders, she was a "passive instrument of God's love for man. . . . . She engaged a few ladies to help her and for convenience' sake they began to take a spare meal on the premises. Religion suggested a garb as grave as their occupation, and a dark costume was assumed. At first the name 'Sister' was playfully applied and spiritual authority was offended at the usurpa-

² Belloc, op. cit., p. 4, Life of Catherine McAuley, p. 111.
³ McGirr, op. cit., p. 21.
⁴ Convent Records.
⁵ Life of Catherine McAuley, op. cit., p. 128.

tion. Soon the casually associated band had insensibly come within the circle of monastic feelings and habits; its spirit had insensibly stolen in among them, and shaped their lives and ordinary practices, until at length they stood on the threshold of the sanctuary."

In 1829 the position of the institute was somewhat anomalous. It was not a convent, its members were bound by neither rule nor vow. It could not with propriety, be styled a secular house, for already it had appointed hours of silence and recreation, of labor and rest, of prayer and study. Yet not one of those concerned ever thought of the Baggot Street house becoming the cradle of a new religious congregation. Miss McAuley in modern parlance was simply acting in "response to the social claim"; she was mistress of her own possessions, and retained her place in society. In the summer of 1830, however, ecclesiastical authority took a definite step and decided that the band of twelve young women associated in Miss McAuley's settlement should either appear as religious or as seculars. The ladies in question unanimously chose the former, and arrangements were made for the foundress and two of her companions to make their novitiate with the Presentation Sisters. One year later, the three novices made their vows according to the Presentation form, with the proviso that the Vow of Obedience might include whatever the Church should subsequently approve for the new congregation. Though the Institute had been in constant operation from the feast of Our Lady of Mercy 1827, the day on which the foundress became a religious, December 12, 1831, is considered the foundation date of the Congregation. On January 23, 1832, six of the ladies who had conducted the settlement during Mother McAuley's absence were clothed in the religious habit, and a year later among those who vowed themselves to God by the rules of the new congregation was Frances Warde,[6] who was to lead the first Sisters of Mercy to the United States. Only five years of Mother Warde's life as a professed religious were spent at the Baggot Street house. In 1837 the foundress took her with four younger Sisters to Carlow where a successful foundation was made. After the confirmation of the rules of the new congregation by Gregory XVI in 1840, requests for foundations came from all quarters, and it was in Carlow that "the foundress of the Sisters of Mercy in the United States" was to answer the "call of the West."

CALLED TO AMERICA

The invitation to "the Iron City" came through the Rt. Rev. Michael O'Connor, its first bishop. As a student in the Propaganda

---

[6] *Life of Mother Warde, op. cit.,* p. 47.

at Rome he had been given the task of translating the Rules of the Order into Italian. The task deeply interested the young Irish student, who seems to have realized how ably women living under the Rule of Catherine McAuley could meet the growing needs of the Church in the country of his adoption. Later as pastor of St. Paul's Church, Pittsburgh, he reverted to this in letters to his friend Dr. Cullen, head of the Irish College in Rome, and Dr. Cullen was in close communication with his nephew, Father Maher of Carlow. Father Maher read his uncle's letter to the Sisters in June of 1843 but they did not pay much attention to it. "Bishop England, Bishop Clancy of Demerara, and other prelates, had visited Carlow for Sisters and nothing had come of it."[7] But late in September, 1843, the appearance of a clerical stranger of magnificent physique in the streets of Carlow created unusual comment. It was Right Reverend Michael O'Connor who had been consecrated in Rome on August 15. In the evening of October 4, the bishop accompanied by Father Maher called at the Convent. It was only when he begged a few nuns for his mission that his visit assumed a serious aspect. . . . . In clear eloquent language he set forth the advantages he hoped would accrue from the labors of the Sisters in his diocese where the need of them was so great. He dwelt particularly on the immense good to be done by teaching the young in a rapidly growing country, where it was all-important to establish Catholic Schools.[8] Every one of the twenty-three Sisters who formed the Community "was willing to sacrifice to God her love of country and community and embark for the distant West." Six Sisters and one postulant were selected from the volunteers. Mother Francis Warde was appointed Superior, the dowries of the Sisters were transferred to the Pittsburgh house, and in less than one month after the Bishop's application, the band of seven began the long journey to the United States aboard the "Queen of the West." This vessel, one of the largest three-masters then crossing the Atlantic, set sail November 10, 1843 and hove in sight of New York the tenth of the following month. Bishop O'Connor and several other gentlemen went ashore the same evening, but the Sisters remained on board until the following day when the Bishop and Father Quarter, Bishop-elect of Chicago, came for them.[9]

As Assistant Pastor of St. Peter's, Father William Quarter had been instrumental in establishing the first colony of the Emmitsburg Sisters of Charity in New York, and later as Pastor of St. Mary's

[7] Cf. *Annals of Sisters of Mercy*, Vol. III, pp. 43-44.
[8] *Op. cit.*, p. 45.
[9] *Life of Mother Warde*, p. 96.

Establishments for Sisters...............20,000f.
Establishments for Schools..............10,000f.

The Community in Pittsburgh had grown in the meantime. Bishop O'Connor had officiated at the first ceremony which took place February 22, 1844[13] To Miss Margaret O'Brien, the postulant who had come from Carlow, he had given the white veil and the name, Sister Mary Agatha. Of importance for the completeness of this record was another reception in St. Vincent's Church, Youngstown, Pennsylvania on July 26, 1845. On this occasion Miss Mary Anne McGirr of Youngstown received the name of Sister Mary Vincent, and Catherine McGuire, a native of Philadelphia, was known afterward as Sister Mary Gertrude. These two novices together with two postulants, Eliza Corbett, and Eva Schmidt, were destined for Chicago

---

[10] McGirr, *op. cit.*, p. 33.
[11] Cf. *Annals*, Vol. III, p. 227.
[12] *Diocesan Journal* kept by first two Bishops of Chicago. Usually referred to as "Bishop Quarter's Diary."
[13] Sisters of Mercy, Pittsburgh, Pa., (1843-1918), N. Y., 1918, p. 22.

under the superiorship of Sister Agatha O'Brien, who pronounced her vows on the fifth of May, 1846.[14]

SISTERS COME TO CHICAGO

Friday, September 18, 1846, these religious set out for "the City of the Plains" accompanied by Mother Frances Warde and very Reverend Walter J. Quarter, who had been commissioned to conduct the Sisters to their future home. For the traveler of those days there were about four regularly established routes to Chicago.[15] The longest, but by far the most comfortable, was by way of the Great Lakes. Bishop Quarter planned the lake trip from Cleveland to Chicago by one of the well-appointed steamers about which travelers of those days have given interesting accounts. The journey of about thirty miles from Pittsburgh to Beaver, Pennsylvania was made by boat. For the stretch of some fifty miles, between Beaver and Poland, Ohio, it was necessary to charter a stage. After putting up in Poland for the night, the journey to Cleveland was continued by stage. The latter was reached Saturday evening, and on the evening of the following day, the party boarded the "S. S. Oregon" which they hoped would bring them to Chicago; but disappointment awaited them in Detroit. Their reservations were disputed and they were obliged to disembark to make way for the other passengers. Their forced stay in Detroit was made pleasant by the Bishop, Right Rev. Peter Paul Lefevere, and on Tuesday, they set out for Kalamazoo by stage which they reached Wednesday morning. From Kalamazoo they journeyed to St. Joseph, Michigan where they boarded the little steamer "Sam Ward." After a stormy night and a bright cool day on Lake Michigan, Chicago was sighted on the eve of the Feast of Our Lady of Mercy, September 23, 1846.

Crossing Michigan had shortened the trip so that the early arrival of the Sisters in Chicago was unexpected. No one awaited them at the landing place, but Father Quarter led them to the Episcopal cottage which was at the northwest corner of Michigan Avenue and Madison Street, just opposite the wharf. The tender heart of the Bishop was touched when he saw the five young Sisters who had come from a big prosperous city to a place that had scarcely the necessaries of life to offer them. Mother Agatha, the only professed Sister and the eldest of the band, counted but twenty-four

---

[14] There was a third Sister in this reception band. Cf. *U. S. Catholic Magazine*, Vol. IV, p. 610.

[15] Cf. *The Story of the Great Lakes*, Channing & Lavisna, N. Y., 1909.

years. Bishop Quarter immediately vacated his poor one-story house to provide a temporary· convent for the Sisters. Poor as it was, it was a palace compared to the shack to which he and Father Patrick J. McElhearne, the rector, removed. His biographer says: "Could you have seen him as he passed that round, ·watching to catch but one expression of satisfaction upon the countenances of the Sisters. you would have pitied him had it not been given. That night he did not retire at all; his anxiety banished sleep from his· eyelids; for he feared that they might be disappointed at not finding things in better order for their coming. Next· morning, however, while seated conversing with their Superioress, he heard in their· Community room the joyous laugh which could only come from the contented heart; clasping his hands as he rose· from his seat. he exclaimed, 'Now indeed I am satisfied; that laugh could not have come from the dissatisfied.' ''[16]

THE CHICAGO FOUNDATION

The Sisters immediately set to work to prepare the old church which was back of their temporary convent for school purposes.[17] Reverend Ŋother Francis Warde and the Sisters arranged and beautified this inside, "with the help of the Bishop's private purse, until it was, perhaps, the prettiest and best equipped school building on the shores of Lake Ŋichigan. . . . .

"As Divine Providence would have it, nearly all the Chicago foundresses were possessed of much ingenuity and energy, with artistic taste and abilities. . . . .

·'On parchment, which was sent to Reverend Ŋother in large supplies by her friends·in Ireland, the Sisters sketched maps of the different countries, with geographical plans of study and illustrations annexed, in a series adapted to the different grades of classes. These, when finished in water-colors, were not only artistic, but clear, instructive, and interesting. . . . .

"For globes they made sphere-frames of willow branches, over which they neatly fastened parchment, sketching ·distinctly the map-work of the hemispheres, and arranging thereon the mechanism of the ordinary school globe. The blackboards were made of plain timber formed in squares, fastened to the wall and then painted in the old-fashioned way of producing a blackboard surface.

---

[16] McGirr, *op. cit.*, p. 95.
[17] The old church erected at Lake and State had been moved to Madison Street near Michigan. Father O'Meara had extended it. It was St. Mary's Parish Church until the brick edifice at Wabash and Madison was ready for occupancy.

"The Sisters made their own numeral frames on squares of delicate elm framework, with strings of wire stretched horizontally, on which were strung small spools painted in the primary colors. "The community-room, with its rough board walls, was, during these days, a veritable warehouse of school supplies. In variety and design, to suit all wants, might be seen hand-made maps and charts, solar systems and globes, ball-frames and color plans; . . . , and all necessaries for teaching form; collection of minerals, sponges, coral, etc., and specimens of the vegetable kingdom for object lessons."[18]

The November number of the United States Catholic Magazine quotes the following concerning the Diocese of Chicago from the *Pittsburg Catholic:* "The interesting ceremony of taking the veil, by two nuns of the order of the 'Sisters of Mercy,' took place in this city (Chicago) on Friday, the 9th of October. A pontifical high mass was celebrated on the occasion, and a beautiful and appropriate discourse delivered by the Rev. Mr. Kinsella. The cathedral was crowded, aisles and all, and all present seemed devoutly impressed with the exercises. Numerous Protestants were there.

"A school for young ladies is this day opened by these Sisters of Mercy (than whom none are more competent to teach) in the old chapel, in the rear of their residence on the lake shore.

"They also visit the sick and distressed, and dispense mercies to the wretched, and those whom poverty has chained to her car.

"They will also soon establish a hospital in the city, and take the entire burden of nursing the sick, and management of such charity upon themselves.

"Ere long, too, they contemplate forming an orphan asylum.

"What citizen is there who will not hail the coming of these Sisters of Mercy as among the choicest of blessings for our city?"[19]

PROBLEMS TO BE SOLVED

Since the Sisters had no dowries other than their spiritual and intellectual qualifications the question of their support had to be settled. In a frontier state they could not hope to fill the ranks of the community with dowered subjects and they could look to no mother house for support. This was indeed a problem for the daughters of Mother McAuley, who had come to Chicago. The Sisters of Mercy were supposed to support themselves from the funds brought to the community by subjects at their entrance. Had the foundress

---

[18] *Life of Mother Warde, op. cit.,* p. 140 ff.
[19] *United States Catholic Magazine,* Vol. V, p. 620.

lived longer she doubtless would have modified this plan. Shortly before her death she opened private day-schools in addition to the poor schools so that the income from the former might support the latter. A select school which was later chartered on February 27, 1847, as the Saint Francis Xavier Female Academy of Chicago, Illinois, was, therefore, organized.[20] Announcements of this select school were circulated and on October 12, 1846, it opened its doors to ten boarders and forty day pupils. St. Mary's Parochial School for Girls, which began its career the same day, had an attendance of fifty girls the first month.[21]

These schools were in advance of their day. Dr. J. E. McGirr of the University of St. Mary of the Lake, brother to Sister Mary Vincent McGirr and one of the finest scholars of his day, helped the Sisters to organize the academy and the free schools.[22] He devoted much of his time to teaching the sisters chemistry, physiology, and other branches not then commonly taught. In all that pertained to the schools the Bishop was at once the keenest and kindest of examiners. Sister Mary Vincent McGirr and her sister, Sister Mary Xavier, were accomplished musicians, and like their distinguished brother, had enjoyed unusual educational advantages. Miss Mary Monholland, who was one of the first postulants, was just what the young community needed. She was the daughter of a successful New York merchant, and "association with trade in her father's counting house had given her a methodical business training that few Chicago men of that day possessed." The temporal affairs of the community were placed in the hands of this mature young woman of thirty-five when she was received as Sister Francis de Sales.[23] She gave systematic courses in mathematics and commercial subjects. Art needle work and other subjects included in the curricula of the academies of those days were in equally skilful hands, and the schools had a patronage which was remarkable.[24]

---

[20] Convent Records. One of the original circulars in the archives.

[21] Andreas, *History of Chicago*, Vol. II, p. 407.

[22] Dr. McGirr was a member of the committee appointed in 1852 by the Inspectors of Public Schools of Chicago "to enquire into the expediency of presenting a plan" for a school where the ordinary academic studies could be taught. Cf. Andreas, *op. cit.*, Vol. I, p. 218. Dr. McGirr was an M. A. from St. Mary's College, Emmitsburg, Md., had attended lectures in the Medical Department of the University of Pennsylvania and was a graduate of Rush Medical College. He removed to Chicago in 1847 and was appointed Professor of Botany, Chemistry, Anatomy, Physiology and Hygiene in the University of St. Mary of the Lake.

[23] *Life of Mary Monholland, a Pioneer Sister of the Order of Mercy.*

[24] The state of the public schools of this period is given in the "Report of

Sister Mary Gertrude McGuire was the first Sister to be professed in Chicago. The solemn ceremony took place in the Cathedral on November 21. Bishop Quarter preached to the crowded audience, explaining in clear and elegant language the origin and scope of the religious life. Six days later Mother Warde bade farewell to Mother Agatha and the little community by the lake and made her perilous return trip to her Sisters in Pittsburgh.[25] Then followed anxious days. "Only the incessant occupations of the community kept the sisters from imagining themselves at the end of the earth. For their daily supplies they had frequently to depend on the generosity of the early settlers."[26] The poverty and self-denial of the Bishop animated their zeal. They were proud to second, in their way, his anxious efforts in behalf of his flock. The Bishop advised Mother Agatha to write to Lyons to the Society for the Propagation of the Faith for pecuniary assistance. In reply the Society sent four thousand dollars ($4,000.00) and three large oil paintings.[27] In the meantime the community was increasing and a second story was added to the temporary convent. The Bishop was at the same time building next to the Cathedral at 131 Wabash Avenue. This brick house had two stories and a basement and was intended for the Cathedral Rectory.[28] When it was ready for occupancy in November, 1847, he directed the Sisters to move into it until a suitable place could be had for them. The old schoolhouse back of the first temporary convent on Michigan Avenue was then divided, and on November 10, half of it was removed to the rear of the Cathedral.

The first Sunday of January, 1848, Mother Agatha organized the Children of Mary Sodality for the girls of St. Mary's Congregation.[29] A little later instruction classes for converts and a night school for adults were organized. In the night school were old toilers

Mr. William Wells, Supt. to the Board of Education, bearing date March 20, 1858. The Fourth Annual Report of the Superintendent of Public Schools of the City of Chicago: In January, 1841, the public schools were taught by four male teachers. In January, 1846, five years later, there were three male teachers and six female teachers; in January, 1851, four male teachers and twenty female teachers; . . . . '' *Chicago Antiquities* by H. Hurlbut, Chicago, 1881.

  [25] Cf. *Life of Mother Warde*, p. 146 ff.

  [26] Cf. *Life of Mother Warde*, p. 139 and *Annals*, Vol. III, p. 233.

  [27] Cf. *Annals*, Vol. III, p. 246. It is probable that the donations of the Society were made to the Diocese and then distributed by the Bishop. The oil paintings here referred to were among the few things saved from ''the great fire'' of 1871.

  [28] *Annals*, Vol III, p. 299.

  [29] *Diocesan Journal*, p. 66.

in the labor world, and "young girls commencing to earn wages; all, determined to read and write, for two purposes,—assisting properly at Mass, and corresponding with their friends in Ireland."[30] An employment office in connection with a boarding-house for working girls was another channel of Mercy opened by these pioneer sisters. Mercy in the meantime was quietly working for the individual in the almshouse and in the jail; and the only social worker who sought out the sick in their own homes in those days was the Sister of Mercy of St. Xavier Academy.

DEATH OF BISHOP QUARTER

The sudden death of Bishop Quarter on April 10, 1848, deprived the Sisters of Mercy of their earliest and best friend. The Bishop's demise was a severe blow to the Sisters in more ways than one. His agreement with Bishop O'Connor "to provide amply for the Sisters" had never been carried out, and he died intestate. Whatever money had come to the Sisters above that used to supply their daily needs had been put into repairs and additions to the buildings they occupied, but to which they held no title. The Bishop's intentions in regard to the Sisters of Mercy were, however, well known to his brother ,who became Administrator of the diocese on the death of Bishop Quarter. The Very Reverend Walter Quarter considered it his duty to carry out his brother's plans for the Sisters. He gave them the ground intended for them, seventeen acres lined along the shore between the lake and the old Catholic cemetery, just back of the present Episcopal residence at the entrance to Lincoln Park.[31] The lake afterward receded and the seventeen acres became twenty. The deeds for the house and property in Galena to which the Sisters sent a foundation in May, 1848, were also transferred to the Sisters by Father Quarter as Administrator of the diocese.[32] Galena was the leading village of the West in 1848. There were many who prophesied for it a future greater than that of Chicago. "On May 29, 1848, Mother Agatha, in compliance with the wishes of the deceased Bishop Quarter and at the request of the Pastor and chief people of the town, opened a branch house in Galena, on the confines of Wisconsin and Iowa. . . . . They were most cordially received, donations of provisions and furniture aided them materially to establish the house and their schools opened with bright pros-

[30] *Life of Mother Monholland*, p. 45.
[31] *Annals*, Vol. III, p. 269.
[32] *Diocesan Journal*, p. 78.

pects."[33]   Sister M. Gertrude McGuire, who was appointed local Superior, did not bear the responsibility long. In August Father Walter Quarter wrote in the *Diocesan Journal:* "Died on the night of the 14th inst., at the Convent of St. Mary of the Sisters of Mercy in the City of Galena . . . . the saintly Sister Maguire, in the 22nd year of her age. . .. . . Never have we witnessed such a death as that of Sister Gertrude. . . . . So much resignation. Such piety. Such confidence in the mercy of God."[34]

Death, however, was not the hardest of the trials sent to the young community. Only Mother Agatha's wonderful prudence preserved her daughters from taking any part in the deplorable dissensions that began to disturb ecclesiastical Chicago during the incumbency of Bishop Van de Velde.[35] Bishop Quarter's successor said the community Mass daily in the convent when not absent on visitations of his diocese. He was "kind to the Sisters and insisted they should call him not Bishop but father.[36] But Bishop Van de Velde had peculiar ideas about religious holding property even in common, and questioned the right of the Sisters to the property conveyed to them by Father Walter Quarter. The Sisters refused to give him the deed. Mother Agatha, who was charity personified, for peace sake thought of yielding rather than have any misunderstanding. Mother Frances urged her to hold the deed. Mother Agatha's courage failed. It was not that she could not bear the brunt of trials, but she felt her responsibility for the community and would not yield to any demand that would compromise its interests. After consulting with Bishop O'Connor she decided to return to Pittsburgh. Bishop Van de Velde, who was on his way to Baltimore, accompanied her as far as the parent house.[37] Mother Francis Monholland was left in charge of the Sisters in Chicago, and it was she who was at the helm when cholera broke out in July, 1849. During this awful epidemic Catholic priests and the Sisters were seen early and late caring for those who otherwise would have been thrown upon the streets.[38]

---

[33] *Annals*, Vol. III, p. 267.
[34] *Diocesan Journal*, p. 77.
[35] Clarke; *Lives of the Deceased Bishops of the Catholic Church*, N. Y. 1872. Vol. II, p. 384.
[36] Cf. Notes, p. 314, Vol. III, *Annals*.
[37] *Diocesan Journal*, p. 94. "At six o'clock P. M. left for Pittsburgh and Baltimore via New Buffalo, and Detroit on S. B. Samuel Ward, Mother Agatha, Superior of the Order of Mercy, being recalled by Bp. O'Connor of Pittsburgh, accompanied the Bp. to the latter place."
[38] *Andreas*, Vol. I, p. 596.

The question of the care of the orphans was one of the first placed before Mother Agatha when she returned to Chicago on August 7. A large frame house on Wabash Avenue near Van Buren Street (the Cumberland House) was rented, and Sister Vincent McGirr and three other Sisters took charge of it on August 16. There were at this time one hundred and twenty-five children in the Institution.[42]

On May 13, 1850, a free parochial school was opened on the North Side in the parish of the Holy Name, and in the autumn of the same year, the first effective move in the founding of a general hospital was made.[43] The city needed such a hospital and Dr. N. S. Davis, who had been offered the chair of Principles and Practice of Medicine by Rush Medical College, did not wish to accept the proffered position without the facilities for bedside clinics. Doctor Davis says under date of September 26, 1850: "The trustees have engaged a building adequate for the accommodation of fifty patients. . . . . " The hospital was opened in the old Lake House at Michigan and

---

[*] McGovern, *Life of Bishop McMullen*, p. 29 ff.
[**] *Annals*, Vol. III, p. 268.
[41] *Life of Mother Monholland*, p. 36.
[42] Andreas, *History of Chicago*, Vol. I, p. 299.
[*] Andreas, *History of Chicago*, Vol. I, p. 598.

Rush Streets. Rooms were rented, twelve beds were procured and soon occupied, but the doctors were puzzled about the nursing of the patients. A woman who kept boarders in the Lake House agreed to look after the domestic wants of the patients. The medical students were to do the nursing. The arrangements were not satisfactory and became a source of anxiety to the doctors. The chief surgeon, Dr. Daniel Brainard, lived on Wabash Avenue, just north of the convent. A little wooden fence separated his garden from that of the sisters. He and Doctor Evans applied to the Bishop regarding the possibilities of securing sisters for their institution which had been chartered as the Illinois General Hospital of the Lake.[44]. They were referred to Mother Agatha, but she had just opened a new school and the care of the orphans left her no sisters to spare. She objected that the sisters were not trained for hospital work. Notwithstanding all her arguments, the Bishop and the doctors prevailed, and on February 22, 1851, Sister M. deChantal, Sister Mary Patricia, Sister Mary Ann, with Sister Mary Vincent McGirr as their superior were sent to take charge of the hospital at the Lake House. The fact that Sister Vincent's father was a practicing physician and that her only brother was also a medical doctor seems to have given her courage and zeal to undertake hospital work.

The sisters, even by doubling the number of beds, could not accommodate all who applied. The lease for the Lake House expired after three years, and the owners would not re-rent it for hospital purposes. In May, 1853, the Sisters removed their patients to Tippecanoe Hall, a rickety old frame building on Kinzie Street, fronting the river. Mercy Hospital and Mercy Orphan Asylum were incorporated on June 21, 1852,[45] and it was agreed that if the Sisters would build a hospital, a number of doctors would assist as a regular medical board, leaving the control of affairs to the Sisters. A green stagnant swamp on Wabash Avenue between Harrison and Van Buren Streets was on sale at the time, and Mother Frances Monholland proposed buying it. The undesirable lots were accordingly purchased as a site for the new hospital. Urged on by an indomitable will, Mother Frances, "in the sweat of her brow, and with the strength of her woman's arm," assisted in filling up the swamp while she superintended the work of erecting the first Mercy Hospital owned by the Sisters of Mercy. To defray a part of the expense a few fairs were held.

---

[44] Convent Records.
[45] Ibid.

Bishop Van de Velde was in Rome at the time of the purchase, but on his return he recorded the hospital as diocesan property.[46]

A renewal of the troubles and difficulties which had arisen in the diocese had such an unfavorable effect upon the Bishop's health that he petitioned Rome to relieve him of his responsibilities. Early in November he was transferred to the vacancy at Natchez and left Chicago on the morning of November 4, 1853.[47]

The hospital did not pay expenses. The poor, its chief patients, were often boarded gratuitously, and it was with difficulty kept open. But for the exertions of its firm friends, the doctors, Mercy Hospital would have been closed. In the nature of things, the Orphan Asylum was not self-supporting. The sisters gave their services gratuitously; they assisted these charities from the revenue of the Academy, and collected money for them. Yet when more room was needed in all their institutions, they hesitated about making additions or further improvements upon buildings to which they held no deeds. To avoid any further unpleasantness about property, Mother Agatha decided to buy a strip of prairie in a suburb known as Carville. A generous contractor offered to construct the building with his money and wait for compensation. The purchase of the land, which cost six hundred dollars, was made by Mother Francis Monholland. As if by magic, a new academy arose at the corner of Calumet Avenue and Twenty-sixth Street. Then the venturesome Mother Francis purchased fifty acres of unbroken prairie in the suburbs of South Chicago. Mother Francis' notes of this latter transaction are interesting[48] as samples of the way in which the Sister did business in the early fifties.

---

[46] *Life of Monholland*, p. 41 ff.
[47] *Diocesan Journal*, p. 162.
[48] Bought from Stone, Aug. 8, A. D. 1853, Chicago: Gave the bonds against the corporation of St. Francis Xavier Female Academy to H. O. Stone for $11,-000.00, on property bought of said Stone by us, to-wit: Fifty and thirty-four hundredths acres, at $175 per acre.
Amount of purchases $8,809.50
Eight acres, donation to the Academy............................... 1,250.00

Amount due Stone $7,559.50
Aug. 8, 1853—First payment then made........................... 2,000.00

Amount now due $5,559.50
And real value of bond now given to H. O. Stone, payable as follows, at 6 per cent. interest, every 8th day of August, until all is paid for, with interest:
First payment, Aug. 8, 1854, $1,111.90; interest, $333.54; less orphans' donation of $10.00, $1,101.90; total, $1,435.44.

THE DEATH-GRAPPLE WITH CHOLERA

. But the shadow of the. cross, in the form of death, was again approaching. In the summer of 1854 Asiatic cholera broke out in Chicago; it spread with frightful rapidity. The sisters laid aside all duties to visit and care for the sick; Reverend Mother Mary Agatha took her turn as faithfully as the others. On July 7 she visited the hospital, which was overcrowded, and after spending some time with Sister Mary Veronica, who was ill,. she walked back to the convent. It was a warm day and she was exhausted and overheated. On entering the convent she asked for a drink of water. . In a short time she was seized .with violent symptoms and died the morning of the 8th. Sister Mary Bernadine Meagher and Sister Mary Louise Conners died the same day. Sister Mary Veronica Hickey, whose coffin was carried out of the hospital on the 11, was the fourth victim of the cholera of 1854.[49]

Mother Agatha was but thirty-two when she gave up her sweet soul to God as a martyr of charity. ''In appearance Mother Agatha was of medium height; her complexion was a dark olive and her beautiful brown eyes most expressive. Her manner was bright and animated.''[50]   Bishop O'Connor often said that he never knew anyone to surpass her in common sense.[51] She was exceedingly loved and revered by her young community, who recognized that she was eminently fitted by remarkable gifts of nature and grace to direct the difficult work of the young foundation.

ST. AGATHA'S ACADEMY

Reverend Mother Paula Ruth, who succeeded Reverend Mother Agatha as superior, opened the new Academy, which was called St. Agatha's, in honor of the first superior. From its opening, December 3, 1854, until 1863 this boarding-school was in a flourishing condition.[52] Several of the first families of the city sent their daughters

---

Second payment, Aug. 8, 1855, $1,111.90; interest, $266.85; less orphans' donation of $10.00, $1,101.9; total, $1,368.75.

Third payment, Aug. 8, 1856, $1,111.90; interest, $200.14; less orphans' donation of $10.00, $1,101.90; total, $1,302.04.

Fourth payment, Aug. 8, 1857, $1,101.90; interest, $133.40; less $10.00; total, $1,235.30.

Fifth payment, Aug. 8, 1859, $1,101.90; interest, 66.71; less $10.00; total, $1,168.61.

[49] *Annals*, Vol. III, p .271.
[50] *Ibid.*, p. 245.
[51] *Annals*, Vol. IV, p. 549.

to it. On the register appeared the names of pupils from Missouri, Ohio, California, and other states. St. Agatha's outrivaled the older St. Xavier Academy and was the largest brick building in the southern part of Chicago. People called it the "big brick house on the prairie."[53] It was a boon to the Sisters, who had always lived in the great throbbing heart of Chicago. They enjoyed the quiet and peace of this country place during their retreats and looked upon a trip to 2525 Calumet Avenue as an excursion. Death claimed the second superior rather suddenly August 3, 1855; she was succeeded by Reverend Mother Vincent McGirr. It was during Mother Vincent's term of office that Bishop O'Regan asked the Sisters for the North Shore property, the title to which had been questioned by Bishop Van de Velde. The first official discussion of the matter on record came up March 20, 1856.[54] The community finally agreed to an exchange of the North Shore property for the deed of the convent and lot at 131 Wabash Avenue. When the transaction was closed it was found to be a shade worse, for the sisters were obliged to give a note for four thousand dollars ($4,000.00), in addition to their property. Mother Monholland notes the transaction as follows:
"Nov. 2, 1856. Purchased from Rt. Rev. A. O'Regan 40-foot lot on which the convent now stands, viz., situated on Wabash Avenue, for the sum of $8,000.00; gave in part payment a deed of lot on North Side, $4,000.00; balance still due, $4,000.00. Payable in thirteen years, fourteen years, fifteen years, at 6 per cent interest, payable annually."[55]

---

[53] There is a copy of the prospectus of St. Agatha's Academy in the archives. It reads, in part: "St. Agatha's Academy for Young Ladies, Corner of Rio Grande and Calumet Streets. . . . Under the charge of the Sisters of Mercy. This institution, which is a branch of the Saint Xavier Academy, incorporated by an Act of the Illinois Legislature, 1846, is situated at the corner of Rio Grande and Calumet Streets, two miles, or twenty minutes' ride, from the Center of the City of Chicago, about one square distant from Lake Michigan. . . . Board and tuition (including bed and bedding, washing and mending) varies according to studies, from one hundred and fifty to one hundred and eighty and two hundred dollars ($150 to $180 and $200), payable half yearly in advance. Extra charges for the French, German, Latin and Italian languages; for drawing and painting; for music on piano and guitar and for use of the same; . . . Ordinary tuition embraces the English language. Plain and Ornamental Writing, Practical and Rational Arithmetic, Principles of Algebra, Geography, with Maps, Globes, etc. and etc., Civil and Natural History, Mythology, Moral and Natural Philosophy, Astronomy, Chemistry, Embroidery, Tapestry, . . ."
[54] *Annals*, Vol. III, p. 268.
[54] Convent Records.
[55] Convent Records. "When he left Chicago he did not remove this obliga-

The panic of 1857 left money scarce and the expenses incurred by the sisters going to and from Galena were heavy. Other local causes were unfavorable and the sisters were badly needed in Chicago. Following the closing of the Galena mission in 1857 a school was opened on the West Side in St. Patrick's parish.[56] In connection with this free school, there must have been a private school of some kind. There are accounts for the receipts from the West division schools dated from May 4, 1857, and Sister Mary Angela was in charge of them.

Complications which had arisen in Bishop Van de Velde's time were carried over into the administration of Bishop O'Regan, and the actual finances of the diocese were not adequate to the many demands made on the third Bishop of Chicago. The Sisters' dealings with him had not been so personal as with his predecessors, both of whom had acted as their Chaplains. It was during the incumbency of Bishop O'Regan that arrangements were made to furnish the Sisters with a Chaplain from the local parish.[57] Finding the duties of the Episcopacy uncongenial, Bishop O'Regan left the diocese for Rome in 1857, and the following year took up his permanent residence in London.

Rt. Reverend Clement Smith, as temporary administrator, following the departure of Bishop O'Regan, was a kind friend to the Sisters. It was he who on May 31, 1858, presided at the election of Reverend Mother Monholland. Eliza Allen Starr said truly that the footprints of Mother Francis in Chicago were "the footprints of God's loving Providence toward us as a City."[58] No woman ever worked more unselfishly for the honor and glory of God and the good of souls in Chicago than Mother Francis. From the day of her entrance until that on which she left Chicago to extend the work of the Sisters of Mercy in Iowa she was "a hewer of wood and a drawer of water" for her Community. No task was too menial, none unsurmountable where the welfare of her Sisters was con-

---

tion, and they were obliged to pay the first thousand to Bishop Duggan. When he left, the remaining three were paid to Rev. Thomas Halligan, administrator, from a bequest of three thousand dollars left the Sisters by Bishop O'Regan. This amount was subscribed by him to the Mercy Hospital, but never paid except in this way. It came to the Sisters in Father Halligan's time. He released their notes for the three thousand due by Bishop O'Regan's arrangement, thus balancing accounts."—*Annals*, Vol. III, p. 270.

[56] Convent Records. The Sisters had taught the Sunday School for girls from their coming to Chicago. Cf. *Annals*, Vol III, p. 269.

[57] St. Xavier's has never had a resident chaplain.

[58] Obituary notice which appeared in the *New World*, 1888.

cerned. She was quick, aggressive, and unattractive in appearance, but no one with whom she dealt could withhold respect from her. No metal was ever tried harder and none ever rang truer.[59]

THE PRECURSOR OF THE HOUSE OF THE GOOD SHEPHERD

For the August retreat of 1858 Mother Francis secured a Jesuit to give the exercises. This was the first bit of spiritual indulgence .the Community had ever enjoyed.[60] At the request of Dr. McMullen, she opened an unpretentious refuge for erring women in a house rented by him on Market street. This refuge was kept by the Sisters of Mercy until the Good Shepherd nuns came in 1859. Her next move was to enlarge the Convent at 131 Wabash Avenue by adding a third story. Improvements were made in the Mercy House at the same time. In August, 1859, she sent a colony of five Sisters under Sister Xavier McGirr to make a foundation in Ottawa, Illinois.[62]

AMONG THE "NUNS OF THE BATTLEFIELDS"

Then came the war and soon after it broke out Colonel Mulligan, who organized the celebrated Irish Brigade, determined to secure the service of the Sisters in behalf of his sick and wounded. Before his departure from Chicago he called upon Mother Francis and obtained her promise to send Sisters to the aid of his regiment. Bishop Duggan gave the necessary permissions and after the regiment was stationed at Lexington, Missouri, Lieutenant Shanley of the "First Brigade," returned to Chicago to conduct the Sisters to the scenes of battle. On September 2, 1861, "Mother Francis with Mother Mary Borromeo, her assistant, accompanied five Sisters and several nurses to the South. Not being able to reach Lexington, they were placed in charge of the Jefferson City Hospital, which soon became overcrowded with the sick, wounded and dying." After a fruitless attempt to reach Lexington, Lieutenant Shanley brought the Sisters back to Jefferson City where they remained in charge of the hospitals until April, 1862. The regiment was then ordered to another division. They then took charge of the hospital department of the steamboat Empress on the Mississippi and Ohio rivers. Their five weeks service on the hospital boat ended when they brought "the last cargo of sick and wounded from the terrible

---

[footnote] *Life of Mother Francis Monholland.*
[footnote] Convent Records.
[footnote] Cf. Thompson, *Archdiocese of Chicago,* p. 747.
[footnote] Convent Records.

battle at Shiloh" to Louisville where they were placed under proper care. The Sisters in Chicago had their opportunity of aiding the soldiers when, after the fall of Fort Donaldson, the southern prisoners were brought to Chicago.

"Companies of Federal troops with squads of Confederate prisoners often passed the convent en route to Camp Douglas. This Camp was in charge of Colonel Sweet, and it was said the poor Southern prisoners might be more humanely treated; it was also said that there was a great dearth of food in the Camp." The undercurrent of feeling in the city was strong when Colonel Sweet refused admission to an investigating committee. The committee appealed to Mother Francis who, armed with a note from the Mayor went to the camp with her Sisters. Colonel Sweet received them courteously and permitted them to do what they could for the prisoners.

During the war time Mother Francis opened two new schools; one at Sherman and Polk Streets in the parish of St. Louis, the other at Wabash Avenue and Eighteenth Street, in Father John Waldron's parish. In the year in which the Sisters undertook the charge of educating the girls of St. John's parish, the Rev. Dr. Denis Dunne asked that the Sisters who taught at St. Patrick's be allowed to reside there. Rev. Mother Francis would not agree to this arrangement whereupon Dr. Dunne invited the Sisters of Loretto to take charge of the education of the girls of his parish. This necessitated the closing of St. Angela's select school for girls of the West Side, which was conducted in connection with St. Patrick's parochial school.

It was then arranged to exchange the West Side property for the lot on Wabash Avenue adjoining the convent. Later Bishop Duggan wanted the Community to erect an orphan asylum on this ground; the Sisters not being able to do this offered to appropriate two acres of their farm for the orphanage. The building of a new hospital was also discussed at this time, but collections for the purpose were not sufficient. Although the accommodations for the orphans and the sick were poor and inadequate, it was difficult to come to any definite decision with the Bishop concerning ways and means. Holding no deed to the hospital and orphanage property, Rev. Mother Francis could only voice a feeble protest when Bishop Duggan offered both hospital and orphanage for sale. The orphans were given in charge to the Sisters of St. Joseph and were moved into the buildings vacated by the University of St. Mary of the Lake. Mother Francis was told to find a place for her patients.

There was nothing to do but move the students from the new academy at Twenty-sixth Street back to the already crowded building at 131 Wabash Avenue. The vacated academy was then converted into a hospital..

A PERIOD OF EXPANSION

Larger quarters for the Saint Xavier Academy and the mother house at) adison Street were demanded by this new order of things, and it was decided to erect a new academy on the lots at 133 and 135 Wabash Avenue, which had been taken in exchange for the community property on the West Side. The new St. Xavier Academy then erected at a cost of thirty-five thousand dollars had every convenience afforded during the sixties. It was a monument to the creative genius of Mother Francis. Progress had been made in every department. St. Xavier's had developed along traditional lines. At first it had aimed to do little more than supply the educational needs of the immediate neighborhood, but the course of study widened as it drew teachers and pupils from a broader field. The music and art departments reached a high degree of efficiency between 1860 and 1870 when a number of remarkably talented young American women entered the community. Sister) ary Pius Teats, whose clever sketches of teachers and pupils were appreciated by) other Francis, studied under Mr. George P. A. Healy, the celebrated Chicago portrait painter. To him she owed the success of her studio which was up to date in its appointments and a source of revenue to her community. The young Paul Wood who worked under Gregori in the decoration of the Sacred Heart Chapel of Notre Dame University was one of her discoveries.

From almost every standpoint St. Xavier's never enjoyed such prosperity as at this time. The Ottawa foundation had succeeded and had been made an independent community in September, 1861, and when) other Francis resigned her superiorship in 1867 there was not a cent of debt on any property held by the community.

Mother) ary Scholastica Drum, the fifth superior, sent out two foundations, one to DeWitt, Iowa, and the other to Harrisburg, Pennsylvania. She also leased the corner lot of Mercy Hospital grounds, Prairie Avenue and twenty-sixth Street, to the Chicago) edical College, and the faculty of this college agreed to furnish medical and surgical attendance to the hospital for the privilege of holding clinics. On the occasion of the laying of the corner-stone of the new) ercy Hospital, July 25, 1869, Doctor Davis, who had

lectured for the benefit of the Illinois General Hospital of the Lake
at the time the Sisters of Mercy first took up hospital work, and
who had been associated with them since that time, was the speaker.
In epitomizing the history of Mercy Hospital, he said:

"Its growth has been steady and uniform, until it now lays the foundation
of a magnificent structure which will remain for ages an ornament to the city, and
a perpetual monument to the liberality and charity of its founders, and an asylum
for the suffering and afflicted of many generations. During its past history, without the aid of public appropriations or private endowment, and constantly embarrassed by the temporary structure it has occupied, it has accommodated and
. kindly treated more than six thousand human beings suffering from serious diseases, at least one-fourth of whom were cared for gratuitously. Its doors have
been opened alike to every class and creed.

"It has received the professional services, always gratuitously, of the most
eminent members of the medical profession, among whom have been Drs. Brainard,
McGirr, Herrick, Blaney, Boon, Johnson, Andrews, Byford, Nelson, and your
speaker.

"In regard to the ability and faithfulness of the Sisters of Mercy in the
management of the hospital, I can speak in terms of the fullest commendation.
Having visited it professionally from its incipient organization to the present
hour, I must say that in cleanliness, good order, kindly attention, and Christian
liberality, I have not seen them equalled in any other public hospital in the
country. . ."[68]

IN THE WAKE OF THE DESTROYER

After investing the sum of one hundred and fifteen thousand
dollars in the hospital, Reverend Mother Scholastica purchased
property at 2834 Wabash Avenue for a new Motherhouse and
Academy. The location at 131-135 Wabash Avenue was no longer
suitable for academic purposes, and the frontage had risen
enormously in value. She therefore mortgaged the downtown site
to make a payment on the new purchase and negotiated for its sale.
The papers were ready to be signed October 7, 1871, but the
transaction was transferred until the ever-memorable ninth. Everything was ready for a whole burnt-offering. "In the vacation of
1871, the Sisters had spared no labor or expense in their schools.
The study had been newly fitted up; maps, charts, globes, philosophical instruments were selected irrespective of cost; the studio was
furnished with new models; everything was polished up." The
great fire swept away all. The lots covered by the ashy ruins of
"dear old St. Xavier's" were sold later for sixty-one thousand dollars
subject to a mortgage. After deducting taxes, interest and fees,
there remained only three hundred and seventy dollars.

*Cf. Annals, Vol. III, p. 260.

Just one month before the fire when the Silver Jubilee of the Community was celebrated, there were forty-five boarders, eighty day scholars, and ten teachers in the Academy. Twelve Sisters had charge of parochial schools in St. John's parish, at Clark and Eighteenth Streets, in the parish of St. Louis on Clark Street near Polk, in St. Mary's Wabash Avenue and Madison Street, and at St. James', Prairie Avenue, near Twenty-sixth Street. Of these, only St. John's and St. James' escaped the flames.[64]

Mercy Hospital served as the Motherhouse and Novitiate for the Sisters until the new building at Twenty-ninth Street was ready, while the Rotheberger Mansion at Thirty-fourth Street and Cottage Grove Avenue was used as an Academy.

The financial predicament of the Community was made public when Reverend Mother Genevieve succeeded Mother Scholastica. The Sisters took possession of the new Academy August 28, 1873, but every brick in it, every bit of furniture it contained was mortgaged. Bishop Foley[65] advised the Sisters to sell the Academy and the Hospital at auction. One of his representatives bought them and the deeds were in the Bishop's name at the time of his death in 1879. Reverend Mother paid the interest semi-annually, and a small portion of the principal each year. It was like beginning all over again.

Even the cholera did not absent itself. A committee represented the deplorable condition of those attacked by the disease who had been isolated in the Small-Pox Hospital. Bishop Foley addressed himself to Reverend Mother and pleaded for Sisters to visit the cholera-patients and if possible to remain to nurse them. Sister Mary Alphonsus Butler and Sister Mary Jane Duggan tended the sick in the old Isolation Hospital, then located on Wentworth Avenue between Thirty-seventh and Thirty-eighth Streets, until the epidemic abated at the end of the month of August.[66] When Doctor McMullen became Administrator, the interest on the community debt was lowered from ten to seven per cent. Later the deeds of both Academy and Hospital were returned to the Sisters by Archbishop Feehan who cancelled what remained of the debt,—about ten thousand dollars.

---

[64] Andreas, *History of Chicago*, Vol. II, 407.
[65] "The first school the Bishop visited after coming to Chicago was the St. Xavier Academy, and he always proved himself a tender father and a faithful friend to the Sisters. . . . Whenever the kind Bishop had noted visitors from Baltimore or other cities, he always brought them to see St. Xavier's. . . . These visits were always a surprise, so there was nothing formal about them, and they were all the more enjoyed."—*Reminiscences of Seventy Years.*
[66] *Reminiscences of Seventy Years*, Sisters of Mercy, Chicago, p. 99.

There were those who were firmly convinced that the Community
could never surmount these financial difficulties, but good Reverend
Mother Genevieve always said "God will provide."
No foundations outside the diocese were made during Rev. Mother
Genevieve's time. On one occasion Bishop Foley of Detroit "announced that he would soon ask for a colony, as he was about to build
a Mercy House, and, of course, he wanted no other Sisters if it were
possible to procure them. Several volunteered. Sister Mary Ignatius
was very enthusiastic and this pleased the good Bishop. About six
months later, when the home was built, he wrote to Mother Genevieve
asking that she keep her word and send some Sisters at once. In
good faith she went to Archbishop P. A. Feehan and told him all
about it, asking permission to send the mission to Detroit. To her
surprise the Archbishop said, "No! We have enough of work at
home for the Sisters. We have none to spare."[67] Rapid as was the
growth of the Community the supply of Sisters was not sufficient
to meet the demands.

DEVELOPMENT OF ST. XAVIER ACADEMY

In the first annual catalogue of the St. Xavier Academy issued
in June, 1874, the one hundred ninety-five students registered during
the Academic year, 1873-1874, are divided into seven classes. No
outline of the course of study is given, but it embraced "the various
branches of a solid and useful education." The cost of board and
tuition in English and Music for the academic year was three-hundred
dollars. Before the opening of the next year, classes were organized
on another basis; graduate class, second class, third class, fourth class,
and a Second Division. Miss Nellie C. Dore[68] was the only student
to receive the "graduate medal" and academic honors in June, 1875.
"Having completed the Course of Study prescribed in the Academy,
given evidence of her proficiency at the recent Annual Examination,
and distinguished herself for amiable and correct deportment" Miss
Dore was entitled "to the highest honors of the Institution, namely,
a Crown and Gold Medal; also to the following Premiums:

First Premium—Grammar and Composition.
"   "   Arithmetic, Algebra and Geometry.
"   "   Penmanship and Bookkeeping.
"   "   Philosophy and Natural History.
"   "   Botany and General History.[*]

[*] Ibid., p. 214.
[*] Mrs. Ellen Reynolds, whose son Edward is a Jesuit.
[*] Catalogue of St. Xavier Academy, Vol. I, p. 13.

From the Course of Study outlined in the third annual catalogue
it is evident that the Senior Department had two divisions. "Reading
(Young Ladies' Reader), Orthographic Dictation (Creery's Gram.
School Speller), Penmanship, Composition, Grammar (Brown's Institute), Arithmetic (Robinson's Practical and Mental), Physical
Geography (Mitchell's) Sacred History (Gilmore's), Familiar Science (Peterson's), English Literature" were the subjects assigned
for students of the Second Division. After spending two years in
the first half of the Senior Department, successful students were
given places in the First Division where they set themselves to master
"Reading, Penmanship, Rhetoric, and Composition; Algebra, Geometry, Chemistry, Geology, Philosophy, Natural History, Physiology,
Botany, and Bookkeeping." It is quite evident from this that St.
Xavier's, as far as the secular branches were concerned was quite
on a par with the only Public High School then in Chicago. The
Course of Study differed from that of the Public High School in
only one respect, a language was not required though both French
and German were taught. Astronomy was added to the Curriculum
in 1876, and in 1877, French or German was made obligatory. Quite
in contrast with most of the schools offering secondary work in the
seventies, St. Xavier's laid great stress on the Sciences. The study
of science had always been given a prominent place in the subjects
taught by the Sisters in the upper classes at old St. Xavier's for the
spirit of the Community's first great teacher, Doctor John E. McGirr
had passed to the entire teaching corps. The Doctors in attendance
at Mercy Hospital were among the chief lecturers on scientific subjects in the forties, fifties, and sixties. No one was more hungry
for what they had to give of knowledge than their co-laborers in
the hospital. At one time or another almost every Sister of Mercy
before 1873 had taken her term in serving the sick, and Mother
Gabriel O'Brien, who was back of every progressive educational movement in the history of the Academy in her day, was on duty at
Mercy Hospital from 1870 until the new St. Xavier's was opened in
1873. The Chicago Medical College had its laboratories of Bacteri-
ology, Physiology, Chemistry, etc., next door to Mercy Hospital, and
these were a never ending source of interest and profit to Sister Mary
Gabriel. Her special province was the drug room, where she worked
with Sister Mary Ignatius Feeney, in a most scientific fashion. When
then in 1873 she was assigned to the senior classes at St. Xavier's
she brought with her the scientific spirit. In a short time her "drug
room" was as complete a scientific laboratory as was to be found in
the Chicago High School. The catalogue of 1883-1884 outlines a

Course of Study made by Mother Gabriel to bring the work of the Academy into greater harmony with that of the Chicago Department of Education for many of the girls graduating from St. Xavier's desired to qualify as teachers in the Public Schools. The divisions then made of eight grammar grades and four distinct years of High School are still retained at St. Xavier's. Latin was taught at the Academy for the first time during this period, and Physics as well as Chemistry was given a distinct place in the Curriculum. The school publication, *The St. Xavier Echo*, came into existence in Mother Gabriel's time and it was she who organized the Alumnae Association in 1887.

During the difficult times following the fire most of the land in Hyde Park known as "the farm" had been sold. It was decided to establish the Novitiate on the five acres which had been retained. For this purpose a large residence in the neighborhood was bought and moved to the corner of Forty-ninth Street and Evans Avenue in 1890. A boarding and day-school for girls known as St. Agatha's Academy was opened in connection with this Novitiate.

Important improvements and extensions were made in Mercy Hospital in 1892 and again in 1896. In the former year the Mercy Hospital School for Nurses, which was regularly organized in 1889, received a Charter from the State; and in 1901, the year in which the Nurses Alumnae Association was organized, a change was made from the old two-year course with one month's probation to a three-year course with two month's probation.

THE LIBERTYVILLE FOUNDATION

In 1896 St. Mary's Convent, Libertyville, was erected on a tract of twenty acres, a gift to the Community from Mr. C. C. Copeland. Mother Gabriel, its first local Superior, organized St. Mary's Academy. The building at 4928 Evans Avenue erected at a cost of over three-hundred thousand dollars serves as the present Mother House. Novitiate, College, and Academy; but no single work developed during Mother Genevieve's time made the strides marked by the progress of the parish schools to which she sent her Sisters. St. Patrick's School in South Chicago was opened September 10. 1883 with an enrollment of two hundred and seven pupils. From the start there was a high school in connection with the grammar school, and it was the first Catholic Parochial High School in the diocese. Miss Minnie Dougherty, teacher in the Sheridan School, who resides at 2728 East 75th Place, Chicago, has the distinction of being the first graduate of a Parochial High School in the diocese. The late

Rev. Father Van de Laar presented to Miss Dougherty a Diploma of Graduation at the Commencement Exercises held on June 30, 1887. St. Elizabeth's Grammar School was opened by Father Daniel J. Riordan in September, 1885, with an attendance of two hundred pupils. In 1891, he added the high school department for girls. St. James' School, which had been in charge of the Sisters of Mercy since 1866, housed four hundred pupils, when the new school building was opened in 1884. The High School organized by the late Rev. Hugh McGuire in 1890 became the model Parochial High School. No energy or expense was spared by Father McGuire to make it perfect in every department.[70] The Sisters were supplied with everything necessary for doing efficient work, and the laboratories, museum, and libraries in the building specially erected for the High School were on a par with those of the contemporary Chicago Public High Schools. In 1897 the late lamented Reverend Maurice J. Dorney added a High School for boys and girls to the Grammar School which had been in charge of the Sisters of Mercy since 1880. "The marvelous success of the School may be attributed, in the natural order, almost entirely to the energy and ability of Sister Mary Philomena, who, as Superior, guided the destines of the Students of the school for thirty years. Her former pupils gladly testify to her untiring zeal and self sacrifices."[71]

The Institutions listed in 1890 as under the direction of the Sisters of Mercy when Archbishop Feenan celebrated his Silver Jubilee are:[72]

St. Francis Xavier Academy—Mother Genevieve, Superior......... 200 pupils
Academy of St. Agatha—Mother Theresa, Superior.............. 35 pupils
House of Providence—Sister M. Angela, Superior............... 80 boarders
Mercy Hospital—Sister M. Raphael, Superior....................
St. Agnes—Sister M. Agnes, Superior.......................... 305 pupils
All Saints—Sister M. Sebastian, Superior...................... 800 pupils
St. Elizabeth's—Sister M. Baptist, Superior................... 438 pupils

---

[70] On his death this princely priest and great educator bequeathed "To the Sisters of Mercy, St. Xavier Academy, Chicago, the property owned by me in St. Charles Township, Kane County, Illinois, known as Villa Maria—five islands, including about 64 acres, with buildings, vehicles and boats and household furniture. It is my will and wish that this place be kept and maintained as a summer residence and recreation place for the Sisters of St. James' School, and any other Sisters whom the Superior of the Community may send there. It has always been my earnest desire and wish to do something for the Sisters who worked so zealously and faithfully in the cause of education. This is the only opportunity I have had and it gives me great pleasure to do it."—*Reminiscences of Seventy Years*, p. 251.

[71] Cf. *Archdiocese of Chicago*, p. 477.

[72] *The Catholic Church in Chicago*, p. 250.

St. Gabriel's—Sister M. Philomena, Superior..................... 375 pupils
Holy Angels'—Sister Mary Mark, Superior..................... 239 pupils
St. James—Sister M. de Sales, Superior........................1100 pupils
St. John—Sister M. Mercy, Superior........................... 200 pupils
St. Patrick's (South Shicago)—Sister M. Borromeo, Superior...... 232 pupils
St. Rose's—Sister M. Euphrasia, Superior..................... 185 pupils

If Reverend Mother Agatha O'Brien enkindled the spirit of Mercy in her children, it was Reverend Mother Genevieve who fanned the flame when untold obstacles threatened to extinguish it. Her knowledge of the past history of the Community together with her straight thinking and great trust in God made her fit to cope with the difficulties of her trying position. She kept her troubles to herself, and was wise enough to let her children serve the Lord in gladness so that their work for the Master might not be vitiated by worry. Though her call was sudden, she was amply prepared for death which came to her the evening of April 26, 1904. On that day she had assisted at the Community exercises from Meditation at 5:30 A. M. until Benediction at 4 P. M.

Reverend Mother de Sales Ryan, who came into office after the death of Reverend Mother Genevieve, had been a student at "old St. Xavier's." As a novice she had been one of its teachers, and for twenty years had been in charge of St. James' School. The wealth of possibilities for the development of the works of Mercy must have been embarrassing for her, but she wisely took up the great responsibilities of her position where her much-revered predecessor had laid them down. The splendid new addition to Mercy Hospital was erected in her time and she seconded every new plan launched by Sister Mary Raphael McGill for the expansion of the work to which that good Sister devoted over forty years of her religious life. At the suggestion of Archbishop Quigley, Rev. Mother de Sales purchased the five acres in front of the new motherhouse for a campus. In 1906 the Sisters, at her direction, took up the care of the orphans—after a lapse of forty-two years—at St. Mary's Training School. On July third Mother de Sales accompanied the first band of her community to this diocesan home for dependent children of Des Plaines, and the novices who gave their vacation that year to this foundation work have a fund of stories to hand down to their followers. The late Sister Mary Borromeo who was the first superior of St. Patrick's School, South Chicago, and who directed it for twenty-three years was given charge of this new undertaking in August. Later she became acting superintendent of the Training School and served as such almost to the time of her death which

occurred October 15, 1911.[73] Among the new schools opened at this time were St. Ita's, St. Mary of the Lake, and Corpus Christi. The Sisters also continued to teach School at St. Mary's Church (Paulist) and until the coming of Mother Drexel's Sisters, two Sisters went regularly to St. Monica's Church to instruct the colored children and to visit the sick colored people.

The munificence of the late Mr. Ferris S. Thompson of New York, with whom the Sisters were unacquainted but who had learned of the needs of the Hospital from a friend, made it possible to erect the Home for Nurses which was completed in 1914. A bequest of the late Mr. Charles Haines of St. Charles, Illinois, whose sister Malvina had been a pupil at the old St. Agatha's Academy, encouraged the Sisters to incur the debt for the new wing of the hospital on Calumet Avenue.

SOCIAL WORK

When Rev. Mother Xavier Flanagan became superior in 1910 she recognized that the problems before her were not those of either the founder or the savior of the community. It was quite clear that the lives of the poor lacked the simplicity usually attributed to them. The truly poor were not so easy of access as in the pioneer days. If they were to be reached, it was to be by training young women for leadership to vie with the "social-worker" of non-Catholic denominations. Mother Xavier encouraged the Sisters to continue their studies, and sent several to the Catholic University at Washington, D. C., and others to Europe. Although the original charter for St. Xavier's gave power "to confer on such persons as may be considered worthy such Academical or honorary degrees as are usually conferred by similar institutions" Mother Xavier applied for a new charter for the Saint Xavier College for Women in March, 1912. Post-graduate students had been on the Academy register at various times, but no systematic undergraduate course leading to a degree was offered previous to this. The Home for Working Girls, which had occupied the old St. Agatha's Academy after the fire, and which had been removed to 2834 Wabash Avenue when the building in Xavier Park became the mother house, was incorporated at the same time as the "Convent of Mercy and the Mercy Home."

In 1916 when Mother de Sales took up the duties of Superior for the second time her efforts were mainly directed to a systematization of the many splendid grammar and high schools which the Sisters

[73] *Archdiocese of Chicago*, p. 744.

of Mercy now controlled. The new schools opened in 1917 were in the parishes of Our Lady of Solace, at St. Mary's, Lake Forest, in the Italian parish of the Holy Rosary, and St. Justin Martyr's. No advantage was denied the Sisters that would increase their efficiency in the classroom. A sister supervisor was appointed and all the Sisters who were graduates of a High School were regularly classified in the College so that they might work toward a degree. The World War made the erection of a proposed new college impossible, but the purchase of the annex at 649-651 East Forty-ninth Street gave increased laboratory facilities.

When the United States entered the World War a unit of doctors and nurses was organized from Mercy Hospital. The Liberty Loans were advocated in the parish schools and the War Saving movement furthered. The Sisters and children made hospital garments and knitted-wear. A St. Xavier Red Cross Auxiliary was chartered in November, 1917, but it was later found more convenient for the members of the Alumnae to meet at the rooms of the International Federation of Catholic Alumnae and the charter for the St. Xavier Auxiliary was surrendered.

The present superior of the Sisters of Mercy of St. Xavier's is Reverend Mother Sophia Mitchell, formerly supervisor of the schools, and for twelve years directress of Holy Angels School. She had handled her problems ably and successfully during the past two years but the "housing question" which is begging an answer from our great growing city has also come up to this Mother of over four hundred children. Since 1901 when the present mother house was built the community has practically doubled. Then there were 200 Sisters, now there are four hundred and seven. The academic enrollment of 325 students in that year has grown to 700. There is not a room to be spared in Mercy Hospital and a Novitiate in the country is an absolute necessity. The proposed new home for the novices is to be erected on the twenty-acre tract in Libertyville just seven miles east of the new University of St. Mary of the Lake. It is the wish of His Grace, the Most Rev. Archibshop George W. Mundelein, D. D., that the Sisters build a central high school on the South Side. The college is growing rapidly, having at present a registration of one hundred and two. There are 865 students in the high schools conducted by the Sisters, and the total number of children in their grammar schools is 11,387.[74]

---

[74] In the communities of Sisters of Mary in Iowa and Illinois, which were founded from St. Xavier's there are over seven hundred Sisters.

The very latest work taken up by the Sisters is the management of the new Diocesan Maternity Hospital, the Mater Misericordiae, at Forty-seventh Street and California Avenue, to which Rev. Mother Sophia has sent four Sisters from Mercy Hospital. The latter institution is just about closing negotiations to transfer affiliation from Northwestern University to Loyola. In future the internes and nurses of Mercy Hospital will take their degrees from Loyola University.

IN RETROSPECT

At the close of seventy-five years the Sisters are encouraged at the retrospect. The pioneer members who partook of the bitterness of the first trying days are tasting the sweet reward promised to those who leave all for Christ's sake. When every thing has been said on the subject of what the Community could have done this fact remains true, the Sisters themselves have given their all—whatever they had of this world's goods, their talents, their very lives. No one knows better than they what they could have done with just a little more material wealth to dispense to the needy with whom they have always been in contact. They shared the hardships of the pioneer days when those for whom they labored gave freely and willingly of their much needed earnings. The Catholics during the first decade of the Sisters' work were making desparate efforts to establish their homes, and it is certain that there was scarcely one of them who had it not in his heart to help the Sisters as soon as he had cared for those directly dependent upon him. Then came the rapid growth of the city and the multiplication of parishes. Oftentimes the generous Catholic of those early days had his home in territory which, due to the rapid division of parishes, supported successively two or three different pastors, each with his new problem of church and school. Next followed the great influx of religious communities to meet the demands of a developing Catholic School system in Chicago, and to help with the work of social relief. The Sisters of Mercy soon realized that there was little to be expected from the heavily-taxed people for whom they had borne "the heat and burden of the day." They have tried to work out their own problems and the kind friends who have come forward with unsolicited help have been many. To these the gratitude of the Sisters is unbounded and the prayers of the Community for those who have done it good in Christ's name shall never cease.

'Tis God's blest will that onward we should go.
Few magic words of commendation meet

E'er sweetly chime to keep our hearts aglow.
What matters this! While toiling here below
With quenchless love, our faith will e'er respond
To One awaiting in the Great Beyond
With sweet award which He will there bestow.
Whoever saves his life for self alone
Shall lose it. And who gives his life for God
And souls, shall find it happily indeed,
So true it is we reap as we have sown.
But while we bow beneath love's chastening rod,
We trust our all to Him in Time of Need."

A SISTER OF THE COMMUNITY.

" Mother Gabriel O'Brien, who died April 29, 1918.

SEBASTIEN LOUIS MEURIN, S. J.

II

(Continued from January Issue)

Father Meurin was thus spared to the missions; he was now sixty-one years of age; he had never been well during the twenty-two years he had toiled in the wilderness. All the property of the Jesuits had been sold; he had no home, no resources, no income, no means of live-lihood. What comfort could he derive from the assurance that efforts would be made at the court of Louis XIV to secure for him an annual pension of 600 livres, some $120? The king was too preoccupied with wars, and politics, and building, to give thought to the fortunes or welfare of an obscure missionary, and, even supposing the pension would be granted eventually, what was the missionary to do mean-while? Prospects as dark and forbidding as these could not daunt his noble spirit, because his only thought was of the danger to the faith and morals of the Indians and French if they remained long without a missionary. There was one more delay; the Council was still to be reckoned with and Father Meurin was not allowed to proceed up-stream till he was informed by this august assembly that the diocese of Quebec no longer included Louisiana, for they had assumed power to define ecclesiastical provinces and jurisdiction. Meurin was there-fore obliged to sign a document to the effect that he would reside at Sainte Genevieve and "recognize no other ecclesiastical superior than the Superior of the Capuchins at New Orleans."[53] But he was in no wise baffled by their intrigues; he signed these stipulations without delay, for what mattered it to him from what source he derived his faculties, providing they were genuine. Nevertheless, he took certain other precautions to insure to himself these same faculties.

About this time he made application at Rome for very extensive powers which were granted the following year when on Sept. 4, 1765, the Holy Office decreed that His Holiness should be asked to grant the power of dispensing in cases of marriage which involved 'disparitas cultus' to Father Meurin, who had petitioned for this power. That same day the Holy Father "granted for a triennium, from the date of cultus in matrimoniorum celebratione'"[54] "for the relief of a mission

[53] Conway, J. J., S. J., *The Catholic Church in Saint Louis*, p. 12. *Missouri Historical Publication*, No. 14.
[54] Hughes, Thomas, S. J., *The History of the Society of Jesus in North Amer-ica*. Text. Vol. II, p. 589.

receipt, this extraordinary faculty, 'dispensandi super disparitate cultus in matrimoniorum celebratione' ''[54] ''for the relief of a mission almost destitute of every aid, and for the spiritual comfort of a Christian flock, so far remote by sea and land.''[55] In this way Father Meurin "received from the Holy See for his country of the Illinois extraordinary faculties, such as had never been granted to any 'bishops, vicars apostolic or missionaries in America.' ''[56]

After all these distressing delays our missionary left New Orleans the middle of February, 1764. During the trip upstream, he baptized thirteen persons as "the archives for the station of Arcana, now in the possession of the Bishop of Little Rock"[57] attest. He must have returned to the scene of his former labors by mid-summer, for on July 29 he baptized in Kaskaskia the son of Baptiste LaChapelle and Louise Lalumandiere, on August 14th he baptized another child and on August 30 he baptized three children. (Records, p. 69.) Meanwhile events of great importance had occurred farther up the Mississippi. Colonel Auguste Chouteau landed on the site of St. Louis about the time Meurin left New Orleans; he cleared the ground and awaited the arrival of Sieur Laclede and his party, who founded the city of Saint Louis, February 15, 1764.[58] We have every reason to suppose that if Father Meurin had been allowed to leave New Orleans when he desired he would have witnessed this historic act. But though he was not present at the city's birth, to him nevertheless belongs the distinction of being the pioneer priest of Saint Louis by virtue of his visits in 1766, and his frequent visits in the three following years. On these occasions he must have said Mass in a tent or private residence since the first Catholic church, a small log house, was not erected

[54] Hughes, Thomas, S. J., op. cit., p. 589.
[55] Hughes, Thomas, S. J., op. cit., p. 598.
[57] Conway, J. J., S. J., op. cit., p. 5.
[58] Houch, Louis, op. cit., Vol. II, p. 7-9.

"On February 14th Chouteau landed there, and he says that on the next day he put the men and boys who came with him on the boat to work. Madame Chouteau and her children came up from Fort de Chartres in a cart through the American Bottom, accompanied by Laclede and arrived at Cahokia about the same time that the boat reached the site selected for the trading post. Laclede, after securing a place of residence for her at Cahokia, came over the river and spent the summer in erecting his establishment, and after the completion of his building, brought up his goods from the Fort, and finally, in September following, he also brought Madame Chouteau over to the new village to the home prepared for her—her family being considered Laclede's family. But, during the summer, a number of other settlers from Cahokia crossed over and established themselves, building houses and making other improvements, and these, too, with their families, brought over their goods and merchandise. The total number of persons forming the new settlement in the first six months aggregated about thirty."

till 1770,[59] when it was blessed by. Meurin himself on June 24. It is an established fact that as early as 1698 Father St. Cosme and companion said Mass on the site of the present city of Saint Louis, which was then covered with virgin forest. Again, early in July, 1673, Father James Marquette passed by the same place while exploring the Mississippi, and later in the same month he passed again after having proceeded as far south as the Red River. We have no records to show that he said Mass or administered the sacraments here; the venerable explorer mentions the Missouri and the Ohio rivers but makes no mention of a village where today thrives the metropolis of the Mississippi Valley. Hence we have no misgivings in styling our hero ''the pioneer priest of Saint Louis.''

For four years Sainte Genevieve was our missionary's place of abode; nevertheless, the parish records of Kaskaskia establish the fact that he was frequently in his beloved Kaskaskia, sometimes for several successive days.[60] Sainte Genevieve, in those pioneer days, was not the quiet little village we know today, but a much smaller place, about three miles south of the present location and some distance from the limestone bluffs which line the Missouri side of the river. When threatened with destruction by the Mississippi flood of 1785, the citizens had the good sense to remove farther north to higher ground, an act which saved them from the catastrophe which befell Kaskaskia in 1885, and preserved to us the historic houses of which the citizens of today are justly proud. So effectually did they transplant their original village that practically no traces of it remain today. Originally Sainte Genevieve was an Indian mission, but white men soon found their way to it and made it their home.[61]

The parish records of Sainte Genevieve bear witness to the activity of Father Meurin in his new home. As priests were not numerous in the Mississippi Valley, many of the people who came for baptism were from the former missions across the river or from more distant places even. Complete strangers sometimes found their way to Sainte Genevieve as we learn when in a funeral entry in the parish records Father Meurin writes:

[59] Garraghan, Gilbert J., S. J., *Unpublished Manuscript*, p. 36.

[60] For example: in 1765 he conferred baptism on the following dates: February 2, 7, 8, 9, 19, 19; March 22; April 22; May 8, 9; June 3, 12, 12, 21; July 6, 7, 22, 22; September 17; November 17, 22; December 15, 15, 15, 15. In 1766 he conferred baptism on the following dates: January 6, 6, 8; March 10, 10, 10, 10; April 8, 9, 15, 15; June 6, 12, 12, 13, 13; October 7, 7; November 14; December 8, 8.

[61] Various dates have been assigned for the beginning of Sainte Genevieve as a white settlement. See *Jesuit Relations*, 70:316.

• "I know neither the family, nor the parish, nor where or when he was born."

The first entry in the St. Genevieve parish records is a baptism conferred May 13, 1764, on the son of Louis and Janette, negro slaves of Jean Baptiste Beauvais of Kaskaskia—the child was christened Louis. The first marriage, of which Meurin makes record under date of October 30th, 1764, is a very interesting case, the parties being Mark Constantinot [62] of Canada, and Susan Henn, of German parentage, who had settled in Pennsylvania. As both had been carried into slavery by the Shawnee Indians some five years previous, they contracted a natural marriage, which was blessed with two daughters. Availing themselves of a favorable opportunity for escape, they fled from captivity and on October 30th presented themselves to Father Meurin to have him pronounce the church's blessing on their union. It is of interest to note that Father Meurin styles himself "pretre missionaire," or "cure aux Illinois," or finally "cure aux pays des Illinois" while he designates the church in Sainte Genevieve as "l'Eglise de Saint Joachim aux Illinois," or "en la paroisse de St. Joachim de Ste. Genevieve aux Illinois," or "St. Joachim village de Ste. Genevieve" and finally "a Ste. Genevieve." The years 1766 and 1767 mark the period of his greatest activity in Ste. Genevieve as is evidenced by the parish records, for in 1766 be baptized thirty-one persons and married five couples, while in 1767 he baptized twenty-eight persons and married eight parties. A comparative study of his duties and activities at Sainte Genevieve and at Kaskaskia. as recorded in the official documents of both places is not without interest.[63] By a very curious mistake he records a marriage for June 31, 1766; as he uses numerals in the margin and words in the text his mistake is final. How would the courts regard a marriage registered in this erroneous manner? The last entry for this period in Father Meurin's hand is a baptism on October 22, 1768, after which Father Gibault cared for the spiritual wants of the people and Meurin kept away from Saint Genevieve, save on two occasions to be referred to later.

---

[62] An examination of the *Records of Sainte Genevieve* shows that the name of the man was Mark Constantinot of Canada, not Mark Constantino Canada as Houck has it in his *History of Missouri*, Vol. II, p. 297. Note 29.

[63] Baptisms, Kaskaskia, 1764. 11; 1765. 25; 1766, 21; 1767. 23: 1768. 14. Ste. Genevieve, 1764, 13; 1765, 14; 1766, 31; 1767. 28; 1768. 23. Marriages. Kaskaskia, 1764, 1; 1765, 6; 1766, 1; 1767, 5; 1768, 3. Ste. Genevieve, 1764, 2: 1765, 6; 1766, 5; 1767, 8; 1768, 5.

In a long letter to Bishop Briand of Quebec, dated March 23, 1767, Father Meurin testifies to his joy upon learning at Kaskaskia that his lordship had taken possession of the see of Quebec, asserting that his joy was so great that it almost made him forget his old age and his infirmities. After a sentence or two about the Illinois country he continues:

The country of the Illinois is nothing more than six villages of about fifty to eighty fires each not including the slaves whose number is sufficiently great. Each of these villages, on account of the distance between them and their situation, demands a priest; namely, in the English territory, the parish of the Immaculate Conception at Kaskaskia, that of St. Joseph at Prairie du Rocher, and the parish of the Holy Family of Cahokia or Tamaroa and that of the savages with the title of Holy Family. . . . . In the French or Spanish territory beyond the river are situated the villages of Ste. Genevieve with the title of St. Joachim on which are dependent the salines and the mines; and thirty leagues above is the new village called St. Louis which has been formed out of the ruins of St. Philippe and Fort de Chartres. These two villages are as large as the first in inhabitants or in slaves red or black. .

St. Joachim or Ste. Genevieve is the place of my residence as it was ordained by the conditions of my return to the country. It is from there that I come every springtime and go through the other villages for Easter. I return thither again in the autumn and every time that I am called for the sick. This is all my infirmities and my means can permit me. Still this is disagreeable and prejudicial to the people of Ste. Genevieve who alone nourish and support me; and they complain of it. With only these visits the people, and especially the children and slaves, are lacking sufficient instruction; and since they are deprived of the pastoral vigilance they are insensibly losing piety and abandoning themselves to vices. There are here still many families in which religion rules and who fear with reason that it will become extinct with them. They join in prayer with me that you have pity on their children and send them at least two or three priests if your highness cannot send the four or five that are needed. One of these should have the title of grand vicar of your highness. I try to maintain in my absence the use of the offices and prayers to assist in the sanctification of Sundays and saints' days. There are already a number who no longer attend church or who seem to come there only to show their lack of respect for it. Some intractable and insolent people say, haughtily enough, that I have no title, and that I am not their pastor, that I have no right to give them advice, and that they are not obliged to listen to me. They would not have dared to speak thus in the time of MM. Stirling and Farmer, commandants, from whom I had every protection. Under the command of these two first no person dared to attempt the least indecency.

The church of Ste. Anne has, for almost a year, been without roof, doors and windows and with walls broken or badly closed, because the church wardens have changed their home and village without informing me or having others elected; and they left the keys to the beadle who withdrew also and left them with an inhabitant and thus they pass from one to another. When finally I was informed I went there and demanded and obtained from the English commandant his consent to the removal of the furniture of the church of Ste. Anne

to the chapel of St. Joseph at Prairie du Rocher. I myself carried the sacred vessels, accompanied by the one to whom the keys had been given. Since I was unable to stay longer, I gave, by written commission, to the captain of the militia and three others named the right to betake themselves to the church of Ste. Anne and make there together an inventory, and to carry away the said furniture, etc., to their chapel where it was to remain in deposit until one could receive an answer and order from the ordinary. The commissioned men set out, wished to execute their commission, and met with opposition. There was petition upon petition from the two single inhabitants who remained there and assured the commandant that the church and furniture belonged to them personally. An order was given me to bring back the sacred vessels and to leave them all in the said church of Ste. Anne. I did not believe it my duty to go there. I wrote in the form of a petition drawn up in the name of your chapter, since I did not know that it should be done in the name of your highness; I was obliged to stand a suit; my adversaries insisted upon I know not what yet; I lost your suit; I wrote again; English judges were named and the process will be ended when it shall please God and your highness. The church is getting always in a worse condition; open on every side it has served, I am told, as a den for beasts during winter. The furniture and ornaments are still there and I know not in what state. I await your orders and the repentance of the opponents. The sacred vessels are still at Prairie du Rocher.

Post Vincennes on the Wabash, among the Miami Piankashaw, is as large as our best villages here and has still greater need of a missionary. Disorder has always been great there, but it has increased in the last three years. Some come here to be married or to make their Easter duty. The majority do not wish to, nor can they do it. The guardian of the church there[44] publishes the the banns for three Sundays; to those who wish to come here he gives a certificate of publication without opposition which I myself republish before marrying them. Those who do not wish to come declare in a loud voice in their church their mutual consent. Can such a marriage be permitted? Since there is no exception to the formal decree of the holy council of Trent on the reformation of marriage, I pray you instruct me. Does clandestinity render the marriage of heretics null, as it does that of Catholics? Can their resistance to the church exempt them from the laws of the church?

Before I returned to the Illinois, I was assured at New Orleans that Louisiana was not and would no longer be in the diocese of Quebec. I was made to promise and sign that I would no longer recognize other ecclesiastical superior than the reverend father superior of the Capuchins who alone had and would have all jurisdiction, that on the first occasion they would give me a certificate of it if I required. It is on this condition that I signed, adding that when it should please his holiness to give the jurisdiction to the highest chief of the Negroes I should be submissive to him as to one meriting more than bishops consequently as my signature was given upon the promise of a confirmation which has not yet come, I am bound no longer with any relations either with Rome or with Quebec. That is what has hindered me up to the present from writing to the grand vicars of the diocese, especially since I have not found a safe opportunity by land as I have today by MM. Despins and Bauvais, who are going to Montreal and should return this next autumn. They have volunteered to bring

[44] This was the faithful Philibert to whose work reference will be made later.

at their own expense the missionaries you appoint for this place and the parishioners have promised to reimburse them. The great need of missionaries for this country has forced me to strike at all doors in order to obtain some. . . . . While I am awaiting for the effects of your pastoral charity I shall continue to make use of the former powers which I received from M. Mercier twenty-five years ago, which have been continued by MM. Laurent and Forget the latter of whom verbally left me at his departure all that he had received. The grand vicar whom you will send to us will limit them as he shall judge fitting and will find me, as did his predecessors, with all zeal and all possible respect, by lord, your highness' very humble and very obedient servant, Sebastian Louis Meurin, missionary priest.[65]

This long detailed letter enables us to form some concept of the spiritual and moral havoc wrought by the decree which expelled the missionaries, and of the unique difficulties which confronted Father Meurin upon his return. It is indeed a sad picture that the devoted priest paints for his bishop. In the light of the facts and conditions revealed here we can readily perceive that Meurin's insistent and persistent appeals for immediate help were the only logical course of procedure if the souls of these people were to be rescued from perdition. The danger was great and called for instant relief.

Notwithstanding the fact that the people of his chief parish took exception to his apostolic journeys, Father Meurin continued his visits to Kaskaskia, Cahokia and Prairie du Rocher.[66] We have already seen something about his activity at Kaskaskia. He likewise cared for the numerous Indian villages on either side of the great river, but he appears not to have journeyed to Vincennes.[67] His conduct does not occasion surprise when we become acquainted with the condition that obtained; indeed, any other line of conduct would have been at variance with his previous solicitous regard for the missions, and the withdrawal of M. Forget du Verger and the Fathers of the Foreign Missions from Cahokia—an act characterized by Bishop Briand as criminal,[68] there had remained but two priest to the Cath-

---

[65] Alvord and Carter, *The New Regime*, pp. 522-529.
[66] Father Meurin's first baptism recorded in the Prairie du Rocher Records is for February 5, 1765, his second for May 16, 1766. Previous to February 5, 1765, and between that date and May 16, 1766, a number of entries were made and signed by Ayme Comte and later countersigned by Father Meurin. Comts appears to have made the entries for Father Luke and Father Hypolitte Collet; he knew that these two Fathers were Recollects; he does not seem to have taken the trouble to inquire to what religious order Father Meurin belonged; hence he likewise calls him a recollect priest. Later on Father Meurin countersigned these entries in which he is styled a "recollect priest."
[67] Shea, *op. cit.*, Vol. II, p. 117.
[68] Alvord and Carter, *The New Regime*, p. 559.

olics of Indiana and Illinois, Father Hippolyte and Luke Collet of the order of Saint Francis, stationed at Fort Chartres. Father Luke occasionally administered the sacraments during Father Meurin's absence in New Orleans and during his subsequent residence at Sainte Genevieve, but when Father Luke passed to his reward Sept. 10, 1768, a year after the death of his brother, Father Meurin was the only priest between the Great Lakes and New Orleans. This was his singular privilege, this his burden till the arrival of Father Gibault. But no one man, however zealous and active he might be, could give each of the missions the attention or the attendance it required under the circumstances; still less could an old man, worn out by the hardships of long years of missionary life do it. That the people realized the grave danger which confronted them we learn from a letter of Captain Thomas Stirling to General Gage:

> The Inhabitants Complain very much for want of Priests, there is but One now remains, the rest either having died or gone away, and he stays on the other Side, he was formerly a Jesuit & would have been sent away likewise if the Caskaskias Indians, to whom he was Priest; had not insisted on his Staying, which the French allowed him to do upon his renouncing Jesuitism and turning Sulpitien, this Priest might be of great Use to us, if he was brought over to this Side, which I make no doubt might be effectuated, provided his former appointments were allowed him, which was 600 Livres pr Annum from the King, as Priest to the Indians.[*]

Now if we bear these facts in mind we can understand why Father Meurin, who was thoroughly aware of the conditions prevailing, should write to Quebec and urge Bishop Briand to send "at least two or three priests if your highness cannot send the four or five that are needed," or that he should at the same time have sent letters of like import and insistance to the Capuchin Fathers, to the Jesuit Fathers in Philadelphia,[70] and to the Abbe de l'Isle Dieu in Paris. For the same reasons he expressed the hope that of the priests to be sent one be appointed vicar-general to facilitate work in the missions. This letter was followed by another two months later, May 9th, in which he once more pleaded with his bishop and besought him to send help at once, complained of the obstacles raised by some malicious persons, called attention to his physical infirmities and his consequent inability to accomplish the impossible task assigned him.

* Alvord and Carter, op. cit., p. 124-125.
70 Unsuccessful efforts to find this letter have been made at Saint Joseph's College and Church, Philadelphia, at Loyola College, Baltimore, at Georgetown University, and at Woodstock College, Woodstock, Maryland.

I represented to your highness my situation, in part, in the country of the Illinois where I have been the only priest, without name, without acknowledgment, without protection from any government, temporal or ecclesiastical, for three years without redress, receiving succor only from God alone who has sustained me against the calumnies, the wickedness, and ungodly acts of several persons who, thanks to God, have not triumphed but whom also I have not been able to repress so much as would have been good for their welfare and, perhaps, for that of many others.

I am sixty-one years old, but I am exhausted and ruined by mission work in this country for twenty-five years, for nearly twenty years of which sickness and infirmities have shown me day by day the gates of death, so that it is only for the last five years that I have been able to make use of life. I am no longer capable of long application or bodily fatigue. I can no longer supply the spiritual needs of this country where the most robust man could not serve long, especially since it is divided by a very rapid and dangerous river.

Four priests are necessary; if you can give only one, he should be appointed for Kaskaskia. At this moment I am called on to go to a man who is dangerously ill at Ste. Genevieve, thirty leagues from Cahokia where I have been only three days. I am forced to leave undone more than three-fourths of the work to be done here. I beg you, my lord, to have pity on this part of your flock and on me who have the honor to be with all possible respect and submission, the very humble and very obedient servant of your highness.[71]

But before this second letter could have reached Quebec the bishop had already answered the previous letter by appointing Meurin himself to the position of vicar-general. Who can picture the astonishment of the lowly missionary when in August he himself received the official notice of appointment as vicar-general! The bishop begins his letter of April 28, written in French, by testifying to his joy at learning that there "was a Jesuit left in the unhappy countries of the Illinois and Mississippi."[72] Then after a few words concerning his grief at the dismissal of the Jesuits, his fears for the fate of the missions because of the retreat of the other priests and "his consolation at having learned that the poor inhabitants of Illinois are not entirely deprived of spiritual succor" he continues in a strain very complimentary to Canada's new masters:

I bless the Lord a thousand times for inspiring the English with goodness and veneration for you so that they permitted your ministrations. We enjoy the same favor, and hardly notice that we are under a Protestant prince. It must be admitted that no nation like the English possesses humanity and all the virtues which flow from it.[73]

We may remark here in passing that Father Meurin's subsequent experiences forced him to differ somewhat from the sentiments ex-

[71] Alvord and Carter, op. cit., pp. 568-569.
[72] Alvord and Carter, op. cit., p. 559.
[73] Alvord and Carter, op. cit., pp. 559.

pressed by his bishop, at least as regards life under a Protestant prince. Here follows the notice of appointment to the dignity of vicar-general:

> I send you letters of appointment as grand vicar in the most extended terms; you will use them wherever you may chance to be throughout this part of my diocese whose limits are immense and unknown even to myself; at least it is certain that they extend to all lands which the French have possessed in North America.[14]

After some remarks about the Capuchins and Ursulines in New Orleans his grace continues:

> If you think that the government authorizes and supports you, you could use your powers even in New Orleans, and exercise there your authority over the whole secular and regular clergy which may be there, and nominate for the sisters the confessor whom they wish, and give limited letters as grand vicar to one of the Capuchins whom you judge most worthy[15]

The official Latin document, which was probably enclosed with the French letter, enumerates in detail the extensive powers conferred on the lowly missionary whose sole ambition was to secure the salvation of the souls of the Indians, French colonists and their negro slaves. The translation runs as follows:

> By divine mercy and the grace of the Holy See, bishop of Quebec and honorary canon of the church of Tours to our beloved in Christ, Father Sebastian Meurin, priest of the Society of Jesus, salutation and benediction in our Lord.
>
> It is impossible in this, our so large and widely scattered diocese, to accomplish directly through our own efforts everything that belongs to the office of the episcopal ministry. Wherefore, because we desire to satisfy in the best way we can our obligations towards the people committed to our care, we have taken care to select some men to whom we believe we could intrust our power which we have a right to delegate. Therefore, we, moved by these causes and reasons most powerfully and trusting in your knowledge, prudence, honesty, and integrity, especially in the Lord, and hoping that you will exercise with zealous solicitude those things which we are induced to commit to your charge, make, constitute, create, and ordain, by these presents, you who are beloved by us in Christ, Father Sebastain Meurin, priest of the Society of Jesus, our vicar general both in spiritual and temporal affairs for everything and for single things in places which are commonly known as Tamaroa, Illinois, and New Orleans; and we give you power to rule and govern all the adjacent places and whatever other ones lie adjacent and are dependent on these whether they are under the power of the French, the English, or the Spanish, yet only in so far as they are contained within the limits of our diocese. We give you the power of visiting and correcting, of conducting and executing everything which pertains to the duty of such visitation, of determining and deciding, not only of those things which

---

[14] Alvord and Carter, *op. cit.*, p. 560.
[15] Alvord and Carter, *op. cit.*, p. 561.

are necessary but useful, of preaching the word of God, and to this preaching
we add the power of hearing the confessions of the faithful and even of the
moniales (1) [sic Alvord] and of appointing confessors to hear these, of examining and approving both the secular and regular clergy and of imposing ecclesiastical censure, of absolving from the same censure even of cases reserved for
censure by us, by yourself and others to whom you may wish to concede this power
of administering all sacraments, with the exception of the confession and ordination[16] and of conceding the right to administer them, of giving dispensation in
vows and oaths where there is just cause, of blessing chapels, cemeteries, and
other places dedicated to divine worship, of restoring those places which are
polluted or profamed or of performing through yourself or others all and every
kind of benediction even those reserved to us, of giving dispensation in all cases
of impediments prohibiting or preventing marriage, especially blood relationship
and affinity of the second grade, and besides in the case of the publications of
banns, finally, of saying, carrying on, deciding and executing in the aforesaid
places to prevent delays, as much for the secular and regular clergy as for the
laity, everything which we ourselves if we were present would say, do, determine,
and execute; and we promise that we shall hold as settled whatever shall have
been done or put in execution by you, our beloved Father Meurin of the Society
of Jesus, our vicar general. The present power shall be valid even up to the
time of its revocation by command.

Given at Quebec under our sign and seal and the subscription of our
secretary and witnesses called for this purpose, April 28, 1761.

JEAN OLIVIER, Bishop of Quebec.[17]

Father Meurin's letters of March 23rd and May 9th evoked from
his ordinary a brief reply on August 7th, as well as a vigorous pastoral
of the same date, addressed to the people of Kaskaskia. In the letter
the bishop exhorts the missionary to perseverance in his apostolic
work despite the obstacles encountered and the sorrows occasioned
by the behavior of certain wayward members of his flock; he urges
him to suffer all this for the sake of God; he makes known his
intention of sending two priests the following year; finally, he replies
to the questions concerning marriage.

In regard to the case of conscience which you propose to me about the
secret marriages, I have no doubt, on authority of the doctors of the Sorbonne
consulted on the question, that the secret marriage of Catholics in your parts
is invalid, except in case of the impossibility of contracting before you. Now
according to the map of your parishes which you made for me, they have always
been able to come and present themselves before you or at least they could have
waited for you, since you have visited them every year. You must make them
renew their consent in your presence according to the rules of the Church and

---

[16] The original Latin document reads: "sacramenta quaecumque confirma-
tione et ordine exceptis adminstrandi aut ad illa administranda licentiam con-
cedere." Evidently, therefore, Mr. Alvord is seriously in error in denying to
Father Meurin the power of administering the Sacrament of Confession.

[17] Alvord and Carter, op. cit., pp.562-565.

I know that you will act in this with the discretion which I discern in you. You must not judge the same about the marriage of the heretic with the Catholic; it is valid even if secret *positis aliunde ponendis.* Such is the decision of the same doctors based on a declaration of the late Pope Benedict XIV about the year 1741 deciding both cases for Holland.[18]

The pastoral letter to the people of Kaskaskia is a model of forceful language; the purpose of his lordship is unmistakable.

About two months ago, my very dear children, I wrote to Rev. Father Meurin to intrust to him my powers of grand vicar. I write to him again to confirm them anew. My will is that you obey him as you would me. I intend to send you in the coming spring one or two missionaries to help him in uprooting among you the vices which I know exist there, because I have been told that the spirit of piety was indeed dim among you. When Father Meurin gives himself the trouble to visit you, many do not go to church, or go there only to show lack of respect. There are even disobedient persons who in some parishes where he officiates refuse to recognize him as a priest, saying he has no right to give them advice and that they are not obliged to listen to him. Others have the boldness to get married without having their marriage blessed by the priest. I am writing to Father Meurin to put a stop to all these disorders; or rather, my dear children, it is to yourselves that I address myself with confidence; it is to those among you who are most Christian—for I hear with comfort that there are among you families where religion shines with brilliancy— it is those, I say, whom I wish to remind here that Jesus Christ has confided to everyone of us the care of his neighbor.[19]

The remainder of the pastoral is an earnest exhortation to virtue and righteous living and a threat by the bishop to send no more laborers to this portion of the diocese of Quebec if the Kaskaskians disregard his counsels or fail to pay due respect and obedience to his vicar.

His new dignity soon involved Father Meurin in difficulties with the Spanish officials at Ste. Genevieve, when, in accordance with episcopal instructions he proceeded to celebrate a jubilee to commemorate the accession of Bishop Briand to the see of Quebec. Although he resided in Spanish territory he enjoyed jurisdiction from Quebec; consequently his jurisdiction was first challenged, then denied. As is evident from one of his letters, the bishop of Quebec, now a British subject, claimed jurisdiction over all lands which the French had formerly possessed in North America, whether they happened to be under the power of the French, the English or the Spanish, because the Holy See, the only competent authority in the matter, had not altered the boundaries of his diocese upon the

18 Alvord and Carter, *op. cit.,* pp. 588-589.
19 Alvord and Carter, *op. cit.,* pp. 589-590.

ratification of the peace terms. But the Spanish authorities, considering the question as political rather than canonical, would recognize
no English bishop and no ecclesiastical jurisdiction save that of the
archbishop of San Domingo, because they contended that all territory
west of the Mississippi now belonged to the jurisdiction of his grace
of San Domingo.[80]

Such was the attitude of the ill-starred Philippe François de
Rastel, Chevalier de Rocheblave,[81] commandant at Sainte Genevieve;
He declared Father Meurin a state criminal because he recognized a
jurisdiction not admitted by Spain, and issued a warrant for his
arrest, an act for which the holy missionary secured the revenge
becoming a priest of God when he returned to Sainte Genevieve
some years later to baptize the infant daughter of his persecutor.
Warned in due time by a faithful friend among the authorities,
Meurin fled from Sainte Genevieve, sought refuge among the English,
who seem to have welcomed him, took without delay the oath of
allegiance to the English government, and made his home at Kaskaskia. When did all this occur? It is difficult to establish the precise
date of Meurin's flight from Sainte Genevieve, but as his last marriage entry in the parish records is for May 17, 1768, while the last
baptisms recorded in his hand are for October 19 and 22, 1768,
when he styles himself "pretre missionaire aux pays des Illinois,"
we must conclude that he fled about the end of October. In his
letter of June 14, 1769 to Bishop Briand he says he came to Cahokia
in the autumn. It is true that three baptisms are recorded for
August 7, one for August 8, and two for August 20, but it is highly
improbable that if he left after this date he would have returned
in October and defied the Spanish officials so shortly after the issuing
of the warrant for his arrest.

---

[80] Houck, Louis, op. cit., Vol. II, p. 296.

[81] Houck, Louis, op. cit., Vol. I, p. 340. "Philip de Rocheblave was in command at Kaskaskia when General George Rogers Clark invaded Illinois, and
conquered the Northwest; sent as a prisoner to Williamsburg, Virginia, where
he broke his parol and fled to New York; he was a member of the noble
Canadian family, Rocheblave de Rastel. After the transfer of Upper Louisiana
to Spain, he seems to have returned to Kaskaskia; entered the British service
and attained the rank of colonel in the British army. The mother of Rocheblave
was Lady Diana Francoise Elizabeth de Dillon; his father's name was Jean
Joseph du Rastel. . . . . In 1773 Father Meurin, then Parish priest at Ste.
Genevieve, baptized his infant daughter, Rosalie, and Father Hilaire a son in
1774 named Henri." Houck is not quite correct in styling Father Meurin parish
priest of Sainte Genevieve in 1773; our text demonstrates that if any one
enjoyed this title it was Father Gibault.

The action of the Spanish authorities has given occasion to an interesting discussion as to the source from which Father Meurin actually derived his jurisdiction to exercise the ministry west of the Mississippi. The Rev. James J. Conway, S. J., who has treated this subject learnedly and at length contends "that there never existed any misgivings in Father Meurin's own mind as to the source of his jurisdiction on the west bank of the Mississippi."[82] Father Conway observes that previous to the destruction of the missions and the journey to New Orleans, Meurin and every priest in the Mississippi Valley was under the episcopal jurisdiction of the bishop of Quebec. Nor had the peace treaties affected ecclesiastical boundaries; indeed, Briand's episcopal jurisdiction was acknowledged by the Treaty of Paris and the Quebec act and was everywhere recognized in what was formerly French dominion in North America.[83] Though the west bank of the Mississippi had become Spanish territory politically it did not follow that nore but prelates of Spanish nationality or sympathy could exercise jurdistion there. Being fully aware of the possibility of dangers and difficulties arising in the future, Father Meurin, before his return from New Orleans, took all possible precautions by obtaining a verbal renewal of faculties from the Rev. Duverger, vicar-general of Illinois for the secular clergy, and sought and obtained a renewal of the same faculties from his former superior, Father Watrin, vicar-general for the Jesuits in Illinois,[84] in addition to the paper he had signed recognizing the superior of the Capuchins at New Orleans. After a lengthy discussion of this interesting case Father Conway concludes, "Look at it as we may the jurisdiction which Father Meurin possessed when he returned to the Illinois Mission in 1764, and which he exercised for the first time in Saint Louis in April and May 1766 was not a two-fold jurisdiction, but a single jurisdiction emanating from Quebec, and delegated to him from his former religious superior, Watrin, or from the former vicar-general, Duverger, or, as is most probable, from both, as the vicars-general of the bishop of Quebec."[85] Of course the exceptional powers granted him by the Sovereign Pontiff on the advice of the Holy Office were his independently of local superiors.

At Kaskaskia Father Meurin enjoyed liberty, no Spanish authorities could molest him or interfere with his ministry, but the English Protestant authorities would not bind themselves to the observance

---

[82] Conway, J. J., S. J., op. cit., p. 8.
[83] Conway, J. J., S. J., op. cit., p. 9.
[84] Conway, J. J., S. J., op. cit., p. 12.
[85] Conway, J. J., S. J., op. cit., pp. 15-16.

of certain ecclesiastical customs which had obtained under the French regime. He was growing old; the arduous labors of a long period of service had sapped his vitality, and, alone, he had to attend to the spiritual needs of a vast territory. These facts, together with a partial acquaintance with colonial conditions, banish all suspicion that he was given to exaggeration or stressed unduly the difficulties he had to face. A man of his years and experience was more apt to judge the situation correctly than a young or less experienced man.

In a long letter to Bishop Briand, on June 11, 1768, Father Meurin acknowledges the receipt of his lordship's letters and the unexpected appointment to the dignity and duties of vicar-general. After calling attention to the physical infirmities which interrupted and impeded his work, he touches upon the mooted question of jurisdiction in New Orleans, communicates the reasons which neces-situated his precipitate flight from Sainte Genevieve, makes known the misunderstandings and friction which have arisen over the property formerly belonging to the Jesuits and the missions, recounts several instances of divergence of opinion with the local British authorities, and, finally, questions his bishop concerning the priestly office, the use of the Protestant Bible in administering oaths, etc., etc. He writes:

I would almost wish that my self-esteem might prevent me from telling you, Monseigneur, that I am as unworthy as anyone can be of the honor which you confer on me; and more than ever incapable of such an office, of which I know but the name. I have never been acquainted with any jurisprudence, either notarial, pontifical, or any other. I have been too long left to myself, and I barely know the duties of a simple priest. It is no longer possible for me to learn anything else.

My letters of last spring must have omitted to inform you of my age, and of my weakness of body and mind. I retain only a small portion of a weak judgment, have no memory, and possess still less firmness. I Need a guide for the soul and for the body; for my eyes, my ears, and my legs are likewise very feeble. I am no longer good for anything but to be laid in the ground. · · · · ·
About a month ago, having learned that Sieur Jautard' (second purchaser of the property of the mission of ste. famille among the Kaskias,[bb] sold to sieur Lagrange by monsieur Forget, vicar-general of your predecessor, and missionary curate in the said parish, etc.) was bargaining to resell it to an Englishman, I went to oppose the sale on behalf of the gentlemen of your Seminary, who claim this property as still belonging to them, through its having been sold, without their power of attorney and without their knowledge, by the person who was but the steward thereof. I also undertook to support by the use of

[bb] The property here referred to was that of the mission among the Kaskias Indians at Cahokia.

your name, Monseigneur, my contention for the preservation of all property belonging to the Churches for their maintenance and that of the missionaries whom You deign to employ. Mr. forbes, the commandant (there is no civil government here, as yet), asked me for the letters containing my commission; I showed him your letters, and those of Monsieur the superior. As regards the letters conferring the appointment of Vicar-general, he replied that, inasmuch as Monsieur de gages had given no instructions respecting the episcopacy and the office of vicar-general, he could not take cognizance of them; and that this seemed purely a scheme on your part and mine. He therefore expressly forbade me to use the letters, or to assume the title of vicar-general in any letter, or deed, or in public, until he should receive an answer from his general regarding both your jurisdiction in the country, and the Kaskias property. He promised me, however, that the latter should not be offered for sale until then. Sieur jautard goes to Canada, and thence to new york or london, to obtain release from the possession of the said estate. The land at fort chartres is also, for the same reason, in danger of being carried away by the river. . . . .

There is also in this village of the Kaskias, the property of the Jesuits which was unduly seized, confiscated, and sold by the french government after the cession of the country to england. If your lordship or Your missionaries in Canada wish to revindicate it. [sic.] As for. myself I ask nothing; I am too old. But I would always be grieved to see the chapel and Cemetery profaned, being used as a garden and storehouse by the english, who rent them from Sieur Jean Baptiste Bauvais—who, under the decree of confiscation and the contract of the sale and purchase of the property, etc., was obliged to demolish the chapel and leave its site and that of the cemetery uncultivated under the debris. He says that the subdelegate, the executor of the decree, has since sold the property to him. By what Right? The presses used for the vestments and sacred vessels are now used in his apartments, as well as the altar-cruets and the floor, etc.

My continual reproaches to him on that score have kept him away from me and from the sacraments for three years. I beg you to give me a decision on this, and to say whether, in case of his presenting himself to me or to another, he can be granted absolution and be dispensed from handing over the said articles to the parish church. That is my only request; for I believe that he bought the remainder in good faith—but not the chapel and its furniture, which, according to the decree, were to be destroyed and burned. I beg you to decide as judge or supreme authority.

During the four years while I have administered to these english parishes, I have received no tithes therefrom: I have received naught but what was given me out of charity by some, and the fees for masses. I have always exhorted them to pay the Tithes to the fabrique[M] for the support of the Churches and the missionary, when one comes. They, I mean the rich ones, have always claimed that they owe nothing where there is no resident pastor. I beg you to decide the Case; otherwise, three missionaries would be unable to live in a suitable manner, or would be compelled to leave some villages abandoned. I shall soon be unable to do anything more. Threatened beforehand, as I am, with being cast out when others come, I wish all the more ardently for them. I have always had the poor on my side. Priests will be at least as charitable as they, and God will assist me through them; or, if he prefer,—and that would be more advantageous

" Jesuit Relations, 71:389 note.

to me,—he will cause me to share his abandonment. If you deem advisable, you will assign me a place or a corner in one of the clergy houses of the country, for which I tender you in advance my most humble thanks,—happy if I can have the consolation of Christians, dying with jesus Christ in the hands of one of his ministers.

This is on the supposition that the government would suffer my presence here; for Father Harding, the superior in philadelphia, wrote me last autumn that there were warnings and signs that the jesuits were about to be trated in england as in france, spain, portugal, and prussia, and he bade me farewell, fearing that he would have no other opportunity of doing so. Why am I not a great enough enemy of the devil to deserve such a treatment for the 3rd time? I forgot last year to ask you whether in the public prayers, at the benediction, etc. The orison pro rege, etc., is said, and the Te Deum, if occasion arise. The question is asked Whether,—this has not happened hitherto,—when oaths are administered, roman catholics can swear on the protestant bible, owing to the falsities in it, etc. The protestants are often present at our holy mysteries, masses, and benedictions, standing during the time of adoration, Elevation, and Benediction of the blessed sacrament, and also when it is carried to the sick, etc. The first two commandants, Messieurs Sterling and farmer, [illegible word in the MS..] prayer, had forbidden their people to attend our prayers,—at least, unless they were willing to do as the roman catholics did. You can perhaps obtain the same order from the government. Our last two commandants in no wise resemble the first two. They forbade me to marry any one without a license, for which Mr. Reed charged 6 piasters,—five being for him, and one for his secretary. The present one charges only for the secretary. Is it the custom in Canada not to marry Catholics without the permission of the magistrate, or of the commandant who fills his office?

Since the English have taken possession of this country, there has been as yet no procession of the blessed sacrament (illegible words in the MS.) on the other side french, spanish, english.) This year, at the request of the inhabitants, I asked messiurs the commandants to allow the militia to turn out under arms, as is the custom among roman catholics, to escort the blessed sacrament. This they refused. The weather was not settled; I was indisposed and fatigued, through having had a procession very early on the other side at ste. genevieve. Here I had one only in the church, and likewise on the day of the octave. . . . . I have on several occasions been puzzled with reference to the quebec calendar, and the transfer of feasts, as I have found no one who could instruct me on the point. The only answer Monsieur forget could give us in our difficulties was, that he knew nothing about it, and that Monseigneur the bishop had often been at fault in the matter. 1st. Do feasts transferred to a sunday retain a double, which is marked therefor? 2nd. Do those which have an octave retain it entire, commencing from the day to which the feast is transferred? . . . . In what does the solemnity of st. thomas consist, on the sunday before christmas? Monsieur forget assured us that the solemnity consisted not only in abstaining from work, but perhaps also in the vestments, lights, sermons, and other things which he did not know. I beg you to decide for us these matters explicitely; for I am very Obtuse and Shortsighted, to say the least, and am quite overcome by the too heavy burden that you have placed on my shoulders."

" Jesuit Relations, 71:33-47 passim.

From this long letter we discover moreover that at this time the Mississippi threatened the chapel at Fort Chartres, over which Meurin had charge, and that because of the imminent peril, he had the remains of Rev. M. Gagnon and Rev. Luke Collet, who had been buried in the chapel, removed to safety to the higher ground at Prairie du Rocher,[88] a work of mercy which found its reward subsequently in the tender care bestowed upon his own remains by those who succeeded him as pastors in this region.

(*To be continued*)

CHARLES H. METZGER, S. J.

St. Louis University,
St. Louis, Mo.

---

[88] Records of the Church of St. Joseph, Prairie due Rocher. ''L'an mil sept cent soixante huit le vingt quatrieme jour du mois de Mai je soussigné prêtre de la Compagnie de Jésus Vicaire Général de Msgr. L'évêque de Quebec ayant (vu) la ruine prochaine de l'église de Ste. Anne au fort de Chartres sur le point (de tomber) dans le fleuve, en ai fait déterrer et transporter en la Chapelle de St. Joseph a la Prairie du Rocher pour y etre inhumés de nouveau les corps de Monsieur Gagnon: prêtre curé du Fort de Chartres et dépendances lequel on a inhumé près du sanctuaire du côté de l'évangile avec les cérémonies accoutuméés. Le même jour (et en) même temps j'ai rendu le même honneur au corps du Révérend Pere Luc que j'ai inhumé du coté de l'épitre près du sanctuaire de la ditte chapelle en presence des habitants qui y ont assistés avec grands sentiments de reconnaisance pour leurs (curés, services?) en foi de quoi j'ai signé le présent avec les srs Barbeau et Lecomte.

            S. L. MEURIN, Vicaire Général.
   Barbau   Ayme Conte.
(In the margin opposite the above):
 24 Mai translation des corps de Mr. Gagnon et du R. P. Luc en la chapelle St. Joseph a la Prairie du Rocher. On mis sure le corps de Mr. Gagnon une pierre gravée
      M + G.
 Sur le corps du R. P. Luc une pierre gravée
      +
     R. P. L.
It should be noted that the pages of this record are not numbered.

DIOCESE OF ST. LOUIS UNDER
BISHOP ROSATI

X. FATHER HILARY TUCKER

We must now once more retrace our course and take up the story of Quincy in 1839. As we have seen there were two parishes in the city, the German congregation under Father Florentine Brickwedde, and the English-speaking one under Father Irenaeus St. Cyr, but for the present, worshipping with their German brethren in Father Brickwedde's humble church. But on the 23rd of May, 1839, there came a momentous change. Father Hilary Tucker, a native American, of Maryland-Kentucky stock, was appointed pastor of the English-speaking Catholics of Quincy and the adjoining missions, and remained their until the close of 1845, two years after Quincy's incorporation in the new diocese of Chicago.

As the Parish of St. Boniface, originally called the Ascension Parish, was the first church in the Mississippi Valley established for German Catholics, exclusively, and as it opened the long series of German-American Parochial Schools, we will have to treat its history in the next chapter. Here we shall confine ourselvse to Father Tucker's activities in Quincy and its dependent missions:

Hilary Tucker was a son of Nicholas Tucker of Perryville, grandson of Joseph Tucker, one of the pioneers of Perry County. Old Mr. Joseph Tucker, as he is called, came to Missouri in June, 1802, on a visit to Isidore Moore, who had established himself near Perryville in 1801. He was soon followed by his sons, among them Nicholas, the father of Hilary and of Lewis, the future pastor of Fredericktown. The first chapel in Perry County had been built and blessed in 1912 by the Rev. James Maxwell, Vicar General, who attended the place from Ste. Genevieve until his death in 1814. Before 1812 Mass had occasionally been said at the home of Old Joseph Tucker. After 1814 the Trappist, Marie Joseph Dunand, visited Perryville at regular intervals, from his parish of Florissant, and made his home, for the time being, with Old Joseph Tucker, who, as Father Dunand states, had eight sons and one daughter, all except the youngest married and "settled about him in good homes." Father Dunand is full of praise for these excellent people. "I enquired," says he, "how they, living in such a secluded place, had passed their Sundays and Holy days

389

without Mass. They answered that on these days all the families of the district assembled three times; the first time they recited the prayers of the Mass; the second time they recited the beads or other prayers, and followed this by singing hymns and canticles; and the third time some one of the better instructed taught catechism, not only to the children, but to the married folks as well. I could not help admiring this beautiful arrangement, which the Holy Spirit, who is the Spirit of righteousness and simplicity, has established among these pious planters, so simple and so free from malice. I imagined myself carried back to that blessed epoch of the birth of the Church. I fancied I saw these first Christians instructed by the Apostles and so united by their charity that they were but one heart and one soul. I would have liked well to have remained with such good people and to have chosen this holy spot for my home, but Divine Providence called me elsewhere."

Coming of such good Catholic stock and falling under the influence of such a *zelator animarum* as Father Dunand was, the youthful Hilary felt himself called to the sacred ministry. What made the project easier of accomplishment was the fact that through the influence of the Trappist monk, Bishop Du Bourg, had been induced to found his Seminary of St. Mary of the Barrens, in the immediate neighborhood of the Tucker settlement. Both Lewis and Hilary Tucker entered the seminary. Hilary was two years younger than his brother, being born in 1808, and whilst Lewis continued his studies at the Barrens, Hilary was chosen by Bishop Rosati to take his course of philosophy and theology at the Propaganda in Rome. Of his stay there the letters will give ample information.

The two young men were to start for Rome in the year 1831, but a delay of one year was brought about by the rumors of revolution in Italy, and the fact that the cholera was raging in Europe. But young Hilary wrote his bishop a reassuring letter, full of the easy familiarity of youth:

The cholera, I think, should not deter us from the journey, for in all probability our own country will be subject to it. So by remaining here we shall run the same risk as by going to Europe and, if it should please God that we should die, Italy can give us a grave as well as Missouri.

Arriving at Rome they were very kindly received by Father Paul Cullen, the future Cardinal Archbishop of Dublin, and treated with distinguished consideration. They soon felt perfectly at home in their new surroundings, though at times a tinge of homesickness colors the flow of their voluble letters:

Think not, writes Hilary Tucker, that the immense ocean and the great distance which now separates us diminishes in the least my love for you all; on the contrary I find by experience that the farther I am removed from you the dearer I find the ties of love and affection for you all without exception. Yet I do not desire to return home, for I see such a field of science before me with so many facilities which I never before imagined, that I cannot permit such a thought to enter my mind at present.

Still the interests of their native diocese and of its bishop, their friend and father, were always uppermost in the hearts of both Hilary Tucker and George Hamilton:

I am really overjoyed to hear of the progress Catholicity is making in my country, and especially in Missouri. Although our Holy Religion is attacked and persecuted by our poor misguided brethren of the Protestant faith, I think that we have reason rather to rejoice than to lament on this account. For our Holy Religion will always flourish and gain strength from persecution, and I should certainly tremble for her had she no enemies. This is a remark made to me by Mr. Connelly and one which first induced him to examine the tenets of Catholicity. For, said he, I thought that a religion persecuted as the Catholic Religion has been, could not stand out against so many tempests, were it not the true one. I am well aware of the disadvantages under which religion labors in my country on account of the great scarcity of native clergy, of which you spoke with so much reason in your last letter. Would to God that more would take into serious consideration the great importance of this object. The American character seems too much engaged in worldly and commercial affairs to think of engaging in the clerical profession. However, notwithstanding all this, I really do yet entertain hopes that, before many years, our country will be able to produce a respectable body of efficient natives for the ministry, for I am persuaded that when they can be convinced of the real importance of this matter, that we will have no longer to lament this great defect. I am sorry that Charles should be the first to dishonor my family by relinquishing so sublime a calling, however, I know not his motives for so doing.

Another short passage from the Roman letters of Hilary Tucker, and we are done with this part of our subject:

The rector was so good as to show me your letter, which you wrote to him. He tells me that he will do all in his power to procure two German priests for your diocese. He desired very much to obtain two from the German College in Rome, for they are all men who have the true Apostolic spirit, and I have no scruple in saying that those educated in the German College in Rome are, generally speaking, the best adapted for our missions of any in the world.

In reading these extracts from Father Tucker's early correspondence we must not expect too much, remembering that the writer was at the time only a student, though of superior talents, yet lacking the wider views of life. One circumstance, however, will please all readers, the familiar tone of the letters, easy and free, yet most respectful, showing in a particular case, the beautiful friendship

existing between the first Bishop of St. Louis and all his co-laborers in the great work.

He was raised to the priesthood in July 2, 1837, and waiting for the delayed ordination of his friend and companion George A. Hamilton, he returned with him to St. Louis, where the privations and hardships of a missionary life awaited them.

Receiving his faculties on November 20, 1838, Father Hilary Tucker was sent to Quincy as pastor for the English-speaking Catholics. Father Lefevre, afterwards Bishop of Detroit, had been at Quincy on various occasions, then Father Brickwedde had established a parish, but being a German, was not altogether acceptable to the English-speaking Catholics. Consequently, the youthful Father Hilary Tucker was sent there to found a separate parish for them, leaving the Germans to Father Brickwedde, May 23, 1839.

Father Tucker's zeal and learning met with immediate success. In a short time he collected $2,000 for a new church; a lot was donated and a brick building begun. The parish was dedicated to St. Lawrence. A good part of the funds came from the Irish Catholics employed on the construction of the so-called Northern Cross Railroad, and the hopes for the future prosperity of St. Lawrence Church were based on the same railroad venture. But the Northern Cross Railroad Company failed; and the church was hardly completed when it was sold under a lien by the contractor, Brittenham. Still, by some amicable arrangement, the church continued to be used by the congregation, and Father Hilary Tucker remained as pastor until 1846. In 1840 Father Tucker received permission to go on a collecting trip for the benefit of his church, on which he achieved good results, so that the parish soon recovered from its early disaster.

We have a number of Father Hilary Tucker's letters covering the period of his ministry in Quincy from June 13, 1839 to September 27, 1840. According to our plan in the sketches we will publish them just as they were written, adding here and there a word of comment or elucidation:

Quincy, June 13, 1839.

Rt. Rev. Sir:

I write to you now to give you an account of the manner we are proceeding in. As soon as I returned we immediately began to make preparations for the building of our new church.

The laying of the corner stone, as you may judge, was not as grand as that of Trinity Church in St. Louis. I simply blessed it according to the prescriptions of the ritual, and there was but little ceremony about it. The foundations are fast progressing, and the stonework will be completed in seven or eight days from this. Contracts have been made, signed and sealed for the

brick and carpenter work. Messers Davidson, Hicks and McCombs will do the brick work, and Messrs. Osburn and Brittenham the carpenter work, the last mentioned do it at the rate of 70 per cent on the dollar (Cincinnati price bill) which is 20 per cent cheaper than ever done here before. The bricks are laid at the rate of three dollars per thousand, making the whole cost of brick work nine dollars per thousand, which is cheaper than ever done here before. Messers S. C. Rogers and S. Kelly are directors of the work. I have no fear of any trouble, the contracts being worded in such a manner as to prevent anything of that kind. I hope we shall have the church ready for consecration by the middle of October when I hope we shall be able to have some display here also; for I shall come down for you and several other gentlemen of the clergy. The Germans are also making preparations for commencing their church. They would have done better to postpone a little, but they seemed anxious to commence. We have rented a large room in which we can have Mass decently on Sundays until we get our church. All seem very anxious and generously contribute what they can towards its completion. The subscription now amounts to nearly $2,000 cash, which will about cover the church in. After which we will open a new subscription, for all say they will give more. I think it is possible that this summer I shall, with Mr. Kelly, go to Galena with the hope of getting some aid, as the prospect from that quarter is good, and Mr. Kelly is personally acquainted with most of the men there. The whole expense of the church will be about 4000 1.00. If you could send either to me or Mr. Samuel C. Rogers your subscription you would do us a particular favor, because we must make payments as the work progresses. I do not know when I shall be able to come to St. Louis, for I cannot now leave here. I have received petitions from Kelly, 20 miles above; from Warsaw 35 miles above, and from Pittsfield 40 miles below this, from various Catholic families praying us to come and visit them, which I must do as soon as possible.

If those articles which were promised us by Card. Fransoni should arrive, I must bespeak for the church of Quincy an incensor, ostensory and whatever else may be most essential.

In the meantime I remain your most obedient and humble child in Xto,

H. TUCKER.

At the Synod held in St. Louis, April 21, 1839, Father Tucker reported the number of souls at Quincy as 385, baptisms 27, funerals 4, and converts 4.

Quincy, June 20th, 1839.

Most Venerable Bishop:

Although it has been but a few days since I wrote to you, still I can not let this occasion pass by, without sending you a few lines. Judge James will acquaint you of the manner we are getting on here. I hope we shall be able to commence next week the brick work of our church, the stone foundations are almost finished, and if we have no more contradictions, I hope that it will be covered in by the 20th of August. I don't think that Mr. Brickwedde has acted altogether a charitable part. For he has gone with his list among most of the Irish Catholics, which was not looked upon here as very genteel. We have not offered our subscription to a single German, as we knew they had the intention of building. However, be this as it may, the church is progressing very well,

and before winter will be fit for consecration. The only thing is, that I wish Mr. Brickwedde would be a little more communicative than he is with me. We have rented a place in which we keep church Sundays. At nine o'clock there will be catechism for those who will dispose themselves for their first communion, but we have got very few children. We will also open up next Sunday a Sunday-school. Mrs. Rogers and two or three other ladies have offered their services to teach the girls. I must find some men for the boys. At 10 we have Mass and sermon. At 3 o'clock P. M. I will on every Sunday, in place of vespers, give an explanation of Christian doctrine which I write and read to the people. The plan I pursue is that laid down by the Catechism of the Council of Trent, commencing with the Creed. With the divine assistance I will continue until all be explained. Next week I shall go to Tully and Warsaw where there are Catholics who have begged me to visit them. I have just this moment also received a petition to go to Pittsfield 40 miles from this where there are 5 families. I must also visit Louisiana where there are two or three families.

I have just received a letter from Mr. Hamilton. He seems to be greatly encouraged, and to have cheering prospects before him. Would you have the kindness to procure for me a book called *Faith of Catholics*, and Hornihold, *On the Commandments and Sacraments.* They are at Danises. And send them by some occasion to Mr. Samuel C. Rogers. I will satisfy for them when I come. I have great need of them.

With true respect I remain yours most affectionately,

H. TUCKER.

Quincy, July 19th, 1839.

Rt. Revd Sir:

I have just returned a few days ago, from a mission to Santa Fe, about 30 miles above this place, on the Missouri side. I found about 35 Catholic families, almost all Kentuckians, some Irish. They have not seen a priest since last September. They are farmers after the old Kentucky manner, good simple and harmless people, and have a delightful country, and will in a few years be doing very well in the temporal sense of the word. They have a church raised and covered, made of hewn logs and very well put up, being 40 feet by 25. After Mass I called a meeting, and we took measures for continuing the work. I hope they will have the flooring in by the middle of August, on which day I promised again to visit them. I will endeavor to give them Mass once a month. I baptized five persons, some of them Protestant, and received two couples into the church, who were married out of it. The church stands on a beautiful piece of ground belonging to the church, of 80 acres, the deed in your name. I think, if we can find some good and trusty farmer to place on it and to make some improvements, it would be well. The people are of the same opinion as it would be a means of support. I have just received a letter from a lady in Pittsfield, 40 miles from this, who wishes me to come there to make some arrangements for a church. She offers a lot in the town for a church. I must endeavor next week to go. Pittsfield is the county seat of Pike county. The lady is of Baltimore, was formerly the wife of a naval officer by the name of Long. She has her two daughters and their families with her.

Here in Quincy we are getting on but slowly with our church. We have been disappointed in getting bricks two or three times. So many buildings are

at present going on in the place, that all are immediately used up. I hope, however, we shall soon be able to have a sufficient quantity not to be delayed more. The joists for the flooring are already in. The church is 48 feet long by 35 wide in the clear, the walls 16 inches thick and 24 feet high. The steeple is 12 feet square on the end and to be carried up from the ground in order to support the bell when we get one. When I come down I will bring the inscription put in the corner-stone. I wish to come to St. Louis about the end of next month, for we must take some more vigorous measures, or else I fear we cannot more than cover the church before winter, as money here is very scarce. I received your subscription.

At present we have some sickness in Quincy, but the place cannot be called unhealthy. I am not very well; but my breast does not pain me as usually in hot weather; preaching greatly fatigues me.

I was lately at Warsaw about 35 miles above this place, where the old Fort Edward stands. Just before, in digging a well, they found the grave of a person buried there probably for 60 or 70 years, and in it a silver crucifix of considerable size. I was very desirous of getting it but it fell into the hands of a protestant lady who would not part with it, she is now in Cincinnati. I will be careful to gain what information I can, that might be interesting to religion or history, in this place.

I wish to know your advice with respect to a penitent who in some points of faith doubts strongly; for example not being fully convinced of the necessity of infant baptism, of the propagation of original sin, or the benefit of prayers for the dead. Can such a penitent continue the use of the sacraments? or must he be refused? At times this penitent is willing to abide by the decision of the church and to make a firm act of faith; at other times is shaken and very wavering and somewhat inclined to abandon all. If you please let me have your decision on this as soon as convenient.

I continue to live with Mr. Rogers who has granted me a very convenient and retired upper room. Until we get means of building a house for the priest, I will continue here. I must be very grateful to this very worthy man; for he furnishes me with every convenience gratis. He is not a Catholic, but I hope will be. I ask your prayers for his conversion.

In the meantime I remain your most obedient and humble,

H. TUCKER.

Quincy, August 29th, 1839.

Rt. Revd Bishop:

I will not let the occasion pass without sending you a line to let you know that I am doing something. I have written to you twice without getting any answer. I will come to St. Louis as soon as I can, but just now I do not like to leave Quincy, because there are too many sick. I have this moment returned from Warsaw, 35 miles from here, where I was called two nights since, I have not slept for the last 50 hours and rode 85 miles. Our church gets on slowly. I must see if I can do nothing at St. Louis when I come. The railroad system of this state will ruin us, I am afraid. I have now no time to say more, but hope soon to be in St. Louis. In the meantime, asking your paternal benediction, I remain your most affectionate,

H. TUCKER.

Quincy, Nov. 3d, 1839.

Most Venerable Father:

I write to you, judging that this will find you, at Bardstown, to communicate to you several plans which I think will greatly progress the cause of
religion in this part of the diocese.

I did hope to see you before this in St. Louis to consult with you *viva voce*
but sickness and occupations have prevented me. Of late I have been confined
for eight days by an inflammation of the throat and breast, which caused me to
spit considerable blood, and yet I have a severe pain in the breast. Our church
is up, ready for the roof, but it must now remain so till spring, for we have
no funds to proceed. We are now owing about $800, but I hope we will be
able to pay this in a month, as we expect near $600 from the railroad, which is
daily expected. But this will not be enough. I have thought of going on a
begging expedition. The winter is now approaching, and I can do nothing here
and would be obliged, at all events, to spend the winter in St. Louis, I have
thought of going to New Orleans this winter to see if I cannot do something
for this and three other congregations, the one at Santa Fee and Pittsfield. The
Doctor tells me, I ought to spend the winter in the South. I must have a
little respite, for I have been utterly harassed and kept in a continual state of
painful anxiety by the church builders, and many other causes of domestic
trouble.

I have just returned from Santa Fee. This will shortly be a flourishing
congregation. There are now 31 families of Kentucky stock, but poor. They,
however, live in great simplicity of manners and resemble much the people of
the Barrens. The church there must be finished next spring. I really intend
establishing there a convent of the Sisters of Loretto. There are now at least
40 girls ready for schooling, and many are even married without any instruction
whatever. There are 80 acres of good land, belonging to the church. It will
be very easy to open a farm and maintain a good school.

In Quincy, also, there are but few Catholics; yet a female school is
absolutely necessary and we must have one. The Governor Carlin, Judge Ralston
and some of the most influential men of Quincy have urged it on me much.
I even believe they will provide a good home and contribute largely to the support. Next spring I will make them some proposals. The Governor's daughters
go to church and, I believe, before long they will openly profess themselves
Catholics, for they are so in heart. At Pittsfield, next Spring, we will commence a small brick church. A lot, and liberal subscription have been given
for that purpose. There are 12 families.

This is only a commencement of what may be done with patience and
perseverance. I, on my late tour on the river, in Lewis and Clark counties
(missions) baptized four protestants.

I hope you will not object to my going on the expedition, and that you
will give the necessary letters for that purpose which, as I may not see you in
St. Louis, I wish you would leave at the Priest's Residence in Louisville.
Mr. Rodgers will defray my expenses on this intended voyage, if I can make
it convenient to take Cincinnati on my route, in which place Mrs. Rogers will
spend the winter. Since they have furnished me a home since I have been on
this mission, I think it would be wrong to refuse this request.

Till I see you I remain your most obedient and sincere servant,

H. TUCKER.

P. S.—Mr. Whitney has made me an offer of his lot and many other properties after his death. I believe next year he will give a deed.

H. TUCKER.

Quincy, January 11, 1840.

Rt. Revd. Sir:

I now write to you to inform you of the course I am pursuing so that nothing may be unknown to you. When I was at St. Louis I informed you that I wished to go eastward, for the purpose of endeavoring to collect for the church, to which you gave your consent. Mr. Rogers, on account of ill health, is obliged to leave for a time for Cincinnati: so that I am left without a home. I thought of coming to St. Louis for a few weeks. But as Mr. Rogers has offered me a place gratis in his private conveyance to Cincinnati, I thought it better to proceed immediately to that place where we will arrive about the 20 of this month. I will wait there till the spring opens. I don't see what I can do better than this, as this will cost me nothing, and I could not remain here. In the mean time I pray you to send by mail to the care of Bishop Purcell my letters, as ample as you think yourself justified in granting. I will thus gain time and will proceed as soon as the river opens. I hope to get back to St. Louis by Easter. I will get Lefevre to come here once a month to give the people Mass. Mr. Hamilton (at Alton) also will visit them. With respect to establishing an academy for females here, I have received the most flattering prospects. Four of the most influential men of the town say they will purchase a lot for a permanent establishment. Judge Rallston even thinks that $3,000 could be raised in the Spring for that purpose. I dont think so much can be done, but a good house can easily be rented and a good school commenced; in the mean time a house of their own could be built. Governor Carlin is of opinion a part of the state school-fund may be obtained from the Legislature, at least next Spring, if we would make the attempt. The Governor's four children, Judge Rallston's two sister-in-laws and Dr. Roger's family, at my return, in all probability, will all be received into the church, as they are now receiving the necessary instructions. But some of them have not yet the courage to declare themselves publicly. Mr. Conyers, the County Treasurer, to whom we are owing about 150 dollars. talks of putting an attachment on the church to secure himself. Should he do so, the only thing you have to do, as the deed is in your name, is to make use of what the law allows, which is eighteen month's grace. As soon as possible I will send Mr. Conyers the money. He is an excellent and upright man and will do nothing but what is right, but he, like many others, is greatly pushed for cash. The river here is entirely closed.

Asking your benediction for the success of the present undertaking, I remain your most affectionate child in Xto.

H. TUCKER.

P. S.—Do not forget the letters.

On the 21st day of April, 1840, Bishop Rosati communicated all his faculties, ordinary and extraordinary, to the Very Rev. P. J. Verhaegen, S. J., for the time of his absence from the diocese, and on April 27th he left St. Louis in company of Father Peter P. Lefevre and Joseph C. Lutz for Baltimore where they were to assist at the Fourth Provincial Council, announced for May 17th, 1840. After

the close of the Council, Bishop Rosati set sail for Havre, thence he journeyed to Paris and Rome, securing there from the Holy Father his coadjutor and successor Peter Richard Kenrick. Whilst in Rome, Bishop Rosati receives the following letter from the pastor of Quincy:

Quincy, Sept. 27th, 1840.

Rt. Revd. Father in Christ:

I know not if it is the custom for any of your clergy, or all of them, to keep in correspondence with you, now that you are away. I for my part, as I am now on the point of complying with my obligation of writing to Propaganda, have thought it proper to address you also, more especially as I have many interesting items to communicate to you. It has been with the greatest pleasure that I read in the papers the notice of your safe arrival in Paris. May God grant you a speedy and propitious return. Here in our city (for Quincy is now by law entitled to that appellation) Catholicity is prospering. Indeed it seems that the hand of God is with us, and that He intends shortly to bring to light something great for the cause of religion here, for certainly we have lately had some signal triumphs. You should recollect that a little more than a year ago, when I came here, I found but a few Catholics in the midst of the most bigoted class of New England Presbyterians that can be imagined, and in the very hotbed of abolitionism. I scarcely dared show myself in the streets for fear of them, and indeed I have often been pointed at as an emissary of Anti-Christ. A great change has been effected in the public feeling in my regard. And now it is only by a certain number of Presbyterian Abolitionists that I am hissed at.

About three weeks ago 500 of the Pottawatomie Indians passed through this place on their way to the Far West from the graves of their fathers whence the stern arm of an unjust power has driven them. 300 are Catholics. They remained with us two days. The Rev. Mr. Baignin was with them. I caused them to come all to the church, and at 10 o'clock I sang for them the High Mass, at which they assisted with an air of piety, devotion and simplicity, which covered many a Catholic with confusion for his own conduct. After Mass their pastor addressed them in a discourse to which they listened with the same attention. At his request I immediately repaired to their camp and commenced hearing confessions by means of an interpreter, and did not leave my place till mid-night, having heard 150, among whom was their chief. Next morning being Sunday they repaired to the church as many as could, and received their Savior, after which they immediately crossed the Mississippi and pursued their journey. All the city witnessed all this, and it has been productive of good to our religion. But it has pleased God to grant still greater triumphs. I think you are acquainted with Miss Emily Carlin, eldest daughter of Governor Carlin. She delivered before you and Bishop Loras an address at Kaskaskia. She is now no longer among the living, but thanks to God, her death was signally glorious to Catholicity. Ever since her return from the convent she has always taken the defense of Catholics in this place. In fact, she was only waiting your return, publicly to embrace it in a solemn manner, as she had often told me. She had thoroughly prepared herself, and when she was taken sick, she immediately sent for me, earnestly entreated to go to confession and

be baptized. I told her that confession, in her case was unnecessary. She then received baptism at my hands in the midst of her family and many friends, with the sentiments of an angel. From that time till her death, two days after, her thoughts were all in God: She longed to die and be with Him. At her earnest request I did not leave her presence till death, when on the morning of the 14th of September she sweetly gave up her soul to God. Before her death she gave orders. for her burial, all according to the rites of the church, and her interment in our new cemetery. She spoke of you in her last moments and called you her dear bishop. All the city was covered with gloom; for she had been the admiration of all. The Supreme Court of the State was then in session. It immediately adjourned to attend her funeral, the order of which was as follows: At 8 A. M. on the morning of the 16th of September all met on the great square before the residence of the governor (hand bills had been printed and sent around the day previous to this fact). Then a large company of foot-men led the way, then a numerous company of horse, then the mounted pallbearers proceeded by the marshal, all with their appropriate garb of mourning, twelve in number; then came the corpse, next myself in soutan, surplice and stole, with attending physician in a carriage; then the family of the Governor, then Senator Young and family, then the lawyers of the court, and at least 100 carriages. We repaired thus to the church. where the funeral rites were performed, after which I briefly addressed the multitude. Then we proceeded in the same order to the grave-yard and returned, in like manner. Such has been the death of this eminently talented young lady. All the papers have vied with one another in their eulogiums on her. I have no doubt but that I shall soon receive the whole family in the church. I am now almost every day with them. The death of Emily has had a thrilling effect on many. Reports have been already circulated by the Presbyterians, that I forced her to embrace the Catholic religion. Their envy is insatiate and finds no relief but in calumny. Indeed, I have been solicited by some of my Protestant friends here to prosecute one, who stands high in society, for a libel on me. If much more is said, I will certainly do so, for I know it would at once cause them even here to be cautious in regard to Catholics, and I fear nothing from them, as all has been public. Judge Young, the Governor, and many of the most influential lawyers would ardently wish it. The person who has been so officious in this case is a Mrs. Tillson, wife of the wealthy brother of John Tillson, agent of the Illinois Land Company, whose lady and family is a very different person from the one in question.

But God has not stayed his hand even here, the Rev. Mr. Dowan, German Lutheran minister of this place, a man well known in all the eastern cities will soon declare himself publicly a Catholic. He will set out next spring for Belgium, where he wishes to receive the priesthood. He is not willing yet that anything should be said about it, as he thinks the impression on his heretofore brethren would be too great. Such, dear bishop, are some of the items that I have to communicate to you. I have established a branch of the Temperance Society, similar to those in Ireland. For, at the last election our Irish disgraced themselves in a public riot, so much that the civil force was called to quell it. I have restored things to order, and on the next Sunday I published from the altar my intention. Altho there have been threats made by some wealthy German dealers in liquors that, if I said any thing, they would drive me from Quincy. I told them from the altar that I knew what had been said, and that I was

ready to suffer even death if necessary in discharging my duty, and that I would raise my voice against such excesses. They have attempted nothing so far. Our little society in the meantime increases, and we now have about 30 members. It is called the Roman Catholic Temperance Society of Quincy. But, dear Bishop, do not imagine that I am free from troubles of the most distressing kind. I assure you I am harrassed beyond measure. I have been grossly slandered even by those who bear the name of Catholics. Letters have been sent to F. Verhaegen long before I knew of it. I then laid my case before him, and he wrote me a consoling letter and encouraged me to go on. May God pardon all, is my prayer. But slander is indeed very dampening to my courage. Dear bishop, our church must be finished. I hope we will have it ready for consecration by the end of October. It is the prettiest one in Illinois, but we shall be in debt. You really must assist us. It weighs heavily on my mind. I have written to the Cardinal Prefect asking some assistance. I hope you will advocate my cause with him, which is your cause. I think he will do something. There is no doubt that this place is destined to be shortly a city of 15,000 inhabitants, and we must rise with it. This is the opinion of the most intelligent here, who, tho protestants, wish for the success of Catholicity. The Presbyterians are straining every nerve to get the ascendancy. Some of their most distinguished ministers have endeavored to entrap me, but above all Dr. Nelson, the abolitionist: Oh, that our church was finished, and that some distinguished controversialist could spend a month with me. I have some hope of having Bishop Purcell here to consecrate the church, as he will be on a visit to St. Louis to see his sister. I shall have a comfortable parsonage finished before winter. Mr. Rogers and Mr. Whitney deserve the eternal gratitude of the Catholics of this place; but they cannot do all. I pray you then to do what you can for me, for my health is really sinking under anxiety. Not long since my horse fell and rolled over me and much injured my breast; but I hope that it will not prove fatal.

Asking your blessing I remain your most obedient,

H. TUCKER.

This passage of a large band of Indians through Quincy in September, 1840, was not the first one in the city's history. As early as 1838 there was a mission established among the Pottawatomies on Sugar Creek, or the Lake of Swans in Kansas and another on Missouri River near Council Bluffs. Two Jesuit Fathers and two lay-brothers commenced this establishment, as Father Verhaegen, S. J., the Provincial of the Order writes to the Bishop assembled in the Fourth Provincial Council. The accounts given by the missionaries is of the most cheering character, discribing the happy dispositions of thousands of these poor children of the forest, particularly of the women and children.

"In the same year, 1838," continues Father Verhaegen's report, "six hundred Catholic Pottawatomies from Indiana, who were accompanied in their removal by the late Rev. Mr. Petit, on reaching their destination were transferred by him to the care of one of our Fathers.

Their location is on the banks of Sugar Creek, about seventy miles southwest of the Kickapoo nation. This is the most flourishing of all the Indian missions, and realizes the accounts which we read of the missions of Paraguay. The story of the unwilling exodus of this band of Pottawatomies from their ancient seats around the southern shores of Lake Michigan, is sad, yet sweet and edifying as related in the letters of their black gown, Father Benjamin Mary Petit, who accompanied them on the long weary journey through Illinois, and across the Mississippi at Quincy, until they reached their destination. Father Petit was born at Rennes in France, April 8, 1811, was admitted to the practice of law in his native city, but after a few years followed the call of God into the apostolic ministry. Bishop Bruté of Vincennes, also a native of Rennes, encouraged the young man in his vocation. Engaged in the study of Theology at the Seminary of St. Sulpice in Paris until 1836 the youthful missionary came to Vincennes and was raised to the holy priesthood in 1837. Immediately after his ordination he was sent to the Indian missions in the vicinity of South Bend in Indiana. At that time the Government of the United States was engaged in removing the remnants of the Indian tribes and nations beyond the Mississippi River: The Pottawatomies too, were doomed to go. As they were almost all Catholic Christians, the Government was anxious to have their Missionary Father go with them on their exodus, and Bishop Bruté gave his consent. Father Petit in one of his letters mentions the hearty reception he and his spiritual children received from Father Brickwedde and his people in Quincy.

"In Naples, when we crossed the Illinois River," says Father Petit, "I took a carriage and hurried to Quincy, to have a few days of rest before crossing the Mississippi. I there found a German priest, Mr. Brickwedde, and a German congregation, who received me with indescribable kindness. I found the same courteous reception with some of the Catholic Americans, and a few of the most prominent Protestants of the city, who offered me their hospitality. When the Indians arrived at Quincy the inhabitants comparing this wandering people with former passing bands of savages, could not refrain themselves from expressing their admiration in regard to the modesty, quietness and good conduct of our Christians. A Catholic lady, probably the Mrs. Rogers of Father Tucker's letters] accompanied by a Protestant friend, made the sign of the cross to show her union in faith with the Indians. Immediately a number of women of the tribe took her hand and joyfully pressed it. This the savages never omit whenever they meet with Catholics." The collection of Father

Petit's letters containing a number of most touching details of his wanderings with the Pottawatomies of St. Joseph's may be found in the *Catholic History of Quincy*, by the Reverend Theodore Brunner, Chicago, 1887.

A brief notice of Father Petit's untimely death may not be out of place here: Having left his dear Indians in the care of their new Fathers, the Jesuits of Missouri, sick in body unto death, the heroic soul was ready to depart from the scene of hard labors. Coming to the St. Louis University, he was received with truly brotherly hospitality. On the eve of the Feast of the Purification he begged that an altar might be installed in a room adjoining his sick-chamber. The wish was gratified, and on the following day Father Petit said Mass in honor of the Blessed virgin. It was his last Mass. He died on the 10th day of February, 1839, in the 28th year of his life.

In concluding this chapter on the early days of Quincy, we would give the few dates we have gathered on the later period of Father Hilary Tucker's life.

Up to 1844 Quincy, together with all Western Illinois, was both de facto and de jure a part of the diocese of St. Louis. But in that year the diocese of Chicago was organized, including the entire state of Illinois. Father Tucker thus, as pastor of Quincy, exchanged his membership in the diocese of his old friend Rosati for that of Chicago; and in 1845 Bishop Rosati died in Rome. A number of the older clergy retired from the western missions; and as Father Hilary's companion, Father George Hamilton, followed a call to the more cultured East, he himself asked to be released from the diocese of Chicago. In 1846 we find Father Hilary Tucker in Boston, Mass., in 1847 in Lowell, from 1848 to 1852 in Providence, and from 1852 to 1872 at the Cathedral in Boston, where he died March 15, 1872.

Father Hilary Tucker was a man of strong character, even impulsive at times, with a high idea of his calling, and filled with zeal for the conversion of souls. His early missionary life at Quincy and the surrounding stations was a sore trial to him; yet he held to his post of duty until the disaster was repaired and all went smoothly once more.

He was a man capable of deep and lasting friendships. What drew him to Boston and the East was not so much a desire for an easier life, but rather the friendships he had contracted in the early Roman days. The saintly Father Lewis Tucker of Fredericktown was, in some respects, the very reverse of his brother Hilary. Unassuming, abstemious, careless of comfort and personal appearance, good old Father Lewis Tucker never wrote a letter except on com-

THE FIRST CHICAGO CHURCH RECORDS

So many records and writings possessing a deep interest are lost, that when a really important old record is found it is the cause of rejoicing.

In spite of the many pointed remarks that have been made about preserving records, and in spite of diocesan rules and ordinances, it is undoubtedly true that even if records have been made they are very frequently not well preserved. The great destroyer, fire, is the most malignant enemy of records, and although parish records of the Catholic church are perhaps more faithfully kept under all circumstances than almost any other records, the nature of the early church buildings and parochial residences was such that they were peculiarly subject to destruction by fire.

Hence when a search for the early records of any church of some age is entered upon, one is almost invariably met by the results of the fire fiend, and baffled at the outset.

As has been seen, and particularly in the January, 1921, number of the ILLINOIS CATHOLIC HISTORICAL REVIEW, the Catholic Church was duly organized in Chicago in 1833. Rev. John Mary Iraenaeus St. Cyr became the first pastor, officiated for the first time on the 5th of May 1833, and entered actively upon the duties of pastor.[1]

Father St. Cyr was a young Frenchman, but a short time in America, and ordained Priest only a month before arriving in Chicago.[2] He had never before performed any pastoral duties, but evidently knew the importance of a parish record, for he begun keeping one at once, and kept it faithfully, even if he did mingle French and English, and violate many of the lexicographer's laws.

And strange as it may seem, Father St. Cyr's parish record is still accessible in spite of the fact that every vestige of the Church property connected with the parish which Father St. Cyr established (St. Mary's) was destroyed in the great Chicago fire of 1871.

In his lifetime William J. Onahan, one of the most distinguished Catholic laymen of Chicago, told the writer that he had come upon the parish records of St. Mary's for the very earliest years of that parish, and fearing their loss or decay or disintegration, he had had copies made of them. After his death the writer asked his family

---

[1] Garrighan, ILLINOIS CATHOLIC HISTORICAL REVIEW, 1-140.
[2] See certificate of ordination by Right Rev. Joseph Rosati, Bishop of St. Louis, in ILLINOIS CATHOLIC HISTORICAL REVIEW, 2, 326-7.

to make a search of his voluminous library for this copy, which was done accordingly, and with the happy result that the records were found. Fortunately, also, the original record is still in existence and in a splendid state of preservation. Through the kindness of the present pastor of St. Mary's, Rev. Edward J. Mullaly, C. S. P., the writer has been privileged to examine this precious document and to have photographs made therefrom.

On the fly leaf of the book appears the following:

This record of baptisms and marriages solemnized from the year 1833-39,— the first record known in the city of Chicago—was collected and bound by me in the year 1880.

(Signed)   Jos. P. Roles, *Rector.*
St. Mary's December 7, 1880.

This set includes the records of baptisms and marriages and a reference to several funerals of the Parish of St. Mary's of Chicago, and extends from the earliest ceremony, which was a baptism performed on the 22nd of May, 1833, twenty-two days after Father St. Cyr's arrival in Chicago, to the middle of October, 1839. In the period covered by these records there were three different resident priests, viz., Father St. Cyr, Rev. Bernard Schaeffer and Rev. Timothy J. O'Meara. During that time there were also visiting priests and also a Bishop, who performed spiritual ministrations, as, for instance, Rev. Francis Plunkett, who was sent here by the Bishop of Vincennes, and took charge of the territory around Joliet. Right Rev. Simon William Gabriel Bruté, the Bishop of Vincennes, made more than one visit, and administered baptism.

There is so much of interest to Chicago people in these early records that we have felt justified in publishing them in tabular form, cherishing the hope that through their publication we will be able to arouse interest amongst descendants or relatives or acquaintances of the persons named that will bring out a body of historical facts that might otherwise remain undeveloped. All those who shall have the opportunity of examining these lists and who have any information concerning any of the parties named, are urgently requested to communicate their information to the Illinois Catholic Historical Review.

The baptismal record is the longest, and begins earlier than the marriage record. It may be said too to be more interesting, since it embraces a wider range of names. It is, therefore, given first place, and as analyzed and put in tabular form appears as follows:

BAPTISMS IN ST. MARY's CATHOLIC CHURCH, CHICAGO

DATE	PERSON BAPTIZED	PARENTS	SPONSORS	PRIEST
5-22-1833	George Beaubien	Mark Beaubian / Monique Nadierne	Mark Beaubien / Marianne Arriage	• J. M. I. Saint Cyr
5-26-1833	Joseph Meyo	Michael Meyo / Margaret Mollard	Joseph Laframboise / Arluge Beaubien	J. M. I. Saint Cyr
5-15-1834	John Logdson (Bear Creek, Sangamon County)	Matthew Lodgson / Elizabeth Logdson	John Durbin / Louisa Simper	J. M. I. Saint Cyr
5-15-1834	Elizabeth Pinter (Bear Creek, Sangamon County)	Sylvester Pinter / Ann Pinter	Phillip Durbin / Eliza Logdson	J. M. I. Saint Cyr
5-15-1834	Marguerite Durbin (Bear Creek, Sangamon County)	Phillip Durbin / Elizabeth Durbin	James Logdson / Marguerite Durbin	J. M. I. Saint Cyr
1-31-1836	Maria Murphy	John Murphy	John Kelly / Bridget Forester	J. M. I. Saint Cyr
3- 6-1836	T. B. George Beaubien	Medard Beaubien / Mary Boyer	J. M. I. Saint Cyr / McIntie Boyer	J. M. I. Saint Cyr
4-10-1836	Henry Gollgark	Henry Gollgark / Bridget Gollgark	Mary Conly	J. M. I. Saint Cyr
4-30-1836	Peter Worden	Peter Worden	Jack Carroll / Mary Carroll	J. M. I. Saint Cyr
5- 1-1836	Mary O'Neil	Patrick O'Neil / Mary Jano	McHenry Kauer / Appolino Kauer	J. M. I. Saint Cyr

Date	Name	Parents	Sponsors	Officiant
		Mary Plane	Ann Plane	J. M. I. Saint Cyr
6-19-1836	Henry Wagner	Frederic Wagner / Maria Wagner	Henry Berg / Maria Ann Mondweller	J. M. I. Saint Cyr
6-20-1836	Christian Goodman	George Goodman / Catherine Cure	Christian Goodman / Barbara Sauter	J. M. I. Saint Cyr
7-14-1836	Sarah Elizabeth Walsh	John Walsh / Elizabeth Curran	J. M. I. Saint Cyr / Mary Foley	J. M. I. Saint Cyr
7-15-1836	Louis Taylor	Anson Taylor / Elizabeth Leahy	J. M. I. Saint Cyr	J. M. I. Saint Cyr
7-16-1836	Helena Oheron	Dory Oheron / Helena Kelley	Davis Vurny / Helena Vurny	J. M. I. Saint Cyr
7-17-1836	Mary Ann Furlong	Michael Furlong / Mary Ann Fellway	Thomas Dooly / Marguerite Silver	J. M. I. Saint Cyr
7-22-1836	Elizabeth Sexton	Steven Sexton / Ann Gaughan	John Gaughan / Bridget McGill	J. M. I. Saint Cyr
7-24-1836	Henry Ward	Bernard Ward / Ruth Ward	John Walsh / Ann Ward	J. M. I. Saint Cyr
7-24-1836	Clariey Ward	Bernard Ward / Ruth Ward	John Lyon / Virginia Gaughan	J. M. I. Saint Cyr
7- ?-1836	Eliza Marguerite Deschamps	Benjamin Deschamps / Marie Louise Deschamps	Francois Lebeau / Marguerite Guion	J. M. I. Saint Cyr

DATE	PERSON BAPTIZED	PARENTS	SPONSORS	PRIEST
7-30-1836	Thomas Carroll	Thomas Carroll / Ann Dover	Thomas Carroll / Mary Green	J. M. I. Saint Cyr
8-22-1836	James White	Thomas White / Bridget Malody	Edward Lalley / Catherine Burk	J. M. I. Saint Cyr
8-23-1836	Amelia Elizabeth Raferty	Thomas Raferty / Rose Carly	Delphine Choulet	J. M. I. Saint Cyr
9- 5-1836	Catherine Muller	James Muller / Catherine Baumgarden	Daniel Muller / Elizabeth Baumgarden	Bernard Schaeffer
9- 6-1836	Francis Agnes Donovan	Simon Donovan / Anastatius	John Horney / Louise Taylor	J. M. I. Saint Cyr
9- ?-1836	Marguerite Tranche	Antoine Tranche / Charlotte Roi	Alexis Gagneaux / Josette Tranche	J. M. I. Saint Cyr
9-11-1836	Charles Hard	John Hard / Mary Fitz-Martin	Martin Dollmanns / Mary Flaherty	Bernard Schaeffer
9-16-1836	Catherine Forestorn	Thomas Forestorn / Bridget Finukane	Patrick O. Miller / Catherine Forestron	Bernard Schaeffer
9-20-1836	August Michael Peter Chapperon	Augustin Chapperon / Mary Bourgeois	Claudine Choulet / Michael Choulet	Bernard Schaeffer
9- ?-1836	Marie Tranche	Antoine Tranche / Charlotte Roy	Augustin Bonin / Josette Tranche	J. M. I. Saint Cyr
9- 5-1836	Robert Holley	Robert Holley / Anna Wobs	Charles Carroll / Bridget Wobs	J. M. I. Saint Cyr

Date	Child	Parents	Sponsors	Officiant
10- 8-1836	Catherine Smith	Lawrence Smith / Mary Welsh	Thomas Master / Mary Ann White	Bernard Schaeffer
10- 8-1836	Mary Cunningham	Henry Cunningham / Ann Cratty	Patrick Heckins / Mary Burk	Bernard Schaeffer
10-13-1836	John Monaghan	James Monaghan / Eliza Lane	Patrick Monaghan / Mary Jane Strong	J. M. I. Saint Cyr
10-16-1836	Eugene Salavin	Daniel Salavin / Mary Nancy	Eugene Salavin / Bridget Burk	Bernard Schaeffer
11-10-1836	Julia Rose Carney	Michael Carney / Bridget Carney	Patrick McDonnel	J. M. I. Saint Cyr
11-26-1836	Cicily Josephine Talley	Alfred Maurice Talley / Mary Monica Taylor	Rev. James Fitton / Mary Josephine Taylor	J. M. I. Saint Cyr
11-27-1836	Thomas Charles Brown	George Brown / Sarah Smith	Samuel Ferry / Louisa Taylor	J. M. I. Saint Cyr
11- ?-1836	Joseph Branehean	Joseph Branehean / Julie Brusseau	Eloi Bergeron / Adelaide Bergeron	J. M. I. Saint Cyr
12- 1-1836	John William Beaubien	T. B. Beaubien / Josephine LaFramboise	William Egan / Aurelia Hotchkiss	Bernard Schaeffer
12- 4-1836	Edward Patrick Keenan	John Keenan / Elizabeth Ann Ferguson	Joffrey Power	J. M. I. Saint Cyr
12-11-1836	Catherine Canavan	Daniel Canavan / Bridget Hynes	Edward Rae / Bridget Eagan	J. M. I. Saint Cyr
12-11-1836	Agnes Ann Gardner	Robert Gardner / Catherine Gardner	John Walsh / Mary McIntyre	J. M. I. Saint Cyr

Date	Person Baptized	Parents	Sponsors	Priest
12-19-1836	John Michael	John Michael Catherine Swiney	Thomas Duquoin Janet Donley	J. M. I. Saint Cyr
12-22-1836	Richard Welsh	Patrick Welsh	Charles McDonell Ann Charles	J. M. I. Saint Cyr
1-28-1837	Mary Anne Flynn	Abraham Flynn Sabinia Miles	Joseph Brown Catherine Flynn	Bernard Schaeffer
2-15-1837	John Peter Dolesey	Peter Dolesey Matilda Leibe	John Dolesey Mary Dolesey	Bernard Schaeffer
2-19-1837	James Nichol	Michael Nichol Johanna Vehan	James Lane Anne Carroll	Bernard Schaeffer
2-20-1837	Michael Standberge	Michael Standberge Mary Flanigan	Thomas Fitzgerald	J. M. I. Saint Cyr
2-20-1837	Patience Meeds	John Meeds Anna Durbin		J. M. I. Saint Cyr
2-20-1837	Ann Durbin	Thomas Durbin Susanna Johnson	William Durbin Ann Durbin	J. M. I. Saint Cyr
2-20-1837	Sarah Kinney	Michael Kinney Ann Flynn	Michael Odill Bridget Odill	J. M. I. Saint Cyr
2-20-1837	John Johnson	Thomas Johnson Mary Doyle	Joseph Finen Helena Curran	J. M. I. Saint Cyr
2-20-1837	Patrick Loughney	Patrick Loughney Sidney Hearn	John Donaghen Julia Murphy	J. M. I. Saint Cyr

Date	Child	Parents	Sponsors	Minister
3-19-1837	Philip Andrew Walter	John Walter / Magdalen Gruber	Phil Andrew Smith / Appolonia Minier	Bernard Schaeffer
3-19-1837	Patrick Murphy	Michael Murphy / Margaret Flynn	Patrick White / Catherine Welsh	J. M. I. Saint Cyr
3-28-1837	Barbara Toni	James Toni / Catherine Schindler	Jacob Toni / Barbara Sauter	Bernard Schaeffer
4- 9-1837	Jeremy Foran	James Foran / Helena Daniel	Keldey Salavin / Mary Salavin	Bernard Schaeffer
4-20-1837	Mathilda Juneau	Solomon Juneau / Josette Vieau	Andrew Vieau / Rachael Lasse	Bernard Schaeffer
4-20-1837	Eugene Andrew Juneau	Solomon Juneau / Josette Vieau	Lewis Franchere / Mary Bourassa	Bernard Schaeffer
4-20-1837	Abraham Peter Juneau	Peter Juneau / Angelica Vieau	Lewis Lafariese / Angelica Remond	Bernard Schaeffer
4-20-1837	Margaret Clark	(Born amongst the Indians)	Mary Bourassa	Bernard Schaeffer
4-20-1837	Mary Hayes	Wm. Hayes / Johanna Fannel	John Furlong / Mary. Falby	Bernard Schaeffer
4-23-1837	Helena Prindeville	Maurice Prindiville / Catherine Morris	Eugene Slavin / Marguerite Corly	Bernard Schaeffer
5- 2-1837	Francisca Raferty	Patrick Raferty / Josepha Finnigan	Thomas Fox / Catherine Manghan	Bernard Schaeffer
5- 2-1837	Mary Anne McDonnell	Henry McDonnell / Mary Stollar	Charles McDonnell	Bernard Schaeffer
5- 5-1837	Daniel Manning	Daniel Manning / Honora Doran	Daniel Work / Margaret Duggan	Bernard Schaeffer

DATE	PERSON BAPTIZED	PARENTS	SPONSORS	PRIEST
5- 7-1837	Mary Daley	John Daley Mary Conaty	Mary Laeser	Bernard Schaeffer
5- 7-1837	James Madden	Thomas Madden Mary Graham	James Graham Mary Anne White	Bernard Schaeffer
5 -7-1837	Catherine Slavin	John Slavin Mary Winehan	John Hurley Mary Kittow	Bernard Schaeffer
5-20-1837	Anne Ryan	John Ryan Sara Corley	Michael Flory Margaret Bartlet	Bernard Schaeffer
5-2-1837	Mery McCarty	Denis McCarty Margaret McLaughlin	Patrick Nagle Bridget Tully	T. O'Meara
6- 1-1837	Anne Maria Harny	Richard Harny Maria Walker	Brian Smith Anne Chago	Bernard Schaeffer
6- 1-1837	Margaret Duffy	James Duffy J. Winnefred	Bridget Cahill Hugh Duffy	Bernard Schaeffer
7-14-1837	Marguerite Murphy	Patrick Murphy Mary Halpin	James Carney Anne Timoney	Bernard Schaeffer
7-16-1837	Marie Clare	Michael Clare Marguerite Clare	Thomas Carroll Maria Tully	Bernard Schaeffer
7-17-1837	Eionisius Hearn	John Hearn July McCaughey	James Sorin Margaret Toomey	Bernard Schaeffer
7-24-1837	John Thomas Robe	John Robe Susan Game	Peter Peltier Marie Hard	Bernard Schaeffer

Date	Name	Parents	Sponsors	Officiant
7-30-1837	Mary Jane Loppin	Richard Lappin / Ellectitia Strickland		T. O'Meara
8- 7-1837	Robert Erwin	Wm. Erwin / Bridget Power	William Dorsey / Ann O'Meara	T. O'Meara
8-23-1837	John Brown	Joseph Brown / Mary Tiernan	William McDonald / Bridget Mungen	T. O'Meara
9-24-1837	Mary Ryan	Wm. Ryan / Jane Pearse	James Ryan / Mary O'Brien	T. O'Meara
9-25-1837	Thomas Murphy	John Murphy / Harriet Day	Thomas Finnan / Lucy Kennedy	T. O'Meara
9-30-1837	John Lenghorn	Hugh Lenghorn / Mary Dentz	William Curry / Catherine Forest	T. O'Meara
9-30-1837	Denis Donchen	John Donehen / Mary Ann Spencer	James Martin / Jane Reed	T. O' Mrs
9-30-1837	Louise Caroline Miller	Jacob Miller / Catherine Baumgarten	John Gerhart / Anastasia Teman	T. O' Mrs
10- 1-1837	Ann Dwyer	Cornelius Dwyer / Joanna Joyce	Christopher Baumgarten / Louise Joseph Dunne	T. O' Mrs
10-12-1837	John Murray	John J. Murray / Elleanor Ryan	Patrick Higgins / Catherine Timoney	T. O'Meara
10-13-1837	Edward McLaughlin	Thos. McLaughlin / Rosamond Benehan	James Lane / Honora Kinane	T. O'Meara
10-18-1837	Esther Edge	Samuel Edge / Catherine Borew	Edward McLaughlin / Margaret McLaughlin; Timothy O'Meara / Bridget Egan	T. O'Meara

Date	Person Baptized	Parents	Sponsors	Priest
10-19-1837	John O'Connor	Thomas O'Connor Mary Hogan	Michael Halloran Mary Murphy	T. O'Meara
11- 5-1837	Ann Gaffy	Hugh Gaffy Mary Ryan	Michael Devine Mary Kieran	T. O'Meara
11-12-1837	Catherine Fitzgerald	Thos. Fitzgerald Margaret McDonald	† B. Beaubien Susanna Beaubien	T. O'Meara
11-19-1837	Gaend Yond	John Yond Margaret Cure	† F. Gie Josephine Salamon	T. O'Meara
11-29-1837	James Clinton	Michael Clinton Mary Sullivan	John Malady Bridget Mangan	T. O'Meara
11-30-1837	Elizabeth Shea	William Shea Elleanor Mahony	Thomas Rooch Elleanor Heavy	T. O'Meara
12- 3-1837	Charles Merrick	Lewis Merrick Mary McIntire	Peter Peltier Mary Militard	T. O'Meara
12- 3-1837	Peter Merrick	Lewis Merrick Mary McIntire	Seraphin Leonard L. Ann Poupard	T. O'Meara
12- 4-1837	Margaret Lorden	Denis Lorden Jude Bohan	Patrick Lane Mary Cooney	T. O'Meara
12-10-1837	Johanna Glavin	Thos. Glavin Mary Power	Patrick Lane Margaret Banin	T. O'Meara
12-24-1837	John McCowen	Peter McCowen Elleanor Heally	John Higgins Mary Cavanaugh	T. O'Meara

Date	Name		
12-25-1837	Johanna Healy	Jeremiah Healy	Mary Duggan
12-31-1837	Thomas Carrol	Thos. Carrol	Bridget Hogan
1- 1-1838	Catherine McNight	Robert McNight	Rose Traynor
1- 4-1838	John Flannery	Michael Flannery	Adaline M. Sibley
1- 9-1838	Michael Bannon	Patrick Bannon	Bridget Haley
1-14-1838	Thomas Jordan	John Jordan	Elleanor Canty
1-14-1838	James Hart	John Hart	Mary Fitzmorris
1-17-1838	Catherine Donnelly (From Virginia Settlement)	Andrew Donnelly	Anna Short
1-20-1838	Peter Tyler	Laurence Martin Tyler	Caroline Larsen
1-20-1838	John McLaughlin	John McLaughlin	Sarah Melody
1-26-1839	Patrick Henry Jackson	Gideon M. Jackson	Bridget Matilda Gaughan
1-30-1838	Charles May	John May	Mary Neeson

Date	Person Baptized	Parents	Sponsors	Priest
2- 2-1838	Elizabeth Collins	H... ...hs / ...ne Beecher	James Lowry / Mary Dawson	T. O'Meara
2- 4-1838	Adeline M. Sibley	David Sibley / Elizabeth Hextel	Timothy O'Meara / Catherine Rowan	T. O'Meara
2- 6-1838	Pat Ween	Thos Ween / ...et Hallan	Peter Nary / Sarah McDonough	T. O'Meara
2- 6-1838	Thos Moll	Thos Maxwell / S r.h McDonough	Denis Daley / Margaret Fallon	T. O'Meara
2- 6-1838	Mary Ann Malloney	William Malloney / Mary Tilly	Henry Michland / Elleanor McClean	T. O'Meara
2- 7-1838	Bridget Furlong	Michael Furlong / Mary A. Falvey	Michael Burk / Margaret Kerby	T. O'Meara
2- 7-1838	Tim thy Crowley	...s Crowley / ...ra Toomy	Timothy Crowley / Catherine Crowley	T. O'Meara
2- 7-1838	Dennis He by	Denis Healy / Joannah Leahy	Denis Toomy / Hanora Toomy	T. O'Meara
2-10-1838	Mary Banigan	Christopher Banigan / Bridget Cahill	John O'Connor / Catherine Cahill	T. O'Meara
2-18-1838	Thos Man	Thomas Man / Catherine the	Mark Smith / Catherine Ready	T. O'Meara
2-19-1838	Michael Murphy	...el Murphy / Catherine ...ly	David McCarty / Bridget Donavan	T. O'Meara

August 5th 1838 & the undersigned priest baptized James son of ~~John~~ Thomas Gawan and Mary Connolly. Sponsors John Flanagan and Bridget Mulloy. Child aged three weeks

T. O'Meara

September 1st 1838 baptized by the Right Rev. Dr. Bruté Francis son of John Bush and Mary Penolet. The sponsors were Francis Penolet and Agnes Berge. Child aged 3 mths.

+ Simon G. Bruté Bp. of Vincennes

September 1st 1838 I baptized Adam son of Joseph Scheinegar and Magdelen Swab, born on the 31st of Augt. 1838 — Sponsors Adam Berg and Elizabeth Engel —

+ Simon G. Bruté Bp. of Vincennes

Sep[t] 2nd 1838 I the undersigned priest baptized Thos son of Edward Horan & Mary Gawan. The sponsors were Mich[l] McBride and Hannah McGillicuddy. Child aged 4 weeks

T. O'Meara

BISHOP BRUTÉ OFFICIATES AND WRITES A BAPTISMAL RECORD.

June 15th 1858 I the undersigned priest baptized ~~priest~~ Mary daughter of John Whistler and Esther Baillie. The sponsors were Timothy O'Meara and ~~Twentstein~~ Whistler. Child age twenty months.

T. O'Meara

June 15th 1858 I the undersigned priest baptized William son of John Whistler and Esther Baillie. The sponsors were William Whistler and Julia Henson. A Child age 7½ years

T. O'Meara

June ___ I the undersigned priest baptized Elizabeth, daughter of Thos ~~Varby~~ and Eleanor Alvin. Sponsors Thomas Melvin and Anastasia Fitzgibbon. Aged 2 weeks

— T. O'Meara

Rev. Timothy O'Meara Baptizes the Whistler Children.

Date				Officiant
2-18-1838	Elizabeth Lantry	Michael Lantry / Elizabeth McDonough	Patrick Gilligan / Sarah McBride	T. O'Meara
2-24-1838	Mary Trimble	William Trindle / Honorah Mahony	Wm. Mahony / Margaret Mahony	T. O'Meara
2-24-1838	Elleanor Mahony	Daniel Mahony / Margaret Cronan	William Sheehan / Joannah Driscol	T. O'Meara
2-24-1838	Catherine McAllister	Daniel McAllister / Catherine Higgins	John Dompsey / Rose Kenny	T. O'Meara
2-26-1838	Thomas Cody	Patrick Cody / Mary Horan	Andrew Barry / Ellen Downey	T. O'Meara
2-25-1836	John Dwyer	Patrick Dwyer / Mary Quin	John Doyle / Ann Murphy	T. O'Meara
2- 7-1838	Sarah Rock	Thomas Rock / Mary White	James Egan / Elleanor Mahony	T. O'Meara
2-29-1838	Denis Murphy	Denis Murphy / Mary Keally	David McCarty / Bridget Donovan	T. O'Meara
3- 2-1838	Margaret Ferris	James Ferris / Elleanor Dwyer	Owen Curly / Elleanor Ferris	T. O'Meara
3- 5-1838	Julia Murphy	John Murphy / Bridget Rodgers	Henry Cunningham / Catherine Flynn	T. O'Meara
3- 6-1838	Mary Doolan	Maurice Doolan / Mary Desmond	Jeremiah Donoghue / Elleanor McCarty	T. O'Meara
3- 7-1838	Mary Elizabeth Monahan	James Monahan / Elizabeth Lane	John Carrol / Mary Quin	T. O'Meara

DATE	PERSON BAPTIZED	PARENTS	SPONSORS	PRIEST
3-20-1838	Mary Duggan	Thomas Duggan / Jane Donnolly	Richard Lappin / Ellecti Strickland	T. O'Meara
3-21-1838	Patrick Sullivan	John Sullivan / Mary Hogan	Maurice Prindiville / Margaret Bouderin	T. O'Meara
3-24-1838	William Molden	John Molden / Lena Groubre	William Lebocak / Barbara Williaman	T. O'Meara
3-25-1838	Ferdinand Pogd	John Pogd / Catherine Molden	Ferdinand Sebisky / Lena Fisher	T. O'Meara
3-26-1838	John Herod	William Herod / Catherine Sauter	John Sauter / Barbara Sauter	T. O'Meara
3-26-1838	Maurice Savage	Maurice Savage / Mary Walsh	James Ferris / Catherine McClean	T. O'Meara
3-28-1838	Edmond Delay	Edmond Delay / Bridget Cavanaugh	Philip Sheehan / Margaret MacShea	T. O'Meara
3-31-1838	Elleanor Boles	Hugh Boles / Bridget Dealy	John Boles / Mary Higgins	T. O'Meara
3-31-1838	Mary McGovern	John McGovern / Elizabeth Duffy	John Duffy / Margaret McGovern	T. O'Meara
- 1-1838	Thomas Conron	Michael Conron / Bridget Lynch	Patrick Carroll / Rose Carroll	T. O'Meara
4- 8-1838	Nathaniel Reed	William Reed / Ann Rafferty	Patrick Crowley / Ellen Duggan	T. O'Meara

Date	Name			Priest
4-12-1838	Mary Kelley	Daniel Kelley / Catherine ?ghlin		T. O'Meara
4-15-1838	Ann Fitzgibbons	Patrick Fitzgibbons / Mary Hoolahan	John Mahony / Mary McDonough	T. O'Meara
4-17-1838	?ael ?dy	James Malady / Margaret Cavanaugh	William Regan / Jane Rohan	T. O'Meara
4-19-1838	Emma Mul?d	Edward Harris Mulferd	James Lackin / Catherine Colkin	T. O'Meara
4-22-1838	Michael ?rol	O?en ?ol / Eli?th Rieley	T. O'Meara / Elleanor Ryan	T. O'Meara
4-22-1838	Edward ?	?rd Hughes / ?Karns	Michael Fitzsimons / Catherine McCarty	T. O'Meara
4-28-1838	Robert A. Kinzie Age 28 years		Thomas Peters / Mary Berger	T. O'Meara
5- 3-1838	Mry Ann Davelin	Edward Davelin / Rose McDonnell	T. O'Meara / Rose Bailly; John Davelin / Ann Finnerty	T. O'Meara

Date	Person Baptized	Parents	Sponsors	By
5-26-1838	Hannah Dunnegan	Michael Dunnegan Elizabeth Walsh	Patrick Law Hannah Riorden	.T. O'Meara
5-29-1838	Maria Lane	Cornelius Lane Bridget McCarty	Patrick Theny Catherine McCarty	T. O'Meara
6- 2-1838	Jane Callahan	John Callahan Ann Wellon	John Callahan Bridget Doyle	T. O'.
6- 6-1838	Eleanor Bedelia Halligan	Samuel Halligan Mary Mary	Owen Burke Mary Burke	John F. Plunkett
6- 6-1838	James Wall	Bt Wall Catherine Owly	Patrick Carney Bridget Higgins	T. O'Meara
6-13-1838	Elleanor Dwyer	Wm. Dwyer Mary May	John Dwyer Catherine Dwyer	OMeara
6-15-1838	John Whistler	John Wr Br Baillie	John B. Deaublen Rose Baille	T. OMeara
6-15-1838	Mary Whistler	John Ber Esther Baillie	Timothy O'Meara Gwenthlean Whistler	T. O'Meara
6-15-1838	William Whistler	John Ber Eher Baillie	William Whistler Julia Horson	T. O'Meara
6-17-1838	Elizabeth Kerby	Ths. Kerby Br Alpin	Thomas Melvin Annstitia Fitzgibbon	T. O'Mara
6-17-1838	John Healy	Thomas Hly Margaret Sullivan	Thomas Leo Julia Stuart	T. O'Meara

Date	Name	Parents	Sponsors	Priest
6-18-1838	Margaret Tierney	Pat rik Tierney / Mary Kelly	James Lane / Bridget Barkley	T. O'Meara
6-23-1838	Catherine Reedy	gh Reedy / Rose Higgins	Patrick Egan / Bridget Fahey	T. O'Meara
6-24-1838	Catherine Carroll	Ed Coll / Christy McDonald	John Breen / Mary McDonough	T. O'Meara
6-24-1838	John Walsh	Patrick Walsh / Elizabeth Cn	Patrick Conlan / Bridget Corcoran	T. O'Meara
6-24-1838	Elleanor Cunningham	Mry Cunningham / An Finnerty	Edward Gibbons / Ann Flynn	T. O'Meara
6-25-1838	Susanna Drum	Ed Drum / Ann McT ge	John McGork / Margaret Tehan	T. O'Meara
7- 1-1838	Eridget Joyce	Patrick Joyce / M ria Cn	Michael King / Bridget Jordan	T. O'Meara
7- 1-1838	Elizabeth Heavy	E el Heavy / Elleanor Burk	James Lane / Mary Dawson	T. O'Meara
7- 2-1838	William McCanna	Patrick McCanna / Bridget Duffy	Patrick Gallagher / Rose Walsh	T. O' Ma
7- 2-1838	Henry uffy	John Duffy / Margaret Walsh	Henry Walsh / An Morris	T. O'Meara
7- 8-1838	Martin Bulger	Patrick Blger / Anty M phy	Etrick Fzgerald / Eh Gr	T. O'Meara
7- 8-1838	Ei nrd Fit zgld	co Fitzgerald / II corn gs	s Tully / Sa th Grlin	T. O'Meara

Date	Person Baptized	Parents	Sponsors	Priest
7- 8-1838	Elleanor Neagle	Michael Neagle Johannah Vaughn	Daniel Vaughan Jane Carrigan	T. O'Meara
7- 9-1838	Elleanor Maria Leahy	Silveth Leahy Elleanor Kelly	Peter Tyler Mary Murphy	T. O'Meara
7-10-1838	Jchn McConnell	Antony McConnell Mary Ryan	T. O'Meara Mary Sayers	T. O'Meara
7-11-1838	Mary ahe Gah	Stephen Cash Elleanor Grace	Michael O'Keeff Ann Leery	T. O'Meara
7-12-1838	Cat the ting	Hugh Young Catherine Herly	John Kennedy Bridget Mahon	T. O'Meara
7-12-1838	Methew Scanlon	Michael Scanlon Margaret M. Annestray	John Byrnes Catherine Byrnes	T. O'Meara
7-14-1838	Andre Shore	the Shore Catherine J.	Morty Miller Magdalena Miller	T. O'Meara
7-22-1838	Catherine Deelenty	Michael Deelenty Elleanor Armstrong	Michael McGuire Elleanor Ryan	T. O'Meara
7-23-1838	James Fagan	James Fagan Catherine Murry	James Bolan Catherine ah	T. O' Mra
30-1838	Cornelius Wren	J . luh Wo n lnh Rierden	Mi uhel O'Brien Bridget Kerby	T. O'Meara
- 5-1838	James Ganghan	Th m ao (in Mary Connolly	John Flanigan Bridget Mulloy	T. O Ma

Date	Name	Parents	Sponsors	Celebrant
9 -1-1838	Francis Bush	John Bush / Mary Periolat	Francis Periolet / Agnes Berg	Simon G. Bruté Bishop of Vincennes
9- 1-1838	Adam Scheinegar	Joseph Scheinegar / Magdalen Swab	Adam Berg / Elizabeth Engel	Simon G. Bruté Bishop of Vincennes
9- 2-1838	Thomas Horan	Edward Horan / Mary Gahan	Micl. White / Hanora McGillicuddy	T. O'Meara
9- 2-1838	Micl. Meagher	James Meagher / Mary Boyle	John Boland / Sarah Byan	T. O'Meara
9- 2-1838	Thomas McQuade	Mutrough McQuade / Ann McQuade	Jeremiah Healy / Bridget Fitzmorris	T. O'Meara
9- 2-1838	Elleanor Sullivan	Oen Sullivan / ----- Mrin	John Keenan / Eileanor McCarty	T. O'Meara
9- 2-1838	Oan Harriet Kinzie	Robert Kinzie / G. Harriet Whistler	T. O'Meara / Listy Hotchkiss	Rt. Rev. Dr. Bruté
9- 2-1838	Oet Gahan	Thos. Oan / Margaret Boglan	Owen McManinis / Margaret Timoney	Rt. Rev. Dr. Bruté
9- 3-1838	Alexander Miller	Daniel Miller / Oline Onie	Michael Alexander Jelet / Catherine Bomgarton	T. O'Meara
9- 4-1838	Edward Healy	Robert Healy / Ann Wallace	Thmas Masterson / My Quin	T. O'Meara
9- 5-1838	John Jordan	Richard Jordan / Dolly Hickey	Patrick CeCarty / Mry Jordan	T. O'Meara
9- 9-1838	Mary Harkin	William Harkin / Cathⅽrin McCauley	Francis H. Lawless / Catherine Dawson	T. O'Meara

Date	Person Baptized	Parents	Sponsors	Priest
9-16-1838	Elleanor Redden	Edward Redden Bridget Garity	John C. Lawrence Catherine McCarty	T. O'Meara
9-16-1838	Susan J. Beaubien	Medore Meaubien M ria E. By r o	T. O'Meara Monica Beaubien	T. O'Meara
9-22-1838	William Collins	John Collins Margaret Bondrin	John Thornton Mary Thornton	T. O'Meara
9-22-1838	John Conlan	Patrick Conlan My O 'lhd	Patrick Kelly Mary Flaherty	T. O'Meara
9-22-1838	John Beauvel	John B uvel Barbara Moldre	John Moldre Anna Long	T. O'Meara
9-22-1838	Thomas White	Thos. White Bridget Melody	Thomas Melody Mary Cowen	T. O'Meara
9-22-1838	Charles Muldery	John Muldery Ann Clappy	Edward Horn Mary Gaunan	T. O'Meara
9-22-1838	John Bays	Patrick Bays Julian Bergen	Thomas Keating Alice Larkin	T. O'Meara
9-25-1838	Michael Harney	John Harney Mary Lonergan	Terry O'M ra o Bridget McGrath	T. O'Meara
9-26-1838	Mel King	James King et lls	William Morgan Mra Corcoran	T. O'Meara
9-30-1838	lor Hyde	Patrick Hyde Margaret F rrelh	John Higgins Ann Kelley	T. O'Meara

Mai 22 1833.

1er Bapte

L'an mil huit trente trois, le soussigné ai baptisé George Beaubin fils de ... Beaubien et de Monique Nadeau né le 19 août 1832 ... a été Monsr Beaubien père de l'enfant baptisé marraine Orianger Beaulieu née du père de l'enfant
H. R. F. J. aint Cyr
prêtre

On the 26th of may Eighteen hundred thirty three I, the undersigned, baptised Joseph Son of Michel Mayo one of Marguerit Malore ... 1833 ... gransors were Joseph Lafranboise and Orianger Beaubien.
H. Rbf J. aint Cyr

L'an ... mil huit cent trente trois, ... ai baptisé Augustin Potier fils de Jean Potier et de Victoire Nadeau née ... le ... 1832 ... Augustin ... Marraine Monique Nadeau
H. Rbf J. aint Cyr
prêtre

On the fifth of ... Eighteen hundred and thirty three I, the undersigned, baptised Caroline ...

Chicago
Mary anne
McDonnel

On the second of May 1837 I the undersigned baptized Mary anne, seven months old.
Henry McDonnel & Mary Hollar's daughter,
her sponsors were Charles McDonnel
                                        Schaeffer
                                        cath priest

Mary
Duley

On the seventh of May 1837 I the undersigned
baptised Mary six weeks old of John Duley
and Mary Kanisty Godmother was Mary
Lever
                                        Schaeffer
                                        cath priest

James
Madden

On the seventh of May 1837 I the undersigned
baptised James eleven days old of Thomas
Madden and Mary Grayham his sponsors
were James Grayham and Mary anne White
                                        Schaeffer
                                        cath priest

Cathrine
Salerin

On the seventh of May 1837 I the undersigned
baptised Cathrine thirteen days old of John Salerin and Mary Mimnon her sponsors were John
Hurley and Mary Kittoe
                                        Schaeffer
                                        cath priest

Date	Name	Parents	Parents	Officiant
9-30-1838	Mary Ann Hogan	John Hogan / Elizabeth Missaden	Robert Slattery / Mary Ann Chapman	T. O'Meara
10- 3-1838	Bridget Dalton	Edward Dalton / Mary Farrell	Thomas Brennan / Hanora Fenton	T. O'Meara
10- 3-1838	Rose Brennan	Thos. Brennan / Margaret Donohoe	John Connolly / Eliza Connolly	T. O'Meara
10- 4-1838	Margaret Lumbard	Laurence Lumbard / Catherine Hennerty	Thomas Havey / Mary Phelan	T. O'Meara
10- 4-1838	Catherine Smith	Patrick Smith / Rose Carret	Patrick Cashen / Janet Cavanagh	T. O'Meara
10- 4-1838	Elizabeth McDermott	James McDermott / Ann Hughes	Michael McDermott / Ann Malony	T. O'Meara
10- 4-1839	Ann Davelin	Michael Davelin / Ann Fegan	Patrick Brennan	T. O'Meara
10- 4-1833	Harriet Murphy	John Murphy / H rriet F. Hay	—— McDonald / Mary McIntire	T. O'Meara
10- 5 1838	Margaret Keffe	James Keffe / Mary Shaughnessy	James Lane / Mary S v ga	T. O'Meara
10- 7-1838	Mary McGuire	Michael McGuire / Bridget Hartney	Patrick Higgins / Mary (Ann	T. O'Meara
10- 7-1833	Anne Carrigan	Gen Carrigan / Mary McCarty	Patrick Byrns / Jane Carrigan	T. O'Meara
10- 7-1838	Sarah Ann McNamara	James McNamara / Catherine Cahil	John Sweeney / Bridget Hartney	T. O'Meara

DATE	PERSON BAPTIZED	PARENTS	SPONSORS	PRIEST
10- 7-1838	Catherine McNamara	James McNamara Catherine Cahil	William McCarty Elizabeth	T. O'Meara
10- 9-1838	James Killalea	John Killalea Bridget Keeley	Michael Reilly Jane Costello	T. O'Meara
10-11-1838	James Murphy	Dennis Murphy Mary Keally	Daniel Gaughan Mary Higgins	T. O'Meara
10-14-1838	John Gleason	Edward Gleason Honorah Gleason	Cornelius Dwyer Mary Quin	T. O'Meara
10-16-1838	Julia Connel	Denis Connel Catherine Keilleher	Laurence Sullivan Bridget Splane	T. O'Meara
10-21-1838	Michael Cure	Michael Cure Barbara Goolman	Michael Cure Mary Sopse	J. Benoist
11- 2-1838	Edward Conoway	Michael Conoway Am O'Neil	John Callen Catherine Stanton	T. O'Meara
11- 4-1838	George H. Brown	George Brown Sar h dSmith	George C. Collins Louisa Taylor	T. O'Meara
11- 4-1838	Eleanor O'Hearn	James O'Hearn Mary Flynn	Owen O'Neil Bridget Duffy	T. O'Meara
12-10-1838	John Short	Francis Short Catherine Donnelly	Patrick Murphy Elinor Foley	John F. Plunkett
11-10-1838	Catherine Donnelly	Andrew Donnelly Ann Short	Wm. Fanning Catherine Dunne	John F. Plunkett

12-0-1838	Abegail Burke	Owen Burke Mary Glass (The four above are from the Virginia Settlement).	Patrick McCabe Mary Halligan	John F. Plunket
4-27-1839	Catherine Murry	Michael Murry Mary French	John French Ann Sinnot	T. O'Meara
4-27-1839	John Wilkinson	George Wilkinson Ann Kirkwood	Owen Sullivan Ann Shaw	T. O'Meara
4-27-1839	Julia Beaubien Woodville	—— Woodville Susanna Beaubien	Horace E. Taylor Catherine Byrne	T. O'Meara
5-9-1839	John McCanna	Bernard McCanna Catherine Byrns	John Healy Margaret McNevin	T. O'Meara
5-10-1839	Catherine Fogarty	Edward Fogarty Catherine Armstrong	Joseph Haslet Maria Doran	T. O'Meara
5-14-1839	Henry Meyrose	Henry Meyrose Agnes Burger	Henry Burger Mary Sonderson	T. O'Meara
5-15-1839	James O'Brien	Daniel O'Brien Mary Kelley	Michael Kelly Rosanna Kenney	T. O'Meara
5-19-1839	Sarah Keogh	Peter R. Keough Sarah Saul	William Laughlin Mary Coen	T. O'Meara
5-26-1839	Elleanor Shea	Wm. Shea Elleanor Mahony	John Donnolan Julia Lally	T. O'Meara

Date	Name	Parents	Sponsors	Priest
6- 9-1839	James Henry	Patrick Baxter / Mary Soyer	John Ryan / Catherine White	T. O'Meara
6-12-1839	Mary E. Murry	John Murry / Mary Brennan	Timothy O'Meara / Margaret Timoney	T. O'Meara
6-13-1839	Winifred Battle	John Battle / Alice Doyle	James Carney / Alice Dwyer	T. O'Meara
6-16-1839	John Carney	John Carney / Mary Linehan	James Leonard / Bridget Flynn	T. O'Meara
6-16-1839	Rose Andros	⸫n Andros / Delaide Bouchard	Brien Coughlin / Mary Hartigan	T. O'Meara
6-16-1839	Catherine McCarty	⸫. McCarty / Elizabeth Hanlon	Andrew McCarty / Catherine ⸫ M	T. O' Mra
6-17-1839	John Ryan	John Ryan / Jane Byrns	Henry ⸫ingham / Ann Flynn	T. O'Meara
6-25-1839	Elizabeth Beaubien	Mark Beaubien / Monica ⸫u	T. O ⸫Mra / Julia Lafromboise	T. O'Meara
7- 7-1839	Thomas James Byan	⸫m Ryan / Sarah Carlan	Jmes Mahor / Ann Bogly	T. O'Meara
7- 1-1839	Cathorine O'Connor	Th s.O ⸫for / Mary Hogan	Jeremiah Connor / Mary Holl ard	T. O'Meara

Date		
7-21-1839	Paul Masey	Bernard Masey
		Josephine Bey
7-21-1839	Margaret Ivens	Denis Ivens
		Catherine Trumble
7-25-1839	Catherine Lane	James Lane
		Mary Higgins
7-31-1839	Jane Patwell	Thomas Patwell
		Anna Montgomery
8- 8-1839	Mary A. Crowley	P. Crowley
		Ellen Duggan
8-16-1839	Bernard Malser	Louis Malser
		Mary Beamer
8-19-1839	Mary Carney	James Carney
		An Tim ney o
8-30-1839	Margaret Dwyer	Cornelius Dwyer
		Hanorah Joyce
9- 1-1839	James Mrn	John McGovern
		Elizabeth Duffy
9-15-1839	Nicola Murry	John Murry
		Alice rfor
9-15-1839	Ni dhas Cliff rd o	Thomas Clifford
		Mary Campion
9-16-1839	James Mrn	Hugh Mrn
		Bridget Donn dly

Date	Person Baptized	Parents	Sponsors	Priest
9-22-1839	Gana Fitzpatrick	John Fitzpatrick / Ann McGrath	Thomas McCleud / Catherine Devine	T. O'Meara
9-22-1839	Catherine Dalton	Michael Dalton / Bridget Buckley	James Simmons / Eleanor Powers	T. O'Meara
9-24-1839	John Mattle	Joseph Mattle / Mary A. Astell	Peter Rice / Catherine Chandler	T. O'Meara
9-29-1839	William Carty	Andrew Carty / Catherine Noonan	William McCarty / Elizabeth Hanlon	T. O'Meara
9-29-1839	Timothy Bennet	James Bennet / Catherine Collins	Martin Russell / Catherine O Brien	T. O'Meara
10- 6-1839	James Lappin	Richard Lappin / Electi Strickland	John Fitzpatrick / Christiana Tierney	T. O'Meara
10-11-1839	John Murphy	John Murphy / Bridget Rogers	Edward Gibbons / Margaret Feeney	T. O'Meara
10-13-1839	Catherine Gable	Peter Gable / Maria Maloney	Fernandis Lebnke / Catherine Malta	T. O'Meara
10-16-1839	Martin Shenagre	Joseph Shenagre / Catherine Shaub	Martin Shelle / Catherine Berge	T. O'Meara

NOTE—It is morally certain that we have misconceived many of these names. The difficulty of a correct rendering may be judged from the entry "Hirn" found on the record. We have rendered it Hearn, thinking the writer meant to write "Hirn."

There are many names amongst the foregoing that are very
familiar in Chicago and Illinois. Everybody knows of the very early
family of Beaubiens, and almost everybody gives the pioneer of that
family, Jean Baptist Beaubien, the credit of being virtually the first
substantial permanent resident of Chicago. It is certain that he was
here as early as 1805, and it is known certainly that he lived here
from 1817 until his death.[3] His brother Mark came later, but must
also be considered amongst the founders of Chicago, and for many
years one of its most substantial citizens.[4]

The name of Laframboise also is familiar, and has been borne by
worthy people from the earliest inhabitants of that name to the
present time.[5]

The appearance of the name Kinzie in these records is a surprise
to some, and when we note that the name of Robert A. Kinzie appears
on the baptismal record under the date of April 23, 1838, with the
notation that the baptized was 28 years of age, it sets us thinking.
Upon diligent search it will be revealed that the said Robert A. Kinzie
was married back in 1834[6] to the beautiful Gwenthlean Whistler,
one of the most charming and cultured of the early maids and matrons
of Chicago.

Robert was born in Chicago on February 8, 1810, and is said to
have retained a recollection of the Fort Dearborn Massacre, although
he was only two and one-half years old when it occurred. When nine
years old he is said to have made a trip to St. Louis with his father.
He was sent to Detroit to attend school, and in reaching Detroit went
by way of the Lakes, but returned on horseback. In 1825 he went
to work in the fur trade at Prairie du Chien. Here he remained two
years, and returning to Chicago in 1827, soon went to Detroit. In
1829 he joined his brother John at Fort Winnebago, and became
sutler to the Fort. He was back in Chicago in 1831 and in 1832 built
a frame store, the first frame store in Chicago, on the west side. All
prior structures were of logs.

---

[3] Franck G. Beaubien's account of *The Beaubiens in Illinois* in the July,
1919 and January, 1920 numbers of the ILLINOIS CATHOLIC HISTORICAL REVIEW
is the best that has been given of this distinguished family.

[4] Mark undoubtedly took the lead in helping to secure the Priest and establish
the first Church.

[5] There are the names of three families of this unusual name in the Chicago
telephone directory. Some of them are unable to tell me just how they are related to the pioneers of that name.

[6] See, Note 11.

About this time, although we have found no record of the marriage, Robert married Gwenthlean Whistler, the daughter of Major William Whistler, who, as has been stated, was in command of Fort Dearborn, and who was a Lieutenant in his father's force when his father, Captain John Whistler, in 1803, first came to Chicago and erected Fort Dearborn.

In 1835 Robert Kinzie became a member of the firm of Kinzie, Davis & Hyde, Hardware Dealers. In 1840 he moved to a farm at Walnut Grove, Illinois, and remained three years. In 1845 he was at Des Moines, Iowa, and from thence went beyond the Missouri River in Kansas to trade with the Indians.

In May, 1861, he was appointed paymaster in the army, with the rank of Major, and remained in the service until the time of his death. From 1861 to 1864, during the war of the Rebellion, he was in Washington, D. C. From 1864 to 1868 he was in New Mexico, and after that was in Chicago.[7]

Although a man of apparently excellent health he died suddenly at his residence on 35th Street, Chicago, on Saturday afternoon, December 13, 1873.

The funeral services were conducted by Rev. Patrick W. Riordan at St. James Catholic Church.[8]

A little incident in the life of Major Kinzie, related rather incidentally, has to do with one of the first fires that ever occurred in Chicago. Shortly prior to the Black Hawk War a large number of Pottawatomi Indians had been drawn to Chicago for the annual payment, and upon receiving their annuity all of the Indians departed, except a number of Chief Big Foot's Band, who then lived where Lake Geneva now stands. On the night following the payment there was a violent storm, and the part of old Fort Dearborn, which was then occupied by the garrison, known as the Barracks, was struck by lightning, and destroyed, together with the storehouse and a portion of the guard house.

The alarm of fire soon roused the settlers, and men and women to the number of forty, came to the scene of the fire. It was seen that the barracks and store house could not be saved, and so all efforts were directed to saving the remaining buildings. In the emergency Robert Kinzie, wrapped in a wet blanket, mounted to the roof of the guard house, which already on fire, while the others formed a line to the river, along which water was passed to him in buckets and

[7] Hurlbut, *Chicago Antiquities*, consult index.
[8] *Ibid.*

CHICAGO'S EARLIEST FAMILIES UNITED.

Above—Major William Whistler and wife. Below—Major Robert A. Kinzie and
Wife. Mrs. Kinzie was the Daughter of Major Whistler and Wife.
Robert A. Kinzie was the son of John Kinzie.

other available utensils. Despite his burns and the danger he ran, Kinzie maintained his position until about dawn, when the fire was brought under control.[9]

Gwenthlean Whistler Kinzie was born in 1818, and was married to Robert A. Kinzie, in 1834. This charming woman was still living and residing in Chicago when Joseph Kirkland wrote his short history of Chicago under the title "The Story of Chicago," published in 1892. The author states that she was consulted with reference to the narrative of the Whistler family, and in a footnote states that upon mentioning her name to Judge John D. Caton, who was also still living at the time, Judge Caton said: "Yes, I remember the marriage, and that the bride was one of the most beautiful women you can imagine. I have never seen her since that time. Ladies were not plentiful in this part of the world then, and we were not over particular about looks, but Gwenthlean Whistler Kinzie would be noted for beauty anywhere at any time." The author in his note continues: "And on looking at the lady herself one can well believe all that can be said in praise of her charms in her girlish years—sixteen when she was married."[10]

Mr. Kirkland in his story of Chicago has this to say about the Kinzie Whistler wedding:

It was in 1834 that a marriage took place, memorable in several ways. It joined together the two historic races, Kinzies and Whistlers. Robert Allen Kinzie married Gwenthlean Whistler, grand-daughter of the builder and first commandant of the first fort, and daughter of one of the last commandants of the second. The wedding took place in the fort, and was, of course followed by a dance. The beauty of the bride has already been spoken of, and the interesting fact that she today is in Chicago, in full virgor of her faculties, as are also two at least of her early contemporaries, Judge and Mrs. Caton, whose latest portraits are kindly placed at the disposal of this "Story," which would scarcely be complete without them. In vain do we try to get the bill of fare of the wedding feast. Of ice-cream and oysters there were surely none. Home-made confectionery, cakes, pies, sweetmeats, perhaps a few precious Eastern apples, cold meats, poultry and game, and such convival liquids as the garrison could furnish—this was probably all that the union of all the housewifely forces could provide, and good and ample it was, and laughter.'"[11]

Mrs. Gwenthlean Whistler Kinzie was a devout Catholic all her life. Throughout her residence in Chicago she was active in all the progressive and humanitarian movements of the parishes in which she lived and in a larger way assisted with all church work in the

---

[9] *Ibid.*
[10] Kirkland, *Story of Chicago*, p. 51.
[11] *Ibid.*, pp. 137-8.

city. She has to her credit several liberal donations of property and funds for Catholic churches and other Catholic institutions. It should be said that her distinguished husband was equally zealous in the Catholic cause and that all the children were reared Catholics.

Mrs. Kinzie died near the end of the nineteenth or the beginning of the twentieth century—of the exact date we are not at present informed. She was buried from St. James' Church as was her husband and laid to rest in Graceland Cemetery in the Kinzie family burial ground.

Farther down we come across quite a list of Whistlers. On July 15, 1838, John, Mary and William Whistler were baptized by Father Timothy O'Meara. They were, according to the record, the children of John Whistler and Esther Baillie Whistler. John Whistler was the son of Major Whistler, in command of Fort Dearborn at that time, and the grandson of Captain John Whistler, the founder and father of Chicago. The sponsors for John Whistler were John E. Beaubien and Rose Baillie. The sponsors for Mary Whistler were Father Timothy O'Meara and Gwenthlean Whistler, while those for William Whistler were William Whistler and Julia Herson.

Yet other names on the record deserve more attention than they may be given here. John McGovern's name appears for the first time on the parish records of Chicago as of March 31, 1838. It was the occasion of the baptism of Mary McGovern, and John McGovern and Elizabeth Duffy are recorded as parents, while John Duffy and Margaret McGovern were the sponsors.

The name of McGovern was from this time on a familiar one in Catholic records and circles of Chicago. This pious layman was the willing and able assistant of every bishop and priest who needed lay help during his lifetime. Moreover, he was the father of one of the most distinguished clergymen of the Chicago diocese, the Rev. James J. McGovern, D. D. Worthy representatives of his family still survive in his two daughters, Mrs. Anna E. Young of Rogers Park, and Mrs. Margaret Walsh of Hyde Park, and their accomplished children.[12]

The McGoverns through marriage became united to another worthy Catholic family, whose names appear on these records. One of John McGovern's daughters, Margaret, a sister of Father McGovern, married John L. Walsh, the son of Patrick Walsh. Patrick Walsh was the son of Michael Walsh or Welch, who had been written down in

---

[12] The name of McGovern has undergone some changes. It is variously spelled in the records as McGauren, McGouvren and McGovern.

history as the first Irishman of Chicago. This baptismal record shows
that John Walsh was baptized on June 24, 1838; that Patrick Walsh
and Elizabeth Corcoran were his parents, and that Patrick Conlon
and Bridget Corcoran were sponsors, and Father O'Meara administered the sacrament.[13] Michael Walsh, the grandfather of the baptized infant, was a United States soldier or sailor, and after his discharge bought 160 acres of land situated along the south branch
of the Chicago river. He enlisted in the Blackhawk War, and was
probably killed in that war, as no subsequent trace can be found of
him. Patrick, as stated, was the son of Michael Walsh and became
owner of the land purchased by Michael, known as Walsh's woods.
In turn the property came to the two sons of Patrick, John L., and
Hugh. Hugh died before reaching fifty years of age, unmarried.
John L. married Margaret McGovern. John L. Walsh died on March
23, 1890, but his widow is still living in Chicago with her daughter,
Mrs. Margaret Kidder, and a son and granddaughter.

It is most interesting to trace these worthy pioneers through their
descendants, and especially through those that have reflected credit
upon their ancestors, having remained true to the faith of their
fathers, and to the best interests and traditions of their land.

Another interesting name found on these early records is Sauter.
The first members of the Sauter family to reach Chicago came in
1835. Two or three members of the family who first came became
associated in business with the pioneer Kinzie family. The patriarch
of the family, Elogyus Sauter, came to Chicago in 1837, accompanied
by his wife, whose maiden name was Beck, and several sons and
daughters.

Of the sons and daughters who survived to manhood and woman-
hood and lived in Chicago may be named Charles, Vincent, and Jacob,
sons, and Barbara, Catherine, Victoria and Dominica, daughters. The
son Jacob remained in Chicago until his death, and was the father
of Charles Jacob Sauter, still living in Chicago, and still quite
prominent amongst a large circle of friends and acquaintances.
Charles Sauter is the father of Louis Edward, Frank, and Frederick
Sauter, and Mrs. Mary Louise Westrich and Mrs. Clara Alice Finn.

Louis Edward Sauter is a prominent lawyer well know in Catholic
circles, and was State Deputy of the Knights of Columbus in 1906
and 1907.

The first appearance of the name Sauter on the parish records of
St. Mary's is the baptism of John Herod, on March 26, 1838. The

---

[13] This family was called variously, "Welsh" and "Walsh."

parents of the child were William Herod and Catherine Sauter, while the sponsors were John Sauter and Barbara Sauter, with Father ʼMeara as officiating clergyman. We next find the Sauters getting married at a rather wholesale rate. On August 4, 1838 Father O'Meara had a big double wedding, the principals in which were Joseph Claus and Barbara Sauter and Andrew Schaller and Victoria Sauter. Andrew Schaller and Victoria Sauter did the honors as best man and bridesmaid for the first couple, and in turn Joseph Claus and Barbara Sauter did the honors for the second couple.

The Sauter family would be a delight to the genealogist. In tracing the root and branches of the family tree he would encounter titles and distinctions and coat-of-arms; would find the sturdy old pioneer of the family leaving his native land for the greater liberty to be enjoyed in a new and strange world. As he followed the progeny he would find good soldiers fighting for the Union—none better than the respected septuagenarian, Charles Jacob Sauter, still living in Chicago and in like manner he would find others gracing the professions, in general true to their rearing and valuable and respected citizens of their several communities.

A long list of Irish names will be found, sufficient to furnish the oldest settlers topics of interest, conversation and investigation for many moons.

(To be continued)

JOSEPH J. THOMPSON.

Chicago.

PETER REINBERG

A distinguished Catholic in the person of Peter Reinberg, at the time of his death President of the Board of Commissioners of Cook County, is added to the Bead Roll of the ILLINOIS CATHOLIC HIS-·TORICAL SOCIETY.

The most satisfactory expression of appreciation of the deceased which has come to our attention is contained in a memorial address delivered by Mr. Charles H. Wacker at a meeting held to honor the memory of Mr. Reinberg on Thursday, March 10, 1921.

Mr. Wacker spoke as follows:

Mr. Reinberg was a Chicago product. He was born March 5, 1858, sixty-three years ago, in the town of Lake View on the corner of Robey Street and Balmoral Avenue, now a part of the City of Chicago.

He was an ideal citizen and a thoroughly well rounded character. All exalted characters must be well rounded, men who are developed on all sides of their character, physical, mental, moral and spiritual.

As a business man his ability was shown in his career as a florist. He was a pioneer in that line and had been given the title of the "Rose and Carnation King." At the time of his death his greenhouses covered an area of twenty-five acres.

Although a successful business man, he was a practical idealist with a keen sense of the beautiful in nature.

All—rich and poor—looked upon him as an able man; as one above reproach in public life; as an exemplary citizen; and as a charitable, big-hearted, public-spirited man, broad and big enough for all regardless of color or creed.

He enjoyed the confidence and good will of everyone, and his exceptional qualities of mind and heart were fully appreciated by his fellow-citizens.

He will be remembered as a true, loyal friend, hospitable, kind and generous; as the exemplary head of his family and as a citizen of the highest type—a man of sterling qualities who well performed all the duties which as a citizen he owed the community in which he lived.

A striking example of the confidence the voters of Chicago had in him is shown by his election four times as Alderman of the 26th Ward; twice without opposition, despite the fact that that is a strong Republican ward.

437

He served as president of the County Board and Forest Preserve District for six years, and as president of the Board of Education for two years.

Numerous examples could be cited to show that he was courageous and fearless, and that he always put the public good above individual gain or political prestige.

Peter Reinberg died happy and contented. In a letter to a friend written but a few days before his death he said, "I am well and happy and in looking out of the window I am enjoying the birds flitting about. Even a political enemy passed me today and smiled."

It was one of his outstanding characteristics that he never carried grudge.

The outpouring of people from every walk in life who paid him the tribute of affection is conclusive evidence of the place he held in the hearts of his fellow-citizens. His death was a great loss, not only to his family and a host of friends, but also to the City and County.

He was a devout Christian gentleman, faithful and devoted to his parish. Never did he fail to attend church on Sunday mornings nor during the season to visit with the children, whom he came to call "his children," in the forest preserves,—little ones sojourning at the fresh air camp which bears his name.

The pictures in the annual Forest Preserve and Charity Service reports are impressive, nay inspirational, and teach a wholesome lesson. They show Mr. Reinberg surrounded by a lot of laughing little tots grateful for the generous gifts of candies and dainties he was always sure to bring. Instinctively these children knew that Mr. Reinberg was their friend and the pictures show his face beaming with joy and love as he played and romped with them.

He had hobbies, but the predominating ones were centered in the love of children and a compassionate and tender feeling for the down-and-out.

It was inspiring to discuss with him the Oak Forest Institutions, the County Hospital, the Forest Preserves and the Zoololigica Garden. His heart and soul were wrapped up in the humanitarian activities of the County Board.

His last accomplishment was the creation of a Zoological Board ready to undertake making the Chicago Zoological Garden one of the finest in the world.

As time goes on our people will realize more and more the value of increased health and happiness to the millions that have already visited the Forest Preserves and the millions upon millions that will

continue to enjoy the healthgiving and elevating pleasures of these great country playgrounds.

The Forest Preserve system when completed will have no equal in the world and will forever stand out as a monument to the men who have conducted its affairs in a manner which has met with universal commendation.

The history of Chicago abounds in periods of great accomplishment.

In the short span of approximately eighty-five years, Chicago has grown from a village to a city of nearly three million people. During this period there have been a number of outstanding epochs.

In the early '60's, the city was raised fourteen feet for drainage purposes, a tremendous undertaking for the time.

Then in 1869 our splendid system of parks and boulevards was established.

Next came the rebuilding of the city after the destructive fire of 1871.

Following that occurred the never-surpassed World's Fair of 1893.

1900 witnessed the opening of the drainage canal.

In 1909 the Commercial Club of Chicago presented to the city the Chicago Plan replete with commercial and humanitarian suggestions for the public good. This resulted in the creation of the Chicago Plan Commission by the City Council.

The last great epoch in Chicago's history was the creation by the State Legislature of the Forest Preserve District of Cook County, with which our friend will always be associated as the first president and in reality the founder.

Chicago has risen to every emergency. Whenever needed, men of the hour were not wanting,—men like Peter Reinberg—men of vision and foresight—stalwart men, who recognized the potentialities of and had implicit confidence in the future of their city. Such men feared no obstacles and aroused the civic patriotism that put "I Will" upon the shield of Chicago.

Peter Reinberg did not live in vain. He set an example well worth emulating and it may truly be said of him "the world is better for his having lived in it."

Illinois Catholic Historical Society
617 ASHLAND BLOCK, CHICAGO

Illinois Catholic Historical Review
Journal of the Illinois Catholic Historical Society
917 ASHLAND BLOCK, CHICAGO

EDITOR-IN-CHIEF
Joseph J. Thompson..............*Chicago*

ASSOCIATE EDITORS
Rev. Frederick Beuckman........*Belleville*   Kate Meade ....*Chicago*
Rev. J. B. Culemans.............*Moline*.   Rev. Francis J. Epstein...........*Chicago*
William Stetson Merrill.............*Chicago*

EDITORIAL COMMENT

Conclusion of Volume Three. With this, April, 1921 number we conclude the third volume of the ILLINOIS CATHOLIC HISTORICAL REVIEW. The ILLINOIS CATHOLIC HISTORICAL SOCIETY was organized on February 28, 1918, in the very midst of the World War. The pendency of the war added difficulties usual to the establishment of a new institution in a community generally assumed to be already over-crowded, nor have general conditions bearing upon such an undertaking improved very materially to the present. Although two years distant from the end of actual fighting, we are still influenced by the results of the war. These results have naturally had an influence upon the finances of all enterprises, and especially upon those that are more or less of a cultural nature and not strictly within the domain of necessities. One drive succeeding another, prosecuted for urgent needs, has deterred many who under other conditions

would have given liberal support to such an undertaking, from enthusiastic co-operation. We feel, however, under all the circumstances, that we have been fortunate in being able to launch this enterprise and to maintain it with a substantial degree of success. Looking back over the three years of endeavor and glancing at the accomplishments of the Society, as best exemplified in the three substantial volumes which have become the inheritance of the generations to come, every member of the Society will, we are sure, experience a pleasurable sensation that he or she played some part in achieving the result. That our work is appreciated by the public is evidenced especially by the frequent inquiries received from librarians expressing sometimes an uneasiness in connection with the late delivery of the magazine. Interest in such quarters is especially gratifying, since, aside from the actual individual distribution of the REVIEW, the library and reading room are our special objects of conquest. Were we permitted as a reward for striving faithfully to have granted three requests, one for each year of the life of the REVIEW, they would in their order run something like this: 1st: a large, new life membership; 2nd, a wide individual distribution of the ILLINOIS CATHOLIC HISTORICAL REVIEW, and 3rd, a place for the REVIEW on the table of every library and reading room, especially those in the Mississippi Valley. Every reader can help to realize these wishes.

To Get a Hearing.—A recent writer, well qualified to speak upon the subject, has talked pointedly on the subject of history writing. These lines quoted from a very extensive six volume work recently issued under the name of ''Beacon Lights of History'' are interesting:

''A great history must have other merits besides accuracy, antiquarian research, and presentation of authorities and notes. It must be a work of art; and art has reference to style and language, to grouping of details and richness of illustration, to eloquence and poetry and beauty. A dry history, however learned, will never be read; it will only be consulted, like a law-book, or Mosheims 'Commentaries'. We require life in history, and it is for their vividness that the writings of Livy and Tacitus will be perpetuated.''

Wanted: A Story of the Christian Era Written by a Catholic. The lack of historical knowledge in modern times is appalling. It would be dangerous to suggest any percentage, however small, of present day people who have even a superficial knowledge of the history of the past. True most of those who know little of the past are convinced that they are as well off not to be informed in such respect, despite the trite saying of a great American orator that ''The only lamp by which I may guide my feet is the light of the past.'' There are some indications, however, that if history be palatively served it may be interestingly partaken of. The best evidence of this fact recently introduced is ''The Outline of History'' by H. G. Wells. Wells, to begin with, is a popular writer, rather of the newspaper or popular magazine style, something of a phrase maker, and, at any rate, light and easy to follow. For these reasons, more than for any other, we are convinced this Outline of History, which is a simple story of man and life from the first faint glimmerings of civilization to the present, is receiving a wider hearing than any historical work has ever had. Some of the reviewers look upon Wells' story as more than a history as, for example, one says: ''Here is more than history. Here is a philosophy of life. Here is an elaborate explanation

of the origins of ideas and institutions. Here is an attempt to penetrate the darkness of the future." We think the final judgment upon Wells' work will be that it has been depreciated in value by these very features. Had he omitted his philosophy of life and his attempt to penetrate the darkness of the future especially, none would have missed them, and all rational readers would consider the work of greater merit for their omission. A philosophy that acknowledges the very existence of progress and civilization as due to a Divine impulse, but that takes faith and religion out of the plan of the Universe leaves nothing. Without faith and religion man is but one of the beasts of the jungle, and his doings and sayings of no import. As has been well said by the *Literary Digest*: "The historian's attempt to reduce Christianity to a few simple teachings which might easily be accepted by good Buddhists and Confucianists and Mohammedans is not unnaturally met with praise by Unitarians and scorned by Catholics." How the book looks to a trained Catholic mind is well stated in the *Catholic World* by Dr. Henry A. Lappin:

"He refuses all interpretations of Jesus Christ that would transcend the limits of human experience. The tremendous and unique claim of Christ upon the loyalty and submission of mankind, he simply will not recognize. He misses the central fact of all pre-Christian history; that it was a divinely ordained preparation for the adorable mystery of the Incarnation, and that with the coming of Christ and His Death upon the Cross, the sum of human life and human aspiration was instantly carried up to a new and infinitely higher level: that, in short, the Incarnation of the Son of God was a unique and emphatic remedial intervention. Believing Christians will passionately repudiate the whole temper and mind of these chapters. Reason and common sense and human experience reject them. Mr. Wells' arguments will neither wear nor wash. Of the whole exquisitely beautiful and intricately wrought yet sublimely simple structure of the Christian Doctrine of the Trinity, and of the sacraments, and of the Divine Constitution of the Church, Mr. Wells has no faintest glimmering of understanding, or appreciation. Far from being Christian, Mr. Wells' optimism is the shoddiest sentimentalism."

However, as we have before stated, the reception of the book is proof that there is a deep, if dormant, interest in history,—hence our suggestion that a story, especially of the Christian era, written by a Catholic, is needed. The Old Testament can hardly be improved upon as a history of man to the time of Christ, but the story of the Christian era is yet to be written. Those who have made pretentious attempts at writing modern history have consciously or unconsciously distorted the facts. It is not intended, however, to maintain that non-Catholics alone have sinned in this respect. There are no doubt cases of distortion on the Catholic side, but it yet remains true that the properly qualified Catholic is better equipped to write a true story of the Christian era than any non-Catholic. We have grown into the habit of being pleased with favorable mention of the Church and its work in non-Catholic publications, and of pointing with pride to them as concessions, when, as a matter of fact, they constitute but the truth, and should be made as a matter of course. As a rule, however, the non-Catholic writer lacks the viewpoint, and be he ever so fair-minded, he is disqualified by his want of faith to treat truthfully subjects in which Catholicity is vitally concerned. Entirely too little is known of the birth, the early struggles and the development of Christianity under the guidance of the Catholic Church. How many men on the street can tell you anything about the religion which

fostered and reared civilization from the first to the fourteenth century, before any other form of Divine Worship than that followed by the Catholic Church to the present day was dreamed of. How many are informed that Martin Luther was but an ex-priest in the same sense of Chiniquy, Schlatter, and others of our own day? That the inquisition was a political and not a religious institution; that the popes were the leaders of science and education, and that every advance of civilization was prompted and forwarded by the Church. The "dark ages" have been too long taken for granted, and the distinction between spiritual and material progress has been too long obscured. A story of the character indicated, following the style of Wells' *Outline of History* if you will, and written by a Catholic of the attainments and capabilities of a man like Dr. James J. Walsh, would, we are convinced, get, if not a world-wide, at least a nation-wide, hearing.

Philosophy Drawn From History. The late lamented Lord Mayor of Cork, Terence MacSwiney, was a philosopher as well as a patriot. To be convinced of this, one need only glance through his book, *Principles of Freedom* (New York, E. P. Dutton & Co.) and note the constantly recurring passages that bear all the characteristics of high grade philosophy. Speaking of human relations in general and particularly of the Irish-English situation MacSwiney says:

"If the world is to be regenerated, we must have a world-wide unity—not of government, but of brotherhood. To this great end every individual, every nation has a duty; and that the end may not be missed we must continually turn for the correction of our philosophy to reflecting on the common origin of the human race, on the beauty of the world that is the heritage of all, our common hopes and fears, and in the greatest sense the mutual interests of the peoples of the earth. If, unheeding this, any people make their part of the earth ugly with acts of tyranny and baseness, they threaten the security of all."

On the exercise of power we read this sage observation:

"It is the duty of the rightful power to develop the best in its subjects: it is the practice of the usurping power to develop the basest."

Of patriotism we read:

"It is nothing but love of country that rouses us to make our land full-blooded and beautiful."

Of idealism it is said:

"The man who cries for the sacred thing but voices a universal need. To exist, the healthy mind must have beautiful things—the rapture of a song, the music of running water, the glory of the sunset and its dreams, and the deeper dreams of the dawn."

"The end of freedom," we are told, "is to realize the salvation and happiness of all peoples, to make the world, and not any selfish corner of it, a more beautiful dwelling-place for men."

BOOK REVIEWS

Beacon Lights of History. By JOHN LORD, LL. D. New York, Wise & Company; The University of Cambridge Press, Cambridge, Mass. (Current Opinion).

Sets of books are in grave danger of neglect. Everybody is so busy nowadays that effort must be exerted to find time for general reading—hence a work consisting of several volumes is more or less forbidding. There is an attractiveness about the *Beacon Lights of History*, however, that in a measure offsets the disinclination to undertake a new task, and once one has grasped the plan of the author and read briefly from any of the great studies included, it is no longer necessary to cultivate an inclination.

These handy-volume books, (there are six of them), in coat pocket size, are filled with a number of studies, lectures really, on the leading events and personages of all known time. They begin with ancient religion, and make the reader acquainted with Egyptian, Assyrian, Babylonian and Persian beliefs and with Brahmanism and Buddhism, Classic Mythology and Ancient Philosophy.

In separate studies we read of Confucius, Socrates, Phidias and of the Greek and Roman Classics.

Taking up the Old Testament characters we are made intimately acquinted with Abraham, Joseph, Moses, Samuel, David, Solomon, Elijah, Isaiah, Jeremiah, and Judas Maccabaeus.

In other lines we study Cyrus the Great, Julius Caesar, Marcus Aurelius, Constantine the Great, Saint Chrysostom, Saint Ambrose, Saint Augustine, Theodosius the Great, Saint Leo the Great, Mohammed, Charlemagne, Hildebrand, Saint Bernard, Saint Anselm, Saint Thomas Aquinas, Saint Thomas a'Becket, William Wykeham, John Wycliff, Dante, Geoffrey Chaucer, Christopher Columbus, Savonarola, Michael Angelo, Martin Luther, Thomas Cranmer, Saint Ignatius Loyola, John Calvin, Lord Bacon, Galileo, Heloise, Joan of Arc, St. Theresa, Madame de Maintenon, Sarah, Duchess of Marlborough, Madame Recamier, Madame de Stael, Hannah More, George Eliot, Alfred the Great, Queen Elizabeth, Henry of Navarre, Gustavus Adolphus, Cardinal Richelieu, Oliver Cromwell, Louis XIV, Louis XV, Peter the Great, Frederick the Great.

Coming to America, we have studies of Benjamin Franklin, George Washington, Alexander Hamilton, John Adams, Thomas Jefferson, John Marshall, Lafayette, Andrew Jackson, Henry Clay, Daniel Webster, John C. Calhoun, Abraham Lincoln, Robert E. Lee, Ulysses S. Grant and John Hay.

Returning to Europe, we can study Edmund Burke, Napoleon

Bonaparte, Prince Metternich, Chateaubriand, Louis Philippe, William IV, Sir Robert Peel, Cavour, Czar Nicholas, Louis Napoleon, Prince Bismarck, William E. Gladstone. Now a volume is devoted to great writers, and we have intimate studies of Rousseau, Sir Walter Scott, Lord Byron, Thomas Carlyle, Lord Macaulay, Shakespeare, John Milton, Johann Wolfgang von Goethe, Alfred (Lord) Tennyson.

In music, we have a study of Richard Wagner; in art, of John Ruskin; in Philosophy, Herbert Spencer; in Science, Charles Darwin; in Navies of War and Commerce, John Ericsson; in the Far East, Li Hung Chang; African development, David Livingstone; in modern archaelogy, Sir Austen Henry Layard; in electricity and magnetism, Michael Faraday; in medicine and surgery, Rudolpf Virchow.

There are compilations, the work of many authors, that cover a wider range of subjects than *Beacon Lights of History*, but we recall nothing from the pen of a single individual that indicates such a wide range of study and investigation by one mind; and while it is not desired to give the appearance of undue enthusiasm, candor requires the admission that we have been fascinated by these studies.

Of course the Catholic reader will not be surprised to find many of the old charges against the Church repeated in Dr. Lord's studies, and, like most non-Catholic writers, the author falls into the error of charging up crimes and errors of individuals to the Church. He does not, however, place the seal of condemnation upon the Church, but even admitting that faults have been committed, either finds a justification for the act, or advises his readers to look upon it in the light of the age and of the circumstances under which it occurred.

Beacon Lights of History is as delightful as it is substantial and valuable. J. J. T.

The McCarthys in Early American History.—Michael J. O'Brien. New York. Dodd, Mead & Co.

Michael J. O'Brien, Historiographer of the American-Irish Historical Society, and auther of the great work "A Hidden Phase of American History" has produced under the above title another monumental work, illustrating his tirelessness as an investigator.

This latest of Mr. O'Brien's efforts contains ten chapters under the following divisions:

The McCarthys of Virginia; the McCarthys in Maryland, the Carolinas and Georgia; the McCarthys in Louisiana, Illinois and Kentucky; the McCarthys in Pennsylvania and Delaware; the McCarthys in New York and New Jersey; the McCarthys in Massachu-

setts; the McCarthys in Connecticut, Rhode Island, Maine, New Hampshire and Vermont. A chapter on "the Fighting Race," and a most interesting appendix, in which are listed the names from the muster rolls and enlistment papers of the Revolutionary Army and Navy, and the Provincial Militia of the thousands of McCarthys who served their country during the Revolutionary War.

Every line of Mr. O'Brien's book is of intense interest, but a paragraph from his introduction can be read with much profit by all those entertaining a kindly feeling for the Irish race:

> There is no earthly reason why the Irish, like Americans of other races, should not be accorded a place in the history of this country. The Huguenot Society has put on record the contributions of the French; the Holland Society has told of the part played by Americans of Dutch descent; the Thistle Society has related the story of the Scotch; the Spaniards have a well-established place in American history, and the English have had numberless historians who made it a business and a trade to supply the world with histories of their own making and from their own point of view; in short, nearly every race which made up the population of this country with the exception of the Irish, has supplied historians who have put on record the creditable deeds of men and women of their own blood. Thus, the American people have had opportunities to learn what each nationality has contributed to the greatness and progress of their country, but, although the Celtic element was numerically important in the Colonies, the general public knows practically nothing of the history of the Irish immigrants or their American descendants.

This much said, Mr. O'Brien suggests the cause and the cure:

> Irish-blooded Americans are, however, themselves to blame if their people have been relegated to a place of no importance in American history. For many years they have been complaining that the 'historians have kept us out of history,' unmindful of the fact that the fault is all their own, since the real facts are readily obtainable if they would only devote to the work a part of the energy they waste in denouncing unsympathetic historians. Since a nation is but an aggregation of individuals and families, it has been well said that 'the history of a country is but the history of its people,' and in the numerous published geanealogies of American families and the biographical works of historical societies are found some of the most interesting items of the nation's history. American genealogists, however, have devoted their attention mainly to families of English or Dutch descent, because the demand for their work came chiefly from those sources.
>
> There is a strong and ever increasing reason, therefore, to see this state of affairs remedied, to look into the emigrant ancestry of Americans of Irish blood. It is highly desirable that their history should be traced as far as practicable, but it can be done only by consulting the records of the towns and parishes and the official documents of the Colonial governments, and if the proper spirit were displayed this work would result in making many valuable contributions to the historical literature of the country.

May Michael J. O'Brien be long spared for the excellent work in which he is engaged.

RELICS OF FATHER MARQUETTE

To the Editor of AMERICA:

The present writer recently called the attention of your readers to a newly found letter of Father Marquette. Since the publication of that contribution in *America* for November 6, several inquiries have come to him in regard to this missionary-explorer, and particularly in regard to his mortal remains. Nearly all of these latter questioners disclosed some misapprehension of fact; one a strange misconception, as you will see, which spoke of his skeleton; and more than one, a painful error, since it reflected unjustly on the guardianship that the faculty of Marquette University has exercised over the relics in their possession. Perhaps a general statement in your pages will interest others as well as these inquirers.

In the twenty-sixth volume of the *Catholic World*, John Gilmary Shea tells, with a great historian's exquisite detail, of the discovery at St. Ignace, Michigan, of the site of the old Jesuit mission chapel, and beneath its floor of a charred bich box in which were found several minute fragments of human bones. Father Edward Jacker, the discoverer of the mission site, and Dr. Shea likewise, were convinced that these ashes were undoubtedly all that remains on earth of the gentle Marquette. On August 25, 1882, Father Jacker wrote to Marquette University, Milwaukee: "Here are all the bones [of Marquette] left in my possession after sending about seven fragments to Father Killian [O. M. Cap.] at St. Ignace."

I have not inquired about the seven fragments sent to St. Ignace; but the nineteen pieces consigned to Marquette University have been guarded with the most sacred care at all times; they have been uninterruptedly in the safety-vault of the treasurer of the school since its removal some years ago to its new location on Grand Avenue. The longest piece is one and a quarter inches in length, and weighs about one-eighth of an ounce. The combined weight of the nineteen fragments is not quite an ounce.

The Rev. H. B. MacMahon, S. J., of Marquette University, writes me that this "treasure is kept in a box eleven and a half by nine inches of polished black walnut, inlaid with an elaborate design in some hard light-colored wood. The interior is lined with white satin, padded, and has under the thick outer cover, whch s hinged and locked, a heavy glass plate, kept in place by a frame that must be unscrewed before the 'relics' can be reached. Under this glass can be seen a small box, apparently of tin, four and a half by three by one and a quarter inches, bearing a label in the handwriting of Father Jacker: 'Fragments of bone from the grave of Father Marquette. 1877.'"

Whoever has not read Dr. Shea's article in the *Catholic World*, referred to above, is scarcely justified in holding an opinion adverse to the authenticity of these remains. It must be added, however, that not all who have read it are entirely convinced. No miracles, wrought through the application of the fragments, have been recorded.

LAURENCE J. KENNY, S. J.

St. Louis.

STATEMENT OF THE OWNERSHIP, MANAGEMENT, CIRCULATION, ETC., REQUIRED BY THE ACT OF CONGRESS OF AUGUST 24, 1912,

Of ILLINOIS CATHOLIC HISTORICAL REVIEW, published quarterly at Chicago, Illinois, for April, 1920.

STATE OF ILLINOIS, COUNTY OF COOK, ss.

Before me, a Notary Public in and for the State and county aforesaid, personally appeared Joseph J. Thompson, who have been duly sworn according to law, deposes and says that he is the Editor of the ILLINOIS CATHOLIC HISTORICAL REVIEW and that the following is, to the best of his knowledge and belief, a true statement of the ownership, management, etc., of the aforesaid publication for the date shown in the above caption, required by the Act of August 24, 1912, embodied in section 443, Postal Laws and Regulations, printed on the reverse of this form, to-wit:

1. That the names and addresses of the publisher, editor, managing editor, and business managers are:

Publisher, ILLINOIS CATHOLIC HISTORICAL SOCIETY, Ashland Block, Chicago, Illinois.

Editor, Joseph J Thompson, Ashland Block, Chicago, Illinois.

Managing Editor, Joseph J. Thompson, Ashland Block, Chicago, Illinois.

2. That the owners are: THE ILLINOIS CATHOLIC HISTORICAL SOCIETY, Ashland Block, Chicago, Illinois (a corporation not for profit. No stockholders.)

3. That the known bondholders, mortgagees, and other security holders owning or holding 1 per cent or more of total amount of bonds, mortgages, or other securities are: None.

4. That the two paragraphs next above, giving the names of the owners, stockholders, and security holders, if any, contain not only the list of stockholders and security holders as they appear upon the books of the company but also, in cases where the stockholder or security holder appears upon the books of the company as trustee or in any other fiduciary relation, the name of the person or corporation for whom such trustee is acting, is given; also that the said two paragraphs contain statements embracing affiant's full knowledge and belief as to the circumstances and conditions under which stockholders and security holders who do not appear upon the books of the company as trustee, hold stock and securities in a capacity other than that of a bona fide owner; and this affiant has no reason to believe that any other person, association, or corporation has any interest direct or indirect in the said stock, bonds, or other securities than as so stated by him.

JOSEPH J. THOMPSON.

Sworn to and subscribed before me this 30th day of April, 1921.

[SEAL]   ANNA M. SHEEHAN,

(My commission expires, August 5, 1922).

ILLINOIS
CATHOLIC HISTORICAL
-REVIEW

lume III   JULY, 1920   Number 1

$19\,\overset{3}{\leq}0 - 3.\,1$

CONTENTS

PUBLISHED BY THE ILLINOIS CATHOLIC HISTORICAL SOCIETY
617 ASHLAND BLOCK, CHICAGO, ILL.
Issued Quarterly
Annual Subscription, $3.00   Single Numbers, 75 cents
Foreign Countries, $3.50
red as second class matter July 26, 1918, at the post office at Chicago. Ill.,
under the Act of March 3, 1879

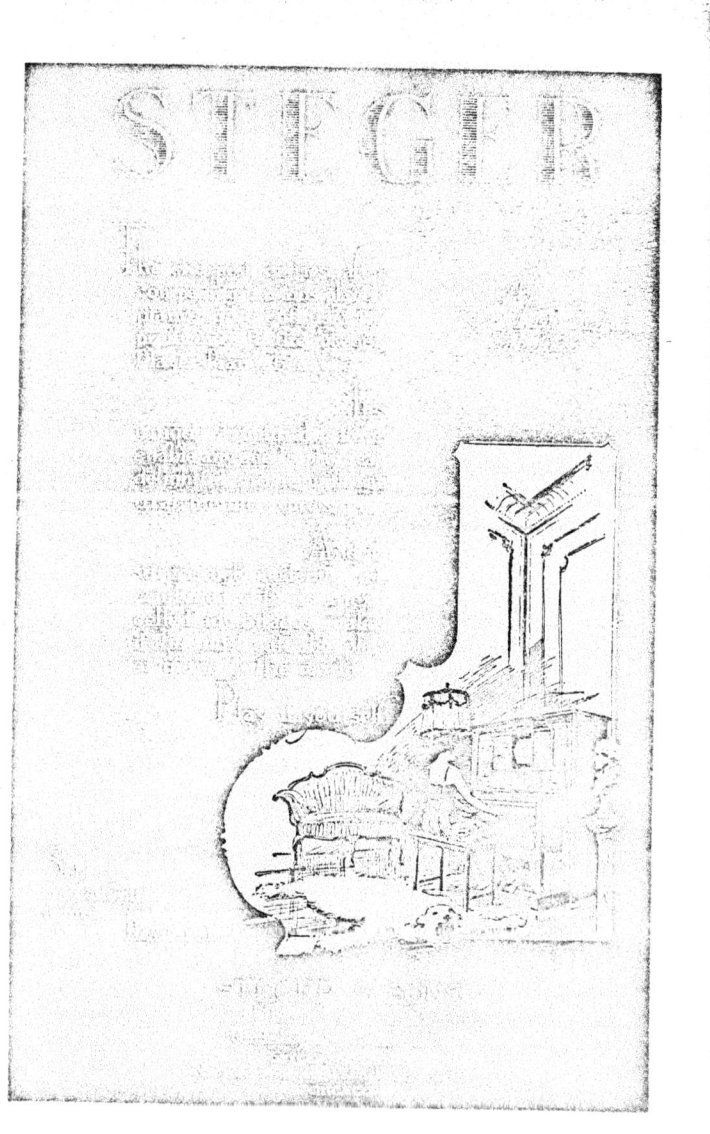

Loyola University
Chicago, Illinois

2945 STUDENTS   157 PROFESSORS

Conducted by the Jesuits

College of Arts and Sciences

St. Ignatius College, Roosevelt Road and Blue Island Avenue.

Sociology Department

Ashland Block, Clark and Randolph Streets.

Law Department

Ashland Block, Clark and Randoph Streets.

Engineering Department

1076 Roosevelt Rd., W.

Medical Department

Loyola University School of Medicine, 706 So. Lincoln Street.

High School Departments

St. Ignatius Academy, 1076 West Roosevelt Road.

Loyola Academy, Loyola Avenue and Sheridan Road.

In the Departments of Law and Sociology energetic students will have no difficulty in securing work that will cover the expenses of board and lodging.

There is a call for Catholic lawyers, doctors, and social workers throughout the country. Women are admitted to the medical and sociological schools. Graduates of the Department of Sociology heve been able to obtain positions at once.

Come to Chicago, prepare for your life work in law, engineering, medicine or sociology.

In writing for Information give name and full address (as above) of the department in which you are interested.

Lightning Source UK Ltd.
Milton Keynes UK
UKHW021329170119
335636UK00009B/937/P